AMERICAN FILM

A HISTORY

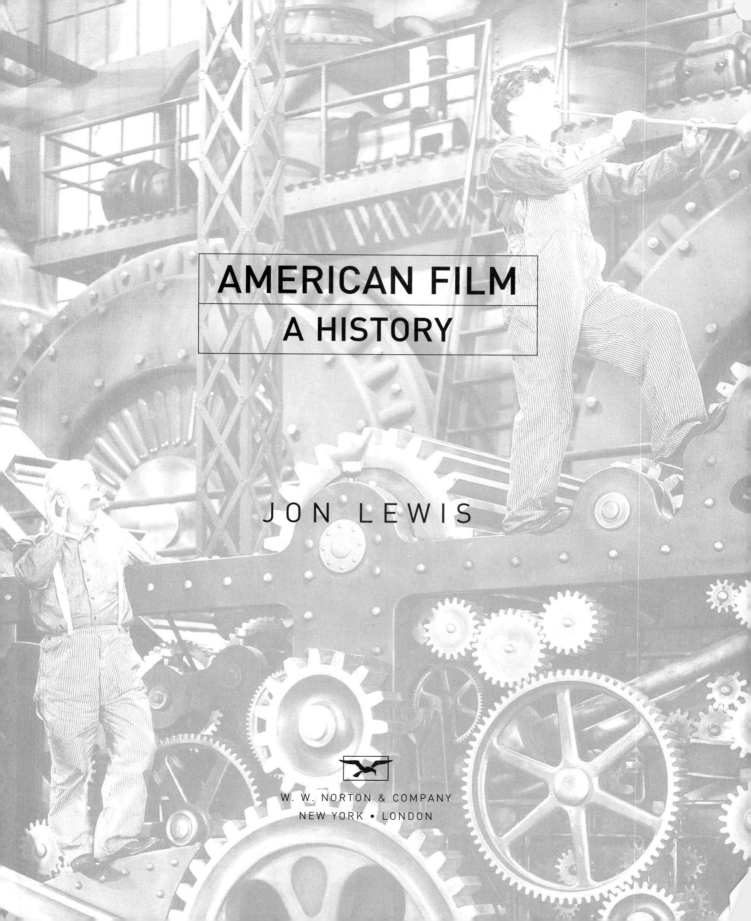

AMERICAN FILM

A HISTORY

JON LEWIS

W. W. NORTON & COMPANY
NEW YORK • LONDON

W. W. Norton & Company has been independent since its founding in 1923, when William Warder Norton and Mary D. Herter Norton first published lectures delivered at the People's Institute, the adult education division of New York City's Cooper Union. The Nortons soon expanded their program beyond the Institute, publishing books by celebrated academics from America and abroad. By mid-century, the two major pillars of Norton's publishing program—trade books and college texts—were firmly established. In the 1950s, the Norton family transferred control of the company to its employees, and today—with a staff of four hundred and a comparable number of trade, college, and professional titles published each year—W. W. Norton & Company stands as the largest and oldest publishing house owned wholly by its employees.

Editor: Peter Simon
Managing Editor—College: Marian Johnson
Associate Managing Editor—College: Kim Yi
Senior Production Manager: Benjamin Reynolds
Copy Editor: Abigail Winograd
Page Layout and Book Design by Lissi Sigillo
Composition by Matrix
Art file manipulation by Jay's Publishers Services, Inc.
Manufacturing by the Courier Companies—Westford division

Printed in the United States of America.
First Edition

Library of Congress Cataloging-in-Publication Data

Lewis, Jon E., 1961–
    American film : a history / Jon Lewis. — 1st ed.
        p. cm.
    Includes bibliographical references and index.
    ISBN 978-0-393-97922-0 (pbk.)
    1.   Motion pictures—United States—History.   I. Title.
    PN1993.5.U6L46 2008
    791.430973—dc22
                                    2007018214

W. W. Norton & Company, Inc., 500 Fifth Avenue, New York, NY 10110
        www.wwnorton.com

W. W. Norton & Company Ltd., Castle House, 75/76 Wells Street, London W1T 3QT

1 2 3 4 5 6 7 8 9 0

About the Author

J on Lewis (Ph.D., 1983, University of California, Los Angeles) is a professor in the English Department at Oregon State University, where he has taught film and cultural studies since 1983. He has published six books: *The Road to Romance and Ruin: Teen Films and Youth Culture* (Routledge, 1992); *Whom God Wishes to Destroy . . . Francis Coppola and the New Hollywood* (Duke University Press, 1995); *The New American Cinema* (Duke University Press, 1998); *Hollywood v. Hard Core: How the Struggle over Censorship Saved the Modern Film Industry* (NYU Press, 2000); *The End of Cinema as We Know It: American Film in the Nineties* (NYU Press, 2001); and, with Eric Smoodin, *Looking Past the Screen: Case Studies in American Film History and Method* (Duke University Press, 2007). In the past two years, Professor Lewis has appeared in two theatrically released documentaries on film censorship: *Inside Deep Throat* (Fenton Baily, 2005) and *This Film Is Not Yet Rated* (Kirby Dick, 2006). From 2002 to 2007, he was the Editor of *Cinema Journal*.

CONTENTS

2

3

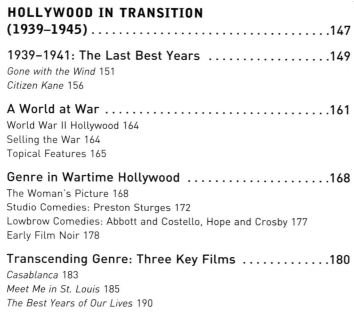

8

9

Preface

There are things in films that make us laugh, cry, wince, dig our nails into a friend's arm, walk out (and then maybe peek back in), dream of a different life, make resolutions, fall in love. Though intellectually we know that what we are seeing isn't real, that knowledge is routinely suspended in favor of a unique sort of emotional engagement. There are scenes in films that are unaccountably exhilarating and euphoric and stories in even the most disposable of genre pictures that satisfy our desires and our needs in ways no other, smaller, softer art form can match. We seldom say we like a movie; it's a matter of love or hate.

We go to the movies to escape the humdrum, the pressures of everyday life, to see a certain star or the work of a director or producer we like. There is a ceremonial exchange of cash; movies are something we pay to see, so there is a value attached to the experience than can be measured in dollars and cents. Movies take up time in our lives, time that adds up, time we anxiously surrender for one more look, one more evening in the dark.

Going to the movies is a communal ritual that has endured for over a century in the United States, and movie theaters remain one of the few places (along with sports stadiums, megachurches, and casinos) where Americans from "all walks of life" share time together. When the lights go down and the movie begins, everyone is equal for an hour or two. And there in the dark, in a hall full of strangers, we perform an odd little ritual as we, together, engage in a phenomenon that appeals nakedly to our emotions, aspirations, and fears.

Although the meaning of movies is often deeply personal, the history of film tells us a lot about ourselves not only as individuals but as a culture as well. My aim throughout this book is to provide a historical perspective on film, to insist that movies have a historical significance. Films from decades past tell us things about the world into which they were released—how people looked, how they talked, what they cared about, what they dreamed, what they wanted. Furthermore, movies don't simply reflect their times; they also shape them. Sometimes art follows history; sometimes it's the other way around.

The American film history told here begins in the last decade of the nineteenth century with the medium an uncertain product of the Industrial Revolution and an emerging form of popular entertainment in American society and ends, for the time being at least, with its present incarnation as a global cultural phenomenon. How we got here from there is the challenge this book takes on.

To account for the medium's swift evolution, *American Film: A History* embraces a simple binary: that in the United States, film history reveals a delicate if not always productive balance between art and commerce, between entertainment and commercial enterprise. Approaching the history of American film from this perspective allows for a close look at not only the important films and filmmakers of a given time (the focus of most film histories and an important part of this one) but also the sometimes complex and always fascinating business that is conducted behind the scenes by producers, financiers, lawyers, technicians, politicians, censors, and a cast of other characters as varied as that in any movie. Film history is, after all, the history of completed, screened movies produced by a system that censors its own products, a system that molds, advertises, and thus characterizes its products in advance of their distribution and exhibition, a system that, at bottom, is designed to make money.

For the most part, the nine chapters that constitute *American Film: A History* follow a similar pattern: each one begins with a general cultural and historical overview, which is followed by a close look at the business, a close reading of exemplary studio films (organized as the studios themselves organize them, by genre), and finally, in-depth coverage of important films and filmmakers, the "great books" and "great authors" of American cinema. Such an organizing strategy—such a historical method—accommodates the notion that from its very beginnings, American filmmaking has been a collaborative undertaking that requires dozens—nowadays often hundreds—of people to produce a single film. Consequently, the mythology of the lone genius in the garret working in anonymity—the prevailing portrait of the painter, poet, or novelist—does not suit the production model here. With so many people involved and so many ideas, expectations, and interests hovering over the production of every movie made in America, a complete history of American film must examine both the work up there on-screen and the process that made that work possible.

Although it is safe to assume that readers of this book will know a thing or two about the movies, I have endeavored to outline something approximating an American film literacy. I believe that such a literacy is not based on a short list of "classic" titles but instead should be grounded in a broad understanding of the role that films have played and continue to play in American culture. This book introduces readers to a range of American movies in a range of genres. Many of the films discussed played an important part in the cultural life of their times, though they are not by any critical consensus acknowledged to be among the best movies of all time. Others are widely regarded as classics, though in their day they went into and out of release without much fanfare. If there is a canon here, it is very, very big.

As will become evident in the pages that follow, I view film history less as a matter of dates and facts—less as a matter of reading closely a handful of key titles—than as a collection of stories and film readings that alternatively parallel, overlap, intersect, and occasionally even contradict one another. Film history is a complex thing regarding industry and artifice, economy and entertainment, money and movies. This book embraces that complexity.

As I suggested at the outset, our responses to specific movies grow out of our experience, knowledge, and temperament. What we make of the movies in our lives is a product of our personal history. Mine took shape on a snowy night at Hobart College in tiny Geneva, New York, sometime in the winter of 1976. Bored and cold, I ducked into a free screening sponsored by a class in American studies: a 1947 film noir, *Out of the Past*. That night more than thirty years ago marks the date on which—the precise ninety-seven minutes during which—I fell in love with the movies. What brought me to that part of campus, to that screening that night, I'll never know. But my life has not been the same since.

Movies mark significant moments in our lives: a first date, a first kiss. I have made a career out of going to the movies—and I go to the movies a lot—so some of the most significant—indeed, some of the best things—that have happened in my life have happened at the movies. I first flirted with Martha, now my wife, in the moments before a screening of *The Blue Angel*. And I finally got the courage to ask her out during the intermission between *Now, Voyager* (coincidentally my mother's favorite film) and *Leave Her to Heaven*. I have chosen, in the twenty-plus years since that night, to ignore the ominous signs: that our first significant conversation was followed by a film about a professor who is ruined by a showgirl with great legs and a heart of stone and that our first date was set during the intermission between two annihilating melodramas, one that ends with a reminder that love is sometimes not enough and another that ends with the notion that life is so crazy love is probably more trouble than it's worth.

If you ask me about the first movie I ever saw—*Pinocchio* in rerelease—though it was well over forty years ago, memories of the movie and the whole day come to mind immediately. I saw the film with my father at the Syosset Theater on Long Island, a thirty-minute drive from our house, in what the studios in those days called a hard-ticket road-show engagement. That is, a big film was first released—and even rereleased—to select showcase theaters, with tickets sold in advance for assigned seats. Those days are, alas, long gone. Big movies today get saturation releases so extensive that multiplexes tie up as many as half their screens to show them. When *Independence Day* opened in July 1996, the ads read, "At theaters EVERYWHERE"—and they weren't kidding.

In 1963, my parents took me to see *Bye Bye Birdie* at Radio City Music Hall in New York City, at the time the nation's most famous movie palace. And for the first time in my life, I fell in love (with Ann-

Margret biting her lip as she sang the film's opening number). Every time I've seen that film since then, I've forgotten all I know about musicals and 1960s youth culture and have remembered what it was like to be a little boy and to want Ann-Margret, though I was too young to know why.

This book to a great extent chronicles my life at the movies and as such regards not only a life's work thus far—I have taught, researched, and written about American film history since 1982—but also a life's infatuation, a relationship with the movies I just can't (and have no desire to) kick. More than anything else, I hope that this book evinces my enthusiasm and affection for American movies and my fascination with the industry that produces them.

Acknowledgments

First, I would like to acknowledge my debt to the film scholars whose work has influenced my teaching and my writing: Richard Abel, Tino Balio, André Bazin, Gregory D. Black, David Bordwell, Eileen Bowser, Andrew Britton, Nick Browne, Kevin Brownlow, Robert L. Carringer, Noël Carroll, Stanley Cavell, Carol J. Clover, David A. Cook, Timothy Corrigan, Donald Crafton, Richard deCordova, Tom Doherty, Richard Dyer, Thomas Elsaesser, Neal Gabler, Douglas Gomery, Barry Keith Grant, Ed Guerrero, Tom Gunning, Miriam Bratu Hansen, Brian Henderson, John Hess, Sumiko Higashi, J. Hoberman, Gerald Horne, Pauline Kael, E. Ann Kaplan, Chuck Kleinhans, Robert Kolker, Richard Koszarski, Julia Lesage, Peter Lev, Gerald Mast, Lary May, Toby Miller, Tania Modleski, Paul Monaco, Charles Musser, James Naremore, Victor Navasky, Bill Nichols, Fred Pfeil, Dana Polan, Jonathan Rosenbaum, Andrew Sarris, Eric Schaefer, Tom Schatz, Robert Sklar, Eric Smoodin, Janet Staiger, Kristin Thompson, David Thomson, Andrew Tudor, Gregory A. Waller, Robert Warshow, Janet Wasko, Linda Williams, Robin Wood, Will Wright, and Justin Wyatt. No doubt these historians and critics—or their students—will recognize their work condensed, translated, reconfigured, and recontextualized here; I hope that I have done their work justice and that this book will mean half as much to future film historians and critics as their work has meant to me.

I also want to express my gratitude to my teachers, who taught me not only how to read and watch but also how to write: Jim Crenner, Talbot Spivak, Dan O'Connell, Eric Patterson, Grant Holly, Brian Henderson, Raymond Federman, Alan Spiegel, Stephen Fleischer, Nick Browne, Thomas Elsaesser, Howard Suber, Robert Rosen, and Steve Mamber. I know how much I owe you guys.

This project dates to a casual dinner I had with David Cook, Peter Brunette, Dana Polan, and Pete Simon in Dallas in March of 1996. I forget who first suggested that I write a history of American film; I know it wasn't me. In fact, it took me a long time to get started—six years!—to convince myself that this was something I could do and something teachers and students of American film history might want. And then it took almost five years to get it all down in a way that fully represents how I think about—and, more important—how I teach American film history.

I have had considerable help along the way. First and foremost has been my editor at Norton, Pete Simon, whose unflagging devotion and unrelenting editorial commitment made this book happen. Several colleagues read various versions of the book and offered thoughtful, useful commentary. The book is a lot better than it would have been without their input. So, big thanks to my buddies Eric Smoodin, Dana Polan, Tom Doherty, and Henry Sayre, all of whom contributed significantly (and differently) throughout the duration of the project. Thanks also to the formerly anonymous readers who waded through early drafts that (for good reason) don't much resemble the book in its final form: Todd Berliner, Cynthia Felando, M. Allison Graham, Brian Henderson (with whom, coincidentally, I took my first film theory class back in 1978 at the State University of New York, Buffalo), Charles J. Maland, and J. Emmett Winn. You all saw me naked and were kind enough not to laugh.

From start to finish, the editorial and production staff at Norton was terrific. In addition to Pete Simon, I'd like to thank the managing editor, Marian Johnson; project editor Kim Yi; photo researcher Kelly Mitchell; interior and cover designer Lissi Sigillo; production manager Benjamin Reynolds; editorial assistants Birgit Larsson, Annie Abrams, and Conor Sullivan; and my intrepid copyeditor, Abigail Winograd, whose painstaking work scouring the final draft made the book stylistically cleaner and more factually accurate.

This book took almost five years to research and write. I have lived with it, intimately, through its various incarnations. So has my family—Martha, Guy, and Adam. They're no doubt as happy as I am that I've finished it. So, thanks big time to Q and the Lewis boys, for being quiet (a lot of the time) while I worked and for understanding all along what that work means to me.

For Martha and the boys, Guy and Adam

AMERICAN FILM
A HISTORY

May Irwin and John Rice in
Edison's *The Kiss* (1896).

Early Cinema

1893–1914

By the end of the nineteenth century, the United States had become a major player on the world stage. The mid-nineteenth-century faith in "manifest destiny" had fueled the acquisition and conquest of a large portion of the North American continent, and colonial expansion beyond the nation's continental borders had increased the American sphere of influence. Accompanying this geographic expansion was an economic boom. In the first few years of the twentieth century, the total economic output of the country increased by more than 80 percent, and by 1913 the United States accounted for a third of the world's total industrial output. The American century—as the twentieth century would be called—had arrived.

The emergence of cinema as a modern American industry and pop-culture pastime at once accompanied and punctuated the nation's transformation into a mature industrial society. Emblematic of this transformation was a series of modern industrial inventions that culminated with the cinema: Alexander Graham Bell's telephone (1876), Thomas Edison's phonograph (1877), Henry Ford's first "horseless carriage" (1896), and finally Edison's first projected and screened moving pictures (also 1896). The rapid accommodation of these inventions in daily life came to symbolize America's newfound prominence and wealth.

The nation's embrace of industrial progress—the key to its transformation into a global superpower—prompted a number of changes in American social and economic life. First among those changes was a dramatic population shift. Between 1880 and 1920 the proportion of Americans living in urban centers grew from 26 to 51 percent. Modern city life was essential to the early development of the movies; indeed, cinema's initial appeal was keenest

3

among the cities' newest and poorest inhabitants. Cultural historians routinely connect American industrialization and urbanization to the advent of a consumer society. For the urban poor participating only partially in this new American economy, cinema quickly became a cheap and accessible consumable product.

In the early years of the twentieth century, several of the nation's biggest cities absorbed huge new immigrant populations. By 1920, for example, 76 percent of New York City's population was foreign-born. Similar percentages were found in Boston (72 percent) and Chicago (71 percent). It was in those cities that the early studios made most of their money, and it was among the immigrant population that they found their most ardent moviegoers. For recent immigrants the embrace of (silent) cinema—a medium that did not require a working understanding of English—was crucial to fitting in, to taking part in the popular culture of the day.

As the early filmmaking enterprises began to make money in the first few years of the new century, they modeled themselves on other successful companies operating within the burgeoning industrial sector of the American economy. Consolidation was commonplace at the time; between 1897 and 1904 over four thousand small companies were assimilated by a handful of conglomerates. By 1902 a select group of companies—including Northern Securities, Standard Oil, United States Steel, and International Harvester—controlled over half the nation's total financial and industrial capital. That imbalance applied to individuals too: at the turn of the century, the wealthiest 1 percent of Americans accounted for the same total income as the remaining 99 percent. Although such a concentration of economic resources and control over industrial production exaggerated the divide between labor and wealth, many in the business world viewed it as a necessary stage in the development of more efficient companies and industries. It was the age of Henry Ford, after all, and the dream of a streamlined assembly-line American economy was in vogue among the industrial elite.

The first move toward a consolidated, modernized, and standardized movie industry came as early as 1908, when a cartel headed by Thomas Edison, the Motion Picture Patents Company (MPPC), monopolized the production and distribution of American movies. The MPPC tried to make cinema fit the Fordist principles of standardization and efficiency, but in the end the trust failed to understand and appreciate the medium's audience. By the second decade of the twentieth century, the MPPC had lost its hold on the industry, and in its place arose another cartel, a group of first-generation immigrants, men quite like the audience they served, who ventured west and "invented" Hollywood.

The struggle between the MPPC and the so-called independents was a logical consequence of the industry's astonishing growth; it became clear early on that there was lots of money to be made in the movie business. But success in moving pictures also brought increased public scrutiny. Film censorship became a fact of everyday life in this early period as two distinct American impulses—a spirit of social progressivism and a continued legacy of early-American Puritanism—contended with each other. As the industrial economy evolved, much of the nation embraced new ideas of social reform. But a late-Victorian social conservatism persisted. The movie industry felt the effects of both social realities from the very start.

Early efforts to regulate motion pictures were also characterized by the trenchant racism and ethnocentrism that were endemic to American life at the time. Initial attempts to censor American movies were based on stereotypical assumptions about impressionable, ignorant immigrants who constituted a significant portion of the silent-film audience. Even its opponents could see that cinema offered transcendence, or at least escape, for those who needed it most, but its very accessibility and its apparent persuasive power worried those in power, those for whom the sweaty masses were an appalling threat.

Censorship may well have been troublesome, but it did little to slow the development of the art of moving pictures. Indeed, the speed with which the industry achieved financial and cultural success was matched by the pace of the medium's artistic development. Although films made during the 1890s were mostly slices of everyday life or simple gags or skits lasting less than a minute, by 1902 innovative filmmakers such as Edwin S. Porter were producing longer and more ambitious story films, like the groundbreaking *Great Train Robbery* (1903). Pioneering filmmaking during the first decade of the twentieth century hinted at a future in which movies would take on even bigger subjects and more complex story lines.

A second wave of filmmakers, led by D. W. Griffith and Mack Sennett, emerged near the end of the century's first decade. Griffith explored a new cinematic grammar, a language composed of camerawork (changes in camera position and movement and expressive use of different lenses), lighting, set design, and editing to create more ambitious and more sophisticated films. Conversely, Sennett reduced cinema to its basic elements—he simply set bodies in motion—and in so doing he mined the commercial bottom line in American cinema: he entertained his audience.

In 1931, Edison famously mused that he was astonished by the amount of money being spent on the making of movies and the amount of money being made by the movie studios. Edison lived long enough to witness (and miss out on much of) the medium's rapid evolution—he witnessed the relatively short amount of time it took for cinema to advance from a technological novelty to a national pastime. The hectic pace of its development suited the age much as the medium itself—an undeniably industrial art—suited America at the time. By the end of the era of early cinema (1893—1914), movies had become so important to the national economy, so absolutely vital to the national identity, that it was hard to remember the time—not so long before—when they hadn't existed at all.

PRE-CINEMA

As an idea—the idea of triggering in people a sense of motion, action, and narrative—cinema's roots stretch all the way back to prehistory, to the drawings made thousands of years ago on the walls at Lascaux Cave, in present-day France. In fact, the entire history of human accomplishment in the visual arts—in drawing, sculpture, painting, and other forms—seems to reveal a deep-seated desire to represent time, space, and action visually—and as vividly as possible. For much of that history, the technological problem of setting images in motion was a hurdle that forced visual artists to devise ingenious methods to suggest or simulate movement and the passage of time in their otherwise static images.

Minor successes in projecting realistic images and then putting them in motion date back at least five hundred years, to various parlor games and divertissements that, in one way or another, animated still images. Image projection began with the so-called magic lantern, a device employing a lens, shutter, and persistent light source that projects images on glass slides onto a flat white wall or cloth drape (hung like a screen) in the dark. At first the images were painted or etched on the slides. Later, photographs were printed on the glass and then highlighted with paint. The glass plates would then be mounted on a rudimentary slide projector that utilized a light source and a single lens to focus the picture on a distant screen.

The faster the projector could be made to move from one image to the next, the more it simulated modern moving pictures.

During the nineteenth century a variety of substances (most notably lime—hence the term *limelight*) were heated to create sufficient illumination to project the images. Other combustible substances were used as well: hydrogen, coal gas, ether, and oxygen. Needless to say the heating of those substances required a degree of expertise on the part of the magic-lantern operator, and the risk of explosion or fire loomed over every show.

Magic lanterns were used as parlor entertainments for adults and as educational devices for children and occasionally by scientists to display scientific procedures (so-called live experiments). Missionary workers (for example, the Band of Hope mission in the United Kingdom) used the seeming magic of image projection to spread the "good word."

During the early nineteenth century the magic lantern was modernized in conjunction with motion-toy technology. Motion toys included the thaumatrope (a round card bearing multiple images that appear as one when the card is spun), the phenakistoscope (a platelike slotted disc spun to simulate moving images), the zoetrope (a bowl-like apparatus with slots for viewers to peer through), and the praxinoscope (essentially a zoetrope using mirrors). The devices were marketed as children's toys—made for the entertainment of children if not for their own play—and as

The Zoetrope, one of the early motion toys that prefigured cinema.

parlor entertainments (toys for wealthy adults). When the two technologies were combined—when glass magic-lantern plates were mounted and spun (or otherwise set in motion) to simulate movement—audiences got their first glimpse of multiple continuous moving images—their first glimpse of what would soon be a new mass medium.

Photography

The advent of photography in the nineteenth century made pictorial representation a matter of mechanical precision. The next step—from images captured in time (photography) to images that moved and simulated real life (cinema)—was inevitable and was accomplished swiftly. A practical apparatus for the production of photographs preceded cinema by only about fifty years; the introduction of a consumer-grade camera preceded it by only about a decade. Cinema was in many ways the logical end point of photography, an end point reached in a hurry thanks in part to

the spirit of industrial progress of the time and in part to the seemingly instinctual human desire to see images move.

Between 1816 and 1818 a Frenchman named Joseph Niepce produced the first fuzzy images from metal plates, what historians have come to regard as the first crude photographs. Along with Louis Daguerre, Niepce continued to experiment with the photographic process. In the early 1830s the exposure time was about 15 minutes: models had to hold a pose for that amount of time in order for the photographer to produce a clear photograph. Moving pictures were thus very much the stuff of science fiction, as they still were five years later when Daguerre reduced the exposure time to approximately 3 minutes.

Photography began as an industrial art best left to experts. But research and development worked to make the medium more accessible. When George Eastman introduced the first consumer-grade Kodak camera in 1888, he cleverly exploited a simple yet brilliant commercial slogan that signaled the shift from a technical and complicated process to a democratic art form: "You push the button, we do the rest." As the nineteenth century came to a close, photography was quite suddenly a proletarian medium, something pretty much anyone and everyone could engage in.

Simulations of movement using still photographs—the most direct antecedent of true motion pictures—date to 1828, just a decade after the first crude photograph was produced and only four years after the Frenchman Paul Roget first described the phenomenon of persistence of vision (or *positive afterimages*, the preferred term today), the phenomenon produced when a sequence of still photographs passes in front of the eye at considerable speed. To dramatize his "discovery," Roget introduced the thaumatrope, a device composed of a disc and a string (so the disc could be twirled). Each side of the disc contains an illustration (let's say a bird on one side, a cage on the other). The act of twirling the disc merges the two illustrations (the bird appears to be in the cage), making it seem as though there's only one image.

In conjunction with a few other features of visual perception, persistence of vision explains why movies work, why we're able to see them as a continuous record of movement rather than a series of thousands of discontinuous still images.

The hard work of matching Niepce's and Daguerre's innovations with Eastman's cameras and Roget's theory of physics would be accomplished with dispatch.

Eadweard Muybridge and Étienne-Jules Marey

The history of true moving pictures began with a silly moment in California history. None of the principals involved could have known that they would play a crucial role in what would become film history. Leland Stanford, a railway magnate, one-time governor of California, and inveterate gambler, got into a disagreement with a fellow horseplayer about whether all four hooves of a horse are ever off the ground at the same time. Stanford bet that they were; his rival insisted that they weren't. To settle the bet, Stanford hired Eadweard Muybridge, a British-born entrepreneur and renowned photographer. Muybridge set up a row of cameras along a racetrack straightaway and timed exposures to capture the many stages of a horse's gallop. It was Muybridge's good

fortune that Stanford was right and that one of his photographs proved it. Stanford collected his cash, and Muybridge became a minor celebrity. More important, Muybridge's "battery-of-cameras" technique brought photography one giant step closer to cinema.

In 1875, Muybridge was involved in a scandal, the first of many in what would become the film colony in California: he caught his wife in an adulterous affair and killed her lover. He was eventually acquitted—the crime was deemed a justifiable homicide—and after a year in Central America (to allow the gossip to cool) he returned to the United States and began exhibiting his "series photographs."

Among other things, Muybridge's series photographs—printed, traced, or drawn on glass plates designed to enable projection on a screen—featured naked women performing simple household tasks and leisure-time activities. These early "motion pictures," with titles like *Woman Walking Downstairs* and *Woman Setting Down Jug*, were essentially cast as figure studies along the lines of high-art nudes rendered in pencil sketches and

Eadweard Muybridge's series photographs, taken with his "battery of cameras," simulated movement and thus foreshadowed cinema. The photographs, mounted on glass plates, could be affixed to a zoopraxiscope, a motion toy that doubled as a moving still-frame projector.

The pre-cinema entrepreneur and series photographer Eadweard Muybridge.

and attractive (the islands of the South Seas were popular subjects, for example) or distant and foreboding (expeditions to the polar regions). Ostensibly educational, these illustrated lectures brought the world to the people in an era (prior to air travel) when bringing people to the farthest reaches of the world was impractical.

Muybridge was neither an explorer nor a performer by nature, so he was a curious fit in the illustrated-lecture circuit. Unlike the legendary explorer Robert Edwin Peary, whose slideshow "Land of the Eskimos" presented a sober study of an untamed wilderness and the "primitive" people who lived there, or Joseph Boggs Beale, who traveled with a slideshow presentation based on Edgar Allan Poe's "The Raven," Muybridge presented an act that was less about showmanship or the content of the pictures themselves than it was about the technology he'd "invented" to produce them. Although Peary's and Beale's slides were fascinating, they were just still photographs. Muybridge's slides, although relatively mundane, simulated movement. There was a gee-whiz aspect to the early shows, and Muybridge cleverly exploited it.

Thomas Edison attended one of Muybridge's stage shows and met with Muybridge afterward.

paintings. But whereas *Woman Walking Downstairs* and *Woman Setting Down Jug* seem at least superficially rooted in museum culture, series studies like *Woman Throwing a Baseball* and *Woman Jumping from Rock to Rock* veer toward the carny peep show. The models in the latter two titles smile, even laugh, as they look back at Muybridge's camera, at once acknowledging the act of voyeurism and taking an apparent exhibitionist's delight in being seen. Like many of cinema's pioneers, Muybridge was primarily an entrepreneur and only secondarily, even incidentally, an artist. His series photographs reveal a keen sense of his audience as well as a prescient understanding of the ways in which motion pictures might someday conflate the very different worlds of the museum and the midway.

In 1878, Muybridge took his show on the road, exhibiting and talking about his work and the technology that produced it. So-called illustrated lectures had already become quite popular. Many of them were travelogues that included projected images of places that struck audiences as exotic

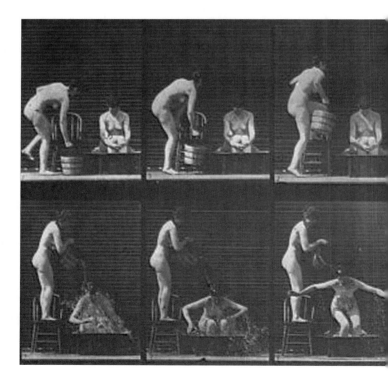

We will never know how much help Edison got from Muybridge, but we do know that Edison was interested in producing a more sophisticated simulation of movement on film than Muybridge's series photographs could ever have produced and that he had plans to develop a system that might sync serial images with recorded sound played back on the Edison phonograph.

After his meeting with Muybridge, Edison traveled to France to meet with Étienne-Jules Marey, who as early as 1882 had used a shotgun-shaped camera to shoot sequential photographs. Marey's invention seems a bit like the popular disc cameras of the 1980s. A single disc enabled him to shoot multiple images on a single load of film. But unlike the more refined 1980s version, Marey's shotgun camera produced overlapping images, often gorgeous but surreal impressions of movement.

Edison returned from France and immediately got to work on a camera that could take a sequence of pictures with a single load of film. To do so, in 1889 he enlisted the help of one of his employees, an electrical engineer and gifted photographer named William Kennedy Laurie Dickson, the man who would become the company's motion-picture expert. At Edison's behest, Dickson experimented

Thomas Alva Edison, photographed in 1904.

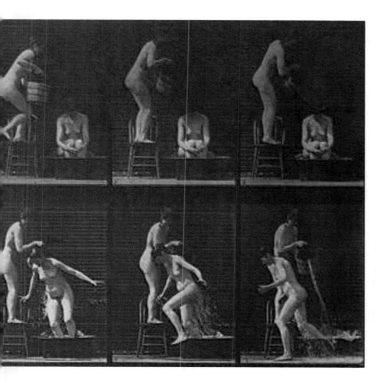

Eadweard Muybridge's *Nude Woman Pouring Water on Another Woman* (c. 1884–1887).

with film size and speed in order to design a practical method by which film might be moved through a camera. After experiments with a smaller gauge that moved horizontally through the camera (as in Marey's shotgun), Dickson settled on the 35-millimeter (mm) uniform width (which is still the standard today) set in motion vertically through the camera at the astonishingly fast rate of 40 frames per second (fps; the film speed was later reduced to 16 fps for silent film, 24 fps for sound).

Dickson also introduced sprocket holes (perforations running lengthwise along the sides of the film stock), enabling the stable movement of the film through the camera and the projector. This innovation was part of his work on an early version of sound film, in which sprockets helped regulate the speed at which the film moved through the gate in sync with recorded sound. William Heise, a telegraph expert and fellow Edison employee, helped Dickson develop the vertical-feed mechanism. It was Heise's idea to mimic the movement of paper tape through the stock-market Teletype to facilitate the movement of the perforated film stock through the camera. In 1891, Edison secured a U.S. patent on his company's version of moving-picture technology. And with that patent, movies in America were born.

The Edison Manufacturing Company and America's First Films

After securing the patent, in 1891, for his Kinetograph (the photographic apparatus that produced the pictures) and his Kinetoscope (the "peep-show" viewing machine that exhibited them), Edison set out to reach an audience. The first public demonstration of Edison's motion-picture apparatus followed soon thereafter, at the Brooklyn Institute of Arts and Sciences in May 1893, the place and date of what most experts agree was the first public exhibition of moving pictures. Attendees were able to see the technology up close and view a number of short Kinetoscope programs, including "Blacksmith Scene," which showed three men, all Edison

employees, hammering on an anvil for approximately 20 seconds.

Edison had fully outfitted a production studio in New Jersey by the time the Brooklyn Institute showcase was held. Dubbed the Black Maria after contemporary slang for a paddy wagon because, like the police department's van, it had windows covered with tar-paper strips, the studio was the site of the first slate of Edison movies shot for release to the general public. The movie from this series that is traditionally seen as Edison's first has a clunky title: *Edison Kinetoscopic Record of a Sneeze*, also known as *Fred Ott's Sneeze* (Dickson, 1894). Shot in front of a flat black backdrop, like most of Edison's early work, the film shows Fred Ott, an Edison employee, in the process of sneezing. All of the early Edison films were similarly simple: documenting movement (the 1894 *American Gymnast*, for example, shows a young woman performing a somersault) or preserving for posterity the gestures of day-to-day life (*The Barber Shop*, 1894).

The Kinetoscope, a boxed peephole-style viewing device, was designed by Thomas Edison to show the films produced by Edison's early Kinetograph cameras.

In the spring of 1894, Edison founded the Edison Manufacturing Company. As the name makes clear, Edison's business model focused on making (and selling) his Kinetoscope and Kinetograph equipment. But it also clarified Edison's vision of the medium and his role in it. In Edison's vision, movies were produced not by artists but by experts in the technology of motion-picture production (like Dickson and Heise). Movies were made much as other products of industry were made. The pretenses to art, even the pretenses to museum culture courted by Muybridge and Marey, were left for another day.

In April 1894, Edison spun off a subsidiary of the Edison Manufacturing Company—the Kinetoscope Company—to begin marketing short films and exhibition equipment. By the middle of the month, Edison had fully outfitted the Holland Brothers' Kinetoscope Parlor on Broadway in New York City, and film exhibition in America officially began. At this first commercial film venue, patrons paid 25¢ a ticket to view a row of five peephole machines. A second 25¢ got patrons a look at a second row. The Holland Brothers' Kinetoscope Parlor was a major attraction, and its success spawned a brief Kinetoscope boom. A second parlor opened in Chicago in May, followed by parlors in Atlantic City, New Jersey; Washington, D.C.; Boston; St. Louis; and San Francisco.

Initially the peephole Kinetoscope viewers and short films sold briskly: in 1894, Edison boasted sales approaching $200,000 and profits of over $85,000. But the Kinetoscope craze proved brief. Sales and profits fell off significantly in 1895; storefront theaters with rows of peephole viewers proved to be little more than a fad. The real thing—moving pictures projected on giant screens in what came to be known as movie palaces—was still a year away.

Of the Edison films made in 1894 with an eye to commercial exhibition, two series emerged. The first features the Prussian-born muscleman Eugene Sandow, who is said to have agreed to appear in the films in exchange for a chance to meet Edison in person. The films, which have been preserved and can be seen today, show Sandow in front of a flat black background, striking various poses designed to show off his physique. They are in essence figure studies, stylistically not unlike the sort of stuff Muybridge had shown ten years

Edison Kinetoscopic Record of a Sneeze (also known as *Fred Ott's Sneeze*. W. K. L. Dickson, 1894). Shot in front of a flat black backdrop, the film shows Fred Ott, an Edison employee, sneezing.

earlier. Much the same can be said about the second series, which focuses on the popular dancer Annabelle Whitford (also known as Peerless Annabelle). With titles like *Annabelle Serpentine Dance* and *Annabelle Butterfly Dance*, these early films document a performance (again set in front of a flat black backdrop) and rather obviously cater to the interests of an anticipated (mostly male) audience.

In 1896, Edison produced and released *The Kiss*. Shot by Heise, the film depicts a clumsy, closed-mouthed kiss between two stage actors, May Irwin and John Rice. It was the first screen kiss ever shown; a still photograph taken during the filming became the first photograph of a kiss ever published in an American newspaper. Though hardly erotic or obscene by contemporary standards, the film prompted a call for censorship of the medium.

Other early works include the comic boxing vaudeville skit *The Glenroy Brothers* (Dickson and Heise, 1894); *Cock Fight* (James White and Heise, 1896), which shows a fight between two roosters staged in front of a camera strategically mounted to show the cocks in full figure; *Feeding the Doves* (White and Heise, 1896), which used Edison's first portable camera to capture the movement of the birds' wings; and the comic *Seminary Girls* (White and Heise, 1897), which is composed entirely of a pillow fight among a handful of young girls dressed in nightgowns. The simplicity of these films—none

The muscleman Eugene Sandow was the subject of several of Thomas Edison's early films. Legend has it that Sandow agreed to star in the films in exchange for a chance to meet the inventor.

28, 1895, the Lumières rented out a basement room in the Grand Café and thus became the first film-makers to screen a program of projected motion pictures to a paying audience. The total take for that very first screening was a modest 35 F (francs): all of thirty-five patrons showed up for the event, each paying 1 F to see the show. The first film on the bill, *La sortie des usines Lumière* (*Leaving the Lumière Factory*) depicts, as the title suggests, the workers at the filmmakers' factory, in Lyon, leaving after a day's work. The film is little more than an advertisement for the Lumières' company and a celebration of the plant that enabled the production of the first projected motion picture. But its visual style—its mise-en-scène (the look of a film as it is created by the ways in which set design, lighting, camera position, focal length, and theatrical blocking are used)—is far more careful and aesthetically interesting than anything the Edison Manufacturing Company had produced for its Kinetoscope to date. *La sortie des usines* employs a stationary camera placed strategically to depict two doorways, one large and one small, from which the workers exit. There is a neat symmetry at play, with two distinct fields of movement framed by the doorways. But despite its staginess—the scene was no doubt rehearsed: the workers walk out to a specific spot and then exit either screen right or screen left—the impression is one of three-dimensionality, of some sort of depth to the image, of, in the final analysis, a cinematic realism.

Another film from the Grand Café show was *Repas de bébé* (*Baby's Meal*). Though this is little more than a home movie of Auguste Lumière, his wife, and their child, the camera is positioned cleverly to highlight movement in the foreground (the child eating, the parents doting) and in the background (leaves of a tree rustling in the wind). Also in play is a clever use of a wall, presented at an angle from the bottom right to the top center of the frame, thereby calling our attention to the image's vanishing point, ably implying depth. *Repas de bébé* was meant to be a model for consumer-made home movies. As manufacturers of photographic equipment, the Lumières were

is longer than a single load of the camera (20 seconds), and none even begins to tell a story—speaks to cinema's novelty status; it was enough in the 1890s that Edison could make pictures move.

The Lumière Brothers and Robert Paul: Filmmaking Begins in Europe

Edison never bothered to secure an international copyright on his Kinetograph and Kinetoscope; as a result, cinema was "invented" all over again in France and Great Britain. In 1894, about the time the first Kinetoscope parlors opened their doors in the United States, two brothers in the photographic-equipment business in France, Auguste and Louis Lumière, patented a motion-picture camera. The Lumières' *cinématographe* was a more portable and more practical machine than Edison's. It combined camera, film processor, and projector in a single unit and ran at 16 fps, the eventual standard for silent film.

In March 1895 the Lumière brothers showcased their *cinematographe* before an invitation-only audience in Paris. Nine months later, on December

looking to a future in which they might supply consumer-grade film equipment for families wanting to record the precious moments in their own and their children's lives.

By far the most famous Lumière picture is *L'arrivée d'un train en gare à la Ciotat* (*The Arrival of a Train at la Ciotat*). The film simply depicts the arrival of a train at a station. But as with *La sortie des usines* and *Repas de bébé*, it takes full advantage of camera position. The camera is placed at an acute angle and at eye level, as if it were a person waiting on the platform. As the train comes to a stop, it seems to be heading directly at the camera. Legend has it that early audience members cowered in their seats, mistaking the filmed image for the real thing.

Two months after the Lumières' Grand Café show, the British-born inventor Robert Paul, using a projector of his own design, exhibited his first motion pictures in London. With the cameraman Birt Acres, Paul produced a series of documentaries that capture quintessentially British events and scenes: *The Oxford and Cambridge University Boat Race*, *The Derby* (a popular horse race), and *Rough Sea at Dover* (all 1895). Separately and together, Acres and Paul experimented with narrative film well before Edison did. Acres's *Arrest of a Pickpocket* (1896), for example, is a docudrama of sorts: it re-creates dramatically an everyday event. Paul's 1898 *Come Along Do!* was one of the earliest two-shot films (a film composed of two shots spliced together).

The Lumières, Paul, and Acres all seemed keenly aware of the expressive potential of motion pictures. And obviously they recognized that movies viewed by an audience en masse were potentially more attractive than movies viewed by one person at a time. The success of their first public screenings (which preceded Edison's by a few months) caught the American inventor-entrepreneur's attention and spurred him to take action.

April 23, 1896: Edison's Vitascope Debuts

The main stumbling block in the years leading up to Edison's first public screening was the frustrating technical problem of film breakage in his early projectors. A solution surfaced late in 1895, when Edison was tipped off to a new device in a crude stop-motion projector that was being showcased by two inventors in Atlanta: C. Francis Jenkins and Thomas Armat. The stop-motion projector that Jenkins and Armat were using employed a technology newly designed by the Latham family (father Woodville and sons Gray and Otway), who were successful Kinetoscope exhibitors. Their invention was called the Latham loop, and it provided a simple answer to a vexing and complex problem. Through the use of two gears, one above and one below the projection lens, the Lathams were able to minimize the inertia or tension created by the take-up reel and thus reduce the incidence of film breakage. The loop allowed for the screening of films longer than 100 feet, something the Lumières, with their more primitive hand-cranked machine, could not accommodate in 1896.

Edison's first projector, the Vitascope, which used the Latham loop technology, made its premiere on April 23, 1896, at Koster and Bial's Music Hall on Broadway in New York City, the first exhibition of projected moving images in the United States. On the program were *Umbrella Dance* (Edison, 1895), which shows, as the title suggests, two dancers holding an umbrella; a comic boxing bout (most likely *The Glenroy Brothers*); a handful of newsworthy shorts (with patriotic themes); one in the series of serpentine dance films produced by

The Lumière brothers' *L'arrivée d'un train en gare à la Ciotat* (*The Arrival of a Train at la Ciotat*, 1895).

The Vitascope, billed (in this advertisement at least) as "Edison's greatest marvel."

Edison; and a seacoast scene depicting undulating waves (Paul's *Rough Sea at Dover*). A live orchestra was on hand to accompany the films, thereby setting a trend—silent movies would be watched not in silence but instead to the accompaniment of an orchestra (at the larger venues) or a pianist or an organist (at the smaller sites)—and contextualizing the new medium in terms of a music-hall-type popular entertainment.

Commercial Film Exhibition and the Birth of the Movie House

The commercial exhibition of motion pictures began with the opening of the Holland Brothers' Kinetoscope Parlor in New York City in April 1894. Though film historians distinguish that first commercial exhibition, during which patrons watched films by peering into a Kinetoscope, from the first

projected, screened films by the Lumières in 1895 and by Edison in 1896, it is worth noting that the history of commercial American cinema exhibition began on Broadway (a full two years before Edison's first projected films), signaling at once early cinema's roots in the theater and establishing from the start New York City as the capital of American cinema exhibition.

The Holland brothers charged 25¢ a ticket, with each ticket entitling a patron to view a row of five machines, each loaded with a different short feature. By the summer of 1894, the boom in Kinetoscope parlors was under way in several big cities on the East Coast, in the Midwest, and at smaller summer resorts, like the New Jersey shore.

In the late nineteenth century and through the early twentieth, vaudeville shows were the most popular form of public popular culture. Those traveling variety shows featured a diversity of attractions: comedy acts, dramatic readings, singing, dancing, acrobatics, and animal acts. Short film programs were eventually added. Cinema soon supplanted vaudeville in the affections of the popular audience, a shift that got an unintended but significant boost in 1900 when variety-show performers went on strike to protest the percentage of their salary routinely claimed by theatrical managers. Without the live acts with which to stage live performances, theater owners booked full film programs to keep their venues from going dark. To the theater owners' happy surprise, the all-film showcases proved extremely popular. The success of film screenings during the vaudeville strike created a trend that was especially strong in small towns, where, prior to moving pictures, theaters routinely went dark for months at a time as their owners awaited the next traveling revue. After the vaudeville strike most small-town theaters filled those downtimes with the exhibition of moving pictures.

Films in those early days were also shown in saloons (over and over again, in many cases), at the penny arcades at amusement parks, and as a diversion during intermission at theater productions. Between 1905 and 1907 increased production of story films gave rise to the specialized storefront theaters called nickelodeons, so named because it cost a nickel to view a program of short motion pictures. In 1906 a trade magazine counted a total of 313 nickelodeons in thirty-five states. Two years later a survey found more than 600 nickelodeon parlors in New York City alone. Exhibition was big business in New York, but nickelodeon parlors were hardly restricted to big cities. By 1910 nickelodeon parlors were prospering in Oklahoma, several having opened when it was still Indian Territory.

A row of Kinetoscopes (*bottom left*) offers audiences a diversion between bicycle races at Madison Square Garden, in New York City, c. 1895.

Nickelodeons were often located in busy shopping districts so that shoppers might stop in and take in a show during a day's visit to the stores. Many of the storefront parlors did terrific business. In New York City, for example, nickelodeon parlors boasted a combined daily attendance of between three hundred thousand and four hundred thousand. Annual ticket sales in New York City in 1908 topped $6 million (roughly 118 million in 2005 dollars).

As more and more cinema-only venues prospered throughout the country, the movie house emerged as a permanent site for film exhibition. Such venues expanded in size and splendor as entrepreneurs realized that the popularity of the movies would endure. As early as 1905–1906, theaters accommodating as many as 250 patrons opened in New Orleans and other cities in the South, and many movie houses in New England sported nearly 1,000 seats.

Early cinema began as a novelty, a curio of the machine age. As the medium grew more sophisticated and more popular, it became a significant pop-culture attraction, something to see and do in one's brief leisure time. The notion of cinema as an attraction prompted outfits like Hale's Tours and Scenes of the World to contextualize cinema as something of a theme-park ride. Patrons of Hale's Tours paid a uniformed "train conductor" and entered a theater that was designed to look like a railroad car. Films displayed by rear-screen projectors played at the front as the cars rocked to simulate an actual train ride. The essential thrill-ride aspect of those early venues lives on in various theme-park attractions at Disneyland and Universal Studios and in the revamped movie houses of the early twenty-first century, where sound systems are so powerful they rock patrons in their seats.

The movie house quickly became an important public space in working-class American culture. Nickelodeons and other early film houses provided cheap entertainment that was accessible to everyone. There was an egalitarianism inherent in the early film exhibitions that was seldom evident in the larger class-based, gender-divided American culture. The movie-theater experience that supplanted the nickelodeons became one in which the public, vast and various as it was, sat together in the dark, sharing laughter and tears with an abandon that would be unseemly anyplace else. The movie house enabled immigrants to assimilate not only an American way of life (evinced in slice-of-life documentaries and cautionary melodramas warning of the evils attending alcohol and extra-marital sex) but also an emerging consumer culture, in which one paid one's money and got in return some sort of amusement, some sort of escape from the daily grind.

The early movie house quickly earned a loyal audience. That audience in turn created a need for more and more product. Film programs were composed of as many as fifteen short movies. Audience demand forced program changes weekly at the very least; at some venues, changes were made two or three times a week.

There was money to be made in the film-exhibition business, obviously, but it was a hazardous, arduous enterprise. Most theaters depended on hand-cranked projectors. Pity the poor operator who had to crank a projector in the same carefully modulated motion for hours on end. The projector's arc light raised the temperature in the projection booth to well over 100 degrees. The nitrate film stock itself posed an alarming risk: it ignited easily. Theater fires were commonplace, so much so that groups attempting to suppress or regulate cinema routinely cited concerns of public health as well as public morality.

Though it was hazardous to work as a projectionist, there was a certain creativity to the job. Because the projectors were cranked by hand, the projectionist controlled the speed at which the film moved through the gate. The move to more complex story films in the silent era put an end to this degree of control and in so doing prioritized production over exhibition. But in the early days, exhibitors had a great deal of influence over the motion-picture show.

AN AMERICAN FILM INDUSTRY

In the wake of Edison's 1896 screening and the success of the early movie houses, it was clear that there was money to be made making and showing movies. By the turn of the century, there was no shortage of men with money and vision to take a risk on the new medium.

(*right*) Havlin's Theatre, St. Louis, 1910.

The American Mutoscope and Biograph Company

Thomas Edison's first real competitor was the American Mutoscope Company, later renamed the American Mutoscope and Biograph Company and routinely referred to simply as Biograph. Biograph was a particularly irksome competitor for Edison for two reasons: one of its founders was W. K. L. Dickson, who had resigned his position at the Edison Manufacturing Company in 1895 (as the story goes, feeling disenchanted and neglected), and the company worked in 70mm, a superior film format, providing four times the image surface of the Edison (and international industry) standard of 35mm.

The size of the image produced by Biograph's 70mm projector was an attraction in itself, as it presented not only a bigger but also a clearer image than Edison's Vitascope. And since the projector did not use the Latham loop design and the 70mm stock had no sprocket holes, the films lacked the "flicker and jump" that were characteristic of Edison's 35mm screenings.

President William McKinley (*right*) in an 1897 Biograph short shot outside his home in Canton, Ohio.

The founders of the American Mutoscope and Biograph Company, photographed in 1895. *From left to right:* Henry N. Marvin, William Kennedy Laurie Dickson, Herman Casler, and Elias Koopman. Biograph is still in the movie business today.

Biograph prospered in ways Edison could only envy. As early as 1899, Biograph founders Henry N. (Harry) Marvin, Herman Casler, Elias Koopman, and W. K. L. Dickson began thinking multi-nationally, entering into an international cartel with affiliated companies in Great Britain, France, Germany, the Netherlands, Belgium, Italy, South Africa, and India. Its machines (and thus its movies) were mainstays at amusement parks, on resort boardwalks, in saloons, and in train stations. Dickson's research and development paid off quickly with the production of a panning-head tripod that enabled rudimentary camera movement from side to side. Camera movement, a monumental technical and aesthetic advance, was put on display in two early Biograph films: *In the Grip of the Blizzard* and *Panoramic View of Niagara Falls in Winter* (both 1899). Biograph's interest in moving-camera studies was also on display in *The Georgetown Loop* (1903), which features a camera mounted on a moving railroad car in order to explore and exploit further the notion of *moving* pictures.

Prominent among the early Biograph films were documentary shorts, like *President McKinley at Home* (Dickson, 1897), which shows the twenty-fifth president of the United States strolling on the grounds outside his home in Canton, Ohio. In an age before movie newsreels and television, this short film showed McKinley as no other medium could: it gave him life; it animated him. Dickson could not have guessed how history would soon make his film invaluable: McKinley won by a landslide in 1896 and was a popular president, but early in his second term (in September 1901) he was assassinated by the anarchist Leon Czolgosz. Dickson's film, one of a handful of short films of the popular president, became a significant historical document fairly soon after its production.

Many of Biograph's early films featured boxing bouts and demonstrations of firefighting equipment. Other films were retreads of Edison short subjects featuring players—such as the strongman Eugene Sandow and the dancer Annabelle Whitford—who had worked with Dickson before. Also among the early Biograph titles were crude gag films, several with race-based subtexts. *A Hard Wash* (Dickson, 1896), for example, depicts an African American woman scrubbing her child. The implication, and the reason many white audiences found the film amusing, was that no matter how hard the woman scrubbed, she was unable to make the child "clean," or white. *A Hard Wash* and similar pictures—like *A Watermelon Feast* (Dickson, 1896) and *Dancing Darkies* (Dickson, 1896)—provide disturbing evidence of late-nineteenth-century American racism. Set in front of flat black backdrops, the African American actors seem captured onstage, like curiosities in a carnival sideshow.

Biograph began making story films as early as 1900. These early melodramas are brief moral tales about the evils of drink, infidelity, promiscuity, and prostitution—the seductive evils of modern city life. Their titles tell us nearly all we need to know about their content: *The Downward Path* (Arthur Marvin), *She Ran Away with a City Man*, and *The Girl Who Went Astray* (all 1900). But lest we take this civic-mindedness too seriously, also among Biograph's early titles was a series of burlesque shorts, including *From Show Girl to Burlesque Queen* (1903), *Troubles of a Manager of a Burlesque Show* (1903), *A Fire in a Burlesque Theatre* (1904), and *Airy Fairy Lillian Tries on Her New Corsets* (1905).

The competition from Biograph forced Edison to rethink his company's role in the marketplace. However much Edison believed that the long-term future of cinema lay in education, at the turn of the century he had to acknowledge that its short-term future was tied to popular culture. Out of necessity, Edison expanded his range beyond documentaries and sketches of everyday life, and by 1900 roughly 40 percent of his total output consisted of story films. Titles like *Maude's Naughty Little Brother*, *The Clown and the Alchemist*, and *Why Mrs. Jones Got a Divorce* (all 1900) fit snugly into popular turn-of-the-century film genres. But despite those concessions to the marketplace, the production of popular genre films did little to help Edison compete successfully with Biograph's better-looking, bigger, and more risqué films.

Biograph was not Edison's only competitor. As demand for motion pictures increased, several other film companies emerged. Selig (later Selig Polyscope), a 35mm production-distribution outfit based in Chicago, began releasing films around 1900. Selig's "stockyard series" reflected life as it was lived in the Windy City at the time. Selig also produced crude "comic" narratives similar to those produced at Biograph: *Shooting Craps* (1900), *A Night in Blackville* (1900), *Prizefight in Coontown* (1902), and *Who Said Watermelon?* (1902). A number of smaller film outfits emerged, all cause for Edison's alarm and for his continuing (and mostly

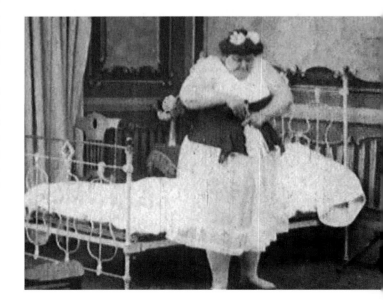

An early blue movie from Biograph: *Airy Fairy Lillian Tries on Her New Corsets* (1905).

The founders of the Motion Picture Patents Company (MPPC) Trust photographed on December 18, 1908. *Front row (from left to right):* Frank L. Dyer, Sigmund Lubin, William Rock, Thomas A. Edison, J. Stuart Blackton, Jeremiah J. Kennedy, George Kleine, and George K. Spoor. *Back row:* Frank J. Marion, Samuel Long, William Selig, Albert E. Smith, Jacques A. Berst, Henry H. Marvin, William Singhi, and Peter Huber.

futile) attempts to protect his patented equipment. In the first few years of the 1900s, the Philadelphia-based Lubin Company, the New York–based Kleine Optical, and perhaps most significantly, the New York distribution house Star Film, which handled the exclusive U.S. runs of the films made by the French magician turned filmmaker Georges Méliès, began distributing movies.

The Motion Picture Patents Company Trust

By 1908, at a point when his importance in the motion-picture industry seemed to be on the wane, Edison decided to embrace rather than fight his competitors. In December of that year, the Motion Picture Patents Company (MPPC) was born. The MPPC was a trust that linked the interests of Edison and nine of his competitors: Biograph, Vitagraph, Essanay, Kalem, Selig Polyscope, Lubin,

Star Film, Pathé Frères, and Kleine Optical. The MPPC effectively exploited key industry patents on motion-picture technology to fix prices, restrict the distribution and exhibition of foreign-made pictures, regulate domestic production and control film licensing and distribution. The trust was supported by an exclusive contract with the Eastman Kodak Company (then the principal and only dependable provider of raw film stock), which was signed the same day the MPPC trust agreement was signed.

Joined in a vertical and horizontal monopoly, the ten film companies constituting the MPPC owned and controlled the technology necessary to the making of movies and maintained exclusive access to the requisite raw materials. To say that this cartel put many independent companies out of business would be a gross understatement. Indeed, the unstated goals of the cartel were simple: to consolidate control over the industry by limiting domestic competition and to create a distribution-exhibition apparatus that would greatly disadvantage foreign filmmakers and distributors.

The MPPC was an immediate boon for its ten member companies. It enabled them to expand and enhance their facilities and thus made possible the emergence of cinema as a big business. In 1909 virtually all of the MPPC members built bigger and better studios in the New York area, updated their laboratories, and streamlined production. The trust guaranteed profits for the MPPC members and standardized their product lines. It provided a hint of things to come: trust arrangements and industry collusion in general that would characterize the American movie industry for the entire century.

In 1910 the General Film Company became the key middleman in the film production-distribution equation and made an already strong cartel even stronger. The General Film Company was the largest of a number of companies that served as distribution brokers, buying prints from the studios and then leasing them to theaters. Before that system of distribution was established, in 1903, studios routinely sold positive prints of their films to theaters. Direct sale was particularly expensive (for the exhibitors) and wasteful (for the production units). An "exchange system" enabled theater owners to change their programs more quickly and more systematically and significantly reduce their risk. That was good news for the production studios as well. Demand for product increased as the cost of operating a theater decreased.

But despite the organization and intra- and interindustry cooperation, the MPPC's domination of the movie business was brief. Within a year of the formation of the trust, a group of independent film producers organized themselves into a combine of their own: the Motion Picture Distributing and Sales Company (known as the Sales Company). By the summer of 1910, non-MPPC production units accounted for approximately 30 percent of the film market, a reasonably large piece of the pie, especially considering the absence of fair and free trade. The independents were led by Carl Laemmle, William Fox, and Adolph Zukor, who, in an effort to compete with the MPPC, established affiliations with rival film exchanges (the Sales Company colluded with the Greater New York Film Exchange; the MPPC with General Film), challenged in court the various collusive arrangements between the MPPC and other industry groups, and perhaps most important, introduced an alternative product: multireel motion pictures. The independents realized that the MPPC's biggest weakness was its strict single-reel (approximately 15-minute) standard and planned from the beginning to offer the market multireel and, eventually, feature-length films.

The independents' first big break came in February 1911, when Kodak, miffed that it did not have a profit interest in the trust, exploited a clause in its agreement with the MPPC and began to sell film stock to the newly organized independents. A second break came in August 1912, when a court case, *The Motion Picture Patents Company v. IMP*, reached a U.S. district court. The case involved the use of the so-called beater-type camera by the Independent Moving Picture Company (IMP): the trust claimed that the camera infringed on its members' shared patents. The court did not share the trust's

view, however, and decided in favor of IMP, thus throwing out the Latham loop patent. The effect of the decision was immediate, with independents more freely using formerly licensed and restricted equipment.

The victory for the independents in what became known as the Latham loop case preceded by a year or so the U.S. government's suit against the MPPC, a suit filed partly in response to the lobbying efforts of the independents. By the time the government got around to breaking up the MPPC, Edison's cartel had already lost its hold on the industry, and the independents were well on their way to establishing Hollywood.

The Move West

When the MPPC trust agreement was signed in the winter of 1908, film production was concentrated in New York and Chicago. Both cities were centers of American industrial production and finance, but neither had a climate conducive to year-round outdoor shooting, a necessity by 1910, when many theaters were changing their film programs daily. To meet the increased demand for motion-picture product, several film companies established traveling outdoor production units that followed the sun. Those units increased productivity, but the maintenance of multiple production sites proved complicated and expensive.

The search for a permanent site that might support year-round filming prompted a series of early ventures in Southern California. Los Angeles—with its 320 days of sunshine a year, dozens of beaches, and nearby desert and mountains, as well as an emerging urban center—provided easy access to exterior sites suited for work on a variety of film genres. It was a natural choice.

The first two companies to try their luck in Southern California were Essanay and Selig. G. M. "Broncho Billy" Anderson, who had helped produce and appeared in *The Great Train Robbery* (Edwin S. Porter, 1903), headed the Essanay contingent. After brief stops in El Paso, Texas, and northern Mexico, Anderson and his crew settled in Niles, California, in Alameda County, where a rugged headquarters was set up for the production of movie westerns. Like Essanay, Selig initially went to Los Angeles to produce more-authentic-looking westerns. Francis Boggs,

By 1915 (the approximate date of this photograph) pretty much everyone making movies was making them in Southern California. The men, women, and children in the crowd outside this Hollywood employment office were no doubt looking for work in the movies.

an actor, led the West Coast Selig contingent in 1907. By 1908, Boggs's Selig unit had two California-made productions in the can: an adaptation of *The Count of Monte Cristo* and *The Cattle Rustlers*. In 1909, Boggs rented the back lot of a Chinese laundry on Olive Street in what is now Hollywood; it was most likely the first Hollywood studio. In 1910 a more permanent facility was erected in an L.A. suburb, and in 1913 the company moved much of its operation to yet another site, in Lincoln Park in East Los Angeles. Boggs was a cinema pioneer, an important player in the industry's move west. But as fate would have it, he did not live long enough to see just how big the West Coast industry would get: Boggs was murdered in 1911 by a man authorities identified simply as a "crazed" gardener.

Though Essanay, Selig, and Biograph (which arrived on the West Coast in 1910) found what they were looking for on the West Coast, not all the MPPC production companies were immediately sold on Los Angeles. In 1910, Kalem took advantage of cheap real estate and cheap labor in Jacksonville, Florida. Lubin began filming in Jacksonville as well, making comedies, many of which starred Oliver "Babe" Hardy, who would later join with Stan Laurel to form a popular slapstick comedy team.

Other film companies tried their luck elsewhere. Georges and Gaston Méliès set up shop in San Antonio in 1910, where the French brothers began producing American westerns. They abandoned Texas in 1911 for Southern California, which they then abandoned in 1912 for a series of ventures in the Far East. In a move that seemed to strangely complement Méliès's move to Texas, Vitagraph built a studio in Paris. The Mutual Film Corporation tried its luck in Mexico (where it found warm weather and a civil war).

For a variety of reasons, the studio sites in Florida, the Southwest, and overseas never worked out, and by 1915 pretty much everyone who was making movies was making them in California. Just seven years after the first studio ventured west, 80 percent of all the films made in the United States were produced in the Los Angeles area. The move west established a bicoastal model, with Los Angeles the center of film production and New York the headquarters of the business and financial end of things. That bicoastal division of labor would remain in place until well after the end of World War II.

Movie Moguls and Movie Stars

Before the former independents William Fox (founder of what would become 20th Century–Fox), Adolph Zukor (Paramount), Marcus Loew (Metro Pictures, which through a merger became Metro-Goldwyn-Mayer, or MGM), Sam, Harry, Jack, and Albert Warner (Warner Bros.), and Carl Laemmle (Universal) ventured west and "invented" Hollywood, they were all successful players in the East Coast exhibition business, first with nick-elodeons and then with movie theaters. Having worked their way in from the outside (from showing films to making them, from struggling on the margins of the legitimate business as outlaw independents to running the show as successful mainstream studio managers), they had come to understand the American film-going audience and to appreciate the rich future cinema offered to those with the vision to exploit it.

Laemmle spearheaded the organized move against the MPPC, and in many ways he was the driving force behind the new industry cartel. Ambitious from the start, he had emigrated from Germany to Chicago and found work as the manager of a clothing store but made a quick transition from haberdashery to the burgeoning film business by making a smart investment in a handful of storefront theaters. Laemmle was very successful in Chicago—so successful that in 1909, in order to be where the action was, he moved to New York, where he established his own distribution exchange: the Independent Moving Picture Company of America, or IMP. Three years later Laemmle consolidated his (and IMP's) interests with several other independents and formed Universal, a studio that remains in operation today. In 1915, Laemmle moved west and opened Universal City, a model studio facility built on 230 acres of ranch land just north of Hollywood. It, too, remains in operation today.

Carl Laemmle (*foreground*), founder of Universal Pictures, photographed in 1912.

America's first movie star: Florence Lawrence.

Laemmle is also credited with jump-starting the Hollywood star system with a remark that he made to the press in 1922: "The fabrication of stars is the fundamental thing in the film industry." Laemmle, along with his fellow independents, had come to appreciate the value of movie stars during their struggle with the MPPC. Stars gave their studios a recognizable identity, and they gave production a direction and a form. Stars were especially valuable in advertising and promotion. As the movie moguls quickly realized, telling audiences they should see a film because it is funny or sad or thrilling is a challenge, since only buying a ticket and sitting through the movie can prove or disprove the claim. But telling folks they should see a movie because a certain star is in it is an easier and surer sales pitch.

The first real movie star was Florence Lawrence. Lawrence first appeared on-screen in 1906 in a Vitagraph short titled *The Automobile Thieves* (J. Stuart Blackton). In 1908 she was featured in a D. W. Griffith short, *The Girl and the Outlaw*, billed simply as "the Biograph Girl," a title subsequently held by Mary Pickford.

The studio handling of Lawrence's brief career foreshadowed the ways in which stardom might be used to promote not only individual motion pictures but also the industry as a whole. Lawrence became a trademarked commodity of sorts, the face of IMP. But such celebrity proved a double-edged sword for the actress and set in motion a familiar, darker star paradigm: Lawrence's career peaked in 1914, just as silent shorts gave way to features. She made over 250 short films between 1906 and 1914, then fewer than 20 features from 1915 to her death (by suicide) in December 1938. She was undeniably famous for a time, but her moment in the sun was brief. From the start, movie stars were at once invaluable and temporary, for a moment indispensable but ultimately disposable.

Early Film Censorship

From the very moment movies were first exhibited publicly, there were calls to censor or ban them. A key concern early on was who went to the movies (immigrants and others from the lower classes) and what effect the movies might have on them. Might seeing a man crack a safe provide the poor and disenfranchised with ideas? Might licentious behavior on-screen make sin appear all too attractive? From the end of the nineteenth century to today, censorship of one sort or another has been a fundamental aspect of American cinema.

The speed with which cinema's popularity grew as a leisure activity prompted would-be censors to fear the medium's persuasive, narcotic influence over its huge loyal audience. The stylized depictions of violence and eroticism, essential elements early on, subtly combined antisocial behavior with commercial leisure. *Dorolita's Passion Dance* (Edison, 1894), one in a series of early "erotic-dance" Kinetoscopes, was pulled from circulation in Atlantic City in response to public pressure. May Irwin and John Rice's clumsy closed-mouthed kiss in *The Kiss* (Edison, 1896) was met with calls for its and the medium's prohibition. The flap over the film was considerable, only making it more popular. *The Kiss* played for over a year on the vaudeville circuit and offered a hint of how controversy might be used to promote movies.

Short features depicting sporting events, especially boxing matches, hinted at cinema's promising future as a means of documenting important and interesting events. But many of those films, especially the early boxing films, struck would-be reformers as not only too violent (for children, women, and the impressionable masses) but of a kind with the widely distributed circus-act Kineto-scopes of bearded ladies, strongmen, and trapeze artists. Cinema seemed in those early years firmly rooted in the carnival tradition, the very low culture entertainment that purported to exploit the sucker born every minute.

Concerns were also raised about the uniquely social aspect of the theatrical-film experience. The movie theater afforded the lower classes, who constituted a significant portion of the early film audience, a safe place in which to express themselves physically and emotionally with laughter, tears, or sexual longing. Film-going quickly became something for adults and youngsters to do on dates, and as a result Victorian moral codes were routinely defied on theater balconies nationwide. What could be done there in the dark (and ostensibly in public!) suggested that the problem lay not only in film content but also in the theatrical experience itself. Reformers feared that movie theaters afforded a certain element of the population a place of escape as well as lessons in criminal violence and sexual seduction.

Reformers also expressed health and safety concerns, some real and some imagined. Attempts to enjoin theatrical exhibition called attention to the very real fire hazard posed by early film projection in what were in many cases unsafe buildings. Such legitimate safety concerns were accompanied by cockamamy theories contending that exposure to flickering cinema images might cause epilepsy in otherwise healthy filmgoers.

The first organized local government effort to regulate the exhibition of cinema came on Christmas Eve 1908, when New York City mayor George McClellan closed all the nickelodeons in the metropolitan area. By instituting the ban on one of Christian America's most important holidays, he highlighted the fact that those most affected by the

shutdown were Jewish theater owners, men who did not celebrate Christmas.

The ethnic-religious divide was hardly a small thing at the time. At that point in film history, the producers of American films were quite like the members of the mostly church-based "reform" groups—they were mostly upper-class white American Protestants. The exhibitors, including most famously the men who opposed the MPPC (such as Laemmle and Zukor) were mostly Jews. Beginning in 1908 and continuing through the end of the era of early cinema, the target of censorship was inevitably the exhibitors, who, like so many of their patrons, were more often than not recent immigrants. The MPPC trust was formed in part to diminish the role of that mostly Jewish cadre of independent exhibitors. The MPPC's failure not only gave rise to the modern studio industry but also put in power in what would soon become Hollywood the very Jews whom the trust had endeavored to restrict.

New York City nickelodeon owners challenged McClellan's ban and took their suit to court. They won, and the nickelodeon parlors reopened, thanks in large part to a sympathetic judge, William Gaynor. Judge Gaynor and Mayor McClellan were bitter political rivals; Gaynor subsequently opposed McClellan in the mayoral race and won in part because of a campaign promise to protect the fledgling movie industry. Then as now campaign

The popular dancer Annabelle Whitford in *Serpentine Dances* (1895), a short film shot for Thomas Edison by W. K. L. Dickson and William Heise. Early critics of the medium found *Serpentine Dances* unseemly.

New York City mayor William Gaynor, the first in a long series of politicians to take sides publicly in the film-censorship debate, shaking hands in 1912 with the celebrity athlete Jim Thorpe.

financing played a significant role in the election, with local motion-picture companies and exhibitors financing Gaynor's campaign.

Less than a month after McClellan made his move against the Jewish theater owners, a meeting of Christian clergymen was held at the Marble Collegiate Church in New York City in order to develop a strategy to force theater owners to stop screening films on Sundays. Theater owners tried to improve their public relations by adding educational films and uplifting speakers to their Sunday programs, but pressure from church groups continued. When it became clear that the theater owners would not shut down on Sundays (it was, after all, the one day of the week when just about every working stiff had the time to go to the movies), some churches decided to compete by screening uplifting movies of their own as part of their morning service.

In an attempt to reach a compromise among the various religious and political forces at play in film censorship, the liberal-reformist People's Institute in New York City announced in March 1909 its intention to establish a censorship board. The People's Institute brought together Christian clergy (the Reverend Walter Laidlaw of the New York Federation of Churches and the Reverend G. W. Knox of the Ethical Social League), local educators (Gustave Straubemiller and Evangeline Whitney, two members of the city's board of education), the leader of a women's group (M. Serena Townsend of the Women's Municipal League), a blue-collar labor leader (Howard Bradstreet of the Neighborhood Workers Association), and nationally recognized artists and authors (the initial group included Mark Twain). Set up more like a think tank or a book club than a bureaucracy for censoring movies, the People's Institute proposed a forum for "discussion" of film content. However promising its board may have been, it never raised the level of public debate, nor did it protect cinema from the pressure of state and local censorship.

The exhibitors themselves did not oppose censorship per se. They were all too practical for that. Instead, they put their faith in the federal judiciary, supporting federal constitutional guidelines. But the producers and distributors of the Motion Picture Patents Company opposed such federal oversight and instead supported a national system of *self*-regulation. To that end in 1909 the MPPC lent its support to the self-regulatory National Board of Censorship. All the members of the MPPC agreed to submit their films to the board, and all agreed to make appropriate cuts in accordance with the board's decisions. Independent film companies were not required to submit their films to the board, but board approval significantly increased the number of theaters willing to screen their films.

In the first few years of its operation, the Censorship Board had a reputation for reasonable administration of content censorship, but it had no real authority. Local law enforcement, at the behest of so-called reformers, routinely seized and/or banned board-approved films because they did not meet local standards. As early as 1914, at a National Exhibitors' Convention held in New York City, local censorship was cited as the biggest problem facing theater owners nationwide. Some cities were strict but consistent; others, like Chicago, were decidedly erratic. Major Metellus Lucullus Cicero Funkhouser of the Chicago Police Department banned films that included dancing but licensed *Henry Spenser's Confession* (1913), which details the life and times of a notorious serial killer.

The mostly reasonable National Board of Censorship was too weak to stem the tide of grassroots reform, so in an attempt to devise a system by which the industry might regulate its own movies, it was revamped and renamed the National Board of Review in 1915. The Board of Review took as its primary objective the maintenance of "quality" production standards. The relevance of quality production standards to actual ("moral" or "Christian") film content was left, for the time being, purposefully vague.

The *Mutual* Case: Movies and the First Amendment

The fledgling industry's various attempts at self-regulation failed to establish national guidelines. As a result, communities across the United States established their own peculiar censorship guidelines and used local law enforcement to ban films, seize prints, and occasionally jail theater owners and managers. The problems posed by local censorship proved so troublesome and so costly to the studios that a legal confrontation between community censors and film producers became inevitable.

That confrontation came in 1915, when *Mutual Film Corporation v. Industrial Commission of Ohio*, the so-called *Mutual* case, made its way to the U.S. Supreme Court. The case involved a conflict between a film production and distribution company, the Mutual Film Corporation, and Ohio's motion-picture censorship board, which by 1915 was routinely prohibiting the screening for profit of movies it found offensive and/or a threat to public safety and welfare. Mutual's attorneys claimed in the suit that the Ohio board's actions unfairly inhibited interstate commerce and violated guarantees of free speech. Moreover, Mutual contended

that the board's standards for censoring and/or prohibiting the screening of films were vague and inconsistent: the prohibition of certain films based on "overbroad criteria" amounted to an unlawful prior restraint of expression and trade.

In a unanimous decision, the Court found in favor of the Industrial Commission of Ohio and in so doing empowered other state boards of censorship nationwide. Writing for the majority, Justice Joseph McKenna concluded that cinema must be treated differently from the press (which enjoys free-speech guarantees) because it panders to a very different audience. Movies, McKenna opined, appeal to and excite prurient interest in its mass audience. He also expressed concern that such a persuasive medium might be "used for evil" and cautioned in general terms against the "insidious power of amusement."

The *Mutual* case required the Court to weigh constitutional protections of free speech against the state and federal government's right and obligation to protect the public from harm. In the end the Court's concern about the effects of cinema as "an unregulated social force" outweighed the First Amendment and the guarantees of free and fair trade sought by the studios. The decision in the *Mutual* case hinged on the Court's view of cinema as an entertainment business "pure and simple" and as an art form secondarily, even incidentally. The justices viewed cinema the way most of the well educated did in the early years: as an entertainment most suited to the hoi polloi, the unruly and uneducated masses. Censorship was thus a matter of protecting us from them—protecting those likely to dismiss cinema as an empty divertissement from those, so the court assumed, all too likely to be influenced by the stories and characters up there on-screen.

MAJOR FILMMAKERS IN EARLY AMERICAN CINEMA

Filmmaking in the first few years of the twentieth century was not a glamorous occupation. Most early American filmmakers worked in obscurity, and many opted for anonymity because filmmaking was not seen as a reputable enterprise. Such anonymity was easy to maintain because the studios did not credit filmmakers on-screen. Instead, they imposed a corporate logo on every print to preserve their copyright and to lay claim, despite varying degrees of creative input, to ownership *and* authorship. But out of that industrial context emerged a handful of filmmakers—Georges Méliès, Edwin S. Porter, D. W. Griffith, Mack Sennett, and Alice Guy—whose work, whose very persistence, gave shape to what historians refer to as early cinema.

Georges Méliès and the French Invasion

The first filmmaker to make a name for himself in America was not American. He was the French magician turned filmmaker Georges Méliès, an aesthetic (as opposed to a technical) innovator who as early as 1901 had dabbled in trick photography and cinematic special effects, all in service of telling or, more accurately, showing an entertaining story. Méliès was a colorful character and a huge influence on this first generation of American filmmakers, especially the early innovator Edwin S. Porter (whose work is discussed below).

Like his countrymen the Lumière brothers, Méliès began his career making actualities. But it was his story films—*Barbe-Bleue* (*Bluebeard*, 1901), *Le voyage dans la lune* (*A Trip to the Moon*, 1902), *La sirène* (*The Mermaid*, 1904), and *Le diable noir* (*The Black Imp*, 1905)—that made him an international star. Of Méliès's considerable output—over five hundred films between 1896 and 1912—the most memorable work is *A Trip to the Moon*. The

film played widely in 1902 and 1903 in the United States, mostly in pirated editions, for which Méliès received no compensation. In some ways *A Trip to the Moon* was like a lot of other films made at the time: it is theatrical in style, the camera is always at a right angle to the action, and the scenery is constructed much as it would be for a stage play. But Méliès ably complicated things visually with the use of scrims that move scenery into and then out of the frame. And to keep the film lively, Méliès included crude special effects, many of which were rooted in his magic act, like a sequence depicting moon men disappearing in a cloud of smoke.

Such camera tricks and special effects became a mainstay of Méliès's cinema: the magical appearance of a mermaid in what we first take to be a household-size fish tank in *The Mermaid*, for example. But the larger relevance of the special effects goes well beyond the gee-whiz attraction of camera and editing tricks. Méliès used optical effects such as the fade-in and fade-out, the dissolve, superimposition (the placement of one image on top of another), and stop-motion photography, along with his bag full of magic stage tricks, as storytelling tools. Thus was born the marriage of visual effects and storytelling technique—a marriage that lives on today with every summer blockbuster.

French films in general enjoyed a great deal of success in the United States in the early years. This "French invasion" was led by Pathé Frères, a company founded by Charles and Émile Pathé. Legend has it that the brothers bought an Edison Kinetograph at a fair in 1894 and began making movies soon thereafter. By 1899 their films were making a splash on the European film circuit. Eyeing the American market, the Pathé brothers opened a New York office in 1904. Between 1906 and 1908, the year the company joined the MPPC, Pathé Frères produced more than a third of the films that played on U.S. screens. Though its influence in the United States waned with the dissolution of the MPPC, Pathé remained an international cineconglomerate into the sound era. Important Pathé films screened in the United States in the early

The bullet-shaped capsule prepared for liftoff in Georges Méliès's *La voyage dans la lune* (*A Trip to the Moon*, 1902). Note the clever game with scale (the capsule looms large above the painted-in rooftops) and the bathing beauties (*top left*) who preside over the launch.

The French film comedian Max Linder, photographed in 1910.

years include *Peeping Tom* (1901), which employs a stencil cutout shaped like a keyhole through which the viewer spies on several hotel residents (including a woman the viewer discovers is a man in drag), and the retelling of the familiar fairy tales *Ali Baba and the Forty Thieves* (Ferdinand Zecca, 1902) and *Aladdin, or the Marvelous Lamp* (1906).

Pathé's biggest star was the French comedian Max Linder, who made over 350 films between 1905 and 1915. His persona—that of a sentimental soul down on his luck, made shabby or just ridiculous by an inability to fit in to an even more ridiculous bourgeois culture—is often cited as an influence on Charlie Chaplin's later, far more famous Little Tramp character. One of Linder's best-known films, *Troubles of a Grasswidower*, which he also directed and was distributed by Pathé Frères in 1908, focuses on a middle-class husband abandoned by his wife, whose endeavor to perform basic household chores, like cooking dinner or washing the dishes, ends in comic disaster.

Pathé Frères also pioneered ensemble slapstick films of the sort that would soon become a staple of silent American film. The 1907 title *The Policemen's Little Run* (Ferdinand Zecca) is composed of a frantic chase of the sort Mack Sennett would later feature in his Keystone Kop series (more on Sennett later in this chapter). *The Policemen's Little Run* begins with a dog stealing a ham. The police, wielding giant nightsticks (which because of their oblong shape and out-of-proportion size are meant to be sexually suggestive), give chase. After the usual pratfalls the police corner their prey. But the dog turns on them and chases them back to their station. The film ends with a shot of the happy dog eating the ham.

Edwin S. Porter

The success of Méliès and Pathé Frères encouraged American filmmakers to make more complete and complex story films. At Edison, Edwin S. Porter, a former telegraph operator and navy electrician who got involved in the film business working as a Vitagraph projector operator, was among the first to meet the challenge. Though his background was not much different from Dickson's and Heise's, Edison's earliest technicians turned filmmakers, Porter was a far more instinctive and natural filmmaker.

Porter's first important film for Edison was *Life of an American Fireman* (1902), a documentary-style account of a particularly interesting and exciting profession. In it Porter cleverly uses editing, an underexplored aspect of the medium at the time, to compress time and establish a creative geography (an understanding of the physical—or geographic—relationship between the various sets and shots), giving the audience a sense of real space within the fictional film world.

Porter had to wait four months to make his next film. Production at Edison was shut down while the inventor and his competitors attempted to sort out what were becoming increasingly complex patent and copyright issues. But after the hiatus,

A daring rescue in Edwin S. Porter's *Life of an American Fireman* (1902).

Porter began work on a follow-up short. His ambitions for the new medium became clear in the spring of 1903 with his adaptation of Harriet Beecher Stowe's best-selling 1852 novel *Uncle Tom's Cabin*. Billed as a "multishot film," *Uncle Tom's Cabin* ran a full 15 minutes, setting a standard for American short features for years to come. A title card (what we now call an intertitle) precedes each scene, and public screenings of the picture featured a scripted commentary read by an actor as the film unspooled. Porter's interest in narrative was obvious.

After *Uncle Tom's Cabin*, Porter went to work on the film for which he is most famous, *The Great Train Robbery* (1903). Inspired by the popular 1896 play of the same title by Scott Marble, *The Great Train Robbery* has long been credited as the first movie western, but a western is not what Porter or Edison had in mind. *The Great Train Robbery* was produced in an attempt to cash in on a trend set by a popular cycle of British-made crime films. But with its train robbery, frequent gunplay, and chase through the woods on horseback, *The Great Train Robbery* has become for filmmakers and filmgoers alike the prototype of the American movie western.

The Great Train Robbery was a monumental filmmaking achievement. It is composed of fourteen distinct (that is, nonoverlapping) and mostly stationary camera shots. Porter cleverly alternated those shots to simulate simultaneous action. In so doing, he took shots that didn't necessarily have much meaning in themselves and gave them meaning in context. For example, a shot of the cowboys dancing is part of a three-shot sequence: shot 1 shows the interior of a telegraph office, where a little girl unties her father, a victim of the robbers' scheme; shot 2 gives us the dancing cowboy lawmen; and shot 3 shows the train robbers on horseback making their getaway. Taken together, the three shots introduce a dramatic narrative of rescue and retribution. Also evident in this sequence is a creative geography in which a geographic relationship is established among the office, the lawmen's station house, and the woods.

The film's final shot, in which a cowboy (Broncho Billy Anderson) faces the camera and fires his gun at the audience, is perhaps the film's most famous. Legend has it that Porter came to regard this parting gesture as a mistake, not because of its violence or shock value but because it suggests awareness on the part of the actor that he is in a movie that is being watched by an audience. Porter finally decided not to cut the shot out of the film, but exhibitors occasionally toyed with its placement: sometimes it was screened at the start of the film; in other venues it was screened at the end (as in Porter's original version) or at both the start and the end. (In the era of early cinema, exhibitors often took such liberties with the films they contracted to screen.)

The release of *The Great Train Robbery*, a film at once nostalgic (for the Old West) and ever so modern and contemporary (in its clever use of film style), came at a particularly auspicious time in American technological and scientific history. Audiences were inclined to appreciate the picture as not only a piece of entertainment but also as yet another example of the sudden and swift modernization of America in the still-young century. The year *The Great Train Robbery* reached American movie screens, 1903, was also the year the Wright brothers took their first airplane aloft and Henry Ford introduced his automobile to consumers. Two years later Albert Einstein would publish a paper on the theory of relativity. It was a time of wonder, a time in which a cinematic attraction might also be seen as a technological wonder.

Porter's subsequent films for Edison were less earthshaking but nonetheless set in motion important trends in early narrative moviemaking. His 1904 film *Buster Brown and His Dog Tige* adapted a popular newspaper comic strip, a formula for many early (and modern) film series. *The Ex-Convict*, also released in 1904, took into account the popularity of nineteenth-century stage melodrama. Porter's 1906 film *Dream of a Rarebit Fiend*—a trick or gag film featuring crude model animation based on a popular Winsor McCay comic strip—was also a big hit. The *"Teddy" Bears*, released the following year, similarly mixed live action with animated special effects.

The decline in the Edison Manufacturing Company's output after 1905 was due in no small measure to Porter, who as the executive in charge of production at the studio micromanaged every aspect of the operation. But the films Porter directed consistently turned a profit, and as we look back at those early years, it is Porter's work at Edison that remains the most interesting.

Broncho Billy Anderson in the famous final shot of Edwin S. Porter's *The Great Train Robbery* (1903).

D. W. Griffith

In an interesting twist of fate, it was Porter, early cinema's first widely known filmmaker, who gave D. W. Griffith, whom many historians credit as the most important director of the silent era, his first break in the film business. D. W. (David Wark) Griffith applied for a writing job at Edison in 1908 after halfhearted attempts at working on a farm and selling encyclopedias door-to-door. He proposed an adaptation of Victorien Sardou's *La Tosca*, a play that had been made into an opera by Giacomo Puccini in 1900. Porter dismissed the idea as too complex and too highbrow. At the time, Porter was working on *Rescued from an Eagle's Nest* (Porter and J. Searle Dawley, 1908), and he needed someone to play the heroic woodcutter who rescues a baby that has been kidnapped by a giant eagle. He asked Griffith to play the part, and Griffith did what he could with the role; the film ends with a magnificently implausible scene of the woodcutter wrestling the big bird to its death and recovering the helpless child. The performance is lackluster—riddled with clichéd gestures. Acting was not Griffith's calling. His future lay behind the camera.

Griffith got his first chance to direct at Biograph in 1908. His first one-reeler, *The Adventures of Dollie*, tells the story of a child who is kidnapped by

A last-minute rescue in D. W. Griffith's *The Girl and Her Trust* (1912).

Gypsies and saved improbably at the end from certain death as the basket she is in plunges down a rapids. Evident from the start is Griffith's ability to navigate the last-minute rescue and render this genre convention in peculiarly cinematic terms. Griffith used crosscutting (also called intercutting, the alternating of shots in more than one locale) not only to compress time and express a creative geography (as Porter did) but also to cut seamlessly from locale to locale. Crosscutting gave Griffith a filmic equivalent of simultaneous action, the literary gesture of "meanwhile . . ."

Alas, also in evidence in this early film is Griffith's narrow-mindedness, his distrust and dislike of immigrants and racial others, here epitomized by the Gypsies. Born in rural Kentucky in 1875, the son of the Confederate army colonel and Civil War hero Jacob "Roaring Jake" Griffith, D.W. would never outlive or outgrow the worldview that his father and so many other rural southerners held at the time.

The Adventures of Dollie impressed Griffith's employers at Biograph, and on its release he was put under contract at $45 per week. At the time, directors did not receive on-screen credit for their work. In fact, all the early Biograph shorts helmed by Griffith bore on their initial release a simple corporate logo (AB, for American Biograph), with no mention at all of the director. Working in anonymity irked Griffith. And he bristled at producing films for the nickelodeon trade, filling the demand for more and more, as opposed to better and better, pictures. When Griffith left Biograph for Mutual Reliance-Majestic, he publicly took credit for the hundreds of films he had made between 1908 and 1913. Griffith's former employers at Biograph made no effort to dispute his claims; in so doing, they helped make Griffith the first auteur celebrity, the first star director.

Several of Griffith's Biograph one-reelers are worth a close look today because they showcase Griffith's rapidly evolving mastery of film technique. For example, his 1908 short *After Many Years* uses intercutting not to propel an action sequence but to tell two connected stories at once. *The Lonely Villa*, made in 1909, matches three simultaneous actions intercut strategically at the end of the film. First we see a band of robbers attempting to break into "the lonely villa." Then we see a frightened mother and her children huddled in the villa, desperately trying to keep the intruders out. And finally we see the father hurrying home from his job in town. Griffith executes the last-minute rescue sequence by progressively shortening the length of each shot, emphasizing the notion that time is running out.

The Girl and Her Trust (1912) features a last-minute rescue punctuated not only by intercut scenes of an exciting race against time but also by the clever use of a moving camera. Griffith and the cameraman with whom he worked most of his career, G. W. (Billy) Bitzer, mounted a camera on a moving locomotive (Bitzer had done something similar in the 1903 film *The Georgetown Loop*). This early moving-camera gesture brought something new to the stock chase sequence at the end of Griffith's film.

Between 1908, when he directed *The Adventures of Dollie*, and 1915, when his feature, *The Birth of a Nation*, took the country by storm, Griffith shot almost five hundred short films, a staggering output and, at over sixty films per year, a staggering rate. In the process of developing a signature style, one as much dependent on technical innovation as on a certain characteristic treatment of plot and character, Griffith engaged in a variety of early-cinema genres. He produced morality plays like *A Drunkard's Reformation* and

From left to right: Lillian Gish, Elmer Booth, and Harry Carey in D. W. Griffith's seminal crime film *The Musketeers of Pig Alley* (1912).

What Drink Did (both 1909); Victorian melodramas, many capped by exciting last-minute rescues, like *The Lonely Villa, The Lonedale Operator* (1911), and *The Girl and Her Trust*; westerns like *In Old California* (1910) and *The Goddess of Sagebrush Gulch* (1912); and a seminal crime film, *The Musketeers of Pig Alley* (1912).

Film historians routinely credit Griffith with inventing a range of technical innovations: crosscutting, for example, and the close-up. It is unlikely that the director invented those techniques, but he was the first filmmaker to establish a working film grammar composed of such techniques; he was the first filmmaker to speak in a language that was purely and simply cinematic. Indeed today what seems most remarkable about Griffith's work is the technique: the alternation of spatial lengths (cutting back and forth among full shots, medium close-ups, and close-ups in key sequences), the systematic use of point-of-view (or subjective camera) shots, the clever use of shot–reverse shot sequences (first showing that a character sees something and then, by reversing the angle, showing what he or she sees), so-called Rembrandt lighting, or chiaroscuro (revealing fields of light and shade in a frame, which was unusual in an era when cinema lighting was mostly uniform), and an effort, despite the limitations of the equipment, to compose shots in depth (in which the action is evident in both the foreground and the background of a single camera setup).

With hundreds of short genre films to his credit, Griffith in 1912 expressed his impatience with the constraints of the one-reel format favored by the MPPC (of which Biograph was a key member) and prevailed on executives at Biograph to make the

Judith (Blanche Sweet) charms Holofernes (Henry B. Walthall) in D. W. Griffith's early multireel film *Judith of Bethulia* (1914).

jump to two-reelers. The most noteworthy of the early Griffith two-reelers is the film spectacle *The Massacre* (1913), a western chronicling an Indian raid on a wagon train. *The Massacre* features expertly staged skirmishes as long shots (of the prairie landscape) alternate with close-ups of the characters involved in the struggle. But to Griffith's profound disappointment, *The Massacre* had little affect on a box office dominated by even bigger film spectacles imported from Europe, including Enrico Guazzoni's *Quo Vadis?* (1912), an Italian film that took the American box office by storm in 1913. Although there is little in it that formally approaches the sort of sophistication Griffith routinely brought to the screen in his one-reel shorts, *Quo Vadis?* introduced a scale and scope that could not be ignored.

Acknowledging the challenge from abroad, Biograph gave Griffith permission to shoot a multireel film, *Judith of Bethulia* (1914). The film adapts the apocryphal story in which the Israelite Judith feigns love for Holofernes, the leading general of the Assyrians, in order to assassinate him and foment a revolt among the Jews. (Griffith complicates the story having Judith [Blanche Sweet] fall

in love with Holofernes [Henry B. Walthall]. Sex without love was out of the question for Griffith, even as a matter of sacrifice.) In the end, Judith kills Holofernes, but she is hardly freed by the act. The film is memorable less for the characters' strange and doomed "romance" than for the grandly staged battles, complete with terrific chariot-fight sequences—a staple of future sword-and-sandal pictures, from *Ben Hur* (William Wyler, 1959) to *Gladiator* (Ridley Scott, 2000). However high-minded Griffith's intentions were in placing the morality play at the heart of the story, audiences exiting the theater were most likely talking about the action sequences.

Griffith's dream of making feature films was realized just as the nasty battle between the MPPC and the independents reached its climax. The moneyed eastern corporations that founded the MPPC viewed their audiences with scorn, believing that film audiences in large measure comprised an uneducated urban immigrant mob that would never be able to sit through feature-length pictures. The independents, much more confident in the filmgoing public's attention span and intelligence, put their money behind feature films. The eventual victory of the independents over the MPPC proved to be good news for ambitious filmmakers like Griffith. After 1914 the feature film would become the American standard.

Mack Sennett and Early Film Comedy

The first American moving picture to receive a U.S. copyright, *Edison Kinetoscopic Record of a Sneeze* (or *Fred Ott's Sneeze,* 1894), was a comedy. Though it is ostensibly a document of a real event and thus consistent with most of Edison's early output, Ott clearly winds up for his sneeze and milks the event for all it is worth, finishing off with a bemused smirk on his face. Among the Lumière brothers' early films, too, was a comedy, *L'arroseur arrosée* (*The Waterer Watered*, 1895), screened as part of their first showcases.

Biograph made a series of 30-second comedies in 1902, including *The Schoolmaster's Surprise*, in which two boys pour flour into a kerosene lantern; the schoolmaster ignites the lantern and gets a face full of flour. Also in 1902, Biograph released *She Meets with Wife's Approval*, an early narrative comedy in which a man's wife visits his office to eye his new secretary. To her delight she finds an ugly woman sitting at the front desk. The wife exits, and the secretary removes her mask. She is beautiful, of course, and in the wife's absence kisses her boss.

Biograph comedies often featured recurring characters—for example, Foxy Grandpa (played by Joseph Hart) in films such as *Foxy Grandpa Tells the Boys a Funny Story* and *Foxy Grandpa Shows the Boys a Trick or Two with the Tramp* (both 1902) and Mr. and Mrs. Jones (played by John R. Cumpson and Florence Lawrence) in such films as *Mr. Jones at the Ball* (1908) and *Mr. Jones Has a Card Party* (1909). Such character-based comedies soon became a staple of early cinema. John Bunny, a vaudeville star who abandoned the variety circuit to make movies for Vitagraph, is a typical example. Between 1910 and 1915, Bunny made over 150 films, all of which exploit his familiar comic persona of a happy fat man whose overindulgence (in food, drink, women, and gambling) leads inevitably to comic disaster.

What Bunny understood was that audiences could not help but root for a character who so cheerfully broke the rules. Though largely simple and crude—gags were repeated in film after film, with characters falling on a banana peel, walking into a door, performing a hazardous "drunk walk" into stationary objects, flirting with disaster at the precipice of a cliff or on a high window ledge— early film comedy deftly lampooned the social and political realities of the time in very pointed ways, offering a commentary on societal hypocrisy while delivering laughs.

The single most important figure in early film comedy was Mack Sennett, American cinema's first important film producer (in any genre) and the medium's first great showman. Legend has it that Sennett's showbiz career began with a vaudeville stint playing the back end of a horse. After a series of similarly insignificant parts, Sennett made the transition from the stage to the screen in 1908, when he took a job as a comedy actor at Biograph. By all accounts he was a lousy hammy actor, and in 1909 he turned to gag writing and in 1910 began directing comedies under Griffith's supervision. Within a year, Sennett was responsible for the majority of Biograph's comedy slate. In 1912, with financing from two New York bookies, he founded Keystone, where he produced over three hundred short film comedies.

All the Keystone comedies were rooted in the crude knockabout world of American burlesque, a

The silent-film comedian John Bunny captured live on the vaudeville stage c. 1915.

A key to Mack Sennett's formula for popular filmmaking was the bathing beauties he routinely featured in his knockabout comedies.

world that Sennett had loved long before he made his first movie. Sennett famously observed that all comedy gags fall into one of two categories: the fall from dignity and the mistaken identity. In both cases the joke is on the player. Scenarios involving city slickers in the country, country bumpkins in the city, and innocent women in distress abound in Sennett's Keystone films. The narrative frame—the simplistic parody of the Victorian melodrama—lampooned the staple of Biograph, Sennett's first employer in the business. But story lines for Sennett were merely a means toward an end, a reason to set bodies and machines in motion.

As the studio chief at Keystone, Sennett "discovered" Charlie Chaplin, Mabel Normand, Fatty Arbuckle, Ben Turpin, Harry Langdon, and Billy Bevan, some of the silent era's biggest comedy stars. The dramatic movie stars Gloria Swanson and Wallace Beery and the sound-era director Frank Capra also got their start working for Sennett. But prodigious as Sennett's gift for discovering talent was, it was largely wasted on him, since his formula for film comedy depended less on character than on caricature, less on individual comedic stars than on his stock ensemble.

Sennett is best remembered today as the producer of the Keystone Kop series, films featuring some insignificant fracas or crime made crazy, silly, or even dangerous by the arrival of clumsy, harebrained policemen lamely attempting to save the day. The Keystone ensemble included a wealth of comic players: the sinister-looking Ford Sterling; the gruff, bald, comic fatty Mack Swain; Chester Conklin, with his huge handlebar mustache and wild eyes; Slim Summerville, an elastic beanpole; and the dour, tight-lipped Phyllis Allen. Those actors were inserted more or less into the same basic roles in film after film. Even Chaplin, Arbuckle, and Normand—Keystone's biggest stars—were typecast and never spared in the comic mayhem.

All told, Sennett produced almost five hundred films between 1911 and 1935. Some of them are more memorable than others, perhaps, but they all share a basic structure and a fundamentally antisocial vision of the emerging modern world. A short list of key Sennett titles includes *The Water Nymph* (1912), introducing Mabel Normand as one of the first in a long line of Sennett bathing

Comic mayhem in a c. 1920 Mack Sennett comedy short.

beauties; the early cop stunt film *The Bangville Police* (Sennett and Henry Lehrman, 1913); the chase film *Barney Oldfield's Race for a Life* (1913); *The Knockout* (Sennett and Charles Avery, 1914), with Arbuckle as a clumsy boxer and Chaplin as a numskull referee; *Tillie's Punctured Romance* (also 1914), which is the first feature-length comedy starring Chaplin, who plays a man with eyes for another woman, and also stars Normand as that other woman and Marie Dressler—who had introduced Sennett to Griffith and gotten the producer into the movie business—as the grotesque woman scorned; *Mabel's Busy Day* (Sennett and Normand, 1914), which features an outrageous sexually suggestive hot-dog gag; *Kid Auto Races at Venice* (Sennett and Lehrman, 1914), a short in which Chaplin appears for the first time as the Little Tramp; the *Mabel and Fatty* series, starring Arbuckle, the screen's best-loved comic fatty at the time, and Normand, who plays his slight and pretty—and incomprehensibly willing—lover; *The Danger Girl* (Sennett and Clarence C. Badgers, 1916), with Gloria Swanson; and *Lizzies of the Field* (Sennett and Del Lord, 1924), which stars Billy Bevan, who comically tries to master the Tin Lizzie, a contemporary automobile.

Appreciating Sennett's films today is something of a challenge. Though they constitute the foundation of silent film comedy, they are crude and sloppy, so clearly improvised as to seem arbitrary and amateur and not nearly so funny as we can assume they must have been in their day. They are, alas, very much of their time and place but nonetheless crucial in the evolution of motion-picture comedy.

Women and Early Cinema

Women played a significant role in early Hollywood, and not just on-screen, an accomplishment that is all the more remarkable given how few women found success in the larger workplace in the early decades of the twentieth century and how few women wield power in Hollywood today. The logical place to start as we recount the role of women in early Hollywood is with Alice Guy (known as Alice Guy Blaché after her marriage to Herbert Blaché, the manager of the Gaumont film studio). Guy immigrated to the United States after directing over 180 short films in France. After directing a series of socially conscious, politically progressive films, Guy became the chief executive officer of the independent outfit Solax and American cinema's first female film executive.

It is hard to recount Guy's American career because so little of her output—fifty-six films as

Hapless immigrants arrive as yet untutored in the American way of life in Alice Guy's *The Making of an American Citizen* (1912).

a director and seventeen as a producer and studio executive between 1910 and 1920—survives today. Her melodrama *The Making of an American Citizen* (1912), one of the few of her films still available, is the film for which she is now best known. It focuses on a Russian immigrant couple. The man is dissolute and unemployed; the wife, the unlucky victim of his frustration and rage. Early in the film we see the couple's arrival in New York, the Statue of Liberty in the background. The wife totes the family's luggage until a local resident persuades the husband to carry the load for her, implying that that's the way things are done in America. Frustrated in the new environment, the husband abuses his wife. The violence escalates, and he is brought to justice. A judge sentences him to six months on a chain gang, during which he repents and is Americanized. On returning home, he embraces his wife, and we see that his attitude has changed completely; even the acting of Lee Beggs, who plays the husband, is more restrained at this point in the film. The husband finds work on a farm, and his daily employment is complemented by his wife's happy performance of household chores: cooking, cleaning, and so on.

To an extent, *The Making of an American Citizen* is a feminist film: it deals frankly with domestic violence, and the perpetrator of that violence is punished for his behavior. But the implicit message is a contrast between the Old World and America: beating one's wife is the sort of behavior that the Old World failed to punish, whereas American men (who constitute the jury that convicts the husband) reject it as barbaric, foreign, and unseemly. The film is thus primarily a story about the socialization of an immigrant in American mores. American mores, Guy's film suggests, involve the fair and gentle treatment of one's spouse, just as they establish domestic roles (husband at work, wife at home), roles that ironically were not embraced by the director–film executive herself.

Guy blazed a trail that was followed by a number of women in early Hollywood. For example, by 1916 Universal had under contract seven female directors: Ruth Ann Baldwin, Grace Cunard, Cleo Madison, Ida May Park, Ruth Stonehouse, Lois Weber, and Elsie Jane Wilson. In retrospect, Weber seems the most important. She is credited as the

Margaret McWade in Lois Weber's *The Blot* (Phillips Smalley and Weber, 1921). Weber was one of a number of successful female directors in the silent era.

director of well over one hundred films, beginning with *A Heroine of '76* in 1911. Her 1914 adaptation of William Shakespeare's *Merchant of Venice* is generally cited as the first American feature-length film directed by a woman.

Women also made significant contributions as screenwriters. The successful actress Gene Gauntier, for example, had more than forty writing credits, beginning with *Why Girls Leave Home* in 1907. Gauntier was primarily a writer of melodramas: her later films have titles like *The Slave to Drink* (1909) and *The Romance of a Trained Nurse* (Sidney Olcott, 1910). The early studios routinely regarded melodrama as a genre that women favored. And the executives at Kalem, Gauntier's studio, no doubt believed that a woman might better speak to those films' predominantly female audiences. Gauntier's brief career (she stopped

writing films before the feature boom began in 1914) also included adaptations of respected literary works: *Tom Sawyer* in 1907 and in 1908 *Evangeline, The Scarlet Letter, Hiawatha,* and *As You Like It* (Kenean Buel). Yet the prestige niche into which Gauntier's work fell also evinced a form of gender bias. Indeed, such prestige films were often assigned to female writers: literary material was seen as women's work; executives believed that the more rugged stuff—westerns, crime films, and the like—was better suited to male writers and directors.

In 1914 Pathé Eclectic introduced two film serials featuring a female hero: *The Perils of Pauline* (Louis J. Gasnier and Donald MacKenzie), starring Pearl White as the heroine Pauline Marvin, and *The Exploits of Elaine* (Gasnier and George B. Seitz), also starring White, again in the title role. In both serials the heroine lives a life of adventure and excitement. And though today's audiences might be put off by the degree to which and the frequency with which the title characters appear to be under duress and threat—each episode ends with a cliffhanger, a seemingly impossible predicament— the point of these serials was that their characters were action heroes: smart, pretty, and capable.

Many early films recount with alternating doses of pride and alarm women's pursuit of the right to vote and the struggle for social and professional equality and freedom. *Daisies* (1910), for example, tells the story of a young woman who forgoes marriage in order to pursue a college degree. In the end she gets her degree (from Vassar, where much of the movie was shot), and her boyfriend learns that having a smart, pretty, and capable wife might not be all that bad.

The flip side of the progressive women's films was a body of work that betrays a discomfort with the increasing visibility of women in public places. Foremost among these pictures were the so-called vamp films that became popular after the box-office success of the 1910 Selig title *The Vampire* (based on a poem by Rudyard Kipling). In this genre, vamps are women who suck the soul out of their men, and they do so with a kind of delight. But vile and dangerous as the vamps may have been, they were also prototypical new women: they were socially and sexually progressive in ways that were characteristic of far less threatening and far less dangerous women of the time. Vamps smoked in public, wore suggestive clothing, promised sex outside marriage with no strings attached. Of course the men who got involved with these women suffered dire consequences: they were rou-

Pearl White and Crane Wilbur in *The Perils of Pauline* (Donald McKenzie, 1914).

tinely left dissolute and penniless, mere shells of their former selves.

Also of considerable interest to early film audiences was the white-slave film, the most famous of which was *Traffic in Souls* (George Loane Tucker, 1913). Despite, or perhaps because of, the film's quasi-documentary take on the topic, the sad lives of the women forced into prostitution became a subject of prurient fascination in a number of early films: *The Inside of the White Slave Traffic* (Frank Beal, 1913), *Trapped in the Great Metropolis* (1914), *It May Be Your Daughter* (George M. Merrick, 1916), and *Is Any Girl Safe?* (Jacques Jaccard, 1916). Virtue was held in the balance in such films, and women's claims to

social emancipation seemed downright foolhardy given the seamier side of turn-of-the-century American urban culture.

Though the "new woman" was a subject of fascination and the industry was initially willing to sign contracts with women who would perform a range of tasks in the movie business, a residual paternalism persisted. The new woman in America, in American films, and in Hollywood posed a problem to be solved. In the increasingly liberal social climate of the early twentieth century, many women made significant inroads into the movie industry, but on-screen such women became a symbol of decadence and temptation, a serious threat to a society struggling with its Puritan roots.

■　■　■

In less than twenty years moving pictures were transformed from a technological curiosity to a viable commercial art form. En route the innovators of cinema (Edison and his cohorts in the MPPC) gave way to the erstwhile independents, the future studio moguls who would invent Hollywood.

Films at the beginning of the twentieth century were simple projects involving just a single load of the camera, a single placement of the camera. But things changed quickly. By 1902 story films composed of multiple camera setups were in vogue. By 1908 a star system was under way, and filmmakers like D. W. Griffith had developed a language (composed of camerawork, lighting, and set design) unique to the medium. By 1911 a Hollywood studio system was taking shape, and a modern era of American filmmaking was poised to begin.

The hectic pace of the early years testified to three important aspects of the new medium. First was the coincidence of moviemaking and the nation's

embrace of industrial progress. Cinema was the art form of the age of invention, the product of a national priority on technological change. Second was the medium's undeniably seductive force. From the start, films were made to meet audience demand. And no one in those early days could have imagined how great that demand would become and how fast it would grow. Third were the medium's commercial value and its apparently sunny fiscal future. For those with the capital to invest in making, distributing, and exhibiting motion pictures, there was lots of money to be made in return. What came to be known as Hollywood dates to this era, and its early success barely hinted at far better times to come.

By 1914 the industry and the American moviegoer were ready to make the transition to features, films that ran for 90 minutes or more and were composed of hundreds of shots. As World War I approached, cinema was a worldwide sensation and Hollywood the planet's cinematic capital.

The Silent Era

1915–1928

The movies came of age in the United States just as the country entered an era of conspicuous consumption: the so-called Jazz Age, or the Roaring Twenties. This modern age saw America in ascent, rebounding from World War I, when the mobilization of troops and industry for the war effort and daily worries about the combat overseas had dominated the American political, economic, and cultural scene. Following its decisive participation in the war, the United States at the end of the second decade of the twentieth century was poised to take full advantage of its newfound global influence.

In concert with the dramatic postwar economic boom, the stock market soared, fueling public confidence in the American dream of prosperity and opportunity. But all was not so simple or so easy on the home front. Indeed, from the end of the war, in 1918, to the crash of the stock market, in 1929, the United States struggled with dramatic social change, its citizens torn between modernization and increased social freedom on the one hand and a grassroots conservatism on the other. This was the era of labor unionism and labor reform and women's suffrage (the Constitution finally guaranteed women the right to vote in 1920). But at the same time this was an era of increased social regulation: Prohibition, a nationwide ban on the manufacture and sale of alcoholic beverages, went into effect in 1920, and the National Origins Act of 1924 severely limited the number of immigrants entering the United States from southern and eastern Europe and prohibited new immigration from Asia.

For the many immigrants who struggled in America's cities at the time, cinema continued to be the most inclusive, the most relevant, and the most inspiring medium available to them. Cinema comprised images

Roscoe "Fatty" Arbuckle and Mabel Normand in *He Did and He Didn't* (Arbuckle, 1916).

that could be understood independent of one's native tongue, and the gestures of the actors on-screen were universally recognizable, no matter where one was from or what language one spoke. In 1920 over three quarters of the residents of New York City, the capital of film exhibition at the time, were either immigrants or the children of immigrants. In Chicago, the second biggest market, 70 percent of audience members were likewise immigrants or children of immigrants.

Stardom became fundamental to the art and business of American movies as stars came to epitomize the new American ideal of beauty, wealth, and conspicuous consumption. Many of the principal players in the rags-to-riches scenarios presented on-screen—Rudolph Valentino and Theda Bara, for example—were themselves immigrants or the children of immigrants. Others—Douglas Fairbanks, Wallace Reid, Tom Mix, and Mary Pickford—represented an all-American ideal to which immigrants might aspire.

At the same time the celebration of movie stars by the national press and the emulation of them by filmgoers became a source of anxiety among conservatives who worried about a loosening of traditional standards and values. The public's struggle with stardom came to characterize a larger, more philosophical struggle with success in general. Could too much prosperity—too much fun—be a problem? The answer to that question came soon enough, as a series of scandals in the early 1920s, involving suicide, rape, murder, drug addiction, and homosexuality, rocked the Hollywood colony. Bowing to public pressure from conservative "reformers" who had predicted all along that the social abandon of the period had come at a price, the studios reined in their stars, and a new era of self-regulation was born. In the wake of the star scandals, the studios formed the Motion Picture Producers and Distributors of America (MPPDA) and hired a former postmaster general, Will Hays, to run the organization. Through the MPPDA the studios set out to accomplish two things: modernize the industry (mostly by controlling the labor force, especially its highest-profile laborers: its movie stars) and establish good public relations by monitoring the content of American movies.

With self-regulation came significantly greater control over the production, distribution, and exhibition of American cinema by studio management. For the men behind the new studio system, the Hollywood moguls, a second rags-to-riches story applied. Carl Laemmle, William Fox, Adolph Zukor, Marcus Loew, and the Warner brothers (Sam, Harry, Jack, and Albert) were eastern European Jewish immigrants who first found success in the exhibition business. They ventured west as part of a larger strategy to challenge the Motion Picture Patents Company trust. But once they gained the upper hand, around 1915, their Hollywood studios—Universal, 20th Century–Fox, Paramount, MGM, and Warner Bros., respectively—quickly evolved into monopolies in their own right. By the early 1920s, with the adoption of the MPPDA, the studios operated much as the MPPC had ten years earlier—as an industry cartel that limited competition and standardized policies, procedures, and product lines.

As we look back on those years, it is important to remember that none of the studio moguls were artists; none were filmmakers. They were instead hard-nosed businessmen with unbridled confidence in the commercial value of the product their companies produced and a keen understanding of the audience they served. The moguls ran their studios by the seat of their pants, sensing that the marketplace comprised lots of folks much like them, or at least much like they had been before their success in the motion-picture business. Self-regulation gave the moguls only more power and more control, making the emergence of a first wave of film artists all the more remarkable.

Hugely influential in this era were the directors D. W. Griffith, Cecil B. DeMille, Erich von Stroheim, and F. W. Murnau, the producer Thomas Ince, and the film-comedy pioneers Charlie Chaplin, Buster Keaton, and Harold Lloyd, all of whom produced work that achieved greatness despite the restrictive system in which they operated. Their films, more than any others, have come to characterize the era, perhaps because they transcended the social contradictions of the age or perhaps because they laid bare those contradictions in ways the American moviegoing audience could understand and appreciate.

A STUDIO INDUSTRY IS BORN

In March 1915, Carl Laemmle moved his company's production facilities to Universal City, a massive studio complex built on a 230-acre ranch in the San Fernando Valley, just north of Hollywood. The studio sported the largest shooting stage in the world (65 feet by 300 feet) and another almost as big (50 feet by 200 feet), several open-air stages with various exterior sets (city streets, a country lane, and so on), a huge back lot for location work, a film-processing lab, prop rooms, editing suites, and even a zoo. If there is a moment in film history that can be said to have begun the Hollywood studio era, this moment in the early spring of 1915 is it.

Like virtually all of the West Coast studios, Universal maintained business offices in New York. Managing a bicoastal company in those days—before commercial air travel was established—was a much more difficult task than it is today. In response to the difficulties, Laemmle decided in 1918 to delegate his authority over the day-to-day operation of the West Coast studio to Irving Thalberg, his nineteen-year-old former secretary. Although impossibly young, Thalberg seemed to have an instinctive understanding of the movie business. He whipped the unruly mess that was Universal City into shape, taking control from

An artist's rendering of Universal City in the 1920s.

Maurice Fleckles and Isidore Bernstein, relatives Laemmle had first put in charge on the West Coast.

Unfortunately, Laemmle's daring decision to promote Thalberg wasn't matched by daring decision making about the sort of films Universal would make. Thalberg brought order to Universal, but the studio lacked a vision to match his managerial skills. He urged Laemmle to take advantage of both the market for A features and the impressive new facilities he had built, but Laemmle remained wedded to the idea of a balanced program. Frustrated by his boss's refusal to profit from the new studio facility and the burgeoning new feature-film marketplace, Thalberg left Universal in 1923 to work for Louis B. Mayer, a move that proved fortunate, for Metro-Goldwyn-Mayer (MGM) would be formed less than a year later (discussed below), and Thalberg would become the key executive responsible for that studio's rise.

Thalberg's exit from Universal was the first in what would become a long line of departures from that studio. It soon became a place where stars were born and from which they then moved on: the actors Rudolph Valentino, Lon Chaney, and Mae Murray and the directors John Ford and Rex Ingram all left Universal to make bigger films elsewhere. Laemmle was a visionary in the struggle with the MPPC but proved to be an uninspired studio mogul, an especially surprising story given the facility he built and the town—Hollywood—he helped put on the map.

Carl Laemmle (*center*) leads the opening-day parade at Universal City, March 1915.

Irving Thalberg, the "boy wonder" behind MGM's success, photographed in 1936.

While Universal clung to the old programming model, the other studios moved headlong into the A-feature market. Fox, for example, which made only four features in 1914, produced seventy-three in 1918. Fox also expanded its holdings in the exhibition business. By the end of the 1920s, Fox owned over five hundred movie houses, many of which were so-called showcase theaters, urban movie palaces at which the studios routinely opened their films. Fox's expansion set the tone for several of the other new studios: from about 1917 to 1923, Paramount, First National, and Loew's all expanded their theater businesses. Universal, the one-time leader in the move west, lagged behind here as well. It was not until the mid-1920s that Universal would have its own chain of theaters.

Another key player in the early years was the showcase-theater entrepreneur Marcus Loew, who integrated his holdings in the film business in the early 1920s to form the first modern studio trust. In 1920, Loew purchased Metro Pictures, a film exchange (a company that brokered licensed film rentals), which, combined with his East Coast theater chain (Loew's Theatrical Enterprises), established significant positions for the future studio in both the distribution and the exhibition aspects of the business. In 1924, Loew expanded further by purchasing first Samuel Goldwyn's production facility in Culver City and then Louis B. Mayer Pictures, thus forming a new production-distribution-exhibition studio, which he named Metro-Goldwyn-Mayer, or MGM. Loew delegated authority over the studio to three men: Nicholas Schenck, his right-hand man; Louis B. Mayer, a tough-talking, street-smart former junk dealer and nickelodeon owner; and Irving Thalberg, Universal's former "boy wonder." MGM became the silent era's great success story, in no small part because of Loew's appreciation for the value of first-run exhibition and vertical corporate integration.

The studio system that evolved during the silent era was built on standardized and professionalized policies and procedures, mainly because the Wall Street investors upon whom the studios increasingly depended were more impressed by bottom-line profits than by the glamour and glitz of the emerging movie colony. Also important was the establishment of a system by which the studios might better control the growing industry workforce. Feature moviemaking was, and is, a labor-intensive undertaking, and the studio system, built on exclusive contracts (with movie stars and movie directors, as well as carpenters, scene painters, and hairdressers), was the best way to keep costs down and profits up.

Movie Stars: Mary Pickford, Theda Bara, and Rudolph Valentino

Laemmle's famous quip about movie stars' being "the fundamental thing" in the industry remained a core studio concept throughout the silent era. Indeed, the studios soon came to value stars not only as a marketing attraction but also as the public face of the industry. Studio moguls at the time were hardly the sort of guys middle America much cared for, so Hollywood's public image as a place where the likes of Mary Pickford, Theda Bara, and Rudolph Valentino lived and loved went a long way toward making the entire industry a site of American aspiration and fantasy.

Mary Pickford became the fledgling industry's second female movie star—a bigger and, by most

Mary Pickford c. 1915.

Theda Bara, silent cinema's notorious vamp.

accounts, happier star than her predecessor, Florence Lawrence. Pickford's rise to fame was a rags-to-riches story, much like the story line of her movies: she was initially noticed because of her youthful good looks, but she succeeded where other pretty girls failed because she had what was called gumption or pluck. By the time she turned twenty, Pickford had made over 175 films. She was twenty-five (but looked much younger) when she appeared in two of her best-known features, *The Poor Little Rich Girl* (Maurice Tourneur, 1917) and *Rebecca of Sunnybrook Farm* (Marshall Neilan, 1917), and twenty-six when she appeared in one of the era's signature melodramas, *Stella Maris* (Neilan, 1918). Pickford continued to be cast as a girl even as she approached thirty. Once such casting became unsustainable, her star status quickly faded.

Pickford is important in the history of stardom because she was so successful in parlaying her celebrity into power in the industry. She began her career in 1908 as a bit player earning $5 a week, eventually landing at Biograph, where she worked with Griffith. Her salary increased along with her popularity. In 1913 her films headlined Adolph

Zukor's Famous Players production company, and her salary soared to $2,000 a week. Zukor gave Pickford, by then earning $10,000 per film, her own label, the special distribution unit Artcraft, so that she could better maintain the quality of her productions. Artcraft came with a guarantee of marketability (based on Pickford's popularity) and a guarantee of a certain quality of production: only the most talented filmmakers at Famous Players—the directors Maurice Tourneur, Marshall Neilan, and Cecil B. DeMille and the writer Frances Marion—were used in Artcraft's films.

In 1919, Pickford took the next logical step. In partnership with her husband-to-be and fellow movie star, Douglas Fairbanks, the comedy actor and director Charlie Chaplin, and the director D. W. Griffith, Pickford founded United Artists, a company that initially promised to give these elite creative moviemakers control over the development, production, and marketing of their own motion pictures. It was a good idea, but the company failed to fulfill its promise. By 1925 the four principals had turned the day-to-day operation of the studio over to a savvy Hollywood player, Joseph Schenck, who helped fashion United Artists into a modern distribution (as opposed to production) company. Much later, in 1951, Pickford and Chaplin sold their shares in the company to the businessmen Arthur Krim and Robert Benjamin, who retained the name but not the spirit of the artists' studio project.

Pickford's popularity made clear that the studios should be in the business of making stars as well as movies. Her name above the title of a film guaranteed audience interest and financial success. In the hunt for a hedge against the vagaries of the film marketplace and the caprice of the American filmgoer, the studios searched desperately for stars. Because demand soon outstripped supply, the studios quickly adopted a more aggressive strategy, "manufacturing" stars to headline their product lines. One of the first studio-made stars was Theda Bara. Born Theodosia Goodman, the daughter of Polish Jewish immigrants living in Cincinnati, Bara was discovered by the film director Frank Powell. She was by then a veteran of bit parts on Broadway and had had stints as an extra in a couple of Hollywood pictures. Although she was already thirty years old when Powell "discovered" her, the director saw star potential in her dark "exotic" look. At Powell's urging, Fox put

Goodman under contract and launched the newly christened Theda Bara as the next new thing, concocting a crazy backstory that described her as the daughter of an artist (her father was a tailor) and an Arabian princess who practiced "the black arts." Bara was a willing player in the studio's far-fetched promotional strategy. She posed for publicity photos with snakes and human skulls, playing a new sort of celebrity game, one in which a nice Jewish girl from the Midwest might be reinvented as an exotic temptress.

Bara's signature role was "the vampire" in Powell's *A Fool There Was* (1915), her first film performance of any substance. The picture tells the story of a woman who lives to seduce and destroy powerful men. Bara's principal target in the movie is an ambassador whose picture in the newspaper captures her interest. When she first comes across his photograph, she is already planning to dump her lover, whom we find doddering around her house, talking about how much he once loved her and how she has destroyed him. When the vamp boards an ocean liner with her eye on her new prey, the old lover follows close behind to declare his desperation one last time—and then blow his brains out.

Two scenes in the film stand out. The first key scene shows Bara in her boudoir in a flimsy nightgown. As it falls off her shoulders, she shows little concern for propriety, as if the Victorian codes that governed women's dress and comportment did not matter to her. The second key scene may come as a surprise to anyone seeing a vamp film for the first time: Well after the vampire seduces the ambassador away from his wife, the man's daughter comes to the vampire's house to beg her father to return home. Despite her tugging at his (and the audience's) heartstrings, he turns her down. The moral is firmly drawn: if you fall for a woman like the vampire in *A Fool There Was*, nothing, not even the love for your own child, can save you.

Among Hollywood's men, the star with the most transcendent sexual celebrity was Rudolph Valentino. Named at birth Rodolfo Alfonzo Raffaelo Pierre Filibert Guglielmi di Valentina D'Antonguolla, Valentino was a former busboy and taxi dancer (hired to do the tango with women for 10¢ a dance) in New York City who was discovered by Adolph Zukor in the early 1920s. He starred in fourteen films between 1921 (his celebrated debut in Rex Ingram's *The Four Horsemen of the Apocalypse*)

Rudolph Valentino, silent cinema's most ardently desired male star.

and 1926, when he died suddenly at thirty-one of a perforated ulcer. Valentino played romantic and exotic characters in most of his films—for example, a matador in *Blood and Sand* (Fred Niblo, 1922) and a wealthy European doubling as a wealthy Middle Easterner in *The Sheik* (George Melford, 1921) and *The Son of the Sheik* (George Fitzmaurice, 1926). His Mediterranean good looks—dark skin, aquiline nose, piercing eyes—served any number of mysterious stereotypes, most notably that of the Latin lover.

Valentino's star persona was from the start more complex than Bara's. Both on-screen and in fan magazines, Valentino was the epitome of male attractiveness and sex appeal as well as a lonely guy lost in a desperate search for the right woman to save him from a life wasted dancing the tango or fighting bulls or playing typecast roles in the movies. Like a number of late-twentieth-century male pop stars (David Bowie and Prince, for example), Valentino played with androgyny. He was astonishingly popular with female audiences through the first half of the Roaring Twenties and decidedly unpopular with male audiences and the

The swashbuckler hero Douglas Fairbanks in *The Thief of Bagdad* (Raoul Walsh, 1924).

tough-guy newsmen from the mainstream press who covered the Hollywood beat. Those journalists routinely referred to Valentino as a "powder puff" and encouraged doubts about the star's sexual preference.

Part of Valentino's appeal to women, no doubt, was the product of his androgynous and conflicted persona. For example, he was lit and shot in ways that had been used by filmmakers to highlight the sex appeal of female stars of the era. Even when he was the sexual aggressor, as in the strange abduction scene in *The Sheik*, female fans saw something behind the façade of the character, something that transcended the film and told them all they needed to know about the man playing the role.

By way of contrast, we can consider the star personae of Valentino and Douglas Fairbanks, the swashbuckling hero in films like *The Three Muske-* *teers* (Niblo, 1921), *Robin Hood* (Allan Dwan, 1922), and *The Thief of Bagdad* (Raoul Walsh, 1924). Fairbanks, like many of the stars of the early westerns—Tom Mix in *The Cyclone* (Clifford Smith, 1920) and William S. Hart in *The Return of Draw Egan* (William S. Hart, 1916)—and all those square-jawed silent leading men—Wallace Reid in *The Affairs of Anatole* (DeMille, 1921), for example—was a quintessential American type: instinctive, rugged, and fiercely independent. Valentino, on the other hand, was Continental and cosmopolitan—decidedly not American. Fairbanks's off-screen romance with Mary Pickford was the stuff of American fantasy: he and Pickford were the perfect happy, rich, fun-loving celebrity couple. Valentino's personal life was the stuff of fascination as well, though the story was neither so happy nor so simple. In 1922 the actor was jailed and then fined for bigamy. After two failed marriages (to the actresses Jean Acker and Natacha Rambova), he took up with his co-star Vilma Bánky and the notorious screen vamp Pola Negri. In the months before his death, Valentino seemed to crack under the scrutiny and pressure of stardom, at one point challenging a Chicago newsman to a fistfight to settle the matter of his manhood once and for all.

Because Valentino died suddenly and young, rumors predictably hinted at death by poison at the hands of a cuckolded husband and other steamy scenarios stolen from one or another of the actor's screen melodramas. Whatever the facts were, many of his most ardent fans believed that he had been killed by the pressures of stardom, by the need to maintain the celebrity of Valentino. Even (or especially) in death, Valentino's tragic image transcended reason, reality, and common sense. Eighty thousand mourners descended on his New York funeral. Women lined the streets to witness the subsequent cortege in Los Angeles, and for a generation after his death his grave was a site for lonely female pilgrims who could not shake his mysterious hold over them.

The public's fascination with movie stars made the studios money, but the glamour industry that sustained stardom was not without its pitfalls. Especially troubling for studio executives was a seeming shift of power within the industry, away from them and toward the celebrity actors. By the early 1920s many stars had their own production units within the larger studios. Their demands had to be taken seriously because their value to the studios and to the industry as a whole was clear. But the moguls were not so eager to surrender their power. A spate of celebrity scandals ensured that they wouldn't have to.

Movie-Star Scandals

As early as 1913, approximately a year before the first features were screened before paying audiences, a fan-magazine subculture had emerged to answer the pressing question, What do movie stars do when they're not working? At first the studios controlled press releases and the distribution of stories about the stars. Thus the stories published in early fan magazines focused on the conventionality, stability, and normalcy of screen performers, echoing the melodramatic scenarios that prevailed in the films of the time: the world is fraught with temptation, and only the stars' virtue, beauty, and talent enable them to endure.

As the aptly named Roaring Twenties approached, however, the fan magazines increasingly celebrated postwar prosperity, touting various stars' extravagance and conspicuous consumption. Stars were spending more and partying more, and fans were eager to learn every detail. Sensing a market opportunity, mainstream newspapers began to run gossip and news items about Hollywood's celebrity culture. Unlike the early fan magazines, the major newspapers weren't dependent on the studios for their stories, so the studios began to lose their ability to control what was reported about their stars.

The first major star scandal involved Olive Thomas, a former Ziegfeld *Follies* showgirl under contract to Selznick Pictures, who died in 1920 of an apparent drug overdose at the Hôtel de Crillon in Paris. Thomas was married to Jack Pickford, Mary's brother (who was also rumored to be involved with drugs), a fact that made her death bigger news than it might otherwise have been. In response to the news of Thomas's death, Archbishop George Mundelein, one of many Catholic clerics who attempted to reform and regulate the early motion-picture industry, published a tract, *The Danger of Hollywood: A Warning to Young Girls,* that proved prescient.

Perhaps the most lurid of the celebrity scandals involved Roscoe "Fatty" Arbuckle, who allegedly raped and murdered the starlet Virginia Rappe during a wild party that began in Los Angeles and ended nearly 400 miles away, at the St. Francis Hotel in San Francisco. Arbuckle was singled out as her killer, but he was never convicted of the crime, largely because no one at the party could accurately recollect much of anything from the night in question. Whatever the actual circumstances of Rappe's death were, Arbuckle became a scapegoat for "crimes" committed by the movie colony against proper American society. He later found work (thanks to Buster Keaton and other friends) as a gag writer and low-budget film director, but Paramount pulled Arbuckle's films from circulation after the trial. Arbuckle's Hollywood career, as a movie star at least, was all but over after 1922.

Also in the news in the early 1920s were the film director William Desmond Taylor's unsolved murder and the movie star Wallace Reid's death from pneumonia, apparently due to a drug overdose. When Taylor was discovered murdered in his Hollywood bungalow, neighbors called his studio to report the crime. Only after going through his rooms themselves did the studio operatives call the police. What the police found in the apartment was surprising because it incriminated Taylor in a romance with the film stars Mabel Normand (whose love letters to Taylor were easily identified) and Mary Miles Minter (whose monogrammed underpants were apparently kept by Taylor as a souvenir). Historians now contend that the studio, in order to cover up the real story—that Taylor was gay—planted the love letters and the underwear and suggest that his murder may well have had something to do with his secret other life. Reid's death from a longtime addiction to narcotics was a disconcerting shock to his many fans, who considered him a quintessentially all-American movie star.

The star scandals prompted editorials nationwide condemning the Hollywood film colony. Women's clubs, religious groups, and other reform organizations threatened boycotts of motion pictures unless the studios got "their" stars under control. The prevailing view held that people in the movie business made too much money and the independence and power that the wealth brought them also corrupted them. Studio moguls used the scandals to rein in their stars, many of whom made a lot of money and wielded a lot of power in the industry. In 1922 the studios began insisting on morality clauses in their contracts with talent. Such clauses called further attention to the overlap in the lives of the stars on and off the screen and protected the studios from having to pay out a star's contract if he or she was involved in a scandal. The lesson of these scandals—one that the studios made sure the actors couldn't ignore—was that no star was too big to be brought down by public outrage.

Will Hays and the MPPDA

In 1922, in response to public pressure following the star scandals, the studios established the Motion Picture Producers and Distributors of America (MPPDA). Chosen by the studios to run this new industry trade organization was a former postmaster general, Will Hays. His mandate—a challenging public relations job—was to convince grassroots organizations and conservative legislators across the country that the industry wanted what they wanted: a scandal-free Hollywood that produced films that were at once entertaining and socially responsible.

The MPPDA's first significant act was to take credit for Paramount's nationwide ban on Arbuckle's movies. When the Arbuckle scandal broke, thirty-six state legislatures were considering film-censorship bills. The MPPDA's swift action in support of the ban on Arbuckle's films, as well as its success in preventing independent exhibitors from screening exploitative retrospectives of Virginia Rappe's films, was a first step in a larger effort to self-regulate film content. The promise of self-regulation under the auspices of Will Hays and the

Fatty Arbuckle in a publicity photograph taken shortly before the scandal in 1921 that ruined his career.

Will Hays, chief of the Motion Picture Producers and Distributors of America (MPPDA), giving a speech during his first "inspection tour" of Hollywood in 1922.

MPPDA succeeded in diminishing the threat of widespread state and local censorship. By 1925 thirty-five of the thirty-six states contemplating film censorship had abandoned their efforts, apparently deciding that the task was best left to Hays and his organization.

Hays's appointment seemed at the time to parallel major-league baseball's selection of Judge Kenesaw Mountain Landis as its first commissioner. Landis's appointment was a consequence of the infamous 1919 Black Sox scandal, in which a number of Chicago White Sox players took money from gangsters in exchange for deliberately losing the World Series. Much as the baseball owners used Landis's sober, no-nonsense image to restore the public's faith in America's pastime, the studios used Hays's squeaky-clean public image to legitimate the movie industry.

Hays's mandate was not just to clean house but to establish the MPPDA as a strong industry trade organization. The newspapers, of course, characterized his appointment as a moral crusade. That the two tasks—modernizing industry operations and self-regulating content—were somehow related, even indistinguishable, would become apparent in the years to come (a matter discussed at length in Chapter 3).

MOVIEMAKING AND MOVIEMAKERS

In the period of early cinema (1893–1914), screen credit for directing a movie was routinely omitted. Films opened with a corporate logo, not a director's name, so corporate ownership more or less equaled authorship. In the silent era (1915–1928), however, crediting movie directors on-screen became more commonplace. A movie was still said to be an MGM film or a Paramount film, and few in the film-going public paid much attention to the director's name as it scrolled down the screen, but the mere fact that directors and other filmmaking personnel were acknowledged was a significant change.

D. W. Griffith was the first American director to be as well known as the films he directed, and he was among the very first to insist that filmmaking was an art form. The only other dramatic film directors as well known at the time were Cecil B. DeMille, who made a range of popular genre films that nonetheless revealed a unique creative signature, and Erich von Stroheim, who as director, writer, and star took full control of his films—and paid dearly for his artistic hubris. Somewhat less well known (but no less important as filmmakers) were the creative producer Thomas H. Ince, who, like Mack Sennett, imposed his signature on his studio's films, and the German-born F. W. Murnau, who brought a Continental style to the final years of American silent cinema.

Film histories tend to focus on those directors whose work transcended the restrictions of the studio system, largely ignoring a number of mostly anonymous "studio directors" who produced the vast majority of motion pictures in the silent era. Among the most important of the lesser-known studio directors were Maurice Tourneur, Marshall Neilan, Rex Ingram, Clarence Brown, Allan Dwan, Mauritz Stiller, Fred Niblo, King Vidor, Raoul Walsh, and Henry King. Finally, behind the scenes in the silent era were the screenwriters, many of whom were women. Indeed, among the most successful writers in Hollywood at the time were June Mathis, Frances Marion, and Jeanie Macpherson.

D. W. Griffith, photographed in the 1920s.

D. W. Griffith

Griffith was the most famous director of the silent era. He was also among the first to demand screen credit for his work and push for the move to feature filmmaking. By 1915, when he made his best-known feature, *The Birth of a Nation*, he was already the industry's most famous cineaste.

The Birth of a Nation premiered in February 1915 in Los Angeles and a month later in New York. It was a sensation—the industry's first blockbuster. The film's initial run in New York lasted an astonishing forty-seven weeks despite an unprecedented $2 ticket price. President Woodrow Wilson screened the film at the White House, ostensibly to see what everyone was talking about, and legend has it he remarked that Griffith was "writing history with lightning."

But while the picture made Griffith famous, it also set him up for controversy. Reviewers were quick to acknowledge the film's undeniable technical brilliance, but many balked at its politics. The public was similarly split: the film was at once a box-office sensation and a cause célèbre. The intran-

sigent racism and bigotry that pervade *The Birth of a Nation* (which was based on Thomas Dixon's incendiary book *The Clansman: An Historical Romance of the Ku Klux Klan*) prompted protests in the Northeast, several of which were organized by former abolitionists. Pressure from the National Association for the Advancement of Colored People (NAACP) forced Griffith to cut a few of the many objectionable sequences, and street protests prompted local licensing boards in Connecticut, Illinois, Massachusetts, Kansas, and Ohio to refuse theaters permission to screen the film.

The Birth of a Nation begins with a prologue that audaciously blames the institution of slavery on the northern slave traders of the seventeenth century. Those men who trafficked in the slave trade were, Griffith muses, the great-great-grandparents of the nineteenth-century abolitionists who helped set the country's course as it headed toward the Civil War. Such northern hypocrisy is juxtaposed with the genteel, idyllic southern way of life, which was destroyed by the war.

The film introduces two families: the Stonemans (whose patriarch is Austin Stoneman, an abolitionist senator played by Ralph Lewis) and the Camerons (South Carolina plantation owners). In what was a predictable melodramatic plot device even in 1915, Phil Stoneman (Elmer Clifton), Austin's son, falls in love with Margaret Cameron (Miriam Cooper), and although all he has to go on is a photograph, Ben Cameron (Henry B. Walthall) falls in love with Phil's sister, Elsie (Lillian Gish). Complications ensue as the North and South go to war.

The long Civil War segment of the film is pure spectacle. But unlike previous film spectacles, like *Quo Vadis?*, which simply parade actors and extras in opulent costumes in front of mostly stationary cameras, Griffith found (and frequently alternated) camera positions that enhanced his film's epic look. In the scene that re-creates William Tecumseh Sherman's march to the sea, for example, Griffith covered the action with a variety of camera shots and positions, including a telling shot from atop a hill overlooking the assembled regiment, which offers scale to the massive onslaught. That Griffith also fully appreciated and exploited the ways in which editing might be used to heighten a scene's intensity is evident in the action editing (the use of multiple camera positions and accelerated intercutting) in the Battle of Petersburg and burning-of-Atlanta sequences. Although they are scenes of war and carnage, they are nonetheless exhilarating to watch.

The war segment ends with the assassination of Abraham Lincoln at Ford's Theater, re-created by Griffith with an eye to historical accuracy. Griffith employed his trademark intercutting to identify the parallel scenes that inexorably culminate in the assassination. Using fifty-five separate shots, Griffith intercut images of President Lincoln (Joseph Henabery) sitting innocently in his theater box, John Wilkes Booth (played by the director Raoul Walsh) biding his time outside, the president's bodyguard asleep on the job, the audience as a whole, Phil and Elsie (in the Ford Theater's audience), and the play, *Our American Cousin,* being performed onstage.

Griffith's painstaking verisimilitude suggesting historical accuracy contrasts with several specious and ridiculous musings on the political history of the late-nineteenth-century South. For example, to illustrate what he saw as the injustice of Reconstruction (the period following the South's capitulation to the North), Griffith offers a shot of the actual South Carolina capitol and then dissolves to a scene of its takeover by itinerant African Americans (played by whites in blackface), whose slovenly, savage comportment betrays a disrespect for this symbol of government and a disregard for the laws and traditions of the South. The African American legislators strip southern whites of their land and, even more dangerously, enact laws allowing interracial marriage. At the introduction of the dreaded subject of miscegenation (race mixing),

D. W. Griffith directing *The Birth of a Nation* in 1915.

(*top*) The rousing Civil War re-creations in *The Birth of a Nation* (1915) ably displayed D. W. Griffith's sophistication as a filmmaker.

(*bottom*) In *The Birth of a Nation* (1915), D. W. Griffith dramatized historical events by means of carefully staged reenactments. Here we see the signing of the South's surrender at Appomattox Court House, Virginia.

Griffith offers a sight-line cut (a shot of someone looking at something followed by a shot of what that person is looking at) that shows an African American legislator leering at a group of young white women in the capitol gallery.

As the film looks at the postwar period, Griffith focuses on Ben Cameron, a loyal son of the South who becomes so frustrated by what the former slaves have made of his home that he forms a secret society composed of similarly disenfranchised and disturbed white men who take to wear-ing sheets to conceal their identity. Those men become vigilantes and endeavor to defend their "Aryan" birthright. The Ku Klux Klan in *The Birth of a Nation* is as violent as its incarnation in the America of Griffith's day, but according to Griffith's version of events the Klan is violent not because of unreasonable hatred but because in the era of Reconstruction violence became necessary to the very survival of white southerners. *The Birth of a Nation* presents the Klan as an organization whose members are characterized by honor and courage and whose raison d'être is justifiable self-defense.

Shifting from the macrohistory of the reconstructed South to the micro- (and fictional) history of the Cameron and Stoneman families, Griffith has an emancipated black man, Gus (Walter Long, a white actor playing the role in blackface) ardently pursue Ben's sister, Flora (Mae Marsh), in a chase scene that culminates in Flora's desperate suicidal leap off a cliff to escape Gus's advances. Critics and historians have often commented on this sequence because it is at once masterfully shot (it's difficult not to appreciate the skill with which it was made), exciting (it successfully enlists us in rooting for the object of the chase), and profoundly offensive (as it in effect justifies the Klan's racist violence, a violence for which we indirectly and perhaps unwillingly cheer). Following Flora's death, Gus is caught and lynched, a scenario that is, for good reason, offensive to today's audiences familiar with the ugly history of American race relations in the post–Civil War South.

The racism that pervades *The Birth of a Nation* makes Griffith a difficult director to appreciate. But to understand, if not appreciate, his importance and influence, we must look past the stories and the themes (and perhaps the man himself) and examine instead the stylistic innovation, Griffith's role in the development of what might be called a modern cinematic grammar or language. More than any other director of his generation, Griffith appreciated how camera position, especially the distance between the camera and its subject, was a matter of primary aesthetic import. In the Civil War battle sequences, for example, Griffith cuts from distant establishing shots offering the battleground as a whole to medium close-ups of individual soldiers. In another part of the Civil War segment, an iris shot (so called because it opens and shuts like an eye) focuses on a sorrowful woman. As the iris opens to fill the screen, we see more of the woman—and the source of her dismay: General Sherman's inexorable and bloody march to the sea. In the exciting rescue of the Camerons by the Klan, Griffith uses alternating focal lengths, multiple camera positions, and an ever-decreasing duration of shots to increase the tension. As offensive as the film is, there is no question that in it Griffith synthesized into a coherent, seamless narrative whole the formal elements of film: focal length, editing (for pace,

for effect), even intertitles (printed titles inserted into films—especially silent films—that speak for characters or to the narrative).

After all the controversy attending the release of *The Birth of a Nation*, Griffith responded not with an apology but with a second provocation, an ambitious four-part film called *Intolerance* (1916). Like *Birth of a Nation*, *Intolerance* is didactic and sentimental. The rough cut ran for 8 hours. Griffith originally wanted to screen it in two parts on consecutive nights, but exhibitors balked, so he cut the film to 3 hours 20 minutes.

Intolerance moves back and forth among four story lines set in different historical periods: ancient Babylon, Judaea during the life of Jesus and at the time of his crucifixion, sixteenth-century France, and the present. Griffith proves equally adept with intimate scenes (with the star Lillian Gish in the film's modern sequence) and panoramic crowd scenes in the famed Babylonian sequence.

The Ku Klux Klan overtakes the Negro militia in *The Birth of a Nation* (D. W. Griffith, 1915).

To appreciate *Intolerance* today, one must recognize the inventiveness of Griffith's aesthetic choices. For the Babylonian sequence, for example, the director erected life-size, detailed sets. Built in Hollywood, the Babylonian set was 1 mile wide, and some of its structures topped 300 feet. Even the extras donned opulent costumes. For the orgies, which shocked audiences with their scantily clad women in lewd poses, and the elaborate battles, Griffith had a cameraman shoot the scenes from a hot-air balloon. The effect, even today, is breathtaking.

Several scenes in *Intolerance* offer lessons in the editing of silent films. The modern story alone contains a number of examples: the strike sequence (composed of shots of steadily decreasing length cutting back and forth among strikers, their families, the armed militia called in to suppress the strike, and the factory owner, who is depicted in a long shot as a tiny figure safely ensconced behind his desk in his cavernous office), the hangman's-test sequence (a medium close-up of the prison guards, a close-up of the strings on the hangman's noose that the executioners cut, a close-up of the man-size dummy weight falling through the trapdoor, and then a long establishing shot of the entire gallows apparatus as the dummy swings below the hangman's platform), and the action-edited, intercut montage sequence depicting a last-minute effort to save an innocent man from execution.

The last-minute rescue that ends the modern story was a staple of silent-film dramas and comedies. However much Griffith saw his work as different from or better than what other directors were doing, such melodramatic elements routinely punctuated his better films. One of Griffith's most

famous rescue sequences is in *Way Down East* (1920), the story of a country innocent named Anna (Lillian Gish) who ventures to the city to beg money from wealthy relatives, only to be tricked into a false marriage to Lennox Sanderson (Lowell Sherman). After having an illegitimate child by Sanderson and then losing the baby to a sudden illness, Anna finds momentary peace (and work) at a farm owned by the simple, God-fearing Bartlett family. The peace is short-lived, however, because through an improbable series of coincidences, Anna comes face-to-face once again with Sanderson. Forced to reveal to her hosts the truth about her sordid past, Anna confesses and then runs wildly out into the night, into a terrible winter storm, gets lost, and falls on the ice. The patch of ice on which she falls cracks free from the shore, sending Anna downriver toward Niagara Falls (and certain death). Fighting the blizzard, David Bartlett (Richard Barthelmess), the son of the farm owner who employs her, leaps across many ice floes and saves her. During the rescue, Anna gets soaked in the river and is ostensibly reborn: the Christian (baptismal) symbolism is hard to miss. She returns to the family farm as David's future wife, saved from the life of sin that inevitably (in silent melodrama, at least) accompanied her venture to the city. The scene is impressive enough as cinema, but even more impressive is the fact that both Barthelmess and Gish, like most other silent-film actors, did their own stunts. Adding to the suspense of the sequence and the drama of the last-minute rescue was the risk the actors themselves took in making the picture.

The plot of *Way Down East* is indicative of so much of the popular genre of silent Victorian melodrama. These films inevitably concern threats, usually of a sexual nature, to a young woman. The city (and the wealth it promises) is inevitably and unavoidably a trap, a place where a more modern culture lies in wait, poised to destroy the very fabric of Victorian morality. There is often a secret that must be kept at all costs—a secret that we know, after seeing a melodrama or two, will nonetheless be revealed. The private must be made

The last-minute rescue was a staple of silent-film melodrama. D. W. Griffith proved himself a master of this genre element in *Way Down East* (1920). Here Anna (Lillian Gish) floats helplessly toward Niagara Falls. At the very last minute she will be rescued by the film's hero, David Bartlett (Richard Barthelmess), who braves the ice floe to prove his love.

public in these films, and matters can be sorted out only after everyone tells and knows the truth.

Griffith made at least four significant silent features in addition to *The Birth of a Nation, Intolerance,* and *Way Down East: Hearts of the World* (1918), *True Heart Susie* (1919), *Broken Blossoms* (1919), and *Orphans of the Storm* (1922). Historians seldom talk about Griffith's work after 1922, and there is little to say about Griffith after the advent of sound. In 1948 the director died in the Knickerbocker Hotel in Hollywood, a relic of a distant and glorious past.

Cecil B. DeMille

Cecil B. DeMille was the silent era's most consistently entertaining—and, in many ways, its most consistently successful—cineaste. He was a major figure in Hollywood from 1915, the year he made *The Cheat,* one of the great silent melodramas, to

(*left*) The Babylonian set built for D. W. Griffith's *Intolerance* (1916) was 1 mile wide, and some of its structures topped 300 feet.

1956, when he directed perhaps his best-known sound film, *The Ten Commandments*. All told, DeMille directed over seventy features over a career that spanned five decades.

From the start, DeMille adhered to a simple principle: one should make movies that audiences want to see. As a consequence, critics and historians have written him off as a panderer to the lowbrow audiences that so adored his silent melodramas and his later overblown biblical epics. And that's too bad. His work, especially during the silent era, was frequently engaging, always stylistically interesting, and never pretentious or boring.

Of the silent features he directed between 1914 and 1927, DeMille showed off his talent best with steamy melodramas—films with titles like *The Cheat*, *The Woman God Forgot* (1917), *Old Wives for New* (1918), *Don't Change Your Husband* (1919), *Why Change Your Wife?* (1920), *The Affairs of Anatol* (1921), *Forbidden Fruit* (1921), and *Fool's Paradise* (1921). DeMille's stories revel in the temp-

The director Cecil B. DeMille, photographed in 1914, the year before he made *The Cheat*, one of the silent era's truly great melodramas.

tations of modern city culture. And although there is a moral of sorts at the end, one gets the sense that DeMille and his audience were much more interested in, and much more entertained by, the sin that precedes the film's moral than they'd have cared to admit.

DeMille cemented his reputation as an A-list director with *The Cheat*, a compact melodrama made at the end of a remarkably productive twelve-month period, during which he directed fourteen films. *The Cheat* tells the story of a young married woman, Edith (Fannie Ward), who can't wait to join the wealthy set. Social mobility is there for the taking, she thinks, so she doesn't see why she should wait for her husband, Richard (Jack Dean), to finish work on a big deal to get her what she wants. Her impatience proves to be her undoing. She indulges in a harebrained get-rich-quick scheme, in which she invests money intended for a Red Cross relief fund. When she loses the money, she turns to a financier, Haka Arakau (Sessue Hayakawa), who gets her out of the jam on one condition—that she pay him back with sex. The film hinges on this familiar melodramatic motif, as well as on DeMille's unapologetic exploitation of racist stereotypes. Arakau is depicted as a typical "yellow heavy" (as Asian villains were called at the time): he is covetous, inscrutable, and devious. He has lots of things, but what he wants most is what he can't have: a white woman.

We see Arakau and Edith together several times before they make their deal, and each time we are made to feel more and more uneasy. One key scene is an overhead shot of Edith exiting Arakau's car. He holds the door for her and then takes her hand. The film then cuts to the origin of the shot: Richard, looking down at the street from their apartment window, catches his wife cavorting with another man.

Later in the film, after Richard's financial deal succeeds, Edith makes one last visit to Arakau's house, to pay back the money he lent her. But he insists on being paid not in cash but in the manner they had agreed to. She struggles to protect her virtue but quickly gives in. To mark his victory—and to suggest sexual conquest—Arakau brands Edith on the shoulder with a Japanese symbol that the villain has used to mark his ownership of the antiques in his home. Now that she, too, bears his mark—an unmistakable symbol of sexual

Edith (Fanny Ward) imagines the worst in Cecil B. DeMille's *The Cheat* (1915): a headline in the next day's paper telling the world about her misguided attempt to use money from the Red Cross to make a bundle on the stock market. The film's villain, Haka Arakau (Sessue Hayakawa) reads her mind and seizes the opportunity, offering to cover the debt in exchange for sexual favors.

violation—Edith resists his claim to ownership, grabs his gun, and fires, hitting him in the arm.

Richard arrives to clean up the mess his wife has made and takes the blame for the shooting, ostensibly to protect her reputation. A courtroom drama ensues, and just as Richard is about to be found guilty, Edith takes the stand. She boldly pulls down the strap of her dress—an outrageous gesture in America circa 1915—and shows the judge, jury, and gallery the brand on her shoulder. She points her finger at Arakau, and we see an intertitle: "This is my defense!" The judge summarily dismisses all the charges against Richard, and the gallery, composed of white men and women, takes over from there: in the riot they foment,

Arakau is swallowed up, his precise fate uncertain, though lynching seems the most likely outcome. Richard and Edith exit the courtroom looking like a just-married couple walking back down the aisle of a church. To DeMille's credit, Edith's and Richard's expressions are hard to read. What we see is not elation or even relief. Instead, we see a profound uncertainty; after all that Edith has done and all that has been done to her, Richard is not sure which is worse, jail or his newfound notoriety as the cuckolded husband.

Like Griffith's *Way Down East*, DeMille's *The Cheat* pivots on a guilty secret (actually two guilty secrets: Edith's deal with Arakau and Richard's false confession). Both films move headlong

Edith (Fannie Ward) bares her shoulder in the courtroom to reveal Arakau's brand. A title card declares, "I shot Arakau and this is my defense." The entire courtroom then turns on the villain as the married couple exit arm in arm in Cecil B. DeMille's melodrama *The Cheat* (1915).

toward the inevitable revelation, the private made public. And both films are about women waiting for the right man to come along or come around. There's a distinct fascination in these melodramas with women's sexuality, which is presented as perpetually at risk. Propriety in the form of behavior appropriate to young women is also at issue. In *Way Down East*, Griffith reasserted propriety by returning Anna to the simple life in the country, where, after some trials and tribulations, she finds redemption. DeMille refused to tie things up so neatly. He leaves us questioning the future of all the principal characters. At the core of both plotlines, however, is the dynamic opposition of city and country, though DeMille complicates it by situating Arakau on rural Long Island while Richard toils admirably—working for a living—in Manhattan. A second dynamic opposition is added in *The Cheat*: white versus nonwhite. Arakau is recognized as a threat the first time we see him because he is Asian, dark, different.

Silent film depended on stereotypes as a visual shorthand. But that hardly excuses the trenchant racism that exists in so many silent films. To say that the times were such that unflattering stereo-

types were taken for granted is a weak excuse as well. Although such stereotypes and stock characters were widely accepted, there were often protests in response to those portrayals. Following *The Cheat*'s first run, in 1915, the Japanese embassy to the United States issued a formal complaint, and in response the Asian villain's name was changed from Tori (an identifiably Japanese name that was given to the character in the original version of the film) to Arakau (the name used in virtually all available prints of the film), thus transforming him into a native of Burma (present-day Myanmar, a country, we can assume, whose consulate in the United States was less powerful than Japan's).

Although *The Cheat* captures our attention with its clever narrative, DeMille made the most of a decidedly theatrical style. He strategically staged key scenes in front of and behind shoji screens in order to represent clandestine conversations by chance overheard (which is how, for example,

The director Erich von Stroheim in character and in costume as Count Wladislaw Sergius Karamzin in a 1922 publicity photograph for his film *Foolish Wives*.

The wedding-banquet scene in Erich von Stroheim's naturalist melodrama *Greed* (1924). Despite the seeming civility and formality, the family tears the flesh from large carcasses. The inevitable descent of basically decent people to behavior governed by base urges is a major theme of the film.

Arakau first learns of Edith's predicament) and to present important confrontations in silhouette. His expressive use of Rembrandt lighting, focusing a very "hot" (powerful) key (front) light on a subject's face while the rest of the frame is dark, became something of a signature style in the silent era. The effect is at once flattering and mysterious.

DeMille was a set-piece director, which is to say that he designed elaborate stage sets and allowed the drama to unravel within the carefully dressed and lit space. He began his movie career as an actor, and he pushed silent-film acting away from the theatrical toward a more realistic style. Whereas his films have an epic or operatic scale and scope, it is clear that his characters are always just people having to find their way out of a world that is full of temptation and confusion. In many ways, DeMille was Griffith's more modern counterpart—no less a film artist in the final analysis, and one with a more modern sensibility.

Erich von Stroheim

The first thing audiences saw when the projectionist unspooled Erich von Stroheim's *Blind Husbands* (1919) and *The Devil's Pass Key* (1920) was an affirmation of authorship: respectively, "personally directed by Erich von Stroheim" and "in its entirety an Erich von Stroheim creation." Like the movie stars whose celebrity he so coveted, von Stroheim was his own best publicist. And like a lot of early movie stars, von Stroheim, by the time he arrived in Hollywood, was armed with a fabricated backstory, which cast him as an aristocrat in exile, the last in a line of Austrian nobility, a part he played to perfection. Von Stroheim was in reality just Stroheim—the *von* was yet another pretense. Like the executives he worked for (and perhaps fooled), he was just a Jewish boy from the old country, descended from generations of working-class folk.

Von Stroheim may have been a phony, but as a filmmaker he eschewed artifice. Evident from the start of his career was an idiosyncratic style focused on visual detail, a cinematic realism that was new to fiction filmmaking. Foremost among the themes of von Stroheim's early features was a divine decadence: debauched life studied closely (for all its affectations and false fronts) by a camera that refused to shy away from anything. Later in his career, von Stroheim would turn his camera on the wretched lives of the poor and the unlucky, and he would do so with a similar attention to detail and commitment to showing life as it really was.

Such a commitment to an absolute realism required a painstaking production process, one that often caused his films to fall behind schedule and go over budget. Since his celebrity depended on an appearance of autonomy, he tended to overplay the part of the fiercely independent director and so frequently clashed with studio executives. A legendary confrontation between von Stroheim and Irving Thalberg occurred in the early 1920s, shortly after Thalberg became the production chief at Universal and von Stroheim had completed work on his third feature, *Foolish Wives* (1922). During the early stages of the production of *Merry-Go-Round*, Thalberg sent a message to von Stroheim, who was on location with his production staff. Seeing no reason to interrupt production to talk to a studio executive, von Stroheim ignored the message. In response to the slight, Thalberg

In the final moments of Erich von Stroheim's *Greed* (1924), McTeague (Gibson Gowland, *left*) murders Marcus (Jean Hersholt). But the crime hardly frees him. In what seems like a sick joke, McTeague soon collapses from the desert heat while dragging Marcus (to whom he is handcuffed) out of Death Valley. True to the film's larger vision of humanity's struggle to survive, both men die, neither getting what he wanted.

halted production on the project. Von Stroheim turned to Laemmle in the New York office, assuming Laemmle would set Thalberg straight. But to the director's surprise, Universal's founder deferred to Thalberg. When von Stroheim persisted in opposition to Thalberg's directives, he was summarily fired and replaced by the studio stalwart Rupert Julian, the director of some sixty shorts and features between 1914 and 1930.

Merry-Go-Round proved to be an object lesson in the emerging business of moviemaking in America. Thalberg's decision to fire von Stroheim made clear that in the studio system, directors were hired to do a job, and when they didn't do that job (according to criteria set by their employers and managers), they could (and would) be replaced. *Merry-Go-Round*, released in 1923, was a huge box-office success, and von Stroheim's name did not appear anywhere on-screen. For everyone who was familiar with the making of *Merry-Go-Round*, it was clear that Thalberg's business model had won over von Stroheim's creative ideal.

After von Stroheim lost face in his confrontation with Thalberg, he left Universal and signed with Goldwyn Pictures, where he began work on *Greed*, an epic adaptation of Frank Norris's novel *McTeague*. But although his productions at Universal had routinely gone overbudget and run long, nothing prepared von Stroheim's new studio for the rough cut of *Greed*, which weighed in at forty-two reels, with a running time of about 9 hours. Clearly something had to be done to cut or at least break up the film (into separate parts for separate screenings). It was indeed bad luck for the director that negotiating a final cut of the film fell to Thalberg, his nemesis at Universal: *Greed* had taken so long to produce that the rough cut became the property of the newly formed Metro-Goldwyn-Mayer, a conglomerate managed by Thalberg.

Faced with an absurdly long film that was in his eyes unreleasable, Thalberg had studio editors cut all but the film's central narrative, concerning a couple, McTeague and Trina (Gibson Gowland and ZaSu Pitts), whose lives are changed dramatically, and for the worse, when she wins a lottery. The release print of von Stroheim's 9-hour film is just over 2 hours.

After the cuts were made, von Stroheim disowned *Greed*. Though the public never saw anything close to the ambitious film von Stroheim had made, what they did see was an unstinting and uncompromisingly realistic work of cinema, a profoundly faithful adaptation of Norris's obsessive naturalism. Like Norris, von Stroheim put on display unadulterated reality—the human condition in all its sinful squalor. Character motivations in *Greed* are simple; in the end everyone is out for himself or herself. McTeague and Trina marry only after McTeague has taken advantage of her sexually in his dentist's chair. He marries her out of guilt and regrets the arrangement from the start. Their marriage begins with a bizarre and ominous wedding banquet, during which Trina's family devours food by tearing the meat from oversize carcasses. (The sense of foreboding is unmistakable.) After Trina wins the lottery, she falls out of love with McTeague and hopelessly in love with her money. At a butcher's shop, Trina buys rancid bones to save money. And in a memorable scene she lets down her hair and undulates on her bed with a bagful of gold coins.

To achieve his vision of realism, von Stroheim composed *Greed* in depth and with very little camera movement; we're allowed to linger in a scene, with time to take in foreground and background, action, gesture, and detail. Von Stroheim paid careful attention to the dressing of his sets: no item is too small, no artifact too insignificant. The realist effect begins and ends with the actors, who were routinely subjected to von Stroheim's naturalist vision. On the set, von Stroheim played the role of the autocratic Prussian perfectionist, and his insistence on shooting multiple takes wore his actors down to the point where they felt much like the unlucky characters they were playing. This effect was particularly evident in the film's final scene, shot in Death Valley, California. McTeague and Marcus (Jean Hersholt), McTeague's rival for Trina's affections (and her money), face off in the desert. They are there to settle an old score, but instead both die of exhaustion, handcuffed together. The actors themselves were as exhausted as the characters they played. The location von Stroheim chose was so remote that it took a full day to reach by car. And in temperatures exceeding 100 degrees, the actors lived the roles they played, wilting under the magisterial power of Mother Nature. Legend has it that Hersholt lost over 25 pounds on the desert shoot and was hospitalized after the production wrapped. One can guess that von Stroheim viewed Hersholt's suffering as further proof of the value of his naturalist vision.

Greed did poorly at the box office, and that was pretty much it for von Stroheim as a movie director. His only important later work was *Queen Kelly* (1929), which, like *Greed*, was never released in a version he could bear. In what may be a fitting legacy, von Stroheim is today more famous than the films he made. He was the first celebrity director to be undermined and ultimately devoured by "the system," and as such he has become the model for the wronged director, the first in a long, illustrious line including, most famously, Orson Welles and Francis Ford Coppola.

Thomas H. Ince

Thomas H. Ince first worked briefly as a director for Biograph in New York and then for Carl Laemmle's Independent Motion Picture Company (IMP), where, stationed in Cuba, he shot several films featuring Mary Pickford. Then, in 1911, Ince moved to California, where he leased an 18,000-acre ranch in what is now Santa Monica and built his own dream studio. He dubbed the site Inceville.

The silent-film producer Thomas Ince, photographed in the 1920s.

Ince believed that for a studio trademark to mean something, the studio chief had to make sure that every movie produced by the studio followed certain basic guidelines. Although a number of talented directors worked at Inceville—Francis Ford, Frank Borzage, William Desmond Taylor, Fred Niblo, and Henry King—Ince believed in hands-on studio supervision. He outlined the action of every film and then handed the outline to the director with a stamped-on order that read, "Produce this exactly as written." When the shoot was complete, the director was sent to another project while Ince supervised proceedings in the editing room.

Ince was among the first in Hollywood to recognize that assembly-line production methods in other industries might be adopted by the film industry. Though he supervised every stage of film production, employees were organized into separate departments (writing, scenery, makeup, and so on). Like autoworkers, these specialists did the same basic task on every production. Like Henry Ford's automobiles, films that bore Ince's name came with an assurance of uniform quality; his logo became a sign of authorship and ownership.

In 1912, Ince purchased the Miller Brothers 101 Ranch Circus, a Wild West outfit that employed real cowboys and Indians and maintained "improvements," such as covered wagons, tepees, a buffalo herd, assorted western gear, and an arsenal of authentic guns. Taking full advantage of his aquisition, Ince became the premier producer of movie westerns. In 1913 alone Ince produced over 150 films, most of them westerns. In 1914 he hired the cowboy turned actor William S. Hart, who with Ince's help became a major star. Hart was a credible cowboy at a time when there were still plenty of cowboys roaming the range that lay just east of the emerging motion-picture colony.

Unlike Broncho Billy Anderson and Tom Mix, the era's other cowboy stars, Hart was not averse to playing a bad guy. His best films for Ince—*The Bad Buck of Santa Ynez* (1914) and *The Return of Draw Egan* (1916)—are like a lot of other early westerns—*The Virginian* (DeMille, 1914), *The Covered Wagon* (James Cruze, 1923), and *The Iron Horse* (John Ford, 1924)—at once nostalgic and sentimental. They are essentially melodramas made for men.

In 1915, Ince signed a deal with D. W. Griffith to join the Triangle Film Corporation. At Triangle,

Ince directed and produced his best film, the anti-war picture *Civilization* (Reginald Barker and Ince, 1916). Although in his time he was considered as important a film pioneer as Griffith, his legacy as a filmmaker has not fared well, in part because westerns have been widely viewed as second-tier projects and in part because he was an unfortunate player in a strange murder scandal involving the comedy legend Charlie Chaplin, the actress Marion Davies, the soon-to-be-famous gossip columnist Louella Parsons, and the millionaire media mogul William Randolph Hearst. The story, assembled over the years through hearsay and circumstantial evidence, goes something like this: Hearst, in November 1924, invited Ince and several other Hollywood celebrities to take a pleasure cruise aboard his yacht. Because his career was on the decline, Ince had hoped to interest Hearst in investing in his films. In the meantime, Hearst was more interested in finding out whether his girlfriend, Davies, was having an affair with Chaplin, a notorious womanizer. In a disastrous case of mistaken identity, Hearst stumbled on Ince and Davies talking. Thinking his girlfriend was having a tête-à-tête with Chaplin, he shot the producer in the head. An alternative version has Hearst shooting at Chaplin, missing, and hitting Ince instead. Yet another version implicates Hearst only in the cover-up. That version has Ince shot by Davies's secretary, Abigail Kinsolving, who, rumor has it, had been raped by Ince earlier in the cruise. Whatever happened, Hearst cut the pleasure cruise short, and Ince, dying, was surreptitiously gotten off the boat. The official story of Ince's death—the version printed in Hearst newspapers—was that Ince died of heart failure following a severe flare-up of stomach ulcers. Neither Davies nor Chaplin, both alleged to have witnessed the shooting, ever talked about the event. Parsons, who was little more than a staff reporter in the Hearst empire, was soon given a lifetime contract to work the gossip beat in Los Angeles for the Hearst newspaper syndicate.

F. W. Murnau

F. W. (Friedrich Wilhelm) Murnau was an internationally respected director when he arrived in Hollywood in 1927. And his first American film, *Sunrise* (1927), a melodrama that fit the familiar and popular genre pattern, evinced a signature

The movie-star cowboy William S. Hart as the outlaw Bowie Blake in *The Devil's Double* (directed by Hart and produced by Thomas Ince).

mise-en-scène, an expressionist style (low contrast, shadowy key lighting, compositions in depth, and long takes) that had characterized his internationally celebrated German films: *Nosferatu* (1922), *The Last Laugh* (1924), *Tartuffe* and *Faust* (both 1926).

Sunrise, the winner of an Oscar for Best Picture, Unique and Artistic Production at the first Academy Awards ceremony, tells the story of a country farmer (George O'Brien) whose peaceful life with his amiable blond wife (Janet Gaynor) and baby is disrupted by the arrival of a dark, seductive woman from the city (Margaret Livingston). The film depicts the city woman as an interloper who cares little about what the locals think of her relationship with the farmer and does little to conceal her plans to leave the country backwater he calls home with the farmer and his cash. She is listed in the credits as the Woman from the City, as if that information alone is all one needs to understand her.

The farmer is depicted as physically rugged but emotionally and spiritually weak. He is clearly overmatched by the woman's cunning, and he is unable to resist the promise of clandestine (and,

The Woman from the City (Margaret Livingston) imploring the Man (George O'Brien) to leave his wife in F. W. Murnau's melodrama *Sunrise* (1927).

by implication) intense and exciting extramarital encounters. The Woman from the City seems to live by night, a vampire of sorts lurking in the shadows. In one scene we see her perched atop a tree in the dark, watching the farmer like a wild animal sizing up its prey. The city woman eventually persuades the farmer to drown his wife and run away to the city with her. As the farmer and his wife go by boat from the island where their community is located to the mainland city, he reaches for her throat, but he cannot go through with the crime and pulls away in shame. When the boat reaches the outskirts of the city, the wife flees her husband, heartbroken. He gives chase and overtakes her, and after an initial hesitation they reconcile and spend a day rediscovering and rekindling their love. At the end of the film, the family's happy reunion is punctuated by the city woman's return to the city alone.

Throughout *Sunrise*, Murnau uses mise-en-scène to depict the inner state of the characters. The wife is depicted initially in soft white light, the husband is in shadow, and the city woman is sleekly key lit in an otherwise dark frame, as if adrift in a moral void. The film embraces familiar genre characteristics, especially the dynamic opposition between the city and the country, here rendered with an equanimity seldom seen in American melodramas. As they rekindle their love, the husband and wife discover the delights of the city: glamour, automation, and consumerism. The city scenes have a kaleidoscopic quality and are lit with far less contrast than the somber country scenes. Unlike the vision of so many other directors of melodramas, Murnau's vision of the city is not one sided: it isn't simply a bad place in which modernity and progress overrun virtue.

Though his German films were so much of their time and place, Murnau seemed to master the Hollywood melodrama instantly, as is evident in *Sunrise* as well as his two subsequent features: *Four Devils* (1928) and *City Girl* (1930). For his fourth (and what would prove to be his last) film, Murnau departed from the successful formula with *Tabu* (1931), a South Sea Island picture begun auspiciously with the famous documentary filmmaker Robert Flaherty. The film was released within months of Murnau's tragic death in a car accident, rumored to be the result of his dabbling with some ancient cursed stones on the island paradise. *Tabu* displays the peculiar genius of both directors: Flaherty's penchant for rendering heroic the day-to-day struggles of his subjects is complemented by Murnau's romantic vision. Exactly what each director did during the production is unclear, but the final shot, in which two doomed lovers drift apart in open waters, is pure Murnau. The closing image of *Tabu*—Murnau's last testament on film— is an apt display of the singular importance of mise-en-scène in his work.

Though European directors enjoyed greater artistic freedom in their own countries, the lure of Hollywood money, worldwide distribution, and top-notch production crews proved hard to resist for such filmmakers as Murnau, Mauritz Stiller, and Josef von Sternberg. Stiller was hired by MGM in 1925 as part of a package deal that included the captivating Swedish actress Greta Garbo. Stiller may have been the talent MGM was paying for, but Garbo was the one who paid off. The "team" of Stiller and Garbo brought with it the promise of sexier, more stylish, more European films. But

Stiller could not abide the Hollywood studio system and ran into problems with his very first film, *The Temptress* (1926), a highly stylized femme fatale melodrama starring Garbo in the title role. Frustrated by Stiller's inability to stick to the studio's production schedule, MGM executives Irving Thalberg and Louis B. Mayer dumped Stiller and hired the ever-dependable studio director Fred Niblo to complete the film.

Stiller lasted less than two years in Hollywood. His final American assignment (and, as things played out, his final film) was *The Street of Sin* (1928), a melodrama starring Emil Jannings and Fay Wray, who would become famous five years later as Ann Darrow in *King Kong* (Merian C. Cooper and Ernest B. Schoedsack, 1933). Stiller

was pulled off the picture after running afoul of Thalberg and Mayer once again. In 1928 he returned to Europe and died later that year, at the age of forty-five.

The Street of Sin was completed by Josef von Sternberg (even though he received no screen credit for his work on the picture), another director whose Hollywood career was linked to a European-born movie star (Marlene Dietrich). But von Sternberg had slightly better luck than Stiller, at least at first. After taking over *The Street of Sin* in Stiller's stead, he teamed with that film's star, Emil Jannings, to make *The Last Command* (1928) and then the legendary German melodrama about a teacher seduced and shamed, *Der Blaue Engel* (*The Blue Angel*, 1930, released with an English sound track

The city scenes in F. W. Murnau's *Sunrise* (1927) have a kaleidoscopic quality, creating the perfect setting in which the country couple (George O'Brien and Janet Gaynor) rediscover each other.

by Paramount that same year). Although the director's later career was tied to Dietrich, he was already an accomplished filmmaker by the time he met her, having directed two gangster pictures, *Underworld* (1927) and *The Docks of New York* (1928), that helped establish the gritty realist style that influenced the gangster films of the early sound era (discussed in Chapter 3).

Studio Filmmaking

Between 1917 and 1928 the studios released approximately 600 films per year, including an industry record of 841 films in 1918. Only a few of those films were made by directors with any name recognition, and fewer still were made by directors whose names remain familiar to us today. The vast majority of the films in general release were made by so-called studio directors, men and women who labored in relative anonymity, often tied to a particular genre or movie star at their respective studios.

Fay Wray and Emil Jannings share a moment in the 1928 melodrama *The Street of Sin*. The director Mauritz Stiller was pulled off the film and replaced by Josef von Sternberg. *The Street of Sin* proved to be Stiller's last film; he died later in 1928 in Sweden, his adopted homeland, at the age of forty-five.

Being a good studio director meant being anonymous, sacrificing one's ego for the greater good of a movie's potential at the box office. Take, for example Allan Dwan. Though his career spanned fifty years and he is credited as the director of almost four hundred films, he is known today to only the savviest of historians of cinema. Dwan was an electrical engineer by training and did his first work in the film business as a lighting technician. In 1911 he began directing short films for a variety of studios, finally coming to the attention of Griffith when he was hiring directors to work for the Triangle–Fine Arts Studio. At Triangle, Dwan's technical expertise came in handy: a perambulating camera tower he designed was used to great effect in the Babylonian section of Griffith's epic *Intolerance*.

Dwan's first big feature was *Robin Hood* (1922), starring Douglas Fairbanks. The director and star teamed up again in 1929 with *The Iron Mask*. Sandwiched between those action films were three melodramas featuring the studio's temperamental star Gloria Swanson: *Zaza* (1923), *Manhandled* (1924), and *Stage Struck* (1925). In the 1930s, Dwan paid the bills by directing Shirley Temple pictures: *Heidi* (1937) and *Rebecca of Sunnybrook Farm* (1938). A decade later he directed a very

Greta Garbo and her frequent co-star, John Gilbert, in the MGM melodrama *Flesh and the Devil* (Clarence Brown, 1926). When Mauritz Stiller didn't work out at the studio, Brown became Garbo's director of choice, helming seven of her features between 1926 and 1937.

different sort of film star, John Wayne, in *Sands of Iwo Jima* (1949), a performance that earned the actor his first Oscar nomination. In every project he undertook, Dwan understood his role in the collaborative filmmaking process, and to put it bluntly, he knew his place in the celebrity culture that lies at the foundation of Hollywood.

Marshall Neilan, another important but now-obscure filmmaker, directed Mary Pickford in her signature melodrama *Stella Maris* (1918) and his wife, the star Blanche Sweet, in an early adaptation of Thomas Hardy's *Tess of the D'Urbervilles* (1924). Despite his anonymity outside Hollywood, Neilan epitomized the Jazz Age artiste. He dropped out of school at age eleven, had a brief run as a movie star, and went on to make over one hundred films, most of them during the silent era. Perhaps because his films and the stars who appeared in them were better known than he was, Neilan occasionally bristled at the inequity. He once famously quipped about his employer, "An empty taxi cab drove up, and Louis B. Mayer got out," a remark

that characterized his frustration at having to answer to the former junk dealer.

Rex Ingram (who directed Valentino in his first major role, the 1921 silent epic *The Four Horsemen of the Apocalypse*), James Cruze (a one-time snake-oil salesman in a traveling show who became one of the highest-paid directors in the silent era), and Roland West (who specialized in horror pictures, including the 1925 Lon Chaney film *The Monster*) were all productive studio directors in the silent era. Ingram directed twenty-nine films, Cruze helmed seventy-five, and West (whose career ended suddenly after his live-in girlfriend, the movie star Thelma Todd, was found dead of carbon monoxide poisoning in their garage) is credited with fourteen.

The internal politics of a 1920s Hollywood studio could be brutal, and sometimes the misfortune of one director proved to be the good fortune of another waiting for his or her turn behind the camera. For example, Mauritz Stiller's problems helped make the careers of two other studio directors, Clarence Brown and Fred Niblo at MGM. After Stiller left Hollywood, Brown became Garbo's director of choice, directing her in seven features, including *Flesh and the Devil* (1926), *A Woman of Affairs* (1928), *Anna Christie* (1930), and *Anna Karenina* (1935). The reclusive, enigmatic Garbo trusted Brown, and that was enough for the MGM brass. Though he is little known and little regarded today, Brown retired with fifty-three features to his credit and five Oscar nominations for Directing.

By the time Niblo was assigned to take over for Stiller on *The Temptress* in 1926, he was an established studio director with a reputation for quality work in several genres. He ably produced vamp melodramas like *Sex* (1920) and racy comedies like *Silk Hosiery* (1920), but his bread and butter was the action-adventure picture: *The Mark of Zorro* (1920), *The Three Musketeers* (1921), and *Ben-Hur* (1925). Like most other studio directors, Niblo was adaptable and versatile, and he understood that the stars he directed—Garbo, Fairbanks, and Valentino—were the reason to see his films.

Studio directors made movies that fit neatly into the studios' "house style" and properly showcased the studios' prime assets—their movie stars. They were willing to sacrifice ego for a steady gig, celebrity for a steady paycheck, and in so doing they produced the vast majority of films in the silent era, many of which were the films that mattered most to American audiences.

Women behind the Scenes

Women were routinely typecast on-screen, and much the same can be said for their work in the industry infrastructure. The men who ran the business had pretty firm ideas about what constituted "women's work": costume design, hairdressing, makeup, and set decoration. Editing and screenwriting were tasks open to women as well, the latter occupation in part because the studios were actively courting a female audience. Among the most influential screenwriters of the era were June Mathis, Frances Marion, and Jeanie Macpherson.

Mathis began her show-business career as an actress, playing mostly ingenue roles in traveling stage productions. When films took over the live-show market, Mathis tried her hand at writing, and her work came to the attention of Metro president Richard Rowland. She quickly earned a certain

From left to right: The actor Thomas Meighan, the screen heartthrob Rudolph Valentino and the screenwriter June Mathis. This photograph was taken in 1922, right after Mathis and Meighan posted bail for Valentino, Mathis's longtime friend, who was briefly jailed on charges of bigamy.

celebrity and by extension some power over production work on the lot. Her best-known film was *The Four Horsemen of the Apocalypse*, an exotic, romantic melodrama, a genre that would become her métier. Yet Mathis's clout at Metro extended beyond her script work. After writing *The Four Horsemen*, she handpicked Rex Ingram to direct the picture and, legend has it, insisted that Rudolph Valentino be signed to star in it. (Valentino and Mathis were close friends. Valentino, upon his death, was interred in the Mathis family's vault. A year later Mathis died, also suddenly, and joined him there.)

After another successful film with Ingram and Valentino, *The Conquering Power* (1921), Mathis held executive positions at Goldwyn Pictures (where she worked with King Vidor, Neilan, and von Stroheim), the newly merged Metro-Goldwyn-Mayer, and finally First National, where she helped produce films for the stars Colleen Moore and Corrine Griffith. Mathis proved to be a unique figure in an industry that seldom veers from tradition. She was a screenwriter who gained power and control over the films made from her work, and she was a woman who, in the male-dominated profession of moviemaking, became an executive with considerable influence over high-profile films.

Frances Marion, another important female screenwriter in the silent era, wrote scripts for Mary Pickford, the most powerful female star in the industry in the early 1920s. It was Marion who helped create Pickford's Little Mary on-screen persona—at once sweet, pretty, confident, and capable, a version of the so-called new woman that proved extremely popular. After her success with Pickford, Marion wrote scripts for popular films featuring a number of female stars: for Marion Davies, *The Restless Sex* (Robert Z. Leonard, 1920); for Lillian Gish, *The Scarlet Letter* (Victor Sjöström, 1926); for Greta Garbo, *Anna Christie* (Brown, 1930); and for Marie Dressler, *Emma* (Brown, 1932).

All told, Marion wrote 325 scripts, over 150 of which were produced and released. She served as vice president of the Screen Writers Guild, the only woman of her generation to hold an executive office in the union. In 1930 and 1932, Marion won Academy Awards for the script of *The Big House* (George W. Hill, 1930) and the original story of *The Champ* (Vidor, 1931). She was still young and at the top of her game when her career stalled: Irving Thalberg's death left her without an advocate at MGM and on the wrong side of bitter infighting.

Though she broke into the industry as an actress and appeared in nearly 140 films, many with the industry's top stars, including Florence Lawrence and Mary Pickford, Jeanie Macpherson is now best known for her screenplays (and for a much rumored romantic relationship with Cecil B. DeMille). Regardless of what may have occurred between Macpherson and DeMille romantically, a significant creative collaboration certainly took place. Between 1914 and 1930, Macpherson wrote some of DeMille's best and sexiest melodramas— *The Cheat* (1915), *The Woman God Forgot* (1917), and *The Affairs of Anatol* (1921)—and his most opulent biblical spectacles—*The Ten Commandments* (1923) and *The King of Kings* (1927).

Among the cadre of women writing scripts at the studios in the 1920s, most notable are Ouida Bergère, who adapted Booth Tarkington's play *The Man from Home* (George Fitzmaurice, 1922); Olga Printzlau, who wrote the first adaptation of Edith Wharton's novel *The Age of Innocence* (Wesley Ruggles, 1924); Margaret Turnbull, who wrote the scenario that turned Mark Twain's *Pudd'nhead Wilson* into a film (Frank Reicher, 1916); Clara Beranger, who did the same for Robert Louis Stevenson's *Dr. Jekyll and Mr. Hyde* (John S. Robertson, 1920); Jane Murfin, who adapted Jack London's *White Fang* (Laurence Trimble, 1925); Beulah Marie Dix, sce-

narist of *The Squaw Man* (DeMille, 1918); Marion Fairfax, who adapted Arthur Conan Doyle's *The Lost World* (Harry O. Hoyt, 1925); Eve Unsell, who wrote an adaptation of the stage play *Three Men and a Girl* (Neilan, 1919); and Sada Cowan, who adapted the novel *The New Commandment* (Howard Higgin, 1925). These women were mostly college educated, and many boasted a background in other (more traditional) forms of writing. Though screenwriters did not earn the sort of money that movie stars routinely made for their participation in the production of motion pictures, they nonetheless made more than most other women in other occupations and more than most other writers, male or female, writing books or articles for newspapers and magazines. Unlike the screenwriters of today, who are seldom mentioned in the critical literature and popular reviews, the screenwriters of the 1920s were viewed with high regard by critics and film historians, who believed that they brought, by their mere presence if not their actual work, a semblance of high art and high literature to a medium sorely in need of such uplift. That women provided that uplift, that literary underpinning, is a point too seldom acknowledged.

The screenwriter Frances Marion and her fellow writer James Hilton in a publicity photograph taken in the 1930s.

THE GOLDEN AGE OF FILM COMEDY

Comedy shorts played an important role in the silent-film program, in part because comedy acts had long been central to vaudeville, whose variety-show format so influenced early exhibition practices. Though comedy skits were just one of the many acts on a typical vaudeville program, which might also include singers, jugglers, acrobats, and animal acts, several comedians emerged as vaudeville's first true headliners. The same proved true in the early years of American cinema as comedy quickly became a key attraction and a select group of comedians became influential movie stars.

The three transcendent silent-film comedy stars were Charlie Chaplin, Buster Keaton, and Harold Lloyd. Each was distinct in style and approach, but all three were knockabouts, willing to risk health and well-being for the sake of a gag. All three were also veterans of or deeply influenced by vaudeville comedy, and their success made clear the new medium's tie to the popular entertainment it would soon supplant.

It is widely believed that the period from 1915 to 1928 was a golden age for film comedy. Such a contention is based not on the sophistication of the material but on the sheer exuberance of the performances and the importance of comedy to popular film at that point. The vast majority of silent-film comedies were decidedly lowbrow. No amount of athleticism or artistry—and there's no doubt that Chaplin, Keaton, and Lloyd brought considerable athletic ability and artistry to the screen—can change the fact that those artists' films were composed almost exclusively of gags and that those gags fell within a limited range of possibilities generally involving a physical calamity, like a crash or a fall. What Chaplin, Keaton, and Lloyd accomplished was to make the most of a limited set of options: they brought an amazing ingenuity to what was at bottom a simple form.

That said, we should not underrate their films' larger social significance. In a world that was guided by a repressive Victorian morality, the violence, the speed, and the complex mechanics of physical comedy offered a challenge to a system that found little variety or humor in the everyday. The social transcendence briefly achieved by the comedy star in this era represented a move to a more modern (a faster and wilder) America. The characters played by Chaplin, Keaton, and Lloyd ushered in this new America with a bemused innocence; like many moviegoers, they were just little guys trying to make the most out of life, moving from one calamity to the next, bouncing back when the world kicked them, trying to find humor in a life that was seldom funny.

Charlie Chaplin

In 1913, Charlie (Charles Spencer) Chaplin left Karno, a British-based traveling variety show, to become an ensemble player at Mack Sennett's Keystone studio. Though the slapstick style of the English stage and the utter chaos of Sennett's crude cine-knockabouts were quite different affairs, Chaplin made the transition from vaudeville stage to moving pictures look easy. During his first year at Keystone, he appeared in thirty-five films and quickly became a key company player, along with Fatty Arbuckle, Chester Conklin, Marie Dressler, Mabel Normand, Slim Summerville, and Mack Swain.

Chaplin debuted what would become his signature Little Tramp character in a Sennett short, *Kid Auto Races in Venice* (1914). Donning oversize pants and big shoes, he clowns his way through a soapbox derby. The Tramp was a sentimental construct: poor but happy, shabby and homely but

From left to right: Phyllis Allen, Mabel Normand, Mack Swain, and Charlie Chaplin, ensemble players in the 1914 Keystone comedy *Getting Acquainted* (directed by Chaplin and produced by Mack Sennett).

In Charlie Chaplin's *Easy Street* (1917) the recently deputized Little Tramp (Chaplin) uses a gas lamp to subdue the neighborhood bully (Eric Campbell).

beautiful inside. He had a signature walk, a toed-out waddle that had much in common with the pantomime style of the circus clown. But unlike the circus clown, whose clumsiness becomes the butt of every joke (falling off a bike, smashing into a wall, getting doused with a pail of water), the Tramp's waddle masks a dancer's grace. What is funny about the Tramp is that in the end he is not what he seems to be: even (or especially) in moments of inebriation, infatuation, or desperation, he is capable of feats of surprising grace and skill. His fellow comic actor W. C. Fields famously described Chaplin as not a comedian but "the greatest goddamn ballet dancer," a remark that speaks to the grace with which Chaplin performed his slapstick stunts and gags.

Like many other silent-film stars, Chaplin followed the money and the promise of greater artistic freedom from studio to studio (he was at Keystone until 1915, at Essanay from 1915 to 1916, at Mutual from 1916 to 1917, at First National from 1918 to 1922, and at United Artists from 1923 to 1952). At Keystone he earned $150 a week; Essanay paid him $1,250 a week. The move to Mutual came with guarantees totaling almost $700,000 annually. When he was not yet thirty years old, First National signed him to a fixed-term contract exceeding $1 million a year. In order to justify such a lofty salary and to maintain the sort of celebrity to which he had grown accustomed, as early as 1918 Chaplin had begun thinking about making feature films. But how he would get from

the 16- to 30-minute short subject—an ideal length for a gag-based comedy—to feature-length narrative comedy was a question he could not easily or quickly answer.

At Essanay, Chaplin serially refined his signature character and moved away from pure physical comedy to work that offered a social or political edge. In one of his best Essanay films, *The Bank* (1915), he explored what would become an important and consistent theme in his films, the absurdity and futility of hard work. The film casts the Little Tramp as a working stiff, a bank janitor who has a thing for the bank manager's secretary. It is an impossible romance—she is clearly out of his league—but he dreams about a life with her anyway. The film gets interesting when a band of thugs enters the bank. Implausibly, the tramp janitor subdues the thieves, and the secretary lands in his arms—but there is a catch. The comic kick-in-the-pants ending reminds us that such dreams of transcendence are just—well, dreams. The film ends as the Little Tramp wakes to find himself cuddling with his mop—and not, as in his dream, the secretary.

A similar social-satirical bent is evident in the twelve films Chaplin made at Mutual. In *Easy Street* (1917), for example, he plays a vagabond who is recruited to work as a beat cop in a dangerous neighborhood. Through dumb luck and a little ingenuity he subdues a neighborhood bully (Eric Campbell) by comically knocking him out with the gas from a streetlight, and then (in what audiences no doubt found an absurd, comic conclusion) he leads the slum dwellers on the road to redemption, or at least down the street to the New Hope Mission.

The eight comedy shorts Chaplin made for First National—*A Dog's Life* (1918), *Shoulder Arms* (1918), *Sunnyside* (1919), *A Day's Pleasure* (1919), *The Kid* (1921), *The Idle Class* (1921), *Pay Day* (1922), and *The Pilgrim* (1923)—toy with audience expectations regarding the Little Tramp. To wring out original gags, Chaplin placed his signature character in implausible situations and settings. The Tramp is cast as a soldier in *Shoulder Arms*, a farmer in *Sunnyside*, a working stiff

in *Pay Day*, and most unbelievably, a preacher in the 59-minute *Pilgrim*. Chaplin hoped that such situation-based comedies might help him make the transition to feature-length narrative films but discovered that the situations offered little more than a frame for his slapstick gags.

Chaplin's first important comedy feature was *The Gold Rush*, released in 1925 amid a paternity scandal (involving Lita Grey) that followed very soon after the Hearst-Ince incident. Despite Chaplin's personal struggles and the fan-magazine gossip, the film was a huge success commercially and artistically.

The Gold Rush begins on Chilkoot Pass, a perilous mountain crossing on the way to the Alaskan goldfields that was first captured on film in a documentary by Robert Bonine and Thomas Crahan for Edison in 1898. Chaplin's Little Tramp is introduced as just one of many hopeful prospectors. But while the other prospectors dress in furs and snowshoes, the Tramp wears his usual tattered suit and oversize shoes and obliviously walks his signature walk on the icy narrow ledge. The Tramp is of course ill suited to both the locale and the lusty, rugged endeavor—and that's the point. The first gag in the film begins with a bit of ballet on the perilous ledge. The Tramp stumbles, then regains his balance. His stumbling awakens a bear that follows discreetly along the ledge. We see the bear as it nears the Tramp, but Chaplin remains, as always, blissfully oblivious. Just as it seems inevitable that the two will cross paths, the bear enters a cave and decides not to come back out. The Tramp travels on, unaware of the danger he has narrowly avoided.

Chaplin cast himself alongside fellow Sennett veteran Mack Swain as the appropriately named Big Jim. Throughout the film, much is made of their size difference—in silent film, comedy depends on simple dynamic oppositions, like big and small, masculine and feminine, ugly and beautiful. Chaplin is immediately cowed by Swain's bulk, and when they team up to prospect for gold, he willingly takes on the role of housekeeper and sidekick. Since the Tramp is systematically made to appear weak and unmanly, we find unlikely his romance with the film's beautiful female lead, Georgia (Georgia Hale), a barmaid accustomed to far rougher company. Here Chaplin fully indulges his sentimental side, but with a key caveat: the

(*left*) Charlie Chaplin and Mack Swain as unlikely housemates in Chaplin's classic silent feature *The Gold Rush* (1925).

(*top*) The house as teeter-totter, one of the classic gags in Charlie Chaplin's *The Gold Rush* (1925).

(*bottom*) At the end of *The Gold Rush* (Charlie Chaplin, 1925), Georgia (Georgia Hale) finally falls in love with the Little Tramp (Chaplin), only to discover he's a millionaire.

reunited after the former finds, and then loses, a site rich in gold (in a struggle he takes a hit in the head and suffers amnesia). When the wind finally subsides, the house is left teetering on the edge of a cliff, and the two men try to keep themselves and the house from slipping into an abyss. After a sequence made brilliant by camera tricks and stunts—the house for much of the time is just a big, heavy seesaw—the exhausted characters find themselves at the very site of Big Jim's claim. As in many other Chaplin films, luck is more important than design or skill, especially where money is concerned.

The final gag finds the Tramp suddenly a millionaire and a celebrity aboard a steamer heading south. No doubt audiences saw this conclusion as a clever bit of self-parody: Chaplin was a celebrity and could afford to poke fun at the unpredictable sequence of events that had made his success possible. On a lower deck is Georgia: feeling bad about the way she treated the Tramp (and unaware of his change in fortune), she is seeking a new and maybe more civilized life away from the frozen north. The press is onboard to celebrate the Tramp's good fortune, and for a photo shoot a newspaperman persuades the Tramp to exchange his millionaire's duds (two big fur coats worn over a neat suit) for his prospector's outfit (his Tramp costume, of course). The Tramp complies, and while posing for photographers, he stumbles backward and falls onto the lower deck, landing just a few feet from Georgia. A ship's officer mistakes the Tramp for a stowaway, as does Georgia. Georgia generously offers to pay the Tramp's fare, to save him from the brig. Her bighearted gesture is met with an even bigger-hearted one on the Tramp's part as he leads her up to the luxury deck as his fiancée. The film ends happily if ridiculously, and many viewers were no doubt struck by the interesting and ironic counterpoint to the way matters were playing out for Chaplin, whose marriage (to Lita Grey) had become a much-publicized disaster.

Chaplin continued making important movies into the sound era, though he took his time adapt-

effeminate and weak male character offers more than meets the eye (just as the roughnecks offer less). In one scene the Tramp spies Georgia waving in his direction. He smiles in anticipation as she walks toward him, only to discover that there's another guy behind him, a rugged prospector with whom Georgia passes the time in the bar. In a later scene, Georgia and some friends stop by Big Jim's house. They poke gentle fun at the Tramp and in jest make a date to stop by for dinner on New Year's Eve. They stand him up, and he compensates for the pain with a comic daydream in which Georgia and her friends find him attractive.

The film's most famous stunt involves a house set adrift in a blizzard. Big Jim and the Tramp are

ing to the advent of synchronous sound. Through the 1930s he made what were for the most part silent features, using sound only to make the music and the sound effects consistent from print to print. In other words, Chaplin made the transition to sound by not making the transition, by insisting that his work transcended technological and social change. Though Chaplin's three most important sound-era films—*City Lights* (1931), *Modern Times* (1936), and even *The Great Dictator* (1940)—seem very much locked in the past, they nonetheless contain some of his most ambitious and most complex work.

City Lights neatly fits subtle physical gags into a larger romantic plot involving a blind woman (Virginia Cherrill) and the tramp she believes to be a millionaire. He's not a millionaire, of course, but he knows one and eventually gets the money to pay for an operation that might restore her sight. The operation is a success, and she is cured, but he, as a consequence, is out of the picture. Now she can

see him not for who he is (a kind man who loves her) but for what he is (a tramp), and he exits the film aware that his good deed has made their romance impossible.

Essential to *Modern Times* are some of Chaplin's best pantomime sequences: the feeding-machine scene, for example, in which the Little Tramp is victimized by automation—slapped in the face, pelted with processed-food morsels, and drenched with hot soup; the jailhouse dance sequence, which culminates in the cocaine-addled Tramp somehow foiling a jailbreak; and a risqué gag in which the Tramp, unable to stop twitching his arms (having been turning bolts all day), can't help but try to undo the buttons on the dress worn by a woman he chases down the street. To Chaplin's credit, the sexually suggestive gag offers a clever critique of Fordist labor methods.

The Great Dictator, Chaplin's last box-office success, presents a political satire—and for once a full-fledged comedy narrative—playing off the physical

From left to right: Buster Keaton, Roscoe "Fatty" Arbuckle, and Al St. John in the knockabout farce *Out West* (Arbuckle, 1918).

resemblance between his Little Tramp and the German chancellor Adolf Hitler. (A rumor at the time held that Chaplin was Jewish, adding further irony to the mix. He wasn't but nevertheless allowed the rumor to circulate.) The best-known scene is a classic Chaplin pantomime in which the Hitler lookalike juggles a balloon that bears on its surface a map of the world.

In the 1940s, Chaplin, no longer a major moviemaker, ran into problems with Federal Bureau of Investigation chief J. Edgar Hoover. After a decade of political accusations and another paternity scandal, Chaplin left Hollywood for Switzerland. He would remain in exile for twenty years, returning finally in 1972 to accept an honorary Oscar.

Buster Keaton

Joseph Francis Keaton debuted on the vaudeville stage at the tender age of three. He joined his parents, Joe and Myra, and the Two Keatons became the Three Keatons. The act consisted of little more than serial brutality performed on young Buster, who would miraculously emerge from every fracas indifferent and mostly uninjured. In some incarnations of the act, Buster would be made up as a little man, complete with mustache and beard. But the essence of the act was always the same: pure knockabout comedy.

By 1917, Buster Keaton was a vaudeville headliner earning $250 a week. When he made the move to film later that year, his starting salary was a scant $40 a week, and he was suddenly very much a second banana to the very popular comedy star Fatty Arbuckle. As things played out, the salary cut was temporary, and Keaton became one of silent cinema's great comedy stars.

Keaton's first appearance on-screen was a memorable bit in an Arbuckle short, *The Butcher Boy* (1917). He makes his entrance walking slowly, back to the camera, changing the pace of the film on the spot. Next comes a comic bit in which he tosses brooms into a bin and then a series of gags involving Arbuckle and some spilled molasses: Arbuckle gets molasses in Keaton's hat. The hat gets stuck, and Arbuckle tries to pull it off. Keaton remains passive and expressionless as Arbuckle tosses him around the set and then hurls him out the door. Here, as in subsequent Arbuckle films, Keaton proved to be the fat comedian's perfect foil, a paragon of restraint and control amid the chaos. As in so many of the later films on his own, Keaton's stone-faced persona is unflappable, untouchable. He is at once the unluckiest guy in the world (the stuff that happens to him could happen only to him) and the luckiest, because he seems so small and inept, yet he emerges unharmed from the most outrageous scrapes and mishaps.

In 1919, after two years of making films with Arbuckle, Keaton became a movie star in his own right. After signing with Joseph Schenck, his wife's brother-in-law, Keaton was given his own

Man and machine: Buster Keaton in a gag from his 1923 feature *Our Hospitality* (Keaton and John Blystone).

Kathryn McGuire and Buster Keaton in the film-within-a-film in *Sherlock Jr.* (Keaton, 1924).

production studio, and in exchange for the promise of eight short films a year the comedy star received $1,000 a week and a good deal of artistic freedom. Working for Schenck, Keaton produced several memorable two-reelers, including *One Week* (Keaton and Edward Cline, 1920) and *Cops* (Keaton and Cline, 1922).

In the closing scene of *One Week,* Keaton tows a strange-looking build-it-yourself house across town (it looks strange because a rival changed the labels on the modular parts). The house gets stuck on some railroad tracks. Keaton positioned the camera so that we see a train approaching and are sure will hit the house. But it doesn't because what we can't see is that the train is on a parallel track. The take continues as Keaton and his co-star, Sybil Seely, breathe a sigh of relief. But the respite is brief, for a second train comes suddenly into the frame and obliterates the house. The gag works because the first time the camera position fools us, and the second time it prevents us from seeing the payoff until it is too late.

Cops offers Keaton's variation on the sort of hectic chase comedy that Sennett made famous at Keystone. Watching the film today, one finds it hard not to be impressed by Keaton's athletic ability in stunts involving swinging ladders and moving vehicles. But in 1922, *Cops* took on a more timely significance: the film, released just as Arbuckle was mired in scandal, focuses on a man who is falsely accused. (Keaton, incidentally, remained loyal to his old friend long after the studios had blackballed him.)

Keaton's transition to feature-length films, in 1923, was less abrupt than Chaplin's, if only because Keaton rarely tried to make a coherent feature-length narrative; for him features just meant bigger and better stunts. At the end of the feature *Seven Chances* (1925), for example, Keaton's film about a young man who must marry within 24 hours in order to pocket his inheritance, the stone-faced hero is chased to the edge of a cliff by an army of eager would-be brides. He runs down the hill just as a rockslide commences. The

Sherlock Jr. (Buster Keaton) setting up the first of several amazing trick shots that all somehow avoid the thirteen ball (in which the villains have planted a bomb). As with so many gags in *Sherlock Jr.* (Keaton, 1924), the bit depends on amazing physical skill and deft sleight of hand, a nod to Keaton's mentor, the magician–escape artist Harry Houdini.

falling pebbles and stones become, by the end of the stunt, giant boulders, which Keaton must avoid in order to survive. With Keaton such an interplay between man and nature lies at the very center of the comic universe. There are forces bigger than we can imagine—rapids and waterfalls, as in *Our Hospitality* (Keaton and John Blystone, 1923), for example, or storms that topple houses, as in *Steamboat Bill Jr.* (Keaton and Charles Reisner, 1928)— but Keaton always manages to keep his cool.

Though it features the slimmest of narratives, Keaton's most compelling feature is *Sherlock Jr.* (Keaton, 1924). The film opens with Keaton portraying a projectionist sweeping up after a show. In classic three-part gag form, Keaton steps on a piece of paper (which sticks to his shoe), removes

it with his hand (to which it gets stuck), and then calmly slaps it onto the back of a passerby (who thus carries it offscreen). Then, as he lackadaisically sweeps up outside the theater, he finds a dollar bill. The dollar, we discover, should come in handy, because he wants to buy the object of his affections (Kathryn McGuire) an expensive box of candy. But before he can leave work for the candy store, a pretty woman shows up saying that she has lost a dollar. Reluctantly he hands over the money. Next, an old woman drops by looking for a dollar that she has lost, and he gives her one of his own two bills. Finally—the joke comes in three parts here, too—a thug arrives, and he also says he has lost something. The projectionist hands him his last dollar, in part because the guy is so big but mostly because everything seems so futile; he is just unlucky. But the thug returns the dollar because, as we discover after he rummages through the pile of debris that the projectionist has swept up, he has lost (but now finds) a wallet filled with cash.

After switching on the projector for the next show, the projectionist quickly falls asleep. Dreaming, he has an out-of-body experience (depicted in a clever use of superimposed imagery). The projectionist's dream self takes a wonderful pratfall, diving into an orchestra pit (a version of a gag Keaton performed many times in vaudeville: the Three Keatons ended their act with Joe tossing Buster into the pit). Keaton quickly segues into a play on film form as the projectionist dives into the movie on-screen, a silly melodrama titled *Hearts and Pearls*. In *Hearts and Pearls* the projectionist falls victim to the film's editing scheme. We see the projectionist fall off a bench in a garden and land in a busy city street. He walks, and the film cuts to the edge of a cliff. He stops in time and looks ahead, and the film cuts to a lion's den. As he slowly backs out of the den, watching the lions all the while, he finds himself in the Old West and is nearly run down by a train. He sits on the ground, and suddenly he is on a rock in the ocean. He dives off the rock and lands headfirst in the snow. He leans on a tree, and he is back in the garden by the bench we saw in the first shot in the sequence.

When Keaton played vaudeville, he shared the bill on occasion with the legendary escape artist Harry Houdini—it was Houdini who gave Buster his nickname. As Keaton told the story, one day when he was very young, he fell down a flight of stairs. Houdini saw the fall, laughed, and said, "That sure was a buster!" The name stuck. In addition to giving him his screen name, Houdini taught Keaton that a well-executed stunt depends on a game of show and tell. That lesson is clearly demonstrated in *Sherlock Jr.* In the film within a film, the projectionist becomes Sherlock Jr., master detective. This alter ego is at once as silly as the projectionist (he is just as shy and fumbling around his girlfriend) but supernaturally athletic and agile (hardly how one would describe the projectionist). He enters the mansion where the drama of *Hearts and Pearls* plays out, where a villain and his cohort (Ward Crane and Joe Keaton) plot to

kill Sherlock Jr. before he can solve the crime (by identifying who stole some missing jewels). The cohort shows us an exploding number 13 pool ball, pours some poison into a glass, and demonstrates a chair rigged with an ax that might be used to eliminate the detective. Sherlock Jr. almost sits several times but gets distracted each time. The glasses get switched, so the poisoning attempt is foiled. Finally, the pool game begins. The villains exit the room and wait for the explosion. But it does not come. First Keaton performs a series of amazing trick shots, in which somehow the thirteen ball is untouched although other balls fly about the table. The gag is dragged out: the detective scratches, and the villains must return to the room and shoot again. At last the detective plays the thirteen ball and banks it in. No explosion. Keaton finally reintroduces the exploding thirteen ball in the film's climactic comic chase, only after several other gags intervene.

Late in the film, Sherlock Jr. allows himself to be captured, but only after placing a woman's dress in a box outside the hideout's window. After a comic scuffle, Sherlock Jr. jumps out the window and through the box. He lands on his feet, having been transformed into what appears to be a woman wearing the dress he had put in the box. Keaton repeats this gag a few minutes later when he seems to jump through the stomach of his trusty assistant, Gillette, who bears a striking resemblance to his waking-life boss in the theater (Ford West plays both roles). The bad guys (and the audience as well) wonder not only where he is but also how he performed the stunt. Having learning his lesson from Houdini, Keaton never lets on.

Like many silent comedies, *Sherlock Jr.* has as its centerpiece a comic chase. The challenge to the comedian is to make the chase different and interesting, and in Keaton's case that translated into making it more dangerous and more risky. Early in the sequence he gets locked on a roof. The bad guys drive away, but the detective grabs hold of a railroad-crossing barrier and uses it to vault into the back of the bad guy's car. In the same sequence, Keaton rides on the handlebars of a motorcycle driven by his assistant. The assistant falls off, but the detective, unaware, rides on. He weaves in and out of traffic, gets pelted with sand by a road crew, crosses a half-built bridge at the precise moment it is made whole by two trucks crossing under the

Harold Lloyd, the bespectacled Everyman, proved irresistible to Roaring Twenties audiences.

unfinished portion, and finally avoids a log in the road when it is dynamited in half just as he drives through it.

Sherlock Jr. is mostly a short expanded to feature length. The longer running time enabled Keaton to set up, execute, and punctuate his gags more painstakingly, but the narrative thread is as thin as it is in any Keaton short. A far better effort at narrative is made in Keaton's subsequent and best-known feature, *The General* (Keaton and Clyde Bruckman, 1927). Though it has its share of elaborate stunts (using as a centerpiece a train hurtling down the tracks) and showcases the comedian's ability to risk life and limb without expressing any emotion, *The General* integrates the gags into a cogent narrative—in this instance about an

unlucky loser who is rejected by the Confederate army and tries to prove himself (to a young woman, of course) by rescuing a train that has been hijacked by the Union army. The film climaxes with a comic chase after the young man steals the train back and tries to return home; it ends with a sweet scene between the comic hero and the girl (Marion Mack).

Just as the silent era was coming to a close, Keaton signed with MGM. There he locked horns with Thalberg and Mayer, both of whom maintained hands-on control over production and regarded actors strictly as employees. Forced to follow scripted scenes closely and prohibited from staging dangerous stunts (Mayer wanted him to use a stuntman!), Keaton became depressed and descended into alcoholism. The last films that billed him as a star were attempts to team him with the nightclub motormouthed comic Jimmy Durante. It was a profound indignity. Keaton appeared in nearly sixty features after the advent of sound, though mostly in walk-on roles, as in Billy Wilder's *Sunset Boulevard* (1950) and Richard Lester's *A Funny Thing Happened on the Way to the Forum* (1966).

Harold Lloyd

Unlike Chaplin and Keaton and so many other stars of comedy films in the 1920s, Harold Lloyd was never a vaudeville performer of any note. He was just an extra, a veteran of cameos and walk-ons. It was while working as an extra that Lloyd first met and befriended a fellow supernumerary named Hal Roach. When Roach inherited some money, he quit working as an extra and took a stab at moviemaking, and he asked his friend and fellow extra to come along for the ride. The rest, as they say, is history. Lloyd became one of the silent era's biggest stars, and Roach became a successful producer, eventually credited with over one thousand short films and features, including several Laurel and Hardy titles and the entire *Our Gang* series (known as *The Little Rascals* when released for television).

(*right*) Harold Lloyd's death-defying high and dizzy in *Safety Last!* (Fred C. Newmeyer and Sam Taylor, 1923).

Working for Roach, Lloyd first experimented with a character named Lonesome Luke, an obvious nod to Chaplin's Little Tramp. While Chaplin wore baggy clothes and huge clown's shoes, Lloyd (as Luke) donned an outfit that looked a couple of sizes too small. The Lonesome Luke pictures were moderately successful, but Lloyd soon tired of playing a stock character. Unlike Chaplin and Keaton, whose screen characters were very much a matter of stylized performance, Lloyd fashioned for himself a far more natural and naturalized persona, a quiet, boyish comic Everyman with an optimism that proved irresistible in the Roaring Twenties.

Lloyd made more than one hundred one- and two-reelers between 1916 and 1919 but became a star only after he ditched Lonesome Luke and began making features and playing a new character with 1922 *Grandma's Boy* (Fred C. Newmeyer). Whereas Chaplin's waddle masked a dancer's grace and Keaton's stony face was a counterpoint to his acrobatic stunts, Lloyd's bespectacled mild-mannered character only appeared to be uncoordinated. Lloyd himself was an amazing athlete. His most famous stunt—and it may be the greatest stunt in silent-film comedy—comes near the end of *Safety Last!* (Newmeyer and Sam Taylor, 1923) as the pale-faced country boy (Lloyd) climbs the face of a skyscraper to win $1,000. His twelve-story ascent is beset by a series of comically perilous encounters—with pesky pigeons, a flying painter's scaffold, a net, a vicious dog, a mouse climbing up his pant leg, a man who is menacingly pointing a gun in his direction (but is actually posing for a

photograph), and finally a giant clock that suddenly comes loose from the building. The gag is a classic high and dizzy, a stunt at once dangerous and funny. Lloyd followed up *Safety Last!* with *The Freshman* (Newmeyer and Taylor, 1925), his much-copied collegiate-sports spoof—see the Marx Brothers comedy *Horse Feathers* (Norman Z. McLeod, 1932), the Dean Martin–Jerry Lewis feature *That's My Boy* (Hal Walker, 1951), and the Adam Sandler vehicle *The Waterboy* (Frank Coraci, 1998) for homages. It was a huge success.

From the start, Lloyd was lucky, like the characters in his features. He met Roach by chance and was with Roach at the right time: when he suddenly got rich. Lloyd's rise to stardom after *Grandma's Boy* occurred at a time when Chaplin was relatively inactive. By the end of the silent era, Lloyd had surpassed Chaplin and Keaton at the box office, and by 1928 he was the most popular and the most wealthy of the big three comedy stars of the era. But the goofy optimist persona that was perfect for the America of the 1920s and made Lloyd in many ways the ideal Jazz Age comedian— a wide-eyed optimist, a go-getter—did not play well after the stock-market crash of 1929, and Lloyd, like Keaton, did not make a successful transition to sound.

Laurel and Hardy

Stan Laurel understudied Chaplin while both were members of the Karno comedy troupe. In 1913, when Chaplin quit Karno for Sennett and Keystone, Laurel quit as well, to try his hand at American vaudeville. After some success onstage, he ventured west to make movies. Success did not come quickly or easily, however. By the time Laurel formally teamed up with Oliver Hardy, in 1927, he had retired as a performer and was earning his living writing gags and directing two-reelers. Hardy was at the time a serviceable screen heavy in melodramas and comedies, which is to say that he was a character actor making a decent living playing tough and bad guys. Alone, neither was anything like a movie star.

(*left*) Stan Laurel (*left*) and Oliver Hardy, the premier comedy team of silent and early sound cinema.

Laurel first appeared with Hardy in a forgettable 1921 two-reeler titled *A Lucky Dog* (Jess Robbins), and the two did not meet again professionally until 1926, when Hardy was cast in *Get 'Em Young* (Laurel and Fred Guiol). During the shoot, Hardy burned himself in a cooking accident, and Laurel left the director's chair to play his part. When Hardy returned to the set, he was asked to play a different role, and something between the two very-different-looking men seemed to click. The following year, Laurel and Hardy co-starred in *Slipping Wives* (Guiol), produced by Roach. The film was a hit, and the duo decided to work as a team.

Putting Pants on Philip (Bruckman, 1927) is the first true Laurel and Hardy picture, and its success led to ten Laurel and Hardy two-reelers the following year, including *Leave 'Em Laughing* (Bruckman), which features a terrific laughing-gas gag in which the two men become intoxicated and cause a horrible traffic jam; *From Soup to Nuts* (Edgar Kennedy), in which they make a mess of a society dinner party; and the brilliant *Two Tars* (James Parrott), which is almost entirely composed of the joyous destruction of property during a traffic jam. The comic formula for the team was simple: the two men aspire to bourgeois society, but their ambitions are thwarted; rejected and dejected, they descend into anarchy. The destruction is cathartic, hilarious, and liberating.

Though Hardy was the so-called brains of the outfit on screen, Laurel was the creative force behind the team. He directed virtually all their films (even as other men got credit for standing behind the camera when Laurel himself was on-screen), and he mapped out the gags as well. Hardy liked to show up on the set, do his job, and head home (or to the golf course).

In 1929, after making yet another popular slapstick two-reeler, *Big Business* (James W. Horne and Leo McCarey), Laurel and Hardy made a smooth transition to sound. Their voices were as contradictory as their physiques: the burly Hardy had a deep voice; the slight Laurel spoke in a squeaky, high-pitched way that made him sound like he was on the verge of crying. Laurel and Hardy, unlike Chaplin, Keaton, and Lloyd, were not making features when sound films became the norm in 1928, and they did not work for a big studio. Though they tried their hand at feature filmmaking as early

Laurel and Hardy's *Two Tars* (James Parrott, 1928) is composed almost entirely of the joyous destruction of property during a traffic jam. Here we see the comedy team tearing the bumpers off of a car.

as 1931, with *Pardon Us* (Parrott, 1931) and *Pack Up Your Troubles* (George Marshall, Ray McCarey, and others, 1932), they were far more successful (artistically at least) making two-reelers for exhibitors still providing full film programs (including A and B features and assorted short subjects) in the late 1920s and early '30s. Their best film in the sound era was the Academy Award–winning *Music Box* (Parrott, 1932), a simple two-reel gag film about two men trying to get a piano up a flight of stairs. *The Music Box* could just as easily have been a silent film.

When the market for shorts diminished and the team turned exclusively to features, Laurel and Hardy's success as comedians and their popularity with audiences declined. Most famous among their features is the silly Christmas film *Babes in Toyland* (Gus Meíns and Charley Rogers, 1934), and there's one great gag involving a piano, a precipice, and a gorilla in *Swiss Miss* (Blystone and Roach, 1938). But otherwise, for Laurel and Hardy (as for so many other comedians whose careers began in the silent-film era), the short-film format proved to be ideal.

■ ■ ■

Between 1893 and 1914, moving pictures were transformed from a technological curiosity into a viable commercial art form. Over the following ten years the transition from an industry controlled by the East Coast MPPC to one managed by the West Coast Hollywood studio system was made complete, and with the transfer of power came a transition from short subjects to features, the first giant step toward a modern film industry.

By the end of the silent era, the studios were run much as they would be through the so-called classical era (see Chapter 3). A system of contracted labor was in force, and the production, distribution, and exhibition of studio films—no less a monopoly operation than the MPPC model had been—was devised in concert with Fordist ideas then prevalent. The founding of the MPPDA in 1922 not only promised to rein in wayward movie stars and establish production guidelines but also made clear the studios' desire to cooperate with one another for the betterment of the industry as a whole. The policies and procedures instituted by the MPPDA and adopted by the member studios went a long way toward making the industry more professional and more profitable.

With increased sophistication in the operation of the movie business came significant advances in artistic accomplishment. While movie stars dominated the fan magazines and remained the reason many folks went to the movies, an elite group of film directors began to explore the possibilities of moviemaking more fully. For the commercial enterprise of American cinema, the balance between movies and money is often tipped in favor of commerce. Only through the ingenuity and persistence of those making the movies can the creative end keep up. Key players in the early evolution of film as art were D. W. Griffith, Cecil B. DeMille, Erich von Stroheim, F. W. Murnau, Charlie Chaplin, Buster Keaton, and Harold Lloyd—filmmakers who, despite the restrictions of such a commercial and industrial art, made movies of transcendent quality and profound influence.

Silent film accounted for the first thirty years of American filmmaking. When sound film was introduced in 1926 and adopted industry-wide in 1928, silent film was still very popular. But as things played out, the two media's peaceful coexistence was impossible. The technology involved in producing and exhibiting sound films was sufficiently different from that used in the production and exhibition of silent film. So in a matter of two years, silent film disappeared forever from the American popular culture, and a new American cinema was born.

3

Technical Innovation and Industrial Transformation

1927–1938

The prosperity and excitement of the early 1920s gave way, in the last year of the decade, to an economic upheaval that touched nearly everyone in the nation. The stock-market crash of October 1929 ushered in a decade-long economic crisis—the Great Depression—that transformed almost all aspects of American life.

With the Great Depression as the backdrop, the motion-picture industry transformed itself during the 1930s. The first and most radical change was a technological one: the introduction of sound. Sound technology was extremely popular with movie audiences from the beginning, despite its initial limitations. A mere two years after the premiere of sound in movie theaters, silent films vanished completely from American screens. Color-film technologies developed in the early sound era pointed the way toward a more realistic and more spectacular film experience, but the conversion to color would take much longer than the conversion to sound. Nonetheless, the direction of American color cinema was established by technological innovations introduced in the 1930s.

Given the extreme financial pressures on the studios—between 1931 and 1933 all the studios suffered significant losses, and three went into receivership—and the fast-moving technological developments occurring at the same time, it is not surprising that the corporate structure of Hollywood went through an equally dramatic transformation at the beginning of the decade. The 1920s were dominated by three companies—First National, Loew's, which owned Metro-Goldwyn-Mayer, and Paramount—but the turmoil and opportunities of the late '20s changed the studio landscape. In control at the end of the

1930s were the so-called **Big Five** studios: Loew's (owner of MGM), Warner Bros., Paramount, 20th Century–Fox, and RKO. Just below the Big Five were the **Little Three**: Columbia, Universal and United Artists. Those eight studios, buoyed by the technical innovations of sound and color, produced practically all the films released domestically, operated worldwide distribution networks, and owned the best theaters in the United States.

The studio system that evolved from 1927 to 1938 resulted in what historians have called the classical American cinema, an approach to filmmaking that strove for an "invisible" style, a seamless look emphasizing narrative continuity over cinematic experimentation. Although the classical Hollywood style sometimes resulted in a programmatic and uniform product, it would be wrong to see the studio system as wholly hostile to individual creativity. Indeed, by the end of the decade, the two conflicting elements of film production in America—the commercial imperative and the creative instinct—seemed equally well served by the maturing system.

One of the many effects of the Great Depression was a wave of cultural and moral seriousness in response to the perceived moral lapses and excesses of the 1920s. In the eyes of many moralists, Hollywood was partly to blame. To bring movies in line with this shift in the larger culture, the studios introduced a series of self-regulatory measures. Given the scale of the film enterprise—the amount of money that the studios had on the line—self-censorship was at bottom a financial decision intended to ensure that studio product lines (films) could move through the national theatrical marketplace free from local censorship, print seizures, and boycotts. Though the regime of self-censorship stifled creativity to an extent, it was nonetheless another sign of Hollywood's maturity as an industry.

The 1930s were not only a time of technological innovation, standardized production methods, and self-censorship in film; they also witnessed the blossoming of American film genres. Genres had existed from the beginning of cinema, of course, but they flourished in the '30s because of the unique convergence of economic and cultural pressures on the industry, coupled with the narrative opportunities that sound made possible. Also, in many important ways the genres that flourished in the 1930s reflected the social and economic realities of their time. For those many Americans hurt by the Depression, the Horatio Alger ideal that anyone in America could go from rags to riches was undermined, if not altogether obliterated. We can see such an abandonment of faith in hard work and its just rewards in, for example, the series of early-1930s gangster films, which show criminality as a perversion of the success myth, a fast and self-destructive shortcut on the all-but-unimaginable road to success. In the era's romantic comedies, which often focus on the lives and loves of the idle and addled rich, audiences were able to laugh for an hour or two at the petty problems irking the inhabitants of trendy Manhattan apartments, posh urban nightclubs, and rambling Connecticut estates. Such problems were both foreign and ridiculous to the legions of underpaid or unemployed men and women who attended those films.

This chapter covers a crucial era in the history of American cinema. It begins with the advent of sound and the transformation of filmmaking that followed the industry-wide adoption of this new technology and ends on the cusp of the golden age of studio-system Hollywood.

TECHNICAL INNOVATIONS: SOUND AND COLOR

First there were silent movies. Then there was sound. That is film history made simple perhaps, but it's not inaccurate. Once the studios got serious about making, marketing, and exhibiting sound movies, there was little reason to turn back, so the transition from silence to sound was abrupt, sweeping, and irreversible. Fully synchronous sound films—films with sound that accurately reproduces the on-screen characters' voices as they deliver their lines or sing their songs—were more modern, more lifelike, and more central to the evolving American experience than their silent counterparts. They appealed to audiences from the start. But sound also required that filmmakers learn new production methods and studios purchase new equipment. Initially, it was both good and bad for business.

As a technical possibility and finally as an industry standard, sound has its own peculiar history, one not always so directly tied to the movie industry. This parallel history dates at least to 1844, the year in which Samuel Morse sent the world's first telegraph message, and continues through the 1870s, when Alexander Graham Bell and Thomas Edison secured patents for the telephone and the phonograph, respectively. It intersects first with movie history in 1888, when William Dickson and Edison timed the operation of the Edison projector and phonograph to simulate synchronous sound on film. The result wasn't perfect, and it was not a practical long-term solution to the challenge of making synchronous sound films, but it makes clear that from the start Edison had intended that films should "talk."

Developments in radio and magnetic-sound research hinted at very different possibilities for solving the practical problem of synchronizing sound and film. During the same year in which Edison and Dickson performed their experiment, the German physicist Heinrich Hertz produced the first radio waves, and an American mechanical engineer, Oberlin Smith, outlined plans for a magnetic recording system, a forerunner of the magnetic-tape recording system used in early sound films. After decades of research, discovery, and invention, the major pieces of electrical sound recording came together in the laboratories of Western Electric, where the first viable sound-film system was developed in 1924. Later called Vitaphone, Western Electric's sound-on-disc technology, like Edison's first experiment, synchronized sound recorded on a disc with the moving images projected on-screen. It was a first step, and its early adoption by one of the smaller studios demonstrated sound's strong audience appeal.

Two Western Electric engineers demonstrate the Vitaphone sound technology in the mid-1920s.

Warner Bros. and the Conversion to Sound

Before sound became an industry standard, film production and exhibition were largely controlled by three major studios: First National, MGM, and Paramount. Operating on more limited budgets were five much smaller companies: the Film Booking Office (FBO, purchased by Joseph Kennedy in 1926), Fox, the Producers Distributing Corporation (PDC), Universal, and Warner Bros. Unable to compete head-to-head with First National, MGM, and Paramount, the smaller studios had to be satisfied with their smaller share of movie revenues. But the advent of sound changed all that.

Armed with a prototype and a patent for their Vitaphone system, Western Electric courted First National, MGM, and Paramount, but found no takers. Finally, Warner Bros. decided to take a calculated gamble. Though the Warner brothers (born Harry, Jack, Albert, and Samuel Eichelbaum) and their studio's business whiz, Goldman, Sachs investment banker Waddill Catchings, appreciated that the technology would not arrive in a mature or fully integrated state all at once, they figured (correctly) that the publicity they'd receive from the introduction of "talking pictures" would be considerable.

In September 1925, Warner Bros. retrofitted an old studio on Flatbush Avenue in Brooklyn, New York, to produce sound films using Western Electric technology. To showcase the new technology, the studio signed licensing agreements with the Metropolitan Opera, the New York Philharmonic, and a number of popular entertainers, including the vaudeville singer Al Jolson. Warner Bros. signed these contracts before it had any use for the talent involved, but in signing classical and pop entertainers well before the transition to sound, the company was able to avoid paying the inflated rates routinely demanded by talent once sound became the norm. The Warners were business mavericks and visionaries of a sort.

The brothers invested in sound because it promised to upgrade their company. Given the studio's lack of movie stars and the relatively small size of its operation, sound offered Warner Bros. a practical means by which to become a major player. Sound was hardly necessary to the industry as a whole, however. The big studios were making plenty of money with silent pictures. In 1926 the studios boasted a combined weekly movie-theater attendance exceeding 100 million. American films had penetrated foreign markets as well. The Hollywood film was, by 1926, already well on its way toward becoming the medium's gold standard. Without competitive pressures pushing them along, the three major studios seemed willing to wait for the development of a more mature sound-film technology before making the move to sound production. But once Warner Bros. introduced the new technology, the bigger studios were inclined, perhaps even obligated, to follow suit.

Early Experiments with Sound on Film

Although Warner Bros. pushed ahead with its commitment to sound-on-disc technology, nearly everyone in the industry acknowledged that sound recorded directly on film had more of a future. Many researchers were racing toward that goal, but by far the most interesting and most controversial of the early players in the development of sound-on-film technology was Lee De Forest.

Sound-film pioneer Lee De Forest, photographed in 1916 demonstrating his Oscillion tube for his radio telephone transmitter. De Forest's Audion tube was an essential component in the amplification of motion-picture sound.

Mary Astor and John Barrymore in the Warner Bros. silent-sound hybrid *Don Juan* (Alan Crosland, 1926).

In April 1922, De Forest announced the development of Phonofilm, a system, derived mostly from radio technology, that synchronized sound on film. But much as Phonofilm proved an important initial step toward synchronized sound on film, De Forest failed dismally in his efforts to interest the studios, in part because he tried to sell sound films as a curio, a short-subject attraction that the bigger studios did not need and thus did not want. The inventor's anti-Semitism got in the way as well; De Forest could not hide his dislike of the Jewish entrepreneurs who managed the industry.

Spurned by the studios, De Forest began releasing his work through his own company, **De Forest Phonofilm**. His short sound-film "reviews" were programmed like vaudeville shows and featured variety-show headliners like Eddie Cantor and W. C. Fields. But although Phonofilm programs proved attractive and interesting, they never rivaled the studios' silent films. Phonofilm was more a medium unto itself, another sort of attrac-tion, and a throwback to the time when just show-casing a technology was enough to get people into a theater. In the end, De Forest devoted himself to the wrong initiative—competing with the studios—rather than attempting to license his promising technology to them.

When De Forest founded Phonofilm, he took as a partner Theodore Case, an innovative sound engineer. A series of poor business moves—attempting to expand Phonofilm into Canada (fur-nishing 250 theaters with the equipment) without sufficient working capital and floating $22 million in stock to finance the move (which got De Forest in trouble with the attorney general of New York)—crippled the company, and in 1925 Case resigned, taking with him the license to use cer-tain key Phonofilm patents. Case turned out to be a far better businessman than his former partner, and he had fewer concerns about the Jews he rou-tinely encountered in the movie industry. Whereas De Forest initially saw his technology as the foun-dation for a rival medium, Case understood that cooperating instead of competing with the studios was the better route, and he profited nicely. In 1926, Case sold his interests to William Fox, a man De Forest openly despised. De Forest never benefited much from his discoveries and in later years became a bitter critic of what the radio, television, and film industries had done with (what he considered were) his audio innovations.

Early Silent-Sound Hybrids

While sound on film was being developed behind the scenes, sound-on-disc technology took center stage in 1926, care of Warner Bros. The first silent-sound hybrid (a silent film that featured a few sound sequences) was *Don Juan* (Alan Crosland, 1926), which went into production as soon as the Warners' Flatbush Avenue studio was ready for use. The film was shot in the traditional silent method, and then, after a series of successful test screenings, a Vitaphone version was readied for distribution. The Vitaphone prints were screened in selected properly equipped theaters, and an alternative all-silent version was released simultaneously. *Don Juan* is not a talking picture in any sense of the term; instead, its use of sound is confined to a standardized musical score and some neatly timed musical cues and sound effects.

On August 26, 1926, in New York City, the studio screened *Don Juan* along with short sound films of a dramatic reading, an operatic number, and an orchestral performance. Although the studio attracted filmgoers for two reasons—*Don Juan* starred the dramatic movie star John Barrymore, who had considerable box-office appeal, and plenty of advertising had heralded the debut of Vitaphone—according to newspaper accounts of the day the highlight of the show was not the Barrymore film but Giovanni Martinelli's performance of the aria "Vesti la giubba" from Ruggero Leoncavallo's opera *Pagliacci*.

Less than three weeks after the Vitaphone debut, Warner Bros. announced its intention to produce all of its forthcoming features (amounting to about twenty-five films) with Vitaphone sound. The films would also be made available in silent versions for theaters not capable of projecting Vitaphone sound pictures. Thus Warner Bros. made clear as early as 1926 that it was committed to sound.

The second Vitaphone feature, *The Better 'Ole* (Charles Reisner), premiered in October 1926. It starred Syd Chaplin, Charlie Chaplin's half-brother, but the premiere was far less significant for Chaplin's appearance than for the star of the musical short on the same Vitaphone program, Al Jolson. In his customary blackface—a traditional vaudeville performance style that does not translate well to today's political and cultural environment—Jolson performed a number of popular songs: "April Showers," "When the Red, Red Robin Comes Bob, Bob, Bobbin' Along," and "Rock-a-Bye Your Baby with a Dixie Melody." Popular demand for more of Jolson ensured the subsequent success of *The Jazz Singer* (Crosland, 1927), which headlined the next big Vitaphone program.

In November 1926, sensing that Warner Bros. had made a breakthrough with movie audiences and may have more up its sleeve, four rival companies (Paramount, MGM, United Artists, and PDC) offered to purchase a 50 percent interest in Vitaphone. Warner Bros. declined the offer; the studio was interested instead in licensing the sound technology to the other studios and theater chains. In so doing, Warner Bros. believed it could benefit financially from the success of rival studios and theaters and in the process further cement its position as the industry's sound-film innovator.

The Jazz Singer: Making the Transition to Sound Necessary

The Jazz Singer premiered at New York City's Warners' Theatre on October 6, 1927. There is considerable debate among historians about its reception. Some describe the premiere as a pivotal event in film history, in which filmgoers gave themselves over to the talking picture. Others insist on the anticlimax of the first few shows. The reviews were indeed mixed: Jolson's singing was widely praised, but his acting was just as widely panned. The box office, especially for its initial release, was good but not inordinately large. Warner Bros. had made the movie quite cheaply, so it profited nicely, but the film's modest success seemed to hardly issue an industry mandate.

However we account for the specifics of the film's initial theatrical run, the rivals of Warner Bros. had to take notice as *The Jazz Singer* completed its second run in 1927. Due in large part to its gamble on sound, the studio's stock rose from $21 a share in 1925 to $132 a share in 1927. Rivals in the industry could no longer afford to ignore the talking film's bottom line.

Though it is routinely thought of as the first American "talking" picture, *The Jazz Singer* was not a fully synchronous sound film. Instead, it was shot as a silent film, and a sound track was added later. Except for the musical numbers, which of course showcase Vitaphone, there are just two brief scenes with dialogue. The first occurs between musical numbers, as Jolson delivers what has since become a historically prescient line: "Wait a minute. Wait a minute. You ain't heard nothing yet." It was a routine part of his stage act to make such a promise, but in the context of film history, the line—delivered as Jolson looks directly into the camera—carries much greater significance. Later in the film we catch a brief conversation at the

piano between Jack Robin (Jolson) and his mother (Eugenie Besserer). Some historians highlight that brief scene as the first time film audiences witnessed something other than a canned performance—the first time they heard (thanks to sound-film technology) a "real" exchange between characters in a film.

The Jazz Singer was an adaptation of a popular stage melodrama about a cantor's son who decides to pursue a career on the stage singing popular songs. Jolson, like the film's title character, was himself a pop singer and a cantor's son, so the film was widely mistaken to be biographical, a filmic look into his life before he became a star. But the facts of the matter undermine such a reading. The stage version of *The Jazz Singer* starred another Jewish singer-comedian, George Jessel, who, legend has it, was the first choice of Warner Bros. to reprise his Broadway role. But Jessel declined to

Al Jolson performs in blackface in *The Jazz Singer* (Alan Crosland, 1927). Though such performances exploited racial stereotypes, they were very popular in the 1920s on the vaudeville circuit (where Jolson was a huge star).

From left to right: The sound-film pioneers Harry Warner, Darryl Zanuck, Jack Warner, Al Jolson, and Samuel Warner, photographed in 1927.

appear in the film adaptation after a dispute with the studio over money (he wanted extra money for the recorded songs) and the studio's choice of the film's director, Alan Crosland (Jessel was holding out for a Jewish director). Jessel's exit worked in the end to the advantage of Warner Bros. The public's fervent interest in Jolson as a celebrity—an interest that preceded his work in the film—was a key to *The Jazz Singer*'s success.

The first Academy Award ceremony, held in 1929 to honor movies released in 1927–1928, proved to be a good night for the silent-sound hybrids. The winner of the Outstanding Picture award, *Wings* (William Wellman, 1927), starring the recently dubbed "It" Girl, Clara Bow, was a silent-sound hybrid shot, like *The Jazz Singer*, as a silent film with selected scenes produced with sound. F. W. Murnau's *Sunrise* (1927), the first and only Academy Award winner for Unique and Artistic Picture (an award that was scrapped in favor of a single Outstanding Picture category, later called Best Picture), was also a hybrid of sorts. Though shot and structured like a silent film, *Sunrise* was released with a lush orchestral sound track. At the same Academy Awards ceremony, Warner Bros. won a special award "for producing *The Jazz Singer*, the pioneer outstanding talking picture, which has revolutionized the industry."

After the success of *The Jazz Singer* and, more important, as a consequence of the sudden surge in the value of Warner Bros. stock, the big studios moved quickly to accommodate sound in their production and exhibition facilities. In 1927 the Warner brothers' rival, William Fox, premiered his studio's sound technology, Movietone (developed after the studio purchased Case's Phonofilm). Movietone was more mobile than the technology that supported Vitaphone, and that mobility made possible on-location shooting, a distinct advantage that Fox's newsreel outfit, Fox Movietone News, would exploit that year to cover Charles Lindbergh's history-making solo transatlantic flight from New York to Paris.

Meanwhile, Western Electric began to develop its own sound-on-film process, in part to circumvent Warner Bros.'s control over its (sound-on-disc) Vitaphone licenses. The rivals of Warner Bros., unhappy as well with the studio's us-versus-them stance, began to work together to develop an alternative. On May 11, 1928, Electrical Research Products, Inc. (ERPI), a subsidiary of Western Electric responsible for developing new sound-on-film technology, signed an exclusive deal with Paramount, Loew's, First National, and United Artists. Soon after that historic deal several other studios, big and small, including Columbia and Universal, signed on as well.

General Electric and its subsidiary Radio Corporation of America (RCA), which produced Photophone, a rival sound-on-film technology, were cut out of the deal. The studios' decision to go with ERPI over Photohone was particularly rankling because it was at the behest of Loew's MGM, First National, Paramount, Universal, and PDC (as part of the so-called five-cornered agreement) that GE had developed the sound-on-film process in the first place. When the studios decided against Photophone in favor of ERPI, GE purchased a distribution outfit (FBO), American Pathé (a production studio that had just taken over PDC), and the Keith-Albee-Orpheum theater chain, forming Radio-Keith-Orpheum, or RKO, an instant major studio.

During the first wave of the industry-wide conversion to sound, Vitaphone and Movietone were marketed most aggressively to midsize theaters, movie houses that during the silent era had been deemed too small to sport a full live orchestra. The recorded-music tracks of the early sound and silent-sound hybrid films promised the smaller venues big-city sound (and presumably more sold-out shows).

The conversion to sound was expensive for the smaller and midsize independent movie houses, which, unlike the studio-owned showcase theaters, had to pay for the changeover to sound without a corporate parent's help. When the stock market crashed, these theaters were unable to pay back the loans that had financed the changeover. In 1930, just months after the crash, the studios swept up many of the failing theaters. In so doing, they extended studio control over exhibition, expanding further the vertically integrated system of production, distribution, and exhibition that remains in effect today, albeit in a significantly more complex form.

Just as the original MPPC had endeavored to centralize and standardize industry operations back when motion-picture technology was in its infancy, the big Hollywood studios of the late 1920s embraced the new sound technology in order to control more completely the three principal aspects of the film business: production, distribution, and exhibition. The better-capitalized and better-organized studios used the shift from silent films to sound to restructure their operations and better consolidate their positions within the fledgling sound-cinema marketplace. The evolution of the modern studio trust—a key first step toward a more modern, more corporate Hollywood—can be traced directly to the transition from silents to talkies, the transition from an industry dominated by entrepreneurs and other ambitious dreamers working more or less in competition with one another to one managed by well-organized media conglomerates working cooperatively and collusively for the betterment of the studio system as a whole.

Tinting and Painting by Hand

Experiments in color film date to 1909. But color took much longer than sound—decades rather than years—to become an industry standard.

Hand tinting, which involved submerging lengths of exposed film in transparent dyes, dates to 1895 in the United States, when Thomas Edison released selected hand-tinted prints of *Butterfly Dance*. In 1905, Pathé Frères introduced frame-by-frame stencil tinting, which allowed for a some-what more standardized and more selective use of tints on film. Using stencils, a director could selectively color a puff of smoke orange, as in Segundo de Chomón's *The Golden Beetle* (1907), or detail costumes, as in Augusto Genina's *Cyrano de Bergerac* (1925), in which characters wear yellow vests over green coats. Uniform tinting—tinting an entire sequence a single color—was used less decoratively and more evocatively, to set a mood, as in the rose-pastel tint employed in a tender scene in D. W. Griffith's *Broken Blossoms* (1919), or to highlight screen action, as in the deep red tint used in the burning-of-Atlanta sequence in Griffith's *Birth of Nation* (1915). But however attractive it was in its various manifestations (uniform or stencil), tinting was not effective as a way of accurately simulating the colors of real life.

Only slightly more realistic was the rarer process of hand painting positive prints. It involved frame-by-frame painting directly on each print, a process made possible by magnifying lenses and fine sable brushes. Though hand-painted films no doubt wowed audiences, the process was hardly practical. There are 16 frames for every second of film, or 57,600 frames for every hour, and every frame of every print had to be painted separately.

Such artisanal processes had little future in an industry moving toward modern methods of mass production. And experiments in refining or standardizing tinting were not the answer. In 1916, for example, Max Handschiegl, an engraver, and Alvin Wyckoff, a studio cinematographer, both employees of Paramount, modernized the tinting process by using color lithography, which allowed filmmakers to "machine-tint" scenes. Machine-tinting graced prints of *Joan, the Woman* (Cecil B. DeMille, 1917), *Greed* (Erich von Stroheim, 1924), *The Phantom of the Opera* (Rupert Julian, 1925), and *The Big Parade* (King Vidor, 1925), all big-budget releases.

Through the 1920s the studios struggled to supply the demand for more and more positive prints. Having to color each print separately was an unreasonable expense (it roughly doubled the production costs) and in the end was an obstacle to keeping up with audience demand. Moreover, filmgoers in the 1920s found color in films decorative, not realistic. The studios quickly came to realize that a more realistic process was necessary if color film was to have a future on American movie screens.

The arrival of sound-on-film technologies made matters worse for filmmakers interested in using the early color processes. The dyes used in the tinting process interfered with the sound tracks of the talkies. Once synchronous sound became the industry standard, tinting was abandoned altogether. The ability to produce color prints from color negatives—in other words, to develop a viable method for mass-producing color films—became not only an aesthetic necessity but also an industrial one.

Technicolor

In 1909 the first practical color film system was introduced by Charles Urban, an American inventor and entrepreneur who was adapting work that had been begun by the British cine-pioneer G. A. Smith. Urban dubbed this first process Kinemacolor. Two years later he began screening complete programs of Kinemacolor actualities, including the popular travelogue series *Roving Thomas* (five films released in 1922 and 1923). Urban was influential and successful, at least at first: his Kinemacolor programs were screened in theaters all over the world. The content of the films was less important than the gee-whiz effect of the projected colors on-screen. As with Lee De Forest's early

Phonofilm, Kinemacolor was an attraction, a curiosity in an era when folks enjoyed seeing the next new thing.

Other experiments in color followed—Gaumont's Chronochrome, for example, and William Van Doren Kelley's Prizma Color—all of which required cameras and projectors with several lenses operating in sync. The key moment in the history of modern color film came in 1915 in Boston, when an industrial consulting firm headed by Herbert Kalmus, Daniel Comstock, and W. Burton Westcott founded the Technicolor Corporation (the *Tech* in the name was a nod to the Massachusetts Institute of *Tech*nology, where Kalmus and Comstock were educated).

The theoretical foundation of color-process film dates to the mid-nineteenth century, when the Scottish physicist James Clerk Maxwell discovered that all natural colors are composed of some combination of the three primaries—red, green, and blue—which, when combined, produce white light. Color-film systems like the one developed by Technicolor were based on a simple principle. To produce color from white light, one must either add or subtract color. Processes that added color were dubbed *additive;* those that subtracted color, *subtractive.* Early film processes endeavored to simplify matters and economize by using just two colors (red-orange and blue-green), but in the end three-color systems became the rule.

Urban's Kinemacolor was an additive two-color system. Among its drawbacks were the inherent restrictions of the two-color process, especially evident in flesh tones, which never seemed right. Technicolor process No. 1, developed by Kalmus in 1917, was a subtractive system (which seemed to work better than Urban's additive system), but since it, too, was just a two-color (red-and-green) process, flesh tones remained a problem.

The technical problems posed by color-film photography were significant. Technicolor process No. 1 required high-speed shooting and projection, roughly doubling the cost of the film needed to produce a movie. Technicolor process No. 2 (1922), also a two-color system, used a beam-splitting camera to produce two separate color negatives that were printed separately on thin film stock and then cemented together, one on top of the other. Loew's produced the first film to use process No. 2 (in selected scenes), *The Toll of the Sea* (Chester Franklin), an adaptation of the Puc-

Herbet Kalmus, president of Technicolor, photographed in 1950.

From left to right: Una O'Connor, Olivia de Havilland, a Technicolor technician, Claude Rains, and Basil Rathbone prepare a color check on the set of Michael Curtiz and William Keighley's *The Adventures of Robin Hood* (1938).

cini opera *Madama Butterfly*, which was distributed to modest success by MGM in 1922. In 1923, Paramount produced and distributed Cecil B. DeMille's (first version of) *The Ten Commandments* with selected color sequences. MGM followed suit with selected color scenes in Erich von Stroheim's *The Merry Widow* (1925).

The clumsy process of cementing one print on top of the other was eliminated in 1928 by Technicolor process No. 3, a two-color system. Although it did not double the cost of the film needed to make a movie, process No. 3 nonetheless added about 30 percent to a movie's budget. The first complete color films—films that are in color from start to finish—used Technicolor process No. 3: Warner's *On with the Show!*

(Crosland, who had also directed *The Jazz Singer*) and *Gold Diggers of Broadway* (Roy Del Ruth), both released in 1929. Over thirty features released in 1930 were in Technicolor, but color did not catch on right away, in part because the final product looked fake. Sound had introduced a deeper realism to motion pictures. Early color processes seemed to move them in the opposite direction.

Finally, in 1932, Kalmus introduced Technicolor process No. 4 (also known as three-strip Technicolor), a three-color system that would become the industry standard in color film production for the next twenty years. Technicolor was able to exploit its process number 4 to monopolize color-film technology and production; studios shooting with Technicolor film had to rent the

A lobby card for the 1934 comedy short *La Cucaracha* (Lloyd Corrigan), the first live-action three-color-process film.

company's proprietary cameras, hire Technicolor camera operators, use Technicolor-brand makeup, and send the exposed film to a Technicolor lab. Technicolor process number 4 was first used in the Disney short cartoon *Flowers and Trees*, a *Silly Symphony* (Burt Gillett, 1932). The comedy short *La Cucaracha* (Lloyd Corrigan), released in 1934, is routinely credited as the first live-action three-color-process short film. The first Hollywood three-color-process feature was Rouben Mamoulian's *Becky Sharp* (1935), an adaptation of William Makepeace Thackeray's novel *Vanity Fair*.

A number of well-regarded films made in the 1930s were made in color, including *A Star Is Born* (Wellman, 1937), Disney's *Snow White and the Seven Dwarfs* (1937), *The Adventures of Robin Hood* (Michael Curtiz and William Keighley, 1938), and most famously, *The Wizard of Oz* and *Gone With the Wind* (both directed by Victor Fleming and released in 1939). As successful and significant as those films were, black-and-white remained the industry standard in the 1930s. Indeed, color films were not the norm until color television sets became widely available. In 1936 only 1 percent of the 362 films released by the major studios were in color. When broadcast television made the transition to color in the mid-1960s, the studios followed suit to better compete with its small-screen

rival and to more easily and more successfully exploit television as a second-run venue for their films. In 1960, 37 percent of the films in general release were in color. In 1968, 100 percent were in a color—that is, every one of the 177 studio films released that year.

THE STUDIO SYSTEM

The management of film production is fraught with complications, unexpected expenses, creative differences, and all sorts of delays and changes on the fly during virtually every stage of development, production, and postproduction. The expense of making, promoting, and distributing movies is prohibitively high, and the risk involved in every motion-picture production requires of studio executives a gambler's cool and an accountant's attention to budget. During the early 1930s, executives at the eight major studios that survived the financial crisis of 1929 and the conversion to sound worked to structure their businesses so that they would be less vulnerable to risk. Among their most powerful strategies was the so-called contract system.

Child star Jackie Cooper (*right*), photographed signing his studio contract with MGM in 1931. Sitting at his side is the MGM executive Louis B. Mayer.

The Contract System: A System of Contracts

The technicians, mechanics, set decorators, costume designers, hairdressers, writers, directors, actors, and (most and best of all) movie stars were all signed to exclusive contracts whose terms were dictated by the studios. Everyone making films at a studio worked for the studio. Films were written and rewritten, actors cast and recast, sets constructed and modified, lighting and sound rigged, footage shot and edited—all using employees on the studio payroll. Executives managed a workforce that could move easily from one project to another, reproducing the same basic task on film after film. The result of all this contracted labor (some five hundred filmmaking professionals spread among the eight studios) was an unprecedented economy of scale and extraordinary efficiency.

The contract system involved what attorneys call consideration, for both the studio and its employees. The studio used its contracts to control production costs and efficiently staff the production teams at work on its slate of films. The contracted talent helped the studios establish a trademark identity; after all, the same talent base produced all of a studio's films. What emerged from the contracted pools of talent were distinctive studio styles—the gritty realism evident in so many Warner Bros. films, for example, or the lavish, glamorous look of the films made at MGM.

To be contracted to a studio meant a guarantee of work and a steady paycheck, participation in a glamorous industry, and job security. For many Hollywood workers—indeed, for most who were not at the very top in their given field—a studio contract was a pretty good deal, especially during the economically challenging 1930s. For movie stars, however, the results were mixed. The studios circa 1928 to 1938 boasted "stables" of stars. The term was not meant to be as insulting as it sounds today, and it was apt. Stars were still "the fundamental thing," and just for them studio executives devised the "option," or "adhesion," contract. That contract compelled a star to work exclusively for a studio, but like Scotch tape it was sticky on just one side. That is, in the standard actor's contract only one party, the actor, was compelled to comply to the stipulations for the contract's duration.

Joan Crawford as a misunderstood flapper Diana Medford in Harry Beaumont's *Our Dancing Daughters* (1928), the film that made her a star. At her side is Johnny Mack Brown, playing Diana's one true love, the millionaire stockbroker Ben Blaine.

At specified intervals the studio had the option of pulling out without cause. At those intervals through the duration of the contract, the studio could review the actor's work and choose to renew the contract (at a specified pay scale) or exercise its option to terminate the actor's employment. The actor, on the other hand, had no option to terminate his or her employment. Furthermore, management assigned films as well as offscreen appearances and publicity tours. Like it or not, onscreen and off, the actor was bound by his or her contract to perform.

During the contract era the studios gave actors their stage names, controlled their public image, and (until the Supreme Court decided otherwise many years later) owned the merchandising rights to their on- and offscreen image. A star was an asset. He or she was "created" and "protected" by the studio.

Consider, for example, the movie star Joan Crawford. Born Lucille Fay LeSeur on March 23, 1904 in San Antonio, she changed her name to Billie Cassin (taking the surname of her second stepfather, a vaudeville manager) in Kansas City, where she worked at a laundry. After winning a dance contest, Cassin ventured west to try her luck in the movies. In 1925 Casssin was "discovered" by MGM, and the studio mounted a nationwide contest to rename its latest star. Lucille Fay LeSeur, later known as Billie Cassin, then became Joan Crawford. Crawford's big break came with *Our Dancing Daughters* (Harry Beaumont, 1928), in which she plays the flapper socialite Diana Medford. Flappers were young women who lived the high life in the Roaring Twenties, seeking an economic, social, and sexual independence that was at once exhilarating and disturbing to the men in their social circle. Portraying Diana Medford was a far cry from being Lucille Fay LeSeur (the product of poverty and a broken home). But Crawford nonetheless made her mark with the part and was subsequently cast in a series of flapper-socialite roles, including *Our Modern Maidens* (Jack Conway, 1929), in which she played Billie Brown—a character also worlds apart from the former Billie Cassin.

Stars rarely went public with complaints about the contract system. The results were inevitably counterproductive. The movie star James Cagney, for example, walked off the Warner Bros. lot in 1932, demanding more money and fewer assignments. The conflict went to arbitration, and Cagney got a modest increase in salary and the promise of *just* four pictures per year. Three years later he again took Warner Bros. to arbitration, claiming that the studio had exceeded the four-picture-per-year provision of his contract. He had another concern, but it was not one that could be framed in a legal argument: Cagney was unhappy that the studio had continued to typecast him in the role of an Irish tough guy—which it had done to foster his particular image; after all, *The Public Enemy* (Wellman, 1931), in which Cagney plays an Irish gangster, had made him a star. Cagney won the early rounds in arbitration, but the contract system was an elaborate and difficult scheme to crack. Any studio hiring Cagney while his case dragged on—while his contract with Warner Bros. was still technically in force—risked owing Warner

Bros. compensation (should Cagney lose his suit against the studio) and, more important, risked destroying the gentlemen's agreement among the studios that prevented one from tampering with another's star.

Bette Davis also walked out on Warner Bros., in 1936, two years after *Of Human Bondage* (John Cromwell), the melodrama based on Somerset Maugham's novel, made her a star. The studio suspended her without pay and deftly used the press to characterize the young star as a spoiled brat. Given the economic conditions for most Americans in 1936, Davis, the studio argued, was already doing pretty darn well. Like Cagney, Davis wanted greater control over her career. She wanted to make fewer and better films, and she wanted her roles in those films to better display her range and talent. (In the mid-1930s, Davis had been typecast as a home-wrecking Jezebel.) Studio executives countered that they knew what was best for her. They certainly knew how best to *use* Bette Davis for the betterment of Warner Bros. Because the risks of taking on the studios were so great, few stars followed the route taken by Cagney and Davis.

Studio Producers and Studio Styles

As it was for actors, the contract system was both good and bad for directors. During the contract era the studios created a production system under which films might be made according to a standard set of policies and procedures. The studios endeavored to put their stamp on certain distinct product lines and styles. Directors signing with a studio knew in advance what sort of pictures fit that studio's style. Working under such a system, directors were afforded ready access to capital, technology, and skilled and talented labor, all without the headache of raising funds to finance the production, paying the weekly bills, keeping the schedules updated, and ensuring that all the right folks showed up for work. All those details of logistics and financing were handled by studio executives, leaving the director free to concentrate on shooting the film. Understandably, for their trouble and money, the studio executives wanted a say in what got released under their company's name.

The so-called classical Hollywood cinema thus took shape at this point in American film history as a consequence of this system of production. It

The Warner Bros. star James Cagney walked off the studio lot in 1932 demanding more money and fewer film assignments. He got a modest bump in salary but failed to break free of his studio contract.

was characterized by linear, third-person story-telling and a seamless, practical visual style that aimed to make audiences forget they were watching a movie. In part the result of conscious decisions made by studio executives, for whom simple storytelling was a mantra, but also a natural outgrowth of the workshop structure of the studio system itself, this type of filmmaking aimed to make movies that seemed simply to unfold before the viewers' eyes, with aesthetic choices made to move the plot efficiently and highlight the movie's stars within the strictures of the relevant genre. Such a film form, such a discernible, accessible film language, served the studios' desire to standardize their product, and it served as well to help predict success in the quixotic theatrical marketplace.

Studio chiefs and production supervisors like Darryl Zanuck, Louis B. Mayer, Irving Thalberg, Jack Warner, David O. Selznick, and Samuel Goldwyn did not perform the day-to-day production tasks expected of a film director. But the systems they implemented, the talent they hired, and the assignment of that talent to particular projects facilitated and influenced production at their studios and defined their studios' signature styles.

Irving Thalberg, Boy Wonder

In the early 1930s, MGM was managed by Irving Thalberg, called the boy wonder on account of his tender age (he was twenty-four when he became one of MGM's top executives) and baby face. Thalberg instituted "a supervisory system," a model for the contract era, in which employees at every level (from stagehands to movie stars) were supervised by hands-on studio management. The success of

Greta Garbo and John Barrymore in *Grand Hotel* (Edmund Goulding, 1932). The MGM production chief Irving Thalberg conceived of the film as a showcase for MGM's stable of stars

his system led to similar management policies industry-wide.

With an eye toward delivering a quality product, Thalberg hired the literary giants Maxwell Anderson, Robert Benchley, F. Scott Fitzgerald, Moss Hart, Ben Hecht, and Dorothy Parker and kept under contract two longtime screenwriters, Anita Loos and Frances Marion. For Thalberg the story was key. Once the story was set, the studio system would take over. With the studio's typecast stars and film crew available for the asking, the story was the only real variable, the only aspect of the production that changed materially from film to film.

Evidence of Thalberg's initial success with his studio system at MGM can be found in the annual box-office lists for the first few years of the 1930s. Of the top six films for 1930, four were produced and distributed by MGM: *Anna Christie* (directed by studio stalwart Clarence Brown, based on a play by Eugene O'Neill, written by Frances Marion, and starring MGM contract players Greta Garbo and Marie Dressler), *Our Blushing Brides* (directed by the studio director Harry Beaumont, written by the studio writer John Howard Lawson, and starring Robert Montgomery and Joan Crawford in yet another flapper picture), *Caught Short* (directed by Charles Reisner, co-written by Eddie Cantor, and starring Marie Dressler), and *The Divorcee* (directed, but unsigned, by Robert Z. Leonard and starring Thalberg's wife, Norma Shearer, and Robert Montgomery).

The development, production, and release of *Anna Christie* revealed Thalberg's deft understanding of the moviemaking business. By the time MGM began developing the picture—optioning (paying a fee for the exclusive right to develop a motion picture based on a book or play) and then refining the script, casting and staffing the picture, scouting locations (if necessary), making the costumes and the sets—sound had been the industry standard for about two years. Garbo, MGM's biggest silent-film star, had yet to speak on screen, and Thalberg used the star's hiatus as a come-on. "Garbo Talks" became the simple, brilliant tagline that promoted the film. Audiences waited two years to hear the star speak and then waited another 30 minutes once the picture began to hear her say her first lines on camera: "Gimme a whiskey, ginger ale on the side. And don't be stingy, baby." The "property" (or story), adapted from O'Neill's Pulitzer Prize–winning play, was the perfect choice for Garbo. The story line of the play includes the sort of melodramatic elements that Garbo had played so well and so often during the silent era: a desperate young woman runs away from home, becomes a prostitute, suffers, and is redeemed. The play's heroine is Swedish, as was Garbo, so her accent, heard for the first time onscreen, fit perfectly.

With its Pulitzer Prize–winning source material, A-list screenwriter, and star casting, *Anna Christie* was clearly a prestige picture. Like all the other studios, MGM made a range of pictures in the 1930s, but Thalberg appreciated the value of identifying MGM primarily with its prestige product line. It was good public relations.

Nineteen thirty-one brought more success, with *Min and Bill* (directed by George W. Hill, written by Frances Marion, and starring Dressler and Wallace Beery as lovable losers on the waterfront) and the jungle adventure picture *Trader Horn* (directed by W. S. "One-Take Willy" Van Dyke and starring Harry Carey), two of the five top-grossing films of the year. Thalberg's signature picture, *Grand Hotel* (Edmund Goulding), was released in 1932, and it, too, was a top-five picture at the box office. *Grand Hotel* was conceived from the start as a showcase for MGM's stable of stars: Garbo, Beery, Crawford, and John and Lionel Barrymore. Though uncredited, Frances Marion worked on the script, an adaptation of a popular novel by Vicki Baum titled *Menschen im Hotel*. *Grand Hotel* perfected the prestige model introduced with *Anna Christie* in 1930. It was based on a well-known work of literature that nonetheless fit the familiar melodrama formula. Its production was staffed by the studio's A list, from the grips to the cinematographer to the big movie stars, as many as Thalberg could get into one picture.

MGM's films under Thalberg were successful at the box office and did exceedingly well when it came time for the industry to congratulate itself for a job well done. The 1929–1930 Academy Awards saw two 1930 MGM films—*The Divorcee* and *The Big House* (Hill)—nominated in the Outstanding Production category. Two MGM contract employees won major awards, Norma Shearer for her performance in *The Divorcee* and Frances Marion for her script of *The Big House*. For 1930–1931, MGM contract players Lionel Barrymore and Marie Dressler won Oscars for their roles in *A Free*

Soul (Brown, 1931) and *Min and Bill*, respectively. *Grand Hotel* took the Outstanding Production award for 1931–1932. That same year, Wallace Beery won for his role in *The Champ* (King Vidor, 1931), Helen Hayes won for her role in *The Sin of Madelon Claudet* (Edgar Selwyn, 1931), and Frances Marion won again, for the original story of *The Champ*. Of all those commercially and critically successful films, not a single one was directed by anyone whose name is familiar to us today. But every one was "handled" from development through release by Thalberg.

Darryl Zanuck and the Warner Bros. House Style

Darryl Zanuck was as much an iconic force at Warner Bros. as Thalberg was at MGM. His production system (more so than any ideology or creative formula) fostered the Warner Bros. recognizable studio style.

Zanuck's past was more colorful than that of the other studio executives: abandoned by his young parents at the age of thirteen, he saw action in World War I just two years later and then put in time as a boxer, steelworker, and garment-factory foreman. Drawing on those adventures, he began writing stories for pulp magazines, soon discovering that they were easily adapted as motion pictures. After writing gags and stories for Mack Sennett and Carl Laemmle (Universal's chief executive), he landed at Warner Bros., where he made his name as the creator of the *Rin Tin Tin* (canine-action) films. At Warner Bros. he was able to churn out scripts at a pace of almost two a month—storytelling came easy. By 1925, Zanuck was head of production. He was all of twenty-three years old.

When Zanuck became a top executive at Warner Bros., it was still one of the five small studios trailing well behind First National, MGM, and Paramount. But it was about to make its bold move with *Don Juan* and the subsequent sound-film productions, and Zanuck's job was to get those films made even though the studio was more strapped for cash than ever. Zanuck fashioned for Warner Bros. a streamlined, cost-effective (some would say cheapskate) production system.

Zanuck was very much a self-made man, driven to succeed despite little or no formal education. He appreciated the importance of writing and, by extension, writers (as did Thalberg), and he was an especially fast and clever storyteller who could step in to fix a film if he felt he had to. And most and best of all for the Warner brothers, Zanuck knew the value of a dollar.

Spending as little of the Warners' money as he could, Zanuck adapted a star-genre formula that suited the company's budget constraints and the talents of the stars the studio had on hand (and under contract) at the time. In so doing, he redefined a popular genre: the gangster film.

In the early 1930s, James Cagney and Edward G. Robinson were two of the most popular male stars under contract to Warner Bros. The dark, unsentimental, hard-hitting style of so many early Warner Bros. films—what became identifiable as the Warner Bros. house style—was the result of Zanuck's canny use of low-budget production values (hence the gritty realist look) and his exploitation of unglamorous ethnic tough-guy stars such as Cagney and Robinson.

A prototype for the Warner Bros. house style was the social-realist *I Am a Fugitive from a Chain Gang* (Mervyn LeRoy, 1932). This early Warner Bros. sound film offered an unflinching view of life on a southern prison work detail. Paul Muni plays James Allen (also known as Allen James), who twice escapes from the work detail. After the first escape, he moves north, marries, and becomes a successful engineer. But when his marriage goes bad, his wife turns him in, and he is sent back to prison. A second escape leads to the film's open-ended final scenes, in which we see James's uncertain life on the lam, indoors by day, on the road at night.

Though the studio's films were foremost made to be entertaining, the movies shot to suit the Warner Bros. house style went a long way toward presenting an earnest and often disturbingly realistic account of the social problems of the Great Depression. William Wellman's *Wild Boys of the Road* (1933), for example, tells the story of the homeless unemployed, depicted as otherwise decent folk brought to a kind of serial brutality by their unhappy circumstances. The so-called wild boys are two decent high-school kids (Frankie Darro and Edwin Phillips) who run away from home so as not to become burdens to their struggling parents. What they find on the road is hardly romantic, as they camp in places like Sewer City,

Paul Muni (*right*) as the unjustly jailed James Allen victimized by a cruel prison guard (Harry Woods) in the Warner Bros. realist melodrama *I Am a Fugitive from a Chain Gang* (Mervyn LeRoy, 1932).

a squalid site they occupy until they are tossed out by the police. When a character in the film remarks, "Jail can't be any worse than the street," it is hard to argue otherwise.

Labor organization and its violent early history in the United States is depicted with signature grit and realistic detail in the Warner Bros. film *Black Fury* (Michael Curtiz, 1935), a film that dares to imply that there is collusion among organized crime, the police, and the mercenary strikebreakers. Ironically, Warner Bros. itself would soon become the site of industry labor unrest, and the Warner brothers became bitter and powerful enemies of the nascent Hollywood labor movement.

An interesting subtext of the Warner Bros. lower-budget house policy is the issue of celebrity, or "name," directors. At MGM, where making pres-

tige pictures was the goal, Thalberg eschewed such directors. At Warner Bros., which set its sights so much lower (at least in terms of production budgets), a number of men we now view as important directors flourished. For the company executives who cut their checks, studio directors like William Wellman and Michael Curtiz were just contract employees. But a look back at those directors' careers reveals a remarkable body of work. Wellman directed the gangster classic *The Public Enemy* (discussed in detail later in this chapter), *The Call of the Wild* (adapted in 1935 from the popular Jack London adventure novel), the melodrama *A Star Is Born* (1937), the romantic comedy *Nothing Sacred* (1937), and the Foreign Legion epic *Beau Geste* (1939). Curtiz directed a series of highly popular pseudo-historical adventure pictures

William Wellman's *Wild Boys of the Road* (1933) tells the story of the homeless unemployed, depicted as otherwise decent folk subjected to an unrelenting brutality. Warner Bros. specialized in such gritty social-realist melodramas.

starring Warner Bros. contract stars Erroll Flynn and Olivia de Havilland: *Captain Blood* (1935), *The Charge of the Light Brigade* (1936), and *The Adventures of Robin Hood* (1938). And though the film is far better known for its stars—Humphrey Bogart and Ingrid Bergman—Curtiz also directed *Casablanca* for Warner Bros., in 1942 (discussed at length in Chapter 4).

CENSORSHIP: REGULATING FILM CONTENT

Film censorship in the United States dates to the beginning of cinema history—to 1894, when a series of "erotic-dance" kinetoscopes were banned and seized in Atlantic City in response to public pro-censorship activism. Organized pressure on the studios increased dramatically in the wake of the star scandals of the early 1920s, and it showed no sign of relenting during that decade.

By the late 1920s most states, cities, and even local townships had established their own censorship boards. The members of those boards had a vested interest in censorship, and they wielded considerable power in their communities. Many of these censorship boards were housed in police departments, making the seizure of banned films easy and routine. What made the local outfits particularly problematic for filmmakers was that there were no set rules governing their decisions. And the different boards did not communicate or cooperate with one another. What might get banned in Cleveland, for example, could play in Columbus or Chicago. Filmmakers and studio distributors had no way of predicting board decisions in advance.

The development of a self-censorship apparatus by the Hollywood studios was foremost an attempt to adjust to the vicissitudes of the local censorship boards. The studios' early censorship policies and procedures, discussed below, were meant in large part to enhance public relations, to create the impression that the studios wanted what the so-called reformers and local censors wanted: good, clean, all-American entertainment. That such a bargain with the mass audience was based on a financial motive—to enable films to move freely through the marketplace without the studios' having to worry about print seizures or boycotts—was consistent with the studios' prime goal—to make money making movies. Lost in the bargain more often than not was the integrity of the content of the films themselves.

1927: The List of "Don'ts" and "Be Carefuls"

The top man at the Motion Picture Producers and Distributors of America (MPPDA), Will Hays, introduced the first industry-wide self-regulatory system in 1927, the list of "Don'ts" and "Be Carefuls." The eleven "Don'ts" included prohibitions on profanity, "suggestive or licentious nudity," and depictions of drug trafficking, white slavery, and childbirth. It also included reminders regarding what today we'd call political correctness: there were expressed prohibitions, for example, on the "willful offense to any nation, race or creed." While tolerance was to be the rule, any suggestion of miscegenation was absolutely forbidden. The twenty-five "Be Carefuls" included a caution against "realistic, potentially informative" depictions of the methods of committing certain crimes. Among those crimes were theft, robbery, safecracking, arson, the dynamiting of trains, smuggling, rape, the branding of animals or people, and cruelty to children or pets.

The list of "Don'ts" and "Be Carefuls" focused on what the uneducated, unwashed masses that consumed motion pictures so avidly might *do* with what they saw up there on the screen. It is noteworthy that MPPDA chief Will Hays supported free speech in other media. Plays and novels, he argued, need not be so strictly censored because the audience and readership of highbrow entertainment knew better. Such was the philosophy behind the 1915 *Mutual* decision, in which the U.S. Supreme Court denied First Amendment protection to cinema (discussed in Chapter 1). And such was the philosophy embraced by Hays and those he hired to devise and execute industry-wide self-censorship of film content.

The list of "Don'ts" and "Be Carefuls" was an interesting document and no doubt well intended, but it was worth little more than the paper it was written on. The producers and distributors who formally resolved to follow its strictures seldom paid much attention to it, especially when censorship promised to make a movie less sensational.

The MPPDA's inability to regulate film content through its "Don'ts" and "Be Carefuls" empowered grassroots censorship outfits like Combat, a Wisconsin-based group, and the colorfully named Mothers of Minnesota. These primarily church-affiliated groups were soon joined by well-established organizations that branched out into film censorship, including the Parent Teacher Association (PTA), the NAACP, the Catholic War Veterans, and even the International Longshoreman's Association. Local police, community boards, and state departments of education joined the effort to force the studios to behave more responsibly.

1930: The Motion Picture Production Code

With the apparent failure of the "Don'ts" and "Be Carefuls," the MPPDA turned to a Jesuit priest, Father Daniel A. Lord, and a devout Catholic journalist, Martin Quigley, the editor of *Exhibitors Herald-World* (later the *Motion Picture Herald*), to write a more comprehensive set of production regulations. In 1930, Lord and Quigley completed their task and handed in a document that, with few changes, governed the production of American films for over thirty years.

As MPPDA chief, Hays was most interested in protecting studio films in the nationwide marketplace. After all, he worked for the studios. Lord and Quigley had no such conflict of interest, however. They were very much in favor of regulating and restricting film content without regard to profits. Thus the complex and comprehensive code they devised was designed like a catechism, a list of lessons and rules, backed by a moral philosophy laid out in detail in the code's preamble. "Motion picture producers recognize the high trust and confidence which have been placed in them by the people of the world," it begins, "and which have made motion pictures a universal form of entertainment." Given such a moral responsibility, the code promised "a still higher level of wholesome entertainment" so that films might support "spiritual or moral progress," "higher types of social life," and "correct thinking."

Given the headache caused by local censorship boards, the studios simply had to comply. Hays did not play a role in writing the code and may not have been on the same page, so to speak, with Lord and Quigley on every aspect of the document. But when Lord and Quigley's work was made public, it was dubbed the Hays Code, a tag that stuck.

Unlike the list of "Don'ts" and "Be Carefuls," the 1930 Motion Picture Production Code was lengthy and detailed. It elaborated twelve areas of concern:

1. *Crimes against the law.* Included were subsections on murder (no instructions please, and no brutality); the methods used by criminals who stole, blew things up, or burned things down (to avoid inspiring copycats in the audience); drug trafficking and alcohol production, distribution, and consumption (which in 1930 were still prohibited under the Eighteenth Amendment).

2. *Sex.* Included were subsections on adultery (never justified), scenes of passion (with a specific prohibition on "excessive and lustful kissing"), seduction or rape (seen as more or less the same thing; a subsubsection prohibited the use of such scenes in comedy films), "sex perversion" (not defined or elaborated), white slavery, miscegenation, venereal disease, and childbirth and children's sex organs (the on-screen depiction of which was strictly prohibited).

3. *Vulgarity.* "Good taste" must prevail.

4. *Obscenity.* Not defined and something of a catchall.

5. *Profanity.* Rough language (expletives, blasphemy) was strictly censored. The list of forbidden words included *alley cat* (applied to a woman), *cripes, fanny, whore, damn, pansy,* and *nuts* (except when meaning "crazy").

6. *Costume.* "Complete nudity" was strictly forbidden. Diaphanous, overly revealing clothing could not be worn. Scenes showing characters getting undressed "should be avoided."

7. *Dances.* No sexually suggestive movement or gesture was allowed.

8. *Religion.* All faiths and denominations must be respected. "Ministers of religion . . . should not be used as comic characters or as villains."

9. *Locations.* "The treatment of bedrooms must be governed by good taste and delicacy."

10. *National feelings.* Reverence for flag and country must be observed and respect given to other nations and nationalities.

11. *Titles.* "Salacious, indecent, or obscene titles shall not be used."

12. *Repellent subjects.* These subjects had to be treated "within the careful limits of good taste": executions, third-degree methods (used by police), brutality, "branding of people or animals," "cruelty to children or animals," white slavery, and "surgical operations."

1930–1934: The Studios Resist the Code

In 1930 the task of enforcing the code was left to two MPPDA functionaries, Colonel Jason Joy and Dr. James Wingate, neither of whom proved willing or able to take on the studios. The system of enforcement was, after all, rigged. If a studio disputed a decision made by the code administrators, it could file an appeal with the MPPDA board, which was composed of executives from the member studios. In the spirit of working together (and protecting their products in case of a future dispute) the studio executives routinely signed off on everything. Much as they did after the list of "Don'ts" and "Be Carefuls" was introduced, the studios took voluntary compliance to mean that they did not have to do anything if they did not want to.

Between 1930 and 1934, in what is routinely (if misleadingly) called precode Hollywood (there was a code, just no enforcement mechanism), the studios mostly ignored the new production guidelines. In fact, a number of films that gained wide popularity in the precode era were precisely what the code was designed to censor. A case in point is Paramount's *She Done Him Wrong* (Lowell Sherman, 1933), starring Mae West, a notoriously risqué stage comedienne, a master of the wisecrack and the double entendre. Before the film was produced, West received a lot of publicity when she was sentenced to ten days in jail on an obscenity charge stemming from the Broadway run of her show *Sex*. (She got out in eight, with two days off, she joked, for good behavior.) The conviction served only to make her more popular and more attractive to Paramount. Hays had been hired to clean things up in the movie colony. West's arrival promised to make his job a lot more difficult.

As much as any film of its era, *She Done Him Wrong* reveals how little the Hays code meant in precode Hollywood. The film opens with a street cleaner shoveling horse manure, a crude joke that sets the tone. There is a nude painting, ostensibly of West's character, Lou, in plain view in the saloon where she performs. Throughout are wisecracks of questionable taste, at least by the standards of the time. A man says to Lou, "You're a fine woman," to which she responds, "One of the finest women to have walked the streets." Later another man says, "I've heard so much about you." And again she cracks wise: "But you can't prove it." She refers to Captain Cummings (Cary Grant), an undercover cop posing as a pastor, as "warm, dark, and handsome." When she delivers the now-famous come-hither line "Why don't you come up and see me?" and then adds, "You can be had," she and we still think she's talking to a man of the cloth. The reasons for her brazen behavior are made clear in a subsequent conversation: Her maid asks her if she's ever felt the "wolf at her door." "I've had him in my bedroom," Lou replies.

Even more risqué is West's on-screen performance of musical numbers from her notorious stage act. The first, "Easy Rider," is about a jockey who knows how to ride. "A Guy What Takes His Time," the second number, rather obviously lays out what she wants in the bedroom. After all, as Lou quips, "When women go wrong, men go right after them."

Early-sound-era gangster films, like *Little Caesar* (Melvyn LeRoy, 1931), *The Public Enemy* (William Wellman, 1931), and *Scarface* (Howard Hawks, 1932), also reached American screens in seeming defiance of the new code. In 1931 nearly 20 percent of the total studio output featured gangster themes, roughly doubling the already high percentage of the previous year. The trend increased public scrutiny and pressure for censorship.

Exotic adventure films, which were very popular in the early 1930s, also defied the new code. Yet *Tarzan, the Ape Man* (W. S. Van Dyke, 1932), which features an all-American star athlete, Johnny Weismuller, winner of five gold medals at the 1924 and 1928 Olympics, ran afoul of the new

Mae West as the singer and nightclub owner Lady Lou, seducing Serge (Gilbert Roland), yet another "warm, dark, and handsome" man, in the salacious precode comedy *She Done Him Wrong* (Lowell Sherman, 1933).

code. Though the film seems tame by contemporary standards, its stars (Weismuller and Maureen O'Sullivan, who plays Jane) wear skimpy costumes and blissfully live together unmarried and mostly unembarrassed.

Monster films, also a popular genre in the precode era, posed problems as well. *Dracula* (Tod Browning, 1931), *Frankenstein* (James Whale, 1931), and *King Kong* (Merian C. Cooper and Ernest B. Schoedsack, 1933) all deal with proposed or attempted sexual violations. Dracula hypnotizes women and enters their bedrooms to penetrate their bodies with his teeth. Frankenstein similarly lurks outside the heroine's bedroom window with more than just revenge on his mind. And Kong, of course, has a thing for a blonde (Fay Wray). The code hardly allowed for that sort of thing.

The all-American hero and Olympic gold-medal-winning swimmer Johnny Weismuller as Tarzan and Maureen O'Sullivan as Jane in W. S. Van Dyke's 1932 adaptation of Edgar Rice Burroughs's adventure novel *Tarzan of the Apes*. The film made industry censors nervous; Tarzan and Jane live in sin and cavort about the jungle wearing as little as possible.

The most egregious code breakers were the early-sound-era melodramas. Cecil B. DeMille's *Madame Satan* (1930) tells the story of a woman who wins back her philandering husband by livening things up in the bedroom. *Young Sinners* (John G. Blystone, 1931) was released with the tagline "Hot youth at its wildest . . . loving madly, living freely." Many precode melodramas ended with scenes that punished sin but otherwise spent the vast majority of the screen time wallowing (and, by extension, visually celebrating) sins and the sinners who commit them. For example, *Call Her Savage* (John Francis Dillon, 1932), a comeback vehicle for "It" girl Clara Bow, exploits tabloid stories about the star herself (stories that Bow had responded to by suing for libel) by re-presenting them (fictionally, of course) on-screen. The film includes a shopping list of vice—infidelity, sadomasochism, kept women—with each instance providing the excuse for frequent flashes of female skin.

In *Unashamed* (Harry Beaumont, 1932), a rich girl (Helen Twelvetrees) is seduced by and then marries a money-hungry cad (Monroe Owsley). Her brother (Robert Young), who holds a deep and vaguely incestuous affection for her, kills the cad and stands trial for the murder. Just when things look their bleakest, the sister acts the part of the unrepentant party girl. He and we know this is an

Fay Wray and Bruce Cabot in a publicity photograph for the 1933 film *King Kong* (Merian C. Cooper and Ernest B. Schoedsack). Though the film seems innocent—even quaint—today, in 1933 it raised problems with the fledgling Hays Code.

act, but her plan succeeds: for her sacrifice (of reputation, of a future with somebody—anybody—else), the brother is saved.

The studios packaged even the wildest, sexiest, most code-defying melodramas with come-ons to the women in the audience. For example, an over-the-top melodrama about a wild girl (played by Miriam Hopkins) in a small southern town, *The Story of Temple Drake* (Stephen Roberts, 1933), sported the tagline "A love story understandable to every woman." The notion that every woman might "understand" Temple Drake—who is raped and then forced by her circumstances to fake affection for her assailant until she finds an opportunity to murder him and, after a strange courtroom drama, is acquitted and then forgiven by the man she truly loves—seems far-fetched, but the marketing message trumped the reality.

The failure of the code between 1930 and 1934 revealed two things about the early studio system. First, it made clear that the studios were willing to work together. When films as outrageous as *The Story of Temple Drake* were brought to the MPPDA board on appeal, the studio representatives routinely reversed the findings of the code administrators. They did so not because they liked or disliked the films in question or because they thought such films should not be censored but because they appreciated that someday they might have a film with a code problem and they might need their fellow MPPDA board members to see things their way. Second, before 1934 the studios

Miriam Hopkins as the ill-fated southern belle Temple Drake, who falls in with a gang of bootleggers in the lurid precode melodrama *The Story of Temple Drake* (Stephen Roberts, 1933). The film was based loosely on William Faulkner's southern gothic novel *Sanctuary* and seemed to defy the production code at every turn of the plot.

simply did not take seriously the depth of so much of their audience's contempt for the Hollywood film colony and the films in such questionable taste that were made there. It took four years for the MPPDA to appreciate the extent of its public relations problem. Once it did, it moved quickly to establish self-censorship policies and procedures that might satisfy even its most ardent detractors.

1933: The Catholic Legion of Decency

From the advent of the theatrical exhibition of motion pictures, the Catholic Church played a significant role in censorship activities, especially in the nation's most lucrative urban markets: New York, Chicago, and Detroit. A balance of power of sorts among the nation's three major religions emerged, an informal system of checks and balances: Protestant money to a large extent financed the film business, Jews managed production and exhibition, and Catholics, shut out of the profit and production ends of the business, made their voices heard as consumers, demanding certain types of products—or else.

That is an oversimplified model, of course, but it is not necessarily inaccurate. American Catholics, most of whom lived in urban centers, where the studios' showcase theaters made a lot of money, were avid moviegoers. Threats of an organized boycott of certain films or, worse, of entire slates of films at the showcase theaters gave well-organized church-sponsored pro-censorship activists a lot of power. The Catholic Church's influence over American cinema lay in its followers' fervency and organization and in their economic clout. Two prominent Catholics in particular boasted significant economic influence: George Mundelein, by then cardinal of Chicago, controlled a huge account with the Wall Street firm Halsey, Stuart, which handled mortgages for several studios, and A. P. Giannini, a prominent American Catholic, was president of the Bank of America, which financed, through short-term loans, hundreds of motion pictures. Their distaste for so much of what got made in Hollywood no doubt worried the mostly Jewish studio executives.

Increasing public activism supported and financed by the church and wealthy American Catholics culminated in the formation of the Catholic Legion of Decency in 1933. Acknowledging the failure of the industry's self-censorship efforts, the Legion introduced its own film-rating system, either A ("all ages") or C ("condemned"). And it was not just a film that was condemned by a C rating: a parishioner caught by his or her priest attending a C-rated film had plenty to confess. The Legion's own filmgoer's pledge, first penned in 1934, included some colorful prose: "I condemn absolutely those salacious motion pictures, which, with other degrading agencies, are corrupting public morals and promoting a sex mania in the land."

In May 1934 the studios got a glimpse of what an organized church-sponsored boycott might look like. In Philadelphia, Dennis Cardinal Dougherty asked his parishioners to stop going to the movies; subsequently box-office receipts in this major urban market fell by 40 percent. After the Philadelphia boycott the studios began consulting with the Legion as they readied films for production, in order to avoid nasty surprises after a film's release.

1934: The Production Code Administration

The defiance of the code between 1930 and 1934 proved to be a dangerous game. Hays was initially unable to persuade the studios to regulate themselves, but as the influence of the Legion of Decency and other grassroots censorship organizations grew, the member studios of the MPPDA began to understand that if they did not institute and, more important, execute some form of content regulation, someone else would. Fear of federal regulation was not that keen, but local censorship was inconsistent and unpredictable and seriously complicated the distribution process. The MPPDA had rules in place, its 1930 Motion Picture Production Code, and those rules promised to clean things up in Hollywood and improve the public image of the industry as a whole. What the producers and distributors needed in 1934 was someone with the energy and the clout to compel the studios to comply with the code. Not incidentally, that someone needed to be Catholic.

Amid fiery rhetoric from influential clerics like Cardinals Mundelein and Dougherty who were threatening boycotts of all motion pictures, the moneymen in New York forced the studio managers in Hollywood to begin abiding by the code. On July 1, 1934, the board of directors of the MPPDA created the Production Code Administration (PCA) to oversee movie production. The PCA operated at the pleasure of the MPPDA, so it could enforce certain basic standards only by having the member studios agree to comply and, moreover, agree, as an aspect of their very membership in the MPPDA, to adhere to the regulatory decisions made by the PCA. Although censorship at the micro level could be troublesome and costly—having to cut a key scene out of a film, for example, could negatively affect the film's overall appeal to audiences and at the very least create extra expense and hassle in the film's production—the studios decided collectively that such sacrifices were worth it on the macro level. They were willing to sacrifice the integrity of individual products (cutting films to suit the code) for the larger goal of maintaining stable public relations between Hollywood and the American film audience.

Between 1934 and 1954 one man, Joseph Breen, a former newspaperman and a Catholic pro-censorship activist, headed the PCA. Breen took his job seriously and was an ardent censor. Behind his PCA was the basic public relations agenda of keeping the nation's Catholics from boycotting Hollywood films and local censorship boards from banning and seizing individual motion pictures. But Breen's efforts were heartfelt. He had clear ideas about what was right and what was not, what people ought to see and what they ought not see. For twenty years, American movies were as much the product of his sensibility as they were the product of any powerful mogul's or influential filmmaker's.

GENRE AND STUDIO HOLLYWOOD

Between 1927 and 1938 the studios placed a great deal of emphasis on genre films, films that fall easily into one familiar category or another: gangster, melodrama, horror, musical, comedy, and so on. All eight of the influential studios sought to balance their release slates in order to diversify their product line. To maintain the diversity, they organized their films in terms of genre, as product types, much like automobile models. And the American audience came to recognize that organizing principle in deciding which movies to see and which to avoid. Though all the studios diversified release slates, several became identified with certain genres. Warner Bros., as mentioned earlier in this

Joseph I. Breen, the film industry's chief censor, photographed in 1946.

chapter, became known for its gritty urban dramas, especially its crime and gangster films. MGM gained a reputation for musicals, and Universal specialized in horror films.

The Gangster Film

Most early-sound-era gangster films were framed by a reformist message or theme: crime is bad, of course, and it is up to law-abiding citizens, the police, and the courts to make the city safe once again. Within this public-service frame one finds the gangster himself, at once monstrous and fascinating, free to live his life independent of social norms and moral constraint. The gangster's life on film is a success story of sorts: rags to riches to rags. His path to glory ends at the end of a rope or at the business end of a rain of bullets. He dies because he was bad; he is punished for his ill-won success. Crime pays, but only for a while.

The gangster film focuses squarely on the social problems of Depression-era America. After all, at its core the gangster film is about capitalism: the accumulation of capital, its risks and consequences. In most of the early sound crime films, the gangster is a recent immigrant—the accent and lifestyle tell us that—and he takes a road to riches on the wrong side of the law because on the right side he has no chance.

The gangster has expensive clothes, an entourage, and a blonde—all the accoutrements of a young immigrant's success in the 1930s. He dies young and still handsome, having lived long enough to enjoy himself along the way. The gangster's adventure in a world of plenty is complex and fraught with temptation and punishment. He succeeds because he is willing to act on impulses that civilized Americans repress. And his downfall is as violent as his rise: he is gunned down, or knifed, or hanged, dispatched in a manner as fast and dirty as his way of life.

During Prohibition, gangsters were all too real. Al Capone, alias Scarface, a notorious Chicago kingpin in organized crime, made the cover of *Time* magazine in 1930, and the thirteen-month crime spree (of bank robberies, kidnappings, and murders) by John Dillinger, Public Enemy Number 1, was front-page news from the summer of 1933 through the summer of 1934. However frightening Capone and Dillinger might have been in real life, they were nonetheless romanticized in an American popular culture that increasingly celebrated such iconoclastic and dangerous characters.

The groundbreaking early-sound-era Warner Bros.' gangster films, *Little Caesar* (Mervyn LeRoy, 1931) and *The Public Enemy* (William Wellman, 1931), ably display the peculiar affinities between the new sound technology and the requirements of

Edward G. Robinson as the Italian mobster Rico Bandello in the early Warner Bros. gangster film *Little Caesar* (Mervyn LeRoy, 1931).

a new, more realistic gangster film: the snazzy gangster argot, the screeching car tires and other sounds characteristic of the urban chase scene, and most and best of all the shocking sound of gunfire, the rat-a-tat of the genre's weapon of choice, the tommy gun.

Both Edward G. Robinson and James Cagney, the stars of *Little Caesar* and *The Public Enemy*, were themselves ethnic city boys. Though Jewish, Robinson easily played the role of the Italian mobster Cesare Enrico (Rico) Bandello in *Little Caesar*. Cagney was part Irish, and as Tom Powers in *The Public Enemy* he came to epitomize the young Irish tough. A close look at these two films offers something of an armchair psychoanalysis of these fictionalized first-generation immigrants whose stories they tell. Both Robinson and Cagney were

relatively short (as was Capone). Gangsterism was thus for their characters a compensation of sorts tied to pangs of physical inadequacy. The gay subtext in *Little Caesar* is difficult to miss. Rico has a thing for his friend Joe (Douglas Fairbanks Jr.). His gunman, Otera (George E. Stone), is loyal, but that loyalty seems grounded in an unrequited desire for Rico. The suggestions regarding sexual desire are, in a politically incorrect way of course, meant to tell us what we need to know about Rico as a man. Audiences in the 1930s came to recognize suggestions of homosexuality on-screen as signs of weakness and decadence. That recognition no doubt reflected popular notions at the time. The point here isn't that Rico is homosexual—he certainly does not act on his desire—but in the film's easy psychology his denial of his homosexual longings or inclinations explains why he's a sociopath.

In *The Public Enemy*, Cagney's Tom is clearly heterosexual, but he regards women with rage and contempt. In the film's most famous scene, Tom gets a call from his boss asking for help in collecting some overdue payoffs. The prospect of violence and random bullying turns him on: Tom can't wait to tell his partner the good news. But his buddy is busy in an adjacent bedroom. Tom has to wait, something he does not do well. He sits down to breakfast, laid out on a tablecloth by a moll (Mae Clarke) who has been around long enough to have started thinking about keeping house. Resisting the domestic restrictions implicit in sitting down to a "nice" breakfast like a proper family man—he is of course neither proper nor a family man—Tom decides it's time to get a new moll. So he jams a halved grapefruit in this moll's face. Later that morning we see him pick up the new moll (the platinum-blond bombshell Jean Harlow), much as he might pick up a new car or a new suit.

What these two precode-era gangster films reveal is the seductiveness of the American gangster as a romantic type. Though both films go out of their way to show the gangster as sociopathic, audiences seemed to look past the disturbing character tics. The gangster's sense of entitlement, his ability to do and say whatever he wants, and perhaps best of all his money (and the things that his money can buy him) spoke directly to an audience suddenly down on its collective luck. Sure, the gangster paid for his crimes in the end. But in the meantime he enjoyed life in ways many people in the film audience could only dream about.

The eccentric millionaire Howard Hughes co-produced *Scarface* (Howard Hawks) in 1932 for United Artists. The film was not as popular as either of the two big Warner Bros. crime films discussed above, but it nonetheless proved significant to the history of the gangster genre in a number of ways.

Unlike *Little Caesar* and *Public Enemy*, which reached the public more or less intact, *Scarface* was pulled from release early in its first run. It returned to theaters with a disclaimer tacked on to the open-

Paul Muni offers up his profile to show off his X-shaped scar in a publicity shot for Howard Hawks's *Scarface* (1932). Hawks based Muni's character on the real-life scar-faced gangster Al Capone.

ing credit sequence (declaring that gangsters are evil and it is up to us to do something about them) and a completely reworked ending. In the first version (what we would call today the director's cut), Tony (alias Scarface, played by Paul Muni) dies in a hail of bullets. We hear the sound of a crowd in a sort of hushed celebration, and then the camera pans up to reveal a neon sign that sums up Tony's motivation, his drive for success: "The World Is Yours." In the revised version, Tony stands trial and is condemned by the judge and hanged.

Tony "Scarface" Camonte is obviously modeled on Capone. He is an immigrant peasant who believes that, as the neon sign outside his apartment suggests, the world is indeed his. After assassinating the rival gangster Big Louis (Harry J. Vejar) at the start of the film, Tony tells his sidekick, Guino (played with panache by George Raft, an actor with reputed ties to underworld figures), how to make the world "yours." There are three simple rules to follow to get ahead, he says: "Do it

(*left*) James Cagney as the Irish gangster Tom Powers in William Wellman's 1931 Warner Bros. gangster film *The Public Enemy*. Punctuating his resistance to all things domestic (and civil), Tom crushes a halved grapefruit into the face of his girlfriend (Mae Clarke).

Tony "Scarface" Comante's sister, Cesca (Ann Dvorak), and Tony's best friend, Guino (George Raft), eye each other in Howard Hawks's *Scarface* (1932). Tony's misguided jealousy of their romance leads to his downfall.

first, do it yourself, and [miming the action of shooting his gun] keep on doing it."

Tony follows through on this mantra, ridding himself of his competition in a rival gang and then killing his boss. One of the spoils of war is his late boss's moll, the blond Poppy (Karen Morley). On his arm she seems to signify, albeit briefly, mainstream success. But like all gangsters—at least all movie gangsters—Tony is doomed by his own methodology, his impatience with the American dream.

Muni plays Tony as a subhuman, asocial monster. His arms dangle to his knees like the arms of an ape, and as he gets a taste of the stuff only money can buy—expensive suits, for example—it becomes clear that wealth is wasted on him because he has such lowbrow taste. Like Rico in *Little Caesar*, Tony also has a sexual problem: He acquired Poppy after he killed the crime boss, Lovo (Osgood Perkins), because that is how the game works, but he can't have the woman he really wants, Cesca (Ann Dvorak), because she is his sister. Early in the film, Tony returns home for a big plate of spaghetti (such ethnic clichés abound) and discovers that Cesca is out with a guy. When she returns, he scares off the suitor and lectures his sister on proper deportment. She asks what gives him the right to lecture her, and he replies simply, "I'm your brother." The line is countered immedi-

ately, first by Cesca, who says, "You don't act like it," and then by his ever-suffering mother, who in a thick accent warns Cesca, "Tony don't like you the way he makes you believe . . . to him you're just a girl."

The film's alternative endings complicate Cesca's eventual reciprocation of her brother's affection. In both the director's cut and the release cut, Tony kills Guino because he thinks he has seduced Cesca. Guino has indeed slept with Cesca, but he has done the right thing first (he has married her), a detail Tony learns only after the fact. Cesca comes to Tony's lair (followed by the cops) prepared to shoot him for killing her husband, but she can't pull the trigger. In the original version she says, "You're not my brother," and quickly softens to his entreaty that they face the cops together like a proper gangster couple. In the edited version she is shot before she gets to say much of anything (except a line or two condemning him first as a killer and then as a coward, which he indeed reveals himself to be when the cops smoke him out of his hideout with tear gas).

Like *Little Caesar*, *Scarface* is unrelentingly dark. It is lit like a 1920s German expressionist film, which is to say that it employs low key lights (lights placed low or on the ground in front of the actors, like narrow spotlights) and limits fill lights (overhead lights) and backlights to create looming shadows. The lighting scheme gives the film an ominous feel: the urban world comes alive only after dark. The gangster himself emerges as a creature of the night both literally and figuratively.

Howard Hawks adopted the antimontage style used by German expressionist directors like F. W. Murnau. Antimontage deemphasizes editing in favor of expressive mise-en-scène and camera movement. The opening of *Scarface* shows Tony's assassination of Big Louis in a single shot. Hawks's mobile camera follows Tony as he enters the club, walks a ways behind a translucent screen, pulls the trigger, drops the gun, and exits, walking out of the frame. The low key lighting and antimontage style became a visual trope for later crime and gangster films.

In the early 1930s, gangster films accounted for almost 20 percent of Hollywood's studio output. But the genre's popularity proved brief. Howard Hughes so shamelessly promoted *Scarface* with a publicity campaign that made clear the connections between gruesome real-life headlines and

Hollywood fiction that politicians, newspapermen, local activists, and so-called reformers called on Will Hays to step in and do something about the gangster films. Once the PCA took over the enforcement of the Motion Picture Production Code in 1934, the studios cut back significantly on the production of films that fit the popular *Little Caesar–Public Enemy–Scarface* formula.

Melodrama

Melodrama, a key dramatic genre of the silent era, remained a staple of 1930s American cinema. Confident in the continued appeal of the genre, studios cast A-list talent and invested considerable resources in the production of melodramas throughout the decade.

For most filmgoers, melodrama is a genre that is difficult to define but immediately recognizable. It is a construct of collective experience and not the totality of constitutive elements, which is to say that it is the effect of the genre more than its narrative or stylistic parts that audiences recognize. Melodramas play mercilessly and shamelessly on our sympathies and antipathies, and audiences tend to read them and the characters in them as more real and more realistic than stories and players in other genres. At the heart of melodrama is the notion that in real life we don't always get what we deserve. Whereas other genres neatly reward the good and punish the evil, melodrama is characterized by serial suffering. What the characters learn in the end is not that things can or will be righted but rather that the world is unfair, suffer-

Live fast, die young (in a hail of bullets). Tony "Scarface" Comante (Paul Muni) is gunned down by the police in the final scene in the release cut of Howard Hawks's *Scarface* (1932). In an edited version released at the behest of industry censors, Tony is tried, found guilty, and hanged. The censors believed that the public death depicted in the original version made the gangster too much of a celebrity, and they preferred instead to let the justice system take care of him.

The African American housekeeper Delilah (Louise Beavers) and the white single mother Bea (Claudette Colbert) become successful business partners in John M. Stahl's 1934 hit melodrama *Imitation of Life*. The film was unusually frank about race relations in America at the time.

ing is inevitable, and people don't always get what they want or deserve. Fate and, to a large extent, bad luck pervade melodrama. The lesson is blunt and clear: good and bad intentions aside, it is impossible to change the course that one's life takes. The ironies and tragedies outweigh the sweet and the good. Heroism lies in the acceptance of that unhappy fact.

Melodramas can be especially trenchant when it comes to the social and political reality of a given place and time. Though the stories themselves seem particularly personal (these are mostly films about everyday people caught in difficult but not necessarily unbelievable circumstances), larger social and political arguments about race, class, and sexuality often enter the mix. Three very dif-

ferent directors specialized in melodrama in the late 1920s and the 1930s: John M. Stahl, Dorothy Arzner, and Josef von Sternberg.

Stahl began directing films in the silent era, shooting melodramas like *Her Code of Honor* (1919) and *Suspicious Wives* (1921). While under contract to Universal in 1932, he helmed *Back Street*. The film was a hit, and Stahl became the studio's A-list director of melodramas. *Back Street* is based on a popular novel by the novelist Fanny Hurst. It chronicles the impossible love of a young single woman (Irene Dunne) for a married man (John Boles), a plotline familiar to audiences at the time.

Stahl's second hit melodrama for Universal was *Imitation of Life* (1934), also based on a popular Hurst novel. That film tells the story of a single mother, Bea (Claudette Colbert), and her daughter, Jessie (Rochelle Hudson). Bea struggles to make ends meet until an encounter with a housekeeper and the housekeeper's daughter changes the four characters' lives forever. The housekeeper, Delilah (Louise Beavers), an African American single mother, agrees to work for Bea in exchange for room and board. As it turns out, Delilah's pancakes so impress Bea that she decides to market the recipe. (The commentary on race is less than subtle as Delilah becomes Aunt Jemima.) The pancake business takes off, and the two women become rich. And despite the color barrier the two women become great friends. The daughters, on the other hand, handle the change in their families' fortunes badly. Delilah's daughter, Peola (Fredi Washington), rejects her mother in the most dramatic manner she can: far lighter skinned, she leaves home passing for white. Bea and Jessie then lock horns when they compete for the affections of the same man. For 1934, *Imitation of Life* is unusually frank about race issues in America and unusually sophisticated in its depiction of the downside of class mobility.

Stahl's *Magnificent Obsession* was released in 1935, his third popular melodrama for Universal. Its plotline is filled with coincidences and ironies typical of the genre. By saving the life of a celebrated playboy named Robert Merrick (Robert Taylor), an elderly doctor gives up the chance of saving his own life. The doctor's young wife, Helen (Irene Dunne), blames Merrick for her husband's death, and the playboy, having been given a new lease on life, endeavors to make up for his transgressions by adopting the late doctor's selfless commitment to helping others—he enrolls in medical school. After Helen is blinded in a car accident, the recently accredited Dr. Merrick finds the perfect object of his new vocation. Of course the two fall in love.

Their relationship has at its heart an insurmountable obstacle: The blinded Helen is in love with Robert's kindness, with qualities that Robert has displayed only since her late husband saved his life. Yet she does not realize who he is, and he

believes he cannot tell her. A revelation becomes inevitable, however—such are the plot turns in melodrama—when a chancy operation that might restore her sight is developed. He encourages her to undergo the operation even though the restoration of her sight spells the end of their love affair.

Stahl's best film was his last major picture, *Leave Her to Heaven* (discussed in detail in Chapter 4), released in 1945. A far more modern film than the 1930s soap operas discussed above, *Leave Her to Heaven* highlights the intersection between prewar melodrama (a genre Stahl had worked in so expertly) and the darker, more psychological film noir (a genre considered in detail in Chapters 4 and 5).

Dorothy Arzner was the only woman employed consistently as a director in the 1930s. She worked her way up through the ranks, first as an editor—she cut the Valentino vehicle *Blood and Sand* (Fred Niblo, 1922)—then as a screenwriter—of, for example, *Old Ironsides* (James Cruze, 1926). Plenty of women were editing and screenwriting films at the time, some no doubt with ambitions to direct, but Arzner was the only one to break through the glass ceiling.

In 1929, Arzner directed the flapper melodrama *The Wild Party*, the first talkie for the former "It" Girl, Clara Bow. The film is on its surface a typical cautionary melodrama. Party girl Stella Ames (Bow) just wants to have fun, but things get out of hand at a local college haunt, and she is saved from

The recently reformed playboy Dr. Robert Merrick (Robert Taylor) tends to Helen (Irene Dunne), the recently blinded widow of the man who saved his life, in John M. Stahl's 1935 melodrama *Magnificent Obsession*.

The director Dorothy Arzner (left) and the movie star Clara Bow review dailies during the production of the 1929 melodrama *The Wild Party.*

a sorry fate by her stuffy anthropology professor (Fredric March). Arzner gives a feminine, if not a feminist, spin to what begins as a typical male fantasy about a bad girl rescued by a good man. The party girl learns a thing or two about life from the professor, but he learns a lot more from her. And though the flapper film was popular at the time, Arzner couples the party-girl-gone-straight melodrama plotline with a message about false accusations (don't believe everything you hear), false assumptions (based on how a woman dresses, for example), and forgiveness (which is, after all, a Christian virtue).

After *The Wild Party*, Arzner directed *Sarah and Son* (1930), *Christopher Strong* (1933), *Nana* (1934), *Craig's Wife* (1936), and *Dance, Girl, Dance* (1940), giving voice to—and a distinct female perspective on—strong female characters played by, respectively (beginning with *The Wild Party*), Clara Bow, Ruth Chatterton, Katharine Hepburn, Anna Sten, Rosalind Russell, and Maureen O'Hara. Perhaps the most interesting of these films is *Christopher Strong*. Though marginally a "fallen-woman" film—thus fitting into a genre that sports such titles as *Beauty for Sale* (Richard Boleslawski, 1933), *A Dangerous Woman* (Gerald Grove and Rowland V. Lee, 1929), *Fast Life* (John Francis Dillon, 1929), *Half Marriage* (William J. Cowen, 1929), *Laughing Sinners* (Harry Beaumont, 1931), *Red-*

Headed Woman (Jack Conway, 1932), *The Single Standard* (John S. Robertson, 1929), *Street Girl* (Wesley Ruggles, 1929), and *What Men Want* (Ernst Laemmle, 1930)—*Christopher Strong* couples the fallen woman's requisite journey from sin to salvation with what can be described only as an action film for girls.

After a dalliance with a married man leaves the aviator Lady Cynthia Darrington (Hepburn) embarrassed and guilt ridden, she engages in risky behavior in pursuit of the world altitude record. The last flight is nothing short of a suicide run, the only solution to the grief her affair has caused. We watch the altimeter from Lady Cynthia's point of view, and then, superimposed on the dial, we see her life (especially her indiscretions) flashing by. In a quintessential melodramatic moment, Lady Cynthia pulls the oxygen mask from her face, and as tears fall down her cheeks, she finds forgiveness in a rapid descent and crash landing on terra firma.

Josef von Sternberg, like fellow émigré Mauritz Stiller, will forever be thought of along with the movie star he helped make famous: for Stiller it was Garbo; for von Sternberg, Dietrich. Though Dietrich had appeared in about twenty films before she met von Sternberg, the director took credit for "discovering" the future star when casting the part of Lola Lola, the femme fatale in the early German sound film *Der Blaue Engel* (*The Blue Angel*, 1930). Like Garbo, Dietrich was androgynous and exotic. She seemed, again like Garbo, at once self-possessed and cold: unattainable and inscrutable. *The Blue Angel* (and Dietrich's performance in it) so impressed the executives at Paramount, von Sternberg's employer before his brief return to Germany in 1929, that they rerecorded Dietrich singing its songs in English, clumsily dubbed over some of the film's dialogue, and released an English-language version under the studio's banner. The film made Dietrich a Hollywood movie star and solidified von Sternberg's reputation as one of the studio's most important directors.

The Blue Angel tells the story of a respected schoolteacher (Emil Jannings) whose life is destroyed by a dalliance with the seductive nightclub performer Lola Lola (Dietrich). The film highlights a handful of musical numbers sung by Dietrich onstage, key among them being "Falling in Love Again." Lola sings the song early in the film as a spotlight is turned on the schoolteacher. The lyrics speak to the narrative at hand: "Falling

Katharine Hepburn as the guilt-ridden aviator Lady Cynthia Darrington in Dorothy Arzner's 1933 melodrama *Christopher Strong*.

in love again / Never wanted to / What's a girl to do / Can't help it." This first performance of the song feels, in context, sincere and plaintive.

Later Lola sings the song a second time, but so much has changed that we know better than to misread it. She is falling in love again, and even if she can't help it, she doesn't much care who gets hurt in the process. Between the two performances of the song, the schoolteacher loses his job and becomes a member of the troupe headlined by Lola. We see him onstage in clown's makeup, earning his keep as a magician's assistant: when the magician pulls an egg out of his ear, the teacher crows like a rooster to the delight of the crowd. Later we see him on the floor of the nightclub, hawking risqué postcards of Lola, selling to sweaty, drunken men the erotic image of the woman for whom he has thrown away his once-respectable life. When Lola sings the song now, she is falling in love with another man. The cycle will begin again, and there's nothing she can—or cares to—do about it.

After the international success of *The Blue Angel*, Paramount set out to exploit the Dietrich–von Sternberg team. Executives reunited the actress-director duo in a series of mostly improbable melodramas: *Morocco* (1930) with its Foreign Legion backstory (featuring a stolid Gary Cooper as Dietrich's love interest), the spy picture *Dishonored* (1931), the exotic adventure film *Shanghai Express* (1932), the code-busting *Blonde Venus* (1932), the sumptuous biopic (of Catherine the Great) *The Scarlet Empress* (1934) and their final film together, the aptly titled femme fatale melodrama *The Devil Is a Woman* (1935).

Von Sternberg was a cine-stylist, a proponent of the German school of antimontage. He privileged the shot, emphasizing mise-en-scène over the more fluid fast-paced editing of the so-called classical Hollywood style. Von Sternberg's sets were characteristically cluttered, a metaphor in many cases of the lives of his featured characters. He liked to shoot scenes by placing a camera behind objects (nets, cages, statues) or diaphanous material—we watch his films like furtive voyeurs. Von Sternberg used lighting expressively at a time when the Hollywood studio style strictly adhered to a three-point lighting scheme that balanced key, fill, and backlights to illuminate scenes perfectly as opposed to expressively (as in von Sternberg's case). Though he worked almost exclusively in melodrama and adhered to its narrative strictures, von Sternberg made films that look like no one else's. At a time when success as a Hollywood director required one to produce films that somehow fit a studio style, von Sternberg, albeit briefly, clung successfully and obsessively to his signature visual style.

After von Sternberg had a row with Ernst Lubitsch, who by the mid-1930s had become a Paramount production executive as well as one of the studio's best directors, the von Sternberg–Dietrich team was broken up. Dietrich went on to star in significant films, such as *A Foreign Affair* (Billy Wilder, 1948), *Stage Fright* (Alfred Hitchcock, 1950), *Witness for the Prosecution* (Wilder, 1957), and *Judgment at Nuremberg* (Stanley Kramer, 1961), and enjoyed celebrity status until her death (in 1992). Von Sternberg was a successful filmmaker before he met Dietrich but he proved unable to make much of his career after losing his muse. In a gesture made late in his life, von Sternberg famously disowned all the films he made after 1935.

The femme fatale Lola Lola (Marlene Dietrich) charms the innocent schoolteacher Immanuel Rath (Emil Jannings) in Josef von Sternberg's *The Blue Angel* (1930).

Horror Films

Like comedies, horror films are defined by their effect. They routinely exploit our gravest fears—of enclosed spaces, castration, disfigurement, possession—and their central figures are monsters of one sort or another fashioned to provoke disgust, repugnance, and fear. Human frailty is on exhibit in these films, so there's the fear of disease and contamination, the fear of death, and the fear of the unknown (especially in the form of people unknown to and somehow unlike us).

The first known American-made horror film is a 1910 version of *Frankenstein*, produced by Thomas Edison. But although the genre did not initially catch on in the United States, it became a staple of expressionist filmmakers in Weimar Germany (Germany from 1919 to 1933). Exemplary among the German expressionist horror films are Henrik Galeen and Paul Wegener's *Der Golem* (1915), which tells the story of a Frankenstein-like monster, animated by kabbalistic Jews in sixteenth-century Prague, who wreaks havoc on the countryside; Robert Wiene's theatrical, idiosyncratically stylized zombie picture *Das Kabinett des Dr. Caligari* (1919); and F. W. Murnau's early Dracula film, *Nosferatu* (1922). These German expressionist films share certain stylistic conventions that later reemerged in early-sound-era horror films in the United States. They are theatrical in their style of acting, blocking, and set design. Editing is used to move from set to set, but what we need to know about the story and the characters is delivered in long takes (shots that play out without interruption for long periods of time, like scenes in a play) performed on expressively designed stagelike sets. There is a heavy reliance on key lights. Fill lights are used sparingly, and backlights, used to obliterate shadows, are also not used much. The films have an ominous look, a look that fits horror perfectly.

In the late 1920s and early '30s a number of German and Austrian directors, writers, cinematographers, and set designers immigrated to the United States, in many cases fleeing imminent political and social upheaval. The upheaval began, of course, in 1933, when Adolf Hitler became chancellor of Germany, and creative filmmaking pretty much came to a stop. Many of the émigré filmmakers found a home at Universal, a

Before the 1931 release of *Dracula* (Tod Browning), Bela Lugosi was just another contract player at Universal. He made a lasting impression with his portrayal of the legendary vampire, highlighting the count's exotic foreign pedigree and his Old World seductive charm.

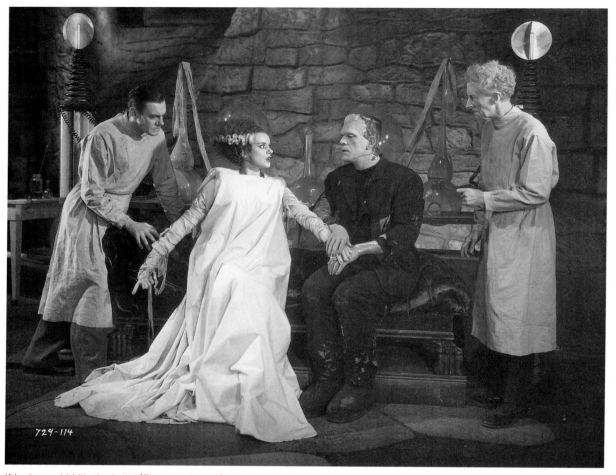

729-114

If looks could kill: the bride (Elsa Lanchester) gets her first look at the groom, and he's a monster (Boris Karloff). Colin Clive (*far left*) reprises his role as the conflicted mad scientist Dr. Frankenstein, and Ernest Thesinger plays his partner in crime, the devious Dr. Pretorius, in James Whale's occasionally comic sequel *The Bride of Frankenstein* (1935).

studio that consequently produced a series of landmark horror films made very much in the expressionist style.

Universal's foray into horror began after the stock-market crash of 1929, when the studio was so strapped for cash it could not afford to make A pictures. Thus its venture into genre filmmaking—and especially the lowbrow genre of horror—was the stuff of necessity, not inspiration. But there is no arguing the significance of the horror films made by Universal in the 1930s.

Dracula, one of the first and best-known of Universal's horror films, premiered in 1931. Directed by Tod Browning, the film was shot and lit by Karl Freund, the Czech-born cinematographer whose expressionist lighting style, honed in such German silent classics as *Der Letzte Mann* (*The Last Laugh,* Murnau, 1924) and *Metropolis* (Fritz Lang, 1925), helped create the house style at Universal in the 1930s. Freund shot over a dozen films at Universal, including *Dracula* and *Murders in the Rue Morgue* (Robert Florey, 1932).

Dracula's star, the Hungarian-born Bela Lugosi, was a contract player at Universal. Before his arrival in Hollywood, Lugosi had acted in a number of German expressionist films, including an early version of *Dr. Jekyll and Mr. Hyde* (*Der Januskopf*) directed by Murnau in 1920. *Dracula* became Lugosi's signature role, and he played it—most say he overplayed it—to highlight the count's exotic, foreign pedigree, his Old World seductive charm. There is precious little violence in the film. The most perilous scenes take place in the heroine's bedroom, where the count visits night after night. This invasion of a vulnerable young woman's private space was already a cliché in the genre (it occurs significantly in both *Das Kabinette des Dr. Caligari* and *Nosferatu*). Given the international turmoil and the growing ethnocentrism and isolationism in American politics and culture, this "home invasion" had, in addition to the obvious sexual suggestiveness, a distinct political import. As in Murnau's *Nosferatu*, part of what makes the vampire so frightening is that he's from a strange, distant place and behaves in ways the locals find weird and scary. Also troubling to the locals is that the vampire's designs are partly, if not mostly, sexual, and despite his strange appearance and accent all the local girls find him irresistible.

Universal's second major horror picture was *Frankenstein*, released later in 1931, directed by James Whale, a British émigré. Legend has it that Whale found the material deeply silly, but if that is true, it did not stop him from making a memorable movie and an even better sequel, *Bride of Frankenstein* (1935). *Frankenstein* stars Boris Karloff, also British-born and, like Whale, not without pretensions to deserving better material. Karloff became, with Lugosi, a steady performer in a number of Universal horror pictures, including *The Mummy* (directed by the cinematographer Karl Freund, 1932), *The Black Cat* (Edgar Ulmer, 1934, co-starring Lugosi), *Bride of Frankenstein*, *The Raven* (Lew Landers, 1935), and *Son of Frankenstein* (Lee, 1939).

Frankenstein has of course become a much remade (and parodied) monster film, but in its original form it was unique in the way it created sympathy for the monster, a trope in many of the subsequent Universal horror pictures. The monster becomes a monster only after the world rejects him for his ugliness, his size, his inability to express himself in words. The one killing the monster plans is an act of revenge. His target is his creator's fiancée. Here again we find the genre convention of the bedroom invasion, complete with scream and swoon. The sequel, *Bride of Frankenstein*, adds loneliness to the monster's list of psychic disturbances, and again the monster kills only after he is wronged.

Karloff's mummy character in Freund's *The Mummy* has his reasons for killing, too—something to do with a curse. But there's no premeditation; the monster exists, like Dracula, in the realm of the undead or the sort-of dead, beyond reason and rationality. The scientist (Claude Rains) who finds a formula to make himself disappear in Whale's *Invisible Man* (1933) goes crazy on an experimental drug. The werewolf in *The Wolf Man* (George Waggner, 1941) is just a good guy with bad luck. The gypsy who looks at his hand to tell his fortune tells him so. He kills because he can't help himself, because he's a monster and that's what monsters do. These somewhat sentimentalized monsters are all vestiges of Universal's expressionist heritage; they are not unlike Cesare (Conrad Veidt) in *Das Kabinett des Dr. Caligari* and the tortured child molester (Peter Lorre) in Fritz Lang's *M* (1931), who commit crimes not because they want to but because they can't help themselves.

The Musical

With the advent of sound film came the adaptation of stage musical reviews and Broadway musical comedies. These early film musicals were very popular in the 1930s. Sound in itself wowed audiences; hearing and seeing performers sing seemed magical, at least initially. Early film musicals gave folks far from the Great White Way of Broadway access to top staged musicals and musical reviews. They also provided audiences with a much-needed escape from the daily grind of the Great Depression by presenting a world in which chorus girls become overnight sensations and people fall so deeply in love they break out in song.

Rouben Mamoulian's *Applause* (1929), the melodramatic story of an aging burlesque star and the daughter she eventually dies for, was the first full-length film musical. It was the renowned stage director Mamoulian's first film, and as things played out, he showed himself to be an eccentric cine-stylist in the making. Mamoulian showed how complex camera movement and expressive editing might make a stage musical more cinematic, how one might choreograph camera movement in concert with stage blocking and dance. The film's soundscape was complicated as well. Mamoulian placed microphones all over the soundstage, mixing (as best as he could in 1929) the central song track along with extraneous noise, sound effects, and dialogue. *Applause* opened to terrific reviews and a strong box office.

Three years later Mamoulian made an even more stylistically ambitious movie, *Love Me Tonight*, a musical featuring songs by (Richard) Rodgers and (Lorenz) Hart (including "Mimi" and "Isn't It Romantic"). *Love Me Tonight* tells the story of a tailor (Maurice Chevalier) who, in an effort to collect a debt from an irresponsible count, ventures to the nobleman's country estate disguised as the count's royal-born friend. En route he meets and falls in love with the princess (Jeanette Mac-Donald), whom he charms first with song and then with his skill as a tailor. In play are several elements that would become formulaic in musical-

comedy films: the easy reconciliation of class differences (it doesn't matter if you're rich or poor so long as you're in love) and the ridiculous notions that attraction is first expressed in immediate dislike and that persistence in love is invariably rewarded. In *Love Me Tonight* no one and nothing can prevent the tailor and the princess's union. In the film's climax the princess mounts her horse and catches up with a train the tailor has boarded to leave her château. It is a grand and ridiculous gesture that Mamoulian smartly plays for laughs.

Mamoulian was a significant and influential director throughout the studio era. He is best known for his musicals—*Applause; Love Me Tonight; High, Wide, and Handsome* (a musical western of all things, released in 1937); *Summer*

Jeanette MacDonald and Maurice Chevalier as the star-crossed lovers in Rouben Mamoulian's innovative musical *Love Me Tonight* (1932).

Holiday (1948, based on a play by Eugene O'Neill); and his last film, the Fred Astaire–Cyd Charisse picture *Silk Stockings* (1957). He was an innovator throughout his career. Of particular note is his landmark work with soundscapes in *Applause* and with Technicolor in *Becky Sharp* (1935), the extended experiment with first-person camera in the 1931 horror classic *Dr. Jekyll and Mr. Hyde,* and the clever choreographed fight scenes in the action-adventure picture *The Mark of Zorro* (1940).

Significant as Mamoulian's early musicals were, the name that most often comes to mind when we think of 1930s film musicals is Busby Berkeley. Born William Berkeley Enos in 1895, the son of show-biz parents, Berkeley became a stage director of musicals and then made the logical (and financially advantageous) leap to motion pictures. In 1930 he signed with Samuel Goldwyn to choreograph *Whoopee!* for United Artists, produced by the Broadway impresario Florenz Ziegfeld and directed by Thornton Freeland, and then choreographed a series of films at the studio that, like *Whoopee!,* featured the popular vaudeville comedian Eddie Cantor.

Berkeley's career took off in 1933 when he signed a seven-year contract with Warner Bros. In his first year at Warner Bros., Berkeley choreographed *42nd Street* (Lloyd Bacon), *Footlight Parade* (Bacon), and *Gold Diggers of 1933* (LeRoy) and, in the following year, *Dames* (Ray Enright and Berkeley), four classics of the musical-comedy genre.

Berkeley's best-known film, and perhaps his best work, is his first at Warner Bros., *42nd Street.* It premiered on March 9, 1933, at the Strand Theater in New York City, five blocks from the intersection of Forty-second Street and Broadway, the epicenter of Times Square. The story behind the making of *42nd Street* is well worth telling. Legend has it that in 1932, Darryl Zanuck, the production chief at Warner Bros., went to Jack and Harry Warner with the simply crazy idea of producing a *big* musical. The Warners rejected the idea out of hand, but Zanuck persevered. He fashioned *42nd Street* as a genre hybrid, a deft combination of backstage melodrama (without music) and lavish musical performance (featuring the creative filming of the live stage revue that the backstage folks produce). With *42nd Street* the so-called backstage musical, a popular subgenre in 1930s cinema, was born. The film was a big gamble for Zanuck. Berke-

ley's costly sets and costumes brought the production budget to $400,000, about 50 percent more than the average Warner Bros. feature. But the gamble paid off: *42nd Street* grossed well over $2 million in its first run.

The film appears to be two films at once because that is exactly what it is: two films directed by two very different directors. In a manner consistent with the gritty-realist Warner Bros. house style, Lloyd Bacon directed the backstage scenes. But what makes *42nd Street* so remarkable are Berkeley's set pieces, the kaleidoscopic and surreal musical numbers that the choreographer shot from a variety of camera placements in front, behind, and above the action. Bacon's and Berkeley's respective contributions to the film don't exactly match up. The result is that the song-and-dance numbers are not integrated into the story line (as they are in Mamoulian's *Love Me Tonight*). The two-director, two-genre split does have its advantages, however. The class conflicts at stake in the story are rendered clear by the differences between the scenes shot by studio stalwart Bacon (which focus on the lives of struggling chorus girls and stagehands) and the iconoclast Berkeley.

The studio cleverly promoted *42nd Street* as "a musical exposé" and—in deference to Franklin Roosevelt's victory over Herbert Hoover in the 1932 presidential election—as a first in "New Deal Entertainment." (The New Deal was a complex plan put forward by Roosevelt to get the nation out of the Depression. It began with a bank moratorium and farm reform and featured a number of public works projects that mated improvements in superstructure with vastly increased government-funded employment). But however much the studio promoted the New Deal angle, in the end *42nd Street* is all about the singing and the dancing. It features three legendary hoofers (tap dancers)—Ruby Keeler, Dick Powell, and Ginger Rogers—and a number of memorable Al Dubin–Harry Warren songs, including "Shuffle Off to Buffalo" and "You're Getting to Be a Habit with Me." The film also features chorus lines teaming with attractive women in revealing outfits who sing suggestive songs and engage in wisecracking dialogue that benefited from the studios' lax attention to the production code at the time.

In 1935, just two years into his contract with Warner Bros., Berkeley found that his luck had

begun to fail him. First there were the pressures of making so many films (three in 1933 alone). Then, in 1935, came a nasty drunk driving–manslaughter scandal, after which Berkeley drank more and worked less. When he was let go from Warner Bros., he was picked up by MGM, reuniting briefly with the man who gave him his first break, Samuel Goldwyn.

Berkeley's move from Warner Bros. to MGM in 1939 marked the end of his run as the genre's single most influential player. At MGM he became little more than a contract choreographer, brought in to spice up single numbers, like the finale in *Broadway Serenade* (Robert Z. Leonard, 1939) and the scarecrow's dance in *The Wizard of Oz* (Flem-

ing, 1939). In the 1940s, Berkeley directed one of the era's top dancers, Gene Kelly, in two films, *For Me and My Gal* (1942) and *Take Me Out to the Ball Game* (1949).

Today Berkeley is known for his wildly lavish kaleidoscopic production numbers featuring revolving sets, overhead camerawork, and lots of leggy women in scanty outfits. Nods to Berkeley's visual style and cinematic rendering of choreography can be found in a number of contemporary films, including the "Springtime for Hitler" number in Mel Brooks's Broadway farce *The Producers* (1968) and the Wagnerian dream sequence in Ethan and Joel Coen's manic comedy *The Big Lebowski* (1998).

(*above*) The vertiginous white-piano production number in *Gold Diggers of 1935* bears the signature of the film's director and choreographer, Busby Berkeley. The film proved to be the impresario's last great musical for Warner Bros.

(*left*) Busby Berkeley (*center*) rehearsing a dance sequence for the Warner Bros. musical *42nd Street* (Lloyd Bacon, 1933).

The sort of dancing normal folks did (only not nearly so well): Fred Astaire and Ginger Rogers cut a rug in Mark Sandrich's *Top Hat* (1935).

While Berkeley's dizzying overhead shots highlighted the precision and teamwork of the chorus lines at Warner Bros., a very different, more romantic sort of song-and-dance movie emerged at RKO. Though the films, starring Fred Astaire, were far less showy than Berkeley's, they had a sophistication and glamour that would come to characterize RKO during this period.

Fred Astaire, the former Frederick Austerlitz of Omaha, Nebraska, was a successful dancer, first in vaudeville and then on Broadway, who since grade school had been teamed on the stage with his sister Adele. When, after fifteen years on the circuit, Adele left the act to get married, Fred took a stab at Hollywood. Things did not go so well at first. The studios' evaluation of Astaire's screen test was pretty pessimistic: "Can't sing. Can't act. Slightly bald. Can dance a little." Fortunately, RKO gave him a chance, and the rest, as they say, is history.

Astaire's first significant film part was in a forgettable musical, *Dancing Lady* (Leonard, 1933), with Astaire on loan to MGM. The film stars Joan Crawford (as a potential dance partner), Clark

Gable (as the man with whom Astaire can't hope to compete), and the Three Stooges (Moe and Curly Howard and Larry Fine, as manic stagehands). Later that year, Astaire was teamed in an RKO feature, *Flying Down to Rio* (Thornton Freeland), with Ginger Rogers, a Broadway veteran known in Hollywood for playing wisecracking dames in precode films like *Hat Check Girl* (Sidney Lanfield, 1932) and *Professional Sweetheart* (William Seiter, 1933). Only her performance as Anytime Annie in *42nd Street* gave any indication that Rogers would become the second half of the decade's most famous dance team.

The Astaire-Rogers team appeared in nine films for RKO and offered a very different style of dance from that of the hoofers who tapped their way through Berkeley's showy numbers. Their smooth ballroom routines, many of which were choreographed by Hermes Pan and accompanied by the popular music of Irving Berlin ("Cheek to Cheek"), Jerome Kern ("The Way You Look Tonight"), or George Gershwin ("A Foggy Day [in London Town]"), was easily integrated into romantic-comedy story lines in which two characters surmount their differences on the dance floor.

Astaire and Rogers engaged in the same sort of dancing that "normal" people did (though not nearly so well), set to music that lots of folks listened to and maybe hummed as they worked. Mark Sandrich, who directed five Astaire-Rogers films for RKO, including *The Gay Divorcee* (1934), *Top Hat* (1935), and *Follow the Fleet* (1936), used an intimate and personal style that at once suited his attractive, sophisticated stars and made them seem real. Sandrich was satisfied to play second fiddle to his stars. He deftly integrated the camera with the dancing, an achievement in a genre that was moving away from the backstage musical (in which musical numbers are set onstage and thus separate from the narrative) toward a more fluid template (in which song-and-dance numbers are integrated into the plot of the film). In Sandrich's films the camera served the stars and not, as in Berkeley's films, the other way around.

Despite the absurdity of folks breaking out in song (and dance) every quarter hour or so and the necessary suspension of disbelief such a formula requires of the audience, the musical proved to be an extremely important genre in Depression-era America. The backstage musicals from Warner Bros. tell stories of people down on their luck, singing and dancing their way if not to success then to some sort of transcendence (in the very act of performance). The RKO films, on the other hand, focus on the lives and loves of rich folks who dress beautifully, move gracefully, and have problems of a romantic—instead of a financial—sort. But whether economic or romantic, the conflicts in the musicals are as real as those in more serious genres. The characters escape through music, and so does the audience. At a time when forgetting the world outside the theater for an hour or two was a popular—and important—activity, the musical transported its audience to a world in which the ecstasy of music and dance is the answer to the world's problems. For a couple of hours, such a ridiculous, glorious notion seemed possible.

Early Sound Comedy

With the exception of Charlie Chaplin, who continued making important and interesting films in the 1930s, like the heartbreaking *City Lights* (1931) and the satire *Modern Times* (1936), the advent of sound was bad news for silent-film comedians. The knockabout, slapstick, chase-based comedy that so dominated the genre's so-called golden age was replaced by animated short subjects made by Walt Disney, Dave and Max Fleischer (who produced the *Betty Boop* and *Popeye the Sailor* cartoons), and the talented corps at Warner Bros. (Tex Avery, Bob Clampett, Bob "Bobe" Cannon, and Chuck Jones, who made cartoons starring Bugs Bunny, Daffy Duck, and Porky Pig). It wasn't that comedy became more refined. It didn't. It just became less physical and more verbal. In part this was due to the audience's fascination with sound on-screen. But that was not all there was to it. The dialogue-based narrative comedy film of the 1930s operated in concert with comedy trends onstage, where actors in plays and stand-up comics cracked wise and titillated audiences with risqué double entendres. The clown tradition, epitomized by the big three comic actors of the silent era—Chaplin, Buster Keaton, and Harold Lloyd—did not vanish altogether and overnight. But as in the more narrative-based romantic comedies, talk as opposed to action became the rule.

The misanthropic vaudeville comedian W. C. Fields. In an era in which the production code kept the studios from offending anyone with their films, Fields seemed to go out of his way to offend everyone.

One of the most popular comics in the early 1930s was W. C. Fields, a former vaudeville comedian with a unique, almost drunken delivery. His routines onstage and on film reveal a decidedly misogynist, even misanthropic streak. In an era in which the production code reminded the studios to avoid offending anyone and prescribed saccharine endings for even the unhappiest and most scandalous plotlines, Fields said what was on his mind. And his mind was not a pretty place. His films—including *The Golf Specialist* (Monte Brice, 1930), *The Dentist* (Leslie Pearce, 1932), *The Barber Shop* (Arthur Ripley, 1933), and *The Bank Dick* (Edward Cline, 1940)—were little more than "situations" that allowed him to reprise his notorious stage act. But however much those films were tied to old (and old-fashioned) vaudeville routines, they were nonetheless extremely popular and funny. The scene in *The Dentist* in which a tooth extraction takes on an outrageous sexual suggestiveness (the patient wraps her legs around Fields's waist as he struggles to pull her tooth) is among the funniest 5 minutes in the history of American sound cinema. It is funny because it's so tasteless, so quintessentially Fields.

Like Fields, the Marx Brothers—Groucho, Harpo, Chico, and Zeppo—were well-known stage comedians who used film, at least at first, to reprise their stage routines. Working mostly for Paramount, the Marx Brothers made frenetic, anarchic films that cashed in on their popularity as a live act—including *Animal Crackers* (Victor Heerman, 1930) and *Monkey Business* (Norman McLeod, 1931), adapted from then current and popular stage shows, and *Horse Feathers* (McLeod, 1932), *Duck Soup* (Leo McCarey, 1933), and *A Night at the Opera* (Sam Wood, 1935).

There's plenty of slapstick in Marx Brothers films, thanks especially to Harpo, whose persistent silence on-screen conceals an innovative and comically destructive force. In *Monkey Business*, Harpo runs amok in a customs office, stamping a number of bald men's heads. In *Duck Soup* he sets alight a munitions dump to great destructive and comic effect.

One of the most memorable of the Marx Brothers' stage routines is reprised in *Duck Soup*. Essentially a pantomime, it features Harpo masquerading as Groucho and Groucho, who stumbles on his look-alike. As the two stand face-to-face, Groucho does a double take, and Harpo plays the gesture right back at him. The mirroring persists through a series of gestures and actions. Finally Groucho reveals a white hat that he has hidden behind his back. Harpo has a hat, too, but it's black. He drops it. Groucho picks it up and hands it to him. The "mirror" is broken by the gesture, but the skit continues as the men change places and continue the pantomime.

All comedy teams have a headliner, and center stage in the Marx Brothers' act was Groucho, a slouching, leering wise guy, a verbal comedian forever winking at the audience, amused, bemused, sometimes even bewildered by a boring, sane world made tolerable—made crazy often enough—by his lunatic brothers. Groucho was routinely comically miscast as an authority figure: a prime minister in *Duck Soup*, a college president in *Horse Feathers*. This casting offered him an opportunity to lampoon propriety, responsibility, and sobriety. He behaved with a carelessness that few in such positions of power in the real world dare display. Groucho, like Fields, said what was on his mind, right when it seemed to cross his mind.

There was never a Marx Brothers "tradition." The brothers had a popular stage act, and like fellow vaudevillians W. C. Fields, Eddie Cantor, and Mae West, they got to make movies because they were already popular. Though the films featuring these popular stage comics used sound to advantage, they were, even upon release, a bit old-fashioned, tied as they were to vaudeville, which, if it wasn't yet dead, was nearly so. In the meantime, the far more modern romantic and screwball comedy films arrived on the scene and offered a first look at what sound might mean to the future of film comedy.

Romantic Comedies

Romantic comedies share a basic structure. The principal characters—routinely a heterosexual couple—desire a change (divorce, some excitement, something new). They convince themselves and others that this change is for the better, that they have suddenly become someone else, someone different. Halfway through the film there's an ah-ha moment. The characters discover that they are not happy with their lives as they have remade them. Instead, they long for things to be, as Lucy (Irene Dunne) remarks at the end of *The Awful Truth* (McCarey, 1937), "like they were before they were different."

By and large, romantic comedies made in the 1930s were blocked and shot as if played onstage. The camerawork does little more than organize

(*left*) The Marx Brothers. *From left to right:* Chico, Zeppo, Groucho, and Harpo sit still for a publicity photograph.

each scene. There are occasional reaction shots (cuts to characters' faces as they react to a remark or an action), but mostly we see in full figure the characters walking and talking their way around sets made to look like apartments, dining rooms, or nightclubs.

Many romantic comedies focus on the life and times of the rich and ridiculous. There are frequent jaunts from posh city apartments to houses on huge tracts of land in Connecticut, a sort of suburban-rural playground for the idle and addled wealthy. The rich have their share of problems in these films. These were not the sorts of problems most of the audience was experiencing during the Depression, of course, but seeing how the other half lived and loved proved to be a tonic for the times. Romantic comedies offered audiences in the Depression the opportunity to have a laugh at the expense of those more financially fortunate.

Trouble in Paradise (Lubitsch, 1932) is often cited as the first sound-era romantic comedy. It tells the story of two high-society thieves who toy with the affections and affectations of the absurdly wealthy in Paris. Gaston (Herbert Marshall) is a thief running a con on a beautiful perfume magnate, Madame Colet (Kay Francis). She has fallen for him, and he, despite having made a play for her only to get access to her safe, has begun thinking about going straight. Warning Gaston against falling for his mark is his working-class, equally light-fingered lover, Lily (Miriam Hopkins). She implores him not to go straight: "Steal, swindle, rob. Oh, but don't become one of those useless, good-for-nothing gigolos." Such screwball logic is not lost on Gaston, who insists to Lily that Colet's "sex appeal is in her safe." When Colet discovers Gaston's true identity and thus also the false pretenses under which their relationship began, she doesn't seem to care. And to an extent, neither does he. "I came here to rob you," he says, "but I fell in love with you." He may or may not be kidding, but in the end he is destined to go back to Lily, a less glamorous woman to be sure, but one more solidly in his social circle.

Trouble in Paradise benefited from the lax enforcement of the production code in 1932. In a clever sequence of social and sexual indecision—should Gaston and Colet go to a party or stay home and find something more intimate to do—Colet finds herself in his room. "When a lady takes off

"Steal, swindle, rob. Oh, but don't become one of those useless, good-for-nothing gigolos." A millionairess (Kay Francis, *left*) and two thieves (Miriam Hopkins and Herbert Marshall) sort things out at the end of Ernst Lubitsch's sophisticated comedy of manners, *Trouble in Paradise* (1932).

her jewels in a man's room, where does she put them?" she asks. "On the night table," he replies. But propriety is hardly the point here, as she offers the scene's payoff: "I don't want to be a lady." Their last scene together is also suggestive. "It could have been marvelous," he tells her, referring to an imagined life in which he is no longer a thief and she no longer his mark. "It could have been divine," she adds. But affirming the socioeconomic reality of the situation—the structural conceit in romantic comedy that prohibits such class mobility—he reminds her that the following day, when the police arrive with an arrest warrant for him, she will be well rid of him and the scandal that any more intimate relationship between them might foster. "But it could have been," she says and then pauses with lots of invitation in her voice. "Do you know what you're missing?" he adds, but the joke is that he's not referring to himself or to their intimacy but to her expensive necklace, which she indeed is missing, because he has stolen it.

Frank Capra's *It Happened One Night*, a second important romantic comedy, was a huge box-office hit in 1934. It is one of the few comedies to win the Outstanding Production (Best Picture) Oscar; it also won Oscars for Directing, Actor (Clark Gable), Actress (Claudette Colbert), and Writing (Robert Riskin). In 1934, when *It Happened One Night* premiered, Colbert was a major star. She was best known for her dramatic performance in two sexy historical epics directed by Cecil B. DeMille, *The Sign of the Cross* (1932), in which she famously bathes in "asses' milk" (a suggestive scene that turned comic on the set when the cow's milk used in the tub curdled under the hot studio lights), and *Cleopatra* (1934), which features Colbert in revealing Egyptian-themed costumes. Gable was on the verge of becoming a star in 1934, and after *It Happened One Night* he became one of the industry's most bankable male attractions.

The film concerns two very different characters: a runaway heiress (Colbert) and a down-on-his-luck reporter (Gable). He stumbles on the heiress and is hired to bring her home so that she can marry a rich creep (Jameson Thomas) she doesn't love. The newspaperman stands to earn $10,000 if he brings her back in time for the wedding, a ridiculously big payoff for 1934. But the reporter's mercenary quest unravels as he falls in love. In the end the reporter proves to be a man of his word: he brings the heiress home. But he turns down the $10,000 and settles instead for $39.60, expense money that is legitimately owed him. True love, in romantic comedies at least, exists independent of the profit motive.

The film features a wealth of clever dialogue, much of which challenged the strictures of the production code. In the film's most famous scene, Colbert and Gable share a room for the night. They string up a blanket to divide the room in half, this after Gable has taken off his shirt to reveal his bare chest (his no-undershirt look proved a groundbreaking style statement aped by a generation of American men). They cleverly refer to the blanket dividing the room as the wall of Jericho, a suggestive allusion since in the Bible story the city walls eventually come tumbling down. Wisecracking dialogue reveals that the characters are aware of the sexual tension in their relationship. When Colbert tries to ditch Gable, she says, "Please keep out of my affairs." Later, referring to an innocent moment in which she dozed off on his shoulder, he says, "Remember me? I'm the fella you slept on last night." She replies, "I already thanked you for that." Like many other romantic comedies of the era—such as *My Man Godfrey* (Gregory La Cava, 1936) and *Nothing Sacred* (Wellman, 1937)—*It Happened One Night* takes into account the hard times of the Depression and the class dynamics made more problematic in an era of so few haves and so many have-nots. When the heiress's money runs out on the road, she learns (albeit briefly) what it's like to be poor, and she doesn't much like it. But she hasn't really enjoyed being rich, either. "I'd change places with a farmer's daughter any day," she says, gesturing at once to the popular naughty jokes about young promiscuous women and convincing Gable that maybe it's not so easy being rich after all.

Like Capra's *It Happened One Night*, Leo McCarey's *The Awful Truth* offers a romantic-comedy template, though one concerned less with class and cash than with the vagaries of romantic entanglements. The film begins with Jerry (Cary Grant) at a men's club taking some time under a sunlamp. A friend wonders why he's so pale and why he needs a quick tan if he was recently in Florida. We wonder, too. Jerry returns home,

Clark Gable as a down-on-his-luck reporter and Claudette Colbert as a madcap heiress on the run share a room in Frank Capra's Academy Award–winning romantic comedy *It Happened One Night* (1934). The characters cleverly refer to the blanket they use to divide the room as the wall of Jericho, a suggestive allusion since in the Bible story the city walls eventually come tumbling down.

and his wife, Lucy (Irene Dunne), is out. Several hangers-on are on hand—such is the way rich folk move about town—and they witness Jerry's surprise when Lucy returns with Armand (Alexander D'Arcy), the handsome music teacher with whom (thanks to a broken-down car) she has spent "an inn-convenient" night (at an inn). Lucy has heard that it has rained in Florida all week, so she wonders why Jerry has a tan. Jerry has heard—maybe he's even used—the broken-down-car story before. So what, this opening scene asks, is "the awful truth"?

As things play out, the awful truth has nothing to do with what either Jerry or Lucy has done in the other's absence—a good thing, since neither comes clean. After the argument over the Florida trip and the music teacher, Jerry and Lucy file for divorce and, while separated, decide to play the field. Lucy finds Dan (Ralph Bellamy), a nice but boring Oklahoman with a big heart, oil wells, and a protective mother (Esther Dale). Jerry meets a showgirl named Dixie Bell (Joyce Compton) who does a revealing and thoroughly embarrassing stage act. After ditching Dixie, Jerry dates a stuffy debutante named Barbara (Molly Lamont) who promises him a calm, socially respectable, and wholly unhappy future.

Lucy discovers early on in her relationship with Dan that she's "still in love with that crazy lunatic"—Jerry—and declares that she can do nothing about it. Jerry comes around soon thereafter. In the end the awful truth is clear enough: Jerry and Lucy are meant for each other. They need to stop talking, stop doubting, stop plotting, and

start having sex (again). The film satisfies this scenario. It ends in a country inn, where Jerry and Lucy spend the night, initially in separate rooms. Eventually, of course, they both end up in Lucy's room, and though we know what will happen next, showing them in bed in 1937 is impossible. Instead, the camera intercuts shots of Jerry and Lucy talking with shots of two figures on a clock that march out the time. The figures look remarkably like Jerry and Lucy (in miniature). The first two times the figures emerge from their doors, they march right back where they came from. But the third time is the charm, so to speak. The clock figures meet, look around, and then march hand in hand through the same door.

There is a famous story about the 1937 Academy Awards ceremony, at which Capra, the winner of the previous year's Directing award for *Mr. Deeds Goes to Town*, was called on to present the Oscar for Directing, which went to McCarey for *The Awful Truth*. Capra pretended to be reluctant to give up the award and playfully wrestled with his fellow romantic-comedy director for the statue. The notion that two directors of comedy might have a hold on the Oscar was unique to the mid-1930s; in no other era was comedy taken so seriously by the Academy. And in no other era was romantic comedy so central to the American film-going experience.

A year after *The Awful Truth* was released, Howard Hawks's *Bringing Up Baby* introduced a screwball variation to the romantic-comedy template. Everyone—the scientist, the heiress, the scientist's fiancée, the heiress's family, the psychiatrist, the police, the milquetoast—everyone in the film is a screwball, a nut, a lovable lunatic.

Bringing Up Baby is based on a *Collier's* magazine story of the same name, by Hagar Wilde. RKO purchased the story for Katharine Hepburn, their critically acclaimed star who at least early in her career had made little impact at the box office. Executives assigned the script to Dudley Nichols, a veteran screenwriter with a wide variety of genre projects under his belt: *The Lost Patrol* (a war picture directed by John Ford in 1934), *The Informer* (about sectarian struggles in Ireland, directed by Ford in 1935), and *The Three Musketeers* (a remake of the oft-remade adventure classic, directed by Rowland V. Lee in 1935). For *Bringing Up Baby*, Nichols collaborated with Wilde, and the two fell in love. The film's attention to the illogic of attraction and its peculiar expression (the funny things we do when we are in love) underscore the very romantic comedy laid out in the film. A line delivered by a pompous psychiatrist (Fritz Feld) whom Susan (Hepburn) meets at the club—"The love impulse in man very frequently reveals itself as conflict"—is rendered all too true in the film, so much so that one wonders what was going on with Wilde and Nichols when they were working on the film and found themselves falling in love.

Hepburn's performance, her first in a comedy, was a jolt for the film's audience. Though the studio bought the story for her, it was her co-star, Cary Grant, who seemed the more obvious choice for a lead in a romantic comedy. Howard Hawks did not find Hepburn a natural comedienne and had her study with the vaudeville veteran Walter Catlett (who plays Slocum, the local police chief) to get her timing down. Her timing, perhaps thanks to Catlett, is fine in the film, but she is so aggressive, so relentless in her pursuit of the overmatched paleontologist (Grant) that in its initial release the film failed to match the critical or box-office success of *It Happened One Night* or *The Awful Truth*.

Screwball comedies are all about turning the world upside down. And in many comedies of that type, we find ourselves in a world run by smart, aggressive women who know what they want and how to get it. A deep understanding of Freud is not required to get the significance of the old bone Susan hides and returns only when the paleontologist, David, finally acknowledges his love for her. "The man who gets you will have a life of misery," he tells her early on in the film, but at least misery is interesting. Susan is fun, if nothing else. David's fiancée, on the other hand, the appropriately named Alice Swallow (Virginia Walker), does not even want a honeymoon; their marriage, she tells David in no uncertain terms, will be all about his work. Susan promises something altogether different—and better.

Susan propels the narrative in *Bringing Up Baby*. She uses every trick she can think of to keep David

(*left*) Jerry (Cary Grant, *left*) and Lucy (Irene Dunne) must overcome a series of obstacles before they can reunite in Leo McCarey's romantic comedy *The Awful Truth* (1937). Here the obstacle is Lucy's bumbling suitor, a millionaire rancher from Oklahoma played by Ralph Bellamy.

In Howard Hawks's screwball comedy *Bringing Up Baby* (1938), David (Cary Grant) and Susan (Katharine Hepburn) meet in a posh nightclub. She professes her love for him, but then things go terribly wrong: she keeps him from meeting a rich museum patron, and he tears her dress. That they fight so much at the start tells us, at least in the world of romantic comedy, that they are destined to be together.

away from his fiancée, and he is, for most of the film, just along for the ride. She gets him to drive her to Connecticut (accompanied by a leopard named Baby), ostensibly to help him get money for his museum. Once at her family estate, she steals his clothes (while he's in the shower) and has her dog, George—who also plays Asta in *The Thin Man* (W. S. Van Dyke, 1934) and Mr. Smith in *The Awful Truth*—hide the dinosaur bone he covets.

David finally acknowledges his love for Susan, atop a high ladder while placing the once-missing bone in a now-complete dinosaur skeleton. Susan climbs up to meet him for the film's inevitable last embrace and in so doing causes the entire skeleton to collapse, wrecking David's life's work. Unlike her competitor, the uptight Alice Swallow, Susan has something else on her mind besides

work. The film ends as David shrugs off this final indignity. In a world where most people take work and career seriously, *Bringing Up Baby* offered a happy alternative.

Hawks directed two romantic comedies after *Bringing Up Baby*: *His Girl Friday* (1940), starring Cary Grant as a fast-talking newspaperman, Rosalind Russell as his ex-wife, and Ralph Bellamy as her overmatched beau, Grant's ever-prudent, boring opposite (a reprise of their roles in *The Awful Truth*), and *Ball of Fire* (1941), about gangsters and academics, starring a fast-talking Barbara Stanwyck and, as her befuddled love interest, Gary Cooper, the least funny actor in American cinema history. To Hawks's credit he makes the pairing work; in a screwball universe, even Gary Cooper can be funny.

■ ■ ■

Between 1927 and 1938, Hollywood changed dramatically. "Talkies" supplanted the silent film and, along with the introduction of color, promised a cinema that would sound and look more like real life. As cinema modernized, so did the industry that produced it. The so-called studio system that matured in the 1930s at once streamlined film production and helped establish monopoly control by the handful of studios that survived the Great Depression.

The studio system had a profound effect on filmmaking. Studios honed signature styles, based in large part on whom they had under contract at a given time. As modern business enterprises the studios appreciated the need for standardization (hence the strictures of the classical Hollywood style) and diversification (which increased the emphasis on genre filmmaking).

The 1930s required of the studios some deft public relations. Increasing public scrutiny of the motion-picture colony and the films made there led to a series of censorship regimes, culminating with the Production Code Administration. But rather than stifle filmmaking, the establishment of the PCA enabled the development of a more modern, more successful, more American moviemaking industry. As we will see in Chapter 4, by 1939 the studio system had neared perfection. Indeed, between 1939 and 1941—between the release of Victor Fleming's *Gone with the Wind* and Orson Welles's *Citizen Kane*—something of a golden age in studio filmmaking emerged. But that golden age was all too brief. In December 1941, World War II intervened. Nearly four years later, when the war ended, there was no way for Hollywood to go back to the way things were "before they were different."

The Wicked Witch of the West (Margaret Hamilton) terrorizes Dorothy (Judy Garland) in the MGM musical fantasy *The Wizard of Oz* (Victor Fleming, 1939).

4

Hollywood in Transition

1939–1945

I n the late 1930s the studio system became more fully streamlined, modernized, and organized. Vertical and horizontal integration—a stake in profits to be made from the development, production, postproduction, and exhibition of motion pictures; control over a contract workforce; and ownership of interior and exterior sites of production—gave the studios monopoly control over the business's industrial process and revenue stream. Such control worked to the advantage of both the corporate interests profiting from the film business and the filmmakers working under contract at the studios. In the last three or four years before the attack on Pearl Harbor, the Hollywood system ably facilitated the making of money and movies.

By 1940 the so-called Big Eight studios (formerly the Big Five and the Little Three)—Columbia, MGM, Paramount, RKO, 20th Century–Fox, United Artists, Universal, and Warner Bros.—produced 75 percent of the films made in the United States and generated 90 percent of the movie industry's total gross revenues. The top three studios (MGM, Paramount, and Fox) boasted annual revenues in excess of $100 million. Seven of the Big Eight averaged a release slate of over forty-five films per year, a simply astonishing output of nearly one feature film per week. These were also banner years for Hollywood filmmakers, a brief golden age in which a number of very talented producers and directors took advantage of the studio system's considerable economic resources and ready access to skilled labor to produce films that remain among the most memorable and the most important ever made in the United States.

Market research, first introduced by the Motion Picture Producers and Distributors of America (MPPDA) in the 1930s, revealed that 80 million people attended movies each week in 1940. A poll conducted in New York City, the industry's top market, indicated that almost 60 percent of the population went to the movies more than three times a month, with almost 30 percent going more than six times a month.

Just as the studio system was reaching its zenith, war consumed Europe. The European war—begun with Germany's invasion of Poland in 1939—was very much in the news and soon became a subject of considerable debate in the increasingly politicized movie colony in Los Angeles. The MPPDA and the Production Code Administration (PCA) held that political films and political activity by movie stars, writers, and directors were bad for business. But controlling the Hollywood workforce proved to be a difficult enterprise, and in the end it took more than directives from the MPPDA or "advice" from the PCA to keep everyone in line. Eventually the politics in Hollywood became a matter of concern for the politicians in Washington, and the first of what would become several key struggles between Hollywood and Washington (covered in this chapter and the next) commenced.

To the frustration of the MPPDA and the PCA, between 1939 and 1941 a number of Hollywood filmmakers made polemical movies that commented on the conflict overseas: *The Great Dictator* (Charles Chaplin, 1940), *Pastor Hall* (Roy Boulting, 1940), *The Mortal Storm* (Frank Borzage, 1940), and *I Married a Nazi* (Irving Pichel, 1940). These films, as well as the offscreen activities of an increasingly political and predominantly Jewish labor force in Hollywood, exacerbated a political rift between an increasingly organized Hollywood Left and a coalition of isolationist (and in many cases anti-Semitic) studio owners, Hollywood talent, and legislators in the U.S. Congress. The isolationists had an all-American celebrity spokesman in the aviator Charles Lindbergh, who made speeches across the nation on behalf of the pro-Nazi isolationist organization, the America First Committee, urging against U.S. involvement in the war and blaming Jews in Hollywood and elsewhere for fomenting American antipathy toward Nazi Germany. For his part the German führer Adolf Hitler counted on American isolationism through the early years of the European war, confidently assuming that "materialist democracy" had made the United States soft and unwilling to fight. "What is America," he famously remarked, "but millionaires, beauty queens, stupid phonograph records, and Hollywood."

The isolationist debate was rendered moot on December 7, 1941, when Japanese airmen bombed the U.S. military installations at Pearl Harbor, Hawaii, and the United States was compelled to enter the war. For the next four years the war brought fundamental changes to American life. The risks of battle made patriotism not only popular but also necessary on and off the screen. A number of topflight Hollywood stars—including Henry Fonda, Clark Gable, and James Stewart—enlisted in the armed services. A-list directors Frank Capra, John Ford, and William Wyler joined up as well. Other movie stars did their part by encouraging folks to buy war bonds or, like Bob Hope, by traveling to entertain the troops. The studios accepted the inevitability of public service by producing war-themed fiction films and documentaries.

But even as the studios were busy producing topical films to help the war effort, America's insatiable appetite for movies of all sorts provided opportunities for other genres to flourish as well. Many of these genre films were not in any obvious way politically relevant, but they were all released against the backdrop of the war to an audience that was well aware of what was going on in the world outside the movie theater. The so-called woman's picture, for example, became very popular during the war, providing stories of selfless sacrifice and casting light on the lives of the women left at home. The broad variety of comedies that provided domestic audiences with an escape from news of the war reminded everyone that such an escape, although important, was all too temporary.

When we talk about the late 1930s and early '40s in Hollywood, we are talking about two American cinemas. One, the classical Hollywood, reached its pinnacle in 1939 and for three years sustained a level of quality production that was unrivaled up to that time. But with our entrance into the war, a second Hollywood emerged, one that forced aside the more selfish, more capitalist enterprise that had financed the brief golden age; this second Hollywood required that all movies have at least one eye on the war. The new industry mind-set produced its share of landmark pictures, including the war-themed suspense melodrama *Casablanca* (Michael Curtiz, 1942), the homespun musical *Meet Me in St. Louis* (Vincente Minnelli, 1944), and the social-realist melodrama *The Best Years of Our Lives* (Wyler, 1946, released just after the war's end), all discussed at length at the end of this chapter. But it also moved the studios away from a system that had served its financial and creative interests. Once the war ended, for a variety of reasons (discussed in Chapter 5), the studios were unable to go back to the way things had been. And they would spend the better part of the next twenty-five years struggling to establish a new Hollywood as successful as the Hollywood they lost during the war.

1939–1941: THE LAST BEST YEARS

Between 1939 and 1941 a number of very talented directors—Frank Capra, George Cukor, John Ford, Howard Hawks, Alfred Hitchcock, Preston Sturges, and Orson Welles—worked within the studio system to make films that could justifiably be identified as much with their artistic signature as with their studio's. This is not to say that dealings between directors and studio executives were routinely amicable. Indeed, it may have been the struggle itself—the give-and-take between directors trying to break away from the strictures of the classical Hollywood formula and producers who believed that they knew best what the American public wanted to see—that gave rise to this brief golden age.

The list of great films released during these years is impressive enough, and even a relative newcomer to film studies will recognize many of them. The classic western *Stagecoach* (the movie that made John Wayne a star), the early Technicolor settlers-versus-Indians drama *Drums along the Mohawk*, and the biopic *Young Mr. Lincoln* (all directed by Ford); the Bette Davis tearjerker *Dark Victory* (Edmund Goulding); the swashbuckler *The Three Musketeers* (Allan Dwan); the romantic melodrama *Wuthering Heights* (adapted from Emily Brontë's novel and directed by William Wyler with revolutionary deep-focus photography by Gregg Toland, whose even more striking work on *Citizen Kane* two years later would change American cinematography forever); the popular adaptation of James Hilton's novel *Goodbye, Mr. Chips* (Sam Wood); the colonial adventure picture *Gunga Din* (directed by George Stevens, based on a poem by Rudyard Kipling); the arch farce *Ninotchka* (Ernst Lubitsch), in which Garbo plays an icy Soviet beauty seduced by the romance and materialism of the West; the romantic adventure picture *Only Angels Have Wings* (Hawks); the populist drama *Mr. Smith Goes to Washington* (Capra); and two films directed by Victor Fleming, the epic adaptation of Margaret Mitchell's epic novel *Gone with the Wind* and the legendary black-and-white and color musical *The Wizard of Oz* reached U.S. screens in 1939.

Nineteen forty brought Charlie Chaplin's political comedy *The Great Dictator,* in which the comedian exploited the physical resemblance between his Little Tramp character and Hitler; Ford's adaptation of John Steinbeck's social-realist novel *The Grapes of Wrath;* Hawks's romantic comedy *His Girl Friday;* Lewis Milestone's adaptation of Steinbeck's *Of Mice and Men;* Raoul Walsh's hard-boiled tale of wildcat truckers *They Drive by Night* and the John Wayne Civil War picture *Dark Command;* Lubitsch's romantic comedy *The Shop around the*

John Wayne as the Ringo Kid in John Ford's *Stagecoach* (1939), the film that made Wayne a star.

Corner; Cukor's romantic comedy *The Philadelphia Story;* Sturges's farce *Christmas in July;* and Hitchcock's adaptation of the Daphne du Maurier melodrama *Rebecca.*

The key releases of 1941, films released during the eleven months before the United States entered the war, include two direced by Hawks, the World War I pacifist picture *Sergeant York* and the screwball comedy *Ball of Fire,* both starring the iconic American strong and silent hero Gary Cooper; the suspense picture *Suspicion* (Hitchcock); the romantic comedy *The Lady Eve* (Sturges); the populist melodrama *Meet John Doe* (Capra), in which a common-man hero played by Gary Cooper extols a free country's ability to win at anything it tries, from "tiddleywinks to war," so long as everyone works together; the classic detective story *The Maltese Falcon* (John Huston); the melodrama *The Little Foxes* (directed by Wyler and scripted by Lillian Hellman); an Errol Flynn picture about General George Custer's last stand, *They Died with Their Boots On* (Walsh); and Welles's stunning debut, *Citizen Kane.*

All of those films are striking examples of what talented filmmakers could achieve within the studio system despite the restrictions that system imposed on them. Two in particular—Victor Fleming's *Gone with the Wind* and Orson Welles's *Citizen Kane*—continue to stand among the most important films ever made, as well as the best examples of the good that can come from the melding of art and commerce.

Gone with the Wind

The person most responsible for the phenomenal success of the Civil War epic *Gone with the Wind* was its producer, David O. Selznick, a second-generation Hollywood mogul with one degree of separation from a houseful of Hollywood royalty. David O. Selznick's father was Lewis J. Selznick, a silent-cinema entrepreneur; his first father-in law was Louis B. Mayer, one of the founders of Metro-Goldwyn-Mayer (MGM); and his brother, Myron, was an agent with a client list that included the movie stars Fred Astaire, Carole Lombard, Myrna Loy, Fredric March, Merle Oberon, Ginger Rogers, and Loretta Young.

Selznick began his career in the story department at MGM in 1926. It was a curious place for him to start, given that Lewis Selznick and Louis B. Mayer (who was not yet David's father-in-law) were once bitter enemies. In 1927, Mayer put Selznick in charge of the production of a series of low-budget Tim McCoy westerns, films routinely shot in less than a month under tight budget constraints. That first assignment would hardly suggest what the producer had in store for American audiences at the end of the 1930s, but it was a start. After an ill-advised showdown with Irving Thalberg, Selznick moved on to Paramount, a studio run by another of his father's former business rivals, Adolph Zukor, but after Paramount's New York–based ownership dictated executive salary cuts, he bolted for RKO.

At RKO, Selznick enjoyed a great deal of authority and autonomy supervising the production of an amazing number of films—seventeen—in 1932, his first full year at the studio. Among them were the steamy teen melodrama *The Age of Consent* (Gregory La Cava); *The Most Dangerous Game* (Irving Pichel and Ernest B. Schoedsack), in which members of a shipwrecked crew on a remote island meet a mysterious count who likes to hunt humans; the socially conscious prison picture

"I'll have some rotten nights after I've sent you over, but that'll pass." Private detective Sam Spade (Humphrey Bogart) turns the tables on the femme fatale Brigid O'Shaughnessy (Mary Astor) in John Huston's 1941 adaptation of the Dashiell Hammett novel *The Maltese Falcon.*

(*left*) Jefferson Smith (Jimmy Stewart, *right*), the populist hero in Frank Capra's *Mr. Smith Goes to Washington* (1939), takes on his boyhood idol, Senator Joseph Harrison Paine (Claude Rains), on the floor of the U.S. Senate. Like most of Capra's films, *Mr. Smith Goes to Washington* celebrates the determination and grit of the common man.

Hell's Highway (Rowland Brown); and the family melodrama *A Bill of Divorcement* (Cukor), starring the Selznick "discovery" Katharine Hepburn.

Unlike the publicity-shy Thalberg, whose supervisory system Selznick instituted at RKO, Selznick gave himself screen credit for the films he produced. He saw himself as a filmmaker and not just a studio manager. And he liked to see his name in lights. Selznick's run at RKO was successful, especially given the budget constraints. In 1933 he added to his production credits *King Kong* (Merian C. Cooper and Schoedsack), the

The producer David O. Selznick on the set of *Gone with the Wind* (Victor Fleming, 1939).

society comedy *Dinner at Eight* (Cukor), and the melodrama *Christopher Strong* (Dorothy Arzner).

Selznick soon left RKO, signing on as a producer at MGM, where he finally seemed to have the sort of financial backing he needed to develop a signature line of films. In 1935 came *Reckless*, a musical melodrama directed by Fleming, and then his first big hit, *Anna Karenina* (Clarence Brown), adapted from the classic novel by Leo Tolstoy and starring the studio superstar Greta Garbo.

In Hollywood, success is often a matter of seizing the day, being ready to make a move just as your fortunes are mysteriously on the rise. And indeed after *Anna Karenina*, Selznick intuited that his moment had come. In one of the boldest moves in Hollywood history, he resigned his executive post at MGM and struck out on his own. With cash from his brother, Myron, and his friend John Hay "Jock" Whitney, Selznick founded Selznick International Pictures, an independent, alternative studio.

Selznick was successful right from the start, producing the oft-remade melodrama *A Star Is*

Born, about an industry couple (Janet Gaynor and Fredric March) coming undone as the young wife's career surpasses that of her mentor-husband, and the clever romantic comedy *Nothing Sacred*, both directed in 1937 by William Wellman. Then came the swashbuckling adventure picture *The Prisoner of Zenda* (John Cromwell, also released in 1937), starring Ronald Colman, Mary Astor, and Douglas Fairbanks Jr., and the romantic melodrama *Intermezzo* (Gregory Ratoff, 1939), starring Ingrid Bergman and Leslie Howard, two films that established Selznick's mature production template, his ability to transcend genre formulas using A-picture production values, clever casting, and expert promotion.

The apotheosis of Selznick's signature production style was *Gone with the Wind* (Fleming, 1939), according to almost every measure (length, box office, public relations) the biggest American film of the first half of the twentieth century. Selznick purchased the rights to the thousand-page first (and only) novel by the Atlanta native Margaret Mitchell for $50,000, the highest sum paid for a book option to that date. The novel, purchased by Selznick just as it reached the bookstores, became a huge success. By the time the film premiered, over 2 million copies of the book had been sold.

At a cost of over $4 million (over $50 million in 2005 dollars) and a running time exceeding 3 hours and 30 minutes, *Gone with the Wind* was fashioned from development through release like a modern blockbuster. During the development stage, Selznick expertly created interest in the film with, among other things, a talent search for the female lead, during which over one thousand actresses were interviewed and over four hundred were auditioned. The role went to the Indian-born British actress Vivien Leigh, whose look Selznick preferred over that of far more famous movie stars like Tallulah Bankhead, Olivia de Havilland, Katharine Hepburn, Carole Lombard, and Margaret Sullavan.

During the production process, Selznick maintained keen interest in the project by leaking to newspapers and fan magazines stories highlighting

(*right*) Rhett Butler (Clark Gable) romancing Scarlett O'Hara (Vivien Leigh) in David O. Selznick's epic production of *Gone with the Wind* (Victor Fleming, 1939).

the film's lavish production. He announced, for example, the start of principal photography before announcing the casting of Leigh and carried on the charade of continuing to search for the perfect actress for the part even as the cameras had begun to roll. We know today that Leigh had been cast fairly early in the development process, but Selznick used the publicity stunt to call even keener attention to a supposed campaign to find the perfect Scarlett O'Hara and to promote himself as the

(*left*) After a much-publicized search for the right actress, the coveted role of Scarlett O'Hara in *Gone with the Wind* (Victor Fleming, 1939) went to the British actress Vivien Leigh. In this scene, Scarlett is fitted for a corset by her maid (Hattie McDaniel). Both actresses won Oscars for their performances.

(*below*) The world premiere of *Gone with the Wind* (Victor Fleming) at the Loew's Grand in Atlanta, December 1939.

consummate high-stakes gambler, the consummate Hollywood showman willing to risk everything on finding the right star for his film.

During the film's long production schedule, Selznick kept *Gone with the Wind* in the news. For the burning-of-Atlanta sequence, for example, which was staged on the MGM lot, Selznick set a real fire, igniting a warehouse full of old sets. The fire caught the interest of Culver City firemen and as a result, of course, the press. The postproduction promotion campaign positioned the film, defining it in advance of its arrival in the marketplace, with a simple tagline: "The most magnificent picture ever!" By the time it came to theaters, in December 1939, *Gone with the Wind* was more of an event than a film; it was, as Selznick had promised, the biggest film ever to hit the big screen.

Due in no small part to Selznick's expert management of the project, *Gone with the Wind* became the highest-grossing film of all time and held that title until 1972, some thirty-three years after its release, when *The Godfather* (Francis Ford Coppola) established a new box-office record. In many ways, *Gone with the Wind* recalled *The Birth of a Nation*, not necessarily in its politics (though both romanticize the civility of the prewar southern aristocracy) but in its scale and scope, in its effort to address—and, to an extent, rewrite—history by focusing on the travails of a single family.

Gone with the Wind tracks the history of the O'Hara family as it progresses from riches to rags to riches. War robs the O'Haras of the Old South, with its cotillions, mint juleps, and Old World chivalry—in short, its way of life. The Yankees lay siege to Atlanta, and the scenes of that southern city burning are among the most memorable in the film. But Scarlett and her beloved Tara (the family estate) nonetheless endure. After the war we see Scarlett, mud strategically smudged on her cheek, working the fields like a hired hand. Her father has lost his mind. Her husband (whom she did not love anyway) is dead. The carpetbaggers have arrived and are pillaging the region. But Scarlett is made of surprisingly stern stuff. And she is—after all, she is the heroine of this melodrama—destined for bigger things and greater sacrifices. Scarlett marries three times, once for spite (after her beloved Ashley Wilkes, played by Leslie Howard, jilts her), once for money (to her sister's beau, Frank Kennedy, played by Carroll Nye), and finally for love (or

Clark Gable (as Rhett Butler) about to deliver one of American cinema's most memorable exit lines—"Frankly, my dear, I don't give a damn"—at the end of *Gone with the Wind* (Victor Fleming, 1939).

something like love), to Rhett Butler (Clark Gable). But even the love match is doomed. Rhett eventually walks out on Scarlett, saying, "Frankly, my dear, I don't give a damn"—surely one of American cinema's most famous and most perfect exit lines (and, incidentally, a line that the PCA wanted changed to "Frankly, my dear, I don't care"; Selznick paid a $5,000 fine to keep the line in the film as written). But while Scarlett ruminates in Rhett's absence that "tomorrow is another day," it will be another day without Rhett and without the Old South and without the wonderful life that seemed hers for the taking at the start of the film. Although in many ways it is the ultimate studio epic, *Gone with the Wind* ends in a very un-Hollywood way, with the heroine abandoned and uncertain.

Gone with the Wind won eight Academy Awards, including Best Picture, Best Director (by Victor Fleming, who had taken over for Selznick's first choice, George Cukor, when Gable refused to be directed "by a fairy"), Best Actress (Vivien Leigh), and Best Supporting Actress (Hattie McDaniel, the first African American to win an Oscar, who chose not to attend the film's premiere in then-segregated Atlanta). Selznick received the coveted Irving Thalberg Memorial Award, an irony given the producer's stormy relationship with Thalberg and his defiance, in going independent, of the very studio system that Thalberg had helped to create.

There can be no debate that *Gone with the Wind* was Selznick's film, but the reality of embarking on such a colossal enterprise made a deal with one of the Big Eight studio distributors inevitable. In order to secure Gable's services and a little over $1 million in financing, Selznick had made a deal with his father-in-law, Louis B. Mayer, and assigned the film's domestic distribution rights (and thus the lion's share of the film's considerable profits) to MGM. In the end most of the money went to his father-in-law's studio. But the accolades went to Selznick, and he became one of the few film executives in Hollywood history to become as famous as the films made under his management.

The cinematographer Gregg Toland (*right*) and the director Orson Welles set up a shot for *Citizen Kane* (1941).

Citizen Kane

Film history offers a handful of truly transformative moments: there is cinema before and after sound, cinema before and after the PCA, cinema before and after *Citizen Kane*. Writing only half in jest well before the release of *Citizen Kane*, the novelist and by-then Hollywood denizen F. Scott Fitzgerald mused that Orson Welles would be the biggest menace to hit Hollywood in decades, that after he made his first film, the studios would have to retool and start all over again as they had after *The Jazz Singer* (Alan Crosland, 1927). Fitzgerald was prescient. *Citizen Kane* redefined the look of modern American cinema and changed forever the way in which American audiences and film historians talk about the movies.

As Fitzgerald's remark suggests, by the time Welles arrived in Hollywood, he was already a well-known talent. He had by then made his mark onstage (as an actor, director, and manager of his own company, the Mercury Theatre) and on radio (thanks mostly to the legendary *War of the Worlds* stunt, for which he adapted the H. G. Wells novel as a news story about aliens attacking the United States). In November 1939, RKO celebrated Welles's arrival in Hollywood with a landmark contract that gave the twenty-four-year-old boy wonder carte blanche—total authority over the production of his first film. Soon after signing with RKO, Welles proposed a film adaptation of Joseph Conrad's novella *Heart of Darkness*. He wrote a two-hundred-page preliminary script (approximately twice the length of a standard feature-length screenplay), built a model for the renegade Kurtz's compound (the film's key set), and presented to the studio a simple visual model with a human eye, an equal sign, and the pronoun *I*. "Eye = I," suggested Welles's planned visual simulation of the novella's first-person narration, the extensive use of subjective camera that Rouben Mamoulian had employed with mixed success in his 1931 adaptation of *Dr. Jekyll and Mr. Hyde*. The proposed budget topped $1 million, about twice what the studio wanted to spend, and the project was scrapped.

(*right*) The larger-than-life Orson Welles as the larger-than-life newspaperman cum gubernatorial candidate Charles Foster Kane in Welles's landmark film *Citizen Kane* (1941).

Orson Welles's evocative use of depth of field (deep focus) is evident in this scene, set at the Kane boardinghouse early in the film. As Thatcher (George Coulouris, seated at the center), explains the trust contract to Charles Foster Kane's mother (Agnes Moorehead) and father (Harry Shannon), we see young Charlie (Buddy Swan) playing in the snow outside. Welles used this visual style throughout *Citizen Kane* (1941).

When the *Heart of Darkness* project fell apart after so much work in development, rumors circulated that Welles might not get to make a movie after all. To help develop another project before RKO lost interest in him, Welles called in Herman Mankiewicz, a respected screenwriter with over fifty feature-film credits. Welles proposed making a film simply titled *American*, focusing at one point on the gangster John Dillinger and at another point on the evangelist Aimee Semple McPherson. Neither subject was viable: telling the story of Dillinger promised to raise problems with FBI director J. Edgar Hoover, and any attempt to portray a religious figure in bad light courted sanctions from the PCA and the Catholic Legion of Decency.

Mankiewicz claimed that it was he who suggested to Welles a third subject: the millionaire media magnate William Randolph Hearst. Welles told a different story—of a dinner party with Hearst, whom he grew to dislike so much that he decided to make a film about him. Whichever version is true, the screenplay that Mankiewicz and Welles wrote was not flattering, and Hearst was well aware of the parallels to his life. To try to stop Welles from releasing the film, Hearst offered to buy the negative from RKO. The studio refused even when Hearst offered to reimburse the studio not only for its out-of-pocket costs but for the potential profits as well. When RKO released *Citizen Kane*, in May 1941, Hearst exacted some measure of revenge by refusing to carry ads for the film or run reviews of it in any of his syndicated papers.

The stand-in for Hearst in Welles's film is Charles Foster Kane (played by Welles), a modern tragic figure who is undone by ambition and pride. Kane, like Hearst, hobnobs with movie stars and presidents, and his life makes front-page news for half a century. But what, the film asks, was he really like? The newsreel that opens the film asks that question and offers a mysterious key to a possible answer, a word Kane uttered as he lay dying: "Rosebud." Though we finally discover the meaning of the word (it's the sled Kane played with on his last happy day as a child in Colorado) and perhaps piece together its significance to the man's life, Welles cleverly leaves the characters at the end of the film no closer to unraveling the mystery of "Rosebud" than they were at the start.

The film posits a clever narrative gimmick: an intrepid journalist interviews several of Kane's former friends and associates, and so these several narrators get their chance to tell him—and us—about the real Charles Foster Kane. Their stories unfold in a series of nine narrative sequences, five of which are flashbacks. It is a fascinating cinematic structure, but it is Welles's contention that the stories are less revealing than we think.

The parallel narrative structure is the first thing most viewers notice the first time they see *Citizen Kane*. But it is not what makes the film so great, so important to the history of American filmmaking. At the heart of the film is not storytelling structure but Welles's evocative use of depth of field, or deep focus, the rendering of film space in depth. Welles himself affirmed the importance of the film's mise-en-scène in the opening credit sequence, which lists the name of the cinematographer, Gregg Toland, last, where one would expect to find the director's name.

Citizen Kane was not the first film to use depth-of-field photography and not the first in which Toland's particular genius was in evidence. Toland had won an Academy Award for Cinematography two years earlier, for *Wuthering Heights* (Wyler), a film that features several scenes composed in depth. But Welles took Toland's deep-focus work in *Wuthering Heights* one step further, conceiving the entire picture in depth-of-field compositions. The effect is at once theatrical—we see figures in the foreground and the background as if they were onstage—and realistic, as the depth of field helps to simulate real living spaces: offices, barrooms, and the grand hall at Xanadu, Kane's "pleasure dome."

Early on in the film, for example, we see young Charles Foster Kane (Buddy Swan) playing in the snow. The camera tracks away from him to reveal in startling size his mother (Agnes Moorehead) at the left corner of the frame, and we realize that like her, we have been watching the boy through a window. The camera continues to track into the room to reveal Charlie's father (Harry Shannon) and Thatcher (George Coulouris), his eventual guardian. Welles blocks the scene cleverly. The mother walks from the window to meet with Thatcher in the foreground. The father stands several steps away, between them and Charles, who is still visible playing in the snow, framed by the window. All the principals are not only in view but also in focus. But they are not equal. Charles, who is outside, can't hear what's going on inside the house, and he isn't involved in the decisions being made there. The father, who stands several feet away from his wife and the banker, can hear every word being said but lacks the authority of the characters who occupy the foreground. Charles's mother is entrusting her son to the banker, ostensibly to give the boy all the advantages the family's sudden wealth can afford and to keep him from his father. The father opposes the decision, but like his son he is powerless. It is a pivotal scene that is staged to tell a story with a minimum of dialogue. Everything we need to know about all four characters is evident in the mise-en-scène.

Much later in the film, when Kane and his second wife, Susan (Dorothy Comingore), inhabit the cavernous Xanadu mansion, Welles uses depth-of-field compositions to express the emotional and physical distance between the couple. One shot in particular, set in the living room, exemplifies Welles's use of film style in the service of narra-

tion. In the foreground of the shot is Susan looking down at a jigsaw puzzle. The camera is placed above her head, and she is lit from the side. The shiny marble floor that forms a V at the bottom of the frame is unlit, as are the walls at the far end of the shot. Our eyes move from light source to light source (Welles holds the shot long enough for us to work through it), from Susan's face in profile to a huge rug at the bottom center of the frame and finally to Kane, seated in a chair made to look like a throne. Four mostly dark windows, all done up with churchlike stained glass, loom on the far wall. The set is gloomy, empty, and gothic. In a single shot, Welles tells us all we need to know about Kane's last days at Xanadu; we see him for what he has become: a lonely, gloomy monarch.

Welles was never generous in crediting directors whose work had influenced him, but it is hard to miss the significance of German expressionism and F. W. Murnau in particular: the chiaroscuro lighting, the theatrical set pieces, the antimontage

A low-angle, deep-focus shot of Charles Foster Kane (Orson Welles, *top left*), whose marriage and gubernatorial aspirations have just fallen apart thanks to some clever sleuthing by his adversary, the political boss James Gettys (Ray Collins), in Welles's *Citizen Kane* (1941).

style, in which long takes and moving-camera, or tracking, shots are used in place of cuts. But much of what Welles does is unique, even revolutionary. The director would later attribute his unusual, radical stylistic choices to his own inexperience. He knew so little about the rules of lighting and cutting in 1941, he later claimed, that his choices were not necessarily governed by the practical or the seemingly possible. For example, when the newsmen gather in the projection room to watch the newsreel telling the (incomplete) story of Kane's life, Welles composes the scene in depth (again using a high-angle shot). He eschews traditional three-point lighting in favor of illumination that comes entirely from behind as light filters onto the set through two square projection-booth windows at the top right of the frame. That is how a room might look at a real newsreel screening, but the lighting makes it difficult for the audience to identify the characters. As one of the journalists gesticulates, his movements are doubled by outsize shadows. There is no narrative significance to the shadows, but the image is nonetheless riveting, another example of how in the film every shot is unique and eccentric; every shot calls attention to the film's author, Orson Welles.

In place of narrative transitions that other directors at the time would have accomplished through continuity editing, Welles used a mobile camera to take the viewer from place to place. When the newsreel reporter leaves Thatcher's library for the seedy barroom where the former Susan Alexander Kane now sings (and drinks), the camera sweeps up and then down again, through the bar's skylight and into the room. It is a dramatic camera move, and it is consistent with the two seemingly oppositional formal goals of the film: to simulate a theatrical look (blocking actors as if they were onstage and moving the camera on a vertical axis, up and then down again, to simulate the movement of stage scrims and scenery) and to create a realist aesthetic (an artistic conception that is meant to reproduce real space as opposed to simulated "movie" space) through compositions in depth.

More subtle, but no less expressive, is the sequence of shots that in a matter of minutes tells the story of Kane's rise and fall as a politician. The sequence begins with Kane's sidekick, Jedediah (Joseph Cotten), shot in extreme high angle, speaking on behalf of Kane, the populist candidate with

no realistic chance of winning the gubernatorial election. The camera closes in to set up a cut to a second rally as the film cuts from Jedediah's face to a giant poster of Kane, and on the sound track Jedediah's unassuming speech is supplanted by Kane's bombast. Two jarring cuts take us further and further from the candidate. As the cinematic space grows increasingly less intimate, we come to appreciate Kane's growing size as a political figure and his increasing distance from the grassroots beginnings of the campaign. The last shot in the sequence places us in a huge hall, with the camera placed at a great distance from the stage. The composition alludes to Leni Reifenstahl's legendary 1935 Nazi documentary *Triumph of the Will*, a bit heavy-handed perhaps, but the effect is very much what Welles is after. In 1941 the iconography of demagoguery packed quite a punch. As the camera tracks in, what at first seems merely a repetition of a move executed by the previous camera placements continues until the camera reaches its subject and then drops down to a low angle that exaggerates Kane's size (as a man, as an American political figure). But just as the mise-en-scène suggests that Kane is at the top of his game, the director offers one of the film's rare sequences constructed in a series of strategic cuts instead of a deep-focus mise-en-scène.

The film cuts from Kane to a low-angle shot of his (first) wife, Emily (Ruth Warrick), and their son, Junior (Sonny Bupp), watching from a box well above the stage. Twelve subsequent cuts explain this segue from the political to the personal: (1) a low-angle shot of Kane speaking; (2) a high-angle shot of Kane speaking; (3) a return to Emily and Junior in high angle; (4) Kane, in high angle, acknowledging his wife and son; (5) a low-angle medium close-up of Jedediah looking on admiringly; (6) Kane, in high angle, talking about "decent, ordinary citizens" (much, we gather, to Jedediah's approval); (7) Kane's cohort Bernstein (Everett Sloane), in low angle, daring like Jedediah, to believe Kane's rhetoric; (8) another reaction shot of the wife and son, this time including a cute personal exchange: Junior asks, "Mother, is Pop governor yet?" Emily responds, "Not yet Junior"; (9) Kane shot "flat" (the camera is level), talking about "keeping promises"; (10) Jedediah, in low angle, still taking in the scene; (11) a high-angle shot of Kane as he talks about investigating the state political machine; and after the camera tracks in, showing a figure we've now seen three times in this scene, (12) a gorgeous deep-focus shot of Kane's political rival, James Gettys (Ray Collins), in the foreground, screen right, looking down to the stage, where Kane seems suddenly very small, completely dwarfed by the image in the poster that hangs behind him and by his rival, who looks down on him. Gettys exits the frame in what is almost a wipe (his exit from screen right to screen left acts like an eraser on a blackboard, taking us out of the sequence). In approximately two-and-a-half minutes, Welles has summarized Kane's rise and fall on the political stage. And in a single shot he foretells a later confrontation—involving Emily, Susan, Kane, and Gettys at Susan's apartment—that ends both Kane's political ambitions and his marriage to Emily.

Drawing on his experience producing and directing for radio, Welles integrated into his signature deep-focus mise-en-scène a cluttered soundscape of live and dubbed music, sound effects, and competing lines of dialogue. In some scenes all the characters talk at once, as if competing for our attention. When Kane celebrates his having stolen the best newspapermen from a rival paper, *The Chronicle*, he emcees a party. He is in control only briefly, though. As showgirls sing a song, the newspapermen joke and his colleagues shout to be heard above the din. By the end of the scene, Kane is singing along with a silly number about himself. He is caught up in the moment, and his voice, once heard above everyone else's, becomes just one of several competing sounds that cannot be distinguished from one another.

Welles's sound work anticipated contemporary sound-film recording techniques that work to complicate the mix. Little of the sound we hear in contemporary Hollywood films is recorded live. Instead, dialogue, sound effects, and music (even if the source of the music is seen in the shot) are added, mixed, and balanced in postproduction. More than any other director of his generation, Welles separated the visual from the aural. The gothic, theatrical mise-en-scène that characterizes much of *Citizen Kane* finds a complement in the deftly engineered layers of sound that make up the movie's sound track.

Welles is a pivotal figure in American film history, but *Citizen Kane* was his only commercially

A gorgeous deep-focus shot of Charles Foster Kane's political rival, James Gettys (Ray Collins, *in the foreground, screen right*), looking down on the stage where Kane (Orson Welles) seems suddenly very small, dwarfed by the political poster that hangs behind him and by his rival, who looks down on him. This shot sets in motion the ambitious candidate's sudden downfall in *Citizen Kane* (Welles, 1941).

successful film. What lay in store for Welles after that movie is a sad but familiar story in the ongoing struggle between the artistic and the industrial, the creative and the commercial, in Hollywood. In 1941, well before Welles's stock would fall in Hollywood, it was clear to everyone that *Citizen Kane* was more than just another movie. But brilliant as it was, after December 7, 1941, the American moviegoing public would have other things to think about rather than Welles and his astonishing debut film. It was not until after the war that the full effect of the film and its radical style was felt.

A WORLD AT WAR

The war overseas cut significantly into the studios' foreign revenues. By 1938 both Japan and Germany had cut off all economic ties to the United States, and by December 1941, when the United States was finally dragged into the war, it was difficult to release a film anyplace in Europe. America's enemies had no use for Hollywood movies, and the Allies had better things to do with their time.

The studios turned briefly to South America, a largely untapped source of revenue. In 1941 three studios released films of topical interest to South Americans: Fox's *That Night in Rio* (Irving Cummings), MGM's *The Life of Simon Bolivar* (Miguel Contreras Torres), and RKO's *They Met in Argentina* (Leslie Goodwins and Jack Hively). This gesture to the south never amounted to much, and after December 1941 the studios focused exclusively on the domestic market.

In the years leading up to the war, patriotism was a complex issue. The country was divided by the question of whether to enter the war, and as a consequence exactly what constituted "Americanism" was unclear. America First championed the isolationist view that the patriotic thing to do was

stay out of the war at all costs. The Hollywood Anti-Nazi League, organized in 1936 by the industry's many left-leaning Jews, held a different view, contending that if America truly stood for freedom and democracy, it had to enter the war against the tyranny of Hitler and his imperialist enterprise in Europe.

Joseph Breen, head of the Production Code Administration, had little affection for the folks in the Hollywood Anti-Nazi League. But although his personal dislike for Hollywood's liberal Left community was hardly an industry secret, his opposition to political films encouraging American intervention in the European war was posed publicly as an economic strategy. Neutrality and isolationism, Breen maintained, were good for business.

Topical films critical of either side in the European conflict were, as Breen argued, difficult to book abroad. One such film was the 1939 Warner Bros. release *Confessions of a Nazi Spy*, a potent anti-Fascist melodrama directed by Anatole Litvak, developed, produced, and released despite steady PCA opposition. After some negotiation the PCA gave the completed film its production seal, only to have its worst fears realized as a wave of anti-Fascist films followed in the next twelve months: *The Great Dictator* (Charles Chaplin, 1940), *Pastor Hall* (Roy Boulting, 1940), *The Mortal Storm* (Frank Borzage, 1940), and *I Married a Nazi* (Irving Pichel, 1940).

The official PCA memo to Jack and Harry Warner concerning the original script for *Confessions of a Nazi Spy* makes for chilling reading today:

> Hitler and his government are unfairly represented in this story in violation of the Code. . . . To represent Hitler ONLY as a screaming madman and a bloodthirsty persecutor and *nothing else* is manifestly unfair. . . . Are we ready to depart from the pleasant and profitable course of entertainment to engage in propaganda, to produce screen portrayals arousing controversy. . . . Where's the line to be drawn? Why not make [pictures about] the Stalin purges, the Japanese rape of China, the Terror of Spain, etc.

Confessions of a Nazi Spy (Anatole Litvak, 1939), starring Edward G. Robinson (*second from the left*), was one of several films that called attention to the Nazi menace well before the United States entered World War II.

Like Anatole Litvak's *Confessions of a Nazi Spy* (1939), the political content of Frank Borzage's *The Mortal Storm* (1940) caused its studio problems with the prewar Production Code Administration (PCA).

Though the memo reveals Breen's personal politics, his official reservations about the movie spoke to the MPPDA studios' declining overseas revenues. Breen wanted Hollywood to stay its course by making inoffensive, apolitical entertainment films. Breen was also concerned about possible problems for the industry in Washington, where anxiety about the politics of the films and filmmakers in Hollywood reached a head on September 9, 1941, when at the urging of two conservative, isolationist senators, Burton Wheeler of Montana and Gerald Nye of North Dakota, Senate subcommittee hearings on motion-picture and radio propaganda—the so-called propaganda hearings—were convened. Wheeler and Nye argued that in the late 1930s, Hollywood had become a "propaganda machine" run by Jews (whom they called the industry's "central agency"). They focused their fellow senators' attention on seventeen so-called "war-mongering features," including *The Great Dictator* (1940) and Alfred Hitchcock's *Foreign Correspondent* (1940).

The liberal Republican Wendell Willkie, a former public advocacy attorney who lost a bid for the presidency in 1940, was hired by the studios to defend the MPPDA. Willkie quickly lured Nye into an embarrassing diatribe against the industry's Jews. "If anti-Semitism exists in America," Nye snarled at Willkie, "the Jews have themselves to blame." How many senators agreed with Wheeler and Nye is something we will never know. The committee's argument regarding Hollywood's warmongering became moot as the attack on Pearl Harbor interrupted the proceedings and guaranteed the country's entry into the war.

World War II Hollywood

During World War II, moviemaking pretty much everywhere except in the United States was governed by the exigencies of nationalism and the scarcity of natural resources. In Germany, for example, Hitler nationalized the film industry under the Office of Propaganda, a division of the state helmed by Joseph Goebbels. Films in the National Socialist interest got made and shown. The thriving commercial industry of the 1920s that showcased the talents of Fritz Lang, F. W. Murnau, and G. W. Pabst was shut down. The Nazi totalitarian government did not risk dissent from artists and intellectuals, especially filmmakers, who had the potential to sway public opinion. Once France was occupied by Germany, beginning in 1940, and a collaborationist government had been established, French filmmaking was subsumed by the Nazi cause as well.

During the war years in Great Britain, the Crown Film Unit was assembled from a handful of directors trained in the 1930s by John Grierson, one of the foremost practitioners of social-realist filmmaking (a working-class documentary project examining the everyday lives of everyday people). Crown Film Unit filmmakers like Harry Watt and Humphrey Jennings (*London Can Take It*, 1940) made sentimental documentaries meant to rally the populace. Given growing political desperation (England was the victim of some of the Nazis' most brutal air assaults) and the rationing of natural resources and food, there was little money or time for commercial divertissements. Many of the commercial feature films to reach British screens were quasi documentaries celebrating heroism on the home front, such as *Went the Day Well?* (Alberto Cavalcanti, 1942), or the glorious exploits of the armed services, such as *The Way Ahead* (Carol Reed, 1944). As in Germany, but of course to a different end, filmmaking in the United Kingdom served national interests as government officials came to appreciate the persuasive power of motion pictures.

Though never interested in nationalizing the film industry, President Franklin D. Roosevelt moved quickly to establish parameters for wartime film production. Eleven days after the attack on Pearl Harbor, the president established the Bureau of Motion Picture Affairs (BMPA), a production unit that, beginning in 1942, was supervised by the Office of War Information (OWI). Patriotism was, understandably, at its zenith, and for altruistic and commercial reasons the Hollywood studios proved eager to contribute what they could to the war effort.

The studios mobilized by creating the War Activities Committee of the Motion Picture Industry and endeavored to make topical and patriotic fictional as well as documentary films. The studios responded favorably to the BMPA's list of suggestions for wartime filmmaking, which urged the studios to (1) make movies that reminded audiences of what was at stake—what might be lost if the war went badly for the United States; (2) render obvious the essential (even natural) evil of those the country was fighting against (their cultural differences, their seeming barbarism, treachery, and so on); and (3) celebrate the history and culture of our allies (as essentially good people with a way of life well worth fighting to preserve).

Selling the War

Though the American film industry was not nationalized during the war years, the government nonetheless used its influence in Hollywood to produce a range of films that were meant to persuade draftees to fight and help those at home understand and support the war effort. The U.S. Army Signal Corps' *Fighting Man* series, for example, was produced by some of the industry's best and brightest filmmakers using studio equipment and labor. These films provided education and advice on topics as diverse as weapons operation, shell shock, and venereal disease—including one titled *Sex Hygiene*, directed by John Ford in 1942.

In the days before TV news coverage, homefront filmgoers got their updates from newsreels, which were carefully monitored and regulated by the War Department. With little on-screen violence (through the first couple of years of the war at least), the newsreels conveyed the impression that the war was being fought someplace else by someone else. Hollywood filmmakers were of course experienced at making movies whose content was strictly regulated, but for the first time the regulator was the federal government, and willingness to cooperate with the censors was a matter of patriotism.

The Nazi deification of Adolf Hitler was put in a new context in the *Why We Fight* film *Prelude to War* (Frank Capra and Anatole Litvak, 1943). This image, from a German newsreel, was used because it promised to offend Christian Americans. Depicting the enemy as blasphemous was just one of many strategies used in wartime documentaries to persuade film audiences to support the war effort.

Also for those on the home front, the War Department enlisted Frank Capra to produce a series of pictures under the apt heading *Why We Fight,* which ran through the duration of the war. With the clever use of newsreel footage (from contemporary studio and news sources as well as enemy documentaries, most released before December 7, 1941, but some seized as the war turned in our favor), these films characterized the enemy as monstrous aliens, the defeat of whom was essential to the preservation of American life. *The Nazis Strike* (Capra and Litvak, 1943), for example, used footage from the pro-Hitler documentary *Triumph of the Will* (Leni Reifenstahl, 1935) to depict the Nazis as just the latest in a long line of German warmongering imperialists. *Know Your Enemy: Japan* (Capra and Joris Ivens, 1945) opens with a voice-over that authenticates the footage used to damn the enemy: "This film has been compiled from authentic newsreel, official United Nations, and captured enemy film." Footage from nationalistic Japanese commercial films was also presented, as were reenactments, mini–war movies staged by the expert Hollywood crew assembled by Capra.

The *Why We Fight* films were clever calls to arms that revealed just how persuasive Hollywood film-makers could be. Perhaps the cleverest was *The Negro Soldier* (Stuart Heisler, 1944). Set in part in a rural African American church, the film employed an actor playing a charismatic black preacher to make the difficult argument that black Americans, who enjoyed few of the freedoms U.S. forces were supposed to be defending, should nevertheless enlist. It is a deft piece of propaganda, neatly staged and slickly argued.

Home-front screenings during the war years also included short recruitment films, often featuring A-list Hollywood talent both behind and in front of the camera. The stars James Stewart and Clark Gable, both serving as officers in the armed forces, hosted several of these films, no doubt with some measurable success.

As the war raged on, the OWI continued to sponsor feature-film production. The most interesting of the OWI features are John Ford's *Battle of Midway* (1942), *December 7th* (Ford and Gregg Toland, 1943), and *We Sail at Midnight* (Ford and Julian Spiro, 1943); John Huston's *Report from the Aleutians* (1943) and the controversial *San Pietro* (1945), which dared to show dead American soldiers, a seldom-seen image in a war-era film; and William Wyler's *The Fighting Lady* (1945). Under the aegis of the OWI, all the studios tried to do their part, including Disney, whose animated shorts lampooned the enemy with grotesque racial stereotypes (offering, for example, images of Japanese with huge buck teeth and thick eyeglasses).

Topical Features

Of the many films that offered support for the war effort on the home front, perhaps the most notable was William Wyler's *Mrs. Miniver,* which swept the Academy Awards in 1942, winning Oscars for Outstanding Motion Picture, Directing, Actress (Greer Garson, a huge star during the war years), Actress in a Supporting Role (Teresa Wright), Cinematography (for Joseph Ruttenberg's work in black-and-white), and Writing (for the screenplay by George Froeschel and others). The film focuses on two very different British families (the Minivers and

Walt Disney produced a number of animated shorts lampooning the enemy with grotesque ethnic and racial stereotypes. In the ominously titled animated short *Education for Death* (Clyde Geronimi, 1943), the German chancellor Adolf Hitler and the Wagnerian heroine Brünnhilde perform a duet.

the Beldons) who persevere despite bombing raids, food rationing, and the daily reminders of the war. The following year brought Victor Fleming's sentimental *A Guy Named Joe*, about a deceased bomber pilot who returns to earth as a guardian angel looking out for a buddy who continues to fight the good fight, along with *Air Force* (Howard Hawks) and *This Is the Army* (Michael Curtiz). All three of these 1943 war-themed pictures (all by A-list directors) broke into the box-office top ten for the year. *Thirty Seconds over Tokyo* (Mervyn LeRoy), a combat film that chronicles (with a formulaic fictional backstory) an actual battle, and the similarly themed patriotic and sentimental action-combat picture *Destination Tokyo* (Delmer Daves) were top-ten films in 1944.

For obvious reasons the spy picture offered a particularly useful frame for war-themed films. Jules Dassin's *Salute to Courage* (also known as *Nazi Agent*, 1942), for example, tells the implausible story of identical twins, one a German officer and the other an American. The American brother is recruited to spy for the Nazis, but he turns double agent and, in the process of doing his bit for the American war effort, kills his brother, success-

fully infiltrates a Nazi spy ring (masquerading as the brother), and aids in its exposure and capture. Hitchcock's *Saboteur* (1942) brought international intrigue home by placing at its center not a professional spy but an everyday workingman who must show his mettle to preserve national security. The film is ostensibly a "wrong-man" picture, one in a long line of similarly themed movies by the director—*Murder!* (1930), *The 39 Steps* (1935), *The Wrong Man* (1956), and *North by Northwest* (1959)—in all of which a man is falsely accused and must, on his own and while being pursued, prove his innocence. *Saboteur* tells the story of a defense-plant worker, Barry Kane (Robert Cummings), who is accused of setting a fire that kills his best friend. To prove his innocence, Kane tracks the real saboteur, a mysterious man named Frank Fry (Norman Lloyd). In the very process of extricating himself from the frame-up set in motion by Fry, Kane chases down and unmasks a Nazi spy ring operating on U.S. soil. The film has two memorable scenes. The first is a wild gunfight set in Radio City Music Hall in New York City, at the time the most famous film theater in the United States. The second shows Kane as he tracks Fry to the Statue of Liberty, which they ascend for a climactic showdown. Hitchcock was fond of ending films in high places: *Blackmail* (1929), for example, ends atop the British Museum, and *Vertigo* (1958) ends with a fall from a bell tower. But the locales for the shoot-out and the climactic scene in *Saboteur*—the first a legendary film palace, the second a monument to American democracy and freedom—were hardly just a matter of auteur or genre convention.

In 1943, Hitchcock followed up *Saboteur* with another wrong-man film, set this time in a small, peaceful town. Unlike *Saboteur*, in which we believe in the innocence of the protagonist from the start, *Shadow of a Doubt* inverts the wrong-man trope and offers us a man we come to know as Uncle Charlie (played by Joseph Cotten), who, if we can believe what we see at the start of the film, is the Merry Widow murderer. It is Hitchcock's sly joke that we kind of wish (and maybe believe) he isn't the killer, and at least until he tries to kill his niece, who also calls herself Charlie (Teresa Wright), we kind of wish he would get away. To avoid detection, Uncle Charlie leaves the city for his family's home in quiet Santa Rosa, a town whose inhabitants are a ridiculous bunch. Hitchcock's quintessential small-town Americans are two men who sit on the porch every night, smoking their pipes, playing armchair detective, scouring gruesome stories they've read in pulp magazines. The urban, urbane, charming Uncle Charlie doesn't fit in. Neither does Charlie, the niece, who yearns for a life in which something interesting might happen to her. Something interesting does come her way, but it's not what she expects or wants. While the men sit on the porch and talk a good game, she solves the real crime in the film. She sees her uncle for who he is and chooses to defend small-town America, the very place she, too, has found ridiculous. What she learns in the end is the importance of sacrifice (of her own selfish yearnings) and the value of fighting to preserve the blissful, peaceful place she calls home. Though the connection to the war is metaphorical, the film succeeds in sending the message that a parallel fight to protect just such a place was being staged overseas.

Unlike Hitchcock, whose political suspense films found an eager audience during the war, the romantic-comedy filmmaker Ernst Lubitsch discovered that art and politics do not always mix so seamlessly. *To Be or Not to Be,* Lubitsch's 1942 film that makes comedy out of the Nazi invasion of Poland, was an interesting failure. It stars Jack Benny, a deadpan comic with a self-effacing, self-deprecating sense of humor built on precise tim-

The cast of characters (in costume) in Ernst Lubitsch's poorly received wartime satire *To Be or Not to Be* (1942). The deadpan American comedian Jack Benny is at the center of the frame; co-stars Carole Lombard and Robert Stack are to his left. Lubitsch discovered (the hard way) that art and politics do not always mix.

ing (the pause between a joke and its punch line is often funnier than the joke itself). In *To Be or Not to Be,* Benny plays a bad stage actor, Joseph Tura, mounting a particularly bad production of *Hamlet.* When Tura comes into conflict with an SS agent (played broadly by the veteran character actor and comedian Sig Ruman), the officer puts Tura's performance in context: "What Tura did to Shakespeare, we are now doing to Poland." The joke, coming from a Nazi SS officer, did not amuse the American wartime audience, nor did much of the rest of the film.

What Lubitsch discovered from the failure of *To Be or Not to Be* was that although comedy is often subversive and some very funny comedy films have a political edge and veer into bad taste, some subjects are taboo. After the commercial and critical failure of *To Be or Not to Be,* Lubitsch (himself a German-born Jew) wisely opted for less political

Fond of ending things in high places, Alfred Hitchcock closes out his wartime spy film *Saboteur* (1942) atop the Statue of Liberty as the wrongly accused hero, Barry Kane (Robert Cummings), and his nemesis, Frank Fry (Norman Lloyd), meet in a climactic showdown.

comedy. His next film was *Heaven Can Wait* (1943), a marital farce that recalls his best film, *Trouble in Paradise* (1932), and marked a permanent turn in his career to more sentimental and distinctly less political fare.

GENRE IN WARTIME HOLLYWOOD

Adhering to a model that proved very successful during the classical era, the studios continued to diversify their product lines throughout the war years. After all, genre films made money, and although the business of running a studio after 1941 involved certain fiscal sacrifices to the war effort, executives could not afford to ignore the bottom line. Between 1941 and 1945, genre films remained the industry's bread and butter; they lent themselves to standardized studio production, they were easy to advertise and promote, and though some of them referred metaphorically to the current catastrophe, they nonetheless harked back to a time when the world was not at war, when going to the movies was something everyone everywhere could enjoy.

The Woman's Picture

With so many men overseas, it is hardly surprising that the studios tried to court the female audience. But to look at the woman's film as mere pandering to a captive audience would be unfair. What many filmmakers who tried their hand at these films discovered was a genre fraught with

opportunities to explore the contemporary circumstances of the world at war. Indeed, many of these films referred either directly or metaphorically to the travails that 1940s American women faced with so many of "their" men overseas: the loneliness, the sacrifice, the temptations, the risks, and on the more positive side, the economic and social autonomy, the possibility of a productive life that did not require the help and support of a man. Many of these films focused on universal themes, showing women making sacrifices for the good of the society at large, women maintaining a civilized society while men are notably absent. In every case these films attended to the lives and loves of women—mostly American women—whose struggle to be happy, to be noble, to be productive, reflected a 1940s American culture that had by necessity counted on women to be similarly happy, noble, and productive on the home front.

There were timely home-front dramas like *Mrs. Miniver* (William Wyler, 1942), and David O. Selznick's story of home-front rationing and romance in *Since You Went Away* (John Cromwell, 1944), which, like *Mrs. Miniver*, deals with the very real sacrifices that women made during the war. Also targeted at women but less directly connected to the war were historical dramas like *Mrs. Parkington* (Tay Garnett, 1944), the story of a frontier hotel maid who becomes a New York City socialite, and Elia Kazan's study of a woman's persistent idealism despite grinding poverty in *A Tree Grows in Brooklyn* (1945). There were also a handful of gothic suspense films, also distant from the war in subject matter, like *Gaslight* (George Cukor, 1944), in which a husband (Charles Boyer) tries to convince his wife (Ingrid Bergman) that she's going crazy, and *Mildred Pierce* (Michael Curtiz, 1945), in which a housewife (Joan Crawford) transforms herself into a restaurant mogul only to be rejected by the daughter (Ann Blyth) for whom she has sacrificed everything.

Bette Davis as Charlotte Vale, an ugly duckling dying to become a swan, and Claude Rains as her no-nonsense psychiatrist in Irving Rapper's 1942 melodrama *Now, Voyager*.

(*left*) The timely home-front drama *Mrs. Miniver* (William Wyler) won six Academy Awards in 1942. Kay Miniver (Greer Garson), her son Toby (Christopher Severn), her daughter Judy (Clare Sandars), and husband, Clem (Walter Pidgeon), huddle together to survive a Nazi bombing raid. The film renders heroic the daily struggle of middle-class families during the war.

Foremost among the women's films were traditional Hollywood melodramas, films that followed a long-standing genre formula but nonetheless spoke to the realities of women's lives during wartime. Exemplary among them is *Now, Voyager* (Irving Rapper, 1942). Like many other wartime women's pictures—George Stevens's *Talk of the Town* (1942), for example, which focuses on a woman (Jean Arthur) who learns to balance ambition and success with romance—*Now, Voyager* focuses on a woman's autonomy, on a young woman who (like so many young women in America in 1942) has to take care of herself without the help of a parent or a man.

Now, Voyager tells the story of a young woman named Charlotte Vale (Bette Davis)—her name is important, as it suggests something concealed, something repressed—who is psychologically abused and manipulated by an overbearing mother (Gladys Cooper). A psychiatrist (Claude Rains) is called in and saves Charlotte by taking her away

"Jerry, don't let's ask for the moon. We have the stars." Charlotte (Bette Davis) and Jerry (Paul Henreid) map out their future at the end of *Now, Voyager* (Irving Rapper, 1942).

to a hospital he administers. At the hospital, Charlotte regains her sanity (in that she learns to take care of herself) and thus is transformed: the ugly duckling in thick glasses, sensible shoes, and frumpy dresses becomes a swan, a trim figure dressed in the height of style. To celebrate her newfound sanity, independence, and attractiveness (the three are conflated in the film), Charlotte falls in love with Jerry (Paul Henreid), a married man whose wife is cruel and most likely insane. Charlotte and Jerry become travel companions, then friends, then (we gather) lovers over several days spent together in one of the world's most romantic cities, Rio de Janeiro.

Charlotte's return home is decidedly bittersweet. She looks good and feels good about herself, but her choices on the home front are dismal: she can live with Mother (who tortures her) or marry Elliot Livingston (John Loder), a decent, rich man who loves her but whom she regards as merely a kind friend. What she really wants, a life with Jerry, is impossible. Jerry is the consummate romantic-melodrama hero: handsome, Continental, polite, and unattainable. Charlotte knows she can't have him but rejects Elliot anyway. Elliot is a decent American guy, and Charlotte decides that he deserves a woman who loves him. She turns down Elliot's marriage proposal by saying, "I don't

think I'll ever marry. You will meet someone. Thank you for thinking it was me."

Soon after Charlotte rejects Elliot, her mother dies. Charlotte returns to the hospital to get her life back in order, but although the film initially suggests that Charlotte has sought therapy because she feels guilty about her role in her mother's death (an argument, she thinks, caused it), it is life without Jerry that requires of her significant psychological adjustment. At the hospital, Charlotte quickly becomes less a patient than a volunteer aide and as such befriends Tina (Janis Wilson), a troubled girl who—this is a Hollywood melodrama, after all—turns out to be her former lover's daughter. Tina proclaims, "I wish you were my mother," and Charlotte endeavors to make that wish come true. When Jerry arrives at the hospital to discover that his daughter and his former lover plan to live together, he's at once thrilled and heartbroken. The films ends as Jerry hugs his daughter, symbolically offering his blessing to the strange domestic setup, and mouths the words "I love you" to Charlotte. These are words that he cannot say out loud but need saying nonetheless. Although Charlotte fails to get Jerry, she emerges an independent woman moving confidently into the future in a world without a man in her (daily) life. She has also, not conversely, become a mother without having to go through all the trouble of producing and delivering her own baby.

A second exemplary 1940s melodrama, John Stahl's *Leave Her to Heaven*, shot in the last months of the war and released in time for Christmas 1945, transformed the romantic (albeit depressing) melodrama of *Now, Voyager* into something significantly more sinister and weird. The film was shot in lush Technicolor (Leon Shamroy won an Academy Award for his cinematography), much of it on location amid dramatic natural landscapes, but the story it tells is hardly light and lovely. It focuses on Ellen (Gene Tierney), a young woman who falls for a writer named Richard (Cornel Wilde). They marry, but Ellen gets more than she bargains for: Richard's brother (Darryl Hickman), who is physically disabled, moves in with them. Jealous of the brothers' close relationship, she takes the boy out on a lake and watches him drown. Her gesture of putting on sunglasses as he screams for help is as profound an image of evil as we have on-screen. Yet the boy's death does not help Ellen's situation as much as she had hoped. Neither does a pregnancy, which she soon fears will make her unattractive. To solve that problem, Ellen throws herself down a flight of stairs, prompting a miscarriage. Meantime, Ellen's adopted sister (Jeanne Crain) and Richard get close, and that makes Ellen crazy too. Things get sorted out in the end: the writer and the sister get together, but only after much suffering and loss.

Leave Her to Heaven was a huge hit, a surprise, perhaps, given its over-the-top narrative. But it was hardly the only annihilating melodrama targeted at women in the late 1940s. Another film in the same vein is Mark Robson's *My Foolish Heart* (1949), adapted by Julius and Philip Epstein (who, with Howard Koch, wrote the 1942 hit *Casablanca*) from a J. D. Salinger short story, "Uncle Wiggily in Connecticut." (The famously reclusive author so

disliked the film that he vowed never to sell another story to Hollywood, which explains why there has never been a film adaptation of his most famous work, *The Catcher in the Rye*.)

My Foolish Heart, made after the war, is tied to wartime themes more obviously than most of the melodramas released during the war. It tells the story of Eloise (Susan Hayward), who says yes to sex before marriage and then loses her lover to a military training accident. She discovers that she is pregnant, of course, and solves the problem of unwed motherhood by seducing her best friend's dumb but decent boyfriend, Lew (Kent Smith). Eloise's plan works out, at least at first. The essentially good-hearted Lew marries her because he believes he is the father of her baby. But marriage hardly makes a decent woman out of Eloise; while

Ellen (Gene Tierney, left) discovers that her marriage (to a writer played by Cornell Wilde, center, in suit and hat) means more than playing house—it means caring for her husband's brother (Darryl Hickman, center, using crutches)—in John Stahl's 1945 melodrama *Leave Her to Heaven.* The look on Ellen's face tells us what she's thinking and foreshadows a simply unbelievable scene in which she coldly watches her brother-in-law drown.

The final scene in Mark Robson's postwar melodrama *My Foolish Heart* (1949) sorts everything out. Eloise (Susan Hayward, *seated*) gets to keep her daughter but loses her husband, Lew (Kent Smith), whom she never loved anyway, to her best friend, Mary Jane (Lois Wheeler).

she was busy seducing Lew to cover up her indiscretion, she failed to consider what marriage with a man she does not love might be like. Eloise goes slowly crazy, and so does her dope of a husband, who eventually realizes he still loves Eloise's best friend, Mary Jane (Lois Wheeler). In the end, Eloise abandons the sham of a marriage and after some wrangling gets to keep her child. In 1949 America, Eloise can't hope to keep another woman's man, but after she sees the errors of her past, she gets a second chance in the form of being a good mother and a good homemaker.

Studio Comedies: Preston Sturges

When historians talk about the important comedy films released during the war years, they inevitably focus on the work of one director: Preston Sturges. At a time when laughs in the real world were pretty hard to come by, Sturges's arch topical comedies were extremely popular and no doubt offered audiences an escape of sorts from the serious and perilous news of the world at war. Sturges first signed a contract with Paramount in 1930 as a scriptwriter. Like other contract screenwriters, he was assigned films in various genres and often saw his work rewritten by a colleague, a director, even a star. Much of his early script writing at Paramount went uncredited, including contributions to

Howard Hawks's romantic comedy *Twentieth Century* (1934) and John Stahl's melodrama *Imitation of Life* (1934).

Sturges's first film as writer-director was the deft political satire *The Great McGinty* (1940), for which he won an Academy Award, for Best Original Screenplay. Told in flashback, the film focuses on Dan McGinty (Brian Donlevy), a Depression-era hobo recruited by a ruthless political boss (Akim Tamiroff) as part of a ballot-fraud scheme. Over time, Dan endears himself to the boss, so much so that he's put forward as a reform candidate for mayor. To aid in his campaign, the boss arranges for a marriage (of convenience) between Dan and Catherine (Muriel Angelus), who, like Dan, works for the boss. Since it's a romantic comedy, Dan and Catherine fall in love, and together they successfully defy the boss. Despite the ruse that got him into office, Dan endeavors to keep his campaign promises to reform city politics. *The Great McGinty* effectively counters the goofy idealism of Frank Capra's populist Depression-era films, *Mr. Deeds Goes to Town* (1936) and *Mr. Smith Goes to Washington* (1939). Capra saw as quintessential American archetypes the likes of Longfellow Deeds (a small-town tuba player who must contend with big-city treachery after he inherits a fortune) and Jefferson Smith (another rural naïf, this one initially overmatched by corrupt politicos in Congress). For Sturges the corrupt political boss was the American politician you'd be most likely to meet.

Sturges's brief run at Paramount ended after seven great films—*The Great McGinty, Christmas in July* (1940), *The Lady Eve* (1941), *Sullivan's Travels* (1941), *The Palm Beach Story* (1942), *The Miracle of Morgan's Creek* (1944), and *Hail the Conquering Hero* (1944)—and one not so great picture, *The Great Moment* (produced in 1942 but not released until 1944).

Christmas in July is a clever satire about a little man with big ideas, a nobody who enters a contest to write an advertising slogan for a new product. His slogan is pretty bad ("If you can't sleep at night, it isn't the coffee, it's the bunk"), but he wins nonetheless and is made briefly rich. Like *The Great McGinty, Christmas in July* seems to be an anti-Capra picture, an unsentimental story about the everyday American's ridiculous dreams of wealth and fame.

The Lady Eve is just as unsentimental. The film moves at a hectic pace and pits a cardsharp named Jean (Barbara Stanwyck) against a wealthy lunkhead named Charles "Hopsi" Pike (played with appropriate nervousness and clumsiness by the rugged dramatic star Henry Fonda). Jean initially takes Charles for a sucker. But much to her

(*right*) The writer-director Preston Sturges, photographed in 1942.

(*below*) "You see, Hopsi, you don't know very much about girls. The best ones aren't as good as you think they are, and the bad ones aren't as bad." The millionaire Charles "Hopsi" Pike (Henry Fonda) falls for a cardsharp (Barbara Stanwyck) and learns a thing or two about love in Preston Sturges's romantic comedy *The Lady Eve* (1941).

The successful movie director John L. Sullivan (Joel McCrea) and a struggling actress with whom he falls in love (Veronica Lake) pose as hobos in Preston Sturges's comic parable *Sullivan's Travels* (1941). Sullivan soon discovers that there's nothing funny about being broke and homeless. Sturges uses Sullivan's travels to affirm the value of comedy, especially in tough times.

disappointment, she falls in love with him for real. The film plays with our expectations and teaches us a lesson or two about judging other folks when love is held in the balance. Such lessons are hard won, and as a result *The Lady Eve* is occasionally hard-hearted; comedy for Sturges isn't always pretty. When Jean is revealed to be a con woman, Charles dumps her, after having declared earlier in the film that "a man who couldn't forgive wouldn't be much of a man." For Sturges such high-mindedness is phony, even un-American. Charles pays for his pretentiousness when he becomes the target of a vicious bit of revenge. Jean tells her father that she needs Charles "like the ax needs the turkey" and concocts a plan in which she poses only slightly disguised as the Lady Eve Sidwich, a houseguest at a neighboring estate.

As Eve, Jean easily gets Charles to fall in love with her, and in short order they marry. Jean (as Eve) then tortures Charles on their honeymoon by telling outrageous, made-up stories about a promiscuous past. The stories are patently ridiculous and clearly drawn from bad society melodramas, but Charles is easily lost in the moment and endeavors to get the marriage annulled. The film ends with the usual abandonment of conversation in favor of long-awaited (sexual) action, but only after both characters face their comeuppance. Although Jean has executed the perfect crime, she feels anything but victorious. Charles has been had twice by the same woman, an outcome that doesn't surprise his father (Eugene Pallette), who has long since given up on Charles as an appropriate heir. But the real complication is that despite everything, Jean and Charles love each other. Like Lucy and Jerry in *The Awful Truth*, they need to take each other for who they really are.

In *Sullivan's Travels*, Sturges's next film, a wealthy film director, John L. Sullivan (Joel McCrea), begins to feel guilty about his recent run of success. While there is so much suffering in the world, he concludes, making romantic comedies is irresponsible. He poses as a hobo to research a proposed serious picture with the working title "O Brother, Where Art Thou" (a title used by the real-life filmmakers Joel and Ethan Coen in 2000 for a prison-break comedy based loosely on Homer's *Odyssey*). While Sullivan is posing as a hobo, he gets conked on the head and then arrested. He suffers amnesia and wakes up in a southern prison, where, working on a chain gang, he learns plenty about the so-called common man. Regaining his memory, he realizes that he is not a hobo but a millionaire Hollywood director, but no one at the prison will pay attention. For Sturges, Sullivan must do more than just remember who he is. He must repudiate his former pretentiousness, his phony (and dangerous) game of playing at being poor. There is no greater crime in Sturges's universe than taking yourself too seriously.

At an all-black church, where the convicts take in a screening of a Mickey Mouse cartoon, Sullivan comes to understand that the world needs a laugh now and then and that it's more than just disingenuous for a rich Hollywood director to make a movie chronicling the life of the poor and the disenfranchised. Sullivan finally returns to his former life, resumes a romance with an actress (played by Veronica Lake), and goes back to making the sorts of films (with titles like *Ants in the Pants*) that had made him famous.

The self-reflexivity of *Sullivan's Travels* is evident again in the clever closing scene of *The Palm Beach Story*. Tom (played by Joel McCrea, who appears in several of Sturges's films) is an idealistic inventor. He is married to Geraldine (Claudette Colbert), who has tired of living on the cheap while Tom tries to make his first big sale. Gerry leaves Tom and quickly finds a millionaire who wants to marry her (played by the singer Rudy Vallee, ably handling the Ralph Bellamy role). Tom of course still loves Gerry and tracks her down. Posing as her brother so as not to expose Gerry as a gold digger (she is a gold digger, but that's OK with Sturges), Tom arouses the sexual interest of the millionaire's sister (Mary Astor). The film ends in a triple wedding, though the three couples seem haphazardly matched: Tom remarries Gerry, the millionaire marries Gerry's identical twin, and the millionaire's sister marries Tom's identical twin. The ending, in which the protagonists' twins appear deus ex machina at the last minute, is meant less to satisfy the strictures of the genre, in which the final scene traditionally brings everyone happily back together, than to lampoon the genre convention as patently screwball and completely unrealistic. That everything might actually turn out OK for anyone is for Sturges the film's final joke.

Tom (Joel McRea) and Geraldine (Claudette Colbert) tie the knot in Preston Sturges's screwball comedy *The Palm Beach Story* (1942).

In 1944, less than five years after the release of his first feature as a writer-director, Sturges grew weary of tangling with meddlesome executives at Paramount and signed a production deal with Howard Hughes, a move that pretty much ended his career. The deal promised Sturges the creative freedom he so wanted, but soon enough it became clear that Hughes was far more interested in airplanes than movies. After Sturges had wasted almost four years working with Hughes, he signed with Darryl Zanuck at Fox, where he made two pictures in rapid succession, *Unfaithfully Yours* (1948) and *The Beautiful Blonde from Bashful Bend* (1949), comedies that after the war seemed pretty old-fashioned. Out of style and out of favor, Sturges left Hollywood for England, where he tried, unsuccessfully, to resurrect his career.

Though he was the highest paid nonactor in Hollywood in the early 1940s, Sturges died, in 1959, penniless and pretty much forgotten. He has since been rediscovered on the strength of the handful of films (discussed above) that he wrote and directed at Paramount between 1940 and

1944. Though the studio system was responsible for its fair share of ruined movies and ruined careers and Sturges no doubt had his reasons for wanting to get out of his contract with Paramount, in retrospect we can surmise that he did not appreciate what he had until it was lost. The studio had under contract a number of gifted comedy actors whom Sturges used again and again (Eric Blore, William Demarest, Joel McCrea, Eugene Pallette, and Franklin Pangborn), and though he bristled at the meddling of studio executives, the workshop-like setup of studio-era Hollywood suited him better than he realized. It is ironic that Sturges was undone by a desire to be taken more seriously in the industry, a tragic flaw for which his film characters would no doubt have paid dearly.

Sturges's oft-repeated formula for comedy is worth repeating here. Like his films, there's an

"A pratfall is better than anything." Charles (Henry Fonda) takes one on the chin in *The Lady Eve* (Preston Sturges, 1941).

element of truth in it, but mostly it's just a gag: "A pretty girl is better than a plain one. A leg is better than an arm. A bedroom is better than a living room. An arrival is better than a departure. A birth is better than a death. A chase is better than a chat. A dog is better than a landscape. A kitten is better than a dog. A baby is better than a kitten. A kiss is better than a baby. A pratfall is better than anything."

Lowbrow Comedies: Abbott and Costello, Hope and Crosby

Though they worked exclusively in formulaic B movies distributed by Universal, a studio known for lowbrow genre entertainment, Bud Abbott and Lou Costello became two of the biggest movie stars in Hollywood at the start of the war. They were on the top-ten box-office list (assembled by prominent U.S. theater owners) in 1941, 1942 (when they placed number 1), 1943, 1944, 1948, and 1949. If historic importance is a matter of popularity, Abbott and Costello were the most important comedy stars of the 1940s.

Abbott and Costello first made their mark on the big screen in *Buck Privates, In the Navy,* and *Keep 'Em Flying* (all directed by Arthur Lubin in 1941), three so-called service farces made in the last several months before the United States entered the war. *Buck Privates* opens as the comedy team enlists to avoid the police and focuses mostly on basic training, which provides just another excuse for the tall and slick Abbott, the straight man, and the rotund, ever-nervous Costello to perform their familiar wisecracking slapstick stage act. Like most of the comedy team's films, *Buck Privates* does not exactly tell a story; instead, it is composed of a series of comedy skits and musical numbers (including the Andrews Sisters' performance of their hit song "Boogie Woogie Bugle Boy of Company B").

In the Navy, the comedy team's next film, follows much the same formula. When Universal forwarded a print to the U.S. Navy, its censors objected to a scene in which Costello, in his usual state of overexcited clumsiness, completely screws up a set of signals he has been ordered to transmit. Though it is clear that Costello is hardly the ideal or typical recruit—indeed the point of the comedy is the implausibility of the lunatic

Costello's comic persona inserted into a situation requiring expertise and cool under fire—the navy was nonetheless concerned that the scene depicted its basic training as inadequate and potentially unsuccessful. To satisfy the Department of the Navy, Lubin left the skit intact but added a clever frame in which we discover that the signal-calling scene is just a nightmare Costello dreams.

In *Keep 'Em Flying*, Abbott and Costello play goofy mechanics who enlist in the U.S. Army Air Corps. The film premiered less than a month before the United States entered the war and thus capped, albeit comically, a series of aviation-training dramas—including *Flight Command* (Frank Borzage, 1940) and *International Squadron* (Lothar Mendes and Lewis Seiler, 1941), starring Ronald Reagan—released before the war. Those pictures, focusing as they do on American servicemen, did little to disguise the growing certainty of our entrance into the war well before the attack on Pearl Harbor.

During the first couple of years of the nation's participation in the war, the studios produced a number of comedy films in the same vein as the

Lou Costello (*third from right*), cigar in hand and belly drooping over his pants, on line for his army physical in the Universal B comedy *Buck Privates* (Arthur Lubin, 1941). Costello, with his comedy partner, Bud Abbott (*in front of him in line*), made light of what during wartime was serious work.

Abbott and Costello service farces, films that ever so affectionately poked fun at the American war effort. The comedy *Blondie for Victory* (Frank Strayer, 1942), for example, shows the comic-strip heroine (played by Penny Singleton) leading American housewives out of the kitchen and onto the streets to do their civic duty. Each woman leaves behind a wholly inept husband (Blondie's Dagwood, played by Arthur Lake, is only the worst of a dumb, clumsy lot) to manage the household in her absence. The men fail, of course, just as the women prove their ability to thrive outside the home.

Like Abbott and Costello, the comedy team of Bob Hope and Bing Crosby had a run of lowbrow comedy hits at the start of the decade, including a series of so-called road pictures, like their 1942 top-ten hit *Road to Morocco* (David Butler). Both Crosby (a singer) and Hope (a comic) were stars on stage and radio. Their pictures together laid the template for a generation of singer-comic duos, such as Dean Martin and Jerry Lewis.

Both Crosby and Hope had considerable film careers on their own in the 1940s. Sandwiched between the road pictures, Crosby starred in his three most successful films: *Holiday Inn* (Mark Sandrich, 1942), in which he famously sings "White Christmas"; the sentimental *Going My Way* (Leo McCarey, 1944), for which he won an Academy Award; and the even more sentimental melodrama *The Bells of St. Mary's* (also McCarey), the number-one box-office film for 1945.

Hope was a popular stand-up comic with an amiable, self-effacing manner and a folksy delivery. He played himself—or at least the celebrity version of himself—in every film he ever appeared in. And it worked well enough on the big and small screen for Hope to remain popular from the 1940s through the end of the twentieth century. He gave his all for the war effort, performing (as he would for five decades to follow) in United Service Organizations (USO) shows, entertaining servicemen and servicewomen overseas. In 1944, Paramount suspended Hope because he was doing too many live shows on the front and did not fulfill his three-picture-a-year obligation. The press got wind of the suspension and made the studio look ridiculous. Studio executives soon came to their senses, lifted the suspension, and wisely exploited Hope's patriotism to promote their star and his films.

Early Film Noir

In the latter years of the war, a series of morally ambiguous urban melodramas matched low-contrast cinematography, skewed camera angles, and an unremittingly dark rendering of the urban landscape with labyrinthine plots that portrayed human beings as treacherous and violent by nature—a worldview whose relevance increased as the war dragged on.

Foremost among these war-era films was Billy Wilder's *Double Indemnity*, a 1944 picture based on a hard-boiled novel by the popular writer James Cain. *Double Indemnity* tells the story of Phyllis Dietrichson (Barbara Stanwyck), an unhappy, amoral woman, and an unscrupulous insurance agent named Walter Neff (Fred MacMurray). Phyllis and Walter meet as he is making a routine sales call. From the moment he sees her, he stops thinking about the sale. She, too, has something besides business on her mind, but as in so many future noir films, it is not exactly—or at least not only—sex. When he makes a pass, she plays coy: "I wonder if I know what you mean." He sees right through the façade: "I wonder if you wonder."

"You'll shriek at these shieks!" Bing Crosby (*center*) and Bob Hope (*right*) in their 1942 farce *Road to Morocco* (David Butler).

Phyllis Dietrichson (Barbara Stanwyck) and Walter Neff (Fred MacMurray) meet clandestinely in a grocery store to discuss the murder of Phyllis's husband in Billy Wilder's early noir *Double Indemnity* (1944).

What begins as an affair ends with a plot to kill her husband and collect the premium on his life insurance. With murder, Walter tells her, three rules apply: it takes two, it takes a plan, and it takes guts. They seem to have all three, but as we come to learn, Phyllis has plans for widowhood that don't include Walter.

Double Indemnity begins well after the plan goes bad, with Walter confessing into a Dictaphone: "I killed him for money and for a woman. I didn't get the money, and I didn't get the woman." The rest of the film takes us from the fateful sales call through the film's famous climactic scene. As light filters into the dark room through half-closed Venetian blinds (a look that comes to characterize noir films), Walter accuses Phyllis of infidelity. "We're both rotten," she says, refusing to defend her actions. "Only you're a little more rotten," he adds. And then she shoots him. The bullet doesn't kill him, and Walter suggests that she try again; death for Walter has become the only way out of the mess he's made for himself. But Phyllis suddenly finds something like grace, and rather than shoot him again, she confesses: "I never loved you, Walter. Not you or anybody else. I'm rotten to the heart just like you said—until a minute ago, when I couldn't fire that second shot." "I ain't buying it, baby," Walter remarks, remaining the cool noir hero to the last. "You don't have to," she says; "just hold me close." He complies, but only so he can shoot her; he has accepted his fate and forces her to accept hers. The gunplay does not end the film, however; Walter lives long enough to return to his office where, as in the beginning scene, we see that the entire film has been his confession, dictated and recorded at his desk.

Barton Keyes (Edward G. Robinson), the insurance-liability investigator who never believed Phyllis's story about her husband's accidental fall from a train, enters the office to express his disappointment in Walter, whom he has treated more or less like a son. Whatever his feelings for his co-worker once were, "Walter, you're all washed up" is all he can say to the sorry mess his dying colleague has made of his life. As Walter turns for the door, Keyes puts matters in perspective: "You'll never make the border. You'll never even make the elevator." We knew from the start that things would end this way.

A number of other 1944 releases follow a similar narrative and visual formula: Otto Preminger's murder mystery *Laura*, George Cukor's *Gaslight*, and Edward Dmytryk's *Murder, My Sweet*, a hard-boiled detective picture based on Raymond Chandler's novel *Farewell, My Lovely*. Nineteen forty-five provided more darkly lit and darkly themed suspense pictures in the film noir mold: Hitchcock's *Spellbound*, Fritz Lang's *Scarlet Street*, and Edgar Ulmer's *Detour*.

Released in the fall of 1945, about two months after the Japanese surrender, *Detour* may well be the prototype postwar noir. It tells the story of a man, Al Roberts (Tom Neal), who hitchhikes across the country to catch up with the woman he loves and en route meets with one disaster after another. While hitchhiking, he is picked up by a shady salesman (Edmund MacDonald) and his young passenger, Vera (Ann Savage). While Al is asleep, Vera kills the salesman, or so we are led to believe, and when he wakes up, she threatens to pin the blame on him unless he agrees to become her boyfriend. When his commitment seems to falter she locks herself in a motel room and tells him she is calling the cops. He tugs on the phone cord through the door. She has unluckily tangled the cord around her neck and is strangled before she can complete the call. Now he really is a murderer. The film offers no denouement, only a nasty little warning that such things happen to people all the time. Such is the worldview of film noir, which seemed at once suited to the American zeitgeist as the war ended and presaged the decade or so of guilt and regret that would follow.

TRANSCENDING GENRE: THREE KEY FILMS

Three very different, very popular studio pictures—*Casablanca* (Michael Curtiz, 1942), *Meet Me in St. Louis* (Vincente Minnelli, 1944), and *The Best Years of Our Lives* (William Wyler, 1946, released just after the war's end)—at once complicated and transcended genre categories during (and immediately after) the war years. All three were top-ten films in the year they were released. But much more important, all three seemed to speak profoundly for or to the American public at different stages of the war.

Casablanca was released in 1942, just after the United States entered the war and, fortunately for the film's distributor, Warner Bros., on the very weekend that President Roosevelt and British prime minister Winston Churchill met in Casablanca, on the Moroccan coast, to discuss the American role in the European war. The film may seem today to stand outside time, but in 1942 it offered a timely message akin to that of the *Why We Fight* films: it explains who is fighting with whom and why.

A lot changed between 1942 and 1944, in Hollywood and in the war. By the time *Meet Me in St. Louis* reached the screen, the war had become something of a structured absence in many films; more and more the studios were making films that took audiences someplace where or sometime when war was not on everyone's mind. *Meet Me in St. Louis* is set at a time (1903) and in a place (St. Louis, of course) where a big problem amounts to figuring out when to eat dinner on a hot evening. The film tells its audience less about why we are fighting and more about what might be lost if we don't fight and win.

The Best Years of Our Lives offers a profound and disturbing early-postwar statement. Victory had its price, and the film attempts to make that point with a cine-realism that convinced viewers they were watching a kind of truth. *The Best Years of Our Lives* is less about why we fought, or what we would have risked losing if we hadn't fought and won, than it is about what lay ahead for those veterans whose physical and psychological pain might be tough to alleviate in postwar America.

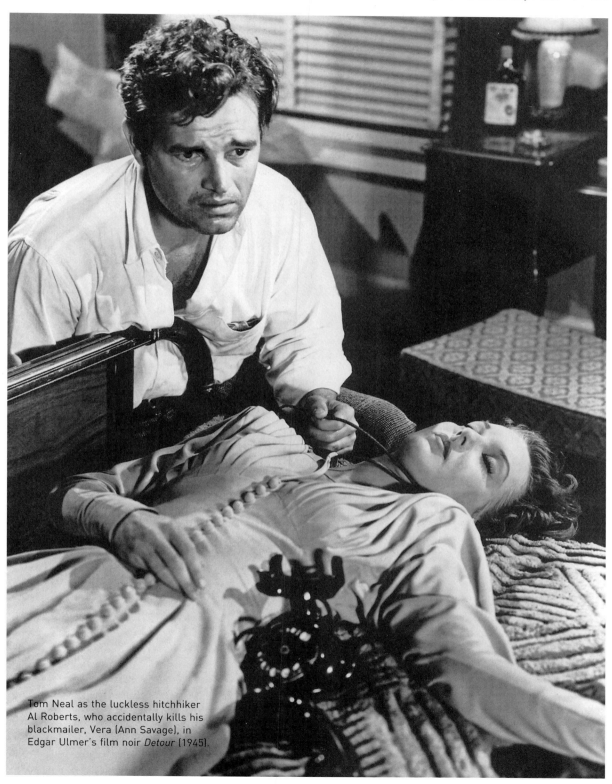

Tom Neal as the luckless hitchhiker Al Roberts, who accidentally kills his blackmailer, Vera (Ann Savage), in Edgar Ulmer's film noir *Detour* (1945).

Casablanca

One of the most recognizable American films ever made, *Casablanca* was based on a little-known play, *Everybody Comes to Rick's*, by Joan Alison and Murray Burnett. (*Casablanca*, it is interesting to note, is the playwrights' only major film credit.) The task of adapting the play to a film was given to twin brothers, Julius and Philip Epstein, both veteran studio screenwriters, and Howard Koch, a Warner Bros. contract writer whose career would be lost to the blacklist in the 1950s (a topic discussed in detail in Chapter 5). Though they produced *Casablanca* as an A feature—the studio assigned the lead to one of its top stars, Humphrey Bogart; surrounded him with an A-list supporting cast (Claude Rains, Paul Henreid, and Ingrid Bergman); and contracted with Michael Curtiz (*The Charge of the Light Brigade*, 1936; *The Adventures of Robin Hood*, 1938; and *Yankee Doodle Dandy*, 1942), their most bankable director—it is fair to conclude that Warner Bros. had no idea the film would hit so big.

Indeed, a close look at the film's trailer, shown in theaters in anticipation of the picture's release, revealed the studio's confusion over exactly what sort of picture it had made. The trailer opens as titles propose: "If you are looking for adventure—you will find it in Casablanca." The come-on is superimposed on an early scene from the film, in which police gun down a man in cold blood because he has outdated papers. Having thus introduced *Casablanca* as a war-themed suspense-and-adventure picture, the trailer shifts gears, and an off-screen narrator intones: "Against this fascinating background is woven the story of an imperishable love." The rest of the trailer shifts between plotlines, selling the film alternatively as a wartime adventure and a romantic melodrama. Bogart (as Rick) is first introduced shooting the German major Strasser (from the film's famous climax) as the titles call him "the most dangerous man in the world's most dangerous city." The trailer then cuts to the big-screen kiss, as Ilsa (Bergman) professes her forbidden love for Rick. As we see them kiss, a title appears that ties the two plots together:

(*left*) Rick (Humphrey Bogart) and Ilsa (Ingrid Bergman), star-crossed lovers in the wartime classic *Casablanca* (Michael Curtiz, 1942).

"where every kiss may be the last." Executives at Warner Bros. knew that Curtiz had made a good picture, but *Casablanca* defied simple genre categories and as such seemed a difficult movie to sell. Of course, as things played out in 1942, the film was not a tough sell at all. It was a sensation, sporting top-ten box-office revenues and Academy Awards for Outstanding Motion Picture and Directing.

Key to the Warner Bros. production of *Casablanca* was a previous Bogart film, *The Maltese Falcon*, directed by John Huston for the studio in 1941. *The Maltese Falcon* made Bogart a star, so the allusions in *Casablanca* to Huston's film were at once intentional and purposeful. Along with Bogart, Warner Bros. recast in *Casablanca* two of the featured players from Huston's film, Peter Lorre and Sydney Greenstreet, and assigned Arthur Edeson, the director of photography on *The Maltese Falcon*, to give *Casablanca* its atmospheric noir look. Edeson's contribution should not be ignored. The famous final scene—in which Rick sends Ilsa and Victor (Henreid) safely off to America (at the very moment we figure he plans to run away with Ilsa himself)—is nothing short of a primer in noir cinematography. Set at an airstrip, things get sorted out as the characters seem to float in a dense fog, lit only from the front. Once Ilsa and Victor's plane takes off and Rick shoots and kills Strasser (Conrad Veidt), Rick and Louis (Rains) decide to depart together. They walk off not into a sunrise, or even a sunset, but into the fog. The film ends as they disappear from view. It is 1942, and though they are doing the right thing, their future is, alas, uncertain.

Casablanca not only looks like a noir film; it plays like one as well. Rick is an existential hero, tortured by a past failed romance (with Ilsa) that has left him alienated from the world around him, in this case a world at war. His predicament is the very sort of bad luck that noir men routinely face. As Rick remarks about Ilsa's arrival in Casablanca, "Of all the gin joints in all the towns in all the world, she had to walk into mine." So much in life is a matter of luck. And in noir one's luck is almost always bad.

Ilsa, too, is a noir woman, at least in some ways. She is willing to use sex to get what she wants. She offers to sleep with Rick in exchange for the letters of transit that will get her and her husband to

"I'm no good at being noble, but it doesn't take much to see that the problems of three little people don't amount to a hill of beans in this crazy world." At the airstrip at the end of *Casablanca* (Michael Curtiz, 1942), Rick (Humphrey Bogart, in trench coat and hat) finally takes a stand. He sends Ilsa (Ingrid Bergman, far right) and Victor (Paul Henreid, behind Bogart) off to the United States while he and Louis (Claude Rains, second from the left) walk off into the fog, leaving their lives in *Casablanca* behind to join the Resistance.

the United States and when that fails, she tries to take the letters at gunpoint (though, unlike a lot of noir women, she can't bring herself to shoot). Ilsa tells Rick, "I don't know what's right anymore," and as she gives in to her passion, she admits, "I wish I didn't love you so much." She finds herself in a plot she can't see her way out of, and Rick is unable and disinclined to help her.

In his refusal to take sides, Rick foreshadows a number of noir heroes, but given the film's plot and its historical context, his neutrality marks him as an isolationist. Romance aside, adventure aside, *Casablanca* tells the story of a man coming to grips with his responsibilities to the war effort and the sacrifices he needs to make for it. Talking with Ugarte (Lorre), from whom he obtains the letters of transit, Rick declares, "I stick my neck out for nobody." Ugarte, a sleazy operator, muses, "That's

a good foreign policy." Soon enough we are told (by more than one character) that Rick was once a freedom fighter. He fought with the Loyalists against Franco in Spain in the '30s and ran guns to Ethiopian nationalists protecting their homeland against Italian imperialism. Rick reflects on this past only to point out the obvious: both the Loyalists and the Ethiopian nationalists lost. The good guys always lose—or maybe Rick has a knack for choosing the wrong side.

The first suggestion that Rick might finally take sides occurs in a scene in which a young woman asks him if she should sleep with Louis in order

(*right*) The piano player Sam (Dooley Wilson) and the club owner Rick (Humphrey Bogart) talk about life, love, and a particular song ("As Time Goes By").in Michael Curtiz's *Casablanca*.

to get exit visas. Her husband is trying to raise the money at the roulette table, but he is losing. She asks Rick if a man can ever forgive such an indiscretion, even one done for such a good reason. But he is clearly the wrong guy to talk to about love. Despite insisting that he sticks his neck out "for nobody," Rick tells his croupier to let the husband win, a gesture that gets the woman off the hook.

In the resolution of things at the airport, Rick affirms duty over love, sacrifice over personal happiness. Rick makes a choice at the end of the film. Everything that happens at the airstrip is his doing, and for his trouble he loses his girl and his club and narrowly escapes with his life. The Vichy-era Frenchman Louis, who had sat on the fence—placating the Germans and making the most of the refugee's desperation by soliciting sex and taking bribes in exchange for visas—appreciates Rick's

sacrifice and suggests that he will join the war effort as well. They become allies, and their cause is bigger than the love story at the center of the film (which ends badly).

Meet Me in St. Louis

Before he was contracted to direct *Meet Me in St. Louis*, Vincente Minnelli had only two film credits as a director, both from 1943: a mostly forgettable star vehicle for the vaudeville-style comic Red Skelton, *I Dood It*, and *Cabin in the Sky*, an adaptation of an all–African American Broadway review, which Minnelli made with the help of the legendary musical director Busby Berkeley. *Cabin in the Sky* benefited from the considerable on-screen talents of a veritable Who's Who in African American musical comedy: Ethel Waters, Louis Armstrong,

Anna (Mary Astor), Rose (Lucille Bremer), and Esther Smith (Judy Garland), in Vincente
Minnelli's nostalgic musical *Meet Me in St. Louis* (1944). The film may have offered a brief
escape from the war, but it also reminded audiences of what might be lost if the United States
did not prevail overseas.

Lena Horne, and Eddie "Rochester" Anderson. In
early 1940s Hollywood, no matter how talented
African American singers, dancers, and comedians
were, they could not have leading roles in the studios' Broadway-style movie musicals. The more
familiar platform for those stars was the all-black
musical revue, a movie with a thin, disposable plot
that advanced a series of set pieces featuring stage
performances by the stars. Along with *Cabin in the
Sky*, the best, or at least the best known, of these
all–African American musical revues is *Stormy
Weather* (Andrew L. Stone), also released in 1943.
Stormy Weather stars Horne and Anderson and features performances by the jazz singer and bandleader Cab Calloway, the blues singer and pianist
Fats Waller, the tap dancer Bill "Bojangles" Robinson, and the simply amazing acrobatic dance team
of the Nicholas Brothers.

MGM musical impresario Arthur Freed
acknowledged Minnelli's potential after seeing
Cabin in the Sky and encouraged the studio brass
to trust the young director with a valuable studio
property—two properties really: *Meet Me in St.
Louis* and Judy Garland. As things played out, Minnelli was the right man for the job, but he was the
studio's second choice, after George Cukor.
Cukor—the director of *Little Women* (1933),
Camille (1936), and *The Philadelphia Story*, which
was nominated for six Academy Awards in 1940—
had a reputation as a woman's director, a term that
refers at once to his ability to direct actresses and
his seeming affinity for what interested female
audiences. The MGM brass had hoped Cukor
would be able to "handle" Garland, who, though
barely twenty-one years old in 1943, was already
a veteran of eighteen feature films—including,

Esther (Judy Garland, right) and her younger sister Tootie (Margaret O'Brien) try to have themselves "a merry little Christmas" in Vincente Minnelli's *Meet Me in St. Louis* (1944).

most famously, *The Wizard of Oz* (1939)—and had lately become a bit of a diva on the set. But while the project was still in development, Cukor was drafted, and the studio turned to Minnelli.

Minnelli filmed the key musical numbers in *Meet Me in St. Louis* as mere extensions of everyday family life. For example, when Tootie (played by a six-year-old Margaret O'Brien) creeps out of bed to watch the older kids and adults downstairs and gets caught by her sister Esther (Garland), the scene calls for a little song ("Under the Bamboo Tree"). But rather than stage the scene as a production number (the way it would have appeared in a more formulaic musical), the two actors perform the song as if they were just hanging out singing, which is, after all, the narrative context for the song. Minnelli treated the scene with restraint, gently moving the camera to follow the performers. Singing is what the girls do together to pass the time. It is how they interact.

Meet Me in St. Louis is divided into four sections, corresponding to the four seasons. The plot concerns the father's proposed move (for work) from St. Louis (depicted in the film as a small town) to New York (suggested to be everything St. Louis is not), and the four seasons are markers in the family's yearlong wait for the father to uproot them. The four-season structure allows for a survey of everyday life at the suitably named Smith household. Summer brings warm nights and seemingly pointless discussions of what and when to eat. There is school, of course, in the fall, but more important is Halloween. Winter brings Christmas and an opportunity for Esther to sing to Tootie the film's best-known song, "Have Yourself a Merry Little Christmas." Spring has the family gearing up for the move—a move the kids absolutely do not want to make. In the end the father decides not to move: he sees that what's best for him professionally may not be best for the family.

The director Vincente Minnelli and his movie-star wife, Judy Garland, on their honeymoon in 1945.

Little of any consequence happens in *Meet Me in St. Louis,* and that is not only its charm; it is the film's principal point. Unlike so many American families in 1944, the Smiths get to enjoy Christmas, Thanksgiving, and Halloween together. The film's happy ending is simple: the Smiths do not have to change for anyone. They get to be the Smiths of St. Louis forever. And that was what we were fighting for in World War II.

Meet Me in St. Louis teems with female energy, and while that is what may have gotten the studio thinking initially about Cukor, Minnelli does well to showcase the female members of the Smith family: Esther, Tootie, Rose (Lucille Bremer), and their mother, Anna (Mary Astor). We get—and again the four-season structure helps with this—a sense of watching the Smith girls grow up, of watching a year go by in their lives.

This, too, has a historical parallel, because much of the film is about expectations: for the Smiths, looking ahead is, for most of the film, worrisome, just as it is for a nation at war. Consider the song "Have Yourself a Merry Little Christmas," which Esther sings to Tootie in a private moment at Christmastime. Beautiful as the song may be, its lyrics, as originally penned by Ralph Blane, were filled with dread. The original version opened with a sentiment that fit 1944 but lacked Christmas cheer: "Have yourself a merry little Christmas, it may be your last." Garland complained that the song was too glum, so Blane rewrote the opening lyrics: "Have yourself a merry little Christmas / Let your heart be light / Next year all our troubles will be out of sight." But although the revised version is less depressing, its promise of a merry Christmas "next year" makes clear that having one this year might not be easy. Moreover, the promise that "through the years, we all will be together"—a reference not to the setting of the film (circa 1903) but to a future reunion with loved ones fighting overseas—is qualified by the subsequent phrase, "if the fates allow." "Until then," the lyrics allow, "we'll have to muddle through somehow"—not exactly a cheery outlook for the Smiths' holiday season.

"Have Yourself a Merry Little Christmas" offers a curious complement to Garland's signature number in *The Wizard of Oz,* "Over the Rainbow." The latter number, written for the 1939 film, is hopeful, a dream about better places (than Kansas, than "here"), whereas the former warns us, three years into the war, in far less pretty terms, that (as Dorothy finally discovers at the end of the yellow brick road) there is no place like home. In *Meet Me in St. Louis,* given Garland's heartbreaking rendition of "Have Yourself a Merry Little Christmas," there is no place like home *right now.*

In his later films, Minnelli proved to be a showy director, fond of grand cinematic gestures—for example, the lush Technicolor work in the musical farce *The Pirate* (1948) and the vertiginous crane shots in the dance musical *An American in Paris* (1951). Though *Meet Me in St. Louis* seems by comparison an exercise in restraint, there are some lovely moments when Minnelli's camera movement makes the most of a mostly stage-bound film. During the Christmas-ball scene, for example Minnelli tracks up, turns right, and then seems to fly through a plate-glass window. When Esther tries to set the scene for a goodnight kiss with John (Tom Drake), Minnelli handles the entire sequence in a single shot even though it involved moving the camera as Esther moves through the set, turning out the lights. The set piece took four days to set up and shoot, and when Minnelli was finished, he realized that the visual made the words superfluous. So he cut all five pages of dialogue from the scene.

In 1944, Technicolor was not a realistic color process. Minnelli seemed to appreciate this and used its very artificiality to further the film's celebration of small-town life: however uneventful the Smith girls' lives may have been, their world is dazzlingly colorful. Moreover, Minnelli changed the palette to represent pictorially the changing sea-

sons: summer is red, autumn is orange and yellow, winter is blue, and spring is white.

As MGM had hoped, *Meet Me in St. Louis* further established Garland as a star of the first order. Yet according to Minnelli, whom Garland later married, the young star did not want to do the film, and when the MGM executive Arthur Freed told her that she had to (per her contract), her behavior on the set was petulant and disruptive. Her tantrums and the assorted delays she caused cost MGM almost two weeks in overtime, but in the end, as is often the case with films produced with "difficult" stars, Garland's performance proved worth the trouble. Like Marilyn Monroe in the 1950s, Garland had difficulties on the set that stemmed from psychological problems she could

From left to right: Three very different men—Homer (Harold Russell), Fred (Dana Andrews), and Al (Fredric March)—get close in the nose of a bomber during World War II in William Wyler's realist melodrama *The Best Years of Our Lives* (1946). Wyler's film showed in unstinting detail the cost of winning the war.

never fully conceal or control. Her drug addiction, which would (like Monroe's) lead to her death well before her time, began with the amphetamines the studio brass gave her to lose weight and was exacerbated by the barbiturates she later took to help herself sleep.

Garland appeared in a handful of entertaining films after *Meet Me in St. Louis*—Minnelli's *The Pirate* and *Easter Parade* (Charles Walters, 1948) are the most memorable—but it was not long before the pills and then the booze took their toll. MGM released Garland from her contract in 1949, firing her on the set of the musical *Annie Get Your Gun* (George Sidney, Busby Berkeley, and Walters, 1950). Garland died of a barbiturate overdose in 1969.

Minnelli's career, in contrast, took off after *Meet Me in St. Louis*. Highlights include a series of terrific adaptations of Broadway musicals: *Brigadoon* (1954), *Kismet* (1955), and *Gigi* (1958), which won nine Academy Awards; collaborations with the

dancer Gene Kelly: *The Pirate* and *An American in Paris;* family comedies: *Father of the Bride* (1950) and *Father's Little Dividend* (1951); and three notable 1950s melodramas: the cautionary Hollywood-based *The Bad and the Beautiful* (1952), the sexually provocative Broadway adaptation *Tea and Sympathy* (1956), and the searing examination of a young man's adjustment to civilian life after the war, *Some Came Running* (1958).

The Best Years of Our Lives

The number 1 box-office film in the first full year after the war was *The Best Years of Our Lives,* directed by William Wyler, whose prewar credits included a series of literary adaptations—*Dodsworth* (1936), *Wuthering Heights* (1939), and *The Little Foxes* (1941)—and the wartime melodrama *Mrs. Miniver* (1942), for which he won his first of three Academy Awards for Directing. *The Best Years of*

Al Stephenson (Fredric March) ponders the changes that occurred while he was fighting in the war, in William Wyler's *The Best Years of Our Lives* (1946).

Our Lives is at once docudrama, social-realist parable, and postwar family melodrama. While it starkly reveals veteran servicemen dramatically affected by postwar trauma, it also presents a soap opera of sorts involving men and women adjusting to life now that the war is over.

At the center of the docudrama is Homer Parrish (Harold Russell), who, having had his legs amputated, is reminded of the cost of combat every minute of every day. Homer's fellow veterans Al Stephenson (Fredric March) and Fred Derry (Dana Andrews) occupy the parallel melodramatic plot as they experience anguish that is more psychological and more diffuse. They return to wives and families who no longer feel quite right to them. Their marriages lack the intimacy of the all-male unit on the front, and their wives have changed in ways they cannot figure out. Al's struggle is muted. His dissatisfaction is mostly internalized, making him perhaps the least dramatic but most realistic character. Fred finds himself at the heart of the film's small-town melodramatic plot, torn between the promise of a happy future with Al's daughter (Teresa Wright), whom he discovers he loves, and an unhappy future doing "the right thing" by staying with his wife (Virginia Mayo).

There is an industry adage—ironically, it is often attributed to Sam Goldwyn, the film's producer—"If you want to send a message, use Western Union." Thus overtly political films are to be avoided, in part because they are seldom entertaining and seldom make money at the box office. Yet the first run of *The Best Years of Our Lives* offered an exception to that industry wisdom. The film earned an astonishing $11 million at the box office and won seven Academy Awards, including Best Motion Picture, Directing, Writing (for Robert E. Sherwood's screenplay), Actor (Fredric March), and Actor in a Supporting Role (Harold Russell, who also took home a special award for offering courage and hope to all returning veterans).

However deeply American audiences were moved by *The Best Years of Our Lives*, by the end of the following year political forces in Washington and Hollywood had mobilized to get the studios out of the business of making message movies. In the first few years after the war, the Motion Picture Association of America (MPAA, as the MPPDA renamed itself in 1945) and congressional players came to associate social-realist and so-called message films with a perceived leftist-Communist influence emerging from the creative ranks of cold war Hollywood. *The Best Years of Our Lives* proved to be a watershed; as the dark years of the Hollywood blacklist played out (discussed at length in Chapter 5), no one who wanted to continue working in Hollywood after 1947 would dare produce another film quite like it.

■ ■ ■

The war years proved to be a transitional period in Hollywood history. Although 1939 through 1941 created for Hollywood filmmakers and the studios that employed them something of a brief golden age, those glory years were experienced on borrowed time. The war, which occupied the attention of much of the rest of the world at the end of the 1930s, eventually occupied the attention of the United States, and by necessity the business of making movies changed.

During the war the studios divided their resources to produce war-themed pictures made in concert with federal agencies and a balanced slate of genre films resembling in many ways their prewar output. Once the war ended, however, the studios found it impossible to resume business as usual. The federal government saw to that.

As we will see in the next chapter, the government forced a thorough reorganization of studio Hollywood, and with that reorganization came the end of the contract era and the classical Hollywood it had created. Making matters worse for the studios were fundamental changes in postwar American material culture. A population shift from cities to suburbs and the introduction of television forced the studios to redefine their role in American culture. Indeed, an enterprise whose function was to create and nourish a significant American pastime appeared to lose its significance within a decade. After finally getting it right at the end of the contract era—we need look only to the stunning studio output between 1939 and 1941 for evidence of success—the studios were forced to find their way in a new Hollywood well before the old one had—for them, at least—lost its luster.

"The Screen Dares to Open the Strange and Savage Pages of a Shocking Best-Seller!" Ray Milland and Doris Dowling in Billy Wilder's trenchant study of alcoholism, *The Lost Weekend* (1945).

5

Adjusting to a Postwar America

1945–1955

When World War II came to an end, a new Hollywood seemed all but inevitable. The nation was on the verge of drastic social changes that promised to have a significant effect on the future of filmmaking and filmgoing. Signs that the studios might be in for a rough time were clear from the moment the war ended. A population shift—the urban flight that took place as folks chased the promise of a cleaner, safer life in the suburbs—took the studios' primary audience out of the big cities and away from the posh showcase theaters where fast returns on limited first runs were a key to the industry's profitability. The birth of suburbia—the destination of choice for so many former city dwellers—is often credited to William Levitt, a navy veteran who helped build airstrips during the war. In 1945, Levitt and Sons purchased some potato fields near Hempstead, New York, on Long Island, approximately 20 miles east of Manhattan. On the site, he initially built two thousand houses and dubbed the development Island Trees, as the location had long been known. By the time the houses went on sale, for $7,900 (for a two-bedroom standard unit), the development had been renamed Levittown. The price proved right, and home ownership in Levittown was made especially accessible to war vets, thanks to the so-called GI Bill of 1944, which guaranteed them home loans with no down payment. By 1950, Levittown housed eighty-two thousand people on 6,000 acres. During the 1950s approximately 1.5 million people left New York City for suburban developments modeled on Levitt's brainchild. Between 1948 and 1958, 13 million new homes were built in the United States, 11 million of them in the newly developed suburbs.

The overall move toward a suburban America was buoyed by rhetoric from the White House. Eager to inspire Americans to greater optimism and industriousness in the postwar era, President Dwight D. Eisenhower touted a vision of America in which citizens could work and play hard, forget the suffering of the Great Depression and the sacrifices of the war years, and enjoy prosperity and leisure with a round of golf or a game of softball. Exactly where movies fit in to this new leisure culture and the economy that produced it was a question film executives could not initially answer.

Exacerbating the effects of urban flight on Hollywood was the advent of television, itself something of a suburban medium. Television evolved from a cutting-edge technology at the war's end to a wildly popular and readily available consumer product in a matter of just a couple of years. Workers tired after a day's work and the daily commute welcomed an evening at home, relaxing in front of the tube. In the 1950s, television was novel, intimate and—best of all—free. Exactly what made movies better—enough better that one would pay to see them—was something the studios had to make clear. And doing so wasn't easy.

With so much happening so fast, it was hardly a good time for Hollywood's relationship with Washington to return to its prewar status, but once wartime propaganda filmmaking ceased, studio-government relations quickly soured. The turn for the worse forced fundamental changes in the policies and procedures that governed the business of making movies. Resuming a legal battle that had begun before the war, the Justice Department filed suit in 1948 to break up the studios' monopoly control over the industry. Industry divestiture—the forced sale of major studio assets in the business of exhibiting motion pictures—which the government accomplished when it prevailed

in *United States v. Paramount Picutres, et al.* (the so-called *Paramount* case, decided by the Supreme Court in 1948)—threatened not only the system by which films were developed, produced, distributed, and exhibited in the United States but also the studios' collective financial base. Prior to the *Paramount* case the studios routinely financed films by using their theater holdings as collateral for short-term loans. Without that valuable real estate, all the studios had to offer the banks as collateral were movies, a decidedly uncertain property, which the banks were reluctant to accept. Complicating matters for the studios was the threat of federal workforce regulation as Congress exerted pressure to rid Hollywood of a supposed Communist conspiracy among screenwriters, producers, directors, and even movie stars. The matter had been taken up just before Pearl Harbor during the Senate propaganda hearings, and resurfaced after the war with an energy that was hard to fathom or forestall. The federal inquiry and subsequent political pressure set in motion the creation of an industry-wide blacklist of workers identified as Communists or Communist sympathizers and complicated an increasingly incendiary climate among the workforce, which was characterized by the two strikes that framed the war years: the 1941 strike by animators at Disney and the 1945 strike of creative personnel at Warner Bros.

Accompanying the increased destabilization of the industry was a sudden and dramatic decline in revenue and profits. After boasting record profits of $120 million in the first full year after the war, the studios saw their profits fall steadily, beginning the following year: to $87 million in 1947, $49 million in 1948, $34 million in 1949, and $31 million in 1950. The decline was particularly rankling because the economy as a whole was booming. Hollywood survived the Great Depression, but by 1950 it was fair to wonder whether it could survive the postwar economic boom.

REINVENTING HOLLYWOOD

There is little room for doubt that the studios were trusts throughout the contract era, just as the Department of Justice contended they were. The studios not only controlled filmmaking from development through release but also exerted almost complete control over theatrical exhibition. Films were routinely released through a two-tier system.

The studios owned most of the first-tier urban showcase theaters outright. The second tier, mostly independently owned theaters, had little choice but to accept the studios' terms if they wanted a chance at a first-run screening of the next big film. Blind bidding (the licensing of films sight unseen), block booking (the licensing of an entire slate of films in order to get access to one or two hit titles), and other schemes perpetrated by the studios kept the theaters under their control whether they owned the theaters outright or not.

When the Justice Department initiated its first antitrust challenge in 1938, the studios seemed to accept that divestiture was inevitable. In fact, the studios' defense had little to do with challenging the government's position. In the first twelve months after the Justice Department's 1938 court action, industry attorneys secured thirteen trial postponements. Then, in order to further forestall a trial date, the Big Five studios—MGM, Warner Bros., Paramount, 20th Century–Fox, and RKO—and the Justice Department signed an interim consent decree on October 29, 1940, a compromise of sorts.

The consent decree temporarily suspended the government's suit. It addressed certain inequities in the marketplace and put in place a system by which conflicts between theater owners and the studios could be arbitrated. But as the government came to understand—and as the independent theater owners of the Motion Picture Theater Owners Association (MPTOA) repeatedly pointed out to Justice Department attorneys—the consent decree did not adequately limit the studios' monopoly control over the marketplace. So in 1941 the studios and the MPTOA hammered out a revised consent agreement: the United Motion Picture Industry (UMPI), or Unity, plan. The UMPI plan closely resembled the initial consent decree; it was a little more complicated and seemed to afford theater owners a bit more choice but did not do enough to satisfy the theater owners. Under pressure from the nation's exhibitors, the Justice Department abandoned its efforts to compromise and returned the case to the courts.

The *Paramount* Decision

In the spring of 1948, just as disappointing box-office numbers were made public in trade publications, the Supreme Court agreed to hear arguments in the *Paramount* case. (Paramount was just the first studio named in the suit; also named were RKO, Warner Bros., 20th Century–Fox, Loew's-MGM, Columbia, Universal, and United Artists.) After ten years of putting off a showdown with the Justice Department, the studios faced their day of reckoning. In a decision handed down on May 3, 1948, the Supreme Court decided

In the 1930s and 1940s all the major studios had their own theater circuits. Here is the Warner Bros. flagship theater, in New York City, in a photograph taken in 1931.

against the studios' interests. Writing for the majority, Justice William O. Douglas made clear the Court's view that the studios were indeed trusts and that the only remedy to the situation was divestiture of the lucrative theater chains. At the time of the decision, Paramount owned 993 theaters; RKO owned 187; Fox, 66; Loew's-MGM, 21; and Warner Bros., 20. Additionally, the studios jointly owned theaters with one another: Paramount-Fox owned 6; Paramount-Loew's, 14; Paramount–Warner Bros., 25; Paramount-RKO, 150; Loew's-RKO, 3; Loew's–Warner Bros., 5; Fox-RKO, 1; and Warner Bros.–RKO, 10. The Big Five held interests in 3,137 of the 18,076 theaters nationwide. In the ninety-two cities with a population exceeding one hundred thousand, over 70 percent of the first-run theaters were affiliated with the Big Five.

The Court found that the defendants in the case had indeed conspired to restrain free and fair trade and to monopolize the distribution and exhibition of films. The decision outlawed price fixing; "run

Like the other big studios, Paramount was a bicoastal operation, with business offices in New York and production offices in Hollywood. (*left*) The Paramount Building, the company's business headquarters, at 1501 Broadway in New York City. (*lright*) The famed Paramount Pictures studio gate at 5555 Melrose Avenue in Hollywood.

clearances," a standard industry practice that favored first-run houses by assuring them first and regionally exclusive access to big studio films; pooling agreements, by which competing exhibitors operated in collusion in order to share in the profits of a given film's run; and block booking.

Although it acknowledged changes in workforce relations, the Court expressed its disapproval of the studios' creative accounting of revenues, especially those earned from block-booking deals. Creative accounting not only affected specific percentage deals between studio distributors and theater owners, a concern relevant to studio-theater relations, but it also systematically undermined management-labor relations, as stars' contracts in the postwar period increasingly called for a salary plus a percentage of a film's profits. Block booking enabled the studios to pool revenues so that a big film's receipts could be combined and confused with those of a bomb, a potentially costly maneuver for a star whose compensation hinged on his or her film's success. That is, the total earnings

from a block-booked theater could be counted against the studio's prorated expenses, and thus even if one movie hit big, the profits might be completely offset by the losses of the studio's other movies in the block, freeing the studios from having to pay points to an actor for his or her successful movie.

The more ruminative sections of Justice Douglas's opinion reveal contempt for the conspiratorial and collusive relationships that prevailed in Hollywood. But just as one door closed, so to speak, another opened. In his opinion for the majority, Douglas wandered a bit off the subject of trusts to comment on the long-standing First Amendment restrictions on cinema that dated to the *Mutual* case in 1915. Douglas, a strict civil libertarian, especially with regard to free speech, took a thorough look at the production code of the Motion Picture Association of America (MPAA), especially the practice of fining theater owners for screening films without a Production Code Administration (PCA) seal. He deemed such fines unconstitutional on antitrust—as opposed to First Amendment—grounds, though either or both seemed to apply.

The effect of the *Paramount* decision was immediate and dire. Industry revenues decreased by over 20 percent over the next few years, reflecting declining attendance, especially for A-budget features in first-run houses (where the studios previously made most of their money). Studio profits declined as well after the war, from $120 million in 1946 to $31 million in 1950.

The only good news for the studios in the late 1940s came from overseas, where Hollywood films dominated the world theatrical market. In 1949 a record 38 percent of the studios' gross revenues came from overseas. This change had come about because most European countries were preoccupied with reconstruction, not moviemaking (yet, with the war over, there was increased demand from potential moviegoers). Germany's industry, for example, was stalled until 1967, when a federally funded program allowed for the emergence of a new German cinema. There was moviemaking in France in the 1950s, but it was not until 1958, and the emergence of the vaunted *Nouvelle Vague* (New Wave), that French film had much of a stake in the world market. In Italy neorealist filmmakers movingly chronicled the realities of Italian life in the late 1940s, but influential as their films ultimately became, at the time they could not compete commercially with the seamlessly produced divertissements made in America.

William O. Douglas, the U.S. Supreme Court justice who wrote the majority opinion in the *Paramount* case in 1948, photographed in 1939, at the time of his nomination to the Court.

The reemergence and rapid growth of foreign demand for American films after the war was of more than just economic import. In the hectic first years after the war, an ideological and military rivalry between the United States and the Soviet Union took shape, and this cold war fueled a new American cinema that was by design and by necessity patriotic. The persuasive power of motion pictures had been proved during the war years domestically and abroad. And filmmaking, something the United States indisputably did better than the Soviet Union (if measured by box-office receipts), became an important tool of American international propaganda.

After 1945 the same federal agencies that had overseen the production and distribution of wartime propaganda films—most notably the Office of War Information (OWI)—cooperated with the MPAA to establish for the studios an ideological and industrial presence abroad. As part of that effort, the MPAA formed the Motion Picture Export Association (MPEA)—later nicknamed the Little State Department—to work closely with the peacetime OWI. For films to get MPEA support, they needed to paint a positive picture of the United States. This subtle but nonetheless effective form of economic and political censorship had a significant impact on the studios, especially at a time when factions within the filmmaking community were becoming increasingly political.

The Hollywood Blacklist

In the fall of 1947, the House Committee on Un-American Activities (HUAC), subpoenaed nineteen studio employees as part of an inquiry into Communist influence in Hollywood. When HUAC convened in October, the committee called to the stand ten of the nineteen, the so-called Hollywood Ten: Alvah Bessie, Herbert Biberman, Lester Cole, Edward Dmytryk, Ring Lardner Jr., John Howard Lawson, Albert Maltz, Samuel Ornitz, Adrian Scott, and Dalton Trumbo. (Eight of those subpoenaed were never called to testify; the committee adjourned early, in part because it seemed to get nowhere with the so-called unfriendly witnesses. The most famous of the original nineteen was the German-born playwright Bertolt Brecht, who appeared before the committee in a closed session. Brecht gave what can only be described as confusing testimony, after which he packed his bags and immigrated to East Germany, where, in a bitter statement on U.S. democracy in 1947, he believed he might find a freer life.)

The congressional committee was interested in the answers to two questions: "Are you now, or have you ever been, a member of the Screen Writers Guild?" and "Are you now, or have you ever been, a member of the Communist Party?" The Hollywood Ten refused to answer the questions directly but also refused to seek Fifth Amendment protection (against self-incrimination), because they believed the questions (regarding union membership and affiliation in a political party) were themselves improper. The conservative congressmen who sat on the committee already knew the answers to the questions anyway. But the hearings were about a lot more than ten men whose leftist politics annoyed the committee members.

What lay under the surface of HUAC's inquiry was not only a passionate fear of Communist influence and infiltration but also a larger distrust and dislike of Hollywood and the Jews who the committee members believed owned and ran the movie business. Indeed, the Hollywood Ten hearings revealed a tendency on the part of HUAC and those

October 27, 1947: Hollywood writers, directors, and producers summoned to appear before HUAC. *Front row*: Lewis Milestone (director), Dalton Trumbo (writer), John H. Lawson (writer), and Bartley Crum (attorney). *Second row*: Gordon Kahn (writer), Irving Pichel (actor-director), Edward Dmytryk (director), Robert Rossen (director). *Third row*: Waldo Salt (writer), Richard Collins (writer-producer), Howard Koch (writer), Albert Maltz (writer), Herbert Biberman (writer-director), Lester Cole (writer), Ring Lardner Jr. (writer), and Martin Popper (attorney).

who shared its politics to conflate communism with unionism and view opposition to racism as a Jewish cause. They further conflated communism with Jewishness, a key issue given the widely held assumption that Hollywood was run by Jews. (Six of the Hollywood Ten were Jews: Bessie, Biberman, Cole, Lawson, Maltz, and Ornitz. Of the four who were not Jewish, two (Dmytryk and Scott) were responsible for *Crossfire*, a 1947 antiracist, anti-anti-Semitic film nominated for five Academy Awards, including Best Motion Picture, Directing, and Writing. The committee steadfastly refused to view films or review screenplays, claiming, in a bizarre twist of logic, that Communists were smart and insidious and thus the political messages they inserted into films were very difficult (for non-Communists) to discern. How, then, the films made by the Hollywood Ten might be dangerous to the uninitiated was a question, for the committee at least, best left unasked and unanswered.

All ten of the unfriendly witnesses called to appear before HUAC in 1947 requested permission to read a statement for the record, but only two of those statements were admitted into evidence. Of the eight statements that were suppressed, five explicitly identified anti-Semitism as a motive behind the hearings, most powerfully and memorably in the closing paragraph of Trumbo's suppressed statement:

> Already the gentlemen of this committee and others of like disposition have produced in this capital city a political atmosphere which is acrid with fear and repression; a community in which anti-Semitism finds safe refuge behind secret tests of loyalty; a city in which no union leader can trust his telephone; a city in which old friends hesitate to recognize one another in public places; a city in which men and women who dissent even slightly from the orthodoxy you seek to impose, speak with confidence only in moving cars and in the open air. You have produced a capital city on the eve of its Reichstag fire. For those who remember German history in the autumn of 1932 there is the smell of smoke in this very room.

When the committee moved unanimously to seek indictments for contempt of Congress against the ten unfriendly witnesses and brought the issue to the House floor, Mississippi representative and HUAC member John Rankin spoke on behalf of

Edward Dmytryk (*second from the right, standing*) directs Robert Mitchum (*in uniform, seated*) and Robert Young (*seated across from Mitchum*) on the set of *Crossfire*, the politically progressive 1947 thriller that piqued the interest of the House Committee on Un-American Activities (HUAC).

the committee. He opened his remarks by referring to the few congressmen who had spoken in defense of the Hollywood Ten as "traitor[s] to the government of the United States" and then segued into a brief speech on Hollywood's "attempt to smear and discredit the white people of the Southern States." Holding up a petition, signed by a number of Hollywood luminaries, that condemned the committee, he announced:

> They sent this petition to Congress, and I want to read some of the names. One of the names is June Havoc. We found from the motion picture almanac that her real name is Joan Hovick. Another one was Danny Kaye, and we found out that his real name was David Daniel Kaminsky. . . . Another one is Eddie Cantor, whose real name is Edward Iskowitz. There is one who calls himself Edward Robinson. His real name is Emmanuel Goldberg. There is another one here who calls himself Melvyn Douglas, whose real name is Melvyn Hesselberg. There are others too numerous to mention. They are attacking the committee for doing its duty in trying to protect this country and save the American people from the horrible fate the Communists have meted out on the unfortunate Christian people of Europe.

Some members of the House Committee on Un-American Activities (HUAC) in the spring of 1948. *From left to right:* John McDowell (Republican of Pennsylvania, *seated*), future president Richard Nixon (Republican of California, *standing*), HUAC chair J. Parnell Thomas (Republican of New Jersey, *seated*), chief investigator Robert E. Stripling (*standing*), and John Rankin (Democrat of Mississippi, *seated*).

Rankin's remarks, no more than racist ravings, served the anti-Communist cause. After the congressman relinquished the floor, the House voted, 346 to 17, to indict the Hollywood Ten.

Initially the MPAA supported the Hollywood Ten. When HUAC made its recommendation to indict the men for contempt of Congress, the MPAA formally assured those under investigation that it planned to stand behind them. "Tell the boys not to worry," MPAA president Eric Johnston stated in a press release on October 18, 1947. "There'll never be a blacklist. We're not going to go totalitarian to please this committee." But just twelve days later—five days before the full House of Representatives was scheduled to vote on the contempt citations—Johnston issued a stunning public reversal: "We did not defend them. We do not defend them now. On the contrary, we believe they have done a tremendous disservice to the industry which has given them so much material rewards [sic] and an opportunity to exercise their talents." Indictments, incarceration (all of the Hollywood Ten went to prison for between six months and a year), and an industry-wide blacklist followed, all with the cooperation—and much of it under the supervision—of the MPAA.

Exactly why the MPAA (on behalf of the studios) complied with HUAC in 1947 is a complex question. One explanation lies in the practical realm of workforce relations. In the fall of 1947, the studios were struggling with fundamental changes in the way films were being staffed and cast. The contract system that had served the studios so well after the advent of sound was in decline, and the union-guild movement was gath-

ering steam. The blacklist—which could make an otherwise successful and talented actor, writer, director, or producer unemployable industry-wide based on a single accusation—had an immediate, sobering effect on the workforce, an effect the studios could exploit if they wanted to. Though it was not begun with such a design in mind, the blacklist provided the means by which the studios could deal with their problems with talent and, by extension, the guilds, agents, and lawyers who represented the talent. Also at stake was a struggle for power in the industry between the New York offices, which supported the MPAA and its president, Eric Johnston, whom they had handpicked, and the erstwhile Hollywood moguls, whom the New York ownership no longer fully trusted.

On November 25, 1947, the day the House voted to approve indictments of the Hollywood Ten, the MPAA issued the Waldorf Statement, so-called because it was delivered at the Waldorf-Astoria Hotel in New York. It was succinct, but in its handful of words it revealed the economic bottom line of the blacklist: "We will forthwith discharge or suspend without compensation those in our employ and we will not re-employ any of the ten until such time he is acquitted or has purged himself of contempt and declares under oath that he is not a Communist." MGM immediately suspended Trumbo and refused to pay him $60,000 in fees (that he was owed per his contract). Fox fired Lardner, and Dmytryk and Scott were dumped by RKO. But the bloodletting didn't stop with the Hollywood Ten. All told, over three hundred writers, directors, producers, and actors were blacklisted between 1947 and 1957. The breaking of contracts and the refusal to pay fees for scripts that had been optioned, developed, and/or produced before the fall of 1947 prompted a number of civil suits that dragged on into the 1950s and 1960s and helped establish the acrimonious relationship between Hollywood management and talent that continues today.

GENRE: FILM NOIR

In the first few years after the war, a single genre—what we have come to call film noir—spoke profoundly to postwar frustration, discomfort, and alienation. Though highly stylized visually, noir is characteristically realistic, so much so that noir films seem to capture something of the American postwar zeitgeist and as such tell us plenty about what folks were thinking about in the first decade after the war.

Though timely, noir is rooted in two 1930s genres: the hard-boiled pulp and pop fiction of James Cain (*Double Indemnity, The Postman Always Rings Twice*, and *Mildred Pierce*), Dashiell Hammett (*The Maltese Falcon* and *Red Harvest*), and Raymond Chandler (*Farewell, My Lovely* and *The Big Sleep*) and the precode gangster films, especially *Little Caesar* (Mervyn LeRoy, 1931), *The Public Enemy* (William Wellman, 1931), and *Scarface* (Howard Hawks, 1932). From the pulps, noir got its hard-boiled ambience and world-weary pessimism. From the gangster films the genre got its characteristic shadow-laden visual style and its larger vision of the intersections of capital accumulation and criminal enterprise.

Though stylistically indebted to the pulps and the '30s gangster pictures, noir is a decidedly modern genre. The noir gangster, for example, is a far more modern villain than the likes of Rico, Tom,

"First is first, and second is nobody." The assimilated gangster as businessman Mr. Brown (Richard Conte, *seated*) explains his success to fellow gangster McClure (Brian Donlevy, *holding hat*) and his chief adversary, police lieutenant Diamond (Cornel Wilde), in Joseph Lewis's 1955 film noir *The Big Combo*.

Expressionist-style lighting, a characteristic of the noir visual style, is used to great effect as police lieutenant Diamond (Cornel Wilde) tries to get information from the concert pianist turned gangster's moll (Jean Wallace) in Joseph Lewis's *The Big Combo* (1955).

and Tony, the gangsters in *Little Caesar, The Public Enemy,* and *Scarface.* Rico, Tom, and Tony are ethnic monsters and pathological criminals. The reasons for their criminality bear out a simple sociology and psychology. Rico, for example, wrestles with doubts about his sexuality. As played by Edward G. Robinson, he seems stuck pathologically playing out the familiar short-man's complex: his violence and bravado are a matter of compensation for his size and latent femininity. James Cagney's Tom Powers is full of booze and rage, a sociopathic version of the public's worst impressions of a young Irishman. The famous scene in which he smashes half a grapefruit in his moll's face in exasperation at any suggestion that he might fit into a bourgeois domestic scene offers visual proof that he can't or won't behave like a civilized American. The gangster in *Scarface* has designs on his own sister. As played by Paul Muni, he is simian, jaw jutting out, arms hanging down to his knees.

By comparison the gangsters in film noir are a smoother lot. They are less obviously ethnic and travel in headier, wealthier, more established circles. The bad guys in noir are modern crooks, like Mike Lagana (Alexander Scourby) in Fritz Lang's *The Big Heat* (1953), whose power derives from ties to urban political machines and crooked law enforcement. The modern noir crooks live in houses or urban penthouses removed from the fray of the city streets, the very streets on which Rico, Tom, and Tony live and die. Whit Sterling (Kirk Douglas), the gangster in the noir film *Out of the Past* (Jacques Tourneur, 1947), lives on Lake Tahoe and runs his criminal empire without leaving his estate. Whit never worries about the cops; he keeps the dirty work of crime at arm's length. But like so many semilegitimate businessman, he does worry about the Internal Revenue Service, because he understands that criminal and corporate enterprise intersect in complex ways. In *The Big Combo* (Joseph Lewis, 1955), a gangster (Richard Conte) calls himself Mr. Brown in a formal disavowal of his ethnicity. He is Italian, but the name he has taken for himself could not be more generic. Mr. Brown sees himself as a businessman. Success, from where he sits, can be measured only in dollars and cents. After Brown first confronts Lieutenant Diamond (Cornel Wilde), the cop who hounds him throughout the film, he speaks of the persistence of his nemesis in the only context he understands—jealousy: "His salary is $96.50 a week. Busboys in my hotel make more than that." Later in the film, when Brown burns a ship's log containing evidence of a murder, a log he has acquired by killing an antiques dealer and then buying his store from the bank, he describes that series of criminal actions as merely a "liquidation of assets." His motto—"First is first, and second is nobody"—echoes Scarface's vow to "do it first, do it yourself, and keep doing it." True to noir form, Brown, like Whit in *Out of the Past,* is undone by a woman, a mysterious blonde both he and Diamond covet. As Brown is taken into custody, the cop and the blonde exit into the fog, like Rick and Captain Renault at the end of *Casablanca* (Michael Curtiz, 1942). The promise at the end of noir is hardly happily ever after.

The Noir Visual Style

Unlike westerns or comedies, noir was not a genre by design. There is no evidence that American filmmakers in the 1940s and 1950s set out to make noir films. In fact the term *film noir,* which in French means simply "black (or dark) film," was coined by sophisticated French film critics writing for a specialized audience in France well after the first wave of noir pictures had played in American theaters. Still, we can find in these films a number of common elements and concerns.

Foremost is a visual style utilizing lighting strategies that originated in Germany in the 1920s. Film noirs are set mostly at nighttime and on forbidding and foreboding urban streets. Key lights are much in evidence, often placed on the ground, rendering figures ominously doubled by their large, looming shadows. As in expressionism, fill lights and backlights, which eliminate shadows and give scenes depth, are used sparingly. The result, as in expressionist and '30s American gangster films, is that characters are depicted as if floating in a (moral, physical) void. Adding to the visual mood are postwar technical advances in film stock that allowed for night-for-night shooting—nighttime scenes actually shot at night. Before 1940 most night scenes were shot day-for-night—that is, during the day, with filters used to imply or simulate the dark of night. Nighttime in noir looks like nighttime, an apt effect for films depicting the hard-boiled urban jungle.

Noir films are mostly theatrical affairs. As such, many noir filmmakers seemed especially sensitive to the antimontage visual style used by Orson Welles in *Citizen Kane* (1941)—distinguished by longer takes and composition in depth. Welles's evocative use of depth of field, or deep focus, influenced noir profoundly, and Welles's penchant for off-angles, camera angles that place the viewer at odds with the action, became a characteristic of noir. As with much of Welles's work, easy identification with characters or easy access to the plotline was discouraged, thanks to the shadowy cinematography and unusual camera angles.

Narrative Form and Ideology in Film Noir

Noir films are rooted in the fundamental social changes that troubled many Americans after the war. The pessimism, longing, and sense of loss and insecurity that reside at the heart of film noir convey the crisis of adjustment experienced by many American men just after the war. *The Blue Dahlia* (George Marshall, 1946), for example, opens as servicemen exit a bus in their hometown. The town has changed, and so have they. One of the men, Buzz (William Bendix) has suffered a severe head injury that causes him to hear things and do things he can't control. The hero, Johnny, played by noir stalwart Alan Ladd, comes home to a wife (Doris Dowling) who has found a new and freer lifestyle with faster, tougher guys. She has entered the noir world in his absence, and he can join her there or get out of town.

Many noir films pivot on a reckless moment, a single bad decision that changes the characters' lives irrevocably: hitchhiking across America in *Detour* (Edgar Ulmer, 1945), for example, or falling for and trusting a gangster's moll in *Out of the Past* (Tourneur, 1947). The past plays a significant role in these films because after such a reckless moment the past is something the characters either lose access to or, conversely, are trapped in forever. The future that looms is a fearful place, as it was for many of the men who returned from the war to an America that had changed dramatically in their absence.

Most noir narratives concern crime and punishment, but they do so with a complexity that was seldom seen before on-screen. Noir films are about characters embarking on a criminal adventure—murder for profit, for example, as in *The Postman Always Rings Twice* (Tay Garnett, 1946). Many men who find themselves on the wrong side of the law in noir films are not professional criminals. They depart from the boring reality of middle-class life into a fictive world of sexual pathology and illegal enterprise, thematic conceits that intersect to the point where they become inseparable in films like *Double Indemnity* (Billy Wilder, 1944).

At the center of many noir films is a devouring woman, a femme fatale. The noir femme fatale seems, in retrospect, like a nightmare version of the economically and sexually emancipated woman of the postwar period. (American women entered the workforce in great numbers during the war, and the money they made gave them greater freedom to move out on their own, to live without the help of a man. That a woman might be reluctant to settle down after the war and surrender her freedom was a significant concern of many men in the postwar period.) The femme fatale is inevitably beautiful (these are Hollywood films, after all), sexually promiscuous (though she does not necessarily enjoy her promiscuity, or at least pleasure is somehow besides the point), and willing to protect herself and her freedom at all costs. When sex is no longer effective or necessary, the noir woman, like male heroes and villains in other

Alan Ladd as an American soldier who returns home after the war to discover that his wife (Doris Dowling) has found a new life with faster, tougher guys in *The Blue Dahlia* (George Marshall, 1946).

genres, reaches for a gun. Take, for example, the femme fatale Elsa (Rita Hayworth) in *The Lady from Shanghai* (Orson Welles, 1947), who draws her gun when she discovers that her plot to frame the film's hero, Michael (Orson Welles), has failed. In the end, Michael is spared by the sudden appearance of Elsa's cuckolded husband, Arthur (Everett Sloane). As seems only fitting, Elsa and Arthur kill each other, she expressing her rage at men and he finally making clear that he is a man despite his disability (he needs crutches to walk) and his failure to hold on to his wife. When all else fails at the end of Jacques Tourneur's *Out of the Past*, the femme fatale, Kathie Moffat (Jane Greer), reaches for her gun and shoots her former lover, the private detective Jeff Bailey (Robert Mitchum), between his legs. In so doing, she embraces her role as a castrating woman.

Noir women are astonishingly pragmatic about sex. Wheras their men give in to passion and obsession and thus find ruin, for the noir femme fatale, as for the vamps in the silent melodramas, sex is merely a means to an end. *Double Indemnity* opens with a telling, reflective voice-over delivered by the film's central male character, the insurance agent Walter Neff (Fred MacMurray): "I killed him for money and for a woman. I didn't get the money, and I didn't get the woman." Walter is hooked the second he sees Phyllis (Barbara Stanwyck) descend a staircase in her house, his eyes (with ours) drawn to her ankle bracelet. Despite lots of hard-boiled banter, he is an easy mark. As Phyllis and Walter go through with the crime (of killing her husband), it becomes clear that she is running the show. "She was perfect," Walter reflects in voice-over, "no nerves." But soon enough her confidence begins to worry him, and the sexual thrill she gets from killing her husband proves downright terrifying. "Aren't you going to kiss me?" she asks after they kill him, clearly turned on by the murder. Walter is not so sure; he's more scared than excited.

Doomed as heterosexual relations seem to be in these films, it is no surprise that families, the formation of which is the closure for so many genre films, are simply not part of the equation in film noir. Although plenty of good-hearted women are offered in counterpoint to the femmes fatales—women who offer a nice, quiet life in the suburbs or, further removed, in the country—noir men seldom choose, or are allowed to choose, such a safe alternative. Once the male hero departs for the noir

Jane Greer as the femme fatale Kathie Moffat in Jacques Tourneur's film noir *Out of the Past* (1947).

world, there is no escape, a fact of noir life made clear by some of the titles themselves: *Detour*, *Caught* (Max Ophüls, 1949), *D.O.A.* (Rudolph Maté, 1950), *Quicksand* (Irving Pichel, 1950), and *Tension* (John Berry, 1950).

In counterpoint to the beautiful and dangerous noir female villain, the noir hero is hardly glamorous. He may be tough in a world-weary sort of way, like Humphrey Bogart in *The Big Sleep* (Hawks, 1946) or Robert Mitchum chain-smoking his way through *Out of the Past*. His pessimism passes for heroism because—just look at his face—he has seen it all. His skills may be considerable, but, alas, they don't help as much as they should because he is not in a fair fight.

The flip side of the world-weary tough-guy hero of so many noir detective pictures—*The Big Sleep*; *Out of the Past*; *Murder, My Sweet* (Edward Dmytryk, 1944)—is the milquetoast. The mild-mannered man—like Edward G. Robinson's Christopher Cross in Fritz Lang's *Scarlet Street* (1945), who seems even on first glance a con's perfect victim—is rendered vulnerable, even impotent by his unwill-

Robert Mitchum as the private detective Jeff Bailey (also known as Markham) and his nemesis (and sometime lover) Kathie Moffat in Jacques Tourneur's *Out of the Past* (1947)

ingness to challenge the authority of the postwar woman. In noir, tough guys and milquetoast alike fare similarly, which is to say badly. The crisis of masculinity in noir is not so much about the difficulty of figuring out what it takes to be a man. In the end, it doesn't really matter.

In a lot of noir films—*Double Indemnity, Out of the Past,* and *Gun Crazy* (also known as *Deadly Is the Female*; Lewis, 1949), to name just three—the male hero must sacrifice his life in order to stop the evil woman. Such suicidal intentions abound, so much so that death for the hero seems to be a welcome reprieve from a world that no longer has much use for "real men." The death of the hero is prefigured in the opening scene of several noir films. *D.O.A.*, for example, unfolds as a man who has been fatally poisoned spends his last days alive tracking his killer. He solves the crime but dies anyway. Billy Wilder's Hollywood noir *Sunset Boulevard* (1950) is narrated by a screenwriter lying dead, facedown in a swimming pool. *Double Indemnity,* narrated by a man about to die, perfectly expresses the nihilist impulse of noir.

Noir and the Hollywood Left

Noir became the genre of choice of the Hollywood Left after the war, and a number of noir films offer progressive takes on postwar capitalism, race relations, and even the blacklist itself. *Crossfire* (1947), directed by Edward Dmytryk and produced by Adrian Scott, two of the Hollywood Ten, tells the story of a confused, vicious ex-GI, Monty (Robert Ryan). He kills a Jewish man he has met

The 1947 film noir *Crossfire* was directed by Edward Dmytryk and produced by Adrian Scott, both of whom were subpoenaed by the House Committee on Un-American Activities (HUAC) in the fall of 1947. The film stars (*from left to right*) Robert Ryan as the anti-Semitic killer Monty; Robert Mitchum as Sergeant Keeley, a World War II vet; and Robert Young as police captain Finlay, a cop who takes a firm stand against prejudice.

by chance because he hates Jews. It's that simple. When the law closes in, Monty dupes a dim-witted buddy and tries to make him the fall guy. But the slow and easy Irish cop (Robert Young), whose father was a victim of anti-Irish prejudice in the 1920s, sees Monty for who and what he is. In the end, the murder is only one of the crimes that are punished.

When HUAC posed the argument that leftist Hollywood writers, directors, and producers were using films to espouse a particular point of view, they were right. Take, for example, the eventually blacklisted Abraham Polonsky, whose *Force of Evil* (1948) tells (in dialogue that appears to be in blank verse) of two brothers, an attorney named Joe (John Garfield), whose sole client is a mob boss, and Leo (Thomas Gomez), a hardheaded, soft-hearted small-time crook with ties to the community that complicate his role in the numbers racket. The film systematically reveals the intersections between criminal and capitalist enterprise, so much so that the two enterprises seem distinguished by style, not content. Leo ends up dead because he is too pigheaded to understand that capitalism consumes everything, that the criminal cartel will, whether he likes it or not, prevail. Joe is forced to rat out his boss, the gangster Tucker (Roy Roberts), and then turn himself in. "If a man's life can be lived so long and come out this way . . . ," Joe says in resignation, "then something was hor-rible and had to be ended one way or another." *Force of Evil* is an unrelentingly political film. For Polonsky all complicity in capitalism, no matter how "legal," is unethical, immoral, and ultimately criminal. Both Leo and Joe come to realize this, but as in most noir films the epiphany does them no good.

Betrayal is an important theme in many film noirs. Given the times, this plot point seems hardly incidental. In Polonsky's film, Freddie Bauer (Howland Chamberlain), an accountant who works for Leo, rats out his boss to rival gangsters. He is depicted as a sniveling, pitiable coward. He becomes a rat because he sees no other way to survive, but in the end ratting earns him a future no brighter than that of those he has betrayed. When Freddie is no longer useful to the gangsters who are making a move on Leo's operation, he is gunned down in cold blood. In such a bad situation (whether a gang war or the blacklist) there are no right decisions; there is only the possibility of dying or suffering with honor.

The pairing of a left-wing political sensibility and noir seems only logical when we consider the crime film's inherent class-conscious drama. For the political right, crime is a sure sign of social disintegration, and the purpose of the crime film is thus a call for law and order. For the political left, however, crime is the inevitable result of the capitalist accumulation by the wealthy and the inequality that results from it. Men turn to crime as a consequence of everyday disappointments and humiliations brought on by unemployment, poverty, or other unforeseen reversals of fortune. For those who were left of center politically in postwar America, noir crime films evinced the desperation of the underclass and were based on the notion that criminality on-screen says less about the individual criminal than it says about the circumstances that led to his sorry fate.

Abraham Polonsky's 1948 film noir *Force of Evil* offered a number of timely references to the Hollywood blacklist. In this key scene the stool pigeon Freddie Bauer (Howland Chamberlain) is murdered by the very gangsters he is paid to help. In 1951, Polonsky was called before the House Committee on Un-American Activities (HUAC). Unlike Freddie he refused to name names, and he was subsequently blacklisted.

Two working-class pugs, one black (Canada Lee), one white (John Garfield). Both men learn about class mobility the hard way in the boxing picture *Body and Soul* (Robert Rossen, 1947, from a script by Abraham Polonsky), one of several progressive film noirs that gave narrative form to the politics of the Hollywood Left. Many of the principals involved in *Body and Soul* ran into trouble as the blacklist era unfolded: Polonsky was blacklisted; Rossen was as well (until he named names). Both Lee and Garfield died young (of heart attacks—or, as legend has it, of broken hearts) while under investigation by the House Committee on Un-American Activities (HUAC).

When Polonsky was blacklisted, he had a lot of company among the writers, directors, and performers in film noir, including the directors John Berry (*Tension; He Ran All the Way*, 1951), Jules Dassin (*The Naked City*, 1948, and *Night and the City*, 1950), Edward Dmytryk (*Murder, My Sweet; Crossfire*), Cy Endfield (*The Sound and the Fury*, 1950), Irving Pichel (*Quicksand*), and blacklistee turned rat Robert Rossen (*Johnny O'Clock*, 1947, and *Body and Soul*, 1947, from a Polonsky script); screenwriters John Bright (the proto-noir gangster picture *The Public Enemy*), Hugo Butler (*He Ran All the Way*), Ben Maddow (*The Asphalt Jungle*, 1950, directed by John Huston), and Dalton Trumbo (*He Ran All the Way*); and actors John Garfield (*Body and Soul; Force of Evil*), Mickey Knox (*Knock on Any Door*, 1949, directed by Nicholas Ray, and *White Heat*, 1949, directed by Raoul Walsh), Canada Lee (*Body and Soul*), and Lionel Stander (*Unfaithfully Yours*, 1948, directed by Preston Sturges).

TRANSCENDING GENRE, TRANSCENDING HOLLYWOOD

In the 1950s and 1960s many influential film critics, film reviewers, academic film historians, film-studies students, and movie buffs embraced the auteur theory—the notion that films are in large measure the product of a single author: the director. A "cult of the director" thus emerged. Films released just after the war were categorized not according to chronology or genre but instead as part of the oeuvre (the body of work) of a given director. In the struggle between the commercial and the creative, it seemed that the artist had finally won.

Auteurism quickly became the prevailing model for a new sort of film history, one similar to art history (in which the works of the masters are routinely studied) and literary history (in which the so-called great books are emphasized). The auteur historical model thus gave film history a legitimacy by association with these established disciplines.

Although auteurism made a certain practical sense, especially since cinema studies was, and still is, widely taught in universities, it remains something of a convenient fiction. After all, the first image one sees at an American film screening is the corporate logo of the film's distributor (the woman with the torch, for example, when it's a Columbia Pictures film). The director's name may well appear above the title, and then again so might the name of the film's star, but the bottom line is that the film is owned, and the copyright controlled, by the studio distributor and the corporate logo runs first to make that point clear. Complicating matters is the reality of film development and production, the collaborative process by which films get made in America. The long list of credits that runs after every contemporary American film reminds us that films are made by lots of people, specialists working together to produce a single product. Exactly what a director does or doesn't do varies from film to film. The notion of authorship or even authority (over the production as a whole) is elusive, debatable, and impractical.

That said, as we look back on American film in the first ten years after World War II—on the films from those years that seem important today—we can't help but see the logic in the convenient fiction of auteurism. To a great extent we still value

The director Orson Welles and the star Anne Baxter on the set of *The Magnificent Ambersons* (1942).

the work of a handful of masters whose films somehow transcend genre categories and the limitations of studio film production. This section, then, discusses a few of those masters.

Orson Welles

Orson Welles's career provides an object lesson in the uneasy relationship between art and commerce that lies at the heart of American filmmaking. Welles was an important filmmaker in his day because of just one film: *Citizen Kane* (1941). The rest of his output—ten complete films, including one released posthumously—is characterized by interesting, sometimes dazzling work, but by and large Welles's movies meant little at the time of their release.

Welles's follow-up to *Citizen Kane*, *The Magnificent Ambersons* (1942), is a fascinating, beautiful mess of a film, adapted from Booth Tarkington's genial Pulitzer Prize–winning novel, published in 1918. Much of what made *Citizen Kane* important formally and stylistically is in evidence in this film: the emphasis on set design, lighting, and other aspects of mise-en-scène, especially the depth-of-

field compositions and cinematography of Stanley Cortez; the systematic nods to the theater (Welles's employment again of key Mercury Theatre Company actors: Agnes Moorehead, Joseph Cotten, and Ray Collins; his several weeks of preproduction rehearsals, as if he were putting on a play; and the long takes and theatrical blocking of scenes); and the deft layering of competing lines of dialogue, music, and sound effects (vestiges of Welles's roots in radio). But however beautiful the film is to look at, however fascinating it is to take in the soundscape, when Welles delivered a 2-hour 12-minute rough cut of the film and then promptly left for Rio de Janeiro, where he planned to shoot *It's All True* (a film that did not see the light of day during his lifetime), relations between the director and the studio producing and distributing the film, RKO, quickly soured.

After the rough-cut screening, RKO executives asked Welles to fix the film's "problems." The request was hardly unusual. But for reasons we can only guess at, Welles refused to return from Rio and instead sent detailed notes to the film's editor, Robert Wise. Wise followed Welles's instructions and then screened a second rough cut for the RKO executives. They still found it too long, too slow, and (thematically and visually) too dark. Wise and the film's star, Joseph Cotton, wired Welles begging him to come back to finish the film. Again Welles declined, and the studio took the film out of his hands. What was released in the summer of 1942 ran for 1 hour 28 minutes—44 minutes shorter than Welles's director's cut.

Most of the studio's cuts were made with an eye to the clock, so to speak. The film today (as cut by the studio) seems hectic, whereas Welles's original version was purposefully slow in an effort to match the leisurely pace of small-town life. The scenes that were cut did not necessarily propel the narrative, but they had a narrative function, relating—in terms viewers could not miss (in the experience of time passing in the theater)—a nostalgia for a simpler rural life that had been lost in the headlong move toward modernization and urbanization (a key theme in the novel and in Welles's 2-hour 12-minute rough cut). Most critical of all the changes was the studio's new ending, shot by an uncredited studio hack in a style that does not match the rest of the film. Welles's ending was heartbreaking: the principal characters, shown in a single classic Wellesian deep-focus shot, acknowledge that everything that had once mattered to them is lost. The studio ending, on the other hand, is hopeful, complete with serene movie music playing in the background as the characters look to the future.

Nine days before the release of *The Magnificent Ambersons*, Mercury Productions, Welles's production unit, was ousted from the RKO lot. Welles's career, after just two films, only one of which was completely his, was nearing its end. While his contemporaries—Frank Capra, John Ford, Howard Hawks, and Alfred Hitchcock, for example—were finding ways to *use* the studio system to their advantage, Welles simply could not abide the studio process at all. It moved too slowly and required

continued attention to projects long after he could generate any interest in them. Welles's defiance at RKO went a long way toward establishing his legacy in Hollywood. The mythology regarding Welles after 1942 was that he was too much of a genius for the studios to handle. The facts may well be a lot less romantic. Indeed, it is fair to ask whether Welles was a victim of studio caprice or his own impatience, his own carelessness with regard to his films, his co-workers, and finally his legacy as a filmmaker.

Welles's next film was *The Stranger* (1946), about a Nazi war criminal posing as a college professor. It is a good studio suspense picture and nothing more; it displays little of the director's signature style. *The Lady from Shanghai* (1947),

The evocative use of deep focus that characterized Orson Welles's stunning directorial debut, *Citizen Kane* (1941), is used to great effect in his second feature, *The Magnificent Ambersons* (1942). In this scene, Welles uses a deep-focus shot of the ballroom in the empty Amberson mansion to reveal what the spoiled brat George Amberson (Tim Holt) has done to his once happy family.

Welles's fourth major film, is another matter entirely. The story focuses on a working-class seaman, Michael O'Hara, who falls in love with Elsa, the wealthy wife of a criminal attorney, Arthur Bannister, who is crippled emotionally and physically. Though her motivations are never clear, Elsa (played by Rita Hayworth, who was married to Welles when the film was made and divorced from him by the time it came out) traps Michael (Welles) in a strange murder plot. At the start of the film's final act, Michael is on trial for murder, defended—though it makes sense only in the cockamamy world of *The Lady from Shanghai*—by the cuckolded husband (Everett Sloane). Michael is found guilty but escapes and in the end reveals that the attorney and his wife are the real criminals (and maybe the real murderers, too). He walks off-screen promising to forget or die trying, a fairly typical male posture in a noir suspense film.

As the plot summary suggests, *The Lady from Shanghai* is not a coherent story. The rough cut of the film was about 2 hours long; the release print is a mere 87 minutes. No doubt plenty got lost in the editing. But although the film may not hold together well, the version we have today offers some terrific examples of Welles's innovative mise-en-scène. In one scene, Elsa and Michael meet clandestinely at an aquarium. As they discuss running away together—a scheme she declines to get involved in since she has other plans for him—predatory fish swim in the huge tanks behind them. Welles uses the rear-lit tanks to full advantage as the giant fish swim behind the lovers, who appear in the foreground in silhouette. We see what Michael can't or doesn't see: that a predator is lurking, that he is about to be devoured. The kiss that punctuates the scene is thus undercut; the scene is not an introduction to a seduction but the prelude to something far less pleasurable.

A second memorable scene occurs at the very end. Michael, who is on the lam, is abducted by Elsa's henchmen in Chinatown; it's the first we see of them, but careful plotting is beside the point here. Michael wakes up, appropriately, in the fun house. He staggers to his feet and stumbles past a row of Coney Island mirrors and some shadowy scenery (painted to resemble Pablo Picasso's legendary *Guernica*, a tribute to the Spanish Civil War, reminding us that Michael fought against Franco, a fight Welles himself undoubtedly admired).

Michael then falls down a slide, which drops him into a hall of mirrors, where he, Elsa, and Arthur face off. During the climatic shoot-out between Arthur and Elsa, Arthur tries to explain the plot, but it is hard to pay attention as we try to figure out which image is real and which is a reflection. The metaphor for the characters' duplicity may be obvious, even ham-handed, but the technical execution of the mise-en-scène is inspired.

Welles followed *The Lady from Shanghai* with two eccentric Shakespeare films: *Macbeth* (1948) and *Othello* (1952). The first took years to complete, in part because Welles could not secure a distribution deal for it (not suprisingly, given that he was pitching not just a Shakespeare film but one with the actors speaking in a Scottish brogue). *Othello* is only slightly less eccentric. It is lit to look like a film noir and features beautiful location work in a ruined castle. Welles, playing the lead in blackface, reworked Shakespeare to suit his own autobiography. Rather than focus on the machinations and motivations (lust, racial prejudice, and ambition) of Iago (Micheál MacLiammóir), Welles's version highlights Othello's victimization, his persecution and paranoia, about which Welles, who perceived himself to be a victim of the power brokers in Hollywood, knew plenty. Welles's cinematic Shakespeare may well have been ahead of its time: his adaptations played fast and loose with the plays and favored eccentric staging over historically accurate representation. But the two films fared poorly with audiences, especially in comparison with the reverent, stage-bound adaptations directed by and starring Laurence Olivier: *Hamlet* (1948), which won the Oscar for Best Motion Picture, and *Richard III* (1955).

Welles briefly returned to studio filmmaking in 1958 with *Touch of Evil*, a seedy-border-town whodunit made for Columbia Pictures. Once again the film seems memorable for a couple of key scenes, scenes that could have been made by no one else. The film opens with what is perhaps Welles's best-known sequence, an extended tracking shot. The camera pans left to reveal the placement of a bomb in a car, tracks back to a long shot establishing a

(*right*) The glamorous movie star Rita Hayworth as the femme fatale Elsa Bannister in a publicity shot for *The Lady From Shanghai* (1947), a film noir directed by her by-then estranged husband, Orson Welles.

The seaman Michael O'Hara (Orson Welles) and the femme fatale Elsa Bannister (Rita Hayworth) in the hall-of-mirrors finale of *The Lady from Shanghai* (Welles, 1947). This final set piece is an apt metaphor for the film's labyrinthine plot.

fuller view of a seedy town on the Mexican side of the border, and then cranes up and takes in the scene from an extremely high angle. The car begins to move and briefly passes out of range of the camera. The camera catches up to the car, and we gather that this long moving camera shot is establishing not so much the town as some drama involving the car and the bomb we've seen placed in it. Without a single line of dialogue, without establishing any sense of the people in the shot, Welles tells us what we need to know about the drama at hand.

The long tracking shot is a piece of bravura filmmaking. It exists in part to introduce the director, the man in charge of the mise-en-scène, but it is also a deft piece of visual storytelling. The shot will end. We know that. And when it does, the bomb will go off. Welles fulfills this promise and uses the explosion to take the characters from one side of

the border to the other and from one state of being (life) to the other (death). He also uses the explosion to introduce the film's first cut.

For the release print of *Touch of Evil*, the studio stupidly superimposed credits on the opening sequence and added a jazzy number by Henry Mancini that spoils the intended effect of seamless movement and realistic sound (Welles had intended that we hear ambient sound filtering onto the streets from various nightclubs, mixed with the sounds of car horns, people walking, and distant conversations). A 1998 restored version of the film (brilliantly realized by veteran sound engineer Walter Murch) is now available, and the opening sequence can be seen as Welles intended it. That his best-known scene was screened for over forty years with the studio's handprints all over it seems at once ironic and indicative of Welles's career as a director.

That career after *Touch of Evil* can be summed up in a sentence or two. There were to be no more studio films. The best of Welles's later work is *The Trial* (1962), his adaptation of Franz Kafka's neurotic nightmare about a man unjustly persecuted by an insane bureaucracy. Produced entirely in Europe with foreign backing, the film offers an analog to Welles's life and times in Hollywood—at least as Welles himself had spun it—that is hard to miss.

What we have today from Welles are a handful of films with scenes of such genius—the deep-focus shots in *Citizen Kane,* the aquarium and hall-of-mirror scenes in *Lady from Shanghai,* the amazing tracking shots at the start and end of *Touch of Evil*—that it is fair to wonder what he might have made if he only could have learned to play the studios' game. Ironically, Welles's significance to American cinema is now built as much on what he did not do as on what he did, as much on what has been forever lost on the cutting-room floor as what has survived the studios' final cuts.

Orson Welles looms large in *Touch of Evil* (Welles, 1957) as the corrupt (but in the end instinctively astute) police captain Quinlan (*left, holding the gun*). Here he compels the godfather of a Mexican crime family, Uncle Joe Grandi (Akim Tamiroff), to help him complete the frame-up of Susie Vargas (Janet Leigh), the wife of Quinlan's nemesis, a Mexican police detective.

Howard Hawks

Howard Hawks made movies of a consistent quality in a variety of genres with a number of stars while working for different studios with different executives and different house styles. In the very process of remaining invisible, both as a public personality and as a cine-stylist, which is to say in the very process of adhering to the rule of studio filmmaking that values story over style (and studio over director), Hawks proved to be the medium's storyteller par excellence.

Though with Hawks there is little of Welles's insistence that the audience notice the director's work behind the camera and nothing of Welles's celebrity as an auteur notorious for his dysfunction within the studio system, we should note that auteurism is a flexible concept, and it is a common misperception that the label *auteur* applies only to filmmakers who consistently produce work that counters studio trends, as opposed to those who have the ability to tell a good story consistently

The director Howard Hawks (*left*), the cinematographer Gregg Toland, and the actress Frances Farmer on the set of *Come and Get It* (Hawks, Richard Rossen, and William Wyler, 1936).

using a style that suits the material at hand. We should not diminish Hawks's accomplishments simply because he operated successfully within the conventional structural conceits of classical studio Hollywood. Nor should we canonize every film-maker who, like Welles, is unable to flourish under the same circumstances.

Hawks's résumé reveals a body of work that is difficult to overrate. A selective Hawks filmography includes the groundbreaking gangster picture *Scarface* (1932); the romantic-screwball comedies *Bringing Up Baby* (1938), *His Girl Friday* (1940), *Ball of Fire* (1941), and *I Was a Male War Bride* (1949); the quintessential noir detective picture *The Big Sleep* (1946); two very different musicals, the melodramatic *A Song Is Born* (1948) and the broadly comic *Gentlemen Prefer Blondes* (1953); a thoughtful and ambiguous war picture, *Sergeant*

York (1941); and the character-based western *Red River* (1948). Hawks worked in both color and black-and-white, on location and in the studio. His films feature movie stars, all far more famous than he, who in many cases found under his direction the quintessence of their on-screen personae: Humphrey Bogart as the tough but moral detective Philip Marlowe in *The Big Sleep*, for example, or Marilyn Monroe as the seemingly dim-witted but world-wise showgirl Lorelei Lee in *Gentlemen Prefer Blondes*.

Unlike the more famous auteur stylists of his generation—Orson Welles or Alfred Hitchcock—Hawks preferred to present information on-screen with a minimum of fuss. For example, he liked to shoot scenes from eye level, a camera placement that suggests a casual, human onlooker standing and watching the action at hand. He was a mise-

en-scène director—but again, not a fussy one—and used cutting only to segue as smoothly as possible from one action to another. The studios called this style invisible editing, and one can watch an entire Hawks film without noticing more than a couple of cuts. They are there, of course; there are transitions. But the cuts are seldom from one sort of camera placement to another, and they rarely take us out of the world of the film or remind us that we are watching a movie.

Despite a willingness to work in pretty much every film genre and the absence of a showy style, there is an artistic signature to Hawks's work. Like his contemporary John Ford (whose career is discussed at length in the next chapter), Hawks consistently raised questions of ethics and morality in his films, a thematic conceit that gives coherence to his expansive work. Hawks attended the issue of moral responsibility in films as different as *Sergeant York*, about an avowed pacifist country boy who is forced by circumstances to take up arms and becomes, much against his nature, a war hero, and *Gentlemen Prefer Blondes*, which considers why men prefer pretty blondes and why pretty blondes prefer diamonds. Both films trace the evolution of a character not so much from who he or she is but from who he or she appears to be in our eyes. York (played by Gary Cooper) is at first seen scoffing at the very pieties he ultimately embraces. He finds his faith only to lose it again, when he is drafted into combat. War forces York to break faith with his pacifism in the name of a just cause, but he does not make the change lightly. The film ends as York is rewarded for his expertise in the field, but to Hawks's credit York seems to recognize the irony, the futility that lies at the heart of his heroism.

Lorelei Lee in *Gentlemen Prefer Blondes* seems at first little more than a gold-digging showgirl (with novocaine in her lipstick, we're told), but we eventually discover that she has an instinctive understanding of the inequities of male-female relationships. She is a showgirl who understands what her performance means and, more important, appreciates what her performance can get for

Marilyn Monroe in the spotlight as the pragmatic showgirl Lorelei Lee in Howard Hawks's 1953 musical comedy *Gentleman Prefer Blondes.*

her if she plays her cards right. Lorelei is a pragmatist and an unapologetic capitalist. For example, when Gus (Tommy Noonan), the homely millionaire she plans to marry, dumps her after a private detective spreads tales of her apparent improprieties on a cruise ship, Lorelei gets a job as a headliner in a Paris club with her sidekick, Dorothy Shaw (Jane Russell), and makes money to buy clothes and put food on the table. When Gus goes backstage to demand an apology, there is none coming. Lorelei heads for the stage (to sing "Diamonds Are a Girl's Best Friend," a song that very much tells her story), but not before delivering the perfect exit line: "It's men like you who have made me the way I am." In a world in which men overvalue female beauty, Lorelei sees nothing wrong with what she wants to acquire: a millionaire. And as Lorelei later tells Gus's suspicious father (Taylor Holmes), of course she is attracted to Gus for his money, but she also appreciates the fact that he's "nice."

(*left*) Humphrey Bogart as the private eye Philip Marlowe and Lauren Bacall as the heiress Vivian Sternwood Rutledge in Howard Hawks's adaptation of Raymond Chandler's *The Big Sleep* (1946). Hawks was an amazingly versatile director, able to capture the essence of any genre and any movie star.

Three's a crowd: Cary Grant as the newspaper editor Walter Burns plotting to win back his ex-wife, the former crack newspaper reporter Hildy Johnson (Rosalind Russell), who for the moment is engaged to marry Bruce Baldwin, yet another solid but boring foil played by Ralph Bellamy, in Howard Hawks's romantic comedy *His Girl Friday* (1940). When Walter gets Hildy hooked again on the newspaper biz, it's just a matter of time before she dumps a settled life with Bruce for a chaotic one with Walter.

Hawks was a master of pace, which is to say that he was very conscious that films exist in and take up real time and that the real time they take up should be paced to match the subject and themes of a film. *Bringing Up Baby*, for example, plays fast even by the standards of the romantic-comedy genre. With *Bringing Up Baby*, Hawks understood that the pace of romantic-comedy dialogue need not match everyday speech but might instead be used to distinguish those few who think astonishingly fast on their feet, folks ever ready with an answer for anything the world might throw at them. Throughout the film, Susan (Katharine Hepburn) talks astonishingly fast, and the rest of the characters struggle to keep up. The psychiatrist (Fritz Feld) she meets in a restaurant early in the film, the bumbling constable (Walter Catlett) who jails her for stealing a leopard, and her mother's loony companion, the self-described explorer Major Applegate (Charles Ruggles), can't hope to match her verbal virtuosity. As a result,

Susan does to them more or less whatever she wants to. David (Cary Grant), with whom she falls in love, is at first overwhelmed by her energy. But he endeavors to catch up and briefly does so when he, too, is arrested. In the end what separates David from the supporting characters is that he succeeds, finally (but only briefly) in shutting Susan up.

In *His Girl Friday*, released two years later, Hawks pushed the pace again. The plot is set in motion when Walter Burns (a newspaper editor played by Cary Grant) sees Hildy Johnson (a crack reporter and Walter's ex, played by Rosalind Russell) with Bruce Baldwin (her basically good but slow-witted fiancé, played by Ralph Bellamy). Jealousy kicks in, and Walter decides that he must have Hildy back. For the moment, Hildy is sure that Bruce, a steady but boring hunk, is the answer to her problems, which for the most part are caused by the undependable newspaperman she once loved and the career in the newspaper business that had formerly deprived her of a so-called normal woman's life. In the end, Walter wins Hildy back by speeding up the narrative—talking and thinking and plotting too fast for Bruce to keep up. Bruce throws up his hands in frustration; he can't compete with Walter because he can't keep pace with what's going on around him. Walter, of course, knows exactly what's going on; he's behind it all.

Because of his willingness to retreat behind his films and the stars who appeared in them, Hawks never received his due in his lifetime. Though everyone knew his films, no one seemed to know the director. In 1974, just three years before his death, the Motion Picture Academy presented Hawks with an honorary Oscar. Technically, the Academy Award was for a lifetime's achievement, but more than anything it was a belated apology. Despite a filmography that was all but unrivaled in the studio era, Hawks had been nominated just once for the Directing Oscar and did not win it. Howard Hawks just made movies—really good movies. And he did it so easily that even his colleagues underestimated his talent.

Billy Wilder

Samuel "Billy" Wilder began his career as a screenwriter in Germany in the 1920s. He got out before Hitler made emigration difficult, if not impossible, and eventually settled in Hollywood, where—though he did not speak a word of English when he arrived—he found work as a writer for fellow émigré Ernst Lubitsch. Wilder was a quick study—of English and of Hollywood filmmaking—and by the end of the '30s he had made his name as a crack comedy scriptwriter. His early credits include a number of memorable romantic comedies directed by other cineastes: *Bluebeard's Eighth Wife* (Lubitsch, 1938), *Midnight* (Mitchell Leisen, 1939), *Ninotchka* (Lubitsch, 1939), and *Ball of Fire* (Hawks, 1941).

Wilder's first Hollywood assignment behind the camera was a modestly successful light comedy starring Ginger Rogers: *The Major and the Minor* (1942), the story of a young woman who masquerades as a child to avoid paying full fare for a train ride from New York to Iowa. When, early in the film, the conductor discovers her ruse, she takes refuge (still in disguise) with a military-school instructor, Major Philip Kirby (Ray Milland). Complications ensue when Major Kirby finds himself falling for his fellow passenger, whom he at first takes to be just twelve years old. As a rookie studio director, Wilder had the job of getting out of Ginger Rogers's way—she was a big star at the time—and by all reports he did just that.

As would become clear just two years later with the release of the seminal noir film *Double Indemnity* (discussed in Chapter 4), Wilder was destined for bigger, greater things. In the thirty-seven years after the release of *Double Indemnity*, he made cautionary melodramas like *The Lost Weekend* (1945) and *Sunset Boulevard* (1950); a number of romantic comedies, including *Sabrina* (1954); two star vehicles for Marilyn Monroe, *The Seven Year Itch*

The paperback-book publisher Richard Sherman (Tom Ewell) takes a tumble for the gorgeous young woman upstairs (Marilyn Monroe) in Billy Wilder's comedy *The Seven Year Itch* (1955).

(1955) and *Some Like It Hot* (1959); a World War II prison-camp picture, *Stalag 17* (1953); and a courtroom-melodrama whodunit, *Witness for the Prosecution* (1957).

Wilder was a director who did not necessarily put a distinct artistic stamp on all of his films; indeed, he had the sort of flexibility as an auteur that Hawks displayed in his long career and placed the same emphasis on telling a good a story. That said, there is still a thematic unity to the work, one that has come to characterize his oeuvre. What most unites Wilder's films is his sense of humor. Even his more serious films—*Sunset Boulevard*, for example—seem on close examination to be satires. Set in postwar Hollywood, *Sunset Boulevard* tells the story of a down-on-his-luck screenwriter, Joe Gillis (William Holden), whose car breaks down outside a dilapidated Sunset Boulevard mansion owned by the former silent-film star Norma Desmond (played by Gloria Swanson, herself a former silent-film star). When Joe enters Norma's mansion, he is mistaken for a funeral director sent to dispatch Norma's pet monkey's casket to a pet cemetery. Though played with dead seriousness, the scene satirizes the excesses of Hollywood stars (the mansion, the pet monkey, the fancy monkey casket) and the larger absurdity of self-possessed Hollywood celebrity culture. Also in play are the class dynamics of Hollywood, in which some (movie stars like Desmond) enjoy outrageous wealth while others (struggling screenwriters like Joe and like Wilder himself at one time) live just one step ahead of the bill collector. Joe becomes Norma's lover and confidant, a kept man in a town where selling out is a prerequisite for success. Norma—though Joe fails to understand this fully—is herself an object lesson in Hollywood success. She has the money and the (old) fancy car, but she is a shut-in with virtually no contact with the real world.

Wilder's satirical comedies focus on American mass culture. *The Seven Year Itch*, for example, takes aim at an easy target: 1950s American pop culture. Adapted from a play by George Axelrod

Billy Wilder (*right*) receiving (from fellow director William Wyler) the 1945 Academy Award for Directing, for *The Lost Weekend*.

(who also wrote the similarly satiric *Will Success Spoil Rock Hunter?*, directed by Frank Tashlin in 1957), *The Seven Year Itch* is about "a girl" (she has no name in the film), played by Marilyn Monroe, who becomes an object of obsession for a married man (Tom Ewell) who publishes popular paperbacks. He dreams that he rescues her after her big toe gets caught in a bathtub fixture, a scene stolen from a bad paperback novel. Her unselfconscious, unrepressed remarks—for example she tells him that she keeps her undies in the refrigerator on hot summer afternoons—are easily mistaken for seduction, a scenario that scares him more than he could ever have imagined.

In contrast to Hawks, who seemed to disappear behind the films he made, Wilder was one of the first sound-era auteur celebrities. And in part because of his celebrity, he was serially celebrated by his peers in the Motion Picture Academy. All told, he was nominated for twenty-one Oscars, and in 1987 he received the Irving Thalberg Memorial Award for lifetime achievement. He won Directing and Writing Oscars for *The Lost Weekend*, a Writing Oscar for *Sunset Boulevard*, and Directing, Writing, and Best Motion Picture Oscars for his

(*left*) "All right, Mr. DeMille, I'm ready for my close-up." The former star of silent movies Norma Desmond (played by the former star of silent movies Gloria Swanson) in her last scene, making a grand gesture of leaving her house in police custody after killing her young lover in Billy Wilder's dark Hollywood satire *Sunset Boulevard* (1950).

Jerry (Jack Lemmon), posing as Daphne, lands a millionaire, Osgood (Joe E. Brown), in Billy Wilder's comedy *Some Like It Hot* (1959). When asked, "Why would a guy wanna marry a guy?" Jerry replies, "Security."

last important film, *The Apartment* (1960), the story of a spineless middle manager, C. C. Baxter (Jack Lemmon), who facilitates an affair between a young woman (Shirley MacLaine) with whom he eventually falls in love and his boss (played by Fred MacMurray). At a time when the social critics William H. Whyte, C. Wright Mills, and David Riesman were railing against "the organization man," "the power elite," and "other-directed" middle managers (who surrender their identity for the good of an organization), *The Apartment* unflinchingly examined the price so many workers pay for a small taste of success.

Throughout his career, Wilder showed an affection for down-on-their-luck working-class characters, from Walter Neff in *Double Indemnity* and Joe Gillis in *Sunset Boulevard* to C. C. Baxter in *The Apartment*. He was an astute student of social class, and though he was a success story himself (having progressed from obscurity to celebrity in ten years), he seemed to appreciate that social transcendence was not possible for many Americans. What Walter, Joe, and C. C.—characters in three

very different films—had in common was a struggle to achieve social mobility that required a significant moral sacrifice: Walter commits murder, Joe prostitutes himself (in several senses of the term), and C. C. does his boss's dirty work in arranging for, and then covering up, an affair. In the end all three men lose in their quest for a better life because, although tempted, they refuse to be corrupted fully by those around them: Walter turns on his co-conspirator, Phyllis, and then confesses; Joe tries to make a clean break and return to the newspaper business in the Midwest (but is gunned down nonetheless); and C. C. decides to tell the truth in part because he comes to acknowledge that procuring for his boss is wrong. To an astonishing degree, Wilder, for whom English was a second language and America a second homeland, was able to cut to the core of the American struggle for success. He understood what drove Americans to risk everything on crazy plans, and he showed a great deal of sympathy for characters who, having indulged their greed, lust, and ambition, found themselves in too deep.

Like Hawks, Wilder had few problems working within the studio system, and his films were foremost compelling stories told with uncluttered expertise. And like Hawks's body of work, Wilder's speaks to the success of the system itself as it enabled such an expert storyteller to tell his stories so expertly.

Elia Kazan

Though Elia Kazan directed a number of the era's best and most-talked-about films, his decision to name names during the HUAC hearings (essentially betraying his fellow filmmakers) has for many historians diminished the impact of his considerable contributions to film history. Exactly what to make of Kazan's career is often tied directly to how one feels about his cooperation with HUAC.

Kazan arrived in Hollywood from New York after acting in and directing left-leaning stage plays, several of which were produced by the

Group Theatre, an organization targeted by HUAC in the late 1940s. Initially Kazan made politically progressive movies, a logical extension of his politically progressive stage work. He won his first of two Directing Oscars for *Gentleman's Agreement* (1947), a film that condemns anti-Semitism in postwar America, and he followed that up with an incendiary political film, *Pinky* (1949), the story of a light-skinned African American woman who passes for white. Because it deals openly with questions of race and privilege and even miscegenation, it was banned in much of the South.

While his film career took off, Kazan maintained a high profile on the New York stage scene. In 1948, a year after the release of *Gentleman's Agreement*, he helped establish the Actors Studio, where the acting teachers Lee and Paula Strasberg trained many of the best of the stage and screen actors and actresses of the 1950s, including Marlon Brando, Montgomery Clift, Eli Wallach, Kim Hunter, and Eva Marie Saint. In the previous year, Kazan had directed the initial Broadway stage run of Arthur Miller's *All My Sons*, a play about a family torn apart by war profiteering. Two years later he staged Miller's most famous work, *Death of a Salesman*.

Kazan was a marvelous director of actors. He was a proponent of the Method, a style of acting that forsakes the expression of artificial emotions by gestures and other acting techniques for more naturalistic expressions based on the actor's own deeply felt emotions. If you have to play a scene in which your character is sad, to satisfy the Method you analyze your past to discover an experience that made you sad. According to the Method, dredging up that "real emotion" promises a style of acting at once more real and more cinematic than the broader and more technical style grounded in stage performance. The actor James Dunn, for example, whose career had been beset by terrible bouts of alcohol abuse, was urged by Kazan to dredge up the pain he had experienced due to his alcoholism when he played the role of Johnny Nolan in Kazan's melodrama *A Tree Grows in Brooklyn* (1945). For that performance, Dunn was awarded an Oscar. The Method has become the dominant school of screen acting (with the stars Robert De Niro, Dustin Hoffman, and Al Pacino among its devotees), and its prominence today owes much to Kazan's film work in the 1940s and '50s.

In 1951, Kazan made one of his best-known films, *A Streetcar Named Desire*, based on the play by Tennessee Williams. The film is revered partly because of Marlon Brando's memorable portrayal of the rugged, abusive, and charismatic Stanley Kowalski—one of the greatest Method performances of all time. Dressed in a torn T-shirt, emitting a sexual energy the likes of which American audiences had never seen on-screen, Brando was a sensation, and his style of acting took the industry by storm. (Astonishingly, Brando did not win the Academy Award for his performance; he lost to Humphrey Bogart in John Huston's *African Queen*. But virtually everyone else with a major role in the film won—Vivien Leigh, Kim Hunter, and Karl Malden—testimony again to Kazan's skill with actors and the growing popularity of the Method in Hollywood.)

Elia Kazan clutching his Oscar for Directing, for *Gentleman's Agreement*, in 1948. Though Kazan's films remain among the most memorable in the postwar era, his legacy is tainted by his cooperation with the House Committee on Un-American Activities (HUAC).

When Kazan was called to testify before HUAC, he had a lot to lose in Hollywood. But Broadway did not enforce the blacklist, and there seems little doubt that he would have continued working in American theater even if Hollywood had blacklisted him. Moreover, Kazan had considerable clout in the movie industry. He was the biggest fish HUAC ever subpoenaed, and had he refused to cooperate, the studios might have been reluctant to blacklist him. In other words, had Kazan resisted, things might have turned out differently for Hollywood in the '50s.

But he cooperated. And throughout his life he remained steadfastly unapologetic about his complicity. His first film after testifying was the trenchant blacklist allegory *On the Waterfront* (1954). Despite a nod to social realism—its focus on and celebration of the common man, the location work on the rough-and-tumble New Jersey docks—*On the Waterfront* is a deeply reactionary film, as it implausibly celebrates the nobility of naming names. On the waterfront, we're told in a key scene, there is a code of silence. One is "d and d"—that is, deaf and dumb. Such is the code of the streets, of course, the very code that kept a number of Hollywood writers, directors, and actors from testifying in Washington. But in *On the Waterfront*, a film written by the fellow friendly witness Budd Schulberg (who named fifteen names), the street position is untenable because mobsters run the waterfront unions. Thus when the film's punched-out palooka hero, Terry Malloy (Brando), finally stands up for himself against the mob, his actions seem unambiguously honorable. It was hard then,

The stool pigeon as hero: Terry Malloy (Marlon Brando, *center*) rats out the union and takes a beating for his trouble. But it's Elia Kazan's story, so Terry finds vindication (from the local priest, played by Karl Malden, *left*) and true love (with Edie Doyle, played by Eva Marie Saint) in the final reel of *On the Waterfront* (1954).

lywood liberal who credits Kazan with launching his career in *Splendor in the Grass,* stood and applauded. But many in attendance—the actors Ed Harris and Nick Nolte, for example—sat on their hands. For those who followed the story in the press, there was the image of the blacklisted Abraham Polonsky watching the telecast at home. The week before the Oscar ceremony, Polonsky had told the magazine *Entertainment Weekly* that he planned to watch the Oscars for the first time in years, in the hope that someone might gun down Kazan on the stage.

Max Ophüls, Sam Fuller, Nicholas Ray, and Douglas Sirk

Among the lesser-known but extremely talented cineastes working in Hollywood in the postwar period was the German émigré Max Ophüls. His two best American films, *Letter from an Unknown Woman* (1948) and *Caught* (1949), are melodramas of unusual quality and style. Both films are darker than most so-called women's pictures of the time, and both feature Ophüls's penchant for camera movement, a very modern visual style that

as it is now, to distinguish Kazan's personal drama from the one played out by Brando on-screen.

If we can put politics aside—though many film historians have resisted the impulse—we cannot deny that Kazan is one of the most important postwar American film directors. In addition to *On the Waterfront,* his career post–HUAC testimony includes a moving adaptation of John Steinbeck's *East of Eden* (1955), starring the second most famous Method actor of the era, James Dean, in his best performance; *Baby Doll* (1957), a controversial film based on Tennessee Williams's play *27 Wagons Full of Cotton;* the deft and prescient political satire *A Face in the Crowd* (1957); and the heartbreaking melodrama *Splendor in the Grass* (1961).

In 1999, Kazan won an honorary award from the Motion Picture Academy. Martin Scorsese and Robert De Niro, both seeming nervous and embarrassed, presented the award at the televised Academy Awards ceremony. When Kazan took the stage to accept the award, he and everyone else in the hall and in the worldwide television audience got a taste of just how important politics remain in any assessment of his career. Warren Beatty, a Hol-

(*left*) "I coulda been a contender. I coulda been somebody, instead of a bum, which is what I am, let's face it." Marlon Brando (*right*) as the former boxer Terry and Rod Steiger as his brother, the gangster–union organizer Charley "the Gent" Malloy, in Elia Kazan's blacklist parable *On the Waterfront* (1954).

Barbara Bel Geddes (*left*) as Leonora Eames, a former department store model, and James Mason as Larry Quinada, the doctor who tries to save her from a disastrous marriage in Max Ophüls's stylish noir melodrama *Caught* (1949).

Jean Peters as Candy, a B-girl caught in a bizarre espionage plot thwarted by a wily pickpocket
(Richard Widmark), in Sam Fuller's cold war crime melodrama *Pickup on South Street* (1953).

influenced filmmakers like Martin Scorsese and Robert Altman. The opening sequence of *Caught*, set in a narrow apartment shared by two shopgirls with dreams of modeling and maybe landing a rich man, is a particularly noteworthy example of Ophüls's signature style. The interior space is presented in a single fluid camera gesture. What seems initially like an innocuous conversation is given gravity by the camerawork.

Sam Fuller began his media career as a newspaper copyboy at the *New York Journal* at age twelve. He rose within the ranks quickly and soon became the personal copyboy to the editor in chief, William Randolph Hearst. By age seventeen, Fuller was a hard-nosed crime reporter for the *New York Evening Graphic*, a sensationalist tabloid. When the United States entered World War II, Fuller enlisted in the army. He was assigned to the First Infantry Division and saw action on D-Day. His

experience as a crime reporter and as a wartime soldier provides the backdrop for all his films.

Fuller worked on the margins of Hollywood, almost exclusively making B pictures, and enjoyed a degree of artistic freedom because he worked on the cheap and showed little interest in the big time of commercial Hollywood moviemaking. Looking back on his work today, we can see how he defied the narrative and stylistic conventions of his era. *I Shot Jesse James* (1949), his first film, tells a familiar story but from an unfamiliar point of view: that of Bob Ford (John Ireland), the guilt-ridden killer of Jesse James (played by Reed Hadley). *Pickup on South Street* (1953), perhaps Fuller's best film, begins as a story about a working-class pickpocket, but the gritty crime film quickly evolves into something far weirder, about political secrets being passed to the Communists. Fuller's nod to the newspaper business is the nightmarish *Shock*

Corridor (1963), about an ambitious crime reporter who goes undercover in an insane asylum to solve a murder, only to become an inmate himself. Much of the work resists traditional plotting, but it is nonetheless fascinating to watch.

Fuller's war films—especially *The Steel Helmet* (1951), set during the Korean War—are brutal affairs. War really *is* hell, Fuller maintained, for those who know what it's like. Whereas mainstream war films were at their core patriotic, especially in the sensitive 1950s, Fuller made the reasons for waging war beside the point. For men on the front lines, for the men with whom Fuller sympathized, war is about one thing: survival. It is best not to wonder why one fights. In the autobiographical *The Big Red One* (Fuller's comeback film, released in 1980, which recalls his own experiences in World War II), an army platoon tracks some Nazis to an asylum for the insane and mentally retarded in rural France. Tired of fighting, an infantryman suggests to his commanding officer that they call in the bombers. The CO (Lee Marvin) agrees that the bombers would do a quicker job but adds that it's bad PR (public relations) to blow up "maniacs and retards." "But it's OK to kill sane people?" the infantryman reasons. The CO looks him in the eye and in a tight close-up delivers the scene's monosyllabic payoff: "Yep."

In a Hollywood that thrived on the seamless presentation of safe material that would appeal to the widest audience, Fuller saw film as a blunt instrument. He was, as a consequence, never

Life and love on the lam: Keechie (Cathy O'Donnell) and Bowie (Farley Granger) on the run in Nicholas Ray's 1949 film noir *They Live by Night*.

particularly successful with film executives, mainstream reviewers, or the mass audience. His career was both short and, in his day, uneventful. He has become important only now, well after the fact. Thanks in large part to French critics who rescued his films from obscurity, he has become the darling of a new generation of academic film critics and historians, an exemplar of the B-movie auteur: misunderstood in his day because his work was years ahead of its time.

Nicholas Ray had significantly more mainstream success than Fuller, but he, too, began and ended his career making B movies. In the late 1940s and early '50s, Ray made several memorable film noirs: *Knock on Any Door* (1949), *They Live by Night* (1949), *In a Lonely Place* (1950), and *On Dangerous Ground* (1952), making his mark despite directing genre films on modest budgets. Throughout his career, Ray was a socially conscious filmmaker. He made films about juvenile delinquency—*Knock on Any Door* and *Rebel without a Cause* (1955), a film discussed at length in Chapter 6—and drug addiction—*Bigger Than Life* (1956)—when such subjects were difficult to handle in a mainstream, PCA-approved feature film. Like Fuller, Ray made movies that had a message.

Though dismissed in his day by American critics and historians as little more than a studio genre director, Douglas Sirk, who made lush weepies (melodramas lavishly shot in Technicolor and widescreen), was an important auteur of the postwar era. He never received a single Oscar nomination and was largely unknown to the average moviegoer, yet Sirk made five memorable melodramas: *Magnificent Obsession* (1954, a remake of John M. Stahl's 1935 film), *All That Heaven Allows* (1955), *There's Always Tomorrow* (1956), *Written on the Wind* (1956), and *Imitation of Life* (1959, also a remake of a Stahl film). Though he worked mainly in one genre—one routinely dismissed by critics as an empty divertissement—Sirk brought an unusual level of visual sophistication to his movies and smartly used formula as a platform from which to speak out against racism (in *Imitation of Life*) and small-town prejudice (in *All That Heaven Allows*). Sirk's films have been the inspiration for a number of popular and critically celebrated contemporary films, including Todd Haynes's sumptuous interracial melodrama *Far from Heaven* (2002).

BEHIND THE CAMERA, BEHIND THE SCENES: WOMEN IN HOLLYWOOD

In the postwar period the studios continued to contract "starlets," young women, many of them beauty-contest winners, who aspired to movie stardom and ventured to Hollywood in search of fame and fortune. More often than not, they found something else, something altogether less glamorous. Lots of them went home disillusioned, others stayed in Los Angeles and worked at menial service jobs, and still others paid a heavy price for dreaming the golden dream of movie stardom. One such woman was Elizabeth Short, whose 1947 murder and mutilation became something of a national fascination and brought to light for many Americans the darker side of the Hollywood dream. Short never realized her dream career in the pictures. She became a notorious bar girl (though probably not a prostitute, as so many others in her place had become) and then a notorious murder victim: the Black Dahlia.

Stardom was the most elusive of dream jobs in Hollywood. For every starlet who made the transition from bit player to movie star, there were hundreds whose careers ended in disappointment. Steady work for women was more safely found behind the scenes as costume designers, hairdressers, makeup artists, set designers, and screenwriters. There were no women working as film executives and only one woman working behind the camera making major motion pictures, the actress-writer-director Ida Lupino.

Women Screenwriters

Women were employed by most studio story departments in the postwar era. And contrary to the popular assumption, they were not assigned exclusively to women's pictures. Indeed, a number of women wrote scripts for hard-edged films that featured the toughest of tough-guy heroes. Leigh Brackett (along with William Faulkner and Jules Furthman) adapted Raymond Chandler's hard-boiled detective novel *The Big Sleep* for Howard Hawks in 1946. In that film, Brackett helped draw out the quintessential tough, incorruptible, basically moral hard-boiled detective Philip Marlowe, personified by the film star Humphrey Bogart. If there is a woman's touch in the script, it can be found in the way the film departs from the novel with regard to the story's principal female character, Vivian Sternwood Rutledge (Lauren Bacall). Brackett's Vivian, unlike Chandler's, is self-assured, a match for Marlowe. She is a modern woman, verbally adept, confident, and very much in control of her sexuality. Brackett also co-wrote the screenplay for Hawks's western *Rio Bravo* (1959) and later worked on two very different films about men in action, films that one would hardly have guessed were written by a woman: *The Long Goodbye* (a second Raymond Chandler adaptation, directed by Robert Altman in 1973), for which she wrote the screenplay, and the *Star Wars* sequel *The Empire Strikes Back* (Irvin Kershner, 1980), for which she co-wrote the screenplay.

A short list of the significant female scriptwriters of the late 1940s and early '50s includes Betty Comden, who co-wrote the story for *Singin' in the Rain* (Gene Kelly and Stanley Donen, 1952); Olive Cooper, who wrote over twenty westerns in the 1940s; Frances Goodrich, who co-wrote the screenplays for *It's a Wonderful Life* (Capra, 1946), *The Virginian* (Stuart Gilmore, 1946), *Easter Parade* (Charles Walters, 1948), and *Father of the Bride* (Vincente Minnelli, 1950); Isobel Lennart, who co-wrote the screenplay for the Doris Day feature *Love Me or Leave Me* (Charles Vidor, 1955) and on her own wrote the screenplay for the Day feature *Please Don't Eat the Daisies* (Walters, 1960); Ayn Rand, who wrote the screenplay based on her own novel *The Fountainhead* (King Vidor, 1949); Alma Reville, who co-wrote the screenplays for *Suspicion* (1941) and *Shadow of a Doubt* (1943) and contributed to the writing of *The Paradine Case* (1947), all directed by her husband, Alfred Hitchcock; Tess Slesinger, who co-wrote the screenplay for *A Tree Grows in Brooklyn* (Elia Kazan, 1945); and Virginia Van Upp, who co-wrote *Cover Girl* (Charles Vidor, 1944).

Ida Lupino

Ida Lupino began her Hollywood career as a contract player at Warner Bros. She became a star with her performance in Raoul Walsh's gritty crime melodrama *They Drive by Night* (1940). But like a lot of stars, especially female stars, Lupino soon chafed at the restrictions of the studio system. Tired of limiting, stereotyped roles in formu-

Ida Lupino began her career in the 1930s as a glamorous contract player at Warner Bros. She became one of the few women to direct feature films during the studio era.

laic studio films, Lupino formed a production company in 1949 to develop and produce her own films.

Lupino's first film as a producer was *Not Wanted* (1949), and though she was not credited as such on the release print of the film, it is safe to assume that after the director, Elmer Clifton, suffered a heart attack three days into the filming, Lupino took over to keep the production on schedule. She became a director by accident, not by design—in itself a statement about women in Hollywood in the 1940s.

Not Wanted tells the story of a promiscuous teenage girl (Sally Kelton) who frequents bars, gets pregnant, and has to adjust to adulthood and motherhood. Following *Not Wanted*, Lupino directed *Outrage* (1950), about a young woman (Mala Powers) who is raped; *Never Fear* (1950), about a dancer (Sally Forrest) who is stricken with polio (as was Lupino at age sixteen), and her best-known film, *Hard, Fast and Beautiful* (1951), about an ambitious, desperately unhappy stage mother (Claire Trevor) and her tennis-playing daughter (Sally Forrest), through whom she lives vicariously. All three films deal with women's issues, but they are not at all feminist. Though Lupino used her ability as a producer, writer, and director to shepherd films about women (that is, films with interesting, different, complex female roles) through development, into production, and on to distribution through the studio system, there is little in those films that resembles a progressive gender politics.

In *Not Wanted*, for example, the teenager more or less gets what she deserves. The rape victim in *Outrage* finds in the patriarchal legal and medical communities plenty of good men ready to take care of her. When the dancer is stricken with polio in *Never Fear*, her choreographer, a man, nurses her back to health. In the climax of *Hard, Fast and Beautiful*, the daughter gives up tennis for marriage. It is unclear how deeply Lupino appreciated the film's denouement, in which the daughter trades an overbearing mother for a husband who, in the mother's stead, offers to take control of her life. The film plays as a critique of female ambi-

Ida Lupino (*back row, second from the right*) watches dailies during the production of her 1951 feature *Hard, Fast and Beautiful*. As we can see from this photograph, except for Lupino, the entire RKO crew was male.

tion but nonetheless offers terrific roles for the female leads.

Lupino's last film of any consequence was *The Bigamist* (1953). Though the title character (played by Edmund O'Brien) is a philanderer who enters into marriage with two women at the same time, he emerges as a sympathetic figure. His first wife (Joan Fontaine) holds the purse strings in the family business. Her "failure" to get pregnant leads to a kind of careerism that Lupino, herself a capable and ambitious career woman, depicts as unladylike, even antisocial. Lupino's bigamist is just a lonely guy, unhappy with a marriage that plays out as little more than a business arrangement. Lupino cast herself as wife number 2. She is everything that wife number 1 is not: sexy and vulnerable. That the bigamist might have divorced his first wife before marrying his second, that his dissatisfaction with his first marriage might have had something to do with him and not just his wife, are issues not subject to analysis or debate in the film. That Lupino herself plays the object of desire and satisfaction further confuses the morality at play.

The men in Lupino's films are drawn in mostly flattering terms. They're kind and caring in ways that seem less a matter of realism than some sort of wish fulfillment. They are men as women (or at least as Lupino) wished they might or could be. The women, on the other hand, are a troubled lot. Self-doubting or overly ambitious, capable but cold, vulnerable but sexy, they are complex characters of the sort actresses (like Lupino) crave. But they are hardly women anyone watching Lupino's films might want to emulate.

Like other women working behind the scenes in Hollywood, Lupino appreciated her minority status; she was, after all, the only woman director of any consequence in the immediate postwar era. She did not use her position to radicalize her viewers or express a feminist agenda. Instead, she used her position in a more practical way, to write and direct films that featured interesting (albeit conflicted) female characters, then as now in short supply.

■ ■ ■

Because of both the Supreme Court decision in the *Paramount* case and the HUAC hearings, the studios were forced to change their organizational structure and their personnel policies. Those changes came at a particularly difficult time, as they accompanied and exacerbated problems at the box office that had been brought about by urban flight and the advent of television. As a consequence, the studios spent much of the first postwar decade adjusting to a changing American culture and film market, trying to stay in business long enough for the box office to turn around and government interference to recede.

Despite the corporate struggle, some noteworthy filmmaking took place. Film noir, the most influential genre of the era, was in full flower between 1945 and 1955. Noir films at once reflected and refracted the conflicted postwar American society and introduced a more modern film style, which included a new way of lighting and shooting films to accompany more psychologically complex, downbeat story lines. Though not fully appreciated at the time, noir proved to be the postwar period's most influential genre. It has had a significant effect on two generations of American filmmakers, from Arthur Penn, Francis Ford Coppola, and Martin Scorsese in the late 1960s and the 1970s to Quentin Tarantino and David Lynch in the late twentieth and early twenty-first centuries.

A handful of talented movie directors transcended genre during this period: Orson Welles, Howard Hawks, Billy Wilder, and Elia Kazan were the most notable. But impressive as some of their films may have been, as encouraging as the move to a more sophisticated, more idiosyncratic medium proved to be, there was little those talented directors could do to "save Hollywood," a mission that would become even more dire in the decade and a half to follow.

The transition between the classical Hollywood of the 1930s and some successful postwar Hollywood proved difficult, so difficult that several of the studios seemed to be on the brink of collapse a mere decade after the war's end. That a new, very different Hollywood was somewhere out there, on or over the horizon, still seemed possible in 1955; how moviemakers would get there anytime soon was another matter entirely.

Moving toward a New Hollywood

1955–1967

The implementation and enforcement of the Supreme Court's decision in the *Paramount* case in 1948 coincided with a steady decline in box-office revenues: a 43 percent drop from a high of $1.7 billion in 1946 to a low of $955 million in 1961. Average weekly movie attendance suffered a similar decline: in 1947, 90 million people went to the movies every week, but by 1957 the average weekly attendance was down to 40 million. Much of what transpired in the industry between 1955 and 1967 was governed by a single unpleasant fact of life: the once-prosperous studios were no longer so prosperous. It seemed entirely possible, as the 1960s unfolded, that the film industry, which had survived a devastating economic depression and a world war, might not survive peacetime prosperity. The irony was disquieting.

Studio executives came to understand in the mid-1950s that a new Hollywood was necessary and inevitable. The first step toward a more modern movie industry took shape in the form of a truce between the studios and their counterpart in television. By 1960 there were 50 million TV sets in homes across the United States, and lots of people were watching a lot of televison: in 1960 the average daily viewing time for U.S. households with a TV set was over 5 hours a day. In less than a decade, television had gone from a curious gadget to an essential home appliance, from an odd and clumsily delivered electronic signal received by a handful of *Popular Mechanics* subscribers to a viable mass medium that the studios could no longer afford to ignore.

Because the *Paramount* Decision restricted the studios' investment in the television industry, the studios got creative and established what we now term synergies (complex mutually advantageous business relationships) between the two media. Disney led the way, making a

Alfred Hitchcock directing Janet Leigh in the famous shower scene in *Psycho* (1960).

233

deal with the American Broadcasting Company (ABC) that included the production of a Disney TV show that aired weekly on the network. Fox, MGM, and Warner Bros. followed suit, Fox signing an agreement with the Columbia Broadcasting System (CBS), and the other two signing with ABC. By 1956 the once unthinkable had become commonplace: studio movies had found a second life on the small screen.

As the two media learned to work productively and profitably together, the promise of an integrated entertainment industry emerged. This model attracted multinational conglomerates, huge companies interested in diversifying their assets and attracted to the glamour and glitz of the movie industry and to the studios' huge cash reserves (created by the forced sale of their movie houses in accordance with the *Paramount* decision). Once the conglomerates moved in, they established a business model for the production and distribution of motion pictures that was more in tune with their other consumer industries (books, soft drinks, parking lots, and funeral parlors) and thus more predictable. But despite the mutually advantageous deal with the TV networks and the studios' significantly improved access to capital with which to finance film production, one obstacle to prosperity remained: getting people interested in going to the movies again. It was a question studio executives in the mid-1950s had to answer. Initially they looked to their nearest competitors and new business partners in television. What, studio executives asked themselves, distinguished films from television? Foremost were the size and the shape of the image. So the studios began making the big screen seem even bigger, enhancing the theatrical experience with widescreen technologies like CinemaScope and VistaVision, both of which changed the shape of the movie-screen image, with the aspect ratio (the width-to-height ratio) going from 1.33:1 to a new standard of 1.85:1 for "flat," or "non-Scope," prints and 2.35:1 for the various Scope and later Panavision prints; so-called wide-field formats like Cinerama and Todd-AO, which projected an image six times the normal size on curved screens, making audiences feel as if they were somehow "inside" the image; and experiments in 3-D, which simulated depth as long as viewers wore silly plastic glasses. With the advent of stereophonic sound (pioneered in the 1940s and perfected in the 1950s), theaters were equipped with audio systems that were far superior to the 4-inch speakers and tinny

amplifiers used in 1950s TV sets. But none of those dramatic improvements in theatrical exhibition proved significant enough to save the movies from a growing obsolescence. No matter how the studios tried to lure Americans back into the habit of going to the movies, box-office numbers remained disappointingly low.

In order to compete with television, movies needed more than a new shape and a new sound; they needed to present material that could not be found on the small screen. And that meant taking a long, hard look at censorship. The TV networks from the start had adhered to strict enforcement of "standards and practices," a censorship code based on the assumption that television is a "family" medium meant to be consumed by everyone, young and old. Hollywood cinema was still similarly hamstrung by its production code, which had been written in the 1930s by a Jesuit priest and a devout Catholic journalist and, like the TV code, was based on the assumption that all films must be suitable for all audiences. Beginning in 1953—coincidentally the year in which the second of two "reports" by Alfred Kinsey, *Sexual Behavior in the Human Female,* became a best seller (Kinsey's first "report," *Sexual Behavior in the Human Male,* had been published five years before)—a number of Hollywood films were released in defiance of the code. At first these films seemed pretty risky. Would theaters show a film released without a seal of approval from the Production Code Administration? Would people come to see it? Would the production of more adult-themed films risk a reemergence of grassroots censorship? No one knew the answers for sure, but movie attendance had gotten so sparse that the studios were willing to take the risk.

The risk paid off. Theater owners, themselves struggling to survive, anxiously contracted to screen these mature-themed films, several of which were released without PCA seals. And lots of people paid to see the pictures; mature-themed titles that were released despite well-publicized problems with the PCA, such as *The Moon Is Blue* (Otto Preminger, 1953) and *The Man with the Golden Arm* (Preminger, 1955), were top-twenty films. As the success of such films revealed, for a more modern film industry to work profitably, the revamped studios needed more modern films. The filmgoing public was ready for a new American cinema, and a new Hollywood emerged to deliver it.

INDUSTRY SHAKEUP

Between 1955 and 1967, Hollywood was in transition. At the time it was far clearer what the industry was leaving behind than where it might end up. There was no grand design for this transition. Instead, there was a series of stops and starts, a series of moves updating, modernizing, and transforming the movie industry with regard to its relationship with, first, parallel media (like television) and other entertainment- or leisure-related businesses and venues (the music and recording industries and, amusement parks, for example); second, the larger U.S. economy, which was moving inexorably toward greater centralization and conglomeration; and third, the American filmgoing audience, who made clear its interest in films with more mature content just as it expressed its disinterest in what the studios had recently been churning out. A new Hollywood was out there to be found or, more accurately, to be made. But the studios still had some ground to cover before they could get there.

Movies versus Television

By 1956, MGM, 20th Century–Fox, Warner Bros., and the Walt Disney Company had introduced studio shows on network television. The shows put to use otherwise dormant production space on the studio lots and, moreover, helped increase the studios' visibility. All four shows carried their studios' name in the title—*M-G-M Parade* (ABC), *The 20th Century–Fox Hour* (CBS), *Warner Brothers Presents* (ABC), and *Disneyland*, later retitled *Walt Disney Presents* (ABC)—and all four used the broadcast time to promote forthcoming studio features. The studio-network relationship was mutually beneficial: the TV networks needed the studios as badly as the studios needed them. What the networks needed more than anything else was "product," something someone else produced that might fill time, sell a certain sponsor's products, and increase audience interest in the network's overall programming slate.

Disney's move into television was especially significant. After a devastating animators' strike in 1941 and labor problems during the blacklist era, Walt Disney endeavored to diversify, a move that proved timely. In 1952, Disney asked his brother

"Uncle Walt" got into the TV and theme-park business in the mid-1950s, having lost interest in filmmaking after an animators' strike crippled his studio in 1941. By integrating his film business with parallel entertainment and leisure industries, Disney proved to be a visionary.

Roy, who managed the studio's finances, to help him persuade the corporate board to finance a new sort of amusement park: Disneyland. Roy was against the project from the start and came back from his meeting with the board with just $10,000 in seed money. In order to finance the building of the park without the support of his brother and the recalcitrant board of directors, Disney formed a strategic alliance with the smallest of the three TV networks, ABC. The network agreed to back the Disneyland amusement-park project in exchange for a percentage of its future profits and a weekly television show. The ABC-Disney deal was one of the first industry agreements to cross media lines. The establishment of connections among three entertainment venues—film, television, and an amusement park—suggested to the studios that potentially lucrative ancillary markets, or at least ancillary venues, could be exploited even when box-office revenues were in decline.

The American family: Mom, Dad, two kids, and a TV set.

Having lost their first-run theaters, the studios also found in television an opportunity to contract for subsequent (second-run) screenings of their movies. After 1955, movies were offered to the networks under fairly simple licensing or sales agreements. But soon enough the TV contracts were complicated by shifting labor agreements, especially between newly independent movie stars and the studios competing for their services.

In the post–*Paramount* decision Hollywood, stars became more important than ever to a film's and, by extension, a studio's success. To attract stars (who were no longer necessarily under contract to a specific studio), studios negotiated deals with talent agents, who, to boost their clients' (and their own) compensation packages, demanded "points" (a percentage of the profits). Once sales of films to television became a matter of routine, residual schedules (payment schedules for every TV screening of a given film) were drawn up so that stars would get a piece of the TV action as well.

The obligation to pay residuals seemed at first to be bad news for the studios. But film executives soon figured out that prospective residual schedules could be used as a negotiating tool, a means of securing and compensating talent and financing and developing motion pictures. The promise of future residuals—and, moreover, the promise of

a TV sale—provided the studios with a means of deferring payment to stars and guaranteeing revenue for themselves at the end of a film's initial run, revenue that might be used to pay back a production loan or finance a new motion picture.

By the time television had matured enough to provide significant competition to the studios, the two media were inextricably and complexly integrated. Today virtually all the studios have TV divisions; their products move freely and fluidly from one media to another, making money for the parent company at every stop along the way. Just as the *Paramount* decision compelled the studios to dismantle their system of distributing their product to their urban first-run theaters, it drove them to establish new sorts of synergies and to view the larger entertainment marketplace in much the same way they had viewed the movie business before 1948. Studio executives have always had synergy on their minds. But after the *Paramount* decision they traded one sort of synergy (vertical integration of production, distribution, and exhibition) for another.

The Big Hollywood Buyout

Stripped of their flagship theaters and compelled to develop complex new ways in which to finance films and establish synergistic relationships with other media, studio ownership quickly came to realize that the day-to-day business of making and distributing motion pictures required more capital than they had on hand and a more expansive corporate vision than management seemed able to muster. Though industry revenues were down, the value of the studios, especially to large corporations endeavoring to diversify, was fairly high. The studios' film libraries, previously thought of as just inventory, could be exploited on television. And studio lots became valuable as real estate, especially in booming Los Angeles. The studios had little or no debt, since films were routinely financed with short-term loans that were repaid out of film revenues. And thanks to the House Committee on Un-American Activities and the *Paramount* decision, studio stock prices were down. Companies interested in expanding their holdings into the movie business were presented with a rare opportunity to purchase huge blocks of undervalued stock during an economic boom.

The first in what became a series of corporate buyouts involved MCA–Revue Productions and Universal. MCA, originally the Music Corporation of America, was founded by Jules Stein in the 1920s as a talent agency. In the early 1940s, largely under the direction of Stein's ambitious protégé, Lew Wasserman, MCA began representing movie stars. By 1950, Wasserman had so much talent under contract to MCA that the agency resembled a classical-era Hollywood studio. Fully grasping the potential of MCA's talent pool, Wasserman began packaging films. He developed movie projects from scripts written by MCA clients, attached MCA talent to them, and sold the fully developed and cast films to the highest bidder. For his trouble, Wasserman got a percentage of every MCA client's pay and, in the case of MCA's movie stars, a percentage of the profits of the MCA-packaged film.

Just as Wasserman and MCA were emerging as forces to be reckoned with in Hollywood, Universal chief executive officer J. Cheever Cowdin retired, and a struggle for control of the publicly traded studio began. Victory came fast to Decca Records president Milton Rackmil, who planned from the start to institute synergies between Decca's holdings in the music industry and Universal's interests in film. But Decca's control over

the studio was short-lived. In February 1959, MCA bought Universal City, the studio facility formerly owned by Universal Pictures, ostensibly to streamline television production for the MCA subsidiary Revue Productions. At the time, Revue produced approximately a third of the prime-time lineup for the National Broadcasting Company (NBC). These TV shows for the most part featured MCA talent, an arrangement that proved quite profitable for the agency. The MCA purchase of Universal City was a mixed blessing for Decca and Universal Pictures. The deal brought much-needed cash to support studio production, but it made Universal Pictures vulnerable to a takeover and, moreover, dependent on MCA for its production facilities. MCA bought out Decca in 1962, and in its first year in control the former talent agency sported record profits. Under Wasserman's direction, MCA/Universal became a film and television production plant, a motion-picture distribution company, a familiar trademark, and most important, a multimedia company, one that fully exploited a larger vision of the entertainment marketplace.

The MCA/Universal deal set in motion a tide of conglomerate investment in Hollywood. Gulf and Western Industries bought Paramount in 1966. Charles Bluhdorn, the irascible chief executive officer of Gulf and Western, established relationships among his company's various entertainment divisions: film, television, book and magazine publishing, and professional athletics. But unlike MCA's holdings, the bulk of Gulf and Western's were in nonentertainment industries. Through Gulf and Western's first few years in operation, its entertainment companies accounted for only 11 percent of the multinational corporation's gross revenues.

Both Warner Bros. and United Artists turned to conglomerate ownership in 1967. Warner Bros. first merged with Seven Arts Productions (a Canadian film and television distributor) and then was bought out by the parking-lot and car-rental conglomerate Kinney National Service to form Warner Communications. United Artists followed suit, selling out in 1967 to a nonentertainment-industry conglomerate, TransAmerica Corporation, a San Francisco–based insurance company.

Lew Wasserman in a picture taken in the 1950s, when he helped engineer MCA's acquisition of Universal.

The first step taken by the new studio owners was a radical one: they got out of the business of producing movies. With an eye toward downsizing their workforce, streamlining their operation, and limiting their exposure to investment loss, the conglomerate-owned studios focused their attention and capital on distribution, the most profitable and least risky aspect of the movie business. To modernize the industry, the new corporate owners instituted a variety of business practices that were consistent with their nonfilm holdings: a dependence on market research and the development of fewer, more predictably profitable product lines (blockbuster-style films), which exploited relationships with various other conglomerate holdings (merchandising, publishing, television). When Americans finally got back into the habit of going to the movies in the 1970s, the top four studios in terms of market share were Warner Bros., Paramount, Universal, and United Artists, the same four companies that first sought support from conglomerate ownership.

In 1966 the Production Code Administration approved 168 feature films, of which 149 were released by a major studio, evidence of the studios' persistent dominance of the commercial marketplace. But those films were by and large "negative pickups," films made independently and then picked up by a studio for distribution. Of the 149 features distributed by a major studio in 1966, only 38 were produced (that is, directly financed) by a major studio. In 1967 just 43 out of 206 films submitted to the PCA were produced by members of the Motion Picture Association of America. But although the studios produced just 20 percent of the films in general release, they distributed all but 9 (or 96 percent).

In the mid-1960s a new trend emerged involving pickups of European-made films. Popular 1967 releases—such as the 007-spoof *Casino Royale* (John Huston and others), the gritty war picture *The Dirty Dozen* (Robert Aldrich), the bloated musical *Doctor Dolittle* (Richard Fleischer), the Clint Eastwood spaghetti westerns *For a Few Dollars More* and *The Good, the Bad and the Ugly* (both Sergio Leone), the melodrama *A Man and a Woman* (Claude Lelouch), the World War II crime film *The Night of the Generals* (Anatole Litvak), and the James Bond feature *You Only Live Twice* (Lewis Gilbert)—were produced overseas and then distributed in the United States by an American studio. Exactly what might constitute "American cinema" was suddenly subject to debate.

The top four films at the box office in 1967— *The Dirty Dozen, You Only Live Twice, Casino Royale,* and the historical epic *A Man for All Seasons* (Fred Zinnemann, which won Academy Awards for Best Picture, Directing, and Actor for 1966)—were all produced overseas. Two more British imports, the swinging London melodrama *Georgy Girl* (Silvio Narizzano, 1966) and the British interracial teen pic *To Sir, with Love* (James Clavell, 1967) were also listed among the year's top-ten box-office films. But although the European pickups did well with American audiences and won acclaim from newspaper reviewers, they raised problems with the industry's long-standing content watchdog, the PCA. Of the six hit films from 1967 that were made overseas, only one—the prestige title *A Man for All Seasons*—had an easy time with the PCA. As the studios' dependence on foreign-made films increased, their problems with the PCA also increased. In an otherwise dead box office, mature-themed films did fairly well. And the studios could no longer afford to ignore the trend.

Revisiting and Revising the Production Code

Self-regulation (the industry-wide adherence to the PCA's restrictive production code) worked only so long as all the studios agreed to play by the same rules and make the same sorts of films. But when box-office revenues continued to slump through the first few years of the 1950s, it was inevitable that someone would break ranks and try to make some money with a movie that defied the PCA.

The first successful challenge to the PCA was mounted by Otto Preminger, a Hollywood player who, quite like his eastern European predecessor Erich von Stroheim, had a reputation for dogged commitment (at all costs) to the integrity of his films. Through the 1940s and early 1950s, Preminger directed a series of smart, commercial pictures, including the early film noir *Laura* (1944), the costume drama *Forever Amber* (1947, co-directed by John M. Stahl), and the crime film *Angel Face* (1952).

Then, late in 1952, Preminger made news when he purchased an option on a popular risqué Broadway comedy, *The Moon Is Blue,* a play about a young woman's misadventures with two eligible bachelors. Preminger quickly packaged the project with A talent, signing the stars William Holden and David Niven. When news of the project reached the PCA, its director informed Preminger that he had seen *The Moon Is Blue* onstage and that the play was unacceptable from start to finish. Preminger went ahead and developed the project anyway, eventually signing a distribution deal with United Artists.

In April 1953, Preminger completed the film. United Artists submitted it to the PCA and, as expected, was denied a seal of approval. To make clear its dissatisfaction with the PCA decision, United Artists officially (albeit temporarily) quit the MPAA rather than pay a fine for releasing a film without a PCA seal.

The biggest concern for United Artists when it agreed to distribute *The Moon Is Blue* was not the Catholic Legion of Decency or local censorship boards but the theater owners. The studio had no way of knowing whether exhibitors would be willing to book a studio film that lacked a PCA seal. To the studio's surprise, they were. *The Moon Is Blue* grossed over $4 million in its initial release, ranked thirteenth overall for 1953 (tied with the Dean Martin–Jerry Lewis feature *The Caddy,* directed by Norman Taurog) and received three Academy Award nominations.

In 1955, Preminger took on the PCA once again when he optioned Nelson Algren's well-known Hollywood novel about reckless ambition and drug addiction, *The Man with the Golden Arm.* Geoffrey Shurlock, who had just replaced Joseph Breen at the PCA, was more sympathetic than his predecessor to the studios' collective impatience with the continuing box-office slide, but *The Man with the Golden Arm* posed so many code violations that he strongly advised that Preminger not make the film. Having enjoyed success releasing *The Moon Is Blue* without a PCA seal, Preminger went ahead and developed the film anyway. To protect the project, he went after A talent and scored a major coup when he cast Frank Sinatra to play Algren's luckless hero Frankie Machine. Sinatra's participation got United Artists on board again, and Preminger

The producer-director Otto Preminger (photographed in 1956) made two films—*The Moon Is Blue* (1953) and *The Man with the Golden Arm* (1955)—that succeeded at the box office despite running afoul of the Production Code Administration. Preminger's success proved to be the beginning of the end for the old censorship apparatus of the Motion Picture Association of America.

went about making his second film in three years in defiance of the PCA.

On December 14, 1955, United Artists released *The Man with the Golden Arm* without a PCA seal. Theater owners lined up to screen the film, and Sinatra received an Academy Award nomination. (He lost to Ernest Borgnine, who won for his role in *Marty,* directed by Delbert Mann.) Like *The Moon Is Blue, The Man with the Golden Arm* was a top-twenty box-office hit, the second mature-themed, mature-content film released without a PCA seal to find success in a depressed marketplace.

In 1956, due in large measure to the success of Preminger's two films, Shurlock, with the support of MPAA president Eric Johnston, announced a change in the code, the first material change in over twenty years. Failing to recognize the anticlimax, Shurlock proudly declared that under the revised

Two wealthy bachelors (William Holden, *left*, and David Niven, *right*) and one "professional virgin" (Maggie McNamara) spend an eventful evening together in the code-busting romantic comedy *The Moon Is Blue* (Otto Preminger, 1953).

code the words *hell* and *damn* could be uttered, though not in excess and only when relevant. That he viewed such a minor change as significant served only to highlight the PCA's obsolescence.

In 1956 two more controversial stage properties were optioned, again raising problems for the PCA: Robert Anderson's *Tea and Sympathy*, which presents frankly a young boy's sexual coming of age, and Tennessee Williams's gothic melodrama *27 Wagons Full of Cotton* (later retitled *Baby Doll*), the story of a child bride (Carroll Baker) and the struggle over her virtue, such as it is, between her white trash husband (Karl Malden) and an Italian immigrant (Eli Wallach). Shurlock was familiar with both plays and cautioned against their production.

Tea and Sympathy (directed by Vincente Minnelli) reached American screens accompanied by

the movie-poster tagline "Where does a woman's sympathy leave off—and her indiscretion begin?" The advertising slogan made reference to the film's climactic scene, in which a boys'-school house mistress, Laura Reynolds (Deborah Kerr), seduces a young man, Tom (John Kerr, no relation to Deborah), whose life at the private school is made intolerable by bullies (including Laura's husband) who call him "sister boy." Laura helps Tom discover his heterosexuality in the only way she knows how and punctuates the seduction with a classic line: "Years from now when you talk about this—and you will—be kind." Onstage that is the last line of the play, leaving open the short- and long-term consequences of the seduction.

MGM, which had contracted to distribute *Tea and Sympathy*, was unwilling to take the route

"Where does a woman's sympathy leave off—and her indiscretion begin?" We're about to find out as the boys'-school house mother Laura Reynolds (Deborah Kerr) endeavors to "cure" Tom (John Kerr, no relation to Deborah) of his sexual confusion in Vincente Minnelli's *Tea and Sympathy* (1956). Though the screen adaptation of Robert Anderson's play was far tamer than what audiences in 1956 got to see in the stage version, *Tea and Sympathy* became the third mature-themed studio film in three years to make the top-twenty box-office list.

United Artists had taken with the two Preminger films, but it appreciated that it could not cut the scene between the house mistress and the young man, given the press coverage of the play and the film production. Rather than release the film without a PCA seal, MGM struggled to effect a compromise. To please the PCA and keep the seduction scene, MGM added two new scenes, one at the beginning, the other at the end. Thus the film begins and ends with Tom's return to the school, considerably older and considerably wiser. He is no longer a "sister boy," but he has never gotten over his afternoon with Laura, whose life has been all but ruined by her infidelity. Whereas the play ends with the boy's manhood firmly established, the film ends with a reminder that infidelity is bad.

Of all the code-challenging films released in the mid-1950's, *Baby Doll* proved to be the most notorious. But contrary to popular assumption, it bore a PCA seal. Its plot, which posed a problem for the PCA at every turn, regards a sexually ambivalent southern child bride, Baby Doll (Carroll Baker), who exchanges her wedding vows for a promise from her much-older husband that he will not try to have sex with her until she turns twenty. Baby Doll spends most of her time supine in a crib, dressed in a flimsy nightgown and sucking her thumb. (The Baby Doll nightie took the nation by storm. That it became a popular fashion item irked the PCA, which often vetoed such costumes for fear that viewers might want to purchase similarly revealing outfits for themselves.) Baby Doll's virginity and thus her sexuality are the focus of the

The film- and recording-industry superstar Frank Sinatra as the luckless Frankie Machine in Otto Preminger's adaptation of Nelson Algren's *The Man with the Golden Arm* (1955). Though the film was released without a production code seal—the Production Code Administration objected to the film's realistic depiction of the 1950s illicit drug scene—theater owners lined up to screen it.

Carroll Baker in Elia Kazan's code-defying southern gothic *Baby Doll* (1956).

film, and the American South is depicted as a hellish place inhabited by cretinous, sex-starved, larcenous white trash. The code had guidelines prohibiting such negative portrayals of regional America, but the film blithely ignored them.

The PCA had tried to get Elia Kazan, the film's director, and his screenwriter, Tennessee Williams, to make changes to the script to better suit its guidelines. Shurlock wanted a happier ending, or at least an ending in which the good are rewarded and the bad are punished. Williams pointed out that everyone in the film is bad and then proposed an ending in which a typhoon rolls into town and kills everyone. It was meant as a joke, but Shurlock thought it was a good idea.

Baby Doll got a PCA seal not because it in any way satisfied the code but because the MPAA owed Kazan, its most famous friendly witness during the HUAC hearings, and Williams, who had been so cooperative several years earlier when the PCA asked him to change the ending of the screen version of *A Streetcar Named Desire* (Kazan, 1951). In addition, the PCA appreciated the futility of denying the film a seal. Warner Bros. never budged in its commitment to release the picture, and the promise of another Kazan-Williams collaboration made the project difficult to stop. There was so much public interest in the project and so much publicity attending its production (and the various struggles with the PCA) that the film was bound to find plenty of takers among the still-starved theater owners nationwide, code seal or not.

Movie Censorship and the Courts

Just as the PCA seemed to lose control over production in the late 1950s, a series of court cases undermined the autonomy and authority of the state and local film-censorship boards that had made the PCA necessary in the 1930s. Foremost among these cases was *Burstyn v. Wilson* (the so-called *Miracle* case). The film at issue was Roberto Rossellini's *The Miracle*. The New York State Board of Regents had found blasphemous the film's story (about a peasant woman who believes she is the Virgin Mary), seized the print, and banned all screenings. The U.S. Supreme Court overturned the ban in 1952, finding the state board's criteria "overbroad and vague." In so doing, the Court for the first time since the 1915 *Mutual* case examined the subject of First Amendment protection for films. In the *Mutual* case the Court had denied Hollywood such protections. In the *Miracle* case the Court reversed that precedent and thus undermined not only the New York State censorship board but other local censorship boards as well. Following the precedent set in the *Miracle* case, the U.S. Supreme Court reversed specific bans by state censorship boards in the cases of *Gelling v. State of Texas* (also in 1952), *Superior Films v. Department of Education of Ohio* (1954), and most significantly, *Jacobellis v. Ohio* (1964). As local boards became obsolete, so did the production code.

The ban on screen nudity ended in 1957 with *Excelsior Pictures v. Regents of the University of New York State,* a New York State Court of Appeals decision involving a local ban on *Garden of Eden* (Max Nosseck, 1954), a simply ridiculous nudist-colony picture. *Garden of Eden* begins with a fairly pat postwar morality tale: an aggrieved father has become coldhearted due to the death of his son in the war and takes out his anger on his daughter-in-law and her daughter, his only grandchild. Things get so bad that mother and child leave for Florida. En route they take a detour and make a wrong turn, and then their car breaks down miles from anywhere. They are rescued by a good samaritan who takes them to a bungalow park called

Russ Meyer's *The Immoral Mr. Teas* (1959) was among the first feature-length films to give prominence to on-screen nudity. The film tells the story of a man (Bill Teas, *left*) who, after a conk on the head, can mentally undress the women he meets, including the waitress at the local diner (Ann Peters).

Garden of Eden. The Garden of Eden is a nudist camp, and mother and daughter are left inside its gates to wait for a car part to arrive. The woman discovers that she rather likes being nude and likes it when other folks are nude, too. The "story" is accompanied by frequent scenes of nude volleyball, nude sunbathing, even nude water-skiing. Of the 67 minutes of running time, about 20 minutes are devoted to the depiction of nudists enjoying their alternative lifestyle.

Justice Charles Desmond of the New York State Court of Appeals overturned the state ban on the film, ruling that nudity on screen is not in itself obscene. His opinion in the case is amusing but nonetheless significant: "There is nothing sexy or suggestive about [*Garden of Eden*] . . . nudists are shown as wholesome, happy people in family groups practicing their sincere but misguided theory that clothing, when climate does not require it, is deleterious to mental health, by promoting an attitude of shame with regard to the natural attributes and functions of the human body."

The *Exclesior* decision set a precedent regarding on-screen nudity, establishing that the depiction of naked people is not per se obscene. Independent exploitation filmmakers working outside the studio system appreciated the significance of the decision and moved quickly to incorporate nudity into their films. Russ Meyer's *The Immoral Mr. Teas* (1959) was among the first feature-length films to give prominence to on-screen nudity. It tells the story of a man who, having been conked on the head, can mentally undress any woman he meets. Images of undressed women are accompanied by a silly pseudo-documentary voice-over and crude sound effects. *The Immoral Mr. Teas* spawned a brief wave of explicit exploitation films in a variety of colorfully termed new genres: nudie cuties, suggestive, often light comedy pictures with nudity but no touching, with titles like *Mr. Peter's Pets* (Dick Crane, 1962) and *Adam Lost His Apple* (Earl Wainwright, 1965); roughies, which depict antisocial behavior as well as nudity—for example

The Defilers (David F. Friedman and Lee Frost, 1965) and *The Degenerates* (Andy Milligan, 1967); kinkies, with appropriate and revealing titles like *Olga's House of Shame* (Joseph P. Mawra, 1964) and *Love Camp 7* (Frost, 1969); and ghoulies, which merge kink with gruesome horror, as in *Satan's Bed* (Michael Findlay and others, 1965, featuring Yoko Ono) and *Mantis in Lace* (William Rotsler, 1968).

Jack Valenti and the New MPAA

The Motion Picture Production Code that took shape in the early 1930s was designed to make every film suitable for viewers of every age. In the 1930s the studios could afford to make one product for everyone. But as the leisure and entertainment industries changed in the 1950s, the studios began to appreciate that certain films could be profitably marketed to specific segments of the audience. The increasingly well educated adult audience and the burgeoning adolescent audience were easy markets to identify but difficult to serve, given the strict guidelines of the production code. As the success of Preminger's non-PCA-approved films proved, too much money was at stake for the studios to abide by production guidelines that prevented them from exploiting such potentially lucrative target markets.

Talk of a new film rating system that might better acknowledge the ethnic, regional, and generational diversity of the filmgoing public can be found in industry trade magazines as early as 1963, when the MPAA began courting the legendary trial attorney Louis Nizer in the hopes that he would preside over the development and implementation of a new production code. Three years later, when the MPAA made its first decisive move toward changing the code, Universal president Lew Wasserman championed Jack Valenti, an insider in President Lyndon Johnson's White House, over Nizer because Valenti had important Washington contacts and was by trade an advertising man. When Valenti was named president of the MPAA in 1966, Nizer was installed as the organization's special counsel.

The studios had a test case waiting for Valenti and Nizer, a serious, important, potentially very popular adult-themed movie: the Warner Bros. picture *Who's Afraid of Virginia Woolf?* (Mike Nichols, 1966). The PCA had advised Warner Bros. against making the film, having perused the screenplay,

which is faithfully based on a serious, critically acclaimed stage play by Edward Albee. The film went into production in defiance of the PCA or, more likely, in anticipation of a change.

Valenti was by all accounts uncomfortable with the task of censoring a work considered as important as *Who's Afraid of Virginia Woolf?* After a three-hour meeting with executives at Warner Bros., he hashed out a deal: the word *screw* was deleted from the script, and the phrase "hump the hostess" stayed in. Valenti claimed at the time that the process left him uneasy, that it seemed wrong that grown men should be sitting around analyzing every word in a screenplay.

The MPAA had hired Valenti to fix the box-office problem and modernize the PCA. To Valenti's credit he understood that both matters could be addressed at once—that the problems were intrinsically related. After working out a compromise on *Who's Afraid of Virginia Woolf?*, Valenti endeavored to figure out a way, in the name of self-regulation, to enable the production of other mature-themed movies.

Who's Afraid of Virginia Woolf? was released with a PCA exemption. As part of the deal to secure an MPAA-sanctioned release, Warner Bros. agreed to label the film For Mature Audiences and left the task of enforcing the restriction to the nation's exhibitors. In so doing, the studio appeared responsible. But more important for Warner Bros. and for the industry as a whole, the PCA exemption offered a trial run for an age-based exhibitor-enforced regulatory system the chance to see whether a film with an age-restricted release could make money.

The studio (and, by extension, the industry) got its answer when *Who's Afraid of Virginia Woolf?* ranked third on the box-office list in 1966, behind two other mature-themed pictures, the James Bond film *Thunderball* (Terence Young, 1965) and the historical epic *Doctor Zhivago* (David Lean, 1965). By the end of 1966, *Who's Afraid of Virginia Woolf?* had produced over $10 million in box-office

In 1966, Jack Valenti was named president of the Motion Picture Association of America and was charged with modernizing the industry's production code. By the fall of 1968, he had done just that, establishing the voluntary movie rating system, which has been in use ever since.

For mature audiences only: Martha (Elizabeth Taylor) and George (Richard Burton), the dysfunctional academic couple in Mike Nichols's adaptation of Edward Albee's play *Who's Afraid of Virginia Woolf?* (1966).

revenues. Despite Valenti's public assurances that the code exemption was not a precedent, the success of *Who's Afraid of Virginia Woolf?* prompted the production of many more adult-oriented dramas.

Six films released in 1966 received the MPAA's new For Mature Audiences designation: the 007 spoof *Deadlier Than the Male* (Ralph Thomas); *A Funny Thing Happened on the Way to the Forum* (Richard Lester), a zany comedy set in ancient Rome (featuring silent-era star Buster Keaton in his last significant role); the swinging sexual-revolution melodrama *Georgy Girl;* the Civil War picture *A Time for Killing* (Phil Karlson and Roger Corman); *Rage* (Gilberto Gazcón), which tells the story of a man bitten by a rabid dog in the desert; and the rape-revenge western *Welcome to Hard*

Times (Burt Kennedy), based on a novel by E. L. Doctorow. *Who's Afraid of Virginia Woolf?* got its own designation; on all advertising for the picture, an MPAA legend read (in capital letters): NO PERSON UNDER 18 ADMITTED UNLESS ACCOMPANIED BY A PARENT.

The number of films designated For Mature Audiences in 1967 rose dramatically over that for the previous year, from six to forty-four. Among the 1967 mature-themed pictures were the romantic melodrama *A Man and a Woman;* the true-crime blockbuster *In Cold Blood* (Richard Brooks); the revenge-fantasy film noir *Point Blank* (John Boorman); the Hollywood soap opera *Valley of the Dolls* (Mark Robson); the spaghetti western *The Good, the Bad and the Ugly;* the race-reconciliation film and winner of the Best Picture Oscar *In the Heat of the*

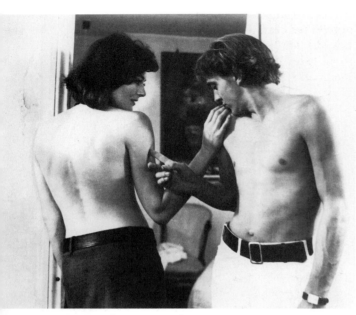

Vanessa Redgrave and David Hemmings in Michelangelo Antonioni's *Blow-Up* (1966), the film that made the rating system not only possible but necessary.

Night (Norman Jewison); the theatrical adaptation *Marat/Sade* (Peter Brook); and the Elizabeth Taylor star vehicle about life on a military base, *Reflections in a Golden Eye* (Huston). A number of films were deemed unacceptable by the MPAA and were never resubmitted for approval. *Belle de jour* (Luis Buñuel, 1967), the story of a bored middle-class woman who moonlights as a prostitute; *I Love You, Alice B. Tok-las* (Hy Averback, 1968), a generation-gap comedy about a middle-aged square (Peter Sellers) who falls for a hippie and decides to drop out; the sexual-revolution melodrama *Petulia* (Lester, 1968), starring George C. Scott and Julie Christie; *Rosemary's Baby* (Roman Polanski, 1968), with its story of the devil's spawn (and its fairly graphic rape scene); and *The Fixer* (John Frankenheimer, 1968), a drama set in the Soviet Union that was scripted by Dalton Trumbo, based on a novel by Bernard Malamud—all were temporarily shelved in anticipation of the new code.

From November 1967 to November 1968, the twelve months preceding the adoption of the 1968 MPAA voluntary film rating system (discussed at length in Chapter 7), roughly 60 percent of the films released by the studios carried the For Mature Audiences tag. But even with the newly available and newly popular For Mature Audiences

designation, some key films were denied a production seal. The most significant of those films—and the final straw for the old MPAA code—was, of all things, a foreign-made art film, Michelangelo Antonioni's *Blow-Up*, an already widely talked about picture contracted for release in the United States by MGM.

When MGM submitted *Blow-Up* to the PCA, it was denied a seal. The controversy that followed spelled the end for the censorship board. The problem with *Blow-Up* was the single nonnarrative and thus (to the censors' eyes, at least) nonessential sequence that featured full-frontal female nudity. As far as Shurlock and Valenti were concerned, the only way for the film to get a seal, even with the For Mature Audiences designation, was to cut the scene. But Antonioni's contract with MGM didn't allow the studio to alter the film to suit the PCA. By the time MGM submitted *Blow-Up* for PCA review, it had already been released to box-office success and critical acclaim in Europe. It was Great Britain's official entry at Cannes and won the festival's Grand Prix. It is difficult to believe that MGM executives were taken by surprise when the PCA refused to grant the picture a production seal, but it is just as difficult to believe that they contracted to release the film (which they knew they couldn't cut) without a strategy for defying or subverting the PCA.

When Shurlock refused to grant the picture a PCA seal and Valenti backed him up, MGM made its move. In order to avoid an MPAA fine and possible sanction—to get the picture out without quitting the MPAA—the studio distributed *Blow-Up* under the banner of its wholly owned and operated subsidiary, Premier Films, which was not a member of the MPAA. MGM's release strategy was a calculated gamble: MGM executives did not know how the other studios would react or how future MGM films might be received by the PCA board as a consequence of their decision to subvert the MPAA's authority. Distribution executives at MGM also appreciated that it might be difficult to contract with venues to exhibit *Blow-Up*, especially if the film did not perform well in its initial urban run.

MGM's gamble paid off, however. *Blow-Up* opened to terrific reviews, the opening-week numbers were strong, and the film eventually grossed seven times the studio's investment. MGM's success with *Blow-Up* exposed the growing irrelevance of the old code. The PCA had been set up to regulate production, but by 1967 the studios had pretty much gotten out of the production business. The PCA advised the studios of potential problems with regional censorship boards, but—again by 1967—the Supreme Court had rendered local board decisions moot. Within months of *Blow-Up*'s release, Valenti began hawking his new age-based rating system, a regulatory apparatus designed to enable the distribution and exhibition of a new generation of films for a new generation of filmgoers.

GENRE

Genre films remained central to studio release slates well into the second decade after World War II. Westerns in particular were popular. In an era that seemed to emphasize conformity, the iconoclastic western hero proved to be a seductive archetype. Along with a revival of the western came the emergence of a new genre, one targeted at an audience demographic that the studios coveted more than any other: the American teenager.

The Western

While the studios suffered through a box-office slump from 1947 to 1968, the western proved to be a consistently if modestly bankable genre. Notable westerns of this era include King Vidor's racy family melodrama *Duel in the Sun* (1947); Howard Hawks's *Red River* (1948), starring the unlikely team of the rugged icon of movies westerns John Wayne and the sensitive Method actor Montgomery Clift; the well-intentioned cowboys-and-Indians détente film *Broken Arrow* (Delmer Daves, 1950); *Winchester '73* (Anthony Mann, 1950), a film ostensibly about a man's love for his gun; the blacklist parable *High Noon* (Fred Zinnemann, 1952), written by the eventually blacklisted Carl Foreman, with Gary Cooper as a marshal who fights to save a town that will not fight to save itself; *Shane* (George Stevens, 1953), starring Alan Ladd as a mysterious gunslinger who descends from the Grand Tetons to prevent a range war; the truly strange *Johnny Guitar* (Nicholas Ray, 1954),

Gary Cooper as Marshal Will Kane fighting to save a town that can't be bothered to save itself in Fred Zinnemann's *High Noon* (1952).

another anti-blacklist parable, which ends w gunfight between two women (Joan Crawford Mercedes McCambridge); the scenic James Stewart cattle-drive picture *The Far Country* (Anthony Mann, 1954); the star-studded *Gunfight at the O.K. Corral* (John Sturges, 1957), one of many films focusing on the life and times of the legendary lawman Wyatt Earp in Tombstone, Arizona; *Rio Bravo* (Hawks, 1959), co-starring John Wayne, the singer Dean Martin, and the pop-music and TV star Ricky Nelson as an unlikely trio teamed against local bad guys bent on engineering a jailbreak; *The Alamo* (1960), a revisionist historical reenactment directed by John Wayne, who also stars as Davy Crockett; the omnibus western *How the West Was Won* (John Ford, Henry Hathaway, George Marshall, and Richard Thorpe, 1962); *Cat Ballou* (Elliot Silverstein, 1965), a parody that won an Oscar for Lee Marvin in a dual role as a ruthless killer and an alcoholic ex-gunfighter; and the modern mercenary western *The Professionals* (Richard Brooks, 1966).

Westerns depend on certain thematic oppositions: progress versus nostalgia, civilization versus the wilderness, violence versus idealism, the male bond (which idealizes loyalty and fraternity) versus the male ideal of isolation. Western narratives

offer a world in which right and wrong are discernible and justice can be had. The genre is by turn antimodern and hypermasculine. At stake in many western films is the relationship between the individual and society, an issue of particular relevance in the postwar years. Men returning from World War II found their country profoundly changed, and many struggled to adapt to the daily grind of middle-class American life. In movie westerns male filmgoers found a nostalgic tribute to a bygone era in which matters were solved according to a strict masculine code.

Though right (and might) mostly win out in movie westerns, the iconoclastic hero struggles and often fails to conform to modern society, much as so many men in the audience had struggled and perhaps failed to adapt to postwar American society. If, as many men at the time argued, postwar America had become feminized and the nine-to-five work routine had become dehumanizing and emasculating, westerns offered an escape and a welcome, if nostalgic, alternative. The western heroes, strong silent types like John Wayne and Gary Cooper, stood tall even as they accepted with grace the inevitability of civilization and their own irrelevance. Though set over half a century in the past, the film western was nonetheless a timely genre in the 1950s.

John Ford (*megaphone in hand*) directing the western *My Darling Clementine* (1946) on location in Monument Valley, Arizona.

John Ford and John Wayne

John Ford, without question the best-known director of movie westerns in film history, was born John Martin Feeney in 1894 in Cape Elizabeth, Maine, about as far from the west as one could get without leaving dry land. Legend has it that he was a sickly child—hardly the rugged type so idealized in his films.

John's brother Francis settled in Los Angeles before him. It was Francis who first changed his surname to Ford, apparently to protect the Feeneys of Maine from the aspersions routinely cast on families whose offspring worked in show business. Under the name Francis Ford, John's older brother acted in and directed well over one hundred short westerns. When John made his way to Los Angeles, Francis got him a job at the studio. John worked his way up through the ranks, as a gofer, then as a grip, and, briefly, as a stuntman.

Ford directed his first film, *The Tornado*, in 1917. Seven years and some fifty short films later he directed Hollywood's first important western feature, *The Iron Horse* (1924). In 1935, Ford won a Directing Oscar for *The Informer*, about the sectarian struggle between Protestants and Catholics in Northern Ireland, and made the penultimate film in the long career of the homespun comic Will Rogers, *Steamboat Round the Bend*. But it was in 1939, with *Stagecoach*, that Ford would become identified so completely with the Hollywood western and with the genre's biggest star, John Wayne, whose first big role was in that film.

Stagecoach was also Ford's first sound-era western. Shot for the most part on location in Monument Valley (in Utah and Arizona), a much-used spot in Ford's later films, *Stagecoach* tells the story of a fateful ride taken by a group of stock western characters brought together by circumstance. Several of them are more or less on the run: a prostitute with a heart of gold (Claire Trevor), a doctor who drinks too much (Thomas Mitchell), a professional gambler who has overstayed his welcome (John Carradine), and a banker (Berton Churchill) who has just embezzled money from his bank. On hand as well are a prim, proper, and pregnant young woman (Louise Platt) off to meet up with her army-officer husband, a meek easterner who wholesales alcohol (Donald Meek), a cowardly and dim-witted stagecoach driver (Andy Devine), and

the local marshal (George Bancroft), who boards the coach at the last minute, to safeguard the passengers and the cargo. The marshal's decision to join the trip is a promise of action that is paid off as the stagecoach meets with two interruptions, the first by an escaped convict named Ringo, played by John Wayne (who is introduced in a shot that marks the precise moment he became a movie star: he comes into, goes out of, and then comes back into focus as the camera, mounted on the stagecoach, dramatically moves into a close-up), and the second by a series of attacks waged by Geronimo and his band of renegade Indians.

What Ford found in the American film western was a frame for an analysis of human behavior under stress. Although there are plenty of the usual western long takes of the open prairie, offering an homage to the rapidly disappearing great American wilderness, the focus of Ford's films is men at the end of their tether, men in search of a place in a West that is changing without them.

For Ford, a devout Catholic, the western framed stories about sin and redemption. In *Stagecoach*, Ringo is a sweet kid who has been rushed into adulthood (and criminality) by Luke Plummer (Tom Tyler), a vicious sociopath who killed Ringo's father and brother. What Ringo must do in the end is risk his life to restore honor to his family name. In *My Darling Clementine* (1946), Ford retells the familiar western story of the gunfight at the O.K. Corral. But instead of focusing on the gunfight, Ford pays close attention to the family ties that bind its adversaries: the Earps and the Clantons. Whatever the reasons for their enmity—it may just be that the Clantons are a bad bunch—family loyalty can't be denied, even at the risk of a perilous gunfight.

Among the best of Ford's westerns is his most ambivalent, *The Searchers* (1956). The film stars John Wayne as Ethan Edwards, a complex character to say the least. Ethan rides into the film still wearing his Confederate army coat, though an intertitle tells us the year is 1888. Throughout the film, Edwards espouses racist opinions of American Indians, whose languages and ways he nonetheless mysteriously understands. He arrives at his brother's homestead with a lot of gold and no explanation for how he got it. Ethan's brother, Aaron (Walter Coy), is from the outset suspicious and cold. And we soon discover why. Just as Ethan is about to ride off to rescue some rustled cattle, we see Aaron's wife, Martha (Dorothy Jordon), affectionately stroke Ethan's coat. The gesture and the look of longing make clear that she and Ethan are more than sister-in-law and brother-in-law.

While Ethan and a handful of other men pursue the lost cattle, Martha, Aaron, and one of their two children are attacked and killed in an Indian raid. The rest of the film tells the story Ethan's search for Debbie (Natalie Wood), his surviving niece, who has been captured by the Indians. The search for Debbie is also a search for vengeance against the leader of the renegade Comanche band, Scar (Henry Brandon), and, more broadly, against the forces of conformity and progress that seem to doom men like Ethan to obsolescence in a less wild and woolly future.

Most westerns, including a number shot by Ford, are profoundly racist in their depiction of Native American "savages." In *Stagecoach* and in *The Searchers*, Native Americans occupy space at the periphery or just offscreen; we see nothing of their everyday lives and thus come to see them solely when they commit violent acts against white settlers. *The Searchers* seems aware of this tendency, and its awareness serves to place its racism at the core of the film.

Predictably, John Wayne's Ethan is the toughest and most capable guy around, but he is also a sociopath. At one point his prejudice so blinds his judgment that he decides to kill his niece because she's "been with" Scar.

Ethan's first confrontation with Scar is a curious affair. Spying the long, jagged scar on the Indian's face, Ethan remarks, "Plain to see how you got your name." Scar affirms that he knows who Ethan is as well. "Broad shoulders," he says in unaccented English. "You speak pretty good American for a Comanche. Someone teach you?" Ethan says, exhibiting his racism. To Ford's credit he gives Scar the payoff line: "You speak pretty good Comanche. . . . Someone teach you?" Scar's remark raises a question that viewers of the film have no doubt already asked. And Ford never offers an answer. In the end, Ethan kills Scar, rescues Debby, and returns her to the farm. But although the job is done and things have been restored to a kind of domestic normalcy, Ethan returns to the prairie wilderness he calls home, reconciled to the notion that he has no place in a civilized setting.

Most of Wayne's best westerns were made after he turned forty; indeed, his popularity as a movie star reached its apex when he was well into middle age. Wayne's name first appeared on the list of top-ten box-office stars in 1949, and he remained on the top ten for all but one year between 1949 and 1974, an amazing run that began when the actor turned forty-two and ended when he was sixty-seven. Many of his most memorable performances were as heroes on their last legs, heroes who are in the process of realizing that the West is changing without them. Though he was an iconic American celebrity throughout the postwar years, his best films were rueful, nostalgic, even existential, including four late westerns for Ford: *Fort Apache* (1948), *She Wore a Yellow Ribbon* (1949), *The Searchers*, and *The Man Who Shot Liberty Valance* (which reached American screens in 1962, when Wayne turned fifty-five). At age sixty-two, Wayne finally won an Academy Award, for his performance in *True Grit* (Hathaway, 1969), in which he plays a caricature of the rugged western hero he had made a career of playing straight. In his last great western, *The Shootist* (Don Siegel, 1976), Wayne plays a gunslinger searching for a quiet place to die. In complex ways the aging star John Wayne and the characters he played spoke profoundly to the western's essential nostalgia and the genre's focus on rugged American masculinity.

Teenagers and Teen Movies

There were of course teenagers before the end of World War II. But Hollywood, Madison Avenue, and the music industry did not discover them until 1953 or so. Hollywood's discovery of the youth audience had less to do with a savvy reading of the zeitgeist, the cultural winds of change, than with a kind of desperation in response to the continuing industry-wide slump at the box office. In the absence of a mass market, certain executives began to experiment with smaller, so-called target-market films. The teen market was particularly attractive because it seemed to transcend class and race; teenagers appeared to be curiously homogeneous and altogether hungry for a culture of their own. Many of them had disposable income and abundant leisure time. For the studios, tapping

John Wayne as the racist hero Ethan Edwards in John Ford's 1956 western *The Searchers*.

into the youth market was also an investment in the future. Getting young people into the habit of going to the movies—any movies—made good business sense.

The Wild One, Rebel without a Cause, and The Blackboard Jungle The first financially successful studio-made film that targeted the youth audience was Columbia's *The Wild One* (László Benedek, 1953), a film loosely based on then-recent headlines about a motorcycle gang that had laid siege to the rural city of Hollister, California. *The Wild One* proved to be at once sensational and documentary, a canny formula that can still be found in a number of teen films.

The movie opens with an overhead shot filmed from a distance that reveals a motorcycle gang on the outskirts of town. Given the rural setting, the gang members appear quite like Indians in a movie western, poised on the horizon to lay waste to this or any other such lonely, peaceful outpost. The film soon makes clear, however, that these marauders are not from some historic or mythic past but are instead American teenagers—disaffected, disillusioned, and out of control.

The opening disclaimer ("It's up to you to prevent this from happening elsewhere") places the film firmly in the message-movie mold, a trope that would mark two more big teen films the following year. But the ripped-from-the-headlines opening gambit also reminded viewers that the sensational events in the film had actually happened someplace quite like the place depicted in the film and warned that unless something was done, it might happen again—in a place closer to the town or city in which the folks in the audience lived.

Johnny (Marlon Brando), the gang's reluctant leader, is introduced on his bike in the opening scene, in a low-angle close-up. He is an inarticulate but nonetheless charismatic villain, and this first image makes clear that he's unlike anyone else in the film. He is, two years before the term was coined in a famous film title, a rebel without a cause. When asked what he's rebelling against, Johnny responds cryptically: "Whaddya got?" It is the most memorable line in the film because audiences find it cool. But as a plot point, it simply denotes Johnny's existential distance and his reluctance to take a stand.

Despite its embrace by the youth subculture of the mid-1950s, *The Wild One* is a politically conservative film. It is structured like a Hollywood western: the bad, uncivilized guys ride into a town populated by weak, civilized adults. The townspeople don't want trouble, and they are willing to make a deal rather than fight the young self-proclaimed outlaws. The town's policeman (Robert Keith) is weak, and he attempts to befriend the gang. His play backfires, however. The bikers see only his fear, and he becomes like the rest of the town's terrified adults, a patsy. When the local café owner sees the gang ride into town, he gleefully remarks to a co-worker, "Better put some beer on ice." But he learns the cost of doing business with outlaws when the gang trashes his establishment.

It takes a sheriff from out of town (Jay C. Flippen) to tame the wild youths. The sheriff arrests Johnny and interrogates him. "I don't get your act at all, and I don't think you do either," the sheriff says. Then, shifting gears, he goes on: "I don't know if there's good in you, but I'm willing to take a chance." As long as Johnny understands the rules, as long as he understands the rationale for conventional adult male authority, he's free to go.

As a teenager in fact or at heart, one cannot watch *The Wild One* without siding with and perhaps even identifying with Johnny. Though the narrative presents the restored adult society as somewhat wiser for having endured the biker gang's siege—few teen films have such an obvious

(left) Marlon Brando as Johnny, the leader of the motorcycle gang in László Benedek's 1953 teen film *The Wild One*. The film was based on an incident in which a gang of young toughs on bikes took over Hollister, California.

tough-love message—Brando's charisma as a star makes *The Wild One* paradoxical to the point of incoherence. Because of Brando, *The Wild One* was widely viewed as a celebration of the very outlaw behavior it purportedly condemns.

Nicholas Ray's *Rebel without a Cause* came out almost two years after *The Wild One*. The film, shot using widescreen technology and lavish Warnercolor, adheres fairly closely to the message-movie melodrama formula that was popular at the time. The message is obvious: American teenagers—even upper-middle-class white suburban teenagers—are not so different from the outlaw bikers in *The Wild One;* unwatched and misunderstood, they are completely out of control.

As *Rebel without a Cause* opens, Jim (played by the Method actor James Dean when he was twenty-four) is drunk in a gutter. It then cuts to a police station, where the film's three principals—Jim; the effeminate and sociopathic Plato (Sal Mineo), who has just shot some puppies; and Judy (Natalie Wood), whose crimes are wearing too much makeup and staying out late—rehearse their particular grievances against adult authority. Jim's tirade is especially dramatic. He tells Ray, the sensitive cop (Edward Platt), that he "just want[s] to hit someone," that he does not know what to do "except maybe die." Later in the scene, Jim adds, "If I only had one day when I didn't have to be all confused—if I felt like I belonged someplace." When his parents (Jim Backus and Ann Doran) finally arrive (from a party, of course), they argue over who's to blame for Jim's problems. Jim tunes them out and repeatedly shouts, "It doesn't matter." The following morning, when Jim and Judy meet again outside her house, they exchange worldviews. "Is this where you live?," he asks. "Who lives?" she responds.

The alienated teenager may well be a cliché in contemporary America. It is certainly a familiar stereotype in the still-popular teen film. But in 1955, when *Rebel without a Cause* was first shown in theaters, the press was only just beginning to sensationalize teen culture (teen alienation, juvenile delinquency, and rock and roll). Much as Nicholas Ray had intended, *Rebel without a Cause* was widely seen as a wake-up call, a warning to parents, even wealthy white parents living in posh suburbs, to start listening to their kids, to start taking care of them. Left to their own devices, as kids inevitably are in *Rebel without a Cause* and so many subsequent teen films, certain disaster awaits. In the course of the nearly 2-hour film, Jim gets arrested for public intoxication and being out after curfew, gets into a knife fight, gets suckered into a "chickie run" with the leader of the tough gang at school (who ends up dying when his car plummets over a cliff), hides out at an abandoned mansion, probably has sex (with Judy), gets shot at, and then gets to watch his friend (Plato) die in his arms.

Jim is handsome, charismatic, smart, and sensitive—he's James Dean, after all. But he is nevertheless lost, and what is more worrisome, he seems fascinated with death from the start of the film. This fascination is tied closely to his profound alienation, his seeming disgust at what his parents have made of the world he is poised to inherit. On a class trip to a planetarium, the elderly curator (Ian Wolfe) gives a particularly depressing presentation of the big bang. "In all the immensity of our universe," the curator concludes, "the earth will not be missed. Through the infinite reaches of space, the problems of man seem trivial and naive indeed. Man, existing alone, seems himself an episode of little consequence." To this chilling speech and the accompanying effects on the plan-

etarium ceiling, Plato adds, "What does he know about man alone?" Jim shrugs; being a teenager, even such a beautiful and smart teenager, is a lonely enterprise. Later in the film, Plato revisits the subject of the big bang, this time alluding to the contemporary anxiety over the atomic bomb. "Do you think the end of the world will come at nighttime?" he asks. Jim responds: "Uh-uh, at dawn."

The "chickie run" is the film's most memorable set piece. Jim and Buzz (Corey Allen), the popular gang leader, agree to meet on a plateau overhanging an abyss. In cars that have probably been stolen, they drive fast toward the edge of the precipice. The first to dive out of his vehicle is "chicken." The last out is the winner. It is a simple game that involves risking death to prove one is truly alive. Buzz has hated Jim from the moment he met him, in part because he is afraid Jim might rival his popularity someday. But the chickie run brings out the best in Jim and brings the two teenagers together. "That's the edge," Buzz says to Jim as they look into the abyss; "that's the end." "Yeah," Jim nods in agreement, "it certainly is." Buzz then confesses that he likes Jim, who asks an obvious question: "Why do we do this?" Buzz's quick reply speaks to the alienation shared by the

Jim (James Dean) gets some last-minute attention from Judy (Natalie Wood) before the fateful chickie run in *Rebel without a Cause* (Nicholas Ray, 1955).

teenagers in the film and in the audience: "You gotta do something, don't you?"

Also released in 1955 was a different sort of cautionary teen melodrama, *The Blackboard Jungle* (Richard Brooks, 1955), a film that convincingly focuses on juvenile delinquency in the inner city. Indeed, it was so convincing that it ran into significant censorship problems. Censors in Memphis, for example, banned the film and dubbed it the most antisocial movie they had ever seen. Before the film's initial American run, it was selected for a screening at the prestigious Venice Film Festival, but it was pulled at the last minute by the State Department, which took the position that it was anti-American.

(*left*) Jim (James Dean, *right*) faces off against "the Wheels," the popular tough kids at his new high school, in Nicholas Ray's groundbreaking teen melodrama *Rebel without a Cause* (1955). For the moment, Judy (Natalie Wood, *center*, wearing a neckerchief) runs with the Wheels.

After the flap over the festival screening, executives at MGM (which distributed the film worldwide) added a disclaimer that ran just after the opening credits:

> We in the United States are fortunate to have a school system that is a tribute to our communities and our faith in American youth. Today we are concerned with juvenile delinquency—its causes—its effects. We are especially concerned when this delinquency boils over into our schools. The scenes and incidents are fictional. However, we believe that public awareness is a first step toward a remedy for any problem. It is in this spirit and with this faith that *The Blackboard Jungle* was produced.

The disclaimer offered instructions in how to read the film, but the studio's attempt at good citizenship did not dilute the film's otherwise sensational treatment of juvenile delinquency in the urban jungle.

"Maybe kids are like the rest of the world today: mixed up, suspicious, scared." Inner-city kids get some tough love from their teacher, Mr. Dadier (Glenn Ford), in Richard Brooks's socially conscious teen melodrama *The Blackboard Jungle* (1955). Standing to the left of the frame is Dadier's principal nemesis in the film, Artie West (Vic Morrow), an unreachable juvenile delinquent who is finally subdued by a classmate wielding an American flag.

The Blackboard Jungle is a topical, progressive film. For example, the writer and director, Richard Brooks, makes reference to the Hollywood blacklist and, rather than simply sensationalize delinquency, takes the time to explain why a teenager might become a delinquent. After the teacher-hero, Mr. Dadier (Glenn Ford), is mugged by some of his students, he steadfastly refuses to name names (it's 1955 after all, and ratting in Hollywood is hardly heroic). The policeman assigned to the case (Horace McMahon) is frustrated by his silence. But he also understands why Dadier won't turn the delinquents in, why he'd rather try to save them first. "I've handled lots of problem kids," the policeman says. He continues, acknowledging the socio-economic roots of delinquency: "Kids from both sides of the tracks—they were five and six years old in the last war—father in the army, mother in a defense plant, no home life, no church life, no place to go. Maybe kids are like the rest of the world today: mixed up, suspicious, scared."

A key scene has Dadier stumble on a robbery planned by his nemesis in class, the gang leader Artie West (Vic Morrow). Dadier steps toward the street to intervene, and West grabs him, at once making sure the robbery goes off without a hitch and Dadier does not do something stupid. "You're in my classroom now," West quips, "and what I could teach you . . . You don't get to flunk out here."

At the end of the film, West pulls a knife on Dadier. But he is easily thwarted as most of the students in the class turn on him. Santini (Jamie Farr), whom the class calls "the idiot boy," delivers the final blow, ramming West in the stomach with a flagpole, from which hangs an American flag. In the film's progressive fantasy, the class is finally more interested in schoolwork than crime.

The Blackboard Jungle begins with an image of the school in a disastrous state, little more than a holding cell for the inner city's future criminal class, but ends with the progressive argument that *all* kids (with very rare exceptions) can be reached through education and that education provides the single most direct ticket out of a life of poverty and desperation.

B Movies for the Drive-in Generation After considerable successes with the teen movie in 1954 and 1955, the studios inexplicably turned their backs on the genre and did not take it seriously again until 1967. The vast majority of teen movies that reached American screens between 1956 and 1967 were produced cheaply and fast by B-movie units within the larger studios or small, independent production companies like American International Pictures (AIP), which was run by the B-movie impresarios Samuel Z. Arkoff and James Nicholson, and its chief competitor in the teen market, Allied Artists.

Notable among the B-unit studio teen films are *Rock around the Clock* (Fred Sears, 1956) and *Don't Knock the Rock* (Sears, 1956), two films from Columbia that tell the story of the disc jockey Alan Freed and his "discovery" of rock and roll; Elvis Presley pictures like *Jailhouse Rock* (Thorpe, 1957); wild-youth films like the drugs-lead-even-good-girls-to-ruin melodrama *High School Confidential!* (Jack Arnold, 1958) and *The Beat Generation* (Charles Haas, 1959), which isn't really about beatniks but instead tells the story of a psychotic teenage rapist; and cautionary melodramas about sex and single girls, like *Where the Boys Are* (Henry Levin, 1960), which begins like a sequel to *Gidget* (a sweet teen-romance picture directed by Paul Wendkos for Universal in 1959, starring Sandra Dee and James Darren) but turns dark and

ominous when a naive but promiscuous col[lege] girl named Melanie (Yvette Mimieux) gets raped. The rape offers an object lesson for all her friends, especially the bookworm Merritt (Dolores Hart), who, having read "too much" of Dr. Kinsey, nearly loses her virginity that same night. Attempting to console her friend after the rape, Merritt suggests that someday Melanie will meet a nice guy and everything will be all right. But Melanie knows better. "Oh, some nice boy," she cries out, "and I'll tell him all about my wonderful spring vacation. He'll like that." The movie makes clear that despite Kinsey's support of greater sexual freedom, sexuality is best left to idle discussions in college classrooms. Acting on a belief in sexual freedom inevitably leads young women to ruin.

Key teen titles from the independent studios include bad-girl films like *Dragstrip Girl* (Edward Cahn, 1957), *Hot Car Girl* (Bernard Kowalski, 1958), and *Date Bait* (O'Dale Ireland, 1960); California beach-culture movies like *Beach Party* (William Asher, 1963) and *Bikini Beach* (Asher, 1964); wild-youth pictures like *Crime in the Streets* (Siegel, 1956), *The Cool and the* Crazy (William Witney, 1958), *Dragstrip Riot* (David Bradley, 1958), and *Riot on Sunset Strip* (Arthur Dreifuss, 1967); and the halfhearted cautionary anti-drug melodrama *Maryjane* (Maury Dexter, 1968).

The teen film between 1956 and 1967 veered from the serious to the sensational, from the

Franklin (Rory Harrity) leers at Melanie (Yvette Mimieux) in *Where the Boys Are* (Henry Levin, 1960). The film begins as a light teen comedy but ends tragically, with Melanie's rape by Franklin's friend Dill

sublime to the ridiculous. After a brief spate of earnest, progressive cultural observations in films such as *Rebel without a Cause* and *The Blackboard Jungle,* Hollywood turned more formulaic. Fast cars and fast girls became less causes for concern than items on a checklist to be included in any self-respecting teen film. It wasn't until 1967 and the release of Mike Nichols's *The Graduate* (discussed below) that the studios would once again take young people seriously. Not incidentally, *The Graduate,* which marks the studios' rekindled attention to the youth audience, was not only the number 1 film of 1967; it was also the highest-grossing film of the decade.

TRANSCENDING GENRE, TRANSCENDING HOLLYWOOD

Throughout American film history a handful of artists have been able to transcend studio genres and impose their peculiar signature on all the films they produced, directed, or starred in. Take, for example, Alfred Hitchcock. His work in the United States between 1940 and 1960 was at once com-

mercially successful and immediately recognizable as his. More so than the works of any other studio director of his time, perhaps of any time, Hitchcock's films form an oeuvre, a body of work with a profound stylistic and thematic unity.

But just as clearly as Hitchcock imposed his signature on his films and became at least as well known as the films themselves, so, too, did stars such as Jerry Lewis, Marilyn Monroe, and Doris Day define "their" films. Filmgoers knew before the lights went down what to expect from a Hitchcock picture, just as they knew what was in store for them in a picture starring Jerry Lewis, Marilyn Monroe, or Doris Day.

Alfred Hitchcock

Alfred Hitchcock was born in London in 1899 and enjoyed a successful career in England before moving to Hollywood in 1940. Hitchcock's first foray into the film business was with Famous Players–Lasky, where from 1920 to 1925 he designed sets and title cards, wrote silent-movie scripts, and worked as an assistant director. In 1925 he began an association with the German expressionist producer Erich Pommer, who co-produced Hitchcock's first complete film as a director, the romantic melodrama *The Pleasure Garden* (1925). The film was shot at Pommer's studio in Munich, as was Hitchcock's second venture, *The Mountain Eagle* (1926), a strange potboiler about a woman who falls for a hermit in the hills of Kentucky.

Hitchcock's apprenticeship in Germany during the 1920s fostered an affection for the antimontage style of filmmaking, popularized by F. W. Murnau, which eschewed the cut in favor of a more theatrical and photographic emphasis on the shot. Rather than depict a scene from a variety of angles, cutting from camera placement to camera placement, Hitchcock used deep-focus compositions or simply moved the camera fluidly through the space of the set. Hitchcock's affection for expressionist-style lighting was very much in evidence through-out his career, from his first important British film, *The Lodger* (1926), which chronicles a series of Jack the Ripper–like killings, to his best-known American suspense picture, *Psycho* (1960).

A quick review of Hitchcock's work in Germany and England offers a useful introduction to his American oeuvre—which is to say that the seeds of the genius that he would display in his American work was evident in many of his early films. *Blackmail* (1929), his next important film after *The Lodger*, is a silent-sound hybrid about a young woman, Alice (Anny Ondra), who ditches her boring policeman boyfriend, Frank (John Longden), in order to embark on a clandestine rendezvous with a handsome painter (Cyril Ritchard) that ends with Alice killing the painter when he tries to rape her. The picture that cemented Hitchcock's international reputation was *The 39 Steps* (1935), a suspense film about a man who is falsely accused of murder and must navigate his way through an espionage plot in order to prove his innocence, a plotline that Hitchcock would use again in his cold war spy film *North by Northwest* (1959). After seeing *The 39 Steps*, David O. Selznick invited Hitchcock to Hollywood to direct *Rebecca* (1940). With that film, Hitchcock's Hollywood career took off.

Hitchcock's American oeuvre is significant in terms of quality and quantity. The films span several Hollywood genres: *Rebecca* is a gothic melodrama; *Shadow of a Doubt* (1943), *Spellbound* (1945), *Rope* (1948), *Strangers on a Train* (1951), *I Confess* (1953), *Rear Window* (1954), *The Wrong Man* (1957), *Vertigo* (1958), *Psycho*, and *Marnie* (1964) are psychological suspense films; *Notorious* (1946) and *North by Northwest* are cold war espionage films; *The Birds* (1963) is a horror picture.

As we look back on Hitchcock's American films, certain themes emerge. Several of the films offer some variation on the theme of mistaken identity—for example, *Shadow of a Doubt*, in which Uncle Charlie (Joseph Cotten) may or may not be the Merry Widow killer; *The Wrong Man*, in which a musician (Henry Fonda) is falsely accused of a robbery he did not commit; and *North by Northwest*, in which a happy-go-lucky businessman (Cary Grant) is mistaken for a spy. For Hitchcock, mistaken identity inevitability carries with it the horror of false accusation and the necessary business of proving oneself innocent.

As in his breakthrough British film, *Blackmail*, in which by the 30-minute mark all the principal characters are culpable in some sort of crime (Alice is a killer, albeit with reason; Frank covers up Alice's crime and then falsely pins the blame on a sleazy blackmailer), several of Hitchcock's American films feature characters locked in an irreconcilable moral dilemma. In *Notorious*, for example, spies trade on the virtue of a young woman (Ingrid Bergman) in order to get to a Nazi on the lam (Claude Rains). Pimping for Uncle Sam soon comes to trouble her handler (Cary Grant), who discovers that he's in love with the woman he has put in the arms of another man. The priest in *I Confess* (Montgomery Clift) becomes a suspect in a murder. He knows the identity of the murderer (O. E. Hasse) but can't betray the killer's confidence even though the killer has confessed to the crime solely to prevent the priest from testifying against him. But lest we idealize the priest, Hitchcock implies that he has had carnal thoughts and may even have acted on them with a former girlfriend (Anne Baxter). Though the priest did not commit the murder, he isn't exactly innocent. In *Rear Window* the hero, L. B. Jefferies, a photo-

The director Alfred Hitchcock in a publicity photograph taken in 1959, the year before the release of *Psycho*.

L. B. Jeffries (James Stewart) in a wheelchair as he spies on his neighbors in Alfred Hitchcock's 1954 suspense film *Rear Window*. We watch the film perversely hoping that what Jeffries has seen across the courtyard adds up to murder.

journalist temporarily confined to a wheelchair (James Stewart), spies on his neighbors. He becomes particularly interested in Lars Thorwald (Raymond Burr), a neighbor with a dark secret to hide. Even though the unfolding drama of Thorwald's crime takes center stage, L. B.'s gaze (aided by a high-powered telephoto lens) tends to wander. Of additional interest are a lonely woman (Judith Evelyn), a songwriter (Ross Bagdasarian), and a woman he calls Miss Torso (Georgine Darcy) because she does contortionist-like exercises in various stages of undress. The film hinges on our developing interest in Thorwald's guilt, a droll, typical Hitchcock joke. For the hero to be right and at least partly justified in his voyeurism, there needs to be a crime; otherwise, the hero is nothing more than a peeping tom.

Despite (or perhaps because of) his Jesuit upbringing, Hitchcock embraced a relative as opposed to an absolute morality. In *Rear Window* we have a peeping-tom hero who in the end solves a murder mystery and prevents a woman from killing herself. In *North by Northwest*, "the professor," a government agent played by Leo G. Carroll, shrugs off the hero's inevitable death as a necessary, albeit mildly regrettable price to pay for freedom. The professor also sacrifices the virtue of a former schoolteacher (Eva Marie Saint) as a necessary casualty of the cold war.

Like a lot of other makers of suspense films, Hitchcock was fond of ending things in high places—the heroes dangling from the faces atop Mount Rushmore in *North by Northwest*, for example. The repetition of a character's ascent to a high

Scottie (James Stewart) rescues Madeleine (Kim Novak) from drowning in Alfred Hitchcock's
Vertigo (1958), only she wasn't drowning and she's not Madeleine. By the time Scottie sorts
things out, it is too late for both of them.

place accompanies a thematic interest in vertigo, not only the disease itself but also a general disorientation, a weakness or fatigue. In the suitably titled *Vertigo*, the hero is Scottie (James Stewart), a cop whose failure to negotiate high places leads to the death of his partner. For Scottie, vertigo manifests itself as a kind of impotence; he retires from the police force and spends his days wandering aimlessly. In what becomes a thinly veiled attempt to regain his manhood, he pursues (first as a detective, then as a lover) a woman he takes to be a former acquaintance's wife, whom he comes to know as Madeleine (Kim Novak). But when Madeleine dies (falling from the bell tower of the San Juan Batista mission, a high place, of course) and an inquest reveals his impotence (his failure to ascend the stairs in time to save her),

Scottie becomes even more downcast than he was before he met her.

In several films, Hitchcock examined a peculiarly psychological view of crime and punishment. Focusing on family dynamics in psychopathology, he explored the notion that some trauma in childhood can make an otherwise decent character a criminal. Norman Bates (Anthony Perkins) in *Psycho*, for example, is the way he is because of his mother (her cloying attention when he was a boy, her abandonment of the adolescent Norman when she meets and falls for another man). The title character (Tippi Hedren) in *Marnie* can similarly, blame her kleptomania and deep fear of intimacy on a crime she witnessed as a child: the murder of a client by her prostitute mother (Louise Latham).

No director before or since has so deftly examined the politics of looking and seeing: the curious allure of scopophilia (objectification through looking) and the seductive kick of voyeurism (a sexual thrill gained by watching in secret). Characters enjoy furtive looking, but their penchant for spying also gets them in trouble. They see something they shouldn't see (a murder, for example, as in *The Man Who Knew Too Much*, made in 1934 and remade in 1956), something that might mean something and then again might not (exactly what does Thorwald have in that trunk in his apartment in *Rear Window*, and exactly what has he got buried out there in the flower bed?), or something that turns them on and then turns them into someone else, someone bad, as in *Psycho*.

Some thematic concerns common to Hitchcock's films verge on idiosyncrasy. For example, there is Hitchcock's idealization of a highly stylized, carefree masculinity and its counterpoint, the effeminate, perhaps homosexual tendencies of the political or pathological criminal. In Hitchcock's world, being macho isn't necessarily an asset, but being quick on your feet and smart in difficult circumstances certainly is. Hitchcock's admiration for grace under pressure partially explains his affection for actors like Cary Grant and James Stewart, movie stars who radiated a cool exterior under fire. Similarly, the most memorable male hero in Hitchcock's British films is Richard Hannay (Robert Donat) in *The 39 Steps*, who casually jokes, after being saved from a bullet to the heart by a hymnbook he by chance has in his pocket, that for the first time in his life he understands the value of songs of praise. In contrast, the prototypical killer of the British films is Handel Fane (Esme Percy) in the 1930 picture *Murder!*, easily identified as a "half-caste," a slang term for a homosexual, who, Hitchcock suggests, kills *because* he's attracted to men. Fane is a model of sorts for a string of Hitchcock's American sociopaths: the thrill killers in *Rope* (played by John Dall and Farley Granger), stand-ins for the notorious real-life killers Nathan Leopold and Richard Loeb, lovers who kidnapped and killed a boy as an intellectual experiment in staging the perfect crime; Bruno (Robert Walker) in *Strangers on a Train*, a mama's boy who wants his father dead and is willing to trade murders to get his wish fulfilled; and Leonard (Martin Landau) in *North by Northwest*,

a henchman with tender feelings for his boss (James Mason), a master spy and killer. And of course there is Norman Bates in *Psycho*. Although he is not gay (so far as we can tell), he is certainly effeminate.

Throughout his years in America, Hitchcock continued to develop his signature style, expanding his use of the theatrical antimontage techniques that inspired him during his time in Germany and England. In *The Wrong Man* the long takes and fluid documentary-style camerawork enable the viewer to inhabit the world of the wrongly accused hero. Such cinematic intimacy is a key to the empathy we come to feel with the character. The theatrical antimontage style is also evident in some of Hitchcock's bigger studio set pieces. The world that L. B. Jefferies watches from his window, for example, is observed through a camera lens in long, fluid takes. The apartment complex across the courtyard is quite like a stage set in a play, a single construction that various characters enter and exit, moving into and then out of view. The cat-and-mouse scenes in railway cars, hotels, and finally the villain's posh modern home in *North by Northwest* are also rendered in this style. Hitchcock was so committed to it that he composed the entirety of *Rope* in a single shot. The only cuts in the movie occur when the camera operator had to reload his film, and those transitions are masked by distractions, like swinging doors or a character walking in front of the camera. In the absence of expressive editing, Hitchcock made the most of simple spatial transitional devices—stairways, for example, which (as in *Psycho*) one ascends or descends at one's peril. Waiting behind a blind corner atop the stairs in the Bateses' family home is Norman dressed as Mother, knife at the ready. Downstairs one finds Norman's mother preserved like one of the stuffed birds in the motel office. Like his expressionist predecessors Fritz Lang and F. W. Murnau, Hitchcock used offscreen space expertly. What we see on film—what the director holds on film in a long take—suggests what we don't and can't see. And in Hitchcock's films, what we don't or can't see can hurt us.

Hitchcock was by popular acclaim American cinema's master of suspense. It was a title that at the very least revealed the American audience's affection for and familiarity with his oeuvre.

Anthony Perkins as the psychotic murderer Norman Bates in Alfred Hitchcock's 1960 thriller *Psycho*.

...s a popular filmmaker ...United States in 1940 ...n the early 1970s, an ...by Hollywood standards. ...uccessful studio director ...ently give audiences and ...they wanted or expected ...im an auteur was an abil... ...and executives in the very process of satisfy...h artistic vision.

Jerry Lewis

Between 1951 and 1960, Jerry Lewis appeared in sixteen top-twenty pictures. No sound comedian before or since can boast such a run of success at the box office. Though today in the United States he is at best regarded as a comedian who once (mysteriously) appealed to children, Lewis's legion of fans in the 1950s included plenty of adults. With his partner, singer-straightman Dean Martin, Lewis made the list of top-ten box-office stars every year from 1951 to 1956 and then on his own (after an acrimonious split with Martin) from 1957 to 1959 and again from 1961 to 1963. Lewis was the single most important, influential, and popular comedy star of his time. Like Chaplin, Keaton, and Lloyd in the silent era, he was able—first as a movie star and then as a director—to impose the stamp of an auteur on all his films.

Martin and Lewis met in New York in 1944, when Martin was a moderately successful club singer and Lewis was a struggling comic emcee. Their collaboration began modestly in 1945 at a nightclub called the Glass Hat. Martin, ever amiable and willing to risk being shown up, let Lewis fool around during his set. While Martin tried to sing, Lewis emerged from the kitchen dressed as a busboy, juggling and eventually dropping a tray full of dishes. As plates scattered across the floor, Lewis shrieked, "I'm sorry, sir." The rest is history.

From the very start of the stage act, Lewis was cast as the stooge, the kid who stumbles on a straight stage act and comically disrupts things. When they got a chance to make movies, Martin and Lewis fell easily into their stage roles. Two of their best films together, the 1953 hits *The Caddy* and *The Stooge* (both directed by Norman Taurog), transparently mythologize Lewis's unlikely rise to stardom, with Lewis playing the oddly talented stooge in both films. *The Caddy* opens with news-

reel footage of a crowd outside a hotel where Martin and Lewis are staying (the 1953 audience no doubt recognized the footage). Inside the hotel are Martin's and Lewis's alter egos in the film, Joe and Harvey. Harvey is clearly the talented one—the comic genius who makes the team work. He is kind, sincere, humble, and childlike, a fascinating combination of virtuosity and virtue. Joe is the typical Martin character: lazy and shiftless with a big ego absent the talent to back it up. Such was the on-screen model of the team through their eight years and sixteen films together.

As a comic playing a comic in *The Caddy* and *The Stooge*, Lewis is afforded the chance to display a wide range of antisocial and self-indulgent behaviors. He is a spastic child lost in the magic of play, which is to say he is completely unselfconscious and self-centered. In this child-man character, which he played in one incarnation or another throughout his film career, Lewis exhibited an irreverence for propriety, for property—destroying a department store in *The Caddy* and a smoking billboard in *Artists and Models* (Frank Tashlin, 1955)—and for professional stage and screen performance—mugging to the crowd or the camera,

Dean Martin and Jerry Lewis mugging for the camera in a publicity shot for their 1953 film *The Caddy* (Norman Taurog).

refusing to acknowledge the boundaries of the stage or the frame of a film. Underneath it all was a strange (especially for the 1950s) pretense to effeminacy. In *The Caddy,* when Joe (Martin) first meets Harvey (Lewis), he remarks, "You're a tomboy aren't you?" When Joe and Harvey travel together, Harvey does the cooking and cleaning and feels betrayed when Joe acts on an attraction to "another" woman. In *Money from Home* (George Marshall, 1954), Honey Talk (a gambler played by Martin) flatters Virgil (the Lewis character) in order to get him to perform a part in a criminal scheme. Virgil boasts of his acting prowess: "I was the John Barrymore of the clamdiggers." Honey Talk foolishly asks, "You played Romeo?" "No," Virgil replies, "Juliet." Lewis's exaggerated effeminacy provides a strong contrast to Martin's insouciant masculinity; they were a good pair because of their mismatched screen personae.

Many of their early films—*The Caddy, The Stooge,* and *Artists and Models,* to name three—mirror the real-life dynamics of the comedy team. The principal drama at play in *The Caddy, The Stooge,* and *Artists and Models* is the question of whether the two buddies will break up. Martin and Lewis's considerable audience seemed awfully interested in that question, and as things played out, there was, even as early as 1953, cause for concern. Their differences became irreconcilable in 1956, and after a flap over the script for *The Delicate Delinquent* (Don McGuire, 1957), Martin terminated the partnership. The conventional wisdom was that Martin would fall flat on his face without his more talented partner and that Lewis, no longer "carrying" Martin, would become an even bigger star. As it turned out, Lewis was a successful Hollywood movie star through 1963 (the date of his last good film, *The Nutty Professor*), but of his mid-1960s films only *The Disorderly Orderly* (Tashlin, 1964) and *The Patsy* (Lewis, 1964) are worth watching today. Neither film had much success at the box office.

Martin, in turn, was hardly lost without Lewis. Between 1956, the year the team broke up, and 1960, the year Lewis directed his first feature, Martin starred in four big films: with Marlon Brando and Montgomery Clift in Edward Dmytryk's World War II picture *The Young Lions* (1958); as an amoral gambler in the unsentimental postwar melodrama *Some Came Running* (Vincente Minnelli, 1958), co-starring Frank Sinatra; with John

From left to right: Dean Martin, Lizabeth Scott, and Jerry Lewis in the 1953 comedy *Scared Stiff* (George Marshall).

Wayne in Howard Hawks's legendary western *Rio Bravo* (1959); and finally with buddies Frank Sinatra, Sammy Davis Jr., and Peter Lawford in the popular Rat Pack comedy *Ocean's Eleven* (Lewis Milestone, 1960). Between 1965 and 1974, Martin hosted a popular weekly TV show and starred in a series of Matt Helm films—*The Silencers* (Phil Karlson, 1966), *Murderers' Row* (Henry Levin, 1966), *The Ambushers* (Levin, 1967), and *The Wrecking Crew* (Karlson, 1969)—gentle spoofs of the popular James Bond movies.

Today Lewis is far bigger in France than he is in the United States, so much so that it is impossible to watch one of his best bits in *The Caddy* without seeing the irony, especially in the scene in which Harvey crashes a breakfast buffet in Santa Barbara, California, posing as Reggie "the Gay Continental," and sings a song that includes the lines "C'est la vie / Now in French that means nothing

Jerry Lewis (*seated at left*) clowning around on the set of *The Geisha Boy* (1958). Seated at the far right is Frank Tashlin, the film's director.

to me." Lewis's reputation in France has never flagged; a generation of film critics and film buffs has found in Lewis's films, especially those made after Martin's exit and during Lewis's brief run as a writer-director, a telling parody of American culture. In the Lewis character's hyperactivity, sexual repression, and seemingly arrested development, the French discovered America. Whether Lewis ever intended to offer such a critique is an unanswered question: after 1970 he could ill afford to let his French fans in on the secret.

A by-product of the French "discovery" of Jerry Lewis is the auteur status granted Frank Tashlin, the director of seven Jerry Lewis films. Before he began directing feature films, Tashlin wrote children's books and directed cartoons. There was a brief stint at MGM making Flip the Frog cartoons. And then came ten amazing years working alongside the legendary Tex Avery at Warner Bros. Among the many 35mm Porky Pig and Daffy Duck cartoons Tashlin produced, ·*Porky's Romance* (1937) and *Plane Daffy* (1944) are among the most memorable.

In the United States, critics and audiences viewed Tashlin's live-action films as little more than competent vehicles exploiting the talents of the featured comedy star—at one point or another Tashlin worked with Bob Hope, Jerry Lewis,

Danny Kaye, Jayne Mansfield, and Doris Day. The French, though, found a trenchant social critique in Tashlin's cartoonlike depictions of American popular culture. *Artists and Models*, for example, lampoons the comic-book industry. *The Girl Can't Help It* (1956), starring Jayne Mansfield (whose body seemed like a cartoon fantasy), pokes gentle fun at show business and early rock and roll. A second Mansfield vehicle, *Will Success Spoil Rock Hunter?* (1957), takes on advertising. And *The Man from the Diner's Club* (1963), with Danny Kaye as a hapless credit-card-company employee who must retrieve a Diner's Club card he foolishly issued to a notorious mobster, is a clever satire of American life on the installment plan.

Tashlin's visual gags are mostly rooted in cartoon exaggeration. He was himself a cartoonishly large man—6 feet 2 inches and 300 pounds—and he seemed particularly sensitive to the grotesque and the ridiculous. In *The Girl Can't Help It*, Mansfield's body, itself an exaggeration of the '50s male obsession with big breasts, is the brunt of a number of jokes. As Jerri Jordan (Mansfield) walks by, one man's eyeglasses crack just from his looking at her. As she enters an apartment building, blithely unaware of the effect she has on men, two milk bottles explode. She complains at one point that her boyfriend, a gangster, doesn't think she's "equipped for motherhood." And in one of the film's best sight gags, she changes clothes at a beach by hiding behind a sapling.

Though they were intended to be lightweight entertainments, the comedy films of Jerry Lewis (and Frank Tashlin) are hard to disregard so easily today. The films feature at times tasteless gags and meaningless slapstick, but the anarchy and irreverence spoke profoundly to a culturally repressed America.

From Marilyn Monroe to Doris Day

Though she starred in only a handful of films, Marilyn Monroe was the most talked about star of the 1950s. Her best films—*Gentlemen Prefer Blondes* (Hawks, 1953), *The Seven Year Itch* (Billy Wilder, 1955), *Bus Stop* (Joshua Logan, 1956), *Some Like It Hot* (Wilder, 1959), and *The Misfits* (John Huston, 1961)—were made by major Hollywood directors who are routinely regarded as auteurs. But it is nonetheless hard to resist thinking about these films as Marilyn Monroe pictures, as films on which she, far more than those directors, left a mark.

Monroe's on-screen persona is a unique combination of wide-eyed innocence and mature sexuality. She is at once the girl next door and the unattainable pinup, a child yet undeniably (anatomically) a woman, an unselfconscious innocent with an alluring wiggle in her walk. She came to represent, even embody, an idealized, deeply complicated femininity, the American man's not so discreet object of desire.

Historians and biographers have tried ever since Monroe's death to make sense of her stardom: Why did she become so important in American popular culture in the 1950s? Why did she become the subject of such fascination on- and offscreen? The intersections of Monroe's biography and the roles she played offer some insight into—if not answers to—those questions. Baptized Norma Jean Baker, Monroe was abandoned by her father, and after her mother was institutionalized, she spent time in an orphanage and several abusive foster homes. She dropped out of high school and later went to work at Hughes Aircraft. After some work as a model, she landed a contract at Fox for $125 a week, the going rate for starlets. The newly christened Marilyn Monroe was given voice and acting lessons—standard operating procedure for studio starlets—and was brought along slowly, given modest walk-on roles in a handful of studio films, in hopes that she might become a movie star. Monroe's Hollywood biography reads like any good American success story: she worked her way to the top, overcoming formidable obstacles on a long and difficult road. But in Hollywood the traditional American rags-to-riches story is neither simple nor happy. For Monroe, stardom was merely a stage in a larger American tragedy; the dramatic heights she reached merely meant that she had much farther to fall.

Monroe made a number of appearances in films from 1950 to 1953, beginning with a bit role in a Marx Brothers film, *Love Happy* (David Miller and Leo McCarey, 1950), in which she walks into Groucho's office, smolders, delivers a single suggestive line ("Some men are following me"), and exits—to Groucho's leer. Bigger roles followed in some very good studio films: *The Asphalt Jungle* (Huston, 1950), in which she plays a languorous moll; *All about Eve* (Joseph Mankiewicz, 1950), a Holly-

Jayne Mansfield holding two strategically placed milk bottles in Frank Tashlin's pop-culture farce *The Girl Can't Help It* (1956). Mansfield plays Jerri Jordan, whose mobster boyfriend hires the press agent Tom Miller (Tom Ewell, *right*) to make her a rock-and-roll superstar. Jerri has other ideas, only she's not so sure she's "equipped for motherhood."

wood melodrama that won six Oscars, including Best Motion Picture; and *Niagara* (Henry Hathaway, 1953), a suspense film set at what was then the nation's most popular honeymoon spot. *Niagara* tells the story of a young, unhappy wife's botched plot to murder her husband. The poster tagline, "Marilyn Monroe and *Niagara*—the high water mark in suspense!" affirmed her stardom.

Just as Monroe's career seemed ready to take off, a photographer who years earlier had taken nude photographs of her for a wartime pinup calendar threatened to release the pictures to the press. While Fox attempted to control the damage—in the 1950s such a story was certain to derail a star's career—Monroe displayed her media savvy. She held a press conference and confessed that she had indeed posed in the nude. She was broke at the time, she said, and needed the $50 she received for the session to get her car out of hock. The reporters also got an earful about her difficult childhood and her mother's emotional breakdown. The story inspired sympathy rather than scorn. Given such a biography to run with, the press embraced her—at least initially.

In quick succession, Monroe nabbed a *Life* magazine cover with an accompanying puff piece and a layout in *Playboy*. Then came her big break, *Gentlemen Prefer Blondes* (1953), a big studio musical comedy based on a popular Broadway play by Anita Loos. Loos's message gets a bit lost in the lavish production numbers, including Monroe's signature performance of "Diamonds Are a Girl's Best Friend," but the film makes clear that in a man's world a woman has to be practical and must be able to exploit her every advantage. As Lorelei Lee, a by-necessity savvy gold digger ("the only girl with a spotlight in her eye who can spot a diamond in a man's pocket") whose breathy, innocent double entendres conceal a pragmatic sexual player ("A man being rich is like a girl being pretty"), Monroe transformed the familiar blond-bombshell walk-on that she played in *Love Happy* into a starring role. The whispery voice, the sexy walk, the seemingly empty-headed witticisms ("Start thinking about happiness and stop thinking about fun") came to define not only Lorelei but Monroe as well.

In an effort to reproduce the success of *Gentlemen Prefer Blondes*, movie executives serially typecast Monroe. She played a model who rendered ridiculous the witticism that "men seldom make passes at girls who wear glasses" in *How to Marry*

a *Millionaire* (Jean Negulesco, 1953), a showgirl in the Otto Preminger western *River of No Return* (1954), a hatcheck girl who becomes a showgirl in *There's No Business Like Show Business* (Walter Lang, 1954), a TV-commercial actress and model in *The Seven Year Itch*, a down-on-her-luck singer in *Bus Stop*, an American showgirl abroad in *The Prince and the Showgirl* (Laurence Olivier, 1957), a down-on-her-luck band singer in the classic MGM comedy *Some Like It Hot* (for which Monroe won a Golden Globe, her only major award), and an off-Broadway actress and singer in *Let's Make Love* (George Cukor, 1960). Monroe struggled with her success in part because it required her to fulfill the studio's relentless typecasting. Indeed, in her brief run as a Hollywood star (from 1953 to 1962), she would never fully escape Lorelei Lee. After the release of *The Seven Year Itch* in 1955 and the press frenzy over the now-famous scene in which her dress billows up and out over a subway grating, Monroe, at the height of her fame, sued to break her studio contract. She moved to New York, enrolled in the Actors Studio to study the Method with Lee and Paula Strasberg, and vowed not to return to Hollywood unless the studio took her more seriously.

During Monroe's brief sabbatical in New York, Fox sought to replace her with another blond bombshell, Jayne Mansfield. But the two films introducing Mansfield as the next Monroe, *The Girl Can't Help It* and *Will Success Spoil Rock Hunter?*, seemed to reveal only how irreplaceable Monroe was. Especially in Frank Tashlin's hands, Mansfield was just a cartoon character, her anatomy the subject and object of crude visual gags. Unlike Monroe, who had genuine comic timing and a voltage on-screen that is hard to define, Mansfield was little more than a cartoon version of the real thing, less a character than a caricature. In 1958, when Monroe decided to return to Hollywood, Mansfield's career stalled.

Monroe's Hollywood comeback, in *Some Like It Hot*, co-starring Tony Curtis and Jack Lemmon, reunited the star with Billy Wilder, who had directed her in *The Seven Year Itch*. Again, however, Monroe was cast as a singer-showgirl, the

Marilyn Monroe as the showgirl Lorelei Lee singing "Diamonds Are a Girl's Best Friend" in Howard Hawks's *Gentlemen Prefer Blondes* (1953).

suggestively named Sugar Kane. The film was hugely successful and is routinely cited as a landmark Hollywood comedy. But upon its release filmgoers and the Hollywood press were more inclined to talk about Monroe's problems on the set than about the film itself.

During the production of *Some Like It Hot*, Monroe gave the press plenty to write about. She was habitually late to the set and took her time preparing herself, often conferring in private with her acting coach while her co-stars and the director waited. When the production wrapped, the press quoted Wilder as saying that Monroe was "the meanest woman I ever encountered in Hollywood." Curtis added, "Kissing her was like kissing Hitler." The bottom line for the gossip rags—in part because it fit a standard Hollywood trope about ambitious actresses with pretensions to more serious roles and partly because the studio, irked by her hiatus, was no longer interested in spinning the story another way—was that Monroe had become an outrageous impaired diva. Making matters worse, Monroe was in poor health in 1958, and her ability to cope with the pressures of film-making and publicity had worn thin. During the production she had suffered a miscarriage, undergone surgery that all but ensured sterility, and become addicted to painkillers; at times she seemed on the verge of a nervous breakdown. The press nonetheless characterized her as an egomaniac movie star, a woman who had seemingly forgotten that less than a decade earlier she was, in Hollywood's cruel parlance, a nobody.

Despite the problems on the set and in her private life, Monroe's performance in *Some Like It Hot* is funny and at times heartbreaking. The film is ostensibly a farcical comedy about two guys who dress up as women so as not to be recognized by mobsters who are on their trail. But the heart of the movie beats when Monroe is on-screen. In her musical numbers, especially "I Wanna Be Loved by You" and "I'm through with Love" (both inspired by her romance with Junior, Tony Curtis's character), the camera—and the audience—love Monroe and only Monroe.

The Misfits, written by Monroe's husband, Arthur Miller, just as their marriage was ending, and co-starring her childhood idol, Clark Gable, and fellow Actors Studio classmates Montgomery Clift and Eli Wallach, was Monroe's last film. She plays

Marilyn Monroe and her husband, Arthur Miller, on the set of *The Misfits* (John Huston, 1961), based on a screenplay Miller wrote especially for her. By the time this photograph was taken, the marriage was falling apart and Monroe was teetering towards self-destruction.

Roslyn, a recent divorcée. The part, written for Monroe by a man who had long sympathized with her struggle to get better roles but was also the cause of her current heartbreak, offered the actress her first (and, unfortunately, her last) chance to escape from the showgirl-model-actress stereotype that so hamstrung her in her years under contract at Fox. In *The Misfits*, Monroe gets to play a real-world woman, who, like the actress, has come to mean different things to the different men who vie for her attention and affection: the rugged cowboy, Gay (Gable), sees Roslyn as an ethereal angel, less a woman than a symbol; the pilot, Guido (Wallach), pursues Roslyn ardently, as a substitute for

Roslyn (Marilyn Monroe) consoles the ailing cowboy Perce (Montgomery Clift) in John Huston's *The Misfits* (1961), Monroe's last complete film.

his late wife; and Perce (Clift), the broken cowboy whose mother has disinherited and abandoned him in favor of a second husband, sees in Roslyn a Madonna figure.

Monroe's behavior on the set of *The Misfits* was even more abominable than it had been on the set of *Some Like It Hot*. She was always late and seldom sober or prepared. Still, her performance was—and is—the best reason to see the film. Although the short story (also written by Miller) on which *The Misfits* is based centers on three men trying in vain to hang on to the cowboy way of life in modern Nevada, the film makes the men's struggle far less interesting than what their struggle might mean to Roslyn. Once again, whenever Monroe is on-screen, the film is about her character, and given the intersections in the lives of the recently divorced and world-weary Roslyn and the

similarly situated Monroe circa 1961, it seems to be mostly about Monroe alone.

Thirty-seven minutes is all we have of Monroe's last production, an aborted film project titled *Something's Got to Give* (Cukor, 1962). The film was conceived as a remake of the 1940 romantic comedy *My Favorite Wife* (directed by Garson Kanin, scripted by Leo McCarey and Bella Spewack, and starring Cary Grant, Randolph Scott, and Irene Dunne). The original tells the story of a wife who remarries several years after her husband is presumed dead. After the wedding the first husband miraculously returns and, true to the romantic-comedy formula, makes a play to get his wife back. The remake promised to switch the genders, putting Monroe in the role of the partner presumed dead. The comedy thus is inherent in the husband's predicament, torn between vows to a new wife and a past commitment to the character played by the country's reigning sex symbol, Marilyn Monroe.

Promising as such a scenario may have seemed, the project was doomed from the start. By 1962, Monroe simply could not handle the daily routine of film production, and her on-set behavior was so problematic that the studio shut the entire production down as a warning to the actress to behave more professionally. Production resumed, but just as things got bad again and a second delay seemed inevitable, Monroe died of an apparent overdose of barbiturates. After her death, Monroe, like her fellow '50s icon Elvis Presley, became a patron saint of devouring stardom, a tragic figure in what is now an all-too-familiar story line in Hollywood.

Soon after Monroe died, the *Something's Got to Give* project resurfaced under a new title, *Move Over, Darling* (1963), with a new director, Michael Gordon, and a very different blond comedy star, Doris Day, in the role written for Monroe. That Day had replaced Monroe as Hollywood's principal blonde is indisputable: between 1960 and 1964, the years leading up to and immediately following Monroe's death, Day was the number 1 female star on the annual poll of U.S. exhibitors in every year but one, 1961, when she ranked second, to Elizabeth Taylor. Day was in many ways the anti-Monroe, an icon of homespun restraint. Monroe projected a wantonness, a torrent of conflicting drives and desires often kept unsuccessfully just below the surface. To the public she was more than anything a movie star: vain and self-important but vulnerable, fragile, doomed. Day, in stark contrast, seemed to be altogether free of movie-star vanity: she was the good girl in her films, and her screen image carried over to her public persona. American audiences took Day at face value: she was pretty, healthy, and a good sport.

Day first became a star while Monroe was in self-imposed exile in New York, with roles in Alfred Hitchcock's thriller *The Man Who Knew Too Much*, in which she sings her signature number, "Whatever Will Be, Will Be (Que Sera, Sera), and the adaptation of the popular musical comedy *The Pajama Game* (George Abbott and Stanley Donen, 1957). In 1959, the year of Monroe's heartbreaking performance in *Some Like It Hot*, Day was cast in the romantic comedy *Pillow Talk* (Gordon, 1959). It proved to be a career-defining role for her, and it came at the moment when Monroe's ability to perform in a feature film was very much in question.

Pillow Talk is a romantic comedy about a cool and practical young woman, Jan Morrow, who is married to her job, a role Day perfected in films like *Teacher's Pet* (George Seaton, 1958) and *Lover Come Back* (Delbert Mann, 1961). Two men vie for her affections: a lothario named Brad (played by Rock Hudson) who vexes her at every turn, and Jonathan, a wealthy mama's boy (Tony Randall), whom she can't take seriously, at least as a lover. Jan first "connects" with Brad because the two share a telephone party line. Every time she picks up the phone to make a call, he's on it, seducing a far less serious and far more glamorous woman than she. Brad gets under Jan's skin, and she tells him off. Brad views Jan as a prig (as do many contemporary filmgoers) and endeavors to teach her a lesson: he masquerades as Rex, a nice guy whom he portrays first as a gallant suitor and then as a

Doris Day playing hard to get with Rock Hudson in Michael Gordon's romantic comedy *Pillow Talk* (1959).

oy, which in '50s parlance means
y. (For Hudson, whose romantic
and carefully managed public
d a private life as a closeted gay
erade must have seemed ironic,
...contemporary audiences, who know the truth about Hudson's private life, it adds an unintended dimension to the humor in the film.)

Eventually Jan discovers that Brad and Rex are the same man. She is of course furious and vows revenge. But at that very moment, Brad discovers that the joke is on him: he admits to himself that he has fallen in love with Jan. Brad destroys his little black book (filled with the names and phone numbers of his many girlfriends) and hires Jan to renovate his apartment, ostensibly to make it more suitable for her to move into with him after their marriage. She misreads his motives and decorates the apartment as some sort of nightmare seraglio, with faux *Arabian Nights* furnishings, vile music at one's fingertips, and a bed that slides out of the wall at the push of a button. After Brad gets a first look at his new apartment, he marches across town to declare his love for Jan. In the end, as Brad carries Jan (in her pajamas) back to his apartment, it is clear that while he is taking her to his lair, she has socialized him, making him into a respectable '50s upper-middle-class man. Unlike Monroe's films, which never promise anything remotely domestic, *Pillow Talk* suggests that Day could tame even the wildest ladies' man. Day subsequently played the same basic role in a series of sweet and light comedies, with Rock Hudson again in *Lover Come Back* and Cary Grant in *That Touch of Mink* (Mann, 1962).

Though the popular press was touting a sexual revolution throughout the 1960s, Day continued to appear in popular films through 1968 playing the same good-girl character. Day, who turned forty-four in 1968, made a smooth transition to television with a popular series called simply *The Doris Day Show*, in which she played the quintessential good girl now in middle age. The series ran from 1968 to 1973, a tumultuous time in American cultural history, framed as it was by the riots at the Democratic National Convention in Chicago and the Watergate scandal. At a time when America was undergoing significant social change and mainstream American values were very much under siege, Day was a model of consistency and the embodiment of those mainstream values. For better or worse, during her heyday on television, Day became an icon of Nixon's purported silent majority (a white God-fearing politically and socially conservative constituency whose members' cars bore bumper stickers with slogans like "America: Love It or Leave It") and as such came to represent an American innocence forever lost in the movie industry's headlong plunge into a new, more modern Hollywood.

TWO KEY FILMS

In 1967, with a new production code in the works and the studios desperate to attract the youth audience, two films pointed boldly toward a new American cinema: Arthur Penn's *Bonnie and Clyde* and Mike Nichols's *The Graduate*. Years before American critics began touting an auteur renaissance, a golden age of Hollywood run by audacious film directors exercising creative autonomy unheard of in the old Hollywood, these two films revealed just how far movie directors might go stylistically and thematically and just how far the American moviegoer, circa 1967 was willing to go with them.

Bonnie and Clyde

When Warren Beatty, the producer and star of *Bonnie and Clyde*, first proposed a film about the legendary Depression-era bank robbers whose two-year crime spree ended in a bloody ambush in 1934, the reaction of Jack Warner (one of the Warner brothers) was lukewarm, but he nonetheless gave Beatty the green light.

Legend has it that when Beatty screened the completed film for Warner, the mogul was aghast: he found the odd mix of comedy and drama off-putting and the violence too extreme. Per his contract with Beatty, Warner dutifully released *Bonnie and Clyde*, but halfheartedly. A handful of bad reviews (from veteran film reviewers at *Life*, *Newsweek*, and *The New York Times*) seemed to support Warner's decision to release the film "small" (to a handful of theaters in big-city markets). But much to Warner's surprise, positive word-of-mouth countered the bad reviews, and the film got legs (it proved popular in the long run). By the end of its second theatrical run, in 1973,

Bonnie and Clyde had grossed approximately $70 million on an investment of just $2.5 million. When *Bonnie and Clyde* became a hit, the seventy-five-year-old Jack Warner and his geriatric Hollywood peers (Paramount's Adolph Zukor was in his nineties and Fox's Darryl Zanuck was in his mid-sixties) got a jolt of reality. They also got a look into Hollywood's future, a future that would not include them.

When we consider the development of *Bonnie and Clyde* and the talent pool behind its production, we can see why Jack Warner never understood the picture or its success at the box office. The screenwriters Robert Benton and David Newman, staff writers at *Esquire* magazine responsible for the monthly's popular satirical Dubious

Achievement awards, first hawked their script not in Hollywood but in Paris, where they tried to interest the French New Wave filmmakers François Truffaut and Jean-Luc Godard. Eventually both French cineastes turned them down, but the trip to Paris revealed that Benton and Newman were after something very different from what was being made in Hollywood at the time. The assignment to direct the film eventually went to Arthur Penn, a novice movie director known at the time for his work on Broadway. Before 1967, Penn had directed just three pictures, two of which did not do well at the box office: the bomb *The Left Handed Gun* (1958), a Billy the Kid biopic scripted by Gore Vidal that Warner Bros. executives recut after Penn had finished his work on it; the hit *The Miracle*

Clyde Barrow (Warren Beatty) may not be much in the "love department," but robbing banks is a lot more fun than waiting tables—the life that Bonnie Parker (played by Faye Dunaway) left behind in West Dallas. Arthur Penn's *Bonnie and Clyde* (1967) offers a curious parallel between their lives on the run and their experiences in the bedroom; just as they find success in bed, they are gunned down by the law.

Faye Dunaway and Warren Beatty as the legendary outlaws Bonnie Parker and Clyde Barrow in Arthur Penn's surprise hit *Bonnie and Clyde* (1967).

Worker (1962), also a biopic (of Helen Keller), this time adapted from a play that Penn had staged successfully on Broadway; and the bomb *Mickey One* (1965), the largely improvised film noir about a failed comic (played by Warren Beatty). To Benton and Newman's delight, Penn brought to their script what they had wanted from Truffaut and Godard: a New Wave sensibility, a willingness to toy audaciously with cinematic convention to make a film that at once defied the strictures of Hollywood genre filmmaking and introduced a distinctive and modern visual style.

The film opens with a nod to the French New Wave; à la Godard, the first images are off-angle close-ups of Bonnie's (Fay Dunaway's) lips, eyes, and face reflected in a dirty mirror. The jump cuts—abrupt, discontinuous segues from one image to another (a style popularized by Godard)—are disorienting; the point of the scene is not to establish a setting (as in a more conventional film) but to create a mood, an ambience. When the camera finally pulls back to show Bonnie from the waist up, we see that she is nude, an image that was consistent with the less restricted French films the screenwriters so adored and would have been unthinkable on an American screen as few as two or three years before. The camera holds on Bonnie as she barely covers up, and then it follows her to the window, where she engages Clyde (Beatty) in conversation while he tries to steal her mother's car.

As in the films of the French New Wave, happenstance in *Bonnie and Clyde* governs action. While the film depicts how Bonnie and Clyde's crime spree captures the Depression-era zeitgeist—when there was little popular affection for the financial institutions that the couple rob—the motivation behind their crimes is not by design political. Clyde robs a store in Bonnie's hometown not to make a statement about class in the 1930s but to impress her. In their first conversation, Clyde tells Bonnie he's been in jail for armed robbery. She doesn't believe him. So he brandishes his gun. The gun is a bigger turn-on than Clyde could ever have imagined: Bonnie fondles it suggestively and says, "Bet you don't have the gumption to use it." It's a telling remark because Clyde plans to use the gun as a threat, but he is reluctant to fire it. For the film viewer the gun stands in for the body part that Clyde is also reluctant to use. In a post-

robbery tryst, Bonnie attempts to devour Clyde sexually, prompting the impotent gangster to remark (in a significant understatement) that he's not much in the "love department."

But rather than exploit this easy psychology—suggesting that Clyde lives a life of crime to compensate for sexual inadequacy—Penn suggests that Bonnie and Clyde make things up as they go along, that nothing they do cuts particularly deep into their psyches. The decision to rob banks, for example, surfaces not after a failed bedroom assignation or some moral conviction vis-à-vis the Depression but after a chance meeting with dispossessed farmers. The couple hide out at an abandoned farmhouse, and the farmer, recently sent packing by the bank that foreclosed on his property, comes by with his family and a former farmworker to take one last look at the life the bank has taken from them. Bonnie and Clyde and the farmer and his family bond, and they joyously shoot holes in the bank's sign (which symbolizes the bank's new ownership of the property). When the farmer is about to leave, Clyde offers the scene's payoff line: "We rob banks." They don't (yet), but Clyde has a pathological need to please, to impress, to ingratiate himself with this stranger he's just met.

Clyde's need to please everyone is his tragic flaw. For most of the film, Bonnie wants one thing from him, and it's the one thing he can't or won't supply. And later in the film, when Clyde tries to comfort Bonnie's mother (Mabel Cavitt) by declaring that someday he and Bonnie will settle down, she sees right through his bluster. She says, "You best keep running, Clyde Barrow, and you know it."

The delicate balance of farce and drama is meant to reveal the truth behind the legend: that Bonnie and Clyde are just dumb kids who quickly get in over their heads. The first bank Clyde tries to rob has defaulted, and there's no money in the safe. The second bank robbery gets them cash, but C. W. (Michael J. Pollard), the grease monkey they take on to drive for them, stupidly parks the car on a side street, and their getaway, which stalls as C. W. tries to get the car out of a tight parking space, takes on the dimensions of a comic disaster. But the comedy does not last long. Once C. W. gets the car back on the road, a bank worker grabs on to the car's running board. In desperation, Clyde shoots him in the face, hardly a comic punctuation to the scene. The film then cuts to a movie theater, where Clyde falls apart, desperately trying to reconcile what he has just done with his self-image. He is hardly a desperado; he is, we are reminded again, just a young man who can't believe how much trouble he's in.

Bonnie and Clyde find a kind of grace at the end of the film not in their newfound celebrity but in their last private moments together. Just as the film is about to reach its inevitable bloody climax, we are given one last scene in bed with Bonnie and Clyde. In this penultimate scene, Clyde finally succeeds. But just as one door opens, another closes. The film cuts to C. W.'s father, Ivan (Dub Taylor), making a deal with the police. It cuts back to the lovers' postcoital conversation: "Do you feel like you're supposed to feel?" Clyde asks Bonnie, who replies, "You did just perfect." This encourages Clyde to try again—again successfully, we gather. Now that they're lovers, Bonnie sees less of a need for them to be criminals; to be crude, she's ready to exchange one gun for another. So she asks Clyde whether he would do things differently if by some magical circumstance they could start all over (as lovers not robbers, she means). "Yes," he replies, and she smiles. But then, after a pregnant pause, he elaborates: he'd rob banks far away from where they live. It's not at all what she wants to hear and reveals again just how clueless this famous desperado is.

Much has been written about the film's final scene, and justifiably so. The slaughter of the counterculture heroes, an ending soon echoed in *Easy Rider* (Dennis Hopper, 1969, discussed in Chapter 7), spoke profoundly to the counterculture audience that flocked to see the film. Even today this climactic scene is remarkable in its depiction of violence, not because it elides the distinctions between good and bad—it doesn't—but because it offered viewers a peek at the future of American cinema, one without strict guidelines governing content, an American cinema less tied to strict genre conventions and suddenly free to show and tell a far wider range of stories than anyone could have imagined less than a decade before.

The Graduate

Mike Nichols was thirty-six years old with just one film under his belt when he made *The Graduate* in 1967. But that one film was *Who's Afraid of Vir-*

ginia Woolf?, a landmark adult-themed picture released for an adults-only audience the previous year. *The Graduate* was only slightly less shocking than *Who's Afraid of Virginia Woolf?* And it did even better at the box office, making all the more clear to the studios that the American audience was ready, indeed eager, for films that defied the thirty-three year-old PCA formula.

The Graduate opens with the film's unlikely hero, Ben (Dustin Hoffman), sitting on a plane about to land at Los Angeles International Airport, looking blankly straight ahead as we hear Simon and Garfunkle's "Sounds of Silence," a song about alienation that begins with the line "Hello, darkness my old friend." (*The Graduate* was one of the first films to take full advantage of a pop-music sound track, a stylistic gesture and marketing strategy employed to great effect in countless films today.) The scene is played without a single line of dialogue as the camera focuses on Ben's benumbed, expressionless face.

Ben has just completed college, and he is returning to his upper-middle-class suburban home as all concerned await his next big move. But any plans for the future are forestalled by an inertia fed by Ben's fear of becoming like his parents and their friends. Not unlike Holden Caulfield, the hero of J. D. Salinger's coming-of-age novel *The Catcher in the Rye*, Ben is tortured to the point of inaction by the phoniness of the middle-class adult world he must inevitably join. Such alienation lands Holden in the nuthouse—the novel's unhappy ending is often missed or ignored by its readers—and a similar estrangement from adult culture hardly provides Ben with a formula for success either.

Early in the movie, Ben's parents throw him a graduation party. But Ben, staring absentmindedly at his aquarium in the first of several images suggesting that he's underwater, refuses to join the festivities. After all, the guests are his parents' friends; he is merely the excuse, the theme of the party. Ben's father (William Daniels) tries to understand his son's behavior. "What's the matter?" he asks impatiently. Ben replies, "I'm just—" And his father finishes the sentence: "Worried?" When asked what he has to be worried about—Ben's father doesn't understand why a young man with everything to live for could be depressed—Ben replies blankly, "I guess about my future. I want it to be . . . different." When Ben finally joins the party, we see why: shot in unflattering close-ups, the upper-middle-class suburbanites are depicted as empty-headed, martini-guzzling phonies. One of his dad's friends, Mr. McGuire (Walter Brooke), takes Ben aside and sums up the future in a single word: "Plastics." Ben nods his head and then seeks refuge in his room.

Refuge can't be had, however; staving off adulthood is just not possible. Indeed, it comes knocking at his bedroom door. Mrs. Robinson (Anne Bancroft), the wife of his father's business partner, interrupts Ben's reverie (he's submerged, figuratively, in the aquarium again) to ask for a ride home. When the film cuts to the Robinson home, Mrs. Robinson's behavior becomes provocative, prompting Ben to blurt out (in what has become one of the most famous lines in American film history), "Mrs. Robinson, you're trying to seduce me." She says she's not, but she is, and the scene ends as she locks the bedroom door and strips, an event that is captured in a series of jump cuts (including one brief shot of the actress's breasts, a risqué image for a pre-rating-system film).

Ben's resistance to the world of his parents seems quintessentially '60s as it regards a generation gap that appears to be insurmountable. A second party scene highlights the generational divide. With his parents' friends assembled poolside, Ben is asked to show off his birthday present: scuba gear. Again he has to be coaxed out of the house. Nichols shot the scene from Ben's point of view: we see through Ben's scuba mask and hear his rhythmic breathing facilitated by the oxygen tank. Ben walks through the gauntlet of his parents' friends (whom he can't hear) and finds escape at the bottom of the pool, submerged again, now literally and figuratively. But underlying the image is the reality of Ben's situation: eventually he will have to come up for air.

Lonely and confused, in search of something that might make the passage of time more interesting, Ben calls his father's partner's wife, and they meet for the first in a series of hotel-room liaisons. The first time is awkward: Ben's entrance into the hotel bar is impeded as a stream of old folks cross his path; he stammers at the hotel desk when he's booking a room, and once upstairs, he tries to back out. Mrs. Robinson bullies Ben into having sex with her, and eventually the affair becomes his rather brutal rite of passage into

Mrs. Robinson (Anne Bancroft) and Ben (Dustin Hoffman) take a moment to reflect on their hotel-room tryst in *The Graduate* (Mike Nichols, 1967).

adulthood. The day after the first hotel liaison, we see Ben lying on an inflatable raft in his pool, no longer submerged. But although he is moving forward, his head finally above water, Ben is, as we see in a subsequent montage of hotel-room scenes, no happier than he was when he first got home. Adult sex, he discovers, can be an alienating experience, and his relationship with Mrs. Robinson is doomed by its inevitable revelation and the inevitable consequences to follow.

The affair ends when Ben takes up with someone closer to his own age, Mrs. Robinson's daughter, Elaine (Katharine Ross). He has to keep his relationship with the mother a secret from the daughter and the depth of his relationship with the daughter a secret from the mother. He can't, of course, and when the truth comes out, Elaine finds the strange romantic triangle too gross for words and dumps him.

The rest of the film follows Ben as he stalks Elaine at college, finally confronting her with his crazy plan to marry her. At first she dismisses him, but in a tender scene in his room in a Berkeley boardinghouse, she offers him some hope, which is dashed in the very next scene, when Mr. Robinson (Murray Hamilton) shows up to vent his disgust at Ben's affair with his wife. The father's visit ruins Ben and Elaine's reunion, and Elaine decides to marry someone else. For Ben and Elaine the rites of passage into adulthood are abrupt and haphazard. Elaine leaves Ben a note that is meant to discourage him, but it doesn't: "I love you but it will never work out."

The film ends as Ben crashes Elaine's wedding and, to everyone's surprise, the bride decides to leave with him. Though the last-minute rescue seems to be the height of romance—and it is the ending that viewers young in fact or at heart have rooted for—the film's denouement brings everyone down to earth. The camera holds Ben and Elaine in a two-shot, and we see in their faces a mix of amusement and confusion. What's next for Ben and Elaine is anybody's guess.

The Graduate was the big Christmas film of 1967. By the time it finished its first run, it had earned almost $40 million, making it the box-office champ of the decade. But for an industry desperately in search of a sign, a formula for the future that might pull the studios out of their generation-long box-office skid, *The Graduate* was initially difficult to read—and difficult to replicate or remake. Though in obvious ways a teen or youth film, *The Graduate* mixed and matched elements of several genres at once: teen pic, romantic comedy, and melodrama. And like *Bonnie and Clyde*, *The Graduate* was stylistically and structurally rooted in the French New Wave, with Nichols making frequent nods to the jump cuts of Jean-Luc Godard and the unsentimental depiction of youth by François Truffaut.

The challenge posed by the huge box-office success of *The Graduate* moved the industry one step

Ben (Dustin Hoffman) and Elaine (Katherine Ross) at the end of *The Graduate* (Mike Nichols, 1967). In this two-shot we see in their faces a mix of amusement and confusion. What's next for Ben and Elaine is anybody's guess.

closer to a simple truth: the old guard running the studios were desperately out of touch, and a new breed of American filmmaker—young and audacious, with an understanding of and an interest in a more international film style and form—had a much better idea of what American audiences wanted than they did. The success of *Bonnie and Clyde* and *The Graduate* made the auteur renaissance—the brief golden age in 1970s Hollywood when directors finally seemed to be the ones to call the shots (an era discussed in detail in Chapter 7)—not only necessary but also inevitable.

■ ■ ■

Between 1955 and 1967, Hollywood was still very much in transition. The old studio model was on its way out, and what might emerge to take its place was still very much, to use an industry term, in development. Two facts of film-industry life dominated the era and drove the various changes that would effect a new Hollywood: first was the box-office slump that began in 1947 and persisted through 1967, and second were the aftershocks of the 1948 *Paramount* decision and divestiture, which dramatically changed the film business and marketplace. To forge a new Hollywood, the studios needed to solve their problems at the box office and adopt a business model that might better exploit the new marketplace.

Though television was not the only source of the studios' box-office woes, by the mid-1950s the studios were resigned to acknowledge that the new medium was a serious threat. So they brokered a peace. In the mid-1950s the détente was dramatically staged with weekly studio-made TV shows that offered a deft combination of original programming and the promotion of Hollywood movies. Once feature films had found a second life on television, the studios began to understand that the new medium was less a rival than a cheap and eager second-run exhibition system.

When the studios were forced to sell their theaters and their real estate—the collateral against which they borrowed the money they needed to finance their films—they became ripe for takeover. It is ironic but nonetheless axiomatic that the conglomeration that has come to characterize the new Hollywood (a subject covered in Chapters 8 and 9) was a direct consequence of divestiture. The Justice Department broke up the studios to create more competition, but the consequent emergence of MCA/Universal, the Gulf and Western–owned Paramount, Kinney National Service's Warner Communications, and Transamerica's United Artists very much countered that impulse. By 1967 a new corporate Hollywood was taking shape, in which the four studios with new conglomerate ownership were in the best position to take advantage of the emerging film markets of the 1970s.

Perhaps the biggest change of all during this period could be seen on the screen. As early as 1953, when Otto Preminger's *The Moon Is Blue* was produced in defiance of the Production Code Administration and succeeded at the box office in an otherwise depressed marketplace, it became clear that something had to be done about the PCA. No doubt America was a different place from what it had been in 1930 when the Motion Picture Production Code was written, but the driving force behind the call for a change was the studios' continuing struggle at the box office. The need to create a fundamentally different product from the shows broadcast on television, new corporate ideas about target markets, and fundamental changes in the demography of the filmgoing public (especially the emerging audience of mostly young viewers hungry for films that reflected their generation's experiences and interests) set in motion a series of challenges to the old production code, challenges that eventually forced the MPAA to adapt or die.

The auteur renaissance that would present something of a golden age in the 1970s found its inspirations in two films released just as the MPAA was dismantling the PCA: *Bonnie and Clyde* and *The Graduate*. Those two films deal with mature themes in a mature manner and evince a visual style rooted in the French New Wave (which was popular with the young, well-educated audience the studios so coveted at the time). The success of those two films came with the unhappy realization that young writers, directors, and producers had a much better idea of what the audience wanted to see than did the aging studio executives—a realization that lay at the heart of the studio's brief embrace of the auteur theory in the 1970s.

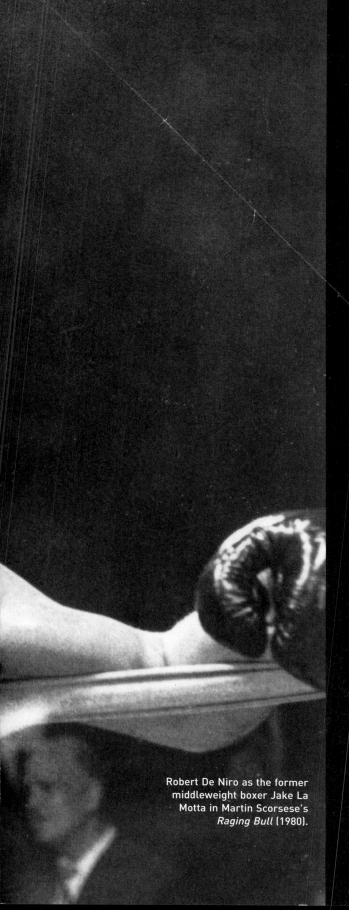

Robert De Niro as the former
middleweight boxer Jake La
Motta in Martin Scorsese's
Raging Bull (1980).

7

A Hollywood
Renaissance

1968–1980

Nineteen sixty-eight was a pivotal year in American film history. The voluntary movie rating system that was introduced that year finally put to rest the Motion Picture Production Code, which had hamstrung filmmakers throughout the sound era, and it completely changed the look and sound of American cinema, making possible more adult-themed films, films that explored in explicit detail formerly regulated subjects like sexuality and criminality.

Nineteen sixty-eight was also a pivotal year in American social and political history. It saw two political assassinations (of the civil rights leader Martin Luther King Jr. and the presidential candidate Robert F. Kennedy) and a dramatic turn for the worse for U.S. forces in the Vietnam War as the Tet Offensive (a surprise attack by the North Vietnamese mounted during the celebration of the lunar new year in Vietnam) made clear to many Americans that the war could not be won. The drama climaxed with riots in Chicago during the Democratic National Convention and ended with the election of Richard Nixon as president. In 1969, Nixon described his election as a victory for the "great silent majority": those Americans who supported the war in Vietnam and proclaimed their confidence in their leaders and their country, right or wrong.

By the time U.S. forces were withdrawn from Vietnam, in 1973, nearly 60,000 American soldiers had been killed and over 150,000 had been wounded in action. Within months of announcing an end to the war, Nixon saw his political career implode when news of his involvement in the criminal cover-up of a break-in at the headquarters of the Democratic National Committee was made public. That scandal, which came to be known as Watergate (after the complex of buildings at which the break-in occurred), forced Nixon's resignation. Such an ignominious ending seemed fitting, given the shadow of dishonesty that hung over his political career and had long before earned him the epithet Tricky Dick. But Watergate also brought public confidence in the establishment to an all-time low.

Domestic protest was a hallmark of the Nixon era. Even before many young Americans organized and marched in protest against the war in Vietnam, movements for the civil rights of African Americans and American women of all races had taken shape. Draft cards, flags, and bras were burned, and America's inner cities erupted in violence. The crime rate skyrocketed (increasing by almost 150 percent between 1955 and 1975), especially in the nation's cities, with much of the increase the result of racial tension.

Against this backdrop of social turmoil, the American economy faltered. Inflation, at least in part a result of rising energy costs, had stymied economic growth. The politics of American dependence on Middle East oil was much in the news throughout the 1970s and reached a crisis in 1979, when a group of students, supporters of Iran's Islamic revolutionary government, seized the U.S. embassy in Tehran and held over fifty Americans hostage for more than fifteen months.

To produce a new American cinema that might reflect or capture this tumultuous era, the studios turned to a coterie of young directors, later dubbed the movie brats. Many of these young cineastes had honed their skills at the nation's top film schools, where they were exposed to not only the best training in production techniques but also film history and film theory. The auteur theory, an argument posed by several French film critics in the late 1950s, which posited that every film has an "author" and that author is the film's director, was particularly attractive to these young directors, all of whom were well aware of the filmmakers before them who had been forced to toe the studio line. The auteurs who came of age in the early 1970s endeavored to place their mark, their artistic signature, on "their" commercial Hollywood films. Those who succeeded in doing so—Francis Ford Coppola, Martin Scorsese, Robert Altman, George Lucas, and Steven Spielberg—became celebrities whose name alone, like that of movie stars of years past, could open (could be used to successfully promote) a film.

These celebrity directors introduced a golden age of American filmmaking, what film historians have come to refer to as the auteur renaissance. Though they pulled Hollywood out of its generation-long box-office slump, the renaissance they initiated was decidedly short-lived. A peculiarly American brand of auteurism was embraced by the studios only so long as the auteurs were able to satisfy the audience's tastes and make money. The new American auteurs tacitly accepted this deal with the devil—embracing the huge budgets and oversize productions of Hollywood filmmaking—partly because they were ambitious and partly because, unlike their French brethren, they did not want to work on small-scale projects or (at least initially) deal with the hassles of independence.

Almost from the start of the auteur renaissance, studio executives were anxious about one day producing an expensive auteur film so personal and so odd that it would bomb at the box office and take the studio management down with it. Their fears were realized in 1980 with Michael Cimino's *Heaven's Gate,* a colossus plagued by budget overruns and production excesses that defied common sense. United Artists lost $40 million on the film, leading its corporate parent, Transamerica, to fire the studio's management. Startled by the disaster, the studios collectively reconsidered their indulgent attitude toward auteur directors and searched for a new model for financially successful moviemaking. An alternative model was already in the making in the late-'70s action-based cinema of Steven Spielberg and George Lucas.

By the time the action blockbuster became the sine qua non of American commercial cinema in 1980, Hollywood had turned things around at the box office. The postwar slump that shaped American film history from 1947 to 1968 was—thanks to the studios' brief indulgence of the auteur theory and the introduction of the blockbuster— finally over. Yet again, Hollywood had been saved from disaster.

REINVENTING HOLLYWOOD

After twenty years of struggle at the box office, the studios made the transition to a new Hollywood guided by a reinvigorated Motion Picture Association of America and its new chief executive, Jack Valenti. The new Hollywood promised to be a place in which filmmakers were far freer to express themselves and the studios were better able to meet the demands of their audience. The first step was a new system of film classification. The second step was an embrace of the auteur theory. The third and final step involved the elimination of competition, especially from an unlikely source: hard-core pornography.

The 1968 Voluntary Film Rating System

On October 7, 1968, MPAA president Jack Valenti issued a press release outlining a radically new motion-picture rating system. The voluntary movie rating system initially comprised four categories: G (suggested for "General" audiences), M (suggested for "Mature" audiences, parental discretion advised), R ("Restricted," no one under age sixteen admitted unless accompanied by a parent or an adult guardian), and X (no one under sixteen admitted). Films rated G, M, and R received an MPAA production seal; films rated X did not. Within a few weeks of Valenti's press release, the voluntary movie rating system was adopted industry-wide. The task of classifying films in advance of their release fell to CARA, the MPAA's newly formed Code and Rating Administration, later renamed (to symbolically eliminate all vestiges of the Production Code Administration) the Classification and Rating Administration.

Though the rating system supplanted a censorship regime that had held sway in Hollywood for over thirty years, it was foremost a business proposition. The studios needed to update their product lines, and the new rating system provided a means toward that end. After 1968 it was no longer a matter of whether a director could or could not shoot a certain scene a certain way, but rather if he shot a scene the way he wanted to, his film might be classified R instead of M (or, later, PG). Either way it would have an MPAA seal and could play in virtually any movie theater without being subject to local bans or seizures. The rating system also

Jack Valenti (*right*), president of the Motion Picture Association of America, with the actor Paul Newman in 1967.

brought together under a single agreement the producers, distributors, and exhibitors of the vast majority of films made for entertainment that were released in the United States. Indeed, when Valenti formally announced the new rating system, he had the support of all the member studios of the MPAA (Columbia, Disney, MGM, Paramount, 20th Century–Fox, United Artists, Universal, and Warner Bros.), as well as NATO (the National Association of Theatre Owners) and IFIDA (the International Film Importers and Distributors of America). Left out of the agreement, significantly, were the smaller American independent film producers and distributors, theater owners who were not members of NATO (approximately 15 percent of the nation's theaters, accounting for barely 5 percent of the domestic box-office take), and the producers, distributors, and exhibitors of hard-core pornography. The new rating system offered a blueprint for a Hollywood in which strategic agreements between MPAA studios and cooperative organizations might further concentrate power among a handful of integrated companies. In this new Hollywood the studios began to challenge the regulatory measures imposed by the *Paramount* decision, which had so crippled the film business in 1948.

From the start, the rating system emphasized parental guidance and studio compliance. Valenti believed that the decision about which films were suitable for children and which were not was best left to parents; hence the change early on from M to GP and then to PG (PARENTAL GUIDANCE SUGGESTED: SOME MATERIAL MAY NOT BE SUITABLE FOR CHILDREN) and then, in 1984, the addition of the PG-13 designation (PARENTS STRONGLY CAUTIONED: SOME MATERIAL MAY BE INAPPROPRIATE FOR CHILDREN UNDER 13). The studios used the rating system less to regulate or censor the content of their films than to differentiate among products to advertise their pictures better and target audiences more precisely.

The Box-Office Recovery

Although the MPAA's voluntary rating system paved the way to a new Hollywood, the studios went through a bumpy transition during the late 1960s and early 1970s. Many of the major releases during those years were remnants of the past, attempts to squeeze the last bit of value out of time-worn formulas that a generation earlier had produced major box-office results. Where the most money was at stake—the movies with the biggest budgets and the highest expectations—Hollywood producers had to accept the fact that they were losing their touch.

Paramount, for one, found itself on the verge of liquidation in 1970. The legions of professionals who depended on Hollywood profits for a paycheck were feeling the pinch, too, as the unemployment rate in Hollywood surged over 40 percent that year. But just as Hollywood seemed to have run out of ideas, the new generation of filmmakers emerged. Working with modest budgets and taking advantage of the new freedom that the rating system provided, they produced movies that were more in touch with the audience and the times.

The top-two box-office films for 1969—the first full year after the adoption of the new rating system—were modestly successful family pictures that seemed very much grounded in the past: *The Love Bug* (Robert Stevenson), a Disney picture released in time for Christmas 1968, and *Funny Girl* (William Wyler), also released in 1968, a big-budget musical in the tradition of such '60s block-busters as *My Fair Lady* (George Cukor, 1964) and *The Sound of Music* (Robert Wise, 1965). For Disney, a company with no interest in testing the waters made safe by the new rating system, *The Love Bug* proved to be a recyclable and mildly profitable franchise film—a movie in a series that tells a long story in several parts or, better yet (for the studios at least), tells the same story over and over again. *Funny Girl* was just another expensive entry in what had become a cycle of at best break-even musicals: *Camelot* (Joshua Logan, 1967), which cost $17 million and grossed $14 million, *Doctor Dolittle* (Richard Fleischer, 1967), produced at a cost of $18 million and grossing just $8 million; *Star!* (Wise, 1968), made for $14 million and returning only $4 million; *Sweet Charity* (Bob Fosse, 1969), produced at a cost of $20 million and returning only $4 million, and *Paint Your Wagon* (Logan, 1969), budgeted at $20 million and grossing $14 million.

Signs of change could be found further down the list of 1969 releases, which included four adult-themed titles: *Midnight Cowboy* (John Schlesinger), a frank studio film about a dim-witted male prostitute and the alcoholic street punk who befriends him, the number 7 film for the year, released with a self-imposed X rating; *I Am Curious (Yellow)* (Vilgot Sjöman), a Swedish soft-core sex film that finished the year with the twelfth-highest box-office earnings; *Three in the Attic* (Richard Wilson), a teen-targeted picture released by the exploitation distributor American International Pictures, which ranked eighteenth; and the independently financed and produced *Easy Rider* (Dennis Hopper), a biker-road picture, eventually picked up for distribution by Columbia, which ranked eleventh. Each of those films took full advantage of the new rating system, exploring prostitution, drug use, homosexuality, the generation gap, and the sexual revolution without apology, without sentimentality, without hedging on detail. Those films earned their R and X ratings and in so doing earned the respect of a new generation of filmgoers.

The number 1 film in 1970 was an old-fashioned big-budget disaster epic, *Airport* (George Seaton), built around the aging stars Burt Lancaster, Dean Martin, George Kennedy, and Helen Hayes. Following the success of *Airport*, the studios produced a series of similarly packaged disaster pictures: *The Poseidon Adventure* (Ronald Neame) was the number 1 film in 1973; *Airport 1975* (Jack Smight) ranked twelfth in 1974; and *The Towering Inferno* (John Guillermin and Irwin Allen) weighed in at number 2 in 1975. But much as the studios might have wanted to look to *Airport* as a sign of good things to come (making money from slightly updated versions of bloated old-style Hollywood pictures), the disaster-picture trend was over in five years.

Signs pointing in the direction that the studios would have to take were evident further down the 1970 box-office list in the form of films that successfully targeted the youth market: *MASH* (Robert Altman), the number 2 earner, balanced bloody operating-room scenes with brief nudity and frank

talk about sex; *Bob & Carol & Ted & Alice* (Paul Mazursky), a parody of wife-swapping swingers playing and losing at being sexually liberated, finished the year at number 4; *Woodstock* (Michael Wadleigh), the rock-festival documentary, was number 5; and the adaptation of Joseph Heller's popular satirical antiwar novel *Catch-22* (Mike Nichols) was number 8.

Each of those films appealed to the youth demographic, but each was unique and could not be reduced to a formula. That fact troubled studio executives because it meant they couldn't reliably repeat the films' success. *MASH*'s success seemed to be the result of an especially talented director, Robert Altman, who enjoyed an unusual degree of

Barbra Streisand as the comedienne Fannie Brice in the William Wyler musical *Funny Girl* (1968). Despite ranking second overall in box-office revenues, *Funny Girl* cost so much, with its opulent production numbers like the one pictured here, that Columbia barely broke even on the film.

Michael Wadleigh's 3-hour look at the Woodstock music festival was the number 5 film for 1970, quite a feat for a documentary. The film captured the spirit of a generation of American youth that mainstream Hollywood struggled to comprehend in the late 1960s.

freedom while making the picture. *MASH* also carried a distinct antiwar message; though set in Korea in the 1950s, it made clear its relevance to the war in Vietnam at a time when the studios were reluctant to criticize that conflict directly. *Woodstock* was a documentary of a unique landmark event in American teen culture that obviously couldn't be repeated. *Catch-22* was an adaptation of a popular and topical antiwar, antiestablishment novel, and *Bob & Carol & Ted & Alice* was a timely and sexy parody of the era's social and sexual experimentation.

Studio executives in 1970 began to realize that an emerging generation of filmmakers making topical movies with a political edge had a much more instinctive sense of what the youth audience wanted to see on-screen than did the executives

themselves. By 1972 this shift in public taste and the ability of young filmmakers to tap into it was impossible to ignore. Although the results for that year suggested that the overall box-office numbers for the industry were up for the first time in a generation, a closer look revealed that one film, Francis Ford Coppola's *Godfather*, had seemingly carried the entire industry on its back. Its record-breaking revenues of $80 million, more than three times the box-office take of the number 2 film, *Fiddler on the Roof* (Norman Jewison, 1971), single-handedly skewed industry data upward. Things were indeed better at the box office, but mostly because of just one studio (Paramount) and just one film.

The Godfather's effect on the studios is hard to overstate. For a brief but crucial period after 1972, studio executives began courting young directors and putting their names above the titles of their films, exploiting a sort of auteur marketing theory. The list of top-twenty box-office films for 1972 provided ample evidence of the value of auteur pictures. Included were eight auteur pictures: *The Godfather* (at number 1), Peter Bogdanovich's *What's Up, Doc?* (number 4) and *The Last Picture Show* (number 6), Stanley Kubrick's *A Clockwork Orange* (number 7) and *2001: A Space Odyssey* (in reissue at number 20), Woody Allen's *Everything You Always Wanted to Know about Sex* (number 10), Franklin J. Schaffner's *Nicholas and Alexandra* (number 13), and Alfred Hitchcock's *Frenzy* (number 14). In the following year, *Deliverance* (John Boorman), *The Getaway* (Sam Peckinpah), *Paper Moon* (Bogdanovich), *Last Tango in Paris* (Bernardo Bertolucci), and *American Graffiti* (George Lucas), all auteur films, hit the top twenty. Like it or not, the executives were forced to accept the fact that auteur directors had a better record of success at the box office than they did. That realization, which should have evoked relief and gratitude, instead struck many studio executives as a rude awakening.

The Astonishing Popularity of Pornography

Another rude awakening came from outside mainstream Hollywood. From June 1972 to June 1973, three hard-core sex features—*Deep Throat* (Gerard Damiano, 1972), *Behind the Green Door* (Jim and Artie Mitchell, 1972), and *The Devil in Miss Jones* (Damiano, 1973)—outearned all but a handful of the major studios' releases. The astonishing popularity of what were clearly hard-core sex films took Valenti and the MPAA by surprise. When he introduced the rating system in 1968, Valenti was reluctant to include the X rating at all, relenting only after the studios pressured him to do so. Even then he chose not to copyright the X (as he had done for the other ratings): he believed Hollywood would have no use for the classification or for films that merited it. Because of that choice, many independent filmmakers and studios freely used the X rating (and later, for emphasis, the XXX label) as a publicity stunt and advertising teaser without submitting their films to CARA for review. The

(*top*) Army surgeons Hawkeye Pierce (Donald Sutherland) and Trapper John McIntyre (Elliott Gould) get ready to tee off in Robert Altman's Korean War comedy *MASH* (1970). The doctors' irreverent attitude toward the war struck a chord with a generation disillusioned with the war in Vietnam.

(*bottom*) Maria Schneider and Marlon Brando share an intimate moment in the X-rated *Last Tango in Paris* (Bernardo Bertoluci, 1972). Despite (or because of) ample nudity, coarse language, and a simulated scene of anal sex, *Last Tango* did big business at the box office.

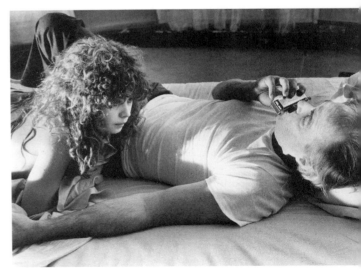

three hard-core hits of the 1972–1973 season made the X rating seem chic.

Deep Throat led the way in June 1972, becoming the first crossover adults-only hit. The film piqued the interest of audiences previously disinclined to patronize hard core, and it even attracted the (favorable) attention of some mainstream celebrities and critics. The film made light of the conventions of stag and previous hard-core films yet did not stint on the extent, duration, or clinical specificity of the requisite hard-core action. True to its roots in the much-publicized sexual revolution, the film maintained that sex and, by extension, sex on-screen need not be taken so seriously.

Deep Throat had an astonishing nationwide fame. It is hard to imagine another 1972 release, besides *The Godfather,* that had wider name recognition. *Deep Throat* enjoyed an astonishing first run that held strong for a full year; after forty-eight weeks in release, it was still ranked as high as tenth in box-office revenues.

As hard-core movies began to sport impressive box-office numbers, producers and distributors of porn movies and, in a less enthusiastic way, the mainstream trades were inclined to argue that legitimacy was less a matter of content than audience share. Films like *Deep Throat* and *The Devil in Miss Jones* competed successfully with mainstream pictures, most of which benefited from wider and more professionally executed release

strategies. *The Devil in Miss Jones* grossed $7.7 million and ranked seventh overall in 1973, just below the James Bond film *Live and Let Die* (Guy Hamilton) and the Academy Award–nominated comedy *Paper Moon. Deep Throat* grossed $4.6 million and ranked eleventh, sandwiched between the controversial studio film *Deliverance* and the Broadway-play adaptation *Sleuth* (Joseph Mankiewicz). The success of hard-core films triggered a trend toward more explicit fare in mainstream moviemaking. Less than a year after the release of *Deep Throat,* the X-rated studio-distributed *Last Tango in Paris* weighed in at number 1; *Billy Jack,* Tom Laughlin's R-rated independently distributed youth-culture picture (which features a graphic on-screen rape) was number 3.

The porn-chic phenomenon was fueled as much by broad social trends (such as the much-discussed sexual revolution) as by the films themselves. But the question of whether the remarkable run of hard-core successes would continue throughout the 1970s, forcing the major studios to respond to a new and unexpected competitor for audience share, was answered not by the marketplace but by the U.S. Supreme Court. In 1973 and 1974 the so-called Nixon court (four of the nine justices having been appointed by President Nixon) rendered five major decisions that effectively banned hard-core movies from public theaters yet shielded mainstream Hollywood studios from censorship.

The pivotal case was *Miller v. California* (1973), and its significance to the industry was lost on no one in Hollywood at the time. *Miller v. California* concerned the mass mailing of an advertisement circular by an erotic bookseller named Marvin Miller. When the circular arrived, unsolicited, at a Newport Beach restaurant, the manager and his mother promptly called the police. They filed a complaint, and Miller was arrested for violating California's criminal obscenity statute. He was tried and convicted, and all his appeals were denied. The U.S. Supreme Court agreed to hear the case, then opted to vacate the judgment and return the case to the California courts with a new set of

Linda Lovelace in her nurse's uniform in the 1972 box-office hit *Deep Throat* (Gerard Damiano). Though the film featured plenty of hard-core action, it crossed over from porno houses to mainstream theaters and proved popular with folks who had never gone to a hard-core film before.

In 1971 the state of Georgia sought a ban on screenings of the R-rated film *Carnal Knowledge* (Mike Nichols) and the Motion Picture Association of America fought back. When the Supreme Court finally rendered its unanimous decision in favor of the MPAA, in 1973, the jurists implied that no film rated R, PG-13, PG, or G could be found obscene by any reasonable legal standard. Pictured here are the film's two stars, Ann-Margret and Jack Nicholson.

prosecutorial guidelines, which virtually guaranteed a conviction. Writing for the 5–4 majority, Chief Justice Warren Berger effectively ceded content regulation to local communities, empowering them—within certain broad guidelines regarding explicit hard-core sexual content—to decide what could and could not play on local movie screens. Had this case been the final word on the matter, Hollywood might have found itself in the same situation as the hard-core producers: in danger of having some of their products shut out of all but the most limited (and unattractive) markets.

But within a year of the Court's decision in *Miller v. California*, the studios got the marketplace all to themselves when a simply ridiculous obscenity case, *Jenkins v. Georgia* (1974), found its way to the Supreme Court. *Jenkins v. Georgia* concerned a local attempt to prohibit the screening of a studio-made R-rated film—*Carnal Knowledge* (Nichols, 1971)—that contains rough language and brief nudity but no hard-core action. Georgia's statewide ban on *Carnal Knowledge* seemed at first a harbinger of more nuisance cases to come. But in the end it wasn't. The ease with which the Supreme Court dispatched the *Jenkins* case (ruling 9–0 to overturn the local ban) seemed to prove the value and utility of Valenti's voluntary rating system. Thanks to the decision in the *Jenkins* case, since 1974 studio films rated G, PG, PG-13, and R have moved through the vast entertainment marketplace with virtual immunity from local bans and seizures.

MAJOR FILMS AND FILMMAKERS OF THE AUTEUR RENAISSANCE

For many film historians and movie buffs, the so-called auteur renaissance is something of a golden age in Hollywood. Indeed, it is hard to dispute the volume of quality studio filmmaking from that time. But as mentioned earlier in this chapter, the

executives' ceding of creative power to so-called auteur directors was from the outset temporary; as soon as another, less demeaning, less risky production model emerged, the auteurs' day in the sun would be over.

Easy Rider

Made for a mere $375,000 and earning an astonishing $19 million in its initial release in 1969, Dennis Hopper's *Easy Rider* made clear just how important the youth audience would be to a Hollywood recovery. Its free-form style and evocative use of a rock- and pop-music score (including one song each by Bob Dylan and Jimi Hendrix and two recorded by Steppenwolf) provided a template for future gestures in the younger generation's direction. But perhaps more significant in the larger history of American cinema, *Easy Rider* is very much an auteur picture, one in which an auteur's eccentric style and form transformed a familiar genre (the road picture) into something undeniably modern and idiosyncratic.

Easy Rider was produced independently by BBS Productions, named for the company's three partners, the co-producers of television's popular musical-comedy series *The Monkees*: Bob Rafelson, Bert Schneider and Steve Blauner. It stars Peter Fonda, the star of the surprise hit biker film *The*

Wild Angels (Roger Corman, 1966) and son of the legendary movie star Henry Fonda, and was directed by the veteran character actor (but neophyte director) Dennis Hopper.

Working closely with Fonda, his co-star and co-writer, and the popular '60s novelist and screenwriter Terry Southern, Hopper fashioned a complex mix of the teen biker picture (borrowing from *The Wild Angels*), the French New Wave (the director's penchant for breaking down narrative structure, toying with genre, mixing and matching styles, and most important, capturing an ambience of cool), and cinema verité or direct-cinema documentaries. The documentary style was especially important to the film's larger appeal as it enticed viewers to sympathize with its counterculture heroes. For example, in one particularly disturbing scene, Wyatt and Billy (Fonda and Hopper) happen on a luncheonette in the rural South, where they are treated with suspicion. The clever use of documentary-style handheld camerawork, unprofessional actors (the other patrons were indeed residents of the small southern town), and unscripted dialogue reveals a truth about this seemingly other America (the film's poster tagline read: "A man went looking for America, but couldn't find it anywhere"). Two truck drivers who observe Wyatt and Billy remark that they "look like refugees from some gorilla love-in. . . . We ought to mate them up with black wenches. . . . That's

The director Haskell Wexler's deft use of documentary film technique in his fictional picture *Medium Cool* (1969) took filmgoers places Hollywood never dared to take them, such as this scene of urban poverty shot in a Chicago ghetto.

as low as you can git." Hopper's willingness to let the scene play out without direction or plan made the conflict in the luncheonette all the more terrifying and made inevitable the film's ending, in which our hippie heroes are gunned down by two rednecks to the strains of Bob Dylan's "It's Alright Ma (I'm Only Bleeding)."

Easy Rider's box-office success and cultural cachet highlighted a brief run of counterculture pictures, none of which was as successful as the original. Notable among these were Arthur Penn's affectionate comedy *Alice's Restaurant* (1969); Haskell Wexler's stylistically innovative, politically complex realist melodrama *Medium Cool* (1969); the notorious X-rated chronicle of campus unrest and the sexual revolution by the Italian Marxist cineaste Michelangelo Antonioni, *Zabriskie Point* (1970); Bob Rafelson's exploration of a young pianist's alienation in *Five Easy Pieces* (1970); the rock-festival documentary *Woodstock* (Michael Wadleigh, 1970); *Joe* (1970), a film about generational unease directed with just the right amount of gratuitous sex and hysterical violence by John Avildsen (who would go on to direct some of the *Rocky* and *Karate Kid* films); *Getting Straight* (1970), Richard Rush's tongue-in-cheek look at campus unrest; Jerry Schatzberg's realist study of two young heroin addicts in *The Panic in Needle Park* (1971), the first film to showcase the considerable talents of Al Pacino; Milos Forman's deft generation-gap satire, *Taking Off* (1971); and the drug melodrama *Cisco Pike* (Bill L. Norton, 1972). What all of these films had in common, besides their focus on youth culture, was their seeming independence from the old Hollywood style and an insistence on a new way of making and looking at commercial motion pictures.

(*left*) Billy (Dennis Hopper, *left*) and Wyatt (Peter Fonda, *center*) in search of America in the quintessential hippie road picture, *Easy Rider* (Hopper, 1969).

The Godfather, Parts I and II

In 1969, executives at Warner Bros. gave Francis Ford Coppola, a relative unknown in Hollywood, $600,000 to develop the next low-budget youth-culture hit. Coppola took the money, bought expensive filmmaking equipment, rented space in an office building in San Francisco, and surrounded himself with a group of talented recent film-school graduates who would all become well-known: Carroll Ballard, who would direct *The Black Stallion* (1979); Willard Huyck and Gloria Katz, who together would write the script for George Lucas's *American Graffiti* (1973); Jim McBride, who would direct a remake of *Breathless* (1983) and the New Orleans–based cop film *The Big Easy* (1987); John Milius, who would co-write the screenplays for *Jeremiah Johnson* (Sydney Pollack, 1972) and *Apocalypse Now* (Coppola, 1979) and direct *Conan the Barbarian* (1982) and *Red Dawn* (1984); the sound engineer Walter Murch, who worked on all

Francis Ford Coppola in the fall of 1972 posed in front of a poster for *The Godfather*. By then the film had won three Oscars (including Best Picture) and Coppola was suddenly the most famous filmmaker in America.

three *Godfather* films as well as Coppola's *Conversation* (1974) and *Apocalypse Now*; and as company vice president, George Lucas. While it is fair to say that Coppola took the studio's money without ever really intending to make the next *Easy Rider*, it is also fair to say that his San Francisco–based dream studio, dubbed American Zoetrope, was conceived to jump-start a new Hollywood.

After a year, Coppola returned to Warner Bros. and pitched four ideas: a dystopian science-fiction film about a populace kept in line by mandatory medication; a thriller based on Antonioni's *Blow-Up* (1966), in which a sound engineer (instead of a fashion photographer, as in the original) unintentionally discovers evidence of a crime; a Vietnam War film about American soldiers who love to surf; and a teen pic about a group of northern California kids on their last night of high school, staring down a future that might well include a tour of duty in Vietnam. None of those films sounded anything like *Easy Rider* to the executives at Warner Bros., so the studio passed on all four.

The failure of Warner Bros. to secure rights to the American Zoetrope slate of films in develop-

ment in 1970 proved to be one of the biggest blunders in modern Hollywood history. All four of those films, conceived and developed at American Zoetrope, made their way to the big screen. The dystopian sci-fi project, *THX 1138* (Lucas, 1971), has become something of a cult film. The proposed remake of *Blow-Up* became *The Conversation*, which won the Grand Prix at Cannes in 1974 and cemented Coppola's reputation as a major international auteur. The Vietnam film was released in 1979 as *Apocalypse Now* to huge box-office success and another top prize at Cannes. And the small-town teen pic became *American Graffiti*, directed by Lucas, with Coppola as executive producer. *American Graffiti* was in its day the top-grossing independent production of all time.

However foolish Warner Bros. looks in retrospect, the unhappy arrangement between the studio and American Zoetrope was emblematic of the times. As the studios had discovered with *Bonnie and Clyde* (Penn, 1967), *The Graduate* (Mike Nichols, 1967), and *Easy Rider*, the only short-term strategy that made any sense for them was to trust young maverick directors whom the aging executives could not fully understand or control. The alternative was to resign themselves to a dwindling market share and an increasing identification with the very sort of film, like *Funny Girl* (William Wyler, 1968) or *The Love Bug* (Robert Stevenson, 1968), that either cost too much to make a profit or made the studios look ridiculous to the youth audience.

After Warner Bros. pulled the plug on American Zoetrope, Coppola paid the bills by making technical films and television commercials. Then, in 1970, he got a big break: an offer to work on the screenplay for the World War II biopic *Patton* (Franklin J. Schaffner, 1970), a commercial hit about the legendary take-no-prisoners general and war hero. That work won for Coppola his first Academy Award (shared with Edmund North). The next year, Paramount Pictures offered Coppola the director's chair for *The Godfather*, one of the luckiest big breaks in motion-picture history, for both Coppola and Paramount.

Coppola got the assignment to direct *The Godfather* only after the project was turned down by Richard Brooks (*The Blackboard Jungle*, 1955; *Cat on a Hot Tin Roof*, 1958; *In Cold Blood*, 1967), Constantin Costa-Gavras (*Z*, 1969), Elia Kazan (*A*

Streetcar Named Desire, 1951; *On the Waterfront*, 1954), Arthur Penn (*Bonnie and Clyde*), Franklin Schaffner (*Patton*), Fred Zinnemann (*High Noon*, 1952; *From Here to Eternity*, 1953; *A Man for All Seasons*, 1966), Lewis Gilbert (*Alfie*, 1966; *You Only Live Twice*, 1967), and Peter Yates (*Bullitt*, 1968). Paramount's production chief, Robert Evans, turned to Coppola for three reason: he had run out of A-list talent, his assistant, Peter Bart, admired Coppola's screenplay for *Patton;* and Coppola was Italian (the studio was concerned about the reaction of the Italian American community to yet another film about the Mafia, and Evans thought that having an Italian American at the helm would insulate the movie from criticism).

The Godfather has become a legendary auteur film, the film routinely identified as the first major picture in the '70s Hollywood renaissance. But although Coppola's signature is all over the picture, *The Godfather* is at its core a traditional genre film. Along with its sequel, *The Godfather: Part II* (Coppola, 1974), *The Godfather* revived the thematic conceits of earlier gangster films: the parallel dramas of assimilation (as immigrants become Americans) and ambition.

In *Scarface* (Howard Hawks, 1932), the classic '30s gangster picture, Tony Camonte's American dream corresponds to the travel-agency sign outside his window: "The World Is Yours." Tony understands what he has to do to realize that dream: "Do it first, do it yourself, and keep on doing it." Vito Corleone (Marlon Brando in *The Godfather*, Robert De Niro in *The Godfather: Part II*) also appreciates what he has to do to get ahead. He pursues the American dream, but unlike Tony he does so less for material reward than for social mobility. Vito, unlike Tony, is a family man. And because he is basically decent, Vito gets to enjoy

Don Corleone (Marlon Brando) addressing a meeting of the five (New York crime) families in Francis Ford Coppola's *The Godfather* (1972). Behind him to the right is his consigliere, Tom Hagen (Robert Duvall). The scene is set as if it were just another board meeting for wealthy executives; the only difference is that the participants discuss recent assassinations and criminal conspiracies involving law enforcement and government officials.

It's lonely at the top: Michael
Corleone (Al Pacino) at the end of
The Godfather, Part II (Francis Ford
Coppola, 1974). He may be the most
powerful man in America, but he has
had to kill his brother to get there.

the material rewards of his criminal empire into old age; he lives far longer and dies far more peacefully (in a garden at his home) than Tony (who is gunned down in the streets while still a young man). But the promise of social mobility, legitimacy, and acceptance in America nonetheless eludes him. In a rueful conversation late in *The Godfather,* well after he has turned over the day-to-day aspects of the family business to his son Michael (Al Pacino), Vito talks about what might have been. He says he has no regrets for what he has had to do to become a success in his line of work; he has done what was necessary to take care of his family. He had hoped that someday Michael might be able to enjoy a life completely independent of the family business. But his dreams of Michael the congressman or senator never pan out. An assassination attempt on his life and a successful hit on Sonny (James Caan), Michael's older brother, force Michael into the family business. And once in, there is no way out.

As the latter half of *The Godfather* and all of *The Godfather: Part II* make clear, Michael is a far more modern gangster than his father; he is by all outward appearances the legitimate businessman Vito had hoped his son would be. But as the business gets bigger and remaining in control becomes more perilous, maintaining a happy family life, something that came easily to his father, becomes impossible for Michael. The business, which was once a means for the family to rise out of poverty, ends up destroying any chance, even late in life, for Michael, his wife, and their children to have what more ordinary folks consider a happy life.

Legend has it that production executives at Paramount bristled when Coppola announced a few weeks before principal photography commenced on the film that in his view Mario Puzo's best-selling novel *The Godfather,* on which the film is based, isn't about gangsters; it is about family. The intersections of the two concerns—the professional life of a bunch of gangsters and the private life of a family (albeit an exceptionally interesting, rich, and powerful family)—are very much at the heart of the *Godfather* films. The conflict between business and family is made clear from the outset, as *The Godfather* opens in a warmly lit office on Vito's estate as an undertaker (Salvatore Corsitto) begs Vito to kill the man who raped his daughter. Vito promises justice and offers to take care of the matter in exchange for an as-yet-unde-

termined favor. A second supplicant asks Vito to help a boy clear immigration so he can marry the man's daughter and stay in the country. Vito offers his hand (for the man to kiss) and his help, again in exchange for a future consideration. Vito delegates both assignments (he is, after all, a businessman), turning over to out-of-town muscle the dirty job of dealing with the rapist and to "some Jew congressman from another district" the immigration problem. That Vito can administer to these two tasks without leaving his den, that he has access to both hit men and politicians (and, we gather, all sorts of people in between), clearly signals the range of his connections and the breadth of his power.

The film then cuts to the sunlit wedding party of Vito's daughter Connie (Talia Shire) in the yard outside his office, a family event that business has temporarily kept Vito from enjoying. The move outside to the party gives us a first look at the importance of family in the film. It also presents in microcosm a larger drama of assimilation that is shared by many immigrants. At the party we first meet Michael with his girlfriend, Kay (Diane Keaton), who stands out because she is not Italian. As she marvels at the rituals of a proper Italian wedding (some of which are decidedly Old World) and sits slack-jawed as Michael tells her a story about Luca Brasi (Lenny Montana), an enforcer employed by his father who once made a bandleader "an offer he couldn't refuse," Michael tells Kay, "That's my family . . . , it's not me." For the moment at least, Michael's remark is a repudiation of not only family but the family business and his ethnic heritage as well. He is an American war hero first—he is introduced in uniform—a Sicilian and his father's son a distant second. The fair-haired Kay on his arm makes clear his effort to break with the past.

The band at the wedding plays Italian songs. When family members and other guests mount the stage, they sing in Italian. When Johnny Fontane (the benefactor of the offer the bandleader could not refuse, played by Al Martino) arrives, he, too, takes to the stage to sing a song from the Old Country. It is probably not part of his professional repertoire, but it is meant as a tribute to his benefactor and host and as an affirmation of the collective roots of pretty much everyone at the party. Conspicuously absent from the festivities are the establishment types with whom Vito does business.

Johnny Fontane (Al Martino) singing a song from the Old Country to Vito Corleone's daughter, Connie (Talia Shire), at her wedding reception at the start of *The Godfather* (Francis Ford Coppola, 1972).

The party commemorating the first communion of Michael's son Anthony (James Gounaris), which opens *The Godfather: Part II*, features a far more ethnically diverse crowd. The Old World types who are so at home at the wedding in the first *Godfather* film, like Frankie Pentangeli (Michael Gazzo), chafe at Michael's family's pretenses to assimilation. First Frankie complains about the food (canapés, which he pronounces "can of peas," instead of antipasto). Frustrated by the orchestra's bland pop tunes, Frankie bounds up to the stage and tries to get the musicians to play a song from the Old Country. But they're not Italian, and when Frankie hums a few bars to get them started, the band members stupidly interpret the tune as "Pop Goes the Weasel." Lost in the move toward legitimacy, lost in the move from New York to Lake Tahoe, are the family's roots, their Italian American heritage. They are finally Americans perhaps, but as the opening of *The Godfather: Part II* makes clear, that may not be such a good thing.

As Frankie vents his frustration outside on the grounds of the family's home at the start of *Part II*, the film cuts to Michael's coolly lit office, again emphasizing the competition between business and family. Inside, Michael meets with Nevada senator Pat Geary (G. D. Spradlin), who is putting the final touches on a deal that may allow Michael to secure a gaming license for a Corleone-controlled casino. Geary, who tries to extort a payoff before signing the deal, makes clear that Michael's pose as a legitimate American businessman is a convenient fiction. "I don't like your kind of people," Geary says bluntly; "I despise your masquerade." When Michael counters that he and Geary are part of "the same hypocrisy," Geary, though he is extorting graft, dismisses the notion as patently ridiculous. From where he sits, Michael is an Italian mafioso, a gangster in a suit. Geary, an establishment politician, the very sort of guy who respectfully declined an invitation to Connie's wedding in *The Godfather*, sees himself as a legitimate American success. The film quickly corrects the misapprehension on his part as Michael's remark about hypocrisy is proved out. With the help of his brother Fredo (John Cazale), Michael frames Geary for a murder at a brothel. He earns—extorts—the senator's loyalty (which comes in handy during a Senate hearing into organized crime) when he offers to keep the story out of the papers and the woman's body away from the police. It is an apparent victory for the family over the ostensibly more legitimate but morally weak American establishment culture; it is also a reminder of the cost of doing business, a cost that serves only to complicate the long-term plan of assimilation and legitimate social status.

What Coppola clearly shows in both films is that in the criminal underworld, family and business intersect. In the first *Godfather* film, threats inevitably come from outside the family: the Jewish gangster Moe Greene (Alex Rocco), their rival for control of a Las Vegas casino; the drug kingpin Sollozzo (Al Lettieri), who fails in an attempt to assassinate Vito; and the rival five (Mafia) families who struggle with the Corleones for control of organized crime in New York. In *Part II*, Michael battles the Jewish gangster Hyman Roth (Lee Strasberg), who enlists Michael's brother Fredo in a move against him. The assassination attempt facilitated by Fredo fails, but because it takes place inside Michael's compound (with Michael and Kay in bed when the gunfire commences), it nonetheless highlights the problematic balance of business and family.

Coppola achieved in the first two *Godfather* films his primary goal as an auteur: to take a mainstream Hollywood genre product and make it his own. His examination of the family business and the business of family and of ethnicity and assimilation was particularly deft and sophisticated. But where Coppola broke out of the genre mold was in his imposition of an idiosyncratic artistic signature. Coppola is primarily a cine-stylist, a director with a fondness for theatrical setups and an attraction to the epic in scale and scope. He is fond of set pieces and places an extraordinary emphasis on set design, lighting, and camerawork.

In a scene about an hour into *The Godfather*, for example, just after the don is shot, Tom Hagen (Robert Duvall) is kidnapped by the don's would-be assassin, the drug-lord Sollozzo. Coppola sets this key scene in what looks like a trailer, and he shoots the principals, at least initially, with a long-

angle lens. The human figures are indiscernible in the dark, and we are given no establishing shot to tell us where we are or what is taking place. We share with Tom, who is held against his will, a profound sense of uncertainty. The suspense is broken when we hear Sollozzo's voice as he negotiates with Tom. The drug lord crosses in front of the camera and is captured in a grotesque close-up, bathed in monstrous orange light. The shot tells us what we need to know about him. When we finally see Tom, he is half lit, half dark (an apt physical portrait of the man who is at once the family's legitimate attorney and Vito's adopted son—the family's non-Italian face in the legitimate business world). The scene ends in darkness outside at a lot where Christmas trees are sold (where, as we have finally discovered, the trailer sits), and though we can't see the faces of Sollozzo's gang members, a key piece of information is revealed:

Young Vito Corleone (Robert De Niro, *right*) with his family on the steps of his New York City apartment building in *The Godfather: Part II* (Francis Ford Coppola, 1974).

the hit has failed; Vito lives. This last part of the scene is rushed and played entirely in the dark, a visual referent for what the sudden change in fortune means to Tom's captors. A later scene has Michael rehearsing his eventual assassination of Sollozzo and a corrupt New York City cop (Sterling Hayden). As the family henchman, Clemenza (Richard S. Castellano), gives Michael some lessons on how to make a successful hit, the two men sit below a framed portrait of the pope. The irony in the set design is hard to miss.

Also important to both films is Coppola's dramatic use of parallel editing. Interestingly, such editing is striking because Coppola uses it much less often than other directors. His commitment to theatrical blocking (for example, in the many scenes in *Part II* that are dominated by Michael seated regally) and to long scenes played out as if onstage, with subtle camera movement leading the viewer through the space of the film, means that when he shifts to montage, the contrast to the rest of the film is striking. The climactic scene in *The Godfather*, for example, shows Michael in the warmly lit interior of a church, attending the baptism of his nephew and godson, intercut with a sequence of shots revealing the perfect execution of a plan to assassinate all of Michael's rivals and enemies. The sequence itself is so well executed that, like the hits depicted on-screen, we come to admire their author's expertise—that is, both the film's author, Coppola, and the author of the assassinations in the film, Michael. The sequence ends with a quick survey of the corpses that have marked Michael's ascension and is punctuated as one of Michael's henchmen whispers in his boss's ear outside the church. So compelling is the filmmaking, so expert the planned killings, that it is hard not to feel a sense of elation at this point, a sense that the right man, through means we can hardly endorse, has made his way to the top.

Though *Part II* is highly theatrical—much of the film is composed of meetings, as if it were about businessmen and not gangsters—Coppola cleverly intercuts scenes of the early days of young Vito on the streets of New York (a time preceding the period covered in the first film) with Michael's struggles as the nation's number 1 crime boss in the postwar era (which take place in the years after he secures power at the end of *The Godfather*). Coppola links the two time periods with elegant dissolves; the film thus moves fluidly back and forth

between the rugged simplicity of the New York streets that Vito eventually controls and the far-reaching sites of the multinational capitalist empire—Lake Tahoe, Las Vegas, New York, Miami, and Havana—that Michael, through business acumen and occasional brutality, supervises.

Both films use warm orange and brown lighting schemes in Vito's and then Michael's offices as an ironic counterpoint to the cold brutality of the business plans formed there. These warm-hued scenes are complemented by the brightly lit sequences in Hollywood, Las Vegas, and Havana, where in both films the Corleones engage in semi-legitimate, mostly nonviolent capitalist acquisition. The family space is warm and soft; the public sphere, cold and harsh.

Though the first two *Godfather* films look back to the 1930s gangster pictures that Coppola no doubt learned to love in film school, they were nonetheless timely in 1972. They explored the myriad connections between legitimate and criminal capitalism at a time when the Vietnam War had increased awareness of the corruption at the heart of the military-industrial complex. A key scene in the second film makes this clear. On a balcony at a posh hotel in Havana, Hyman Roth, Michael, and a handful of other gangsters carve up a cake that was made in the shape of Cuba, fully aware of the act's symbolic importance vis-à-vis American corporate imperialism. The family problems of the Corleones speak volumes about a nation in the throes of dramatic social change and in the midst of what many Americans believed was a doomed colonial mission in Indochina.

While *The Godfather* today is widely acknowledged as one of the best studio films ever made, its historical significance to the industry cannot be overstated. Produced for a mere $6 million, it earned over $80 million in its initial theatrical release, shattering box-office records that were more than thirty years old (going all the way back to 1939 and *Gone with the Wind*). Estimates of its worldwide box-office earnings through its two major theatrical releases (in 1972 and 1997) top out at almost $250 million. *The Godfather* saved Paramount and likely saved Hollywood. Moreover, it set in fast motion the auteur renaissance, clearing the way for the many directors who enjoyed considerable creative freedom in the 1970s. Those directors, and Hollywood itself, owe a significant debt to Coppola.

Chinatown

With the success of *The Godfather* fresh in his mind, Robert Evans bet on *Chinatown* (1974) to be Paramount's next big film. Directing the picture was Roman Polanski, who was then best known in the United States for having been the husband of Sharon Tate (one of the victims of the gruesome 1969 murder spree by the so-called Manson family). Polanski had a solid reputation in Europe dat-

ing back to 1962, but before *Chinatown*, he had only one major American hit. His 1968 horror picture *Rosemary's Baby* earned ten times its production budget in its initial release and received two Academy Award nominations, including one for Polanski for his adaptation of Ira Levin's best-selling novel. Tate's murder derailed Polanski's American career; indeed his only notable U.S. release between *Rosemary's Baby* and *Chinatown* was an exceedingly bloody adaptation of Shakespeare's

The montage sequence at the end of Francis Ford Coppola's *The Godfather* (1972) brings into relief the two aspects of Michael's life that are becoming increasingly irreconcilable: family (represented here by Michael's nephew and godson's baptism) and business (represented by a series of assassinations that have made Michael, played by Al Pacino, the most powerful gangster in New York). (a.) Michael looks down at his godson; (b.) family rival Moe Greene (Alex Rocco) is assassinated while getting a massage; (c.) a hitman (Tom Rosqui) kills one of Michael's rivals; (d.) Don Barzini (Richard Conte), Michael's most powerful adversary, is shot dead; (e.) Michael renouncing Satan in church while his hitmen do his dirty work on the streets; (f.) Al Neri (Richard Bright) delivers the good news (about the assassinations) on the steps outside the church.

The Paramount production chief Robert Evans posing in front of a poster of *Chinatown* (Roman Polanski, 1974), the prototypical studio auteur film.

MacBeth (1971) co-produced by Hugh Hefner's *Playboy Pictures* that seemed all too obviously to allude to the Manson killings. So when Evans chose Polanski to direct this next big Paramount picture, it seemed something of a wild gamble. Polanski was rumored to be "damaged goods" and moreover, the Polish auteur insisted on the sort of creative control he had enjoyed while working in Europe. But Evans believed in Polanski and the gamble paid off. *Chinatown* grossed five times its production budget in its initial release and received eleven Oscar nominations, including one for Best Picture.

Like *The Godfather*, *Chinatown* is a prototypical studio auteur film. It sticks close to a tried-and-true genre and sports the seamless production values that only a big studio's money can buy. Polanski took full advantage of A-list production talent: cinematographer John A. Alonzo, who had shot the counterculture road picture *Vanishing Point* (Richard C. Sarafian, 1971) and the biopic *Lady Sings the Blues* (Sidney J. Furie, 1972); the production designer Richard Sylbert, who had designed the look of such landmark films as *Splendor in the Grass* (Kazan, 1961), *The Manchurian Candidate* (John Frankenheimer, 1962), and *Rosemary's Baby;* and the editor Sam O'Steen, who had worked on *Cool Hand Luke* (Stuart Rosenberg,

1967), *The Graduate*, and *Rosemary's Baby*. Also on hand was an A-list cast: Jack Nicholson, Faye Dunaway, and John Huston. The auteur theory circa 1974 fueled a studio system at its apex: the studios brought together the best talent their considerable money could buy and then stepped back and let the director and his creative staff work with a great deal of independence.

In style and form, *Chinatown* is at once nostalgic and modern. Like previous noir pictures, it features dark, shadowy cinematography and a labyrinthine plot set in motion by a duplicitous femme fatale (Dunaway). But despite period sets and dress, *Chinatown* depicts a corrupt establishment (in government and in business) very much in tune with the times. Like any number of 1940s or '50s noir films, *Chinatown* focuses on a hard-boiled detective. True to genre formula, Jake Gittes (Nicholson) is down on his luck, taking one last stab at respectability but destined to repeat the mistakes of his past. The story, penned by the reclusive screenwriter Robert Towne, is set in Los Angeles's storied past and focuses on two crimes: the murder of a city waterworks official (involved in a scandal involving a real estate scam and the city's access to water reserves) and an act of incest involving a prominent Los Angeles family. That the two plots ultimately intersect is of course inevitable.

Chinatown features a decidedly down ending, following the film noir formula but with a contemporary twist. Jake solves the crime but is duly horrified by his discovery that justice is not forthcoming—a cover-up is inevitable, a timely detail given *Chinatown*'s coincidence with the Watergate scandal. The moral of *Chinatown* is not that justice prevails nor, as in many film noirs, that the bad get punished in the end even if the system itself is corrupt. In *Chinatown*—in this very 1970s look at 1930s L.A.—the rich and powerful get away with even the worst sorts of crimes: murder and incest. In the end the cops must satisfy themselves with clearing the area of unwanted onlookers, including Jake, including us. Their job, after all, is to preserve the peace, a job that in this case does not involve messing with the likes of the powerful millionaire (Huston) who resides at the heart of the film's two crimes. A final smug reminder is delivered by a minor character who utters the film's payoff line as he escorts Jake off the screen:

Jack Nicholson as the private detective Jake Gittes and Faye Dunaway as the femme fatale
Evelyn Mulwray in Roman Polanski's 1974 neo-noir *Chinatown*.

"Forget it, Jake," he says. "It's Chinatown." Apropos Watergate, the film ends with the defeat of a Kennedy-era optimism and idealism, supplanted once and forever by a Nixonian cynicism.

Martin Scorsese

When Francis Ford Coppola and Martin Scorsese burst on the scene in the early '70s, they seemed cast from the same mold. Both were film school educated (Coppola at the University of California, Los Angeles; Scorsese at New York University), and both had gotten their first break in the industry making B movies for the exploitation film producer Roger Corman. Coppola earned his first screen credit as a director in 1963, when he was just twenty-four, with the ax-ploitation (low-budget slasher) picture *Dementia 13*. Scorsese's first widely released picture was the exploitation picture *Boxcar Bertha* (1972), released just before his thirtieth birthday. Both auteurs broke into the A-feature market with gangster films: for Coppola it was *The Godfather;* for Scorsese it was *Mean Streets* (1973).

In many ways, Scorsese emerged in the early 1970s as the East Coast alternative to Coppola. The distinction between the two directors is rooted at least in part in their geographic difference. Key to their visions as filmmakers is their sense of scale and scope. *The Godfather* is from start to finish a Hollywood movie, an epic whose story is rendered in mythic terms. The Corleones are a royal family that exists in the rarefied world of the rich and untouchable. Scorsese's gangsters, in contrast, are unexceptional working-class men mostly on the make. They have the sorts of problems other work-

Baby-faced auteur Martin Scorsese (*center*) directing Robert De Niro (*left, in a white T-shirt*) and Harvey Keitel (*right*) on the set of *Mean Streets* (1973).

ing-class guys have: paying off debts, finding financing for some scheme that might provide a modicum of social ascendance. What the two films mean—what they say about the American experience—reflects the scale and scope of the two projects. When Vito dies at the end of *The Godfather*, his death clearly marks the end of an era; it is less the death of a man than the death of a way of life. The death of Johnny Boy (Robert De Niro) at the end of *Mean Streets*, however, shows us only the murder of a smart-ass street punk who had it coming. His death means nothing to anyone not directly related to him. Coppola's cinema is from the outset grand and at times even grandiose, a Hollywood version of the real world. Scorsese, especially early on, kept the scale intimate and personal. His films are the everyday dramas of the people you might bump into on the streets or meet when you hail a cab.

Scorsese has imbued all his films with a recognizable, personal visual style. His films showcase a handful of signature stylistic tendencies or habits and repeatedly offer insight on the same few per-

sonal, mostly spiritual obsessions. The first 10 minutes of *Mean Streets* exemplifies the Scorsese auteur signature. The film opens with a series of roughly shot vignettes, like a home movie introducing the colorful characters in a low-tech student film. First we meet Michael (Richard Romanus), a slow-witted gangster taking possession of a truckload of "Jap adapters," what he had been led to believe were quality Japanese-made camera lenses. Then we meet Johnny Boy as he bounds toward the camera. He stops to light a firecracker and tosses it into a mailbox. Finally we meet Charlie (Harvey Keitel), whom we find in church ruminating on the meaning of existence, responsibility, causality, and life after death. We follow Charlie from the church to a strip club owned by one of his friends. Charlie floats into the room in slow motion, bathed in red, moving in time to the strains of the Rolling Stones' "Tell Me." The camera tracks one way and then back again, following Charlie as he makes his entrance. After a playful dance with an African American stripper, accompanied by a voice-over musing of what he perceives as the temptation (and sin) of miscegenation, there is a jump cut (inspired perhaps by Jean-Luc Godard, an idol of many film-school-educated auteurs in the early '70s) to Charlie seated with his friends, holding his hand over a flame, a mind-over-matter trick taught to him by a priest.

In this otherwise innocuous introductory sequence—it does little more than introduce the cast of characters; no significant plot points are raised or examined—Scorsese establishes the film's style. The shaky Super-8mm style segues into a more polished sequence delivered by a moving camera and highlighted by occasional shifts into and out of slow motion. The bar itself is at once a real place (it looks like an actual New York City bar) and a surreal, dreamlike space, shot as it is through a red filter (as if we were witnessing Charlie's descent into hell and not just his entrance into

Charlie (Harvey Keitel, *right*) tries to talk some sense to his troubled (and troublesome) cousin Johnny Boy (Robert De Niro) in Martin Scorsese's *Mean Streets* (1973).

"God's lonely man": Travis Bickle (Robert De Niro) cruising Times Square in Martin Scorsese's *Taxi Driver* (1976).

a topless go-go bar). The sound track is stripped of sync dialogue. In its place—in what may be a second nod to early-'70s-era student filmmaking—is the heavy use of diegetic music (music that the characters in the scene hear—in this case, music accompanying both the go-go dancers' performance and Charlie's theatrical entrance into the bar) and Charlie's voice-over. Though the moving camera eliminates a more conventional editing structure, Scorsese uses jump cuts for stylistic effect (and not for plot transitions or scene changes), displaying an affection for discontinuity.

Directors navigate space on-screen to simulate a real, lived-in environment, what theorists call creative geography. Scorsese accomplishes this feat in virtually all his films by incessantly and fluidly moving the camera, making the viewer an active figure within the space of the film. The effect is empowering to an extent: the camera moves and thus we move, which makes us feel, even though we are seated in the theater, somewhat active. But it is also disconcerting. The moving camera is an immersive technique, and what we are immersed in when we watch Scorsese's films is often bloody and frightening. In *Taxi Driver* (1976), for example, the moving camera is used to show us Travis Bickle's (Robert De Niro's) movement through the streets of New York, giving us a sense of drifting along with this troubled character. That we drive through the streets with Travis and see things as he does implicates us in his desperation, his anomie, and finally in the act of violence that inexorably arrives at the end of the film.

Key also to Scorsese's signature style is his affection for the work of the legendary New York independent filmmaker John Cassavetes. Though

better known to the casual filmgoer for his acting work—in popular films like *Edge of the City* (Martin Ritt, 1957), Don Siegel's *The Killers* (1964), and *Rosemary's Baby*—Cassavetes was a relentless, fearless independent filmmaker, a man committed to making films about real people living on the edge of psychic disaster. His films, which include *Shadows* (1959), *Faces* (1968), *Husbands* (1970), *A Woman under the Influence* (1974), *The Killing of a Chinese Bookie* (1976), and *Gloria* (1980), feature a core ensemble of gifted character actors (Cassavetes; his wife, Gena Rowlands; Ben Gazzara; and Peter Falk), all of whom deftly improvise their roles. Scorsese, especially in his early films, similarly strove for performances that captured real people on the edge and employed a core ensemble—most notably De Niro, Keitel, and Joe Pesci—whom he encouraged to improvise to make the action seem spontaneous and real. Cassavetes' influence on Scorsese was at once indirect (Scorsese borrowed some of Cassavetes' filmmaking methods and strove for the nakedly real performances Cassavetes got from his ensemble) and direct (according to an anecdote that Scorsese has related in several interviews, Cassavetes, after seeing *Boxcar Bertha*, admonished the young director to not waste his talents and instead make a film he really cared about; *Mean Streets* was the result).

Scorsese's ability to capture real life on camera—especially the gritty reality of the streets of New York—was rooted in a childhood spent watching the world pass by his window. Scorsese was a sickly child, a sufferer of asthma, forced to linger in his apartment as other children played outside in the streets. Seldom a participant in and most often a viewer of the action, Scorsese came to appreciate city space as if it were framed by a window. What he saw outside his window featured its fair share of colorful characters whose penchant for interpersonal violence was at once striking and disturbing, hence Scorsese's penchant for graphic, explosive violence. Violence in Scorsese's films, even the extreme and graphic violence, is not without its purgative value. The violence at the end of *Taxi Driver* offers a sexual, psychological release

(*left*) In *Raging Bull* (1980), Martin Scorsese shot in black-and-white and used slow motion and stop action to highlight the brutality of prize fighting in general and, in particular, the savage approach by Jake La Motta (Robert De Niro, *right*).

for Travis and something like a purification for the viewer. After the murders, Travis is no longer an anonymous cabdriver but a celebrity vigilante; he becomes something of a New York cult hero, famous for 15 minutes for an act of impromptu violence that is fleetingly embraced by the press and populace as useful and necessary. Such an interpretation and appreciation of his actions proves to be beyond Travis's ability to comprehend, however: he has done only what the streets have made him do.

Bloodletting is never gratuitous or simply sensational for Scorsese. In *Raging Bull* (1980), a film about the former middleweight boxing champion Jake La Motta (De Niro), the brutal battles in the ring are shown in slow and stop motion from angles and camera positions that put us in the ring. Though depicted in black-and-white, these scenes ably capture the savagery of professional boxing. Jake expresses a rage that, like Travis Bickle's, is fueled by a life of frustration on the streets. The sanctioning of that rage in the ring makes Jake a champion boxer and the idol of a generation of Italian Americans. But soon enough, Jake pays the price for his brief stardom and social mobility. Once he's through with boxing (as all the punches take their toll and age slows him down), he struggles outside the ring. The film's ending is anticlimactic and ultimately heartbreaking. It shows Jake, fat and drunk, doling out self-deprecating one-liners to a crowd at a local nightclub. The respect he demanded in the ring has been supplanted by and reduced to parody.

Even though Scorsese's auteurist credentials seemed secure after the release of *Raging Bull*, his career stalled for a long time after that film. Like Coppola and several other '70s auteurs, Scorsese more or less sat out the '80s, directing either commercially unsuccessful but nonetheless interesting films, like *The King of Comedy* (1983), the story of an inept wannabe stand-up comedian (De Niro) who kidnaps a talk-show host (Jerry Lewis) and, like Travis in *Taxi Driver*, becomes a New York celebrity, or far less interesting and only modestly commercial ventures like *The Color of Money* (1986), a sequel to Robert Rossen's 1961 hit *The Hustler*. Not until 1990 would Scorsese make a modest return to form, with *Goodfellas*, a gangster film about working-class guys on the make who don't quite get it right.

The director Robert Altman on location outside Vancouver, British Columbia, during the production of his revisionist western *McCabe & Mrs. Miller* (1971).

Robert Altman

Robert Altman was not one of the movie brats. His route to the director's chair began not with film school but at an industrial-film company, where he made employee training shorts and commercials. In 1955, Altman left the trade-film business and began a successful career in episodic television. Between 1955 and 1968 he helmed episodes of *The Millionaire, Alfred Hitchcock Presents, The Gale Storm Show, Maverick, Peter Gunn, Bonanza, Hawaiian Eye, Route 66,* and *Combat.*

Altman's feature-film career took off in 1970, when he was contracted to direct *MASH,* a film that chronicles the on- and off-duty lives of the doctors and nurses at a mobile army surgical hospital (or MASH unit) during the Korean War. *MASH* was a huge box-office hit, the number-2 picture for 1970, earning well over $20 million. The film also won the Grand Prix at the Cannes Festival, the first American film to win a top prize since 1957 (when William Wyler's now-little-seen 1956 film *Friendly Persuasion* took the Palme d'Or), and scored Oscar nominations for Best Picture, Directing, Actress in a Supporting Role (Sally Kellerman, who plays the repressed career army nurse Hot Lips), Film Editing (Danford B. Greene), and Writing (an award won by the formerly blacklisted Ring Lardner Jr.).

When *MASH* first reached American screens, the war in Vietnam was very much in the news and on the minds of young filmgoers. For that audience, hungry as it was for something relevant on-screen, the sarcastic, hedonistic doctors of the MASH unit were akin to counterculture rebels. The Korean War that the doctors suddenly found themselves part of was shown to be, like the Vietnam War, at once absurd and senseless. Though Altman was considerably older than most of the other Hollywood-renaissance auteurs and had no direct experience with the youth subculture during the tumultuous late 1960s, he nonetheless captured the irreverence and cynicism of America's young and discontented.

Although Altman's TV work was by necessity fashioned to fit the so-called house styles of shows like *Bonanza* and *Combat,* his film work evinced a radically new style. Foremost in that style was a complex layering of sound. In *MASH* there are carefully modulated simultaneous, overlapping conversations and a running commentary on the MASH camp loudspeaker provided by a character who, in a mostly absurd manner, speaks to the daily grind of the war. Altman's layering of sound forces viewers to pay close attention to more than one conversation, more than one "sound field" at the same time.

For Altman this aural technique was part of an effort to achieve larger-scale realism. For example, in order to realistically re-create the look and sound of the Old West, Altman shot the interior scenes of *McCabe & Mrs. Miller* (1971) in low light, simulating the way a room might look if it were lit by kerosene lamps, and he used a gauzy filter to make the barroom appear to be smoke filled. Throughout, he recorded sound as if at a distance, as if the viewer of the film were *witnessing* scenes as opposed to watching them performed. Altman also made narrative use of sound-track music in *McCabe & Mrs. Miller,* as songs performed off-screen by Leonard Cohen speak directly to specific scenes in the film. We hear "He was just some Joseph looking for a manger" when John McCabe (Warren Beatty) rides into town. Later, when the prostitutes arrive to work in McCabe's brothel, we hear a song about "sisters of mercy." And when McCabe and Mrs. Miller (Julie Christie) finally sleep together, the same song tells us "we weren't lovers like that."

In *Nashville* (1975), Altman reprised the aural techniques he used in *MASH* and *McCabe & Mrs. Miller* to simulate the informality of family conversations and to highlight the subtle ways in which personal conversations in the music business evolve into professional negotiations. In several scenes we witness recording sessions or live performances and are asked to pay attention as well to key conversations taking place among the performance's spectators. As in real life the performances, the music, and the conversations compete for attention and occasionally speak directly or ironically to one another. Husbands and wives talk but don't listen to each other, and we can see a dis-

connect as dialogue wanders off the point and characters respond automatically and perfunctorily.

The songs in *Nashville* seem at least superficially to lampoon country-and-western culture. Many of them depict the typical country-and-western family melodramas ("Unpack your bags, and try not to cry / I can't leave my wife, and there are three reasons why / . . . for the sake of the children, I must say good-bye"). Others profess a decidedly absurd American optimism and self-righteousness ("If the doctor says you're through / well, he's a human being just like you / so keep a-going"). Altman is fascinated by such upbeat sentiments, especially those that verge on the patriotic at a time, after Vietnam and Watergate, when such sentiments were indeed embraced by devotees of country music but were held to be ridiculous by the sort of people who went to Altman's films. As in *McCabe*

The cathouse entrepreneur John McCabe (Warren Beatty) might be the famous gunslinger Pudge McCabe, but then again he might not be, in Robert Altman's *McCabe & Mrs. Miller* (1971).

& *Mrs. Miller*, many of the songs in *Nashville* cleverly comment on the narrative at hand. For example, at the end of the film a troubled young man shoots a manic-depressive singer while she is performing onstage. But true to the Nashville spirit, the show must go on. The country-music legend Haven Hamilton (Henry Gibson) shouts, "This isn't Dallas"—a reference to John F. Kennedy's assassination in 1963—"it's Nashville! They can't do this to us. . . . Somebody, sing!" Albuquerque (Barbara Harris), whom we've seen throughout the film—in one key scene she sings at a motor speedway, where no one can hear her—takes the stage and beautifully sings, "It don't worry me." It is hard to miss the ironic relationship between the song and the scene to which it speaks, and it is hard to miss the point that, though the words speak to the images in obvious counterpoint, this finally is the one straight, un-ironic performance in the film.

Irony was indeed a focal point in Altman's work. But Altman's critical distance from the genres he lampooned and from the characters he seemed to regard with amusement was complicated by scenes of terrifying, sudden violence that take us very much out of the safe space of irony and comedy. *McCabe & Mrs. Miller*, for example, ends with a gunfight that leaves McCabe seriously wounded. He bleeds to death in the snow as a fire in the newly constructed downtown distracts the local denizens. *Thieves Like Us*, Altman's 1974 parody of the gangster-on-the-lam genre (his gangsters are all dim-witted losers striving aimlessly for a little happiness in Depression-era America), ends with a massacre much like the one at the end of *Bonnie and Clyde*. In *The Long Goodbye* (1973), Altman's update of the Raymond Chandler novel (resetting the quintessential '40s noir hero, detective Philip Marlowe, in hedonistic '70s Los Angeles), a comic interrogation scene between Marlowe (Elliott Gould) and a psychotic gangster named Marty Augustine (Mark Rydell) is interrupted when Augustine breaks a Coke bottle across his girlfriend's face to make a point. Late in the film, Marlowe, the hero, goes to Mexico and guns down a friend in cold blood. Throughout the film, Marlowe has been a comic figure. The murder at the end reveals what has lain behind the humor: a rage at a more modern world in which Marlowe's code (of honor or morality) no longer makes much sense.

Like a lot of other auteur directors, Altman reused many of the same actors in his films: René Auberjonois, Keith Carradine, Shelley Duvall, Sally Kellerman, Michael Murphy, Bert Remsen, and John Schuck—hardly household names then or now, but capable character actors who worked well within Altman's framework of complex, intersecting narratives that feature as many as twenty significant characters. In his use of a stock company of actors, Altman bucked the commercial-studio tradition of heroic narratives with stars on-screen most if not all the time. The ensemble style forces viewers to pay attention to the story and the characters rather than one well-known actor.

Between 1970 and 1975, between the release of *MASH* and the release of *Nashville*, Altman's ironic dissembling of traditional Hollywood genre film-making was popular. But after the release of the failed parody *Buffalo Bill and the Indians, or Sitting Bull's History Lesson* (1976) and the strained seriousness of the decidedly obscure melodrama *3 Women* (1977), Altman's career stalled. A possible comeback seemed in the offing when he agreed to direct the big studio blockbuster *Popeye* (1980). But despite the film's financial success—*Popeye* ultimately made money, more than twice its bloated $20-million price tag—its troubled production, during which Altman and studio executives battled constantly, led the studio to wonder whether any competent director (one perhaps with less of a stake as an auteur, one with a lot less attitude) could have made *Popeye* a moneymaking film. The answer was there in the asking, and after *Popeye*, Altman became persona non grata in Hollywood. His star continued to fade in the 1980s as he made mostly stage adaptations—*Come Back to the Five and Dime, Jimmy Dean, Jimmy Dean* (1982) and *Secret Honor* (1984)—on B-movie budgets, but in 1992 he made a modest comeback with the Hollywood-set suspense picture *The Player*, a film that, like his work in the early '70s, ably toys with parody and straight drama.

Stanley Kubrick

It is difficult to figure out exactly where Stanley Kubrick fits in the '70s auteur renaissance. By the time *The Godfather* reached American screens,

The ambitious country crooner Albuquerque (Barbara Harris) accompanied by the studio musician Frog (Richard Baskin, who wrote four of the film's songs) sings her heart out as cars race by on a speedway in Robert Altman's *Nashville* (1975). Albuquerque, an unknown in a town of larger-than-life legends, may be the best singer we hear in the film, but we don't discover that until the end of the picture. Here, in just one of the film's many games with sound mixing, her lips move but her voice can't be heard over the racing cars' engines.

The director Stanley Kubrick on the set of his 1971 futurist film *A Clockwork Orange*.

Kubrick already had nine features to his credit, including the pacifist melodrama *Paths of Glory* (1957), the chariot-and-sandal epic *Spartacus* (1960), a tongue-in-cheek adaptation of Vladimir Nabokov's controversial love story *Lolita* (1962), the hilarious cold war farce *Dr. Strangelove or: How I Learned to Stop Worrying and Love the Bomb* (1964), the speculative sci-fi epic *2001: A Space Odyssey* (1968), and the groundbreaking ultraviolent futurist teen pic *A Clockwork Orange* (1971). Though he was only forty-three years old when he made *A Clockwork Orange*, the arrival of the first wave of new American auteurs (Coppola, Scorsese, and Altman) seemed to mark the beginning of a self-imposed semiretirement for Kubrick. Between 1971 and his death, in 1999, he made just four films: the picaresque period piece *Barry Lyndon* (1975), which frame by frame endeavors to reproduce the England we see in nineteenth-century landscape paintings; the psychological horror film *The Shining* (1980), adapted from a Stephen King novel; a harrowing Vietnam film, *Full Metal Jacket* (1987), which follows a group of recruits from their brutal basic training to some in-country action, climaxing with a siege on a sniper's nest that ends as the soldiers discover that the gunman is a young woman; and his last film, the erotic melodrama *Eyes Wide Shut* (1999).

Kubrick apprenticed for the cinema as a still photographer, a career begun when he sold his first picture to *Look* magazine at the tender age of seventeen. A photographic aesthetic dominates all his films, so much so that Kubrick became famous for putting actors through multiple takes in search of the perfect shot. The popular press dutifully reported on his painstaking methods, and as a result he became known as an uncompromising craftsman. The reputation was deserved and later exploited by the director himself. For *The Shining*, Kubrick shot an astonishing 1.3 million feet of film. The film runs long: 2 hours 26 minutes. But the shooting ratio—that is, the amount of film shot to the amount of film used in the final print—was still a whopping 104:1 (10:1 is a generous studio average).

The first important Kubrick film was *Paths of Glory*, a compelling story about World War I enlisted men court-martialled and executed to cover up a general's mistake. To give viewers a sense of what the war's combat might have been like, Kubrick situates them with a series of tracking shots through labyrinthine foxholes. Such an immersion in the space of the film is also a key visual tactic in *2001*, as the spaceship becomes a place we inhabit in simulated weightlessness along with the ill-fated astronauts. And in *The Shining*, we come to know the Overlook Hotel from the point of view of a camera mounted on a Big Wheel tricycle. From that vantage point we experience the place along with the film's young hero, Danny (Danny Lloyd).

While such techniques immerse the viewer in the space of the film, Kubrick's eye for detail and fascination with how things (machines especially) work render realistic even his more speculative exploits. For example, to capture the look and feel of space travel in *2001*, Kubrick hired Douglas Trumbull, a veteran filmmaker for the National Aeronautics and Space Administration (NASA), to supervise the special effects. Kubrick even included a sequence involving a space toilet, complete with instructions on how one might flush in a weightless environment.

To complement the visuals, Kubrick used soundtrack music evocatively. For the Sturm und Drang of the early caveman sequences of *2001*, for example, he used Richard Strauss's bombastic modern tone poem "Also Sprach Zarathustra," a work Strauss composed to tell the story of humankind's development from mute cave dweller to Übermensch (superman). That Strauss's work took on additional ideological baggage thanks to Hitler's mid-twentieth-century embrace of it in a national-istic, racist context was hardly lost on Kubrick. The grandeur of the scene—the images of the cavemen, the bold chords in Strauss's music, the elegant graphic match cut from a club that has been fash-ioned from a bone and is flying through the air to a spaceship floating across the frame—offers an inevitable trajectory from cavemen to astronauts with a notable stop along the way, in 1930s and '40s Germany, hardly humankind's finest hour.

In *A Clockwork Orange* beautiful classical music is a counterpoint to the ugly graffiti-covered gov-ernment housing projects of a London at some unspecified time in the future and the antisocial behavior of the film's central character, an unre-deemable young thug named Alex (Malcolm McDowell). Alex has one saving grace, his affec-tion for classical music, Beethoven in particular. But when Alex is arrested, jailed, and then "cured" of his criminal impulse by an aversion therapy called the Ludovico technique, he loses his taste for music. The doctors who cure him see that as an unfortunate side effect. But Kubrick makes clear that while the doctors make Alex a good cit-izen, they make him much less of a human being. He has lost his freedom to choose right from wrong and, more troubling, his ability to appreciate one of the few things that exalt human beings: beauti-ful music. In the film's ironic conclusion, Alex is restored as a conscienceless thug, a transforma-tion affirmed in voice-over as Alex hears the glori-ous strains of Beethoven's Ninth Symphony and announces that he's been "cured."

If there is a common narrative theme in Kubrick's work, it is a pervasive misanthropy. Though he worked in several genres—crime, war, period melodrama, horror, and science fiction—there is at the core of all the work a dislike and dis-taste for what we humans have made of our lot here on earth. In his adaptation of *Lolita*, Kubrick shrugs off the novel's (albeit ironic) love story. The char-acters in his version are all hideous caricatures: the

Thanks to the work of special-effects wizard and former NASA filmmaker Douglas Trumbull in Stanley Kubrick's dystopian outer-space epic *2001: A Space Oddysey* (1968), scenes like this space walk were both beautiful and realistic.

repressed pedophiliac professor Humbert Humbert (James Mason), the preening Charlotte Haze (Lolita's desperate, horny, and embarrassingly pretentious mother, played by Shelley Winters), and the phony aesthete Clare Quilty (Peter Sellers). Kubrick's disdain for one and all is clear.

In *Dr. Strangelove*, Kubrick makes a joke of nuclear catastrophe. It is a funny film from start to finish, but like *Lolita* it is populated with characters we find stupid and ridiculous, many of whom, alas, are in positions of power: the crazy general Jack Ripper (Sterling Hayden), who prattles on about "precious bodily fluids" and the dangers of water fluoridation as he sets a nuclear conflict in motion; General Buck Turgidson (George C. Scott), who marvels at a pilot's ability to fly under the radar while failing to comprehend that flying undetected guarantees that at least one of the bombs ordered by Ripper will indeed find its target; and finally the aforementioned pilot, Major T. J. "King" Kong (Slim Pickens), who, when the door of the bomb bay fails to open, dons a cowboy hat and rides a warhead into oblivion.

Violence in Kubrick's films is a matter of instinct, an essential aspect of the human animal. The "Dawn of Man" episode in *2001* shows primitive humankind learning about tools and fire. The first man to fashion a club out of a stick uses it to kill an animal and then another man. The violence in *A Clockwork Orange* is set to music and choreographed. Shot in slow motion and accompanied by Gioacchino Rossini's "Thieving Magpie," Beethoven's Ninth Symphony, or the Arthur Freed–Nacio Herb Brown show tune "Singin' in the Rain," the interpersonal violence is made to look aesthetic. But the irony cuts deep. A species capable of producing a Beethoven once in a millennium is capable of producing vicious men far more often.

What is most ironic about Kubrick's filmmaking career is that though the director was something of a recluse (he lived on an estate in rural England), three of his films were embraced in the 1960s and '70s by American youth, a constituency with whom he had almost nothing in common. In the first of those movies, *Dr. Strangelove*, the broad

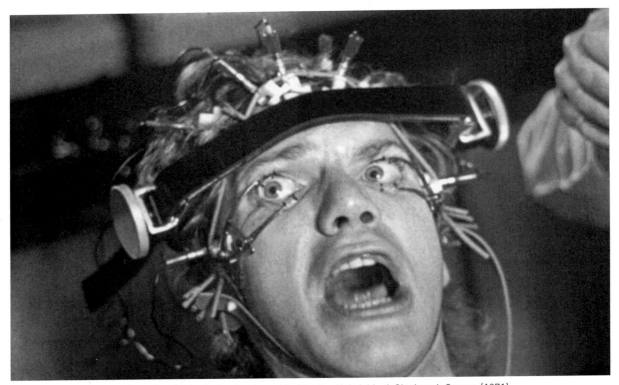

Alex (Malcolm McDowell) getting the Ludovico treatment in Stanley Kubrick's *A Clockwork Orange* (1971).

Peter Sellers channeling Henry Kissinger (at the time the Study Director in Nuclear Weapons and Foreign Policy at the Council on Foreign Relations) and Edward Teller (putative godfather of the nuclear bomb) in Stanley Kubrick's cold war satire *Dr. Strangelove* (1964).

parody struck many young Americans as suitably irreverent, in part because it was co-scripted by the ultimate hipster Terry Southern. The second, *2001*, developed a following among young people attracted to the emerging drug culture of the late '60s. The "waltz" of the spaceships at the start of the film; the endless prattling of the computer HAL, who finally turns on the crew; and the kaleidoscopic sequence at the film's climax seemed, especially to those under the influence of psychotropic drugs, psychedelic, or otherworldly. The third of those films, *A Clockwork Orange*, was embraced by a generation of mostly young male moviegoers: the stylized violence and the hip argot of Alex and his "droogs," seemed in an unhappy way (at an unhappy time) to speak to their desperation and frustration.

After 1975, Kubrick became less an auteur who made movies than a symbol of what Hollywood could not support or contain. For all that he meant to a generation of filmgoers, there is a lingering sense that there could have been, and should have been, much more.

William Friedkin, Peter Bogdanovich, and Terrence Malick

William Friedkin, Peter Bogdanovich, and Terrence Malick were not household names in the 1970s. Unlike the much more famous Coppola, Scorsese, Altman, and Kubrick, they made films that are more famous than they are. But all three filmmakers were nonetheless auteurs, directors who were able to impose a distinct personal signature on a variety of studio projects.

In 1971, at the age of thirty-six, William Friedkin, best known for the gay-themed movie *The Boys in the Band* (1970), won an Oscar for his gritty police saga *The French Connection*. Sporting a fabulous car-and-train chase, *The French Connection* introduced the now-familiar cop-on-the-edge trope. The film stars Gene Hackman, who won an Oscar for his performance as the foul-mouthed Popeye Doyle, whom we see in the film's opening hook

dressed as Santa Claus while beating a suspect senseless. Doyle is hardly your everyday cop on the beat, or at least he was hardly the sort of cop we saw in films made when the PCA was in charge; he has a foot fetish and a drinking problem, and he is willing to take down the bad guys by any means necessary. By contrast, the Frenchman (Fernando Rey), the drug dealer who is Doyle's nemesis, dresses stylishly, behaves impeccably, lives in a beautiful house in Marseilles, and has a beautiful young wife on whom he dotes. The Frenchman is by all visible signs a far nicer guy than Popeye, a guy (unlike Popeye) with whom one might enjoy sharing a drink or a meal someday.

The frenetic, handheld camerawork harking back to the direct-cinema documentaries of the 1960s, the long, silent cat-and-mouse sequences (the opening sequence—a murder in a French port city—plays out without a single line of relevant dialogue), the over-the-top violence, the obscene banter (between Doyle and his partner, Buddy Russo, played by Roy Scheider), and Friedkin's focus on the drug trade as an international corporate enterprise offer a bold variation on the formula typical of the old cop genre. It also, for the first time on American screens, told the truth about crime and punishment in the United States—that it was not so simple (a matter of good guys against bad guys, cops versus robbers) or so easily resolved.

If *The French Connection* was Friedkin's calling card, a dazzling display of what he could do as a director if given a genre framework and left for the most part on his own, then *The Exorcist*, his follow-up film in 1973, revealed just what he could do if he got his hands on a topflight, presold Hollywood property. Like *The Godfather*, *The Exorcist* is based on a best-selling novel that had considerable name recognition in its day. Though in 1973 horror films were generally regarded as B-movie fare, movies that got screened at the drive-in while no one really watched, *The Exorcist* represented a new hybrid, an A-list genre picture that at once clung to the strictures of an old cinematic genre yet transcended those parameters.

The Exorcist is an adult-audience horror film, a significant modernization of the traditionally B-grade, teen-targeted genre. It generates horror not from knives coming out of the darkness or monsters from beyond. Instead, the monster resides in the body of an otherwise innocent girl, Regan (Linda Blair), whose transformation, thanks to the MPAA's new rating system, at once defies nature (her head swivels in a full circle) and good taste (she vomits what looks like gallons of green slime and shouts vile, sexually explicit epithets). The film focuses most of the time on the tireless efforts of Regan's mother (Ellen Burstyn) to save her daughter, a plotline clearly meant to hook parents. True to the horror-film formula, medical experts (representing both technology and science) fail to explain the girl's malady. That failure itself is dramatic and horrifying—nearly as horrifying as the scenes of demonic possession that follow as the doctors subject Regan to medical tests and procedures that verge on torture. We see a spinal tap in all its gory detail, and we get the distinct feeling that the doctors have no idea what they are doing but plod on nonetheless. The failure of science is followed by the triumph of the supernatural as only the efforts of two good priests, Damien Karras (Jason Miller) and Lankester Merrin (Max von Sydow), manage to wrest Regan from the demon possessing her. At a time when many Americans were questioning their faith and church atten-

dance was in decline, *The Exorcist* insisted on the material reality of evil and the astonishing power of prayer.

Only Coppola made more money for Paramount than Friedkin made for Warner Bros. between 1971 and 1974. But despite the financial success, Friedkin's moment in the spotlight was brief. In 1977, after four years without releasing a single feature, Friedkin directed *Sorcerer* (1977), an adaptation of the 1953 French thriller *Le salaire de la peur* (*The Wages of Fear*, Henri-Georges Clouzot), about a ragged band of outcasts who are enlisted to transport nitroglycerin over rough terrain. Though the film features some hair-raising suspense sequences, it failed dismally at the box office. Friedkin's next big film was *Cruising* (1980), a graphic crime picture set in the rough-trade gay underworld. Like *The French Connection*, *Cruising* is ostensibly a cop-on-the-edge movie. But many critics and viewers (especially gay viewers) objected to the way it unflinchingly chronicles the sad and sordid lives of some of the men who frequent gay bars and thus exploits the lifestyle of such men. The critical and box-office failure of *Cruising* pretty much ended Friedkin's run as an A-list auteur. Since then he has made just two films of note: the MTV-inspired caper film *To Live and Die in L.A.* (1985) and the macho military picture *Rules of Engagement* (2000).

Before he became a filmmaker, Peter Bogdanovich was an actor in B movies and, of all things, a film reviewer and critic with published studies of Orson Welles, Howard Hawks, Alfred Hitchcock, Fritz Lang, and John Ford to his credit. In 1968 he got his first chance to direct from Daniel Selznick, David O. Selznick's son. The film, *Targets*, is a low-budget horror picture about an aging horror-film actor (played by the veteran horror-film actor Boris Karloff) who becomes the target of a crazed Vietnam veteran. Then, under the pseudonym Derek Thomas, Bogdanovich directed an exploitation picture for Roger Corman, *Voyage to the Planet of Prehistoric Women* (also 1968). Neither film prepared anyone for what came next, the heartbreaking black-and-white period piece *The Last Picture Show* (1971), based on a novel by the Texas writer Larry McMurtry.

The Last Picture Show is set in a small Texas town in which an old movie palace is about to shut down. The film focuses on two friends, Duane (Jeff

Bridges) and Sonny (Tim Bottoms), who find themselves torn between an uncertain future outside their tiny town and a more certain future at home, managing a second-run theater that fewer and fewer locals bother to attend. It captures the essence of a place and leaves us with an overwhelming feeling of melancholy as we witness a transition from one era to another. As such it bears a distinct resemblance to Orson Welles's original cut of *The Magnificent Ambersons* (1942). Both films are deeply nostalgic laments for a way of life overrun by modernity and progress. *The Last Picture Show* was a popular and critically celebrated film. It was nominated for eight Academy Awards, including Best Picture, Directing, and Writing, and it won two: Cloris Leachman for Actress in a Sup-

porting Role and the veteran western character actor Ben Johnson for Actor in a Supporting Role.

After modest success with his next film, the nostalgic screwball comedy *What's Up, Doc?* (1972), Bogdanovich directed *Paper Moon* (1973), a rural period piece characterized by an unsentimental script and terrific performances by Ryan O'Neal and his daughter, Tatum, then ten years old, who won an Academy Award for Actress in a Supporting Role. This second success on Oscar night again thrust Bogdanovich into the limelight, and by all accounts, even his own, the success nearly killed him. It certainly killed his career.

What had made Bogdanovich especially attractive to the studios from 1971 to 1973 was that, unlike the films of Coppola and Altman, his pic-

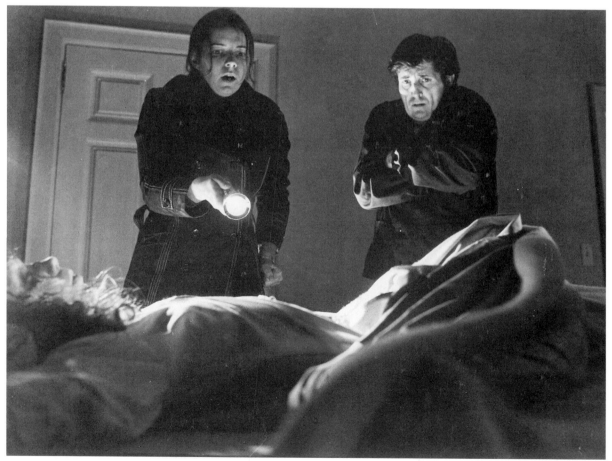

William Friedkin's 1973 horror film *The Exorcist* represented a new hybrid, an A-list genre picture that at once clings to the strictures of an old cinematic genre yet transcends its parameters.

Sonny (Timothy Bottoms) and Duane (Jeff Bridges) get ready to play the jukebox in Peter Bogdanovich's heartbreaking slice of rural life, *The Last Picture Show* (1971).

Holly (Sissy Spacek) and Kit (Martin Sheen), stand-ins for the legendary outlaw couple Caril Ann Fugate and Charles Starkweather, in Terrence Malick's first feature film, *Badlands* (1973)

tures were fairly inexpensive to make, and the productions went smoothly and uneventfully. But that changed in 1974 with his ambitious adaptation of the Henry James novel *Daisy Miller*. For the title role he cast the former fashion model Cybill Shepherd. The press made much of the romantic relationship between Shephard and Bogdanovich, and the party line on the film (that unfortunately preceded its release) was that Bogdanovich had allowed his feelings for Shepherd to cloud his judgment. The film was not as bad as the critics said it was, but the unfavorable publicity ahead of its release killed its chances at the box office.

After 1974, there would be no more A-list offers for Bogdanovich. In 1979, on location and with a tiny budget, he directed *Saint Jack*, a gritty character study of an American huckster on the mean streets of Singapore, starring the veteran Method actor Ben Gazzara. It is a good film that few people bothered to see. Then came the independently produced romantic comedy *They All Laughed* (1981), which was quickly lumped with *Daisy Miller* as the gossip press sensationalized Bogdanovich's relationship with Dorothy Stratten, a former *Playboy* model and the star of the film. Just as *They All Laughed* was being prepared for release, Stratten was murdered by her estranged husband. Rather than exploit the story to promote the film, the studio refused to release the picture at all, and Bogdanovich, in mourning, tried on his own to distribute the film to theaters. Ultimately he didn't have the money or the energy. *They All Laughed* bombed. Since 1981, Bogdanovich has only made two A features, an uneven sequel to *The Last Picture Show* titled *Texasville* (1990) and *The Cat's Meow* (2001), a nostalgic film about the death of Thomas Ince in 1920s Hollywood.

Terrence Malick, the Massachusetts Institute of Technology philosophy professor turned filmmaker, made just two films in the 1970s but nonetheless merits consideration as one of the most important talents to emerge during the auteur era. *Badlands* (1973), his first feature film, stars Martin Sheen and Sissy Spacek, both little known at the time, as Kit and Holly, stand-ins for the legendary teen outlaws Charles Starkweather and Caril Ann Fugate. Starkweather was a mass murderer whose first victim was Fugate's father. Rather than turn her lover in, Fugate joined him on the lam. Together they became pop-culture heroes to a generation of young people during the conformist 1950s. Malick examines the Starkweather-Fugate phenomenon through Fugate's eyes: he has Holly narrate the film even though she is decidedly disaffected and often clueless. In coun-

terpoint to Holly's bland narration and the sudden brutality of Kit's crimes is Malick's dazzlingly beautiful rendering of the badlands they inhabit. Tak Fujimoto's cinematography is breathtaking, especially the slow-motion sequence of Holly's house on fire—a spectacle that we watch in dazed fascination, as does Holly, who is no doubt missing the point that the fire was set to erase the evidence of her father's murder.

Malick's second film, *Days of Heaven* (1978), tells the story of a young impoverished couple, Bill and Abby (Richard Gere and Brooke Adams), who escape Depression-era Chicago and take a chance on reinventing themselves in the farm fields of the Texas panhandle. They pose as brother and sister and hatch a plan in which she woos a wealthy terminally ill ranch owner (Sam Shepard) in order to get his fortune. The plan is found out, and the cou-

Abby (Brooke Adams) tries to find her way on a fateful night that begins with swarming locusts and ends with a raging fire in Terrence Malick's *Days of Heaven* (1978).

ple are hunted down and killed; their story is presented to us in a disaffected voice-over by an emotionless teenager, Linda (Linda Manz), who traveled with them. The sordid story and the comically understated voice-over narration are, as in *Badlands,* juxtaposed against breathtaking cinematography, this time by Nestor Almendros, who won an Oscar for his work on the film.

After *Days of Heaven,* Malick gave up Hollywood to return to academia and did not make another film until 1998, the gorgeous, ruminative war picture, *The Thin Red Line.* Like Kubrick's reclusiveness, Malick's self-imposed exile seemed to many filmgoers a protest against commercial Hollywood. And like Kubrick's voluntary absence, Malick's disappearance from the film community enhanced the director's reputation as a painstaking, uncompromising auteur.

George Lucas and Steven Spielberg

Though initially just as committed to the ideal of auteur filmmaking as their predecessors, George Lucas and Steven Spielberg will forever be associated with the phenomenal box-office success of their films and the dramatic Hollywood recovery their films helped fuel. While Coppola is routinely credited with jump-starting the auteur renaissance, Lucas and Spielberg are saddled with a reputation for hurrying its demise and providing a template for the blockbuster era that replaced it.

Their successes came one after the other. Lucas's breakthrough film, *American Graffiti* (1973), was produced for a mere $750,000, but earned over $21 million in its first run. Spielberg's *Jaws,* released two years later, broke the box-office record set by *The Godfather,* becoming the industry's first $100-million-grossing film. The success of *Jaws* created and defined for the industry the summer season (during which the studios now routinely release mostly action-laced blockbusters). In 1977, Lucas's *Star Wars* broke the record set by *Jaws*—in dramatic fashion. *Star Wars* earned over $210 million in an astonishing first run that lasted from May 1977 to April 1978. Like *American Graffiti, Star Wars* (discussed at length in Chapter 8, along with its sequels and prequels) was a model new-Hollywood product. It was deftly cross-promoted in parallel entertainment and consumer industries and spawned a virtual gold mine in merchandising (toys, logo-emblazoned clothing) and consumer-product tie-ins (at fast-food restaurants and on the shelves of supermarkets).

Although it has become fashionable to view Lucas and Spielberg as marketers first and moviemakers second, their early work—the films that reached American audiences before their names became synonymous with a certain style of entertainment—smacked of the same creative spirit that distinguished the so-called movie brats with whom they shared the stage in the early 1970s. *American Graffiti,* for example, is audacious in concept and execution. Lucas shot the film wild with several simultaneously running handheld cameras to simulate a direct-cinema or TV-news style. The hop scene in the high-school gymnasium, for example, begins with a camera moving from left to right across the bleachers and then up to the stage. As the camera reaches the performers (a band "all the way from Stockton"), it catches a strobelike effect from the lights behind the stage. Pointing a camera directly at a light, as Lucas purposely does in this scene, would be a mistake in most fiction films. But here it generates a realist effect essential to the film's overall conception, creating the impression that the film is documenting (capturing on film) a night in the life of some ordinary American teenagers. To chronicle such an eventful night realistically, Lucas simulated the time span of the narrative by shooting the film exclusively from dusk to dawn. He also shot the entire film in sequence (that is, he shot each scene in the order in which it would appear on-screen). As all-night filming began to weigh on his young cast, the actors began to look and act tired. Like the characters who stay up all night in the film, by the end of weeks of all-night shooting, the actors were exhausted.

Though not known today for his ability to direct actors, Lucas got terrific performances from *American Graffiti*'s ensemble cast, many of whose members—like Richard Dreyfuss, Harrison Ford, and Ron Howard—would go on to become major movie stars. But how much Lucas influenced their performances is subject to question. By the accounts of those who worked on the picture, Lucas was not particularly communicative: he offered little in the way of instruction or motivation. Instead, he simply cautioned the actors that they must always consider themselves

Debbie (Candy Clark), Toad (Charles Martin Smith), and Steve (Ron Howard) in George Lucas's
American Graffiti (1973). Note the reflected light above Ron Howard's head. It's not a mistake.
Instead, it's an autuer signature of sorts, a cue that Lucas shot the film on the fly, in the style
of a documentary.

"on camera"; with several cameras running at once, they could never step out of character. When an actor asked for a narrative or emotional cue, Lucas appeared perplexed and promised only—and vaguely—that the film would come together once the cast and crew went home.

Lucas told his cast that he was "cutting the film in his head," that he instinctively understood how to match the shots from the various cameras. The final product suggests that he was not boasting idly. Especially in evidence is a talent for action editing—at appropriate moments, Lucas picked up the pace of the editing to highlight the multiple camera positions. In the climactic drag-race scene, for example, the camera angles are from above, in front, to the right, then to the left—all just to show

the cars heading away from the starting line. When one of the cars swerves off the road and crashes, the mishap is shown from several more camera positions. And when it explodes—and the car did explode—a handheld camera situates us, like the teenage onlookers at the scene, close to the flames.

Lucas's work with music in *American Graffiti* set a trend for a generation of filmmakers. All the early '60s music that plays throughout the film was of course post-produced, but as we watch the movie, we assume that a source for the music exists within the space of the film—that it comes from the band at the hop, the AM radio blaring from the cruising cars, or the jukebox at the drive-in diner. The songs themselves narrate the film. For example, we hear "Why Do Fools Fall in Love" when Curt (Dreyfuss) first sees the mysterious blonde (the future TV star Suzanne Somers) in the white T-Bird, a ballad about breaking up ("Smoke Gets in Your Eyes") when Steve (Howard) and Laurie (the future TV star Cindy Williams) do their spotlight dance at the hop, "Maybe Baby," when Toad (Charles Martin Smith) tries to get someone to buy liquor for him, "Since I Don't Have You" as Laurie gets into the car with the hot-rodder Falfa (Ford) just before the big race, and "A Thousand Miles Away" when Curt tries to find DJ Wolfman Jack. The ever-present music was of central importance to Lucas's realistic depiction of teen life circa 1962, but—and this would foreshadow Lucas's marketing acumen with the *Star Wars* franchise—the music proved to be more than a narrative conceit: The songs were packaged as a sound-track album and marketed in advance of the film's release. This cross-promotion stimulated a brief nostalgia craze in the music business that supported the film's first run.

Like Lucas, Spielberg achieved his first big success on film with a genre piece, the horror picture *Jaws*. And like Lucas he made the most of the opportunity by making a moribund genre seem suddenly new and exciting. However, while Lucas's approach to the teen film was positively experimental, Spielberg's success with *Jaws* was the result of his fidelity to and expert manipulation of the horror genre's major tropes. *Jaws* is in many ways a prototypical horror picture. In play are several familiar horror themes: progress verus nature (the chamber of commerce versus a monster from the deep), an overriding paranoia (evinced in the tagline "Just when you thought it was safe to go back into the water"), the inevitable panic at the acceptance of the monster's existence (the mad rush out of the water on the Fourth of July), the search for experts to solve the problem (the scientist Hooper, played by Richard Dreyfuss, and the seasoned sea captain, Quint, played by Robert Shaw), the necessary failure of technology (the shark cage) and expertise (Quint's death, Hooper's near drowning) as the seemingly unkillable monster (the shark) gets the better of humankind at every turn. As in so many monster pictures, in the end it all comes down to man versus beast.

Spielberg made the most of the action sequences, especially in the film's latter half. He adeptly places the viewer onboard the boat and makes us comfortable with the men as they drink and trade stories. Slightly drunk, Quint tells a story about the U.S.S. *Indianapolis*, a ship torpedoed and sunk by a Japanese submarine during World War II, an event that left Quint and his mates treading water for days as sharks picked them off, man after man. The story lulls us, only to change pace suddenly (with a shift to multiple camera angles and fast-paced editing) as the shark lays siege to the boat and its crew.

As Hollywood evolved into a blockbuster industry in the late 1970s (see Chapter 8), Lucas and Spielberg provided the formula for what came to be known as high-concept entertainment: films based on ideas that, as Spielberg put it, could be expressed in twenty-five words or less, ideas that one could "hold in one's hand." The simple narratives were easy to condense into a single tagline that might be used to promote the film. Though simple in structure, the films were big and loud, spectacles of commercial and industrial expertise. The emphasis on special effects in *Jaws* and *Star Wars* recalled the so-called cinema of attractions that was popular at the beginning of the twentieth century, when the main attraction of filmed enter-

Steven Spielberg in a publicity photograph for his 1975 hit *Jaws*.

tainment was its gee-whiz quotient, its ability to create a new sensation, bigger and better than ever before.

Lucas and Spielberg gained fame less for a signature style than for a signature product. They were no less tied to an auteur project than the other movie brats, but they conceived a radically different way to realize that goal. Unlike the auteurs among their contemporaries, such as Coppola and Scorsese, who concerned themselves primarily with the production phase of the filmmaking process (performance, lighting, camera placement, camera movement, art direction, and so on), Spielberg and Lucas focused their efforts on postproduction issues: inserting visual and aural effects, using editing to modulate the beats (intervals between action sequences), carefully modulating the rhythm and pace of their films.

Postproduction can be a painstakingly slow and lonely task. But it is the step in the filmmaking process that affords a director complete control over the footage at hand. In an editing booth there are no temperamental actors to contend with, no bad weather to botch a shot. Because so much can change at this late stage in the process, postproduction has historically been the phase during which the battle to control a movie has been keenest. Stories abound about studio executives looking over an editor's or director's shoulder, whispering "suggestions" or, worse, threatening to take a film away if the editor or director does not comply with the studio's wishes.

Because Lucas and Spielberg employed so many electronic, optical, and aural postproduction effects, the rough cuts of their late '70s and early '80s films—Lucas's *Star Wars* and Spielberg's *Close Encounters of the Third Kind* (1977), *Raiders of the Lost Ark* (1981), and *E.T. the Extra-Terrestrial* (1982), all discussed in the next chapter—were mere sketches of the completed films. The task of filling in the effects involved so much work that was well beyond the scope of the studio hired hands that production executives had no choice but to let the two auteurs finish their films on their own. The fact that the postproduction wizardry was a reason so many people paid to see the films further militated against studio interference. If auteurism is all about a director securing and maintaining control of a film from start to finish, Lucas and Spielberg are auteurs par excellence.

The End of Auteurism: *Apocalypse Now* and *Heaven's Gate*

Two films mark the end of auteur Hollywood: *Apocalypse Now* (Coppola, 1979) and *Heaven's Gate* (Michael Cimino, 1980). Both became exemplars of the worst-case auteurist scenario, wherein overindulged egomaniacal directors were given too much money and too much control.

In September 1978, Francis Ford Coppola screened a rough cut of his long-awaited epic *Apocalypse Now* for a room full of United Artists (UA) executives. Coppola's self-proclaimed "ultimate Vietnam film" seemed destined to become a cinematic landmark, but exactly what it would come to mean in the history of Hollywood was still very much up in the air. By 1978 the studios had wearied of the auteur theory; celebrity directors like Coppola were difficult to deal with and notoriously profligate with the studios' cash. Executives had come to understand that the new auteurism presented a fundamental capital risk—one day one of the studios would be caught with its money tied up in an expensive film it could not effectively control or market.

By all accounts, including the director's, the production of *Apocalypse Now* had spun out of control by 1978: the shoot alone covered an astonishing 238 days spread over 15 months. The film's cost, not including optical effects (dissolves and other postproduction visuals), final sound dubbing, and prints (multiple copies of the film made for release to hundreds of theaters nationwide), was already approaching $30 million, approximately double the original budget.

In what can be described only as a colossal misapprehension of the studio's attitude, Coppola had gone into the screening with a plan to ask for more time and more money. But he soon had to rethink his position. By the time the lights came up, the mood in the screening room had turned sour. One UA executive was so disappointed he leaked word to the press that the picture might never come out and then dubbed the film "Apocalypse Never." When the UA executives met again after the September screening to discuss what to do about the film and what to do about Coppola, they agreed on two things: they didn't much like the movie, and they blamed themselves for losing control of the project. Had cooler heads prevailed, the executives

From left to right: Kilgore (Robert Duvall), Chief (Albert Hall), and Willard (Martin Sheen) share a quiet moment during a strange in-country beach party in Francis Ford Coppola's *Apocalypse Now* (1979).

would have realized that they had far less to lose than they thought: they still owned the first film in five years from America's most famous movie director. It would be hard not to make some money. But cooler heads did not prevail, and the UA executives decided to cut their investment in the film. Their reasoning was simple: so long as they could not control the project, so long as they could not control Coppola, they would let the auteur shoulder the risk.

Though the executives can hardly be blamed for their frustration with Coppola, their decision to limit their relationship to the film (and their access to its revenue flow) proved to be one of the biggest blunders in modern Hollywood history. In exchange for a $7.5-million investment, UA retained domestic distribution rights to *Apocalypse Now*. The remaining $25 million in the production budget

was technically lent to Coppola, with his home and his future earnings from *The Godfather* as collateral (though even in combination they were not worth nearly $25 million). In limiting its cash investment, UA surrendered the copyright to Coppola, along with all future rights to pay and network TV, domestic and foreign home rentals and sales, and foreign theatrical distribution. The film became a blockbuster hit, and the studio had so limited its stake in its long-term profits that it lost a fortune (all in a mostly symbolic effort to embarrass Coppola publicly).

Looking at the film today, one cannot help but wonder what the executives were thinking. *Apocalypse Now* is a thrilling film, a spectacular work of entertainment. All the money spent is, in the parlance of the industry, up there on the screen. The film's $32-million budget was at the high end for

Willard (Martin Sheen) about to complete his mission, the assassination of the rogue colonel Kurtz in Francis Ford Coppola's *Apocalypse Now* (1979).

studio productions circa 1979, but *Apocalypse Now* cost less than UA's other big film that year, the James Bond picture *Moonraker* (Gilbert). It is hard to argue that *Moonraker* is a better or bigger film. In the end, *Apocalypse Now* earned nearly $80 million in its initial U.S. theatrical run, had a record-breaking sale to domestic television, and did extremely well abroad. Its success only further embarrassed the UA executives.

Despite the studio's hesitancy at its release, *Apocalypse Now* is uniformly accepted as a major film of the auteur renaissance. Key to its continuing appeal is its scale and scope, thanks to the work of the Academy Award–winning cinematographer Vittorio Storaro, who, with Coppola, fashioned sequences that are among American cinema's most memorable. The most famous of these scenes is the helicopter siege that marks the end of the film's first act. It opens as Captain Willard (Martin Sheen) meets Lieutenant Colonel Kilgore (Robert Duvall) with orders for Kilgore to help him secure passage upriver. To clear the way—and to fit in a bit of surfing on some really good waves—Kilgore's air cavalry crew lays siege to a peaceful village. The setup for the siege is beautiful, a perfect counterpoint to the carnage to follow. As the air cavalry prepares for battle, Coppola offers us a single elegant tracking shot at dawn. The sky is a beautiful natural yellow orange, a color scheme that is recalled at the end of the scene when Kilgore orders a bombing raid and the surrounding woods light up in a sur-

real yellow orange. As Kilgore struts into the rural outpost after killing pretty much everyone there, he delivers one of the film's signature speeches: "I love the smell of napalm in the morning. You know, one time we had a hill bombed for twelve hours. When it was all over, I walked up. We didn't find one of 'em. Not one stinkin' dink body. The smell, you know that gasoline smell, the whole hill. Smelled like . . . victory."

The helicopters swoop in on the village from the direction of the rising sun. We hear soft electronic music in the background, but as the craft near the village, Kilgore turns up the volume on the loudspeakers, and we hear Richard Wagner's "Ride of the Valkyries." It is an at once absurd and gorgeously cinematic gesture. The time it takes for the helicopters to reach their target is condensed through a series of dissolves, soft cuts showing the helicopters in different formations. The tone and pace perfectly match the ambient electronic score. When the air cavalry mounts the attack and the Wagner music is cued, Coppola shifts from dissolves to action editing. The scene ends with senseless devastation that is nonetheless thrilling to watch. As we do when we view the climactic montage at the end of *The Godfather*, we come to appreciate the skill with which the sequence is executed independent of its ideological argument.

The film contains a number of other terrific set pieces: Willard's drunken rant in a Saigon hotel at the start of the film, a USO show featuring Playboy bunnies that ends in a riot, a hallucinogenic scene at the Do Long bridge, where soldiers shoot blindly into the darkness and seem completely confused about whom they're fighting and why. The energy of the film through its first two thirds is relentless: we are immersed in a world that makes no sense, moving headlong upriver to meet Colonel Kurtz (Marlon Brando), the man the war has driven mad. The buildup is so convincingly executed that the long, ponderous philosophical section at Kurtz's compound at the close of the film seems like a segment from another movie.

The last act posed a number of problems for Coppola, especially because Brando arrived on the set overweight and totally unprepared. Forced to improvise the final half hour of the film, Coppola struggled to make Willard's confrontation with Kurtz at the compound fit with what precedes it and then somehow use the improvised scenes to

fit some sort of convincing closure. In all, four endings have been screened over the years, and today video, laser-disc, and DVD versions vary. The rough cut screened for UA featured a ground and air assault on the Kurtz compound stylized to look like the apocalypse of the title. The Cannes Festival version shows Willard completing his mission and killing Kurtz but unsure of what to do next (in the last shot Willard clearly thinks about taking Kurtz's place). The (70mm) limited run has Willard getting back into the boat after killing Kurtz but not calling in the assault. Finally, the print that was screened in most theaters in 1979 shows Willard's exit by boat and then the air assault superimposed on the final credits.

Despite such an anticlimactic third act and Coppola's indecision about the film's final moments, *Apocalypse Now* is in many ways the ultimate auteur picture, the perfect combination of massive

Francis Ford Coppola (*right*) directing Marlon Brando (as Colonel Kurtz) on the set of *Apocalypse Now* (1979). Because the actor showed up terribly overweight and unprepared, Coppola had to improvise, and the long, ponderous, philosophical section at Kurtz's compound that closes the film seems as if it were from another movie.

studio expenditure and equally massive artistic risk. By taking these matters to extremes, Coppola at once exposed the financial and creative risk of auteurism, but to his lasting disappointment the risk proved too great for the studios to bear. In 1972, Coppola created the auteur renaissance with *The Godfather*. Seven years later his last great film, *Apocalypse Now*, marked its end.

Ironically, the very box-office disaster that the UA executives feared when they saw the rough cut of *Apocalypse Now* was already in development at their studio. In August 1978, against the backdrop of mounting prerelease hype for Michael Cimino's Vietnam War film, *The Deer Hunter,* Stan Kamen, Cimino's agent at the William Morris Agency, proposed a movie package to UA: *The Johnson County War,* a low- to moderate-budget western directed by Cimino and starring Kris Kristofferson, another Kamen client. The pitch, made just as UA execu-

tives were in a panic over the budget of *Apocalypse Now,* worked very much to Kamen's advantage because *The Johnson County War* sounded so unlike *Apocalypse Now.* The preliminary budget for the film that became *Heaven's Gate* was a mere $7.5 million; Cimino's salary was set at roughly one fourth of Coppola's. And to soothe the executives' frayed nerves in the wake of *Apocalypse Now's* three-year drain on the studio's resources, Kamen assured UA that he would supervise preproduction himself (by casting and staffing the picture with his own clients) so that the film would be produced in a timely manner.

Three years and $36 million later ($44 million, if advertising costs are factored in), *Heaven's Gate* became the unreleasable disaster that UA executives had feared *Apocalypse Now* would be. An unquestionable failure for the director and the studio, the film nonetheless proved valuable to the

Sheriff James Averill (Kris Kristofferson, *front right*) and Ella Watson (Isabelle Huppert, *skating by his side*), in Michael Cimino's beautifully shot $44-million box-office bomb *Heaven's Gate* (1980).

studios in one important way: after *Heaven's Gate* the studios were able to reclaim control over film production from auteur directors with few howls of protest. Every auteur had the potential to become another Michael Cimino.

It is difficult today to talk about *Heaven's Gate* as an important work of cinema if only because so few people have seen it. And then there are the two versions: Cimino's and the studio's. The original version, released in November 1980 to a handful of theaters, ran 3 hours 39 minutes, but it was pulled before the end of the second week of the run. (The film's opening-weekend take was $12,000, a figure so low that the studio panicked and decided not to lose any more money marketing a picture no one wanted to see.) Several months later UA rereleased the film with almost a third of its running time cut (to 2 hours 29 minutes). This studio version is the one that was most often seen by movie, TV, and video audiences over the next twenty-four years.

A 2005 DVD of the director's cut finally gives us a look at the film Cimino intended us to see. And after taking that look, one ought to wonder why the studio panicked. At the very least, *Heaven's Gate* is a beautifully rendered piece of cinema; the money is again up there on the screen. At 3 hours 39 minutes, it is a mere 19 minutes longer than Coppola's *Godfather: Part II*, a huge hit six years earlier, and just 37 minutes longer than Cimino's previous film, *The Deer Hunter*, winner of the Academy Award for Best Picture in 1979.

One possible explanation for the studio's trouble with the finished film is that more than any other director of his generation, Cimino was far more interested in style than story. In this case the story is the Johnson County War, a bloody confrontation in the late nineteenth century that pitted the wealthy landowners of the Wyoming Stock Growers Association (and their hired guns) against ranchers and immigrant workers. Cimino's focus is not on the scope and sweep of the epic confrontation (between rich and poor, powerful and weak), however. Instead, his focus is the overall look of the film, which thanks to Vilmos Zsigmond's cinematography is breathtaking in the way that only cinematic epics like *Lawrence of Arabia* (David Lean, 1962) or *Heaven's Gate* itself—can be. With an eye for detail that recalls the painstaking productions of another doomed Hollywood artiste,

Erich von Stroheim, Cimino endeavored to simulate the world of the Old West with a specificity never before seen on-screen. Such artistic commitment took time and cost money, and the studio proved unsympathetic to Cimino's claims to an artistic higher ground.

That such a beautiful epic film has been so routinely cited as the ultimate Hollywood bomb tells us less about the filmmaking and the film audience in 1980 than it does about Hollywood's mounting displeasure with auteurism in general and its need, finally, for a big auteur film to fail. *Heaven's Gate* satisfied an industry-wide need for a film that would mark the transition from one new Hollywood to another, from a town controlled by egomaniacal auteurs to one controlled by egomaniacal corporate executives. For the studio executives poised once again to control Hollywood filmmaking, Cimino and his film proved to be the perfect scapegoats.

AMERICAN GENRE CINEMA

The brief Hollywood renaissance required of Hollywood's players a number of artistic and commercial compromises. Executives accommodated themselves to the irksome task of dealing with star or celebrity auteurs whose every demand cost them money. Filmmakers, at least initially, wisely couched even their most ambitious projects in familiar genre, frameworks they then set about dismantling and reassembling. Between 1968 and 1980 many of the popular and important genre films could also be considered auteur pictures; there were routine westerns in the 1970s, of course, but the most interesting westerns were made by one director, Sam Peckinpah. There were run-of-the-mill horror films, but it was the work of two young auteurs, Brian De Palma and John Carpenter, that radically changed the genre to accommodate the permissiveness of the new rating system and the tastes of the burgeoning teen audience that so enthusiastically embraced the genre by decade's end.

Comedy has historically been an auteur's (though not necessarily a director's) genre, and the '70s proved no exception to that rule. Woody Allen, Mel Brooks, and Richard Pryor, all successful comedy performers and writers first famous for their work in nightclubs, onstage, and/or on television, released films very much tied to their own idiosyncratic brand of humor. Auteurism in their case was a matter of branding the material rather than a question of directorial style: audiences knew what sort of humor to expect from a Woody Allen comedy, a Mel Brooks comedy, or a Richard Pryor comedy, and they chose accordingly.

Two new genres—blaxploitation and the modern woman's picture—also emerged in the '70s. Both genres have roots in the silent era but were otherwise tied to timely cultural and political issues. Blaxploitation was a genre of exploitation-style films made by and for African Americans. Reminiscent of the early-twentieth-century race films (like those made by Oscar Micheaux), blaxploitation was at once topical and targeted; the genre dealt with issues of relevance to black Americans and were cleverly marketed to black American audiences. The films were characteristically irreverent in response to the tide of social change sweeping 1970s America as race relations were very much in transition. The other new genre, the revamped woman's picture, spoke volumes about changing gender roles as the sexual revolution and "women's lib" became hot topics of conversation.

The Ultraviolent Western

In 1969, Sam Peckinpah reinvented the Hollywood western with *The Wild Bunch*, escalating the intensity and the duration of the violence that lies at the heart of the genre. Despite such a radical transformation, the film is profoundly nostalgic. Peckinpah's film clings to classic western themes regarding modernity, violence, idealism, and masculinity, but its new style suggested that the director was using the genre to say something profound about America at a particularly violent moment in its history.

Peckinpah began his career directing episodes of the classic TV series *Gunsmoke* and *The Rifleman*. Unlike Francis Ford Coppola, Martin Scorsese, and most of the other movie brats, whose film-school education fueled an intellectual appreciation of genre cinema, Peckinpah was an industry veteran by the time he made his first important feature. He was temperamentally distinct from the new auteurs, too, having a lot more in common with the likes of John Ford and John Huston—two directors of Hollywood genre films with larger-than-life macho reputations—than with his contemporaries. But although his ties to an old Hollywood were strong, his understanding and exploitation of the opportunities that directors enjoyed during the late '60s and early '70s were no less keen than those of his younger counterparts in the auteur renaissance. Peckinpah's evocative use of widescreen and wide-angle lenses and his sudden shifts from an elegiac pastoral mise-en-scène to frantic action-edited gunfights gave a new look to a genre that had begun to stagnate.

The violent sequences in *The Wild Bunch* are choreographed and shot with such loving care that they appear at once horrific and beautiful. By depicting violence in an intentionally hyperbolic way, Peckinpah renders screen carnage as a spectacle of not only macho excess and bloodlust but cinematic talent as well. When the opening scene devolves into a massacre as a bunch of incompetent bounty hunters gun down temperance marchers while the bank robbers they are after get

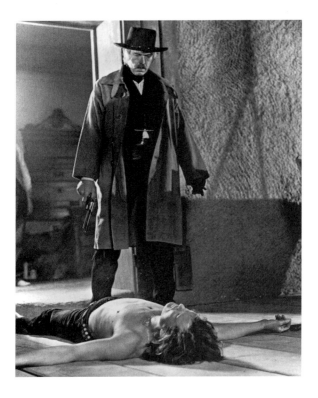

The lawman and hired gun Pat Garrett (James Coburn) guns down a friend, the outlaw Billy the Kid (Kris Kristofferson), in Sam Peckinpah's 1973 western *Pat Garrett and Billy the Kid*.

A gang of seasoned outlaws take a tumble in the desert heat in Sam Peckinpah's ultraviolent western *The Wild Bunch* (1969).

away, Peckinpah flexes his creative muscle. The use of slow motion and deft action editing renders the violence aesthetic and serves mostly to alert us to the director's prodigious talent (as well as the talent of his cinematographer, Lucien Ballard, and his editor, Louis Lombardo). The scene leaves us exhilarated even though all the director has shown us is carnage.

The Wild Bunch, along with Pecknipah's *Pat Garrett and Billy the Kid* (1973), recalibrated the violence of the movie western. No longer are two cowboys facing each other at high noon, ready to draw their guns. Instead, enterprising rival outfits—bounty hunters, trained soldiers, lawmen, and professional outlaws—are armed to the teeth, spoiling for a fight. When confrontation becomes inevitable, the scale and the scope of the carnage

are apocalyptic, genocidal. Never before in the history of the western movie had so many been killed for so little reason.

When *The Wild Bunch* was released, critics were quick to identify a parallel between the violence on-screen and the savagery in Vietnam, which was being aired on the nightly news. Pecknipah was always cagey about this sociopolitical argument, but several scenes in the film make the parallel hard to miss. The wild bunch is led by two American outlaws who leave the United States (for Mexico) in search of adventure and cash. In Mexico they find themselves taking sides in an incomprehensible civil war, where, as in Vietnam, mercenaries and advisers representing various Western powers are also involved. In *The Wild Bunch* we enter into a civil war in medias res, never fully

Clint Eastwood as the rogue cop Harry Callahan in Don Siegel's *Dirty Harry* (1972). In this scene, Harry squares off against his worst enemy, a state bureaucrat.

understanding the reasons for the rivalries but clearly witnessing the deadly intent of the participants. After the wild bunch steals some guns for General Mapache (Emilio Fernandez), the leader of one of the factions in the war, one of their number, Angel (Jaime Sanchez), decides to give a case of the guns to a rival faction. These men are clearly guerrilla fighters (like the Viet Cong, our enemy in Vietnam): they live by their wits and believe in their cause. When Angel's theft is found out, Mapache has him tied to the bumper of an automobile and dragged through the dusty streets of the town. The film's brief denouement begins as we hear a sad Mexican song and see the wounded hobble out of the wrecked town. In 1969 those Mexican refugees looked a lot like the Vietnamese refugees filmgoers were seeing night after night on the TV news.

After *The Wild Bunch*, ultraviolence caught on in American genre cinema. Don Siegel's *Dirty Harry* (1971), for example, opens, like Peckinpah's western, with a scene of senseless carnage, in this case as Harry Callahan (Clint Eastwood) is interrupted from his hot-dog lunch by a melee in the street. Harry is a modern cop who has vowed to protect and serve the citizens of San Francisco. But he is at heart tied to an old-fashioned police ethic, according to which his job is to enforce the law and punish the bad guys, using any means at his disposal. Harry totes a huge handgun (a .44 Magnum) and dispatches justice without abiding by the *Miranda* decision (which guarantees that persons under arrest be informed of certain legal rights and procedures) or consulting the bureaucrats in city hall who have hamstrung the cops on the street. At the end of the opening gunfight, Harry holds the perpetrator at gunpoint. Musing aloud about whether he has fired all six shots in the gun's magazine, Harry suggests that the perp ask himself a simple question: "Do I feel lucky?" He concludes with "Well, do ya, punk?" Harry is a cop brought to the edge by rampant crime and laws that favor criminals; he is ready to pull the trigger, and we are supposed to find that willingness admirable.

Dirty Harry made Eastwood, the stoic former TV actor and star of a string of ultraviolent spaghetti westerns—*A Fistful of Dollars* (1964), *For a Few Dollars More* (1965), and *The Good, the Bad and the Ugly* (1966), all directed by the Italian cineaste Sergio Leone—a movie star and spawned a series of films starring Eastwood as a vigilante cop: *Magnum Force* (Ted Post, 1973), *The Enforcer* (James Fargo, 1976), and *The Gauntlet* (Eastwood, 1977). Variations on the Eastwood vigilante-cop formula followed. The *Death Wish* series, for example—*Death Wish* (Michael Winner, 1974), *Death Wish II* (Winner, 1982), *Death Wish 3* (Winner, 1985), and *Death Wish 4: The Crackdown* (J. Lee Thompson, 1987)—stars Charles Bronson as a regular guy, albeit a regular guy with a propensity for violence, brought to the edge by a crime against his home and family. Another popular variation on the *Dirty Harry* theme, the *Walking Tall* series, is set on rural as opposed to urban mean streets. *Walking Tall* (Phil Karlson, 1973), *Walking Tall Part II* (Earl Bellamy, 1975), and *Walking Tall: The Final Chapter* (Jack Starrett, 1977) tell and retell the story of Buford Pusser (Joe Don Baker in the first film, Bo Svenson in the sequels), a real-life southern lawman who was compelled to take the law into his own hands. *Walking Tall* pivots on a scene (promised on the lobby poster and in the film's trailer) in which the hero, brought to the edge like Harry Callahan, is seen toting a baseball bat, prepared to do what it takes to clean up his dirty town.

Like a number of other films of the late 1960s and early '70s, *Walking Tall* tells us something about the way many urban Americans of that era viewed the rural American South. *Easy Rider* (Dennis Hopper, 1969), for example, ends with a rural southerner, disfigured and bigoted, gunning down its hippie heroes in cold blood. John Boorman's *Deliverance* (1972), which tells the story of a trip upriver by a handful of bored urbanites, similarly depicts the rural South as a haven for idiots and lunatics. The poster tagline—"This is the weekend they didn't play golf"—doesn't begin to suggest all that happens in the film, which climaxes terrifyingly with an on-screen male-on-male rape.

What ties these different genre films together is the scale of the violence. No doubt the new rating system enabled an escalation of violence on-screen, but it is fair to ponder, What was it in American society as the '60s came to a close and the '70s got under way that normalized such on-screen violence? The answer to that question may lie in the reality of Vietnam, or in the terrifying violence on the mean streets of urban America, or in the growing generational and regional divide between young and old, between those tied to a modern urban world and those somehow beyond the ken of American civilization, holed up in some rural backwater waiting for a chance to strike back.

The New American Horror Film

Long the dominant genre in cheap exploitation moviemaking, horror reemerged in the mid-1970s as another arena for the new auteur cinema. The first important new horror film was *Rosemary's Baby* (Roman Polanski, 1968), adapted from Ira Levin's best-selling novel about a coven of New York City witches arranging for the devil to impregnate an unsuspecting housewife (Mia Farrow). The film was shot with a painstaking seriousness seldom seen in horror pictures, except perhaps Polanski's own European thrillers *Repulsion* (1965) and *Cul-de-sac* (1966). *Rosemary's Baby* was the seventh-highest-grossing film in 1968, an astonishing performance for a horror picture.

Polanski's success with *Rosemary's Baby* seemed at first an aberration, but it was instead a foreshadowing of scarier things to come. In the mid-1970s the horror genre was revitalized and retooled by two young American cineastes: Brian De Palma and John Carpenter. De Palma's *Carrie* (1976), a film made on a modest $1.8-million budget, had a fabulous first run at the box office, earning $33 million. Based on a Stephen King novel set in a suburban high school, it tells the story of a lonely girl, Carrie White (Sissy Spacek), who is tortured by more popular and more conventionally pretty classmates on the one hand and by a fanatically religious mother (Piper Laurie) on the other. Carrie's position as an outcast is guaranteed by her mother's controlling parenting and

(*left*) Rosemary (Mia Farrow) faces the awful truth, that her husband's newfound success has been had at her expense: the deal he's made with the devil has her pregnant with Satan's child. Roman Polanski's adaptation of Ira Levin's best-selling novel was the seventh-highest-grossing film in 1968.

by the fact that there's something clearly "different" about her. The torments that her classmates subject her to finally trigger a power that no one, not even she, has foreseen. In the final scenes, Carrie's anger and humiliation at a final, horrifying insult—a bucket of pig's blood raining down on her head during a school dance—propels her over the edge. With her entire body clenched in psychic rage, she enters a fugue state and lays waste to the entire school. A wish-fulfillment allegory for every kid who has ever been bullied or humiliated at school and a cautionary tale for the popular set, *Carrie* was yet another film that targeted the youth audience with material that deftly manipulates and appeals to the anxieties and fears of adolescents.

More than any studio director of horror films before him, De Palma depicted the horror genre as a carnal affair, at once bloody and erotic. For De

Palma naked flesh, amply on display in virtually all his films, is at once a titillation and a sure sign of vulnerability—and the camera in nearly all his films lingers on scenes of extreme brutality to create visually stunning and shockingly vivid tableaux. For many viewers, De Palma's graphic violence carried out against beautiful women and transformed into a stylish aesthetic (a dreamed rape and murder in the 1980 picture *Dressed to Kill*, for example, or an impalement on a power drill in the 1984 *Body Double*) is troublesome and exploitative.

Further complicating De Palma's reputation as an auteur is his reputation as contemporary cinema's most shameless imitator of Alfred Hitchcock. His early spoof *Phantom of the Paradise* (1974) pivots on a parody of the shower scene in *Psycho* (Hitchcock, 1960), in which an effeminate rock singer (Gerrit Graham) is warned off performing the phantom's pop opera. Shower scenes abound in *Dressed to Kill*, in which the killer (Michael Caine), like Norman Bates (Anthony Perkins) in *Psycho*, dresses in drag. *Obsession* (1976), a film about a man (Cliff Robertson) who blames himself

The controversial rape fantasy that opens Brian De Palma's carnal horror film *Dressed to Kill* (1980). Women's groups picketed screenings of the film but succeeded only in drawing attention to it. The inside Hollywood rumor is that the film's producer, Samuel Z. Arkoff, paid actresses to join the picket lines once he discovered the potential box-office benefit of the protests.

The porn-actress heroine Holly (Melanie Griffith) takes the film's wan hero, Jake (Craig Wasson), for a walk on the wild side in a lavish set piece in *Body Double* (Brian De Palma, 1984). Like a lot of the suspense films directed by De Palma, *Body Double* alludes to Alfred Hitchcock's films—in this case, *Rear Window* (1954) and *Vertigo* (1958).

for the death of his wife and years later tries to remake a stranger (Geneviève Bujold) in her image, is patterned rather obviously on Hitchcock's *Vertigo* (1958). *Body Double* blends parts of *Vertigo* (the hero fears tight spaces instead of heights, but the larger themes of impotence and male weakness are the same) with Hitchcock's *Rear Window* (1954), though in De Palma's film the voyeur uses a telescope, and what he sees is a neighbor doing an erotic dance number, the dance's interruption by a break-in, and the dancer's apparent murder.

If *Carrie* introduced a new formula for a stylistically ambitious auteur horror film, John Carpenter, a graduate of the University of Southern California's film school, perfected it with *Halloween* (1978). Shot for a mere $325,000, the film earned over $47 million in its first theatrical run. As a new horror template, *Halloween* proved more

easily reproducible than *Carrie*. It reduces horror to a simple formula (a maniac killer is on the loose, and he can strike anywhere at any time) and presents its story with simple, albeit extremely effective camerawork and sound work.

The signature scene in *Halloween* comes at the very start. While an ominous electronic score matches a heartbeat, the camera, mounted on a Steadicam for maximum mobility, hovers outside a suburban home where a teenage boy and girl are preparing to go upstairs and have sex. They talk briefly about Michael, the girl's brother, but only to affirm his absence and his irrelevance. We soon discover that our point of view is that of a character in the film, and after he (and we) enter the house and grab a big kitchen knife, it becomes clear what he (and we) are about to do. We climb the steps, all the while looking through the eye holes of a Halloween mask that Michael (Will Sandin) has put on. The heartbeat (so to speak) on the electronic score picks up speed, and the sound of Michael's breathing into the mask picks up the pace as well. Without saying a word, the killer attacks his sister. We continue to share his point of view as he goes back down the stairs and ventures outside. The parents arrive, and the camera finally shifts to the third person point of view. The killer, Michael, is unmasked. He is just a boy.

We later learn from the boy's psychiatrist (Donald Pleasence) that Michael is pure evil, a monster beyond reason and redemption. He is placed in an insane asylum after the murder, and it is his escape as a young adult that sets the plot in motion.

Halloween blazed new trails in the horror genre in several ways, but perhaps most notably in its setting: *Halloween* is clearly a suburban nightmare, set in a typical white middle-class community where, as the police chief says, "Families and houses [are] all lined up in a row . . . all lined up for slaughter."

The now-grown-up Michael (Tony Moran) kills the police chief's daughter (Nancy Loomis) as she gets into a car to pick up her boyfriend to have sex. He later kills another young woman (P. J. Soles) just after she has had sex, and he fashions out of her bedroom a strange and macabre shrine, complete with his sister's headstone looming above the dead young woman's head. Obsessed with adolescent sexuality and driven to kill young women who engage in it, Michael (the twenty-three-year-old

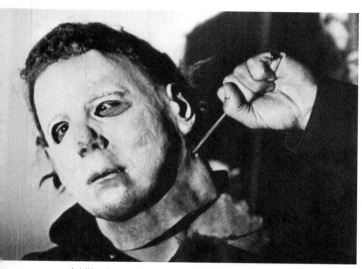

A killer beyond reason and redemption, Michael Meyers (Tony Moran) rises from the dead (for the first of several times) in John Carpenter's hugely popular teen horror film *Halloween* (1978).

Michael who has escaped from the asylum) seems unable to kill Laurie (Jamie Lee Curtis), the one "good girl" he meets. The movie culminates in a drawn-out battle between Michael and Laurie, during which she appears to kill him at least twice (once with a knitting needle in the neck and once with a big kitchen knife). Finally six shots of gunfire ring out from offscreen, and Michael hurdles backward through a bedroom window, falling to what appears to be his death. The scene cuts to the psychiatrist and the smoking gun. "It *was* the bogeyman," Laurie whimpers. "As a matter of fact, it was," he says. The psychiatrist walks to the window and looks out. But Michael is gone. Such evil is apparently indestructible, otherworldly, and beyond our ability to control or comprehend. As in De Palma's *Carrie*, what is at stake in *Halloween* is a young woman's sexuality, here policed by an irrational, super- or subhuman violence. If you have sex, you die. The link that *Halloween* establishes between teen sex and irrational violence became the hallmark of a new genre. Given the target audience for these films, that link is at once perplexing and instructive.

Horror films cast from the *Halloween* mold uniquely feature a female hero who defeats the male monster through moral chastity, smarts, and persistence. Though the films (there are eight *Hal-*

loween pictures in all) are superficially misogynistic—they pay homage to the stalker-film motif of crazed men preying on innocent young women—they also feature a tough, capable young woman. Hollywood cinema is overpopulated with girl sidekicks and love interests and, alas, female victims. But the female heroine of these films is nobody's girlfriend or sidekick. She is a hero, pure and simple.

Two other teen-horror franchises owe obvious debts to *Halloween:* the *Friday the 13th* and *Nightmare on Elm Street* series, the former weighing in with ten films, the latter with seven. Released less than two years after *Halloween*, the first *Friday the 13th* picture (Sean Cunningham, 1980) distills Carpenter's film into its basic horror elements and then increases the amount of sex and violence. The

Halloween's last woman standing, Laurie Strode (Jamie Lee Curtis), whom boogeyman Michael Meyers doesn't and maybe can't kill. John Carpenter's 1978 horror film was the first in a series of teen slasher franchises, including *Halloween*'s seven sequels, *Friday the 13th* (Sean Cunningham, 1980) and its nine sequels, and *A Nightmare on Elm Street* (Wes Craven, 1984) and its six sequels.

Wes Craven's unrelentingly violent B horror film *The Last House on the Left* (1972), a crude forerunner of the teen horror films that would become so popular at the end of the 1970s.

maniac at the center of the *Friday the 13th* franchise, Jason, is a mute killer who dons a hockey mask while laying waste to all the teens who dare indulge their carnal desires. Jason's revenge, like Michael's, is at once simple and ridiculous, but it has also proved of enduring interest, as teenagers for well over a decade have continued to pay to see Jason do his murderous business.

The first *Nightmare on Elm Street* film debuted in 1984. Directed by the veteran exploitation filmmaker Wes Craven—his savage horror films *The Last House on the Left* (1972) and *The Hills Have Eyes* (1977) are notorious in exploitation filmmaking and film-going circles—*A Nightmare on Elm Street* introduced a new sort of horror-movie villain, Freddy Krueger (Robert Englund), a monster of the subconscious who sports razor-sharp fingernails and haunts the collective dreamscape of an entire town's teenagers. Freddy has his reasons for killing, too. Like Carrie and Jason, he was treated badly before he became a monster. His revenge is choreographed and gleefully narrated. Unlike Michael and Jason, Freddy likes to talk as he kills.

Scary as these films may be, teen audiences routinely find them comic. Watching one in a theater full of teenagers reveals a pleasure found in the experience of terror, an experience colored by a profound familiarity with and affection for a genre formula. Even films as outrageous and antisocial as *The Hills Have Eyes* and *The Texas Chain Saw Massacre* (Tobe Hooper, 1974)—films that take the fear and loathing of ignorant men to new and ridiculous heights—make teen audiences laugh. Theaters screening the films resemble a party, a celebration by initiates who get the joke, sick as it may be. An embrace of this film-audience dynamic is apparent in Wes Craven's very popular *Scream* series—*Scream* (1996), *Scream 2* (1997), and *Scream 3* (2000)—films that have as much fun with the teen horror-film formula as their audience does. *Scream*'s poster tagline says it all: "Don't answer the phone. Don't open the door. Don't try to escape." *Scream*'s audience knows why.

Comedy Stars and Comedy Films

The three most influential and most important comedy movie stars of the 1970s were Woody Allen, Mel Brooks, and Richard Pryor, urban ethnic comedians who, in their stage acts and later in their films, exaggerated and celebrated their otherness from mainstream culture. Brooks and Allen joked at their own expense, gleefully constructing caricatures of themselves as neurotic urban Jews. Pryor's stand-up routine comprised long expansive stories about the comedian himself that asked audiences to find a glimmer of humor in the everyday hazards of African American life (poverty, drug addiction, racial prejudice, and prison).

Allen began his career as a gag writer for other comedians (most famously Sid Caesar on the TV comedy series *Your Show of Shows*). Though he enjoyed some success as a stand-up comic, in the 1960s he was primarily regarded in show business as a comedy writer, and it was as a writer that he first made his mark in Hollywood, in 1965, with his script for the sex farce *What's New, Pussycat*, a modest hit for the veteran British director Clive Donner and stars Peter Sellers and Peter O'Toole. Allen's first film as a director was *What's Up, Tiger Lily?* (1966), a silly but often very funny farce with an English-language sound track dubbed over a hokey Japanese spy film.

Allen's second film, *Take the Money and Run* (1969), adapted from one of his stage plays, tells the story of Virgil Starkwell (played by Allen), a would-be thief and desperado. Though the character's name recalls that of the notorious killer Charles Starkweather, Virgil is a feeble crook, the first in a long line of neurotic losers played by Allen on-screen. Following the success of *Take the Money and Run*, Allen made a series of pop-culture spoofs. *Bananas* (1971) pokes fun at television, South American politics, and the Olympic Games. The sex farce *Everything You Always Wanted to Know about Sex* but Were Afraid to Ask* (1972) lampoons a serious nonfiction best seller penned by the psychiatrist David Reuben. The film covers much the same ground as the good doctor's book but with a deep sense of the absurd nature of the task at hand. *Sleeper* (1973), which satirizes the futurist science-fiction genre, has Miles (Allen) waking up from a cryogenic "sleep" to find himself in a strange future world in which people use an "orgasmatron" for sexual pleasure and folks are kept happy in a sterile, empty world. Allen pokes fun at Aldous Huxley's *Brave New World*, George Orwell's *1984*, and—in a particularly clever scene meant to bring Miles back to his senses after he is captured and brainwashed by a totalitarian government—Tennessee Williams's *A Streetcar Named Desire*. In *Love*

and Death (1975), the last of his broad parodies, Allen took on the Russian novel.

For most of Allen's early career, his humor was directed outward, and his films were episodic, constructed of skits that seemed designed less to hold together as a narrative than to provide as many laughs as possible in a 70- to 90-minute film. Those films were widely accessible, and their director seemed unselfconscious. But after a decade of making movies poking fun at an absurd modern world, Allen turned to more autobiographical material in 1977 with *Annie Hall* and then increasingly invested his work in more ambitious narrative themes: interpersonal relationships (*Hannah and Her Sisters*, 1986), fame (*Stardust Memories*, 1980), crime and guilt (*Crimes and Misdemeanors*, 1989), and sexual misadventure (*Husbands and Wives*, 1992).

At first the move to a more story-driven, more adult-themed comedy paid off at the box office. Indeed, *Annie Hall* catapulted Allen to stardom. The film features Allen as Alvy Singer, a comedy writer turned stand-up (like the director) who hates driving, Los Angeles, and industry poseurs and loves New York, the Knicks, jazz, and long movies about the enormity of the Nazis' crimes. The film is particularly revealing (and funny) on the subject of American ethnicity. Alvy's Jewish family lives under the roller-coaster at Coney Island. Family members relate by screaming at one another across the dinner table. A parallel dinner-table scene at Annie's (Diane Keaton's) family's home is sedate but in many ways just as weird, a nightmare vision of rich white Protestant Americans.

Annie Hall won Oscars for Best Picture, Directing, Writing (for an original screenplay, by Allen and Marshall Brickman), and Actress in a Leading Role (Keaton) and established Allen as an auteur and movie star. *Annie Hall* also marked Allen's entrance into the commercial mainstream, a place that seemed to make him uncomfortable, so much so that he followed *Annie Hall* with a straight dramatic film, *Interiors* (1978), grounded in the work of his idol, the dour Swedish filmmaker Ingmar Bergman. The gesture to Swedish melodrama and Allen's decision not to cast himself in the film seemed even at the time a calculated attempt to retreat from the celebrity spotlight.

In his next outing, *Manhattan* (1979), Allen continued his move away from the frantic parodies of his early career with a loving tribute to his home (shot in shimmering black-and-white) that offers a revealing look at the social mores of 1970s New York. Allen plays Isaac Davis, a man whose midlife crisis manifests itself in a romantic triangle involving the mistress of his best friend (Keaton again) and a precocious sixteen-year-old (Mariel Hemingway, who received an Oscar nomination for her performance). Though the parallel to later events in Allen's private life seem today all too close and not particularly funny (in the late 1990s Allen ditched his longtime partner, Mia Farrow, a woman roughly his age, for her adopted daughter, Soon-Yi Previn, thirty-five years his junior), in 1979 no such autobiographical parallel was in play. Instead *Manhattan* gently asked why a sixteen-year-old might find Isaac attractive and why he might find her more than just eye candy. He sees that the relationship is inappropriate and breaks it off but then changes his mind. In the end he gets neither woman because that's just what he deserves. As the director famously quipped only partly in jest, "If my film makes one more person miserable, I'll feel I've done my job."

If *Manhattan* didn't obviously enough mark the transition from episodic parodies to a more serious-minded (and much less zany, much less funny) cinema, then the transparently autobiographical *Stardust Memories* did. In *Stardust Memories*, a film that nods more than once to Federico Fellini's famous autobiographical work *8½* (1963), Allen plays Sandy Bates, a filmmaker tortured by celebrity and hounded by fans at a festival retrospective of his work. The fans beg him to go back to the zany comedies he made early in his career, but Bates, appalled by fame and overwhelmed by the pressures of his private life (wives, girlfriends, children), steadfastly refuses to give in. Anyone familiar with Allen at the time can appreciate the parallel. As the '70s came to a close, he seemed to accept the role of comedy auteur at a moment when the only place to be an auteur was on the margins of Hollywood. *Stardust Memories* made the comedy auteur's position clear: he was moving on, and he didn't care whether or not the studios and his audience came along for the ride.

Mel Brooks's stand-up career began in the 1940s in what was called the Borscht Belt (a swath of nightclubs at popular resort hotels in the Catskill Mountain region of New York State that catered primarily to a Jewish clientele). Modest popularity onstage led to a stint as a comedy writer for Sid Caesar's *Your Show of Shows* (1950–1954). Along with three other comedians—Woody Allen, Carl Reiner, who wrote and directed episodes of *The Dick Van Dyke Show* and directed the 1979 feature film *The Jerk*, starring Steve Martin; and Neil Simon, a playwright whose scripts for comedy films include *Barefoot in the Park* (Gene Saks, 1967), *The Odd Couple* (Saks, 1968), *The Sunshine Boys* (Herbert Ross, 1975), *The Goodbye Girl* (Ross, 1977), and *Biloxi Blues* (Mike Nichols, 1988)—Brooks brought a distinctively urban ethnic (which is to say New York Jewish) sensibility to 1950's prime-time television.

Brooks's first feature, *The Producers* (1968), proved to be a landmark in contemporary comedy. It is crude, lewd, and outrageous, ground zero for the gross-out comedies of John Landis (*Animal House*, 1978) and, later, the Farrelly brothers, Bobby and Peter (co-directors of *Dumb and Dumber*, 1994, and *There's Something about Mary*, 1998). *The Producers* tells the story of two struggling Broadway showmen who, in an elaborate and crackpot scheme, set out to produce a flop. They set their sights on a thoroughly tasteless musical comedy about Hitler and the Third Reich that features a series of bad-taste production numbers, culminating in the showstopping Busby Berkeley–style performance of "Springtime for Hitler," which trots out nearly every cliché about Germans and Germany. The play is so transparently awful that the producers (played by Gene Wilder and Zero Mostel) are sure it will close after one night. But the effete Broadway audience mistakes bad taste for satire, and the play is a huge success.

Brooks's next hit was *Blazing Saddles* (1974), a tasteless send-up of the Hollywood western. Memorable scenes include a farting contest among some cowboys huddled around a campfire and a tough-guy outlaw knocking a horse unconscious.

(*right*) Annie Hall (Diane Keaton) and Alvy Singer (Woody Allen) meet in Woody Allen's Oscar-winning comedy *Annie Hall* (1977).

Sheriff Bart (Cleavon Little, *right*) and the Waco Kid (Gene Wilder) in Mel Brooks's tasteless send-up of the Hollywood western, *Blazing Saddles* (1974).

The film chronicles the arrival of an African American sheriff named Bart (Cleavon Little) in a lawless western town (composed entirely of façades). At a time when race issues were at the forefront of serious debates and conflicts in the United States, Brooks seemed uniquely able to expose and exploit racial stereotypes in his films. For example, at a particularly tense moment, Bart blurts out, "Where the white women at?" His movies ably balance potty humor with an element of social commentary. There is a little Lenny Bruce, a little Richard Pryor, a little Jerry Lewis, a little Milton Berle, and a little Benny Hill all wrapped up in Brooks's topical farces. The '70s were in many ways an angry decade, and with good reason. But Brooks maintained the comedian's critical distance no matter what he aimed his comedy at; in his early films he made some relevant points about the social problems in '70s America while maintaining a goofy smile.

Young Frankenstein (1974), Brooks's last great film, spoofs old Hollywood horror pictures. In the very process of cataloguing genre clichés, it moves from one gag to the next at breakneck speed. Elizabeth (Madeline Kahn), Dr. Frankenstein's fiancée, develops a crush on the monster (Peter Boyle), surmising that his disproportionate height indicates that he is disproportionately big elsewhere. When Igor (Marty Feldman) tells the doctor (Gene Wilder) to "walk this way," the doctor not only follows his new assistant but mimics his limp as well. In the course of the film, Brooks pokes fun at Hitchcock—there's a *Rebecca* (1940) subplot—as well as the Frankenstein and Dracula films and even *King Kong* (Merian C. Cooper and Ernest B. Shoedsack, 1933) as Dr. Frankenstein takes to the stage to introduce his new "discovery," the monster, and news photographers' flashbulbs send the monster into a frenzy. True to Brooks's penchant for tasteless humor—a gag at any cost—the monster performs Irving Berlin's "Puttin' on the Ritz" by screeching a single phrase of the song. He is at that moment less a monster than a child with a disability bleating a phrase to please his father. And yet the scene is excruciatingly funny—to a large extent because it is so insensitive.

Perhaps it was the hectic pace of the early films or the exhausting and exhaustive number of gags necessary to make his sort of comedy work, or perhaps the shock value wore off all too quickly, but Brooks was never able to follow up on *Blazing Saddles* and *Young Frankenstein*, the number 2 and number 7 box-office films for 1974. His later work—including the Hollywood farce *Silent Movie* (1976), the Hitchcock parody *High Anxiety* (1977), and the *Star Wars* spoof *Spaceballs* (1987)—are by comparison juvenile and slapdash.

Richard Pryor was a sensational stand-up comic. But unlike other stage comedians who succeeded in films by playing versions of their stage personae, Pryor was cast at first mostly in supporting roles. He played a financial wizard in the silly but popular B teenpic *Wild in the Streets* (1968, Barry Shear), dramatic parts in the Billie Holiday biopic *Lady Sings the Blues* (Sidney J. Furie, 1972) and Paul Schrader's working-class drama *Blue Collar* (1978), some song-and-dance work in the screen adaptation of *The Wiz* (Sidney Lumet, 1978), and comic roles in a range of films: with Flip Wilson and Bill Cosby in *Uptown Saturday Night* (Sidney Poitier, 1974) and with fellow stand-ups George Carlin and Irwin Corey in the ensemble comedy *Car Wash* (Michael Schultz, 1976). His first important starring role was in the very popular mixed-race buddy comedy *Stir Crazy* (Poitier, 1980), in which he co-stars with Gene Wilder.

As good as many of his film performances were, Pryor was at his best onstage. His series of concert films—*Richard Pryor: Live in Concert* (Jeff Margolis, 1979), *Richard Pryor Live on the Sunset Strip* (Joe Layton, 1982), *Richard Pryor Here and Now* (Pryor, 1983), and *Richard Pryor: Live and Smokin'* (Michael Blum, 1985)—proved to be landmarks in the genre, prototypes for fellow African American stand-ups in films like *Eddie Murphy Raw* (Robert Townsend, 1987) and *Chris Rock: Bigger & Blacker* (Keith Truesdell, 1999). Pryor's four concert films showcase the comedian's irreverent, deeply personal, and honest stand-up style. For Pryor an effective stand-up performance was all about telling the truth, even when the truth was especially painful. "I am no day at the beach," he tells his audience in *Richard Pryor Live on the Sunset Strip*. In *Richard Pryor: Live and Smokin'*, Pryor recounts (as comedy) the fateful day when, in a dope-addled state, he set himself on fire.

Pryor was also brutally frank about racial issues. In the process of describing his work on the popular feature *Stir Crazy*, for example, he details his experiences filming scenes at an Arizona penitentiary. Having met the prison's inmates, Pryor says, "Thank God we have penitentiaries." Then he segues into another point, one of considerable interest to African Americans, wondering why 90 percent of the prison population is black when, according to Pryor, "there are no black people in Arizona." Of course there are, but according to Pryor's monologue, they have to be bused in—that is, to the prison.

In the 1970s, Allen, Brooks, and Pryor targeted adult audiences and thus benefited from the new MPAA guidelines. To find a tamer, more family-friendly brand of comedy in the 1970s, filmgoers turned to a familiar source: Disney. Though the animation unit was not what it had been before the cartoonists' strike in 1941, *The Aristocats* (Wolfgang Reitherman, 1970), the animation–live action hybrid *Bedknobs and Broomsticks* (Robert Stevenson, 1971), and the feature cartoons *Robin Hood* (Reitherman, 1973), *Pete's Dragon* (Don Chaffey, 1976), and *The Rescuers* (Reitherman, John Lounsbery, and Art Stevens, 1977) all broke into the top-twenty box-office lists for their year of release. In a market defined by a new age-based rating

Hollywood's odd couple c. 1980: Richard Pryor (*left*) and Gene Wilder in Sidney Poitier's buddy comedy *Stir Crazy*.

system, there was plenty of money to be made by targeting the G (Geneal Audiences) crowd.

By resisting the industry trend toward making films for a more mature audience, Disney established itself as a niche player and cornered the market on a loyal demographic. Family-oriented live-action comedies like *The Love Bug* (Stevenson, 1968), the reissue of *Mary Poppins* (Stevenson, 1964 and 1971), *Herbie Rides Again* (Stevenson, 1974), *The Apple Dumpling Gang* (Norman Tokar, 1975), and *Freaky Friday* (Gary Nelson, 1976) were all popular family-friendly films in this era.

Disney's success with family fare prompted a predictable response from its competitors. Fox revived (after an eleven-year absence) the accident-prone Inspector Clouseau (Peter Sellers and, in 1983, Roger Moore) in five *Pink Panther* sequels, all directed by Blake Edwards: *Return of the Pink Panther* (1975), *The Pink Panther Strikes Again* (1976), *Revenge of the Pink Panther* (1978), *Trail of the Pink Panther* (1982), and *Curse of the Pink Panther* (1983). To much the same end, Paramount introduced *The Bad News Bears* (Michael Ritchie, 1976), which was followed by *The Bad News Bears in Breaking Training* (Michael Pressman, 1977) and *The Bad News Bears Go to Japan* (John Berry, 1978). These PG-rated films focus on a group of misfits who find success playing organized baseball. The kids in the *Bad News Bears* films are not merely naughty (like kids in Disney films); they can be downright nasty. But in the end they need and want just what Disney kids need and want—an adult who is willing (finally) to care about them. In such a cynical decade such a sentiment proved welcome on the family-movie scene.

Blaxploitation

In the 1970s, African Americans accounted for about 15 percent of the U.S. population. But as market research revealed, they accounted for more than 30 percent of the national first-run film audience. Since African Americans patronized what was essentially white American cinema, many movie-business executives held that producing movies that catered specifically to the African American audience was unnecessary. For others in the business, black America was a largely untapped resource of proven filmgoers, a target audience starved for films about people whose lives more or less resembled theirs.

The studios initially broached the controversial subject of race relations tangentially in films like *Guess Who's Coming to Dinner* (Stanley Kramer, 1967), a film produced by an all-white creative team, starring the very popular black movie actor Sidney Poitier and the legendary white actors Katharine Hepburn and Spencer Tracy. *Guess Who's Coming to Dinner* examines the then-taboo topic of mixed-race marriage. The title gives away the plot, but it does so by design. Audiences flocked to the film (which ranked second in the annual box-office race), already knowing the basic question the film raises: What does a white liberal couple say when their daughter brings home her fiancé and he's African American? And what if he looked like (what if he was) Sidney Poitier—handsome, deeply intelligent, full of integrity? And what if, as the film further poses, he is a medical doctor with a practice in (of all places) Switzerland? Didn't every white couple of that generation dream that their daughter would marry a doctor?

In 1967 two other black-themed films, both starring Poitier, were released to box-office success: *In The Heat of the Night* (Norman Jewison), which won the Best Picture Oscar, and the British-made *To Sir, with Love* (James Clavell). *In The Heat of the Night* tells the story of an African American big-city detective (Poitier) who ventures into the racially segregated South, where he is initially accused of committing a murder and then recruited to help solve the crime. His task is at first complicated by a bigoted lawman (played by Rod Steiger, who won an Oscar for his role), but in the end the two men solve the crime and part company with something approximating mutual respect. *To Sir, with Love*, which is set in London, deftly examines the essential inequality in education for the poor and the rich, an intractable problem in the United States as well.

The sorts of roles Poitier got to play in the 1960s and '70s highlighted his race and revealed how a black person might "fit in" in an integrated America. But a rising tide of African American radical-

Sidney Poitier as Virgil Tibbs (*left*), the well-educated, well-mannered police detective from "up north" and Oscar-winner Rod Steiger as police chief Bill Gillespie, the prototypical southern lawman, in Norman Jewison's politically progressive crime film *In the Heat of the Night* (1967). The two men eventually earn each other's respect, a theme of some relevance given the era's civil rights struggle.

ism in the late 1960s complicated the reception of Poitier in both the black and white communities and to an extent made an alternative black celebrity and an alternative set of black narratives necessary. Such an alternative African American film genre took shape between 1968 and 1974 and came to be known as blaxploitation, a term that affirms the anticipated (black American) audience and celebrates the genre's production style and marketing scheme (exploitation).

Several of the early blaxploitation stars were celebrities before they made movies, like the former professional athletes Jim Brown and Fred Williamson. Brown, a National Football League Hall of Fame running back, made the transition from the playing field to the movie set with a convincing supporting performance in the number 1 Hollywood film of 1967, the war picture *The Dirty*

Dozen (Robert Aldrich). He went on to play a series of uncompromisingly proud black men in mainstream Hollywood films, such as *Ice Station Zebra* (John Sturges, 1968), and in blaxploitation films like the crime picture *Slaughter* (Starrett, 1972) and the revenge fantasy *Black Gunn* (Robert Hartford-Davis, 1972). The former NFL defensive back Fred Williamson followed in Brown's footsteps. His first feature role of note was in the popular Hollywood picture *MASH* (Robert Altman, 1970), as Spearchucker Jones, a doctor recruited to help the MASH unit win a big football game. In a series of blaxploitation films, Williamson patterned his on-screen persona after Brown's: a no-nonsense black man with a sense of personal justice that transcends conventional (and thus traditional white society's) rules. With the title roles in the western revenge fantasy *The Legend of Nig-*

The former professional football player Fred Williamson (*right*), Don Pedro Colley (*left*), and D'Urville Martin in the 1972 blaxploitation western *The Legend of Nigger Charley* (Martin Goldman).

Sworn to avenge the death of her government-agent boyfriend, Foxy Brown (Pam Grier) takes matters into her own hands. With *Foxy Brown* (Jack Hill, 1974), Grier became one of blaxploitation's biggest stars.

ger Charley (Martin Goldman, 1972) and the urban crime film *Hammer* (Bruce D. Clark, 1972), Williamson became one of the biggest stars of the blaxploitation era.

The two best-known blaxploitation films are *Shaft* (Gordon Parks, 1971) and *Super Fly* (Gordon Parks Jr., 1972). Both films chronicle the heroic exploits of handsome and capable men who transcend the immorality and criminality of the urban scene. With an emphasis on action—gunfights and fistfights and a surfeit of sex—and clever tie-ins to the popular African American music scene (*Shaft* features music by Isaac Hayes; *Superfly*, music by Curtis Mayfield), these two films provided a template for a number of subsequent blaxploitation crime and action pictures. Exemplary among the black actioners are *Cleopatra Jones* (Starrett, 1973), with Tamara Dobson playing a secret agent; *The Mack* (Michael Campus, 1973), with Max Julien as a pimp with ambition and Richard Pryor as his loony sidekick; the Fred Williamson gangster picture *Black Caesar* (Larry Cohen, 1973); *Coffy* (Jack Hill, 1973), introducing Pam Grier as a vigilante nurse at war with local drug lords; *Three the Hard Way* (Parks Jr., 1974), teaming Brown and Williamson; and *Foxy Brown* (Hill, 1974), with Grier as a private citizen sworn to avenge the death of her government-agent boyfriend.

Blaxploitation put African Americans behind the camera as well as on-screen. The three best-known black cineastes were Gordon Parks, a photojournalist renowned for his work for *Life* magazine; the actor turned director Ossie Davis; and the wildly creative writer, director, actor, and composer Melvin Van Peebles. Parks directed the semiautobiographical *Learning Tree* (1969), a film that chronicles racial discord in rural Kansas in the 1920s. He then helmed *Shaft* and its sequel, *Shaft's Big Score!* (1972). Davis was a successful movie and TV character actor in the1950s and '60s before his debut as a blaxploitation director with the action-comedy hit *Cotton Comes to Harlem* (1970), about two tough cops, Gravedigger Jones (Godfrey Cambridge) and Coffin Ed Johnson (Raymond St. Jacques), on the trail of a cotton bale filled with cash. *Cotton Comes to Harlem* was one of the most successful titles of the genre, grossing nearly seven times its production budget in its first run.

One of the most compelling and controversial of the blaxploitation filmmakers was Melvin Van Peebles. His first feature film, *The Story of a Three-Day Pass* (1968), was financed by a French company and distributed in the United States by the tiny independent outfit Sigma III. It tells the story of a mild-mannered African American GI stationed in France who celebrates a promotion during a three-day leave. On the first day he meets a white French shopgirl. When she offers to go with him to a resort hotel, he assumes she is a prostitute.

The provocative lobby card for the provocative blaxploitation feature *Sweet Sweetback's Baadasssss Song* (Melvin Van Peebles, 1971).

She's not, but as they discover, both of them would have been better off if she had been. At the end of the film, the GI and his new lover realize the impossibility of ever escaping a society in which mixed-race relationships are taboo.

Van Peebles's next film, *Watermelon Man* (1970), was a commercial hit, a blaxploitation comedy about a bigoted white insurance agent who wakes up one morning to discover that he has been transformed into a black man. Legend has it that the studio commissioned an ending in which the white man discovers that the experience was all a dream but Van Peebles refused to comply. Such independence would become a hallmark of his career. Indeed, just as Van Peebles found himself on the verge of mainstream success, he turned his back on Hollywood, and he and the comedian Bill Cosby, a friend of his, spent their own money to make the alliteratively titled *Sweet Sweetback's Baadasssss Song* (1971). Van Peebles produced, directed, scripted, scored, and starred in the picture, which tells the story of a stud named Sweetback (Van Peebles) who earns a living performing in live sex shows in the ghetto of South Central L.A. It was, to say the least, not the follow-up to *Watermelon Man* that the studios were looking for.

Early in the film, Sweetback witnesses an act of police brutality, the victim of which is a black militant named Mu-Mu (Hubert Scales), and consequently goes on a rampage, first beating up the white cops and then embarking on a series of adventures while on the lam. Sweetback embodies and exaggerates many of the racial stereotypes that have haunted black actors since the silent era. But in blaxploitation those stereotypes (of supersexed studs, drunks, petty criminals, pimps, and the like) offer a commentary on the expectations that white America holds for black men.

Sweet Sweetback's Baadasssss Song was a sensation. The clever promotional campaign highlighted the picture's outlaw status. The film's various taglines included "Rated X by an all white jury," "Dedicated to all the Brothers and Sisters who have had enough of the Man," and "You bled my momma—you bled my poppa—but you won't bleed me." The film is sloppy (in the way that all cheaply made exploitation films are) but fascinating, and throughout Van Peebles refuses to sugarcoat the racial and racist subtext. Though much of the film is funny, it ends with a threat and/or a warning: "A BAAD ASSSS NIGGER IS COMING BACK TO COLLECT SOME DUES."

After the musical comedy *Don't Play Us Cheap* (1973) failed to capitalize on the success of *Sweet Sweetback's Baadasssss Song*, sixteen years passed before Van Peebles got his next major directing gig, *Identity Crisis* (1989), a film cut from the same cloth as *Watermelon Man*. *Identity Crisis* tells the story of a white fashion designer and a black rapper who find themselves in each other's body. The film stars (and was scripted by) Van Peebles's son Mario, who later made a movie about his dad's brief celebrity, aptly titled *Baadasssss!* (2003).

The brief run of blaxploitation films ended in 1980. Today blaxploitation is the stuff of pastiche (*Jackie Brown*, Quentin Tarantino, 1997) and parody (*I'm Gonna Git You Sucka*, Keenen Ivory Wayans, 1988), proof positive that it has achieved full-fledged genre status.

The New Woman's Film

In the 1970s a popular TV ad for Virginia Slims cigarettes touted, "You've come a long way, baby." Though the product for sale was just a slimmer, sleeker, more "feminine" cigarette, the ad campaign celebrated what in the 1960s came to be known as women's liberation, a movement meant to raise everyone's consciousness about women's issues. The ad opened with images from the 1920s, a time when few women dared to smoke in public and those who did were seen as promiscuous. With clever reference to the suffragette movement of the early twentieth century, the ad offered a parallel between a "respectable" woman's freedom to smoke cigarettes and the right to vote. In its claim that women had indeed come "a long way" since they won the right to vote, the ad connected the "right" to smoke with other rights (such as equal pay) that women in the '60s and '70s were fighting for.

If Madison Avenue could use women's liberation to sell cigarettes, it stood to reason that Hollywood could use it to sell movies. But although the studios had a history of embracing social movements if they could be marketed cleverly, women's lib proved to be a difficult social phenomenon to capture on-screen. The studios were far more comfortable with a film like *The Stepford Wives*, Bryan Forbes's 1975 adaptation of Ira Levin's popular

Jane Fonda as the call girl Bree Daniels in Alan J. Pakula's feminist suspense picture *Klute* (1971).

novel about a tony suburb in which a group of men collude to make their wives more compliant and more subservient. The film may well have been designed as a thriller, but as it renders ridiculous both sides of the argument—the women's-lib activists and the male backlash against the women's movement—it plays more like a farce.

Attempts to capture on film the lives of women who struggled to gain a modicum of social and sexual freedom—films like *Alice Doesn't Live Here Anymore* (Scorsese, 1974) and *An Unmarried Woman* (Paul Mazursky, 1978)—are, on close examination, less celebratory than cautionary. In *Alice Doesn't Live Here Anymore* and *An Unmarried Woman*, the widow Alice (Ellen Burstyn) and the divorcée Erica (Jill Clayburgh) discover that being single in the '70s may make them sexually free, but that freedom does not necessarily make them happy. Indeed, they quickly come to regret the absence of romance in such a socially and sexually liberated society—the absence of meaningful social contact in a system in which a connection between sexual intercourse and social commitment is no longer implied.

In Francis Ford Coppola's low-budget 1969 film *The Rain People*, a housewife (Shirley Knight) hits the road because she finds family life in the suburbs boring. But on the road she doesn't "find" herself and instead falls in with men far scarier than her husband. In *Diary of a Mad Housewife* (Frank Perry, 1970), a bright stay-at-home mom named Tina (Carrie Snodgress) married to a pretentious, inattentive husband (Richard Benjamin) discovers that hanging on to a marriage that isn't working isn't such a great idea either. She finds brief solace with a preening, egomaniacal writer (Frank Langella) but recognizes early in their adulterous relationship that he's not going to be around for the long haul. While these films show women caught in a tide of social change, it is not clear exactly where the tide is taking them. Virtually all of these women's films examine a fractured social institution (marriage) without venturing a guess at what might come next for an emancipated woman.

Perhaps the most celebrated of Hollywood's women's films in this era is the urban thriller *Klute*, directed by Alan J. Pakula and produced by an all-male production team in 1971. Though *Klute* was widely hailed on its release as a progressive film, its complex portrait of a high-end New York City call girl, Bree Daniels (Jane Fonda, who won an Oscar for the performance), more consistently serves the strictures of the thriller genre than the politics of feminism. Bree is depicted from the start as a deeply conflicted woman. She uses sex as a means of commerce and claims that in the absence of romance and traditional social ties (dates, engagements, or marriage) she has found a freedom that few women enjoy. The men who solicit her services pay for the experience, and in exchange they get a good performance but nothing more. With one customer early in the film, we hear Bree in what we take to be the throes of orgasm. The man she is with is convinced of her rapture, but we see her check her watch. Like any other worker, after all, she's on the clock and must manage her time. For Bree, sex is just a job.

Bree knows she can't be a call girl forever. She likes the independence, financial security, and

The director Claudia Weill (*left*) and the actress Melanie Mayron on the set of *Girlfriends* (1978).

absence of commitment the job gives her. But such independence, the film posits, makes her vulnerable; when she becomes the object of fascination of a sexual predator (Charles Cioffi) who has already killed two of her prostitute friends, she discovers that she really needs a man. Enter the small-town detective John Klute (Donald Sutherland). Bree realizes that she needs Klute's protection, but depending on Klute troubles her: her gender identity is based on the assumption that she doesn't need a man.

Eventually the stalker is unmasked, and Bree is free again. By this point we have come to realize that Bree is at once independent and needy; she is that rare thing, a complex female character. In the end we find Bree preparing to leave New York for some suburban backwater and a peaceful, conventional life with Klute. Such a rescue by a man and such an acquiescence to a quiet life in the suburbs at first undercut the film's promise of a fully independent heroine. But as she waits for the elevator at the start of her journey with Klute, Bree tells us in voice-over that she may be back in New York

before long. To his credit, Pakula undercuts the easy closure of the requisite Hollywood happy ending because such an ending might not fit a modern woman's story.

However much characters like Bree Daniels came to symbolize an emerging sexual and social freedom for women in the early 1970s and however much characters like Alice, Erica, the housewife Tina, and the call girl Bree represented a much-needed departure from the studios' steady diet of sexpots and sidekicks, Hollywood in the 1960s and '70s was still very much a man's town. Women had been more prominent in Hollywood in the 1920s than they were some fifty years later. A handful of women in the 1970s made movies— Joan Micklin Silver (*Hester Street*, 1975) and Claudia Weill (*Girlfriends*, 1978), to name two of the best known—but their small, low-budget films were at once marginal to and marginalized by mainstream Hollywood. The popular cigarette ad may have proclaimed that "you've come a long way, baby," but quite clearly in the 1970s women in the film industry had gotten nowhere.

■ ■ ■

Propelled by a new film rating system, Hollywood movies changed radically in 1968. Initially the new censorship regime supported something of a film renaissance that served two key functions: it brought Hollywood out of a long-term box-office slump, and it changed the way in which American filmgoers looked at and talked about American movies. To the studios the auteur theory was merely a marketing principle. But prominently displaying a celebrity director's name in promotional material supporting a film's release got filmgoers into the habit of thinking and talking about films as the product of an auteur, or author, and, by extension, as a work of art.

Especially for those in the baby boom generation, the 1970s has come to be considered a golden age of American cinema. Films seemed better than ever because the studios were leaving directors alone to make the sorts of movies they wanted to make. But the golden age was predicated on a fundamental capital risk; one day an auteur film would bomb at the box office, and the studios would have to collectively rethink their dependence on directors, whom

they often distrusted and despised. In 1980 the studios got their auteur bomb, Michael Cimino's *Heaven's Gate*, and the golden age suddenly and officially ended.

With the end of the auteur era came the beginning of yet another new Hollywood, one in which huge corporations (merging and entering into synergistic relationships that made them bigger than ever) held sway and formulaic blockbuster films became the industry's bread and butter. Lost in the translation and the transition were twelve years of terrific filmmaking, a brief era that was perhaps too good to last. Generalizations such as that, about the relative quality of Hollywood films, have come to dominate discussions of post-1968 American cinema. The party line, so to speak, is that there have been two new Hollywoods since the advent of the voluntary film rating system, one in which the director was king, and one in which power was restored to the studio executives and corporate managers. Why the former has been privileged by historians at the expense of the latter is a key to understanding contemporary American cinema.

Uma Thurman as Mia Wallace
in Quentin Tarantino's 1994
hit *Pulp Fiction*.

8

A New New Hollywood

Following the embarrassment of Watergate, a little-little known Democrat from Georgia, Jimmy Carter, ascended to the White House. In 1976, Carter was the right man at the right time: he was at the very least not Nixon, and he was not the former vice president and Repulican incumbent Gerald Ford (who had pardoned his former boss before a public trial could make the embarrassment to the party and the nation any greater). But America's love affair with President Carter failed to survive his first term. In 1980 the former Screen Actors Guild president and California governor Ronald Reagan took the presidency, winning all but four states (and all but forty-nine electoral votes).

Reagan's easy win over Carter in 1980 made clear not only the rising tide of conservatism among the electorate but also an impatience with liberal solutions to the problems of post-Vietnam America. Fears of a decline in American prestige abroad (prompted by the hostage crisis in Iran, brought about when supporters of the Islamic revolutionary government seized control of the U.S. embassy in Tehran and held more than fifty American citizens hostage for over a year) and a loss of confidence in so-called big government entitlement programs (the largesse of the social-welfare state that had come to characterize Democratic liberalism) set in motion what came to be regarded as the Reagan revolution. Ronald Reagan's politics and his affable, unpretentious manner helped to empower a broad coalition of American conservatives comprising Sunbelt suburbanites, foreign-policy hawks, antigovernment libertarians, and the nation's newest political force, the Christian Right.

Reagan was a staunch anti-Communist (dating to the 1950s in Hollywood) with convictions so firm that he glibly referred to the Soviet Union as an "evil empire" (a term taken from George Lucas's 1977 space fantasy *Star Wars*). Such tough talk appealed to his political base and seemed to work on the international stage as the president successfully negotiated landmark arms-reduction deals with the Soviet leader Mikhail Gorbachev. Also during the Reagan years, Gorbachev brought down the "iron curtain" that had separated the Soviet bloc from the rest of Europe. Many Americans believed that Gorbachev's moves toward democracy and free-market capitalism came about as a direct result of Reagan's foreign policy, defense spending, and influence abroad.

Reagan's second landslide victory in 1984, followed by the victory of his vice president, George Herbert Walker Bush, in the 1988 presidential election, cemented the triumph of the conservative politics that had characterized Nixon's "silent majority." Promising to free the federal government from "special interests" and in so doing free the American people from the burden of big government, Reagan supported a "supply-side" (or, as his opponents termed it, a "trickle-down") economic policy that involved reduced spending on federal social programs and tax cuts. In theory, supply-side economics stimulate private investment to such an extent that both big business and the individual taxpayer benefit. In fact, the federal deficit soared during the Reagan presidency, and what came to be known as Reaganomics proved very good only for those Americans with the greatest wealth (the wealthiest 1 percent saw their fortunes increase by over 15 percent during Reagan's presidency) while those in poverty continued to founder.

Reagan's insistence on deregulation enabled big businesses to get even bigger. In the film industry, Reaganomics prompted the studios' move back into exhibition. Lax enforcement by the Federal Communications Commission and the Federal Trade Commission—hallmarks of the Reagan-era deregulation—in many ways made the new Hollywood of the 1980s possible. In the new Hollywood a handful of enormous multinational companies controlled the industry and the larger entertainment marketplace more completely than the old studios ever did. The conglomerates that owned and controlled the stu-

dios viewed the entertainment marketplace expansively, establishing complex vertical and horizontal business relationships, what contemporary Hollywood executives call synergies. The long-delayed postwar box-office turnaround was finally jump-started by the auteur renaissance of the 1970s, but the full-scale Hollywood recovery resulted from what can be described only as a dramatic corporate restructuring.

The beginning of the new multinational Hollywood coincided with a series of seemingly unrelated and isolated incidents in 1979 and 1980: an antitrust case involving the corporate raider Kirk Kerkorian, a failed Screen Actors Guild strike, and a federal court case in which the studios attempted to forestall the retail sale of videocassette recorders. In 1985 a key court case, *United States v. Capitol Service*, pushed aside the 1948 *Paramount* decision, allowing the studios to return to the exhibition business—and monopoly control of the marketplace.

With increased conglomeration came an abandonment of the auteur theory and a growing emphasis on formulaic blockbusters—thrill-ride movies that deliver on a simple promise to entertain. During this era, action-adventure became the genre of choice, and movies were increasingly aimed at adolescent and postadolescent boys. If any vestige of auteurism survived, it was, on the mainstream screen at least, a box-office auteurism dominated by two producer-directors, Steven Spielberg and George Lucas. For those two men, whose work and artistic signatures would intersect throughout the '80s and '90s, auteurism was less a matter of a signature style than a matter of box-office clout.

In the 1980s and 1990s to find something similar to the personal auteur cinema of the Hollywood renaissance of the 1970s, one must look to independent film, the small-scale alternative to Hollywood's big-movie mania. Independent films, produced on modest budgets with modest profit projections, introduced a new generation of indie auteurs (Quentin Tarantino, John Sayles, Joel and Ethan Coen) and offered women (Allison Anders and Nancy Savoca) and people of color (Carl Franklin, Albert and Allen Hughes, Spike Lee) a chance to tell their stories.

A NEW CORPORATE HOLLYWOOD

When historians talk about the new Hollywood, they generally refer to the decline of the auteur renaissance and the emergence, around 1980, of a new industrial system, according to which a handful of companies controlled the vast entertainment marketplace, which was no longer limited to the production, distribution, and exhibition of movies. *Diversification* and *expansion* became catchwords of the newly deregulated industry, and by the end of the twentieth century a handful of companies controlled almost all of the popular media.

In the early 1980s the ability to coordinate and exploit different media outlets promised huge profits, but skyrocketing production costs and high interest rates on short-term loans (used to finance film production) made the movie business an expensive enterprise, so expensive that ten of the leading independent film companies (American International Pictures, Filmways, Jerry Weintraub, Cannon, De Laurentis, New World, Lorimar, Vista, New Century, and the Atlantic Releasing) went out of business at the start of the decade. By the mid-1980s, Hollywood had become the exclusive province of huge, well-diversified companies, and the trend toward consolidation continued through the end of the century.

The billionaire corporate raider Kirk Kerkorian, one of the new Hollywood's most interesting and perplexing players, in a 2002 photograph.

The Kerkorian Case

On April 25, 1979, MGM chief executive Kirk Kerkorian sold 297,000 shares of his company's stock. With the proceeds of the sale, he secured a $38-million loan, which he used to finance the purchase of a block of stock (amounting to 24 percent of the publicly traded shares) in a rival studio, Columbia Pictures Industries (CPI). Those moves enabled Kerkorian to become the largest shareholder in two of the six major studios. Citing antitrust as well as federal trade violations, the Justice Department filed suit in federal court. The suit set in motion a confrontation between federal regulatory agencies and a very new sort of Hollywood player that would change the movie business in dramatic ways.

The key to the Justice Department's argument was that Kerkorian's purchase of such a large block of CPI stock amounted to a hostile move on the company and that his potential dual ownership of

MGM and CPI significantly diminished competition in the marketplace. But on August 22, 1979, the court found in Kerkorian's favor. In an opinion that would kick-start the deregulation of the new Hollywood, presiding judge A. Andrew Hauk admonished the government attorneys for pursuing the case in the first place and dismissed the government's argument even as he acknowledged the corporate structure and operation of what we now call the new Hollywood: "How on earth the government can arrive at the thought that there will be a diminution of non-existent competition is beyond me."

With the courts' seeming approval, Kerkorian made a tender offer in September 1980 to raise his total stake in CPI to 35 percent. But just as Kerkorian prepared to mount a proxy fight for control of CPI, a fight he was poised to win, a catastrophic fire at his Las Vegas hotel, the MGM Grand, killed eighty-four people. Sidetracked by the complex legal and financial ramifications of the hotel catastrophe, Kerkorian allowed Columbia Pictures chief executive Herbert Allen to buy him out. Though he lost out on the opportunity to consolidate two studios, Kerkorian nonetheless netted a neat $137-million profit.

Four months later Kerkorian made an offer to buy Chris-Craft Industries' 22 percent stake in 20th Century–Fox. Studio management backed the millionaire oilman Marvin Davis, who in the end outbid Kerkorian. In 1984, Kerkorian reemerged as a principal in the corporate raider Saul Steinberg's leveraged move on Disney. Kerkorian and Steinberg were well positioned to take over the company but then backed off after receiving a huge greenmail payoff—that is, the Disney ownership bought back Kerkorian's and Steinberg's stock at a premium price ($325 million—a profit of over $30 million) in exchange for the raiders' promise to leave Disney alone. Kerkorian's various attempts to consolidate two studios (MGM with Columbia, Fox, or Disney) in an already consolidated marketplace (in which six companies controlled the vast majority of product and profits) made clear the government's inability (and, after Ronald Reagan's election, its unwillingness) to regulate the business of making movies.

Though he never claimed to be a film mogul—indeed, he made his money in the airline business and then in Las Vegas real estate—Kerkorian emerged as the prototypical new Hollywood player. Through the decade he held significant stock positions at MGM, Columbia, and United Artists; negotiated distribution deals and thus integrated MGM with United Artists, Paramount, and Universal; and made tender offers for Columbia, Fox, Disney, and United Artists. He also spent much of the 1980s trying to unload MGM (and the eventually annexed United Artists)—to the cable-TV mogul Ted Turner, to the producers Peter Guber and Jon Peters, to the Australian multinational Quintex, and finally (and successfully) to the shady Italian entrepreneur Giancarlo Parretti. The deal with Parretti was closed amid accusations of fraud and mismanagement, and in less than a year's time Parretti was forced to relinquish control of the company to his creditor, the French bank Crédit Lyonnais, which maintained control of the studio until July 1996, when the veteran studio executive Frank Mancuso engineered a management buyout financed by—who else?—Kirk Kerkorian.

Kerkorian's shenanigans, entertaining as they may be to recount, were indicative of the new corporate Hollywood, in which the movement of money was at times more dramatic and more compelling than the films made there. After 1979 and the court decision in the Kerkorian case, the big players in Hollywood were no longer necessarily movie people and, as things played out in the 1990s, no longer necessarily Americans.

The Screen Actors Guild Strike

Just as production was set to begin for the 1980 fall TV season, the Screen Actors Guild (SAG) went out on strike. At the time the threat of postponing the start of the fall TV season seemed a decent bit of leverage. But the actors overestimated their clout. In a move later followed by the other major studios, after the actors went out on strike, Universal locked out all of the major guilds (the screenwriters, the directors, the producers). It was a bold and effective strategy, sending SAG leadership (the archconservative but loyal union man Charlton Heston, as well as the outspoken Hollywood liberals Alan Alda, Edward Asner, and Marlo Thomas) into a panic.

The strike was hugely important to the actors because it sought to establish for them contractually a share of revenues from future home-box-office markets (pay TV and videocassette sales and rentals), much as TV residuals (payments every time a TV show is run or rerun) were parceled out at the time. The studios did not contest the importance of the home-box-office discussion. Instead, they argued that the discussion was premature, that the parties involved should wait until the market had established itself before negotiating revenue sharing.

Throughout the lockout the studios held fast. And eventually SAG backed down. Management's victory proved emblematic, demonstrating that after 1980 labor relations in Hollywood would be based on a two simple facts of life: the studios were no longer just studios but were instead diversified conglomerates with many other ways of making money besides making movies, and in the Reagan-

The movie star and Screen Actors Guild president Charlton Heston, photographed in 1980, the year he led the film actors' strike.

Bush era the guilds (especially since they represented what the average filmgoer viewed as spoiled actors and directors) could not depend on public sympathy.

The Battle over the VCR

Diversification within the entertainment industry was a priority after 1979, especially when the notion of competition among studios and studio owners was clarified in the wake of the Kerkorian decision. A future synergy with cable television was simple enough to foresee; after all, as early as the mid-1950s the studios had found a way to profit from strategic deals with network television (despite strict regulations governing film and TV ownership laid out in the *Paramount* decision). But videotapes were another matter, especially since the videocassette recorder (VCR), still new and largely uncertain as a retail item and home-entertainment audiovisual component in 1980, seemed to promise a future in which copyrighted material might be freely copied by consumers with no compensation paid to the studios.

On behalf of the industry, Disney and Universal filed a lawsuit in 1980 against Sony, which had just introduced the Betamax videocassette and video recorder. Citing free and fair trade as well as copyright concerns, the plaintiffs sought financial remedies; they asked that fees be added to the sale of every machine (as much as $100 per VCR) and every blank tape ($1 per cassette) to cover the inevitable "theft of revenue," or copyright violation, by consumers owning the new hardware (VCRs) and software (tapes).

Initially the court was not persuaded by the plaintiffs' arguments. Because VCRs and videotapes could be used in ways that did not infringe on copyrights, the court held that Sony could not be held liable for what consumers might do with the technology. Following that legal setback, the studios quickly moved to promote a prerecorded-videotape industry in which the rental and sale of studio-produced videotapes gave distributors and filmmakers a second opportunity to profit from the same basic product.

The *Capitol Service* Case

In order to move more fully into ancillary markets, the studios needed to figure out a way to get around long-standing regulations concerning exhibition as laid out in the 1948 *Paramount* decision. A window of opportunity opened in 1985 with a Supreme Court case, *United States v. Capitol Service,* which involved an antitrust action filed against four theater chains—Capitol Service, Kohlberg, Marcus, and United Artists—that together controlled 90 percent of Milwaukee's exhibition business and had entered into a collusive agreement not to bid against one another. In industry parlance such a scheme is a split agreement, and it effectively diminishes competition and minimizes licensing costs (the money paid to studios for the right to screen a film). The theaters defended the split agreement by arguing that such schemes were necessary for their survival. But the Court took a dim view of the exhibitors' cries of poverty and found in favor of the studios.

The decision proved devastating for the nation's exhibitors; split agreements were common and indeed necessary to their survival, just as the four Milwaukee theater chains had claimed. In 1986, the first year after the *Capitol Service* decision went into effect, over 4,000 screens changed hands, and in most cases major studios were the buyers. By the end of 1987, MCA/Universal had purchased the Plitt, Septum, Essaness, Sterling, and Neighborhood chains, as well as a 50 percent stake (amounting to some 1,550 screens) in the huge Cineplex Odeon chain. Several other studios moved into the exhibition business as well: Columbia purchased the Walter Reade Theaters; TriStar (owned in part by CPI) picked up the Loew's and United Artist theaters; and Gulf and Western (Paramount) bought the Trans-Lux, Famous Players, and Mann theaters (and, with MCA, Cinema International).

Though the purchase of theaters seemed to be in direct violation of the *Paramount* decision, in July 1986 both the Federal Trade Commission (FTC) and the Federal Communications Commission (FCC) announced that they did not plan to contest the studios' move back into the exhibition business. The announcement fueled further expansion. By the end of 1987, ten companies controlled over 50 percent of the first-run showcase screens. The *Paramount* decision had become moot.

The Time Warner Merger

In April 1989, Time and Warner Communications announced their intention to merge. Despite efforts by Paramount Communications (formed when Gulf and Western split off its mining and manufacturing companies from its various film, TV, music, and publishing divisions) to block the merger and buy Time outright, the merger between

Jack Nicholson as the Joker in Tim Burton's 1989 Warner Bros. blockbuster *Batman*. With this film the newly merged Time Warner took full advantage of so-called synergies in the new American entertainment marketplace.

Time and Warner was sealed in June 1989. At the time the newly formed Time Warner sported combined assets of nearly $25 billion and annual revenues estimated at $7.6 billion. Its holdings spanned a number of related entertainment industries, including film and TV studios (involved in development, production, and distribution), movie theaters, book and magazine publishing, cable-TV delivery systems and pay TV stations, recording-industry operations, and theme parks.

Time Warner's publishing division included the book publishers Warner Books, Time-Life Books, and Little, Brown; the comic-book publisher DC Comics (publisher of *Superman, Batman,* and *Wonder Woman*); and the mass-market magazines *Time, Fortune, Sports Illustrated, Sunset,* and *Parenting.* Its division of publishing services distributed books and magazines for other publishers and owned the Book-of-the-Month Club. The company's music division, the most lucrative and extensive on the planet, included Warner Bros. Records (and its subsidiaries Reprise, Sire, and Paisley Park), the Atlantic Recording Group, Elektra Entertainment (and its subsidiaries Asylum and Nonesuch), and Warner Music International. Its wholly owned subsidiaries American Television Communications and Time Warner Cable made Time Warner the second largest cable provider in the nation, and its cable-software division included some of the better and more profitable premium channels, including the pioneering pay-TV station HBO. Also among the company's holdings was the Licensing Corporation of America (LCA), which managed and protected the copyright on all Warner Bros. characters (Batman, Bugs Bunny, and so on). Products bearing those trademarks were made available for purchase at a chain of Warner Bros. retail stores located in malls nationwide.

To understand how synergies in the new Hollywood worked, consider Tim Burton's *Batman,* a Warner Bros. film released in 1989, just before the merger was finalized. The film grossed more than $250 million domestically. But as amazing as its domestic run was, theatrical grosses accounted for only a small part of the film's overall worth to the company. Because Batman is a DC Comics character and is licensed by LCA, the merchandising subsidiary took its cut from the profits of every Batman T-shirt, coffee mug, book, and action fig-

Ted Turner (*left*) and Gerald Levin announce the merger of Turner Broadcasting System and Time Warner in September 1995. The $6.5-billion merger made Time Warner the world's biggest media company.

ure that was sold. The film appeared on HBO and was delivered to homes across the country via cable systems owned by Time Warner. When the film was released on video, laser disc, and DVD, it bore the Warner Home Video label. The popular sound-track compact disc came out in two versions, both from companies owned by Time Warner. Coverage—constant reminders about the film (as an event, as a franchise)—appeared in Time Warner magazines like *Time, Life,* and—in time for the first sequel, *Batman Returns* (Burton, 1992)—*Entertainment Weekly.* From the perspective of this single movie, the value of the merger is clear.

Before the ink was dry on the Time Warner deal and just as news of another big deal made headlines in the trades—the purchase of MCA/Universal from the Japanese conglomerate Matsushita by the Canadian-born president of Seagrams, Edgar Bronfman Jr.—Disney announced a $19-billion buyout of Capital Cities/ABC—the second-largest corporate takeover in U.S. business history. The Capital Cities/ABC acquisition gave Disney a set of synergies similar to those of the newly formed Time Warner. With the merger, Disney became a company that not only manufactured a product

With his 1981 hit *Raiders of the Lost Ark*, Steven Spielberg set in motion an industry-wide trend toward "event films." Here we see Indiana Jones (Harrison Ford) swapping a bag of sand for an archaeological treasure, setting in motion the film's first action sequence.

that could be routinely reproduced in a variety of forms and formats but also owned a network of venues to which it could distribute that product— for example, ABC and the Disney Channel, theme parks, and retail stores.

In many ways the acquisition was merely a sign of the times, a move that Disney chief executive Michael Eisner had to make to maintain the conglomerate's strong position in the evolving international marketplace. The deal with ABC gave Disney one of the original three TV networks and a second key cable TV station, ESPN. The acquisition of ESPN was strategic—perhaps even the key to the deal. ESPN does not air movies. But its content—round-the-clock sports programming—is fairly neutral and thus as "family friendly" as traditional Disney content. With ESPN, ABC, and the Disney Channel, Disney was able to package its TV stations to cable providers abroad, especially in Asia, where fairly strict programming guidelines (regarding sexual and political content) made it

difficult for Time Warner (with its flagship cable station HBO) to participate.

Not to be outdone by Disney, Time Warner's chairman, Gerald Levin, made the next big move: the purchase of 82 percent of the outstanding shares in the Turner Broadcasting System (TBS), a stock deal worth roughly $7.5 billion. With that purchase, Time Warner projected annual revenues for the combined companies in excess of $19.8 billion, surpassing the new Disney's projected $16.4 billion. In the summer of 1996, the FTC conditionally approved Time Warner's purchase of TBS at the very moment the press began running stories about a strategic alliance between the Chicago-based Tribune Company and the computer information technology company America Online (AOL). As things played out, AOL, which was an unproved Internet outfit in 1996, became a key industry player by the end of the century, eventually merging with Time Warner to create the first of many synergies between the movie and Internet businesses.

GENRES AND TRENDS

While American cinema in the 1970s was dominated by auteurs and films that put on display the particular artistic signatures of celebrity movie directors, the 1980s and 1990s signaled a return to the old Hollywood priority of genre cinema. It also signaled a return to the old Hollywood formula of big films targeted at the widest possible audience.

The most significant trend in '80s and '90s Hollywood genre cinema was the blockbuster, the so-called event film, which provides audiences with a sensational experience independent of such old-fashioned notions as plot and performance. This move toward more sensational entertainment was fueled by the astonishing box-office success of two late-auteur-era action films: *Star Wars* (George Lucas, 1977) and *Raiders of the Lost Ark* (Steven Spielberg, 1981).

Star Wars and *Raiders of the Lost Ark* were by design formulaic and familiar. Their plotlines are clever amalgams of genre entertainment from Hollywood's classical era, at once nostalgic for a golden age of American entertainment and decidedly modern in their state-of-the-art special effects. As the 1980s began to take shape, it became clear that Lucas and Spielberg had established something akin to a template, a formula for success on a scale the studios simply could not afford to ignore.

The Action-Adventure Film

The roots of the contemporary action-adventure film can be traced to the 1962 premiere of the James Bond series and *Dr. No* (Terence Young). John F. Kennedy was president, and the cold war was at its height, but the politics in play were never all that relevant. Through the subsequent 007 films over more than forty years—including *Goldfinger* (Guy Hamilton, 1964), *You Only Live Twice* (Lewis Gilbert, 1967), *Live and Let Die* (Hamilton, 1973), *The Spy Who Loved Me* (Gilbert, 1977), *Moonraker* (Gilbert, 1979), *Octopussy* (1983), *License to Kill* (John Glen, 1989), *Tomorrow Never Dies* (Roger Spottiswoode, 1997), *Die Another Day* (2002) and *Casino Royale* (2006)—the British secret agent James Bond battled a wide variety of über-gangsters bent on world domination, comic-book-style megalomaniacs with strange quirks, fetishes, and gripes against the planet at large.

The scale and the scope of the Bond films are global and apocalyptic; the world inevitably is held in the balance. With ingenuity and skill and the help of all sorts of cool gadgets, Bond inevitably prevails, routinely at the last possible second. The Bond films are by design formulaic: they are spectacles of cinematic excess and repetition. But that is why they have been so popular and so eminently reproducible. Cool gadgets, sexy and sexually available women, loony bad guys bent on world domination, and amazing stunts (beginning with the crucial precredit sequence) were all expected and delivered in abundance. Each film's brief denouement shows Bond with the spoils of war, a beautiful woman for whom he has temporarily ditched one sort of undercover operation for another. Bond is an iconoclast, and although British by birth and Continental in his tastes, he is in many ways an American heroic type, an individual with unusual gifts who instinctively resists institutional authority and never plays by the rules.

The success in the early 1980s of films based on the model of James Bond, Luke Skywalker, or Indiana Jones enabled the emergence of a new breed of auteur studio producer, personified most famously by the action-adventure impresarios Joel Silver, Jerry Bruckheimer, and Don Simpson, three men who updated the action formula for the '80s and the '90s. Silver was a New York University film-school graduate who began his career working with the independent producer Lawrence Gordon. With Gordon, Silver produced the futurist teen-gang action picture *The Warriors* (1979), the action comedy *48 Hrs.* (1982), and the stylized action picture *Streets of Fire* (1984), all directed by Walter Hill. After splitting from Gordon, Silver produced a string of hugely successful action films, all of which bear his stamp as auteur: *Lethal Weapon* (Richard Donner, 1987), *Die Hard* (John McTiernan, 1988), *Lethal Weapon 2* (Donner, 1989), *Die Hard 2* (Renny Harlin, 1990), *Lethal Weapon 3* (Donner, 1992), *Lethal Weapon 4* (Donner, 1998), *The Matrix* (Larry and Andy Wachowski, 1999), and *Romeo Must Die* (Andrzej Bartkowiak, 2000).

Although Silver has produced films directed by a number of talented directors and headlined by action stars as charismatic (and as different) as Mel Gibson, Bruce Willis, Keanu Reeves, and Jet Li, his films all bear his auteur signature. Foremost is the buff male star with a discernible expertise (with guns, with his fists and feet) taking on some sort of cartel or conspiracy (apropos of Reaganism, of the bureaucratic, international, or gangland sort). Inevitably the hero must fight back—he never throws the first punch, of course—and he does so by running wild, which often involves using deadly force in a manner well outside the boundaries of conventional law enforcement (hence the term *male rampage film*, sometimes used to describe these pictures). Silver's heroes disregard the restrictions of proper bureaucratic police work and/or the familiar good-guy code of Hollywood movies. They go about winning by any means necessary.

Silver's films have a time signature just as music does. Action sequences come at prescribed intervals, following beats. A predicament is posed. The situation is made tense. Something explodes or crashes. The first act of a Joel Silver film has the beats (or, as the producer calls them, "whammies") timed to occur at 10- to 15-minute intervals. The second act picks up the pace by decreasing the intervals between whammies. The third act is almost all action, with the whammies coming one after the other. Closure is achieved when the principal good and bad guys face off amid destruction of some colossal and dramatic sort. The hero wins because he is smarter, stronger, and finally angrier than the villains.

Another defining principle of the Joel Silver action-adventure formula involves the bond established between unlikely male buddies. In *Lethal Weapon*, Martin Riggs (Gibson) is a wild white man; he lives close to the edge in all sorts of ways. Roger Murtaugh (Danny Glover), his new partner at the start of the film, is a mild-mannered African American family man approaching retirement. Riggs's style of police work at first gives Roger pause. But soon enough Riggs brings to Roger's moribund life a boost of excitement. Roger in turn tries to rein in Riggs's wilder impulses and succeeds (in part). At the start of the film, we find Riggs with a gun in his mouth, contemplating suicide. By the end of the film, we find Riggs at the door of Roger's house on Christmas, no longer

Bruce Willis as John McClane, the New York City policeman who runs wild in *Die Hard* (John McTiernan, 1988). Released a year after *Lethal Weapon* (Richard Donner), *Die Hard* cemented Joel Silver's reputation as the industry's premier producer of so-called male rampage action-adventure films.

Roger Murtaugh (Danny Glover, *left*), a mild-mannered African American family man, and Martin Riggs (Mel Gibson), a white cop on the edge, team up in *Lethal Weapon* (Richard Donner, 1987).

alone and suicidal. Each man learns from the other, and most and best off all each gives the other someone to care for deeply and an acceptable means of expressing that deep friendship in life-and-death situations.

The *Lethal Weapon* and *Die Hard* films are as much about the love between male buddies as they are about the crime at hand. Riggs's wife's death precedes the action in the first *Lethal Weapon* film, and while it is clear that no woman can ever take her place, Roger does well to fill the void. In *Die Hard*, McClane travels 3,000 miles to see his estranged wife. But although his victory over the bad guys at the end of the film reunites the couple, he is already looking elsewhere, rendering his bond with his all-too-independent wife secondary to the sudden but sure bond he has forged in the heat of battle with the fellow street cop Al (Reginald VelJohnson). The relationship that holds the most promise for McClane and Riggs is the one

with another man—a man who can protect himself, a man who ostensibly understands him and with whom he can fully share his life and his experiences.

Silver's action films end predictably as the hero, beat up but not vanquished, faces off against his smug nemesis. The hero has been outmanned and outgunned and maybe even outsmarted, but he is still hanging in, barefoot and bloody, as we find McClane at the end of *Die Hard*. What the hero discovers in the climactic fight is exactly what he is made of, what he is capable of. The sidekick has a revelation of sorts as well. At the end of *Lethal Weapon*, for example, Riggs faces off against Mr. Joshua (Gary Busey), a fellow dark-operations veteran of the Vietnam War. Though one is a cop and the other a criminal, the two men are more alike than they would like to admit, and both have put their considerable military expertise to work in the only arena stateside that tolerates—let alone

values—it: crime. Their fight in the pelting rain, the climax of *Lethal Weapon,* lasts for several minutes and ends not with one of the two beating the other into submission—such men, after all, cannot be so easily defeated—but with Roger shooting Joshua as he makes one final run at Riggs from behind. The ending of *Die Hard* is similar: McClane guns down Hans (Alan Rickman) and his cohorts, but as he exits the smoldering skyscraper, Karl (played by the ballet dancer Alexander Godunov), a man McClane thinks he has killed, emerges from the smoke, poised to shoot our hero in the back. Al, who has sworn off violence because of a recent on-the-job shooting, pulls out his pistol and kills Karl, saving the hero to fight another day.

Like Silver, the partners Jerry Bruckheimer and Don Simpson have put their particular auteur stamp on the action-adventure film. Though their first film together was *Flashdance* (Adrian Lyne, 1983), a popular picture about a young woman who works as a welder and dares to dream of becoming a professional dancer, they subsequently and profitably turned their attention to a series of action-comedy hybrids: *Beverly Hills Cop* (Martin Brest, 1984), *Beverly Hills Cop II* (Tony Scott, 1987), and *Bad Boys* (Michael Bay, 1995). At the heart of these films are not buff white male action stars but charismatic African American comedians: Eddie Murphy in *Beverly Hills Cop,* Will Smith and Martin Lawrence in *Bad Boys.* The wisecracking heroes in the *Beverly Hills Cop* and *Bad Boys* films scoff at everything and everyone, but in the end they prove themselves able men of action.

The balance between play and work, between taking nothing seriously and finally taking a stand, lies at the center of all the Bruckheimer-Simpson films. Consider, for example, *Top Gun* (Scott, 1986) and *Days of Thunder* (Scott, 1990), films about men who fly or drive fast, proving their manhood in the daily performance of their risk-filled jobs. The films share a central thematic structure: a brash hero (played in both pictures by Tom Cruise) climbs up through the ranks (of military jet pilots or race-car drivers), suffers a setback (because he's not a team player, because he won't play by the rules), and then learns to work well with others. Unlike the Joel Silver films, which valorize macho independence at all costs, *Top Gun* and *Days of Thunder* teach all-American lessons about teamwork and sacrifice.

The Bruckheimer-Simpson man-of-action film cycle reached its pinnacle with *The Rock* (Bay, 1996), a film about a band of disenfranchised elite military men who seize control of Alcatraz Island, imprison tourists, and threaten to douse San Francisco with deadly nerve gas. Three action heroes—

three very different men of action—vie for center stage: the career army officer general Francis X. Hummel (Ed Harris), the former spy John Patrick Mason (Sean Connery), and the scientist Dr. Stanley Goodspeed (Nicolas Cage). Hummel is a war hero and a patriot who turns to terrorism in frustration at the bureaucratic failure of the Veterans Administration to meet his standards of fairness and decency. Mason is a former British spy who has been imprisoned for over twenty years for refusing to rat out the source of some ill-gotten FBI information. His refusal to break under torture or coercion is of course heroic, and he is made to seem all the more masculine in contrast to his nemesis, FBI director Womack (John Spencer), a paper-pushing bureaucrat, the worst of all possible male types in an action film. The third hero is Goodspeed, a government scientist who is at once intellectually smart and physically inept. In the end, of course, it will be Goodspeed who saves the day, but in so doing he must become more like Hummel and Mason: he must act instinctively, learn to use force as well as his wits, and finally become less of a company man, less of a civil servant, and more of an independent man of action.

As in *Lethal Weapon*, the war in Vietnam (the defining historical event for the producers, though not for the audience) underscores the narrative in *The Rock*. Hummel's principle gripe dates to our sad exit from Vietnam in the mid-'70s and to the illegal secret incursions into Laos and Cambodia approved by President Nixon before the war's end. Hummel is brought to a desperate act of terrorism as a matter of honor, as a way to get the government to acknowledge the death of his fellow covert warriors who have been denied a proper military burial (and whose families have been denied proper compensation) as the government persists in keeping their covert actions secret.

In a facile way, *Lethal Weapon* and *The Rock* show men reconciling shared feelings of literal and figurative loss. As such these modern action films have their roots in the *Rambo* series, three 1980s action films starring Sylvester Stallone, the actor who catapulted to stardom in 1976 with the rags-to-riches boxing picture *Rocky* (John Avildsen). The *Rambo* series began with a very strange and fairly minor film, *First Blood* (Ted Kotcheff, 1982), based on a serious novel by David Morrell about a psychologically disturbed Vietnam veteran named John Rambo (Stallone), whose return to the United States after the war is fraught with disillusionment and conflict. In the film, Rambo runs afoul of some small-town cops. He is jailed but easily escapes and uses his military expertise to hole up in the woods. The film was a surprising box-office success, in part because of Stallone but in part because the film struck a chord with Rambo's fellow disillusioned Vietnam vets.

The sequel, much more than the first film, established *Rambo* as a cultural phenomenon. *Rambo: First Blood Part II* (George P. Cosmatos, 1985) has Rambo assigned to a secret mission by his former superior, Colonel Trautman (Richard Crenna): taking pictures of prisoners of war (POWs) still held captive in Vietnam. Rambo takes the assignment but decides early on that taking pictures hardly solves anything. To the consternation of the bureaucrats who, the film suggests, lost "us" Vietnam in the first place, Rambo joins forces with Co Bao (Julia Nickson), a South Vietnamese freedom fighter, to rescue the POWs from a sadistic prison-camp warden (William Ghent) and his vicious Soviet cohort (Voyo Goric).

The poster for *Rambo: First Blood Part II* features Stallone shirtless, buff and greased, a gun belt loaded with bullets draped across his chest. This celebration of the male body became a central trope in the '80s and '90s action picture. Increasingly, personal trainers transformed slim, even slight celebrities into muscled men of action whose every movement carries with it a threat. To take just one example, the slender, mopey slacker Keanu Reeves, best known in the 1980s for the comedy *Bill & Ted's Excellent Adventure* (Stephen Herek, 1989) was transformed in 1994 into the rugged police officer in the action picture *Speed* (Jan de Bont) and then into the future messianic superhero Neo in *The Matrix* (Andy and Larry Wachowski, 1999).

When we consider this focus on the male body, we begin to understand the action-film superstardom of the former Mr. Universe, Arnold Schwarzenegger, who first came to the attention of Hollywood producers in 1977, with his "performance" in *Pumping Iron* (George Butler and Robert Fiore), a documentary on bodybuilding. Schwarzenegger became an action-film star with a series of sword-and-sorcery pictures based on the fantasy fiction of Robert E. Howard—*Conan*

the Barbarian (John Milius, 1982), *Conan the Destroyer* (Richard Fleischer, 1984), and *Red Sonja* (Fleischer, 1985)—and a low-budget science-fiction film, *The Terminator* (1984). Directed by the special-effects postproduction expert James Cameron, *The Terminator* is the story of a killer android sent back in time to murder a woman named Sarah Connor (Linda Hamilton), the mother of the future leader of a human uprising against the machines that we're told rule the world in the future. In the sequel, *Terminator 2: Judgment Day* (Cameron, 1991), Schwarzenegger plays a reprogrammed good Terminator. At the heart of all the Schwarzenegger films is the "man" of few but nonetheless choice words: "Hasta la vista, baby" and "I'll be back" have entered the American pop-culture lexicon to the same extent that "Play it again, Sam," did after the release of *Casablanca* (Michael Curtiz, 1942).

The action films of the 1980s are fast paced. Speed, not suspense, makes them tick. Indeed, the films move so fast that audiences have little to time to think between the stunts that catapult the characters from one implausible situation to another. Action films ask audiences to revel in the experience, in the moment. That so much is held in the balance—the future of the free world in the James Bond films, the future of humankind in *The Terminator* series—is by design left for another time, another day.

Comic-Book Adaptations

An important action-adventure subgenre in the post-auteur era was the comic-book adaptation, a movie type successfully introduced in 1978 by Richard Donner with his big-budget hit *Superman*. The box-office success of *Superman* spawned a series of vastly inferior sequels—*Superman II* (Richard Lester, 1980), *Superman III* (Lester, 1983), *Superman IV: The Quest for Peace* (Sidney J. Furie, 1987)—but it is important not to forget the first film's considerable influence. Given the times, Donner and his successors contented themselves with a jokey treatment of the Man of Steel,

(*left*) "Hasta la vista, baby." The bodybuilder, movie star, and (beginning in 2003) governor of California Arnold Schwarzenegger as the indomitable cyborg who saves humankind in James Cameron's sci-fi action picture *Terminator 2: Judgment Day* (1991).

Michael Keaton, the first in a series of interchangeable Caped Crusaders, with Kim Basinger as Vicki Vale, his love interest, in Tim Burton's premier installment of the comic-book franchise *Batman* (1989).

presenting Christopher Reeve (as Clark Kent and Superman) as a virtuous prude and goody-goody hero fighting for a hokey trinity, "truth, justice, and the American way." Donner appreciated that such a fight seemed outdated in 1978 and maybe not really worth it. *Superman* had, for its day, terrific special effects, the most famous of which simulated the hero's flight over Metropolis, and it recast the very real stakes of later action-adventure pictures in the make-believe world of comic books. The key to its success, then, was its delivery on its promise of escape.

Despite the box-office success of *Superman*, Hollywood took a decade to fully exploit the comic-book action picture. The times, of course, had changed, and the value of escapist cinema seemed only to have increased. The Batman franchise commenced in 1989 with Tim Burton's *Batman*, and it persisted with *Batman Returns* (Burton, 1992), *Batman Forever* (Joel Schumacher, 1995), *Batman and Robin* (Schumacher, 1997), and *Batman Begins* (Christopher Nolan, 2005). Each *Batman* film ably reprises the *Superman* formula, with a marked variation: Batman is no hokey guy in tights. Played first by Michael Keaton, then Val Kilmer, George Clooney, and Christian Bale, Batman on-screen has been portrayed as alternately tortured and brooding. The world he inhabits, the world he protects and serves, is dark and serially under siege and maybe doesn't deserve his help.

The blade runner Deckard (Harrison Ford) on the despoiled streets of some future Los Angeles in Ridley Scott's dystopian science-fiction film *Blade Runner* (1982).

Burton's *Batman* films are moody, dark, and—given the typical pace of an action blockbuster—slow. His low-contrast cinematography, gothic sets, and sweeping camera movements allude to the ominous monster and gangster films of 1920s German expressionism. Schumacher moved the franchise closer to the action-picture formula, staging elaborate stunts and action set pieces. For Schumacher, whose challenge was to keep audiences interested in sequels of sequels (no easy chore), the job required the delivery of an ever-bigger and better "event." And as he learned from the long line of action-adventure films that preceded his, all that matters in the end are the whammies, the effects, and the delivery of a film of suitable size, scale, and noise level.

Coming eight years after the fourth installment, Nolan's 2005 *Batman Begins* is by necessity nostalgic, not so much for Burton's or Donner's work as for a time before action films had been emptied of plot and character development. The hero is no longer stripped of motivation, no longer summarized in a momentary flashback (to a random act of violence perpetrated against his parents, for example). Instead, we are asked to understand what drives a man to such an obsessive, selfless life.

Science Fiction

Science fiction enjoyed something of a renaissance in the 1980s, banking on the success of the first two *Star Wars* films: *Star Wars* and *The Empire Strikes Back* (Irwin Kershner, 1980). As in Lucas's *Star Wars* franchise, the science-fiction films of the 1980s and '90s showcase dazzling futurist effects. But unlike the *Star Wars* films, many of these science-fiction films offer profound political and social commentary with an eye not only to the future but on the present as well.

The most ambitious of these politically conscious science-fiction films was Ridley Scott's *Blade Runner* (1982), based on the Philip K. Dick novel *Do Androids Dream of Electric Sheep?* Set in some future technologically dependent America, the film at once showcases the technology that so permeates contemporary life and plays off the audience's fear of that very technology's evolving unchecked. Like Dick's novel the film explores the fine line between the real and the fake, the human and the artificial.

Blade Runner opens with a moving-camera shot positioned aboard a futurist hovercraft in the skies above Los Angeles in the year 2019. Rain falls throughout the film, a nod to the sci-fi trope of a ruined environment plagued by the aftereffects of years of neglect and abuse. City space is split: in the air is the swift movement of futurist flying vehicles, and on the ground is the slow traffic, made up of pedestrians for the most part. The sound track is crowded with the argot of the ethnically mixed denizens of the city and the ceaseless stream of advertising broadcast over loudspeakers. What is being advertised on the loudspeakers and on the giant billboards includes the usual consumer goods—Coca-Cola, for example—as well as a campaign promoting immigration to "off-world colonies," a futurist suburbia where those healthy enough to leave Los Angeles have "a chance to begin again in a golden land of opportunity and adventure."

The film's stratification of city space clearly mirrors that of 1982 urban America. Tyrell (Joe Turkel), the wealthy android designer and manufacturer, lives in a secure building high above the metropolis. Deckard (Harrison Ford), a cop, lives but a few floors up in a broken-down building that anyone can enter. The suburbs promise a better quality of life, free from the strip joints, the crime, the immigrants, and the homeless, all of which or whom despoil the city streets.

As the film opens, we learn that a model line of androids has "evolved" and poses a danger to humanity's survival. These machines of the future so precisely ape human behavior that they are nearly undetectable. (Tyrell Corporation, the company that makes the androids, has a simple motto: "More human than human.") Indeed, their difference from humans—and this is the key to the film's ironic premise—is a matter of degree and even debate. The test used to identify androids measures empathy, a human quality. But at the end of the film, it is the android villain Roy Batty (Rutger Hauer) who shows empathy when he dies, ostensibly to save Deckard's life. As humans go through the motions of their empty lives, the film suggests, they become less human—less human perhaps than androids programmed with false memories and simulated emotions.

The *Alien* films—*Alien* (Scott, 1979), *Aliens* (Cameron, 1986), *Alien³* (David Fincher, 1992), and *Alien Resurrection* (Jean-Pierre Jeunet, 1997)—are genre hybrids (of horror, action adventure, and science fiction). They offer a host of horror tropes—the fear of contagion and disease, the conflict between the profit motive and the public good, the lone truth teller who is doomed not to be believed, the last woman left behind to fight the monster—and a visual style that accentuates the spaceship's claustrophobia, with tight shots heightening the tension. Of particular nervous interest is the unseen: what lies just outside the frame, what may be lurking inside us or inside a co-worker or

The advanced Nexus-6 androids Roy Batty (Rutger Hauer, *left*) and Pris (Daryl Hannah) hiding out in *Blade Runner* (Ridley Scott, 1982).

Ripley (Sigourney Weaver), a reluctant, apolitical hero, protects the foundling Newt (Carrie Henn) from the alien monster in James Cameron's *Aliens* (1986).

exploitation as a bioweapon. The plan ends in disaster, and the monster menaces distant outposts through three sequels. By the fourth film in the series, Ripley has come to understand the creature: she has been penetrated by it and thus intuits, and on some level admires, its every move. But she never comes to terms with the company whose motivations are greed and political power.

Burke (Paul Reiser), the conniving representative of the company in *Aliens*, lies to Ripley to get her to go on a mission to a remote mining colony recently ravaged by the alien. He endeavors to bring the alien back to Earth not because he enjoys the carnage but because, like a lot of other midlevel employees, he works on commission. The company has done a cost-benefit analysis regarding the alien and has decided that the money to be had in bioweaponry is worth the loss of life of a few employees and bystanders. Burke accepts the company's decision not because he, too, is evil but because he is just a guy trying his best to do a job, and his job does not involve making value judgments.

Taken together, the *Alien* films offered a profound critique of conglomerate capitalism at the very moment Reaganomics had deregulated virtually every major American industry. The films show big companies so dedicated to the profit motive that they willingly risk the lives of their employees and other innocent and unsuspecting citizens. At a time when the accidents at Three Mile Island (1979), Bhopal (1984), and Chernobyl (1986) were very much in the news, that corporations might operate with such disregard for human life hardly seemed the stuff of fiction.

Comedy

The majority of film comedies in the 1980s and 1990s were produced as vehicles for popular nightclub and television comedians. One of the most interesting of those comic performers was Paul Reubens. A comedian known locally in Los Angeles for his sold-out shows at hip venues, Reubens's stage characterization of the bizarre child-man Pee-wee Herman was captured on-screen in the

slouching toward us through the air-conditioning ducts. From action adventure, the era's most popular template, the film gives us a reluctant, apolitical hero on the edge (Ripley, played by Sigourney Weaver), in whose hands the fate of the crew and, eventually, the future of the Earth may well be held. And there are the prerequisite whammies, explosive special effects carefully and the progressively placed throughout the film.

There are two villains in the *Alien* films—one alien, one human. The alien herself and her offspring are horrific creatures, insectlike parasites that devour their human hosts from within. They ooze acid, move with amazing agility, hunt and kill without apparent remorse. The aliens do what instinct tells them to do: protect their offspring, hunt to survive. Though not physically hideous, the men who run the corporation that finances the mission in the first film are ethically bankrupt: they conspire to bring back the monster for

imaginative Tim Burton comedy *Pee-wee's Big Adventure* (1985). The film opens as Pee-wee greets the day. A contraption (based in part on the board game Mousetrap, in which a series of seemingly unconnected devices are linked to make possible a final simple operation: catching a mouse) comes to life and prepares breakfast. As he eats his bowl of Mr. T cereal (named for the buff African American TV star and former bodyguard, a man who could not look or act more different than Pee-wee), Pee-wee sets in motion a zany parody (or perhaps a blissful celebration) of modern-day consumerism.

Pee-wee is chronologically an adult, but his world is all about his toys, especially his fancy bicycle (the theft of which sets the plot in motion) and gadgets that make his world colorful and fun. Though there are the occasional sexually suggestive gags, the Pee-wee character is for the most part presexual. He lives in a world free of the demands of adult entanglements. What makes him funny

and outrageous is his unselfconsciousness; he acts as if he is the coolest kid on the block—despite forays into transvestism and unmanly behavior. Most memorably, Pee-wee runs afoul of a gang of tough bikers in a roadhouse. To get out of the mess, he does a silly dance on a table and somehow becomes the gang's mascot-hero.

Reubens is not a traditional stand-up comic; he is an adept improvisational sketch comic like the comedians featured on the late-night comedy show *Saturday Night Live* who made the jump from the small to the big screen: from the early days of the show, John Belushi in *Animal House* (John Landis, 1978) and *The Blues Brothers* (Landis, 1980), Dan Aykroyd in *The Blues Brothers*, Bill Murray in *Caddyshack* (Harold Ramis, 1980), *Ghost Busters* (Ivan Reitman, 1984), and *Groundhog Day* (Ramis, 1993), and Eddie Murphy in *Beverly Hills Cop*, *The Nutty Professor* (Tom Shadyac, 1996), and *Doctor Dolittle* (Betty Thomas, 1998) on through more recent performers, like Adam Sandler in *Happy*

The better to hear you with . . . Paul Reubens as Pee-wee Herman in Tim Burton's zany farce *Pee-wee's Big Adventure* (1985).

Former *Saturday Night Live* star Eddie Murphy in a fat suit trying out aerobics in Tom Shadyac's 1996 remake of the 1963 Jerry Lewis comedy *The Nutty Professor*.

Gilmore (Dennis Dugan, 1996), *Big Daddy* (Dugan, 1999), and *Mr. Deeds* (Steven Brill, 2002) and Mike Myers in *Wayne's World* (Penelope Spheeris, 1992), *Austin Powers: International Man of Mystery* (Jay Roach, 1997), *Austin Powers: The Spy Who Shagged Me* (Roach, 1999), and *Austin Powers in Goldmember* (Roach, 2002).

Other comics who made their mark on television before "graduating" to the big screen include the frequent *Saturday Night Live* guest host and droll satirist Steve Martin, who appeared in *The Jerk* (Carl Reiner, 1979), *Dirty Rotten Scoundrels* (Frank Oz, 1988), and *Bowfinger* (Oz, 1999); the former MTV comedy star Ben Stiller, who appeared in *Flirting with Disaster* (David O. Russell, 1996), *There's Something about Mary* (Peter and Bobby Farrelly, 1998), and *Zoolander* (Stiller, 2001); and from the popular TV skit-comedy show *In Living Color*, Damon Wayans, who appeared in *Mo' Money* (Peter MacDonald, 1992), Kennen Ivory Wayans, who was in *Don't Be a Menace to South Central While Drinking Your Juice in the Hood* (Paris Barclay, 1996), and Jim Carrey, who starred in *Ace Ventura: Pet Detective* (Shadyac, 1994), *Dumb and Dumber* (Peter and Bobby Farrelly, 1994), *Ace Ventura: When Nature Calls* (Steve Oedekerk, 1995), *The Cable Guy* (Stiller, 1996), and *Bruce Almighty* (Shadyac, 2003).

On the TV show *In Living Color*, Carrey was just one member of an ensemble of terrifically talented comedians, whereas on his own he became the most popular film comedian of the 1990s. Playing outrageous characters whose unselfconsciousness sends up all pretenses of propriety and bourgeois order, Carrey seemed to satisfy audiences' voracious appetite for antisocial, gross-out comedy. At the start of *Ace Ventura: When Nature Calls*, for example, we find the crack "pet detective" Ventura on a retreat in a Buddhist monastery, where, in the process of finding inner peace, he has succeeded in driving the otherwise patient monks crazy. He is lured from the monastery to help solve a case of a missing bat. On the plane to Africa, he eats the way a terribly behaved child might and tastelessly repeats a ludicrous peanuts-penis joke, to the horror of the woman sitting next to him. Later in the film he makes shadow puppets during the screening of an educational film, and at a party with aristocrats he plays with the food and ridicules the guests. Ace not only behaves badly; he also makes everyone around him look ridiculous in the process.

Much of Carrey's humor centers on the body, in part because the actor is amazingly flexible. His face contorts as he mugs for the camera, and he has an uncanny ability to stretch and manipulate his body, moving into and out of tight spaces. In *Ace Ventura: When Nature Calls*, Ace hides inside

Jim Carrey mugs for the camera (with a little help from a friendly monkey) in *Ace Ventura: When Nature Calls* (Steve Oederkerk, 1995).

Accident-prone Ted Stroehmann (Ben Stiller) with a fishhook in his mouth on a date by the shore with his dream girl, Mary Jensen (Cameron Diaz), in Bobby and Peter Farrelly's gross-out comedy hit *There's Something about Mary* (1998).

a metal rhinoceros to spy on some bad guys. There's a malfunction, of course, and he gets stuck in the overheating machine. To extricate himself, he crawls out through the backside of the rhino, to the delight of a child on a photo safari (and all the children in the theater audience). Carrey follows '40s director Preston Sturges's advice on film comedy: "A pratfall is better than anything."

Carrey proved to be the perfect actor for the foremost comedy auteurs of the '90s, the brothers Peter and Bobby Farrelly. The Farrellys' first feature, *Dumb and Dumber*, was a sensation even though it was composed almost exclusively of jokes about flatulence, diarrhea, urination, and vomiting. It was intentionally offensive and politically incorrect. This siege on decorum and political correctness is the common denominator in the Farrelly brothers' oeuvre. In their 1996 film *Kingpin*, a bowling match sets the scene for bad-taste jokes about physical deformity. In *Me, Myself and Irene* (2000), the brothers make jokes of police brutality, miscegenation, and incest.

The Farrellys' biggest hit in the '90s was *There's Something about Mary*, which tells the story of a lonely, hapless man and his endless unrequited

love for his high-school crush, a seemingly perfect young woman named Mary (Cameron Diaz). The film pivots on a scene in which lonely-guy Ted (Ben Stiller) prepares for prom night—with Mary as his date. In his haste he catches his scrotum in his zipper. Paramedics arrive, closely examine his privates, and contemplate how they might safely (or maybe not so safely, but swiftly) extricate Ted's genitals from the zipper. Comedy often involves public humiliation; the Farrellys take the trope to the extreme.

Supporting characters in *There's Something about Mary* sport ridiculous false teeth (the sleezy private detective Pat Healy, played by the usually handsome leading man Matt Dillon), are subjected to rashes (Dom, played by Chris Elliott), and make fun of their own bodies and skin (Magda, played by Lin Shaye, who offers a glimpse of herself half nude as a reminder that everything in the film, even nudity, is a gross-out). The key to *There's Something about Mary* is the folly of sexual desire and the inevitability of disaster striking during the pursuit of the perfect mate. When Ted gets a second chance with Mary, he masturbates, on his friend's advice, because it will supposedly work to his advantage later, should he get lucky. Comically, the ejaculate ends up in his hair and then in hers. That someone as nice and beautiful as Mary (and, by extension, the star who plays her) should be the object of such a gross-out joke shows how far the Farrellys will go in service of a gag.

AUTEUR FILMMAKERS

With the production fiascos of *Apocalypse Now* (Francis Ford Coppola, 1979) and *Heaven's Gate* (Michael Cimino, 1980), the studios' dalliance with the auteur theory had run its course. Francis Ford Coppola, Martin Scorsese, and Robert Altman, filmmakers whose work revolutionized American filmmaking, suddenly found themselves out of favor. In their stead, Steven Spielberg and George Lucas emerged, embodying a new Hollywood auteurism, one in which the goals of the studios (to make movies that appeal to the widest possible audience) coincided with the producer-directors' own ambitions.

With these two directors' unprecedented dominance at the box office, forging an old-school auteur celebrity proved difficult. As a result, on the commercial front at least, only a handful of directors proved up to the challenge. Two of those directors—Spike Lee and Quentin Tarantino—straddled the indie-mainstream divide and in so doing survived assimilation into the Spielberg-Lucas model. Four others—Oliver Stone and, to a slightly less dramatic extent, Tim Burton, David Lynch, and Adrian Lyne—through sheer force of will, made uncompromising auteur studio films that, like the auteur films of the previous decade, had a significant impact on an otherwise blasé American audience.

Steven Spielberg and George Lucas

Steven Spielberg and George Lucas dominated the 1980s box office as no two filmmakers have ever dominated a decade in American film history. The nostalgic action-adventure film *Raiders of the Lost Ark* (1981) and its sequels, *Indiana Jones and the Temple of Doom* (1984) and *Indiana Jones and the Last Crusade* (1989), along with the sci-fi fantasy *E.T. the Extraterrestrial* (1982), all directed by Spielberg, were monumental box-office hits. The Spiel-

Auteurs of the '80s Steven Spielberg (*left*) and George Lucas, photographed in 1985.

berg-produced horror pictures *Poltergeist* (Tobe Hooper, 1982) and *Gremlins* (Joe Dante, 1984), the teen comedy *Back to the Future* (Robert Zemeckis, 1985) and its sequel, *Back to the Future Part II* (Zemeckis, 1989), the live action–animation hybrid *Who Framed Roger Rabbit* (Zemeckis, 1988), and the feature animation pictures *An American Tail* (Don Bluth, 1986) and *The Land before Time* (Bluth, 1988) were all box-office hits. Lucas produced the three *Indiana Jones* films as well as the two blockbuster *Star Wars* sequels, *The Empire Strikes Back* (Irwin Kershner, 1980) and *Return of the Jedi* (Richard Marquand, 1983), the biopic *Tucker: The Man and His Dream* (Coppola, 1988), and with Spielberg the animation picture *The Land before Time*.

Spielberg and Lucas remained key Hollywood players throughout the '90s as well. Spielberg had hits with his Peter Pan fantasy *Hook* (1991) and the science-fiction adventure film *Jurassic Park* (1993), and its sequel, *The Lost World: Jurassic Park* (1997), and earned critical acclaim (and consistently good box-office numbers) for his 3-hour Holocaust film *Schindler's List* (1993) and his World War II epic *Saving Private Ryan* (1998).

Lucas did not direct a film between 1977 and 1999 but remained a key industry auteur thanks to his San Francisco–based production company, Lucasfilm, and at his state-of-the-art postproduction house, Industrial Light and Magic (ILM). Lucasfilm is the production company of record on the *Star Wars* and *Indiana Jones* movies as well as the TV and theme-park spin-offs from those two popular film series. And at ILM, Lucas has done what he does best: postproduction (the work done after the actors and the crew go home). Between 1980 and 1999, ILM became the industry's top effects house, supervising postproduction on over 150 films, including *Raiders of the Lost Ark, E.T. the Extra-Terrestrial, Star Trek: The Wrath of Khan* (Nicholas Meyer, 1982), *Indiana Jones and the Temple of Doom, Star Trek III: The Search for Spock* (Leonard Nimoy, 1984), *Out of Africa* (Sydney Pollack, 1985), *Empire of the Sun* (Spielberg, 1987), *The Witches of Eastwick* (George Miller, 1987), *Who Framed Roger Rabbit, The Last Temptation of Christ* (Scorsese, 1988), *The Abyss* (James Cameron, 1989), *Terminator 2: Judgment Day* (Cameron, 1991), *Jurassic Park, Forrest Gump* (Zemeckis, 1994), *Jumanji* (Joe Johnston, 1995), *Mission: Impossible* (Brian De Palma, 1996), *Titanic* (Cameron, 1997), *Men in Black* (Barry Sonnenfeld, 1997), *Saving Private Ryan, The Mummy* (Stephen Sommers, 1999), and *Sleepy Hollow* (Burton, 1999).

A close look at the films directed and produced by Spielberg and Lucas reveals a set of common thematic and stylistic components. Evident in much of the filmmakers' work is narrative predictability, a thematic emphasis on childhood, and extensive use of special effects that provide view-

Elliott (Henry Thomas) and his new best friend from outer space in Steven Spielberg's heartwarming sci-fi adventure *E.T. the Extraterrestrial* (1982). *E.T.* proved to be one of the most successful films of the 1980s, earning nearly $400 million in the United States and $700 million worldwide.

ers with a visual and aural spectacle. The films are nostalgic and allusive, harking back to early film serials, comic books, and '50s sci-fi and horror movies. The narrative stakes are often apocalyptic—for example, the possibility of the Nazis' gaining access to the ark of the Covenant and winning World War II as a result (in the first *Raiders* film), the Galactic Empire's seizing control of the galaxy (in *Star Wars* and the first two sequels). The films pit rule by force against rule by democracy, or at least rule by popular consent.

Life for almost everyone in these films is characterized by constant locomotion. It is a child's world composed of brief and seemingly meaningless bursts of activity. Heroes and villains alike leave behind a mess they have no intention of ever cleaning up. The heroes—men such as Luke Skywalker and Indiana Jones—have adventures because in the childlike and childish vision perpetuated by Lucas and Spielberg, that is what men do, or would do if they could. The rest is detail, cool gadgets, backstory—stuff to be explained in ancillary materials (books, comics, theme-park rides, computer and video games) purchased between viewings of the movies. The films are so dependent on a rhythm created in the editing room that like so much of '80s and '90s cinema, they fall flat during virtually all the expository sequences. With Spielberg and Lucas, cinema came full circle, and as in the attraction-based cinema of the early twentieth century, moviemaking became an exercise in providing a thrill ride seemingly emptied of political or social commentary.

Such is the legacy of the Spielberg-Lucas cycle of films that so dominated the last twenty years of the twentieth century. The bottom line for the directors, as it has always been for the industry, is the box office; for historians these films and their producers and directors are important because they were so popular. But while it is easy to diminish the importance of their films as simply studio moneymaking projects, it is important to acknowledge how both men used success and popularity to gain a certain independence from studio Hollywood. At the least, they gained the right to make their films without studio interference. After all, what studio executive could presume to know more about popular filmmaking than Spielberg and Lucas?

Though seldom acknowledged, several of Lucas's side projects offer a reminder that Lucas, like Coppola and Scorsese, was in that first wave of film-school graduates to make it big in the film business—a reminder that he wasn't altogether a company man. In addition to all the postproduction work (on mostly blockbuster entertainment films), Lucas worked with Coppola in the 1980s to produce and "present" some ambitious American independent and foreign-made art pictures, including Akira Kurosawa's samurai epic *Kagemusha* (1980), Paul Schrader's biopic *Mishima: A Life in Four Chapters* (1985), and the experimental *Powaqqatsi* (1988), directed by Godfrey Reggio. Even in his higher-profile postproduction work on Hollywood blockbusters, Lucas insisted on an artistic and geographic independence from Hollywood that was rooted in an auteur's distrust of the corporate studios.

Spielberg remained much more ensconced in Hollywood than Lucas and worked within the system. But his later work nonetheless evinces a sensitivity to his legacy as an American auteur, which is to say that after the release of *E.T.*, Spielberg tried to do something about his identification with only one kind of filmmaking. In the mid-1980s he began to use his power in the industry to create a more varied oeuvre, a second line of products that was less obviously tied to the thrill-ride cinema he helped perfect in the 1970s and '80s. Beginning in 1987 with his adaptation of J. G. Ballard's extraordinary autobiographical novel, *Empire of the Sun*, Spielberg made several forays into more serious filmmaking. After *Empire of the Sun*, he split his time between thrill-ride divertissements like *Jurassic Park* and more serious fare, like the Holocaust epic *Schindler's List* and the heartfelt World War II picture *Saving Private Ryan*, both of which won him Oscars for Directing.

In the mid-'70s, when Lucas and Spielberg first came on the scene, directors were under significant pressure to turn the box office around. And that's exactly what those two filmmakers did. Their auteur status was built not on a transcendence of

(*right*) The ultimate 1990s thrill-ride movie: Steven Spielberg's sci-fi adventure *Jurassic Park* (1993).

From left to right: Captain John Miller (Tom Hanks), Private James Francis Ryan (Matt Damon), and Private Richard Reiben (Edward Burns) in Steven Spielberg's sentimental World War II picture *Saving Private Ryan* (1998).

the commercial power structure in New York and Hollywood but on a deft accommodation of that power structure in the very production of their films. But such an accommodation need not cheapen the impact of their films (as films) or the filmmakers' importance as creative American auteurs at the end of the twentieth century.

Oliver Stone

Oliver Stone broke into the industry as a writer, winning an Oscar for his first screenplay, for *Midnight Express* (Alan Parker, 1978), the story of a young American man jailed in Turkey for drug smuggling. He then wrote scripts for a series of macho fantasies: the Arnold Schwarzenegger sword-and-sorcery epic *Conan the Barbarian* (John Milius, 1982), Brian De Palma's remake of *Scarface* (1983), and the Chinese underworld drama *Year of the Dragon* (Cimino, 1985). With the possible exception of *Midnight Express,* there is little evidence in these early scripts of the innovative political filmmaker to follow.

Stone is a child of the baby boom. And his experience of cold war America finds its way into all

the films he's directed. One of Stone's many obsessions is recent American history, which he regards with skepticism. Of particular interest are two seminal baby boom events: the assassination of John F. Kennedy, on November 22, 1963, which occurred when Stone was seventeen, and the Vietnam War, in which Stone distinguished himself as a soldier, earning the Bronze Star and a Purple Heart.

The JFK assassination and the subsequent cover-up in the framing and assassination of Lee Harvey Oswald, retold in detail in Stone's *JFK* (1991), offer the director a moment of truth that bisects the postwar era, a handful of seconds that changed the nation. For Stone, the Vietnam War was one significant result of the assassination; indeed, he makes the case in *JFK* that Kennedy had been planning to withdraw U.S. military assistance from Indochina. Stone's celebrated Vietnam trilogy—*Platoon* (1986), *Born on the Fourth of July* (1989), and *Heaven & Earth* (1993)—is highly critical of what the war did to his generation. *Platoon,* for which Stone received his first of two Academy Awards for Directing (the second came three years later, for *Born on the Fourth of July*), pivots on a civilian massacre that re-creates the much-publicized war crimes at My Lai and a subsequent brutal betrayal and murder in the ranks. The violence and betrayal provide the film's once-naive hero, Chris Taylor (played by Charlie Sheen as an apparent stand-in for the director himself), with life lessons of a sort. *Born on the Fourth of July* chronicles in wrenching detail the life of Ron Kovic (Tom Cruise), a real-life Vietnam veteran who became an activist in the antiwar movement after being severely wounded in battle. Like Taylor in *Platoon*, Kovic enlists in the war because he believes in America. But he soon learns some bitter truths about the country that has sent him overseas and the war that has left him physically disabled. Like Chris Taylor, Kovic speaks very much for Stone himself.

Stone's heroes are often ill-fated truth tellers: Chris Taylor and Ron Kovic; in *Salvador* (1986), Richard Boyle, a journalist (played by James Woods), who discovers the truth about our political and military engagement in Central America in the 1980s; in *Talk Radio* (1988) the doomed free-speaking shock jock Barry Champlain (Eric Bogosian), based on the real-life Denver talk-show host Alan Berg, who was murdered in 1984 by white supremacists; and the New Orleans district attorney Jim Garrison (Kevin Costner) who against all odds tracks the conspiracy behind the Kennedy assassination in *JFK*. Stone's other film heroes are similarly, albeit less tragically, misunderstood: the late rock star Jim Morrison (played by Val Kilmer) in *The Doors* (1991); Tony D'Amato (Al Pacino), the unappreciated coach in the pro-football melodrama *Any Given Sunday* (1999); and even Richard Nixon in the biopic *Nixon* (1995).

Stone's penchant for politically incendiary subject matter (the JFK assassination, Vietnam, American imperialism in Central America) has made the director newsworthy. And he cleverly used his newsworthiness to create an auteur celebrity unrivaled in American cinema in the 1980s and 1990s. But while this celebrity gave meaning to the placement of his name above the title of a film and gained him a degree of clout with the studios, the media scrutiny of his personal politics made it all

Dealey Plaza in miniature: Jim Garrison (Kevin Costner) takes on the "magic-bullet theory" and other political fictions in *JFK* (Oliver Stone, 1991).

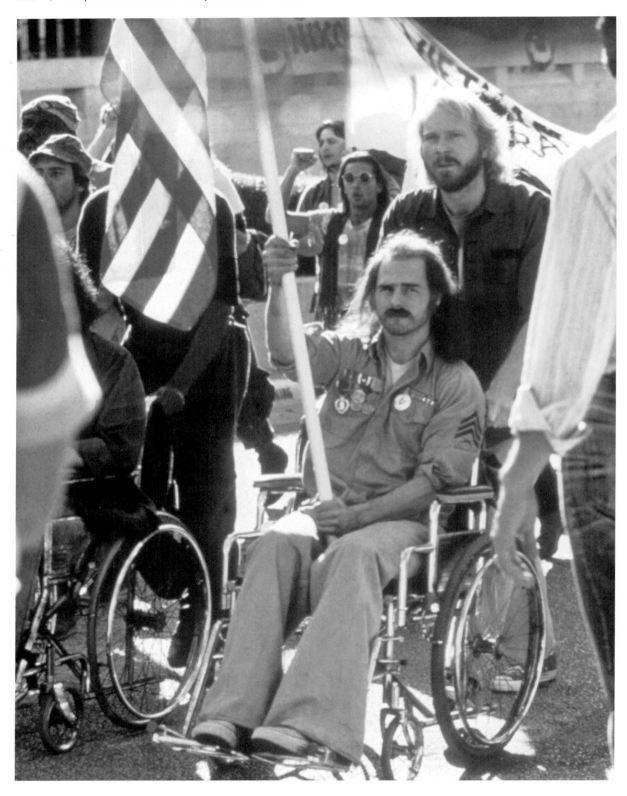

too easy for viewers and reviewers to miss what made Stone an exceptional filmmaker—his astonishing, sometimes overwhelming command of filmmaking technique and style.

For example, in the opening sequence of *JFK*, Stone offers a history lesson composed of various types of footage: real and fake newsreels, actual TV broadcasts, the Zapruder film (a bystander's home movie of Kennedy's assassination), a simulation of the Zapruder film, narration featuring the actors in the movie intercut with documentary shots of John and Jacqueline Kennedy, voice-over (what is called in the trade voice-of-God narration) foregrounding the political events that led up to the assassination, and some deft use of slow and stop motion. What we believe about November 22, 1963, Stone suggests, hinges on how we read these images. At the center of this representation is the Zapruder film. Like the amateur video taken of the 1991 beating and arrest of Rodney King in Los Angeles, the Zapruder film seems to offer ocular proof of a crime: a conspiracy (or at least the existence of more than one gunman) that many Americans have nonetheless chosen to disbelieve. Stone's contention is that we disregard these images at our peril.

Natural Born Killers (1994), Stone's ultraviolent film about a senseless murder spree committed by a young couple, Mickey (Woody Harrelson) and Mallory (Juliette Lewis), begins with a montage sequence similar to the one at the beginning of *JFK*. In the first 10 minutes of the film, we find footage shot in black-and-white and in color 35mm film, shots saturated in red or green, images from a TV broadcast, and other images photographed in low-grade video and then transferred to film. The cutting is so hectic that we lose our bearings—a phenomenon made more acute by off-angle shots and sequences in which the camera rolls off its axis, in effect turning our heads (not away from the action, of course, but to the side, and then upright again). Stone forces the viewer to analyze the origin and, in this case, the emotional power of the violent images on-screen.

Stone matches the hectic imagery with a complex, overlapping sound mix. On the sound track

Mickey and Mallory Knox (Woody Harrelson, *right*, and Juliette Lewis), mass murderers and media darlings, in Oliver Stone's ultraviolent satire *Natural Born Killers* (1994).

we first hear Leonard Cohen's apocryphal ballad "Waiting for the Miracle," then Robert Gordon's oddball rockabilly number "The Way I Walk." Sound and music are deftly integrated throughout the film, so much so that by the time we meet the sensationalist TV producer (Robert Downey Jr.), we have come to appreciate the ways in which sound and image can be manipulated and misunderstood. When the TV producer tries to exploit Mickey and Mallory, he discovers that their rage is real. Mickey and Mallory are not characters in a sensational TV story but real (and really scary) people. This is something the media hound can't understand.

Though he had two Directing Oscars to his credit, as well as a Writing award, Stone became curiously disregarded in Hollywood as the century came to an end. There are reasons why his stock fell so precipitously in the late 1990s: Stone became an important American auteur by making political films in an era when the studios preferred to play things safe. And he made violent films that used violence not just for effect (as in the action-adventure films that were then so popular) but instead to ask audiences to think about what violent images mean. Stone may be a stylist nonpareil, but he is also committed to a cinema of ideas—hardly a commitment that was likely to endear him (for long) to the commercial studios.

(*left*) Tom Cruise (*in wheelchair*) as Ron Kovic, the Vietnam War hero turned antiwar activist, in Oliver Stone's *Born on the Fourth of July* (1989).

Spike Lee

Like Oliver Stone, Spike Lee became a high-profile celebrity auteur because he dared to make politically incendiary films. And like Stone he experienced a decline in popularity because the audience's appetite for challenging fare waned as the century came to a close.

She's Gotta Have It (1986), Lee's first feature, was shot on the cheap and mostly in black-and-white. While the film is ostensibly about the life and loves of a single woman, Nola Darling (Tracy Camilla Johns), it is most memorable for Lee's on-screen performance, his brilliant caricature of the feckless urban youth Mars Blackmon, one of several comical suitors who try to woo the film's heroine. Lee further exploited the Mars Blackmon character in a series of sneaker ads for Nike, co-starring the basketball star Michael Jordan, again lampooning his comic stereotype in the very process of celebrating the charismatic basketball superstar.

She's Gotta Have It and the Nike ads made Lee a celebrity. He made the most of the fame, negotiating a deal with Universal to direct *Do the Right Thing* (1989), a big studio film that deals unflinchingly with racial conflict in urban America. *Do the Right Thing* opens with the provocative rap anthem "Fight the Power" (performed by Public Enemy) and ends with two quotations, one by Martin Luther King Jr. (promoting peaceful protest) and another by Malcolm X (encouraging change "by

any means necessary"), and a dedication to victims of racially motivated police shootings. The context of the film, as these framing devices show, is at once historical, topical, and political.

Set in the heat of a New York summer, *Do the Right Thing* chronicles a series of confrontations between Sal (Danny Aiello), a white pizzeria owner, and the young African Americans who patronize his restaurant, which lead inexorably to a race riot. In the last moments of calm before the storm, a delivery boy named Mookie (Lee) throws a trash can through the window of Sal's pizzeria. This startling action sets the riot in motion, and vandals trash the pizzeria. The police arrive, only to make matters worse, restraining one of the rioters in a choke hold so tight it kills him. Amid the rubble in the film's brief denouement, Mookie demands his salary from Sal. It is an outrageous moment and a final punctuation of the film's title, as no one at the end seems to do the right thing.

Lee examined race issues in virtually all his subsequent films. *Jungle Fever* (1991) dissects an interracial affair between a married black architect (Wesley Snipes) and his single white secretary (Annabella Sciorra). *Get on the Bus* (1996) follows a group of very different African American men en route to a Nation of Islam protest march. *He Got Game* (1998) reveals how colleges exploit African American athletes, and *Summer of Sam* (1999) uses David Berkowitz's 1977 Son of Sam murder spree as a frame for a trenchant critique of social and racial intolerance.

As the century came to a close, Lee was an auteur celebrity famous enough that his mere presence at basketball games (played by his beloved New York Knicks) seemed newsworthy. His films no longer generated the excitement they had in the late 1980s and early 1990s, but his continued celebrity affirmed his importance to a generation of African American filmmakers. Rusty Cundieff (*Fear of a Black Hat*, 1994), Vondie Curtis-Hall (*Gridlock'd*, 1997), Carl Franklin (*One False Move*, 1992; *Devil in a Blue Dress*, 1995), the Hughes Brothers, Albert and Allen (*Menace II Society*, 1993; *Dead Presidents*, 1995), David Johnson (*Drop*

Modern Hollywood's best-known African American filmmaker, Spike Lee, photographed in 1986 editing his first feature, *She's Gotta Have It.*

The staff at Sal's pizzeria in Spike Lee's *Do the Right Thing* (1989). *From left to right:* Mookie (Lee), Sal (Danny Aiello), and Sal's sons, Vito (Richard Edson) and Pino (John Turturro).

Squad, 1994), Darnell Martin (*I Like It Like That,* 1994), and John Singleton (*Boyz n the Hood,* 1991)—all talented black American filmmakers have entered Hollywood through a door opened by Spike Lee.

Tim Burton, David Lynch, and Adrian Lyne

Tim Burton, David Lynch, and Adrian Lyne were among a select group of commercially successful film directors of the 1980s and '90s who could justifiably be called auteurs. Burton began his career as an animator at Disney, where he worked on the saccharine kiddie cartoons *The Fox and the Hound* (Ted Berman, Richard Rich, and Art Stevens, 1981) and *The Black Cauldron* (Berman and Rich, 1985). While in the Disney animation unit, Burton developed two of his own projects: *Vincent* (1982), a clever hand-drawn animation short about a little boy who idolizes Vincent Price, and *Frankenweenie* (1984), a live-action spoof of the Frankenstein films that tells the story of a boy who reanimates his deceased dog. *Vincent* played in a handful of theaters and won a few awards on the festival circuit. *Frankenweenie* was shelved, as studio executives deemed it too weird for kids. Neither film fit the Disney mold. Legend has it that the cult comic Paul Reubens saw Burton's two short films and decided that Burton would be the perfect director of his debut film. Reubens was right: Burton's oddball take on kids' pop culture, evident in those first animated shorts, served him well in *Pee-wee's Big Adventure* (1985), a film that steadfastly resists any critical distance between the filmmaker and his child-man subject, the unique comic character Pee-wee Herman.

Burton has made a career of making movies for and/or about kids in which he refuses to pander or condescend. In *Edward Scissorhands* (1990), he tells the story of a young man (Johnny Depp) who makes the transition from deformed freak to hero in a small suburban town. Edward's transcendence is short-lived, though, as the suburban denizens turn on him after a spurned housewife spreads false rumors about him. Burton's unique take on children's culture is also at the heart of his two big commercial films: *Batman* (1989) and *Batman Returns* (1992). Though both are primarily franchise films, developed and produced to make money for Time Warner in the film, video, TV, music, and comic-book industries, they nonetheless possess the same

The producer Tim Burton poses with his stop-action toys, the stars of *The Nightmare before Christmas* (Henry Selick, 1993).

exuberance, the same oddball chic, that made Burton's earlier, more idiosyncratic films so much fun to watch. After the big-budget *Batman* films, Burton continued to mine the macabre side of children's culture in *The Nightmare before Christmas* (Henry Selick, 1993), a stop-action animation film he produced; his adaptation of Washington Irving's story about the Headless Horseman, *Sleepy Hollow* (1999); and his 2001 remake of Franklin J. Schaffner's 1968 science-fiction picture *Planet of the Apes*.

David Lynch went to art school and trained as a painter before making his first film, *Eraserhead* (1977), the story of a freak whose simple life is complicated when his lover, Mary X (Charlotte Stewart), gives birth to a mutant. Shot entirely in black-and-white and suffused with eerie electronic noise, *Eraserhead* was far too weird to do much business in a conventional first-run release, but it was a mainstay on the midnight-movie circuit for well over a decade, and as a result Lynch became notorious, if not famous. *Eraserhead* hardly prepared anyone for what came next: Lynch's faithful adaptation of the popular stage play *The Elephant Man* (1980), the story of John Merrick (John Hurt), a man horribly disfigured at birth who is rescued

from the carnival circuit by a kindly doctor and transformed into a proper gentleman in Victorian-era England. *The Elephant Man* received eight Academy Award nominations (including Best Picture and Directing) and moved Lynch into the commercial big time, a place from which he couldn't wait to escape.

Instead of exploiting his celebrity, Lynch took four years to make another film, and that film came about more or less by accident. In the early 1980s the producer Dino De Laurentiis hired the notorious British director Nicolas Roeg (*Performance*, 1970) to make *Dune*, an epic-scale adaptation of Frank Herbert's 1965 science-fiction classic. When Roeg and De Laurentiis reached an impasse during the early days of the production, De Laurentiis brought in Lynch, promising to finance a subsequent film over which Lynch would have complete creative control. That film was *Blue Velvet* (1986), a black comedy about what lies beneath the surface of a seemingly normal small American town.

(*right*) "A candy-colored clown they call the Sandman . . ." Ben (Dean Stockwell) lip-synchs Roy Orbison's "In Dreams" in David Lynch's creepy look at the darker side of suburban life, *Blue Velvet* (1986).

Johnny Depp as Ichabod Crane, modern man of science. Donning special glasses in order to snuff out the Headless Horseman, Crane gets more than he can handle in Tim Burton's expressionist *Sleepy Hollow* (1999).

Blue Velvet opens with a series of shots that juxtapose happy small-town residents going about their suburban lives with images of darker underlying realities: a severed ear attracting flies, a heart-attack sufferer collapsed on the ground, a disturbingly amplified flurry of beetles crawling all over one another. The visual dichotomy sets up the film's basic premise about the essential superficiality of small-town life and its hidden contradictions. Neat houses and manicured lawns coexist with sexual deviants and outright sociopaths, such as the film's antagonist, Frank Booth (Dennis Hopper). We first meet Booth as he enters the room of his reluctant lover, Dorothy (Isabella Rossellini), bellowing, "Shut up! It's Daddy, you shithead. Where's my bourbon?" Later, when they engage in foreplay, he interrupts the proceedings by greedily inhaling nitrous oxide, which seems to arouse him more than the sex.

Lynch's subsequent films—*Wild at Heart* (1990, for which he won the Palme d'Or at Cannes), *Lost Highway* (1997), and *Mulholland Dr.* (2001, for which he won an award for Best Director at Cannes)—moved the director even further from the commercial mainstream. Those films resist cause and effect and instead meander through incoherent dreamscapes that seem less like narratives than meditations on illusion and reality.

An interesting contrast to Burton and Lynch is the far more mainstream Hollywood auteur Adrian Lyne, whose *Flashdance*, a working-class success story spiced with erotic dance numbers set to popular disco music, was the surprise hit of 1983. Lyne's subsequent film, *9½ Weeks* (1985), the explicit story of a sado-masochistic affair, introduced an auteur formula of sorts, one that Lyne more or less perfected in his later films. Whereas *9½ Weeks* features ample stylized simulated sex (between the major movie stars Mickey Rourke and Kim Basinger), it also dealt more frankly and explicitly with love, lust, and infidelity than other mainstream films dared. Lyne's 1987 blockbuster hit, *Fatal Attraction*, appealed to more mainstream tastes, but is nonetheless sexually provocative. It tells the story of a basically good guy (Michael Douglas) who cheats on his wife (Anne Archer) and then pays for his sins when the woman with whom he cheated (Glenn Close) decides that she wants him all to herself.

Lyne's *Indecent Proposal* (1993) tells the story of a working-class guy (Woody Harrelson) who agrees to allow a stranger (Robert Redford) to sleep with his wife (Demi Moore) in exchange for $1 million. Absurd as such a plot may be, the film struck a chord with the filmgoing public; its simple premise—what would members of the audience do if they were offered $1 million and a similar deal?—became the subject of conversation at countless cocktail parties.

The $260-million worldwide gross of *Indecent Proposal* cemented Lyne's status as a major player in Hollywood. But rather than produce yet another high-concept adult sexual melodrama as a follow-up, Lyne decided to adapt Vladimir Nabokov's comic novel *Lolita*. Though many industry observers doubted his ability to handle such a complex book, Lyne's film proved to be profoundly faithful to the novel. Released in 1997, it is smart, weirdly comic, and even after the MPAA got its hands on it, disturbingly carnal. But although his timing had been perfect with *Flashdance* (which cashed in on the break-dancing craze), *9½ Weeks*, *Fatal Attraction*, and *Indecent Proposal* (all of which appealed to an adult audience starved for anything that was not made and marketed for teenagers), Lyne's luck dramatically ran out with *Lolita*. Financed independently for $60 million—a reasonable amount, given the fact that Lyne was a popular filmmaker making a movie based on a famous book—the finished film failed to find a distributor. After being rejected by every major studio, *Lolita* premiered on the pay cable channel Showtime and then enjoyed a limited release through the indie distributor Samuel Goldwyn. The U.S. theatrical box office barely broke the $1-million mark. While *Lolita* revealed Lyne's talent with headier material, its failure forced his retreat back to the sort of picture that had made him famous. Hence *Unfaithful* (2002), a film about a happily married woman (Diane Lane) who engages in an affair with a younger man (Olivier Martinez). *Unfaithful* earned a respectable $50 million, over fifty times what Lyne's *Lolita* grossed at the box office in 1997.

Fatal Attraction, Adrian Lyne's cautionary tale of infidelity and obsession, was a blockbuster hit in 1987 and netted six Academy Award nominations. Michael Douglas (*center*) stars as the married man who strays, and Glenn Close is the woman who wants more than he cares to give.

The director-writer-actor Quentin Tarantino as Mr. Brown, one of the five total strangers who botch a bank robbery in Tarantino's breakthrough film *Reservoir Dogs* (1992).

Quentin Tarantino

In marked contrast to the stereotype of the politically conscious, articulate, literate auteur, Quentin Tarantino, a former video-store clerk with a confessed devotion to lowbrow exploitation films and cheesy Asian martial-arts pictures, became the most talked about movie director in Hollywood in the early 1990s. A lot of the talk was generated by the auteur himself, however; from the start, Tarantino had a knack for self-promotion and self-mythology.

For example, in 1996, Tarantino used his new-found Hollywood cachet, based on two successful features, *Reservoir Dogs* (1992) and *Pulp Fiction* (1994), to supervise the rerelease of *Switchblade Sisters*, a B movie directed by Jack Hill in 1975 and initially released with the tagline "So easy to kill. So hard to love." Slumming it with a B movie made for good and colorful press, but, Tarantino's films also reveal the director's appreciation of movies found in the art-house section of the video store, especially the films of the French New Wave director Jean-Luc Godard. (Tarantino's production company is called A Band Apart, a play on the title of Godard's 1964 film *Bande à part*.)

To some film scholars the comparison with Godard credits Tarantino with more than his brief career can support, but it is worth exploring. Godard's breakthrough feature, *À bout de souffle* (*Breathless*, 1960), was—as Tarantino's *Reservoir Dogs* would later be—an homage to the American gangster film. It strips the genre down to its basic elements, recasting them in a package that is part parody, part pastiche. Both directors have preferred, throughout their careers, to work within familiar genres but have done so mostly to exploit and lampoon traditional film structures and styles. Both men are enamored of American pop and trash culture and have found in such "junk" a freedom, a notion of cool that is sadly absent in mainstream commercial fare.

Like *Breathless*, *Reservoir Dogs* proved to be a powerful opening salvo. The film is in spots ultraviolent, and its cast seems juiced on testosterone. But the macho posturing conceals an otherwise faithful adherence to the indie-film mantra: talk is cheap, action is expensive, which is to say that *Reservoir Dogs* is a stagy, talky film in which occasional, albeit hyperbolic scenes of brief and ridiculous violence erupt. The vast majority of *Reservoir Dogs* is set in a warehouse, where the surviving players in a botched heist await backup and rescue. The warehouse doubles as a soundstage, and Tarantino blocked most of the scenes there as if he'd been directing a play. The film's most notorious scene has Vic (Mr. Blonde, played by Michael Madsen) shot in full figure as he sings, dances, and tortures a policeman. We watch the scene as if it were being played onstage. The stylistic simplicity makes the hideous violence all the more effective.

Another scene has Freddy (Tim Roth), the cop who infiltrates the gang, rehearsing his undercover role as a lowlife crook looking for a job on the robbery team. Tarantino sets up Freddy's last rehearsal as something of an audition for his immediate superior. In doing so the director reveals the pretense of Freddy's performance in the film and suggests by extension the importance of performance to the film as a whole.

The bloody climax of Quentin Tarantino's violent caper movie *Reservoir Dogs* (1992).

The clever opening scene of *Reservoir Dogs* is set around a huge table in a diner where the men in the gang first meet. They talk (extemporaneously, it seems) about the meaning of a Madonna video ("Like a Virgin") and the relative ethics of tipping waiters. Neither subject has much to do with propelling the film's story, but the dialogue goes a long way toward establishing a hip ambience.

Much the same technique is used at the start of *Pulp Fiction*, a film for which Tarantino received the Palme d'Or at Cannes in 1994 and a Writing Oscar (with Roger Avary) in 1995. We join two hit men, Jules (Samuel L. Jackson) and Vincent (John Travolta), en route to pick up a suitcase (which contains a mysterious glowing substance) from some young guys who are clearly in over their heads. The hit men have a dirty job to do, but they pass the time talking about McDonald's restaurants in Amsterdam (where a Quarter Pounder with cheese is called a Royale with Cheese) and muse on the question of whether giving a married woman a foot rub constitutes adul-

tery. The street-corner philosophizing does not necessarily humanize the characters; they are, thanks to the performance of the stars, larger than life in many ways. But it is nonetheless interesting and entertaining. At the very moment when mainstream American cinema seemed to be dominated by beats and whammies, by scenes punctuated by things exploding and/or highlighted by catch phrases like "I'll be back" or "Hasta la vista, baby," Tarantino introduced a considerably more articulate action template.

Tarantino's self-awareness as a writer has been evident in his many experiments with narrative form. At its heart, *Reservoir Dogs* is a caper film. But unlike previous caper films it defies the strict chronology of the crime procedural. *Pulp Fiction* is famously framed by two scenes in a coffee shop that depict in two parts a botched robbery. What happens in between those scenes does not exactly fit. In the scenes at the start and the end, we see both Vincent and Jules (who dramatically stops the robbery from playing out). But well before our second look at the scene, Vincent is shot and killed by Butch (Bruce Willis). Even if we ignore the frame, the film seems strangely structured, as if we are seeing Act 1, Act 3, and then Act 2.

Jackie Brown, Tarantino's 1997 adaptation of Elmore Leonard's 1992 novel *Rum Punch*, similarly plays fast and loose with narrative structure. In the film's pivotal scene a suitcase full of cash changes hands. Tarantino replays the scene several times, each time with a slight variation accommodating a given character's point of view. This structure, reminiscent of *Rashomon* (Akira Kurosawa's 1950 film, in which unreliable witnesses recount different versions of the same crime), is mostly a joke, as the various versions differ in only minute and mostly irrelevant ways. Such gamesmanship is yet another nod to Godard, and it works because it effectively suspends (in real time) the film's payoff.

After *Jackie Brown*, Tarantino waited six years before returning to the director's chair. That return produced *Kill Bill*, which was met with a dose of bad press—the sort that had accompanied the most troublesome of auteur projects (like *Apocalypse Now* and *Heaven's Gate*). News and trade reports commented daily on time and budget problems. When Tarantino delivered his cut to his distributor (Miramax), it was about 4 hours, far too long to screen at theaters more than once per night. Miramax first insisted on cuts, then compromised with a two-part release (*Kill Bill: Vol. 1*, 2003, and, in 2004, *Kill Bill: Vol. 2*). The films had modest success at the box office and again on DVD, a medium that allowed the two films to be released as one 247-minute movie.

The *Kill Bill* films offer a departure from the more theatrical style of Tarantino's earlier work. The dialogue-heavy bland-interior set pieces of *Reservoir Dogs* are replaced by long, energetically shot and cut action set pieces. The most exemplary of these is the climactic fight in *Kill Bill: Vol. 1*. Set in a Tokyo club, the Bride (Uma Thurman) fights O-Ren Ishii (Lucy Liu) and her cohorts, including the homicidal schoolgirl Gogo Yubari, played by Chiaki Kuriyama, the star of the Japanese cult classic *Batoru rowaiarut* (*Battle Royale*, Kinji Fukasaku, 2000), one of Tarantino's favorite B pictures. The Bride dispenses with an army of bad

Vincent Vega (John Travolta), hit man (and pretty good dancer) in Quentin Tarantino's *Pulp Fiction* (1994).

guys wielding big swords, lopping off limbs and leaving the disco dance floor drenched in blood. The scene ends as the Bride and O-Ren exit the disco club to duel in a beautiful Japanese garden while snow falls all around them. The scene is at once beautiful and absurd.

In a Hollywood culture that by the end of the twentieth century had effaced, or at least reified, the distinctions between studio and independent films (see Chapter 9 for more on this), Tarantino and his longtime distributor, Miramax, seemed to reside in limbo between the two long-standing categories. With the two *Kill Bill* films, Tarantino cemented his reputation as America's best-known and perhaps best-loved "independent" filmmaker. But given the films' budget ($55 million) and the director's celebrity, it became difficult to continue to talk about Tarantino as an independent, at least as far as filmgoers had come to appreciate the distinction.

INDEPENDENTS AND INDEPENDENCE

The independent-movie scene of the 1980s and '90s emerged to fill the gap created by the studios' collective abandonment of the auteur picture. In the 1980s the identity of the director of a commercial Hollywood film had in most cases become incidental, so long as the film followed the blockbuster formula. This was especially true of the studios' biggest films. In 1984, for example, the most successful studio films were *Ghost Busters* (Ivan Reit-

Roland Emmerich directing *Independence Day*, which grossed over $300 million in the United States and Canada in 1996. Though the film was one of the decade's biggest hits, as was Emmerich's follow-up *Godzilla* (1998), it is unlikely the average moviegoer could pick the auteur out of a lineup.

man), *Indiana Jones and the Temple of Doom* (Steven Spielberg), *Gremlins* (Joe Dante), *Beverly Hills Cop* (Martin Brest), and *Star Trek III: The Search for Spock* (Leonard Nimoy). The top box-office films for 1985 included *Back to the Future* (Robert Zemeckis), *Rambo: First Blood Part II* (George P. Cosmatos), *Rocky IV* (Sylvester Stallone), and the James Bond feature *A View to a Kill* (John Glen). In 1986 the studios offered more of the same: *Top Gun* (Tony Scott), *The Karate Kid, Part II* (John Avildsen), and *Star Trek IV: The Voyage Home* (Nimoy). Of these top box-office films, only Spielberg's *Indiana Jones and the Temple of Doom* could be categorized as an auteur feature.

The trend continued through the next decade. As Hollywood became a place where films were made in response to market research and packaged with stars, music, and high-concept ideas well in advance of principal photography, moviemaking became increasingly systematized and standardized. The most successful directors in American cinema in the 1990s—Michael Bay and Roland Emmerich, for example—were far less known than their blockbuster films: Bay directed *Bad Boys* in 1995, followed by *The Rock* (1996), *Armageddon* (1998), and *Pearl Harbor* (2001); Emmerich directed *Independence Day* (1996) and *Godzilla* (1998). Though their films made hundreds of millions of dollars, it is unlikely that the average

moviegoer would recognize either of those men if he or she bumped into him at the mall. Indeed, considerable as their accomplishments have been with regard to the bottom line of contemporary commercial cinema, Bay and Emmerich have less name and face recognition than independent filmmakers like Joel and Ethan Coen, John Sayles, and Steven Soderbergh, whose movies have never grossed anything close to the box-office revenues of *Armageddon* or *Godzilla*.

The first signs of a new American independent cinema took shape in the mid-1980s with a number of remarkable films made by auteurs working well outside the Hollywood mainstream: Gregory Nava's unflinching chronicle of Mexican "illegals," *El Norte* (1983); Jim Jarmusch's offbeat comedy *Stranger Than Paradise* (1984); John Sayles's race-conscious science-fiction fable *The Brother from Another Planet* (1984); Alan Rudolph's stylish neo-noir *Choose Me* (1984); veteran independent filmmaker John Cassavetes' *Love Streams* (1984); and Robert Altman's adaptation of a one-man stage play about Richard Nixon's last days in the White House, *Secret Honor* (1984); the Coen brothers' first feature, the black comedy *Blood Simple* (1984); Wayne Wang's *Dim Sum: A Little Bit of Heart* (1985), a character study of Chinese Americans; the punk-inspired romantic comedy *Desperately Seeking Susan* (Susan Seidelman, 1985), starring Madonna; *Kiss of the Spiderwoman* (Hector Babenco, 1985), based on a controversial South American novel by Manuel Puig; Joyce Chopra's chilling film about a girl's first time, *Smooth Talk* (1985), based on the Joyce Carol Oates story "Where Are You Going, Where Have You Been?"; Horton Foote's filmed stage play *Trip to Bountiful* (Peter Masterson, 1985); the salsa-music rags-to-riches-to-rags story *Crossover Dreams* (Leon Ichaso, 1985); Martin Scorsese's *After Hours* (1985), a film that tracks a single eventful night in the life of one very unlucky New Yorker; David Lynch's small-town nightmare *Blue Velvet* (1986); Tim Hunter's disturbing teen pic *River's Edge* (1986), which dramatizes the true story of a murder and its cover-up by a handful of disaffected teenagers in northern California; Spike Lee's *She's Gotta Have It* (1986); Oliver Stone's political thriller *Salvador* (1986); Alex Cox's punk biopic *Sid and Nancy* (1986); the sly comedy *True Stories* (1986) from the Talking Heads' front man David

Byrne; and the comedian Robert Townsend's send-up of commercial cinema's stereotyping of black talent, *Hollywood Shuffle* (1987).

Unlike the 1970s, when auteur pictures backed by studio money and muscle were top-grossing films, in the 1980s and 1990s the audience for even the most compelling independent auteur pictures was significantly smaller. Consider for the purpose of argument the following list: *The Addiction* (Abel Ferrara, 1995), *Bodies, Rest & Motion* (Michael Steinberg, 1993), *Box of Moon Light* (Tom DiCillo, 1996), *Clockwatchers* (Jill Sprecher, 1997), *Fear of a Black Hat* (Rusty Cundieff, 1994), *Federal Hill* (Michael Corrente, 1994), *Female Perversions* (Susan Streitfeld, 1996), *Heathers* (Michael Lehmann, 1989), *The House of Yes* (Mark Waters, 1997), *Just Another Girl on the IRT* (Leslie Harris, 1992), *Killing Zoe* (Roger Avary, 1994), *Matewan* (Sayles, 1987), *Men with Guns* (Sayles, 1997), *Naked in New York* (Dan Algrant, 1993), *Party Girl* (Daisy von Scherler Mayer, 1995), *Simple Men* (Hal Hartley, 1992), and *The Underneath* (Soderbergh, 1995). Those well-regarded and well-known films are credited to some of the biggest names on the indie landscape: directors John Sayles, Hal Hartley, Steven Soderbergh, and Abel Ferrara; Quentin Tarantino (as producer of Avary's *Killing Zoe;* and the stars Parker Posey and Winona Ryder. But what all of those films have in common is that they made $1 million or less at the box office, one one-hundredth as much as the average blockbuster, one four-hundredth as much as a franchise heavyweight like George Lucas's *Star Wars: Episode I— The Phantom Menace* (1999).

Keanu Reeves as the slacker hero in Tim Hunter's sobering indie teen pic *River's Edge* (1986).

Many independent titles are what the industry calls niche films, films produced by and for a specific and relatively narrow demographic. Niche films are consistent albeit modest moneymakers because niche audiences are starved for films about people like them. Consider by way of example lesbian-themed films like *Go Fish* (Rose Troche, 1994), *The Incredibly True Adventure of Two Girls in Love* (Maria Maggenti, 1995), and *High Art* (Lisa Cholodenko, 1998), three pictures that share a theme but are otherwise very different in tone and content. All three earned about the same amount: $2 million, suggesting a small but loyal target audience.

Niche films are often written and directed by filmmakers who do not fit the white-heterosexual-male norm of studio Hollywood. At Hollywood studios, women and people of color are, to put it mildly, underrepresented behind the camera and

The indie auteur Abel Ferrara directing Lili Taylor during the production of Ferrara's 1995 grad-school vampire picture *The Addiction*.

behind the executive desk. But the ranks of '80s and '90s indie filmmaking sport a Who's Who of female and/or minority filmmakers: Charles Burnett (*The Glass Shield*, 1994), Lisa Cholodenko, Martha Coolidge (*Valley Girl*, 1983), Rusty Cundieff, Vondie Curtis-Hall (*Gridlock'd*, 1997), Julie Dash (*Daughters in the Dust*, 1991), Tamra Davis (*Guncrazy*, 1992), Cheryl Dunye (*The Watermelon Woman*, 1996), Carl Franklin (*One False Move*, 1992), Leslie Harris (*Just Another Girl on the IRT*, 1992), Nicole Holofcener (*Walking and Talking*, 1996), Reginald Hudlin (*House Party*, 1990), Albert and Allen Hughes (*Menace II Society*, 1993; *Dead Presidents*, 1995), Leon Ichaso, Tamara Jenkins (*Slums of Beverly Hills*, 1998), Spike Lee, Kasi Lemmons (*Eve's Bayou*, 1997), Jennie Livingston (*Paris Is Burning*, 1991), Maria Maggenti, Gregory Nava, Matty Rich (*Straight Out of Brooklyn*, 1991), Nancy Savoca (*True Love*, 1989; *Dogfight*, 1991), Penelope Spheeris (*The Decline of Western Civilization*, 1981), Susan Seidelman, Jill Sprecher, Robert Townsend, Rose Troche, Luis Valdez (*Zoot Suit*, 1981), and Wayne Wang. Add to that list openly gay directors or directors who specialize in gay-themed films, like Gregg Araki (*The Doom Generation*, 1995) and Todd Haynes (*Poison*, 1991).

For a while these directors of indie and niche films thrived under the studios' collective radar. But as the '90s wound down, the studios began assimilating the indie scene, and the margins of Hollywood expanded to contain the independents.

Independent Auteurs: Joel and Ethan Coen, John Sayles, and Steven Soderbergh

The Coen brothers, Joel (who writes and directs their films) and Ethan (who writes and produces them), first appeared on the indie scene in 1984 with *Blood Simple*, a tongue-in-cheek film noir set in rural Texas. The film was the unlikely hit of the New York Film Festival (whose patrons generally prefer artier fare), and the Coens were acknowledged as auteurs overnight. Ever since *Blood Simple* the brothers have straddled the line between independent and commercial Hollywood cinema, making modest-budget films for a loyal fan base. Highlights of their career include the madcap comedy *Raising Arizona* (1987); the neo-noir *Miller's Crossing* (1990); *Barton Fink* (1991), a cautionary melodrama about a Clifford Odets–like playwright hired as a screenwriter by a Hollywood studio in 1941; the Capraesque farce *The Hudsucker Proxy* (1994); another neo-noir, *Fargo* (1996); the madcap comedies *The Big Lebowski* (1998) and *O Brother, Where Art Thou?* (2000); and *The Man Who Wasn't There* (2001), a loose remake of Billy Wilder's *Double Indemnity* (1944).

There are two keys to the Coen brothers' auteur signature: pace and critical distance. *Blood Simple* is dead slow—a complete reversal on the hectic urban noir universe. Much the same can be said about the old-Hollywood satire *Barton Fink* and the neo-noirs *Miller's Crossing, Fargo,* and *The Man Who Wasn't There*. *The Hudsucker Proxy,* a pastiche of 1930s romantic comedies, is breakneck fast, as are the brothers' other slapstick comedies: *Raising Arizona, The Big Lebowski,* and *O Brother, Where Art Thou?*

Virtually all of the Coen brothers' films focus on stupid people doing stupid things. It is thus worth noting that Joel and Ethan Coen are university-educated sons of college professors. Operating from such a safe critical distance, the Coens are all too willing to see their characters suffer through most anything for a laugh, for a cool image, for a gross-out effect. Their characters find themselves in familiar genre predicaments but react in stupid, crazy ways. In *Blood Simple,* Ray (John Getz) finds the corpse of Julian Marty (Dan Hedaya) and mistakenly assumes that his girlfriend (who is Marty's wife, played by Frances McDormand) has done the killing. He tries to clean up the crime scene but succeeds only in making a bigger mess, spreading Marty's blood over every surface in the room. The Snoats brothers (John Goodman and William Forsythe) in *Raising Arizona* stumble through a bank robbery, stupidly leaving behind a baby they've kidnapped and are holding for ransom. Norville Barnes (Tim Robbins), the proxy in *The Hudsucker Proxy,* is a moron from Muncie, Indiana. The film borrows liberally from Frank Capra's *Meet John Doe* (1941): the promise of a holiday suicide, the exploitation of an innocent by a "dame" from the newspapers. (When the Coens allude to or quote other films, as they do here by referring to Capra's populist fable, they do so in service of a gag—it is an insider's game for cinephiles savvy enough to get the references.) Finally, there is Jerry (William H. Macy) in *Fargo,* whose plot to change

John Turturro as the pederast bowling ace Jesus Quintana in Joel and Ethan Coen's comedy *The Big Lebowski* (1998).

the life he has and deserves (as a wimp and a fool) ends the way most plots launched by characters in Coen brothers' films end: with butchered bodies and wrecked cars. Jerry resorts to crime (engineering his wife's kidnapping for ransom) because his plan to get out from under an embezzlement mess goes awry. He has embezzled the money to finance his dream project: a parking lot. But even such a small and simple dream is doomed; there's no shortage of parking in the frozen Midwest. Four important set pieces feature action played out against a background of hundreds of empty parking spaces.

Violence in the Coen brothers' films is pervasive and explicit. The films are routinely marketed with an eye to a college-age and young college-educated audience. Nods to '60s and '70s exploitation fare are hard to miss. In the otherwise manic comedy *The Big Lebowski,* the on-screen violence is so extreme it's funny. Two thugs break into the apartment of the Dude (Jeff Bridges) and find him in the bathtub. When he cannot answer their questions— they have the wrong guy—they drop a marmot into the water, forcing the normally slow-moving Dude to scurry out of the tub. *Fargo,* a film that won two Academy Awards (for Writing and, for Frances McDormand, Best Actress in a Supporting Role) and sports the best production cost to box office

Frances McDormand as the intrepid pregnant sheriff Marge Gunderson in Joel and Ethan Coen's *Fargo* (1996).

revenue ratio of any of the Coens' films, curiously enough goes the furthest into exploitation-style violence. Gaear (Peter Stormare), an almost mute criminal, shoots a policeman in the face in the opening scene. At the end of the film, he kills his partner, Carl (Steve Buscemi), and disposes of the body by feeding the corpse into a wood chipper. The Coen brothers find farcical the everyday violence that other mainstream filmmakers glorify. This perspective forms the foundation of an original social commentary that emerges despite the pervasive irony of their films and their cheeky games with style.

John Sayles is in many ways the model contemporary independent filmmaker, an independent cut in the mold of the New York legend John Cassavetes. Whereas Cassavetes supported his filmmaking with acting work in commercial films,

Sayles initially financed his independent films with the money he made writing scripts for exploitation pictures like *Piranha* (Dante, 1978); *Alligator*, about giant alligators in the New York City sewer system (Lewis Teague, 1980); and *Battle beyond the Stars* (Jimmy T. Murakami, 1980).

Sayles's first film, *Return of the Secaucus 7* (1980), about a handful of twentysomethings set adrift in contemporary America, was a minor arthouse hit. The film is reflective, what popular critics dub "personal." Though it got considerable and positive critical attention, Sayles quickly departed from the strictly personal to the more generally political. From his second film, *Lianna* (1983), which frankly examines a young woman's sexual experimentation, through his 2002 release, *Sunshine State*, which details the impact of upscale developers on a landmark Florida seaside community, Sayles used his independence to make movies that say something about contemporary America. Three of his films focus on discomfiting race relations: the futurist fable *Brother from Another Planet*, the border mystery *Lone Star* (1996), and *Sunshine State*. He is also one of the few directors to focus on workers' rights. *Matewan*, for example, is a period piece about a strike that tears apart a West Virginia mining town. *Eight Men Out* (1988) is a baseball picture that is less about baseball than money, a statement in itself about the great American pastime. The film tells the story of the notorious Black Sox scandal of 1919, in which members of the Chicago White Sox threw the World Series in exchange for a payoff from gangsters who bet on their opponents. Though the story focuses on a moral transgression—the throwing of the World Series—Sayles complicates matters by chronicling the systematic exploitation of the players by team owner Charles Comiskey. Though what the players do is wrong, Sayles renders the story in terms that make one crime an inevitable response to another.

Sayles has a loyal base of fans, for whom his films have come to represent an alternative to all that's gone wrong in Hollywood since 1980 and who appreciate that his films seem to be made independent of the fast-buck profit motive. But while Sayles is a familiar name and face on the American film scene, he has never had a crossover hit.

Art house–to–multiplex crossover hits were a rarity in 1980s and '90s Hollywood, which is why Steven Soderbergh's *sex, lies, and videotape* (1989) merits note here. The film earned over $25 million in its initial domestic release, a previously unimaginable sum for such a talky, quirky, intellectually and formally challenging movie. The picture won for its director, then just twenty-six years old, the Palme d'Or at Cannes and was marketed brilliantly by Miramax, then a fledgling independent distribution company run by two brothers, Harvey and Bob Weinstein.

Soderberg followed up *sex, lies, and videotape* with a bigger-budget film, *Kafka* (1991), that was so confusing and uncommercial it seemed as if the

director were trying to destroy his career just as it got started. Soderbergh's next two films, *King of the Hill* (1993), a family melodrama, and *The Underneath* (1995), a snail-paced neo-noir, seemed only to restate his independence from the commercial mainstream. Though he made some interesting films between 1995 and 2000—*Out of Sight* in 1998 (with George Clooney and Jennifer Lopez), for example—Soderbergh failed to repeat the success he enjoyed with his first film. And then with one film, the Julia Roberts star vehicle *Erin Brockovich* (2000), he forged for himself a unique space in the industry, becoming something of an A-list director on both the indie and the studio circuits.

After the release of *Erin Brockovich*, Soderbergh balanced truly independent fare—the rambling, mostly improvised *Full Frontal* (2002)—with commercial pictures like the star-studded remake of *Oceans Eleven* (2001). Positioned somewhere in between the indie and the commercial worlds, we find Soderbergh's best film, *Traffic* (2000). It features parallel narratives with parallel visual styles to match. Structurally and stylistically, *Traffic* is as challenging as anything contemporary independent cinema has to offer. The picture tells a suspenseful story, did well at the box office, and won for its auteur the ultimate mainstream prize, an Oscar for Directing.

Soderbergh infuses all his work with a signature style. His films are by and large character studies of people in some sort of self-imposed

The indie auteur John Sayles on the set of his historical melodrama *Matewan* (1987).

exile, whether a disillusioned housewife (Andie MacDowell) or an impotent vagabond (James Spader) in *sex, lies, and videotape*, a famous writer (Jeremy Irons) in *Kafka,* a killer (Terence Stamp) in *The Limey* (1999), or a Mexican cop (Benicio Del Toro) in *Traffic*. These characters are curiously, perhaps even pathologically detached, isolated, and lonely. Even Erin Brockovich, played by the vivacious star Julia Roberts, is a fish out of water, battling not only injustice but the sorts of assumptions folks inevitably make about women in the workplace.

Soderbergh toys with time signatures as well; like Tarantino he is fond of playing fast and loose with narrative structure. *The Underneath,* for example, plays out with flashbacks within flashbacks. His experimentation with captured images, like the videotapes of women talking about sex in *sex, lies, and videotape* or the systematic shifts from black-and-white to color in *Traffic,* betrays an independent spirit that has proved to be at once idiosyncratic and commercial, a unique combination in the new Hollywood.

Independent Women Making Movies

Since 1980, women have directed a number of small-budget niche films, most with themes deemed suitable to their gender and sensibility. As such, with the exception of a select few female stars who have parlayed their clout in the industry into the director's chair or the executive suite—women like Jodie Foster, Barbra Streisand, and Goldie Hawn—women working as directors have been mostly ghettoized, limited by small budgets and art-house-only releases.

Such marginalization has its advantages, as Allison Anders and Nancy Savoca have discovered. With a degree of freedom she would not have had working on big-budget studio films, Anders has made a series of pictures about young women on the brink of adulthood, including *Gas Food Lodging* (1992) and the Chicana gang film *Mi Vida Loca* (1993), movies that defy the simple formula of more mainstream coming-of-age films. Also fiercely independent, Savoca has made two trenchant love stories, both of which resist the

(*top*) Jodie Foster: actress, movie star, producer, and director.

(*bottom*) *From left to right:* The groom (Ron Eldard), his groomsman (Michael J. Wolfe), and his uncle (John Nacco) ponder the married life in Nancy Savoca's decidedly unsentimental wedding film *True Love* (1989).

prerequisite Hollywood happy ending. In *True Love* she offers something of a dystopian wedding story. Set during the last days before the wedding of two attractive young Italian Americans, Donna (Annabella Sciorra) and Mickey (Ron Eldard), the film offers a comic commentary on the different expectations of young couples embarking on a life together. The comedy is found not in the actual wedding ceremony or the preceding family interactions, but instead in the more generalized incompatibility of modern young men and women playing at being adults. The complications of adult romance facing young men and women also lie at the heart of Savoca's *Dogfight*, which tells the story of marine recruits who, on the eve of shipping off to train for and fight in Vietnam, hold a "dogfight." That is, each young man searches for the ugliest woman in town and invites her to a party at a local bar. The women think they are the recruits' dates, but they are really contestants in a "beauty" contest, in which the biggest loser wins. Eddie (River Phoenix) tabs Rose (Lili Taylor) as his dogfight date, but during the course of the evening he falls in love with her. Rose discovers Eddie's bad intentions fairly early on, but he works hard to make up for his unkindness, and in the end the two spend the night together.

The film is unusual in many ways. The ugly girl gets the guy. The hero learns that the concepts of manhood valued by the marines and society are selfish and counterproductive. Eddie and his buddies go to Vietnam, but Savoca is far less interested in the war than in what the war does to Eddie and Rose. We get less than 5 minutes in country, during which Eddie sees his friends killed by a mortar round and is badly wounded. The film ends ruefully as Eddie returns from the war literally broken, no longer a dashing, hand-

(*left*) Steven Sodergergh (*left*) directing the actor Peter Gallagher (*center*) in *sex, lies, and videotape* (1989). The film won the grand prize at Cannes and helped make the indie distributor Miramax a major player in Hollywood.

some boy in uniform. Rose still works in the same café, but her life has not been on hold while Eddie has been overseas. When they reunite, neither is sure what to do. After an awkward moment they begin to dance to a song on the jukebox. The moment is sweet enough, but it is unclear what it will lead to.

On the even more distant margins of commercial filmmaking are two African American women, Julie Dash and Leslie Harris. Released almost one hundred years into the history of American cinema, Dash's *Daughters in the Dust* was the first theatrically released motion picture directed by an African American woman. It was financed by the director (who spent five years raising funds) with grants from the National Endowment for the Arts,

Rose (Lili Taylor) and Eddie (River Phoenix) spend an intimate evening together in Nancy Savoca's moving Vietnam-era melodrama *Dogfight* (1991).

the Fulton County (Georgia) Arts Council, the Public Broadcasting Service's *American Playhouse,* and the National Black Women's Health Project. *Daughters in the Dust* is set on the Sea Islands off the coast of South Carolina at the beginning of the twentieth century and chronicles an African American family's trepidations as its members consider a move to the mainland. For Dash the family's move presents the African diaspora in microcosm: still searching for a place in America they can call home, the members of the family at once resist and invite assimilation.

A year after the release of *Daughters in the Dust* came Leslie Harris's critically celebrated debut, *Just Another Girl on the IRT,* a timely film about a young African American woman whose dreams of becoming a doctor and escaping poverty and domestic abuse are waylaid by the arrival of a baby born out of wedlock. Through a series of direct-address monologues that endear the heroine, Chantel (Ariyan A. Johnson), to the audience, Harris demonstrates Chantel's naïveté about the opportunities available to even a smart, charming young black woman. Though the film was widely praised by critics and seemed to be one of those rare movies that fully capture a time and a milieu, Harris, like Dash, struggled in the industry for much of the rest of the decade, finally failing to secure financing for a follow-up film.

Even when we look at women whose films seem closer to the commercial mainstream, we find few who have been able to get steady work as directors. There are exceptions, such as Penelope Spheeris, who has financed her independent documentaries on the punk and heavy-metal subcultures (*The Decline of Western Civilization* trilogy, 1981, 1988, 1998) with studio projects like *Wayne's World,* based on a *Saturday Night Live* skit starring Mike Myers and Dana Carvey, and *The Little Rascals* (1994), based on the early-sound-era shorts produced by Hal Roach. But for most women who have tried to use success on the indie circuit to jump-start a commercial studio career, things have not worked out so nicely or so neatly. Martha Coolidge, whose low-budget teen film *Valley Girl* was a minor hit that prompted her quick graduation to studio A-movie production, is a case in point. In the so-called big time, Coolidge was immediately typecast as a teen-movie director and assigned to *Real Genius* (1985), a sophomoric comedy written by Neal Israel and Pat Proft, the writer-creators of the *Police Academy* series (seven films released between 1984 and 1994). The film failed to hit, and Coolidge was suddenly deemed no longer interesting.

A full eight years later Coolidge finally got to direct an adult-themed drama, *Rambling Rose* (1991), a sweet melodrama with ample local color about a wild young woman (Laura Dern) living with a proper southern family. The film was that rarest of things: a Hollywood movie sympathetic to a sexually adventurous young woman. Coolidge's next big film was *Angie* (1994), a comic take on a young working-class woman (Geena Davis) who must adjust to the changes her baby brings to her life. Though the film exhibits Coolidge's sensitivity to issues faced by young women (as well as the issues of class and interpersonal relations that are evident in *Valley Girl*), *Angie* did poorly at the box office, and Coolidge continued to struggle as a director working for the studios.

Like Martha Coolidge, Amy Heckerling first got noticed for a low-budget teen comedy, *Fast Times at Ridgemont High* (1982), a film now famous for

(right) She may be the smartest girl in her class, but Chantel (Ariyan A. Johnson), the main character in and narrator of Leslie Harris's 1992 debut, is in the end *Just Another Girl on the IRT*.

Sean Penn's hilarious performance as a stoned surfer dude. Based on a book by Cameron Crowe chronicling his reenrollment in high school masquerading as a new student, the film satisfies the episodic structure of a teen hijinks picture (along the lines of John Landis's 1978 *Animal House*) while presenting a startlingly honest look at teenagers' first sexual experiences. Also like Coolidge, Heckerling made the leap to A features but had a hard time getting out of the light-comedy niche. Her most financially successful films have been the forgettable domestic farce *Look Who's Talking* (1989), and its sequel, *Look Who's Talking Too* (1990). A glimmer of hope career-wise came with *Clueless* (1995), a clever update of Jane Austen's *Emma*. The film made Alicia Silverstone a star and grossed about $60 million for Paramount Pictures. But despite its mainstream success, Heckerling went the next five years without making a picture and returned only to helm yet another formulaic teen film, *Loser* (2000), which did absolutely nothing at the box office.

Of all the contemporary women who have tried to make the transition from the indie circuit to mainstream commercial filmmaking, Kathryn Bigelow has perhaps forged the most interesting and most enduring career. A quick survey of her oeuvre reveals that Bigelow has succeeded (to the degree that she has succeeded) in the man's world of Hollywood filmmaking by making the kinds of movies men make. In her indie vampire film *Near Dark* (1987), for example, Bigelow betrays an affection for male-dominated, male-targeted genres: the western (the vampires are cast as misunderstood western outlaws) and the slasher film, complete with allusions to the cult classics *The Texas Chain Saw Massacre* (Tobe Hooper, 1974) and *The Hills Have Eyes* (Wes Craven, 1977). Bigelow followed up *Near Dark* with the ultraviolent policewoman drama *Blue Steel* (1990), featuring the popular actress Jamie Lee Curtis as a police officer cut from the *Dirty Harry* mold—a no-nonsense tough cop, albeit one who, as we see in the opening sequence, wears a lace bra under her uniform. Next

The director Kathryn Bigelow on the set of *Strange Days* (1995).

came *Point Break,* a 1991 commercial feature, which is as butch a film as one might ever encounter. It tells the story of risk-taking young guys who live for the big surf and an occasional big score robbing banks.

Bigelow entered the commercial big time with the $42-million millennial science-fiction film *Strange Days* (1995). As if setting out to prove that she could be as tough as any male action film-maker, she made a film in which the violence—including a grisly scene of sexual violence—is presented vividly and viscerally. The one gender twist concerns a romance in which a woman, a buff bodyguard (Angela Bassett), saves and protects a far weaker man (Ralph Fiennes).

Strange Days did poorly at the box office, earning less than $8 million in its first theatrical run, and briefly pushed Bigelow out of the big time. But after a seven-year hiatus, during which she shot just one film, *The Weight of Water* (2000), a thoughtful adaptation of Anita Shreve's novel about a photojournalist (Catherine McCormack) obsessed with a nineteenth-century murder, Bigelow returned to the action-film template (and commercial success) with the taut submarine thriller *K-19: The Widowmaker* (2002).

■ ■ ■

American cinema celebrated its centennial in the 1990s. And at one hundred, the industry was in better fiscal shape than ever before. The studios had inexorably evolved, assimilating and/or intersecting with parallel media in the television, video, music, and the Internet industries to form vast synergistic entertainment markets through which studio products moved profitably. This cross-pollination expanded what was once just a film market—just movies playing in movie theaters—into a vast information-entertainment marketplace where profits were made not just from domestic and foreign theatrical exhibition but also from domestic and foreign home box office (network and cable television, videocassettes, and DVDs), merchandise (toys, mugs, Happy Meals), video games, and music.

Studio films in the 1980s and 1990s were developed as packages: scripts and stars were put together less to achieve an artistic goal than to match a corporate plan built on data assembled by crack market-research teams. The advertising and promotion of a studio film increasingly resembled the management of a political campaign, with audience surveys and test screenings guiding content. By the end of the 1990s, promotion and advertising budgets were on average a third of a film's overall cost. Considerable attention was being paid to how a film might be positioned in the market, and films were defined in advance of release in a way that might whet the appetite of the filmgoing public. To a large extent, films were produced in concert with strategically planned promotional campaigns, which is to say that production served an advertising scheme instead of the other way around.

With the box-office eminence of the action-adventure genre, the whammy theory supplanted the auteur theory, and films became more spectacular than ever before. Auteur filmmaking, which had saved Hollywood in the 1970s, was summarily abandoned, as all ambitious moviemakers became potential Michael Ciminos. Auteurs were systematically pushed to the margins of commercial Hollywood to make movies for small but devoted niche audiences. More clearly than ever before, American cinema was split between two modes of filmmaking: event blockbuster films that exploited innovations in postproduction special effects and theatrical exhibition drove the industry, whereas smaller projects that exhibited an independent spirit were pushed to the periphery. Despite the chasm between them, by the end of the century both modes were owned and operated by the diversified conglomerate studios.

A single fact of life in the film business prevailed as the century came to a close: anyone with enough money to make movies made money-making movies. Never before in the history of cinema had the bottom line looked so good.

Trinity (Carrie-Anne Moss) poised for action in Andy and Larry Wachowski's *The Matrix Reloaded* (2003).

9

The End of Cinema As We Know It

1999–2006

In 1963 the French filmmaker Jean-Luc Godard famously remarked, "I await the end of cinema with optimism." It was an offhand comment, meant to be provocative and amusing, since the notion of the end of filmmaking seemed impossible at that time. But as the twentieth century drew to a close, a future without cinema—or, more precisely, without cinema as we have known it—no longer seemed so far-fetched. Indeed, it seemed very much a possibility.

The movies turned one hundred years old in the mid-1990s. The studios predictably viewed the centennial as an occasion for nostalgia and self-congratulation, sentiments they have always warmed to. They took stock of their history and for the first time began to appreciate fully the cultural value of their films as well as the fiscal value of their film libraries in the vast consumer market. DVD releases now routinely include quasi-historical data, making-of documentaries, director and star commentaries. Studios have found numerous ways of exploiting and recycling their old(er) films on DVD, on cable television, and in TV advertising.

Beginning in the mid-1990s, the celebration of film's past gave way to the inevitable countdown to the millennium. Films staging the end of the world, like *Strange Days* (Kathryn Bigelow, 1995) and *Terminator 3: Rise of the Machines* (Jonathan Mostow, 2003), proved that global catastrophe could be exciting, profitable, and fun. On film, at least, anxiety over Y2K (year 2000) was subsumed by a cosmic spring cleaning, the notion that we might be better off starting all over again.

The panic over Y2K—founded in the fear that all computer-based industries (banking, for example) would collapse under the weight of a global computer-network crash when the calendar turned from 1999 to 2000—proved unwarranted. But there was still plenty to worry about as we ventured into a new century: terrorism (especially after the attacks on September 11, 2001), the AIDS epidemic, the so-called war on drugs, global warming, and political unrest in Africa and the Middle East (two sites of failed U.S. military ventures). Hollywood filmmakers tapped into those anxieties with films like *Collateral Damage* (Andrew Davis, 2002), *Syriana* (Stephen Gaghan, 2005), *The Hours* (Stephen Daldry, 2002), *Traffic* (Steven Soderbergh, 2000), *The Day after Tomorrow* (Roland Emmerich, 2004), *Black Hawk Down* (Ridley Scott, 2001), *The Constant Gardener* (Fernando Meirelles, 2005), *Three Kings* (David O. Russell, 1999), and *Jarhead* (Sam Mendes, 2005), all of which assessed the political instability of the times.

At the start of the twenty-first century, six companies—Time Warner (and its partner, AOL), Walt Disney (owner of ABC), the News Corporation (owner of 20th Century Fox), Sony (owner of Columbia Tristar and co-owner of MGM), Viacom (owner of Paramount and CBS), and General Electric (partial owner of NBC Universal)—enjoyed more complete control of the entertainment industry than the 1930s-era studio trusts ever did. They dominated not only the mainstream commercial marketplace but also the independent–art film circuit as formerly independent companies like Miramax, along with studio spin-offs like Sony Pictures Classics and Fox Searchlight Pictures, became boutique labels of the major companies.

American cinema in the 1990s became increasingly global as revenues from the foreign theatrical and home box office rivaled those from the parallel domestic markets. As the twenty-first century began, the term *American film* was at best relative, perhaps even obsolete. Increasing globalization was accompanied by significant technological change, a transition as dramatic as the changeover to sound in the late 1920s. Films increasingly employ computer-generated imagery (CGI) to seamlessly simulate real and fictive locations and characters. Actors routinely performed in front of blank screens, and much of filmmaking has been turned over to technicians and engineers. Production is at once more complex, the site for technological innovation of the highest order, and vastly simplified, as the human element has become secondary to the technological.

Technological changes have occurred in exhibition as well. The motion-picture palace—the monument to the classical Hollywood era—became a thing of the past, and in its place have emerged streamlined multiplexes with as many as twenty screens, all equipped with "stadium" seating and some new variant of digital, Dolby, THX, and/or DTS sound. These changes in the theatrical experience have also affected film production as film producers increasingly emphasize action-based visual and sound effects and pop-music sound-track packages. Movie franchises like the *Matrix* trilogy (Andy and Larry Wachowski, 1999 and 2003) were made to suit and exploit the new sound and image capabilities of the modern movie house. As in the pre-cinema and silent eras, audiences flocked to theaters less for a story on a given subject than for a new experience.

This new cinema of attractions proved to be successful at first, but it is fair to wonder whether such a cinema might be a last act of desperation or a sign of exhaustion. In an era characterized by immersive video games, high-definition televisions, surround-sound home audio systems, on-demand content, personal media players, and digital video recorders, one may be prompted to ask why anyone would go to a theater unless he or she were going to see something that couldn't be seen at home.

The good news for the studios is that success in the twenty-first century is no longer simply a matter of getting people into theaters; indeed, income from the domestic theatrical box office has become a small part of a film's overall worth to its studio. Some films have a second life on cable television or DVD, which allows a disappointing showing at the box office to be overcome.

The most financially successful films have been those that speak a universal cine-language, a language that not only travels across the globe but is also easily reformatted as a video game and cross-marketed by the fast-food and toy industries. Billions of dollars have become available in this vastly expanded entertainment marketplace, but not everyone can cash in. The film business at the beginning of the twenty-first century resembled nothing so much as a high-stakes poker game. And as every good player knows, to win a big pot, you have to be willing to gamble a lot of money. In twenty-first-century Hollywood only a handful of players have enough money to play such a high-stakes game.

THE NEW NEW HOLLYWOOD

Six companies, all well diversified in an ever more vertically integrated entertainment marketplace, dominated the corporate landscape of Hollywood—and, by extension, American mass media—at the turn of the century. The following discussion is meant to give a clear, if somewhat overwhelming picture of the extent of their dominance.

Consolidation and Conglomeration

By late 2005, AOL Time Warner was the biggest and most complexly integrated of the entertainment conglomerates. Its vast entertainment holdings included the film studios Warner Bros., Hanna-Barbera Cartoons, Castle Rock Entertainment, New Line Cinema, Fine Line Features, and Turner Original Productions; the television networks HBO, Cinemax, CNN, TBS Superstation, Turner Network Television (TNT), the Cartoon Network, and Turner Classic Movies; the cable delivery outfit Warner Bros. Domestic Pay TV; the Time Warner Book Group (composed of Warner Books and Little, Brown); the magazines *Time, Life, Fortune, Entertainment Weekly, Sports Illustrated, Money, People, Sunset, Popular Science,* and *Mad;* DC Comics; AOL online services and Netscape; the Atlanta Braves baseball team and Warner Bros. Recreational Enterprises (owner and operator a number of theme parks).

The Walt Disney Company, the industry's second largest concern in 2005, owned a handful of movie studios, including Walt Disney Pictures, Touchstone Pictures, Hollywood Pictures, Miramax Films, and Buena Vista Home Entertainment, with Walt Disney, Touchstone, and Buena Vista doubling as TV studios. After a strategic merger with the ABC-TV network in 1995, Disney boasted small-screen holdings that rivaled Time Warner's: ABC, A&E (Arts and Entertainment), ESPN, E! Entertainment, (50 percent of) Lifetime, and of course the Disney Channel, along with a handful of local TV stations, including ABC's flagship KABC in Los Angeles. Along with the Disney-brand publishing imprint, the company owned two book publishers, Hyperion and Miramax Books, and published the popular magazines *Discover, ESPN* and *US Weekly* (which it co-owned). A big part of the company's identity remained the theme parks

Michael Eisner, chairman and chief executive officer of the Walt Disney Company from 1984 to 2005.

and resorts in the United States (Disneyland, including Disney-MGM Studios, and Walt Disney World, including Epcot) and abroad (Tokyo Disney Resort and Disneyland Resort Paris) and the company's line of merchandise sold in its own retail stores. Rounding out Disney's holdings were the ESPN and ABC radio networks (including over fifty radio stations), the Anaheim (California) Ducks professional hockey team (named for a Disney film franchise, which it sold in 2005), and considerable investments in the recording industry (Disney Records, Hollywood Records, and the Buena Vista Music Group) and the Internet (with a variety of sites devoted to Disney and ESPN).

In 1985, Rupert Murdoch's News Corporation purchased the Fox film studio, which by 2005 included 20th Century Fox, Fox Searchlight Pictures, Fox Television Studios, and Blue Sky Studios; the Fox Broadcasting Company (including the Fox Network, FX, Fox News Channel, Fox Movie Channel, Fox Sports Net, Fox Soccer Channel, and the National Geographic Channel); and over forty Fox affiliates in key markets such as New York, Los Angeles, Boston, and Chicago. Two years earlier the newspaper magnate (already owner of the *New York Post* and two London papers, *The Sun* and *The Times*) had become the principal European cable supplier (with Sky). The News Corporation's other holdings included (partial ownership of) *TV Guide,* the HarperCollins Publishing Group (including Avon, HarperMorrow, and

Rupert Murdoch (*right*), chairman and managing director of the News Corporation, answering questions at a 2004 press conference. To his right is his son, Lachlan, at the time the company's deputy chief operating officer.

ReganBooks), a sports league (Australia's National Rugby League), professional sports teams (partial ownership of the National Basketball Association's Los Angeles Lakers and the National Hockey League's Los Angeles Kings) and venues (a 40 percent stake in the Staples Center in Los Angeles, where the Lakers and the Kings play), and the Fox Sports Radio Network.

Sony Corporation, the Japanese electronics conglomerate, has been a Hollywood player since 1989, when it bought Columbia and TriStar studios from the Coca-Cola Company for $3.4 billion. Sony has since added its own trademark Sony Pictures Entertainment and the boutique indie label Sony Pictures Classics and is part of a consortium that acquired MGM. Though it has limited interests in the TV industry, Sony's holdings in the recording industry rival those of Time Warner and Universal: the labels of Sony BMG Music International include Arista Records, Columbia Records, RCA Records, Sony Classical, Sony Music Nashville, and Epic Records. Sony maintains synergies between its film and music companies and between its film and retail electronics products for home theaters, stereo components, and most lucrative of all, console gaming, with its celebrated PlayStation series.

Viacom chief executive officer Sumner Redstone at the world premiere of *K-19: The Widowmaker* (Kathryn Bigelow, 2002).

The venerable film studio Paramount (composed of Paramount Pictures and Paramount Home Entertainment) was purchased in 1994 by Viacom, a cable-TV company headed by Sumner Redstone. Viacom also owned or had strategic corporate relationships with the TV networks CBS and UPN; a host of CBS and UPN affiliates, such as WCBS-TV (New York), KCBS-TV (Los Angeles), WBBM-TV (Chicago), and KPIX-TV (San Francisco); the premium cable-TV stations Showtime, Movie Channel, Flix, and Sundance Channel; the basic cable-TV stations MTV, CMT, Comedy Central, BET, and Nickelodeon; Infinity Broadcasting (composed of over 170 stations); and the publisher Simon and Schuster (including the imprints Simon and Schuster, Pocket Books, Scribner, and MTV Books).

Finally, NBC, itself a subsidiary of the defense contractor and home-appliance maker GE (General Electric), purchased Universal Pictures and most of its holdings from the French media conglomerate Vivendi in 2003, becoming NBC Universal. GE is a multinational conglomerate with considerable interests in the defense, transporta-

tion, finance, home-appliance and health-care industries; NBC Universal and the related entertainment industries are only a small part of GE's holdings. In addition to Universal Pictures and the NBC-TV network, the NBC Universal media group owned the TV network Telemundo; the cable-TV stations Bravo, CNBC, USA, and MSNBC; and a number of local TV affiliates, including both the flagship stations WNBC in New York and KNBC in Los Angeles. Vivendi—now called Vivendi Universal—retained a 20 percent stake in NBC Universal and maintained full ownership of the Universal Music Group (including MCA Nashville, Motown Records, Interscope Geffen A&M, Island Def Jam Music Group, and Verve Music Group) and Vivendi Games (including *Warcraft, Metal Arms: Glitch in the System,* and *Leisure Suit Larry*), along with the French cable-TV and international film company Canal Plus (otherwise known as Canal+), which has financed a number of contemporary American films.

Synergy is the catchword of this new new Hollywood as conglomerates have integrated the operations of their various holdings, distributing filmed products into a variety of markets and venues, all under a single corporate umbrella. Given the number of markets made available through the entertainment synergies and the amount of money to be made in any of the integrated media markets, it became nearly impossible for a film—even an extremely expensive one that fared poorly in American movie theaters—to lose money.

New Marketing Strategies for a New Film Market

With increased conglomeration has come increased dependence on market research. This industry trend is consistent with procedures that the new studio owners used in their primary markets. When Coca-Cola purchased Columbia in 1982, for example, the soft-drink maker used the same market research company (Lieberman Research West) to fashion marketing campaigns for Columbia's motion pictures and its own soft drinks. Coca-Cola was hardly the only studio owner to put its faith in market research. Indeed, in the new new Hollywood, market research begins in the development stage as executives apply numerical values to various aspects of a proposed film project. If after the numbers are tallied, the total exceeds some preselected figure, the film gets a green light and is put into production. If not, it is sent into "turnaround," where it is shelved, most likely forever.

First among the variables considered in market research is casting, with different stars meriting different numerical values (based on each actor's Q rating, a guide to popularity, clout, and/or power rankings as speculated on in popular magazines like *Entertainment Weekly*). Different genres are handicapped differently, and the values vary with industry trends and the recent performance of similar films.

As soon as a film gets a green light at the studio, a marketing strategy is designed and initiated. Before the first shot is set up in the production phase, the studios eye their annual release slate and consider a seasonal release. There are reasons to target one of the big seasons—youngsters off from school in the summer, the nominations made by the Motion Picture Academy during the winter holiday season—especially if market research suggests a studio has a hit on its hands. If the research indicates that it doesn't, there are six other months for which theaters and filmgoers need product.

In this market-driven era, studios have discovered that it is never too early to think about how to sell a movie to the press and the public at large. Newspaper "advertising intensity" is calculated and budgeted well in advance of a given film's release, based on a formula that links the number and size of the motion-picture ads to the projected box-office numbers. The number and type of trailers produced and the venue and time of their airing or screening are also important variables.

Two types of trailers are used for big films. The teaser, released as much as six months before a film is scheduled to reach theaters, enables studios to advertise summer blockbusters during the Christmas season and Christmas movies in the summer. Teaser trailers are designed to reveal little about a movie's content: instead, the focus is on the stars and the genre (the two key factors in the decision to green-light a project). The theatrical, or "story," trailer follows several months later, to position the product in the marketplace more fully. Whereas the teaser is designed to tell audiences that a certain film is so big they need to know about it half a year in advance, the story trailer is

"When danger becomes a temptation . . . When every move brings you closer to the edge . . ." A couple of catchy taglines, a sexy woman with a gun, a car chase, and an indomitable leading man are all you need in a teaser trailer if you're hawking a presold property like the 007 thriller *Die Another Day* (Lee Tamahori, 2002). From the teaser trailer: (*top*) Halle Berry as Jinx (this installment's Bond girl); (*middle*) Bond's Aston Martin Vanquish on thin ice; and (*bottom*) the godfather of contemporary action heroes, James Bond (Pierce Brosnan).

gious affiliation. Test audiences are asked to fill out cards after the screening or may be interviewed by teams of market researchers. The audiences' responses have a significant impact on the final cut of a film. If test groups say, for example, that a film is too bloody (as they said about Francis Ford Coppola's *Bram Stoker's Dracula* in 1992), the studio might compel the director to soften several of the film's more grisly scenes. If an ending doesn't seem to work—a common complaint made by test audiences (in response to Mike Nichols's *Wolf* in 1994, for example)—then the film's release will be held up while a new ending is shot. Although the new Hollywood studios continue to entrust their films to famous directors, they are much more willing than their predecessors to defer creative decisions to randomly chosen test audiences. In American cinema at the turn of the century, customers may not be right, but they certainly are having it their way.

Release Strategies

Thanks to a weak FTC and FCC and a Justice Department disinclined to pursue antitrust cases against the conglomerates that have moved back into theater ownership (a vestige of Reaganism, which is discussed in Chapter 8), in the new new Hollywood it is just like the old days before divestiture, only better. Consider the full-page newspaper ads announcing the release of the 1996 summer hit *Independence Day* (Roland Emmerich). They said nothing about the film or its initial reception by audiences or critics. Instead it touted, "*Independence Day:* Opening at Theaters EVERYWHERE." However good or bad the film might be, the sheer number of prints in circulation and screens devoted to its exhibition virtually guaranteed a successful opening weekend. *Independence Day* grossed $50 million in its first three days of release.

designed—by a studio's market researchers—to tell audiences what the film is about and why they should—or *need to*—see it.

The process of screening rough cuts, which has existed from very early in the history of American cinema, was refined in the 1990s. Following the standard screenings for studio lawyers and executives, screenings for test audiences became increasingly important to the new new Hollywood marketing campaign. Test audiences are composed of folks rounded up at a mall or a busy street corner and herded into a theater for a free screening. Ideally, market researchers seek a diverse sample so that they can approximate a film's performance in a variety of geographic locations (urban, suburban, rural; North, South, East, West; red state, blue state) and with a variety of people codified by gender, education, income, and reli-

By the end of its first run, its domestic gross had topped $300 million. As of September 2001 its total theatrical gross worldwide was a breathtaking $797 million (with a production budget estimated at $75 million).

Because big films by necessity (and definition) open big, the opening weekend has acquired a singular importance. And key to a successful opening weekend is the quality that studio executives call marketability. The relative quality of a film itself—its playability in industry argot—is significantly less important. If a picture can be sold in advance of its release independent of its relative quality—if it has marketability—it will succeed. The auteurs of the new new Hollywood are no longer directors or even producers; instead, they are executive-level advertising specialists who in many cases never bother to see the film they are promoting. Once theatergoers are in their seats, these executives reason, it doesn't much matter whether they like what they see or not.

The degree to which the first weekend foretells a film's success—and the astonishing percentage of a film's total domestic gross that can be attrib-

uted to the first three days in release—reveal just how completely the industry has come to depend on marketable, as opposed to playable, movies. In 1982, when playability still seemed to matter, Steven Spielberg's *E.T.* took in $4,776,000 in its initial week in release. The film grossed $6,014,000 in its second week, an increase of 26 percent. The number 2 film for the year, *Tootsie* (Sydney Pollack), opened at $2,444,000 and then increased 63 percent in its second week, to $3,978,000. *Porky's* (Bob Clark), the year's number 4 film, and *An Officer and a Gentleman* (Taylor Hackford), at number 5, became marketable because they were playable; the films opened modestly but quickly exceeded studio expectations. Of the top ten films for 1982, only two dropped off from week 1 to week 2: *Rocky III* (Sylvester Stallone), which fell 2 percent, and *Star Trek: The Wrath of Khan* (Nicholas Meyer), which fell 9 percent. *Rocky III* and the *Star Trek* sequel were in obvious ways similar properties: both were high-concept franchise films from big studios, films with far more marketability than playability. Both performed predictably at the box office.

Petty Officer Doris Miller (Cuba Gooding Jr.) fights back in Michael Bay's blockbuster *Pearl Harbor* (2001).

At the beginning of the 1990s, studio executives were inclined to believe that playability was a matter of luck. There is, after all, no formula for making good films or films that exceed market expectations. The more formulaic *Rocky* and *Star Trek* films may have fallen off after their first weekend in 1982, but they were easy to handicap in advance of their release, and as sequels they were easy to develop and produce. As an example of the difficulty of forecasting playability, consider 1992, when every one of the top ten films fell off from the first week to the second. *Aladdin* (Ron Clements and John Musker), the number 1 film, sported a negative 48 percent change from week 1 to week 2. The three sequels that placed second, third, and fourth for the year—*Home Alone 2: Lost in New York* (Chris Columbus), *Batman Returns* (Tim Burton), and *Lethal Weapon 3* (Richard Donner)—dropped off significantly as well: by 28 percent, 45 percent, and 25 percent, respectively. All three films did well enough at the box office by year's end ($173.5 million, $163 million, and $144.7 million), and all three turned a profit in the various ancillary markets available in 1992, despite an apparent lack of playability.

Executives' commitment to marketability at the beginning of the twenty-first century is exemplified by the three big films released in the summer of 2001: *Pearl Harbor* (Michael Bay), *Planet of the Apes* (Burton), and *Jurassic Park III* (Joe Johnston). These films succeeded primarily because of well-executed prerelease marketing campaigns and saturation release platforms (like *Independence Day* these films opened "everywhere"). The drop-off from the opening weekend to the second week in release was dramatic and revealing. *Pearl Harbor*, which was budgeted at $152 million, grossed $75 million in its opening weekend. It dropped off to $29 million in its second week, $14 million in its third, and $9 million in its fourth. Of its total first-run gross of $195 million, almost 40 percent was earned in the first three days of general release. The $93-million *Jurassic Park III* opened at $50.7 million. It dropped off steadily, to $22.5 million, $12 million, and $7 million. By September 1, 2001, with the film playing in just a handful of subrun theaters, it had grossed $173 million, 29 percent of which was earned in the first weekend. The most anxiously awaited film of the summer, *Planet of the Apes*, was produced for $100 million. It opened big at $68.5 million but dropped off to $27.5 million, $13 million, and $7 million, for a total gross by the end of the summer of $168 million. Like *Pearl Harbor* and *Jurassic Park III*, a significant portion—in this case 41 percent—of the total gross domestic box office earned by *Planet of the Apes* could be credited to the crucial first weekend. Such are the mathematics of marketability.

Of course, opening-weekend numbers are hardly the whole story. In the new new Hollywood, box office is only the first and fastest money counted. On average (as of 1996), domestic theatrical revenues—that is, box-office receipts in the United States and Canada—accounted for only 16 percent of the total revenue generated by a studio film. The remaining 84 percent was composed of domestic home video (26 percent), foreign theatrical box office (16 percent), foreign home video (20 percent), domestic television (11 percent), and merchandising (11 percent). Success at the box office ensured continued profitability across these ancillary markets, but it wasn't the largest piece of the revenue pie.

The media's increased attention to box-office receipts (published in virtually every local newspaper at least once a week) and the business of entertainment (scrutinized in popular magazines like *Entertainment Weekly* and *Premiere* and on TV shows like *Entertainment Tonight*) fundamentally changed how the film-going public thought about a film's or a filmmaker's success, importance, and value. The twenty-first-century film-going public, thanks in no small part to the success of the complexly integrated media that report on films, can be counted on to consume movies that are big, cost and make a lot of money, and get covered extensively and exhaustively in print and on television well in advance of their release. This new mind-set skews the supply-and-demand paradigm governing filmmaking and film-going.

New Exhibition Formats and Technologies

In the first few years of the twenty-first century, a panoply of audiovisual formats and media has made *film* seem like an outdated name for what Hollywood is producing. American movies are released in various formats (celluloid, a variety of digital media, and the old standby VHS) and

An IMAX film crew captures an F-15 landing at Nellis Air Force Base in the Nevada desert in 2004.

screened on various types of equipment in theaters, at home, in cars and vans, and on tiny handheld screens. Converting films into multiple formats has become a top priority for the studios, as it enables them to expand their revenue base and make money from the same basic product in several parallel markets.

This is not to say that the theatrical experience has become passé; it hasn't. But the stakes of public viewership have changed as the venues have by necessity been modernized. Newly built or refurbished movie theaters are now equipped with sophisticated sound systems tweaked to showcase the volume and energy of the contemporary action genres. Stadium seating, introduced in the mid-1990s, allows theaters to cram more people into smaller spaces and provides customers with improved sight lines and more comfortable seats. An increasing number of theaters are offering more than just a film experience, adding arcade rooms for younger filmgoers and dining for their older customers.

New formats like **IMAX** were introduced, too, offering an alternative to the multiplex experience (with its smaller screens and sound leakage from theater to theater). Whereas IMAX had been used initially for nature shorts screened at science and industry museums, beginning in 2003 selected studio titles were made available to IMAX theaters, including *The Matrix Revolutions* (Andy and Larry Wachowski, 2003) and *Harry Potter and the Goblet of Fire* (Mike Newell, 2005). IMAX offers an immersive widescreen experience much the way Cinerama did half a century ago when the studios were struggling to find an exhibition format that would get people away from their TV sets. IMAX's screening experience is at once big and real and can't be matched or even mimicked by any format sold to individual consumers. The technology is attractive to young viewers already engaged by interactive console and computer games.

Of all the new sites of film distribution and exhibition available at the beginning of the twenty-first century, the Internet is at once the most promising and the most vexing. On the one hand it offers a cost-efficient way in which to distribute filmed product. On the other hand it has created a file-sharing subculture. In the first few years of the

The IMAX 3D Theater adjacent to the Tennessee Aquarium in Chattanooga. IMAX began as an attraction at venues like science museums and aquariums, but as home theaters became more sophisticated and as portable small-screen alternatives became relatively inexpensive, immersive big-screen venues became more commonplace as stand-alone sites, and studios began releasing IMAX versions of their big-budget action films.

century, the MPAA spent a lot of time and money lobbying Congress to protect its members' copyrights against Internet piracy at home and DVD piracy abroad. With so many formats available to consumers worldwide, controlling the flow—that is, establishing systems of compensation as a product moves through the legitimate entertainment marketplace and countering the quasi black market of file-sharing sites and DVD street vendors—has been of paramount importance.

FILMS AND FILMMAKERS: INDUSTRY TRENDS

Two distinct trends marked American cinema in the early years of the twenty-first century: the continued importance of seasonally released "event films," bigger and louder and costlier than ever before, and a complementary increase in "independent" films—or at least independent-minded

films—released by a new generation of American moviemakers, auteurs brought up on movies, television, and video and computer games. Though there has been plenty of talk about the end of cinema, this generation of filmmakers has given cinephiles reason to hope that the rumors of cinema's death are, to paraphrase Mark Twain, greatly exaggerated.

Blockbusters and Box-Office Hits

Blockbusters are defined by two characteristics. The first is immediately recognizable: the size and scope, the speed and sound. The second is empirically measurable: cash spent on production and advertising and cash made at the box office. Foremost among the contemporary blockbusters are the so-called franchise films. Of those that tell a long story in several parts, we find the *Star Wars* franchise: *Episode I—The Phantom Menace* (1999), *Episode II—Attack of the Clones* (2002), and *Episode III—Revenge of the Sith* (2005), prequels directed by the creator of the series, George Lucas. Lucas's return to the director's chair in 1999, after a twenty-two-year hiatus, was widely derided by critics but wholeheartedly embraced by the contemporary film audience. By the time the third prequel had completed its initial global run, the three new films' combined worldwide theatrical gross was an estimated $2.5 billion.

Reviewers complained that the new *Star Wars* films seemed old-fashioned, even quaint. Such a critique was valid, given the competition: Andy and Larry Wachowski's innovative *Matrix* films, which ably combine state-of-the-art special effects, cyberpunk literature, Hong Kong–style kung fu films, and dialogue steeped in Eastern mysticism and postmodern theory. This very contemporary global mix proved seductive to American filmgoers. It also reflected a growing affection among American filmgoers, especially younger ones, for Asian-style action cinema, otherwise evident in the

Keanu Reeves takes aim as Neo, the anointed hero in the popular sci-fi action film *The Matrix* (Andy and Larry Wachowski, 1999).

The Chinese action star and former world martial-arts champion Jet Li in action in Andrzej Bartkowiak's gangland saga *Romeo Must Die* (200).

popularity of films by the Asian-born directors John Woo (*Face/Off*, 1997, and *Mission: Impossible II*, 2000) and Ang Lee (*Crouching Tiger, Hidden Dragon*, which won four Oscars in 2000) and martial-arts stars like Jackie Chan, who appears in such films as *Rush Hour* (Brett Ratner, 1998) and *Shanghai Noon* (Tom Dey, 2000), and Jet Li, known for his performance in *Romeo Must Die* (2000) and *Cradle 2 the Grave* (2003), both directed by Andrzej Bartkowiak.

The mining of popular literature continues to be a staple of Hollywood blockbuster entertainment, as evidenced by the amazing popularity of Peter Jackson's *Lord of the Rings* trilogy, adapted from J. R. R. Tolkien's beloved fantasy novels: *The Lord of the Rings: The Fellowship of the Ring* (2001), *The Lord of the Rings: The Two Towers* (2002), and *The Lord of the Rings: Return of the King* (which won the Best Picture Oscar in 2003). With time and money to give the work a scale and scope that were unthinkable before the era of special-effects blockbuster filmmaking, Jackson made Tolkien's Middle-earth a unique cinematic spectacle, noteworthy especially for the seamless integration of CGI (computer-generated imagery) with live action. Offering nearly 10 hours of entertainment in three monumental films released during three holiday seasons, the *Lord of the Rings* proved to be the perfect modern blockbuster.

Also hugely popular were the films based on the *Harry Potter* novels by J. K. Rowling. The four installments released between 2001 and 2005—*Harry Potter and the Sorcerer's Stone* (Chris Columbus, 2001), *Harry Potter and the Chamber of Secrets* (Columbus, 2002), *Harry Potter and the Prisoner of Azkaban* (Alfonso Cuarón, 2004), and *Harry Potter and the Goblet of Fire* (Mike Newell, 2005)—follow the gifted children of Hogwarts from childhood to adolescence. Although the films target a young audience, as do the books (which have sold over 300 million copies worldwide), like all good blockbusters the *Harry Potter* films consistently appeal to—as the ringmaster of Ringling Bros. and Barnum & Bailey would say—children of all ages.

In the category of blockbuster films that tell the same basic story over and over again (with new stunts and new effects) were three more installments in the James Bond series: Michael Apted's *The World Is Not Enough* (1999), Lee Tamahori's *Die Another Day* (2002), and *Casino Royale* (Martin

(*right*) Harry Potter (Daniel Radcliffe) with Buckbeak, the hippogriff, in *Harry Potter and the Prisoner of Azkaban* (Alfonso Cuarón, 2004), the third installment in the popular young-adult franchise.

Campbell, 2006) three films that ably cast the venerable cold war spy (played by Pierce Brosnan in 1999 and 2002 and Daniel Craig in 2006) into the post–cold war era. Also in this category is the adaptation of episodic TV shows, like *Mission: Impossible* (Brian De Palma, 1996), *Mission Impossible II*, and *Mission Impossible III* (J. J. Abrams, 2006).

Comic-book adaptations continued to do well at the box office after 1999. Among the biggest and best were the mutant-versus-mutant and mutant-versus-human *X-Men* series—*X-Men* (Bryan Singer, 2000), *X2* (Singer, 2003), and *X-Men: The Last Stand* (Ratner, 2006)—and the popular Spider-Man films—*Spider-Man* (2002) and *Spider-Man 2* (2004), both directed by Sam Raimi, based on the Stan Lee–Steve Ditko comic-book series about a misunderstood crime fighter–superhero (played by Tobey Maguire). Less successful at the box office

but perhaps more interesting as a concept was Ang Lee's *Hulk* (2003), adapted from Stan Lee's Marvel comic-book series. Ang Lee tried to complicate the usual CGI-fest with a Freudian backstory, producing a more complex film than the typical comic-book blockbuster. But it disappointed at the box office, earning "just" $225 million worldwide, and it fared poorly with critics, who had otherwise been clamoring for more depth in mainstream American moviemaking. In the end even the newspaper reviewers preferred their blockbusters loud and dumb.

If we take the lofty base figure of $400 million in global theatrical revenue as the criterion for blockbuster status, in addition to the films already mentioned, the following movies, released between 1999 and 2005, qualify as blockbusters: *The Mummy* (Stephen Sommers, 1999), *Tarzan* (Chris

Buck and Kevin Lima, 1999), *The Sixth Sense* (M. Night Shyamalan, 1999), *Toy Story 2* (John Lasseter, Ash Brannon, and Lee Unkrich, 1999), *Cast Away* (Robert Zemeckis, 2000), *Gladiator* (Ridley Scott, 2000), *The Mummy Returns* (Sommers, 2001), *Shrek* (Andrew Adamson and Vicky Jenson, 2001), *Pearl Harbor* (Michael Bay, 2001), *Monsters, Inc.* (Pete Docter, David Silverman and Unkrich, 2001), *Ocean's Eleven* (Steven Soderbergh, 2001), *Men in Black II* (Barry Sonnenfeld, 2002), *Signs* (Shyamalan, 2002), *Bruce Almighty* (Tom Shadyac, 2003), *Finding Nemo (*Andrew Stanton and Lee Unkrich, 2003), *The Pirates of the Caribbean: The Curse of the Black Pearl* (Gore Verbinski, 2003), *The Last Samurai* (Edward Zwick, 2004), *The Passion of the Christ* (Mel Gibson, 2004), *Shrek 2* (Adamson, Kelly Asbury, and Conrad Vernon, 2004), *The Incredibles* (Brad Bird, 2004), *Madagascar* (Eric Darnell and Tom McGrath, 2005), *Mr. & Mrs. Smith* (Doug Liman, 2005), *The War of the Worlds* (Steven Spielberg, 2005), *Charlie and the Chocolate Factory* (Tim Burton, 2005), *Chronicles of Narnia: The Lion, the Witch and the Wardrobe* (Adamson, 2005), and *King Kong* (Jackson, 2005).

If we search for a common denominator in the above list, we find foremost that blockbusters by necessity target the widest audience possible. Only three films—*Gladiator, The Last Samurai,* and *The Passion of the Christ,* all rated R—restricted attendance. The rest availed themselves of the entire American audience independent of age-based criteria. Nearly a third of the films—eight of the twenty-six—were animated, made and marketed for children. Four were sequels, and four were remakes—further evidence of Hollywood's penchant for recycling and further evidence that with blockbusters, plot merely provides a framework, an excuse for special effects and spectacle.

Hugh Jackman as the mutant Wolverine in Bryan Singer's *X2* (also know as *X-Men 2*, 2003).

High Priest Imotep (Arnnold Vosloo) reanimated in Stephen Sommer's blockbuster sequel *The Mummy Returns* (2001).

Twenty-First-Century Auteurs

If there was a surprise among the list of early-twenty-first-century blockbusters, it was the success of two austere horror films, *The Sixth Sense* and *Signs,* directed by the Philadelphia-based, India-born filmmaker M. Night Shyamalan. Both films feature big stars in uncharacteristically unheroic roles—Bruce Willis as a tortured psychiatrist and Mel Gibson as a preacher who has renounced his faith—and both defy the blockbuster formula with their achingly slow pacing and character-based (as opposed to CGI-based) horror sequences. Suspense, in Shyamalan's hands, is all about suspending certain revelations in the narrative. We wait for proof of the alien invasion in *Signs,* for example, and then we wait for the overmatched humans to figure out what to do about it. It is the act of waiting that makes us anxious. Sudden jolts briefly relieve our anxiety—when a face comes out of the dark, for example, or when characters for the first time see what they are up against—but for the most part Shyamalan's films are about people going slowly crazy when faced with what Freud called the uncanny, the horror that resides underneath the commonplace.

Shyamalan was just twenty-nine when *The Sixth Sense* became an international box-office sensation in 1999. Nineteen ninety-nine was a big year as well for a number of other young Hollywood auteurs: Paul Thomas Anderson (also twenty-nine that year, the writer and director of the ensemble melodrama *Magnolia*), David Fincher (then thirty-seven, a music-video director, who made *Fight Club,* a savagely funny and graphically violent foray into the male identity crisis and late-twentieth-century self-help culture), Spike Jonze (who turned thirty that year, is also a music-video director, and directed the wild comedy *Being John Malkovich,* a clever spoof of celebrity culture written by Charlie Kaufman), Doug Liman (then thirty-four, who impressed audiences in 1996 with *Swingers,* his ensemble comedy about wannabe actors in Los Angeles, and in 1999 broke new ground with the complex youth-culture dramedy *Go*), Alexander Payne (who at thirty-eight was a veteran of the indie circuit with his 1996 abortion-activist satire *Citizen Ruth* and in 1999 gained a far wider audience with *Election,* a film that focuses on unselfconscious ambition), and David O. Russell (age forty-one and the eldest of the bunch, whose *Three*

From left to right: Bruce Willis, the child actor Hayley Joel Osment, and the director M. Night Shyamalan at the 2000 People's Choice Awards. Willis won Favorite Motion Picture Actor, and Shyamalan's *The Sixth Sense* (1999) won Favorite Motion Picture.

Kings rendered the Persian Gulf War and its aftermath at once harrowing and darkly comic).

For those directors, 1999 proved the start of something good. Anderson followed up *Magnolia* with *Punch-Drunk Love* (2002), a character study of a lonely geek (Adam Sandler in a mostly straight role) who finally finds romance. Fincher, whose prodigious talent as a cine-stylist was evident in three interesting '90s films—the franchise sequel *Alien³* (1992), the serial-killer mystery *Se7en* (1995), and *The Game* (1997), a hectic fantasy adventure starring Michael Douglas—followed up *Fight Club* with the unrelentingly tense caper film *Panic Room* (2002). From another hilarious script by Charlie Kaufman, Jonze ruminated on the capricious nature of Hollywood moviemaking in *Adaptation* (2002), based loosely (and unconventionally) on Susan Orleans's popular 1998 book *The Orchid Thief*. After 1999, Liman made the leap to the commercial big time with the action hit *The Bourne Identity* (2002) and the farce *Mr. & Mrs. Smith*, a film that grossed over $400 million world-

Edward Norton (*left*) and Brad Pitt as two sides of the same guy in the male-identity-crisis picture *Fight Club* (David Fincher, 1999).

wide despite poor reviews. Its success seemed due in large part to the celebrity romance between its co-stars Brad Pitt and Angelina Jolie.

Unlike Liman, who easily made the transition to commercial blockbuster filmmaking, Payne retreated deeper into character study, directing *About Schmidt* (2002), one of the rare Hollywood films to examine aging (starring the aging super-star Jack Nicholson), and *Sideways* (2004), a character study of two very different men, a lonely divorced wine expert (Paul Giamatti) and a former TV star (Thomas Haden Church) looking for one last fling before he gets married. Russell ventured even further out of the mainstream with *I Heart Huckabees* (2004), a spoof of new-age culture, and a documentary, the suggestively titled *Soldiers Pay* (co-directed by Tricia Regan and Juan Carlos Zaldívar, 2004), for which he returned to Iraq to interview U.S. soldiers fighting in the war that began in 2003.

Other young auteurs to emerge in this period were Wes Anderson, whose quirky comedies *Rushmore* (released in 1998, when the director was not yet thirty) and *The Royal Tenenbaums* (2001) lampoon American family life, and Sam Mendes, whose black-comedy view of suburbia, *American Beauty*, took the Best Picture and Directing Oscars in 1999 for the then thirty-four-year-old auteur. Mendes followed up in 2002 with *Road to Perdition*, a film about an Irish crime family and the hit man (played by the all-American good guy Tom Hanks) who runs afoul of the family's bad-seed heir apparent (Daniel Craig), and in 2005 with *Jarhead*, which focuses on a group of American soldiers hungry for combat in Iraq.

In addition to these young Turks, two veteran auteurs—Robert Altman and Martin Scorsese—made important movies as the twenty-first century unfolded. Altman, who had all but vanished from the commercial scene in the 1980s, reemerged in 1992 with the Hollywood satire *The Player*, followed by the ensemble piece *Short Cuts* (1993), which proposes intersections in otherwise unrelated short stories by Raymond Carver. In 2001, at the age of seventy-six, Altman made the drawing-room mystery *Gosford Park*, a film that features his signature style: overlapping dialogue, ensemble acting, and a moving camera.

Scorsese similarly struggled in the 1980s but regained popularity and significance in the 1990s

Matthew Broderick as an overwrought high-school teacher and Reese Witherspoon as his know-it-all student in Alexander Payne's genre-bending dramedy *Election* (1999).

with two great gangster films, *Goodfellas* (1990) and *Casino* (1995) and with *The Age of Innocence* (1993), based on an Edith Wharton novel set in the auteur's beloved New York at the beginning of the twentieth century. Two of Scorsese's early-twenty-first-century films, his bloody *Gangs of New York* (2002) and his biopic about the legendary billionaire Howard Hughes, *The Aviator* (2004), brought the director commercial success and Best Picture and Directing nominations from the Motion Picture Academy. Like Altman, Scorsese, who was sixty years old when *Gangs of New York* premiered, continued to use his familiar signature style (a moving camera, deft integration of sound-track music, and on-screen action) and continued to explore themes (of temptation, redemption, and salvation, of the cathartic nature of violence) that have haunted his work since the early 1970s.

In 2006 Altman received an Honorary Award on Oscar night, celebrating his long career (and affirming the sorry fact that after so many years and so many good films, he had never won an Academy Award for Directing). Altman died eight months later. Scorsese finally won his first Academy Award for Directing the following year for his Irish gangster epic *The Departed*. On hand to present the award were Francis Ford Coppola, George Lucas, and Steven Spielberg, fellow pioneers of the vaunted Hollywood auteur renaissance of the 1970s.

In 2002 the indie auteur Doug Liman made the leap to the commercial big time with the action hit *The Bourne Identity*, starring Matt Damon as the rogue agent Jason Bourne, seen here clinging to the side of a building in one of the film's many hair-raising action sequences.

A select group of movie stars emerged at the twentieth century's end to lay claim to a kind of authorship of their movies. Foremost in this group was the comedy star Jim Carrey. Boasting a guaranteed salary of $20 million a picture in 1996, Carrey transformed every film he was in and made every film his. That was easy enough in the 1990s, when he appeared in films that existed solely to highlight his peculiar physical and verbal comedy: *Ace Ventura: Pet Detective* (Shadyac, 1994), *The Mask* (Chuck Russell, 1994), *Dumb and Dumber* (Peter and Bobby Farrelly, 1994), and *Ace Ventura: When Nature Calls* (Steve Oedekerk, 1995). It got harder after 1998, when Carrey, like a lot of comic actors before him, endeavored to be taken seriously. Though the dramatic films made nowhere near the profits of his earlier comedies, Carrey proved an able dramatic actor in *The Truman Show* (Peter Weir, 1998), a science-fiction fantasy about a man who lives his life on television, and in the art-house picture *Eternal Sunshine of the Spotless Mind* (Michael Gondry, 2004), a science-fiction parable about a man who tries to clear his mind of a failed romance.

Another $20-million-per-film superstar, Julia Roberts, was the one American actress capable of opening a film on her own—an actress whose name alone would guarantee a successful opening weekend. Roberts became a movie star in 1990 with *Pretty Woman* (Garry Marshall) and exploited that stardom to astonishing commercial and considerable critical success after 1999, the year in which she appeared in two blockbuster romantic comedies: *Notting Hill* (Roger Michell), in which she plays an American movie star who falls for a meek London bookshop owner (Hugh Grant), and *Runaway Bride*, which reunited her with her *Pretty Woman* co-star, Richard Gere, and director, Garry Marshall. In 2000, Roberts won an Oscar for Actress in a Leading Role for her portrayal of the eponymous heroine in the Steven Soderbergh biopic *Erin Brockovich*, and in 2004 she appeared to critical acclaim in Mike Nichols's depressing examination of contemporary relationships, *Closer*.

Perhaps the most interesting and certainly the most perplexing movie-star auteur in early-twenty-first-century Hollywood is Mel Gibson, previously best known for his performances in two action franchises—*Mad Max* (George Miller, 1979), *Mad Max 2: The Road Warrior* (Miller, 1981), and *Mad Max beyond Thunderdome* (Miller and George Ogilvie, 1985) and *Lethal Weapon* (1987), *Lethal Weapon 2* (1989), *Lethal Weapon 3* (1992), and *Lethal Weapon 4* (1998), all directed by Richard

Donner—and a surprising win at the Academy Awards for directing *Braveheart* (1995), a bloody action-packed biopic about the thirteenth-century Scottish hero William Wallace (played by Gibson). At the start of the new century, Gibson proved to be a versatile movie actor able to headline more than just action films, starring in the hit comedy *What Women Want* (Nancy Meyers, 2000) and the science-fiction thriller *Signs*. In 2004, at the height of his stardom, Gibson risked his reputation and his personal fortune on what seemed to be the craziest project in Hollywood history, *The Passion of the Christ,* a $30-million film detailing the final 12 hours in the life of Jesus of Nazareth. The film has all Gibson's peculiar thematic preoccupations—brutality, suffering, martyrdom—all in service of a peculiar and disconcertingly anti-Semitic argument about Jesus's final hours (championed by a small, fundamentalist group within the Catholic

Twenty-first-century Hollywood's $20-million man, Jim Carrey, playing it straight in the art-house hit *Eternal Sunshine of the Spotless Mind* (Michel Gondry, 2004).

The director Mel Gibson (*left*) and the actor James Caviezel filming *The Passion of the Christ* (2004) at the famed Cinecittà Studios in Rome in 2003. Gibson's film, financed in large part by the director himself, grossed a breathtaking $600 million worldwide.

Church). Although the film includes scene after scene of astounding brutality (it may be one of the most unrelentingly violent big-budget films ever screened), the dialogue is all in Aramaic, and its ideology hardly jibes with that of mainstream Catholicism or Christianity, *The Passion of the Christ* was one of 2004's biggest hits, earning a breathtaking $600 million worldwide. In a business where filmmakers guess at what the audience wants, Gibson, making the film he wanted to make, hit the jackpot.

Independents and Independence

In an effort to cash in on the "alternative" market in the 1990s, many of the big studios added boutique indie labels to their corporate rosters: Sony and Paramount spun off so-called classics divisions, and Fox created Fox Searchlight. Time Warner continued to use its three smaller companies—Castle Rock, New Line, and Fine Line—to diversify its annual slate. By the 1990s, two of the era's best known and most highly regarded indie labels, Miramax and Focus Features, had become "specialty units" within their parent companies, Disney and Universal, respectively.

Of these indie–art film companies, Miramax is undoubtedly the best known among the film-going public. Founded in 1979 by the brothers Bob and Harvey Weinstein, Miramax initially achieved success with negative pickups of American independent films and documentaries and a handful of European pictures. Though it would later sport a

production unit, most of Miramax's business came from smart acquisitions of completed films that for one reason or another had not interested the major studios. Best known among Miramax's early films were Steven Soderbergh's Cannes Palme d'Or–winning melodrama *sex, lies, and videotape* (1989); the American release of Peter Greenaway's NC-17 foray into the world of gangsters, sex, and food, *The Cook, the Thief, His Wife & Her Lover* (1989), and his playful adaptation of Shakespeare's *Tempest,* titled *Prospero's Books* (1991); John Sayles's *Passion Fish* (1992), a character study of a soap-opera star (Mary McDonnell) whose life is drastically altered when an accident renders her unable to walk; and Neil Jordon's gender-bending political intrigue *The Crying Game* (1992). Success proved difficult to manage on the small company's bankroll, and in 1993 the brothers sold out to Disney. The deal initially seemed to benefit both companies. The brothers continued to manage Miramax; with Disney's money they were able to release more and bigger alternative films, and Disney got to diversify its moribund film unit.

After the buyout, Miramax found considerable success on the near margins of Hollywood, distributing a number of films that crossed over into mainstream theaters and several that won major Academy Awards. *The Piano,* Jane Campion's 1993 character study, won Oscars for Actress in a Leading Role (Holly Hunter), Actress in a Supporting Role (Anna Paquin), and Campion's screenplay. Quentin Tarantino's three-part neo-noir *Pulp Fiction* (1994) was a huge box-office hit and won the Palme d'Or at Cannes and an Oscar for Best Screenplay (by Tarantino and Roger Avary). *The English Patient,* a 1996 historical drama, won nine Oscars, including Best Picture, Directing (by Anthony Minghella), and Actress in a Supporting Role (Juliette Binoche). Rob Marshall's 2003 adaptation of the Broadway musical *Chicago* won six Oscars, including Best Picture and Actress in a Supporting Role (Catherine Zeta-Jones).

Miramax co-founder Harvey Weinstein with the director Michael Moore (holding the Palme d'Or for *Fahrenheit 9/11*) at Cannes in 2004. Though Weinstein took Moore's film to Cannes under the Miramax banner, Disney forced him to turn over distribution of the film to another company (Lions Gate) and later forced him out as chief executive of the company he founded.

Ennis Del Mar (Heath Ledger, *left*) and Jack Twist (Jake Gyllenhaal), two cowboys with a secret, in Ang Lee's *Brokeback Mountain* (2005).

Despite the success of Miramax under the Disney banner, relations between the Weinsteins and executives at the Mouse became strained. They came to a head when Disney chief executive Michael Eisner refused to support Miramax's planned release of Michael Moore's political documentary *Fahrenheit 9/11* (2004). Though the film was sure to be a hit—it earned over $100 million in its first run, the most money earned by a documentary in American film history—Disney was less interested in the short-term profits than it was concerned about its relationships in Washington (where President George W. Bush's friendship was at stake) and in Florida, where the president's brother Jeb was governor (and where the company owned theme parks). Disney abandoned *Fahrenheit 9/11* (which was picked up by Lions Gate Films) and began negotiating a settlement with the Weinsteins. After distributing well over five hundred films under the Miramax banner, the Weinsteins parted company with Disney in 2005. Disney

kept the company name, and the brothers Weinstein kept the Miramax teen-pic subsidiary Dimension Films.

Miramax's primary rival in the early twenty-first century had been Focus Features, which was formed in 2002 when Vivendi Universal merged two indie outfits, Good Machine and USA Films. In retrospect, it is fair to surmise that Focus was initially patterned on Miramax. The company released a balanced slate of indie films that were as successful at the box office as they were with Motion Picture Academy voters. Among its key titles were the Holocaust-survivor film *The Pianist* (Roman Polanski, 2002), Todd Haynes's retro melodrama *Far from Heaven* (2002), Alejandro González Iñárritu's hectic ensemble film *21 Grams* (2003), Sofia Coppola's spacey melodrama *Lost in Translation* (2003), and Michel Gondry's sci-fi farce *Eternal Sunshine of the Spotless Mind*. Just as Miramax and Disney parted company, Focus hit its stride in 2005 with Jim Jarmusch's droll comedy *Broken*

Flowers, Fernando Meirelles's adaptation of the John Le Carré suspense novel *The Constant Gardener*, Ang Lee's gay-cowboy melodrama *Brokeback Mountain*, and the Jane Austen adaptation *Pride & Prejudice* (Joe Wright).

A quick look at the important contemporary independent films reveals a wide range of auteur pictures, genre movies, and niche-audience projects. Prominent among the auteur pictures were Quentin Tarantino's two-part postmodern revenge fantasy *Kill Bill: Vol. 1* (2003) and *Kill Bill: Vol. 2* (2004). Though Tarantino was something of a household name by 2003 and certainly a Hollywood A-list director, his continued association with Miramax and his self-promotion as a renegade Hollywood player were consistent with the concept, if not the fact, of independence. Much the same can be said for Steven Soderbergh, who con-

tinued to alternate between the studio mainstream (with, for example, the popular biopic *Erin Brockovich*) and the more marginal (the political tour de force, *Traffic*).

Directors similarly interested in forging a place for themselves outside the commercial mainstream and establishing a unique and uncompromised auteur signature followed Tarantino's and Soderbergh's leads. Here again the fact of independence was less significant than the indie reputation a director gained by associating with a real or a boutique indie label or a seemingly non- or anti-commercial project. Key players on the contemporary indie scene include Neil LaBute, director of the surreal comedy *Nurse Betty* (2000); Darren Aronofsky, who made the wildly stylized study of drug addiction, *Requiem for a Dream* (2000); Christopher Nolan, who directed the

thriller *Memento* (2000); and Todd Solondz, director of the sexually explicit drama *Storytelling* (2001). Several female auteurs (who rarely get work on A projects) found a home on the indie circuit. Some delved into contemporary questions regarding gender identity—for example, Kimberly Peirce's *Boys Don't Cry* (1999). Others explored growing up female—Sofia Coppola's *The Virgin Suicides* (1999) and Catherine Hardwicke's *Thirteen* (2003)—or just growing a little older—Nicole Holofcener's *Lovely and Amazing* (2001).

A handful of indie films captured the attention of the youth audience. Indeed, the most popular indie film of all time is the 1999 teen horror picture *The Blair Witch Project* (Daniel Myrick and Eduardo Sánchez), which to great effect apes the style of a typical student film to tell an otherwise familiar story about some kids who get lost in the woods. Myrick and Sánchez's film was made on a minuscule budget—an estimated $35,000—and grossed almost $150 million in domestic theaters alone. Several more polished alternative teen horror films followed, many of them played with equal amounts of thrill and satire: Wes Craven's popular *Scream* series—*Scream* (1996), *Scream 2* (1997),

(*left*) The ill-fated Lisbon girls (*from left to right*: A. J. Cook, Kirsten Dunst, Chelse Swain, and Leslie Hayman) in Sofia Coppola's 1999 adaptation of Jeffrey Eugenides' novel *The Virgin Suicides*.

and *Scream 3* (2000)—and the *Scary Movie* franchise—*Scary Movie* (Keenan Ivory Wayans, 2000), *Scary Movie 2* (Wayans, 2001), and *Scary Movie 3* (David Zucker, 2003). Though these are hardly the sorts of films one thinks of when one thinks of independent American film, they were all distributed by Miramax's indie teen label, Dimension Films. More typical of the indie scene was a series of far darker teen pics: Richard Kelly's exploration of adolescent madness, *Donnie Darko* (2001), the disconcerting coming-of-age film *Igby Goes Down* (Burr Steers, 2002), the nerd satire *Napoleon Dynamite* (Jared Hess, 2004), the antiestablishment druggie road-trip picture *Harold & Kumar Go to White Castle* (Danny Leiner, 2004), and the coming-of-age film *Garden State* (Zach Braff, 2004).

Making a film on the indie circuit became attractive to A-list actors in the early twenty-first century, as it offered these mainstream performers opportunities to showcase their talent playing against type. For example, the beautiful African American actress Halle Berry won an Academy Award for her performance in Marc Forster's *Monster's Ball* (2001). With an unflattering haircut, little makeup, and dingy clothes, Berry plays a waitress who has an affair with a racist jailer (Billy Bob Thornton) after her husband (Sean "P. Diddy" Combs) is executed. Two years later the South African model turned movie star Charlize Theron followed Berry's lead, winning an Oscar for her portrayal of the white-trash serial killer Aileen Wuornos in Patty Jenkins's indie biopic *Monster*.

Independence has always been conditional (one must be independent of someone or something) and partial (the marketplace requires concessions to the commercial mainstream). Though most contemporary indie films have emerged from within the now all-inclusive modern studio system, they have continued to offer directors working outside the commercial mainstream a degree of creative freedom and market access. Independent films have gotten a little bigger perhaps—and the truly marginal films have gotten somewhat

Halle Berry and Billy Bob Thornton as unlikely lovers in Marc Forster's indie melodrama *Monster's Ball* (2001).

more marginal—but the studios' move into boutique-indie distribution has largely proved to be a good thing for the American independent filmmaker and moviegoer alike.

The accommodation of the indie scene has proved beneficial to the studios as well. Diversifying into the small indie market may not have made the studios all that much money, but several boutique titles have added much-needed prestige to industry release slates otherwise dominated by empty-headed action pictures. Prizes won at festivals like Sundance, Cannes, Venice, Berlin, and Toronto, and Golden Globes and Oscars boost a studio's reputation and confer bragging rights. Control over the indie sector has also given the major studios something close to complete control over the entire landscape of American cinema, a degree of control that in the twenty-first century renders the term *independent* not only conditional but perhaps even obsolete.

■ ■ ■

Much as Godard's prognostication of the end of cinema would make for a neat conclusion here, there are few reasons to believe the end will happen anytime soon. A quick look at the box-office numbers for 1999–2004 suggests an astonishingly healthy industry. In 1999 the total combined (worldwide theatrical) gross for American movies was $7.3 billion, and each year after that until 2004 saw an increase: in 2000 the box office topped out at $7.6 billion; in 2001, $8 billion; in 2002, $9 billion; in 2003, $9.1 billion; and in 2004, $9.4 billion. Going to the movies remains an international pastime, and the dominant object of that pastime originates in the United States. Staggering as these numbers may be, it is important to remember that box-office revenue accounts for less than half a film's total value to its studio.

What, then, looms in the future? The industry is moving toward bigger screens and bigger formats and bigger, louder, faster, and more immersive films. But at the same time, studios have their eye on smaller screens: handheld gadgets that render the once-public practice of going to the movies more private.

Challenges to the hegemony of the major studios exist. Internet piracy is at this writing the studios' biggest concern. But the MPAA's lobbying efforts in Washington (where it has successfully pushed for increased protection for its members' copyrights) and public relations campaigns focusing on the notion that piracy hurts everyone in the business (not just movie stars, for example, but key grips and carpenters too) say less about the studios' bottom line than about what the studios would like folks to believe. Increased Internet piracy has accompanied record success at the theatrical box office and astonishing profits across the many sectors that the studios control. And who are those pirates anyway? Many of them are computer-savvy young men and women—high-school and college students—who constitute the studios' most avid customer base. They may be sharing movies online, but they are also going to the movies, renting DVDs, and participating in a movie culture that continues to benefit the companies from whom they steal.

The Internet is also a promising venue for amateur filmmakers, folks working on the far margins of Hollywood, who make movies on the cheap with little hope of compensation. At present few amateur films make the leap from the small cine-workshop sites, such as Ifilm, YouTube, AtomFilms, and Metacafe. Indeed, the artistic possibilities that those online venues make available to undiscovered filmmakers are overshadowed by the public's insatiable desire for the spectacle of "real" sex and violence.

That desire for the real has fueled the success of the few amateur videos that have found a wider audience after postings on the Web, such as the video capture of an incident of police brutality in Los Angeles (the Rodney King video) and celebrity "sex tapes" like the Pamela Anderson–Tommy Lee tape, shot by the celebrity participants themselves, stolen from their home, and surreptitiously distributed via the Web in 1995, and the 2003 Paris Hilton tape, which made the hotel heiress (absent any apparent talent) one of the most talked-about celebrities on the planet.

Unlike Anderson and Hilton, most of the people who appear in amateur videos and most of people who make them are not celebrities and fail to become part of the popular celebrity culture. The legion of amateur sex tapes and blooper reels that are posted on Web sites every day make the participants famous not for the 15 minutes Andy Warhol promised but for closer to 2 or 3—the duration of the average posting on Ifilm, YouTube, AtomFilms, or Metacafe.

A number of theaters nationwide are now screening digitally formatted films. They are doing so not so much to accommodate amateur production but to provide consistent exhibition for the vast majority of the films distributed by the major Hollywood studios. The future of cinema thus may not be cinema exactly—at least it may not involve celluloid for much longer. But that won't mean the end of cinema.

So long as there's so much money at stake, we can shrug off Godard's prediction. If there is to be an end of cinema, we can be sure it will be an event the Hollywood studios have planned for and are now engineering. Even if films will no longer be films as we have known them, even if cinema is once and for all (in some narrow way) really dead, it's not as though there will be nothing for us to pay for and watch in the future. The likes of Time Warner, Disney, Sony, Viacom, General Electric, and the News Corporation will see to that.

Source Material and Suggestions for Further Reading

————. *The Emergence of Cinema: The American Screen to 1907.* Berkeley: University of California Press, 1994.

Sklar, Robert. *Movie-Made America: A Cultural History of American Movies.* New York: Random House, 1975.

Waller, Gregory A., ed. *Moviegoing in America: A Sourcebook in the History of Film Exhibition.* Malden, Mass.: Blackwell, 2002.

CHAPTER 2:
THE SILENT ERA (1915–1928)

Beauchamp, Cari. *Without Lying Down: Frances Marion and the Powerful Women of Early Hollywood.* New York: Scribner, 1997.

Brownlow, Kevin. *Behind the Mask of Innocence: Sex, Violence, Prejudice, Crime; Films of Social Conscience in the Silent Era.* New York: Knopf, 1990.

————. *The Parade's Gone By . . : A Vivid, Nostalgic, Immediate Portrait of an Art in the Making.* New York: Knopf, 1968.

Chaplin, Charles. *My Autobiography.* New York: Simon and Schuster, 1964.

Crafton, Donald. "Pie and Chase: Gag, Spectacle and Narrative in Comedy." In Karnick and Jenkins, *Classical Hollywood Comedy,* 106–119.

Dardis, Tom. *Keaton: The Man Who Wouldn't Lie Down.* Minneapolis: University of Minnesota Press, 2002.

deCordova, Richard. *Picture Personalities: The Emergence of the Star System in America.* Champaign: University of Illinois Press, 1990.

Foner, Eric. *Give Me Liberty! An American History.* New York: Norton, 2005.

Gunning, Tom. "Buster Keaton, or the Work of Comedy in the Age of Mechanical Reproduction." In Krutnik, *Hollywood Comedians,* 73–78.

————. "Crazy Machines in the Garden of Forking Paths: Mischief Gags and the Origins of American Film Comedy." In Karnick and Jenkins, *Classical Hollywood Comedy,* 87–105.

Higashi, Sumiko. *Cecil B. DeMille and American Culture: The Silent Era.* Berkeley: University of California Press, 1994.

Jenkins, Henry, III, "Anarchistic Comedy and the Vaudeville Aesthetic." In Krutnik, *Hollywood Comedians,* 91–104.

Karnick, Kristine Brunovska, and Henry Jenkins, eds. *Classical Hollywood Comedy.* New York: Routledge, 1995.

Koszarski, Richard. *An Evening's Entertainment: The Age of the Silent Feature Picture, 1915–1928.* Berkeley: University of California Press, 1994.

————. *The Man You Loved to Hate: Erich von Stroheim and Hollywood.* New York: Oxford University Press, 1983.

Kramer, Peter. "The Making of a Comic Star: Buster Keaton and *The Saphead.*" In Karnick and Jenkins, *Classical Hollywood Comedy,* 190–210.

CHAPTER 1:
EARLY CINEMA (1893–1914)

Abel, Richard, "Motion Picture Exhibition in Manhattan, 1906–1912: Beyond the Nickelodeon." *Cinema Journal* 18, no. 2 (1979): 2–15.

————, ed. *Silent Film.* New Brunswick, N.J.: Rutgers University Press, 1996.

Bowser, Eileen. *The Transformation of Cinema: 1907–1915.* Berkeley: University of California Press, 1994.

Cook, David A. *A History of Narrative Film.* 4th ed. New York: Norton, 2004.

deCordova, Richard. *Picture Personalities: The Emergence of the Star System in America.* Champaign: University of Illinois Press, 1990.

Elsaesser, Thomas, ed. *Early Cinema: Space Frame Narrative.* London: British Film Institute, 1990.

Foner, Eric. *Give Me Liberty! An American History.* New York: Norton, 2005.

Gabler, Neal. *An Empire of Their Own: How the Jews Invented Hollywood.* New York: Crown, 1988.

Gunning, Tom. "The Cinema of Attraction: Early Film, Its Spectator, and the Avant Garde." *Wide Angle 8,* nos. 3 and 4 (1986): 66–77.

————. *D. W. Griffith and the Origins of American Narrative Form: The Early Years at Biograph.* Champaign: University of Illinois Press, 1991.

Hansen, Miriam. *Babel and Babylon: Spectatorship in American Silent Film.* Cambridge, Mass.: Harvard University Press, 1988.

Koszarski, Richard. *An Evening's Entertainment: The Age of the Silent Feature Picture, 1915–1928.* Berkeley: University of California Press, 1994.

May, Lary. *Screening Out the Past: The Birth of Mass Culture and the Motion Picture Industry.* New York: Oxford University Press, 1980.

Musser, Charles. *Before the Nickelodeon: Edwin S. Porter and the Edison Manufacturing Company.* Berkeley: University of California Press, 1991.

Krutnik, Frank, ed. *Hollywood Comedians: The Film Reader*. New York: Routledge, 2003.

Lang, Robert, ed. *The Birth of a Nation: D. W. Griffith, Director*. New Brunswick, N.J.: Rutgers University Press, 1994.

Mast, Gerald. *The Comic Mind: Comedy and the Movies*. Chicago: University of Chicago Press, 1979.

Neale, Steve, and Frank Krutnik. "The Case of Silent Slapstick." In Krutnik, *Hollywood Comedians*, 57–72.

Riblet, Doug. "The Keystone Film Company and the Historiography of Early Slapstick." In Karnick and Jenkins, *Classical Hollywood Comedy*, 168–189.

Robinson, David. *Buster Keaton*. Bloomington: University of Indiana Press, 1969.

———. *Chaplin: His Life and Art*. New York: McGraw-Hill, 1985.

———. *Hollywood in the Twenties*. Cranbury, N.J.: Barnes, 1968.

Schickel, Richard. *D. W. Griffith: An American Life*. New York: Simon and Schuster, 1984.

Sklar, Robert. *Movie-Made America: A Cultural History of American Movies*. New York: Random House, 1975.

Staiger, Janet. "Dividing Labor for Production Control: Thomas Ince and the Rise of the Studio System." *Cinema Journal* 18, no. 2 (1979): 16–25.

Vasey, Ruth. *The World according to Hollywood, 1918–1939*. Madison: University of Wisconsin Press, 1997.

Wallace, Michelle Faith. "The Good Lynching and *The Birth of a Nation*: Discourses and Aesthetics of Jim Crow." *Cinema Journal* 43, no. 1 (2003): 85–104.

Weinberg, Herman G. *The Complete Greed of Erich von Stroheim*. New York: Dutton, 1972.

CHAPTER 3:
TECHNICAL INNOVATION AND INDUSTRIAL TRANSFORMATION (1927–1938)

Balio, Tino. *Grand Design: Hollywood as a Modern Business Enterprise, 1930–1939*. Berkeley: University of California Press, 1993.

Black, Gregory D. *Hollywood Censored: Morality, Codes, Catholics, and the Movies*. Cambridge, U.K.: Cambridge University Press, 1994.

Bordwell, David, Janet Staiger and Kristin Thompson. *The Classical Hollywood Cinema: Film Style and Mode of Production to 1960*. New York: Columbia University Press, 1985.

Bordwell, David, and Kristin Thompson. "Technological Change and Classical Film Style." In Balio, *Grand Design*, 109–142.

Carroll, Noel. *The Philosophy of Horror*. New York: Routledge, 1990.

Cavell, Stanley. *Pursuits of Happiness: The Hollywood Comedy of Remarriage*. Cambridge, Mass.: Harvard University Press, 1981.

Cohan, Steven, ed. *Hollywood Musicals: The Film Reader*. London: Routledge, 2002.

Crafton, Donald. *The Talkies: American Cinema's Transition to Sound, 1926–1931*. Berkeley: University of California Press, 1999.

Doherty, Thomas. *Pre-Code Hollywood: Sex, Immorality, and Insurrection in American Culture, 1930–1934*. New York: Columbia University Press, 1999.

Elsaesser, Thomas. "Tales of Sound and Fury: Observations on the Family Melodrama." *Film Genre Reader II*, edited by Barry Keith Grant, 350–380. Austin: University of Texas Press, 1995.

Feuer, Jane. *The Hollywood Musical*. Bloomington: University of Indiana Press, 1993.

Gabler, Neal. *An Empire of Their Own: How the Jews Invented Hollywood*. New York: Crown, 1988.

Gomery, Douglas. *The Hollywood Studio System*. New York: St. Martin's, 1986.

Henderson, Brian. "Romantic Comedy Today: Semi-Tough or Impossible." In Grant, *Film Genre Reader*, edited by Barry Keith Grant, 311–313. Austin: University of Texas Press, 1986.

Kindem, Gorham. *The American Movie Industry: The Business of Motion Pictures*. Carbondale: Southern Illinois University Press, 1982.

Lewis, Jon. *Hollywood v. Hard Core: How the Struggle over Censorship Saved the Modern Film Industry*. New York: New York University Press, 2000.

Mayne, Judith. *Directed by Dorothy Arzner*. Bloomington: University of Indiana Press, 1994.

Neale, Steve. *Cinema and Technology: Image, Sound, Colour*. Bloomington: University of Indiana Press, 1985.

Randall, Richard S. *Censorship and the Movies: The Social and Political Control of a Mass Medium*. Madison: University of Wisconsin Press, 1968.

Salt, Barry. *Film Style and Technology: History and Analysis*. London: Starword, 1992.

Sarris, Andrew. *The American Cinema: Directors and Directions, 1929–1968*. New York: Dutton, 1968.

———. *"You Ain't Heard Nothing Yet": The American Talking Film, History and Memory, 1927–1949*. New York: Oxford University Press, 1998.

Schatz, Thomas. *The Genius of the System: Hollywood Filmmaking in the Studio Era*. New York: Henry Holt, 1988.

Shumway, David. "Screwball Comedies: Constructing Romance, Mystifying Marriage." *Cinema Journal* 30, no. 4 (1991): 7–23.

CHAPTER 4:
HOLLYWOOD IN TRANSITION (1939–1945)

Robert Carringer. *The Making of Citizen Kane*. Berkeley: University of California Press, 1996.

Curtis, James. *Between Flops: A Biography of Preston Sturges*. New York: Harcourt, Brace, 1982.

Doane, Mary Ann. *The Desire to Desire: The Woman's Film of the 1940s*. Bloomington: Indiana University Press, 1987.

Doherty, Thomas. *Projections of War: Hollywood, American Culture, and World War II.* New York: Columbia University Press, 1993.

Jacobs, Diane. *Christmas in July: The Life and Art of Preston Sturges.* Berkeley: University of California Press, 1992.

Kaufman, Gerald. *Meet Me in St. Louis.* London: British Film Institute, 1994.

Leff, Leonard J. *Hitchcock and Selznick: The Rich and Strange Collaboration of Alfred Hitchcock and David O. Selznick in Hollywood.* New York: Weidenfeld and Nicolson, 1987.

Modleski, Tania. *Loving with a Vengeance: Mass-Produced Fantasies for Women.* New York: Routledge, 1984.

Polan, Dana. *Power and Paranoia: History, Narrative, and the American Cinema, 1940–1950.* New York: Columbia University Press, 1986.

Rosenbaum, Jonathan, ed. *This Is Orson Welles: Orson Welles and Peter Bogdanovich.* New York: HarperCollins, 1992.

Sarris, Andrew. *The American Cinema: Directors and Directions, 1929–1968.* New York: Dutton, 1968.

Schatz, Thomas. *Boom and Bust: American Cinema in the 1940s.* Berkeley: University of California Press, 1997.

Shindler, Colin. *Hollywood Goes to War: Films and American Society, 1939–1952.* New York: Routledge, 1996.

Thomson, David. "Happiness." In *Beneath Mulholland: Thoughts on Hollywood and Its Ghosts.* New York: Knopf, 1997.

———. *Rosebud: The Story of Orson Welles.* New York: Knopf, 1996.

———. *Showman: The Life of David O. Selznick.* New York: Knopf, 1992.

Warshow, Robert. "The Gangster as Tragic Hero." In *The Immediate Experience: Movies, Comics, Theatre and Other Aspects of Popular Culture.* New York: Atheneum, 1970.

CHAPTER 5:
ADJUSTING TO A POSTWAR AMERICA (1945–1955)

Ceplair, Larry, and Steven Englund. *The Inquisition in Hollywood: Politics in the Film Community, 1930–1960.* New York: Anchor Press, 1980.

Clark, Danae. *Negotiating Hollywood: The Cultural Politics of Actors' Labor.* Minneapolis: University of Minnesota Press, 1995).

Crowe, Cameron. *Conversations with Wilder.* New York: Knopf, 1999.

Drummond, Phillip. *High Noon.* London: British Film Institute, 1997.

Francke, Lizzie. *Script Girls: Women Screenwriters in Hollywood.* London: British Film Institute, 1995.

Hillier, Jim, and Peter Wollen, eds. *Howard Hawks: American Artist.* London: British Film Institute, 1996.

Horne, Gerald. *Class Struggle in Hollywood, 1930–1950: Moguls, Mobsters, Stars, Reds, and Trade Unionists.* Austin: University of Texas Press, 2001.

Kahn, Gordon. *Hollywood on Trial: The Story of the 10 Who Were Indicted.* New York: Boni and Gaer, 1948.

Kazan, Elia. *An American Odyssey.* Edited by Michel Ciment. London: Bloomsbury, 1988.

Lewis, Jon. *Hollywood v. Hard Core: How the Struggle over Censorship Saved the Modern Film Industry.* New York: New York University Press, 2000.

———. "Trust and Anti-trust in the New Hollywood." *Michigan Quarterly Review* 35, no. 1 (1997): 85–105.

———. "We Do Not Ask You to Condone This: How the Blacklist Saved Hollywood." *Cinema Journal* 39, no. 2 (2000), 3–30.

McGilligan, Patrick, and Paul Buhle. *Tender Comrades: A Backstory of the Hollywood Blacklist.* New York: St. Martin's Press, 1997.

Kaplan, E. Ann, ed. *Women in Film Noir.* London: British Film Institute, 1998.

Kazan, Elia. *A Life.* New York: Da Capo Press, 1997.

McArthur, Colin. *The Big Heat.* London: British Film Institute, 1992.

McBride, Joseph. *Hawks on Hawks.* Berkeley: University of California Press, 1982.

Naremore, James. *More Than Night: Film Noir in Its Contexts.* Berkeley: University of California Press, 1998.

Navasky, Victor S. *Naming Names.* New York: Viking Press, 1980.

Polan, Dana. *In a Lonely Place.* London: British Film Institute, 1993.

———. *Power and Paranoia: History, Narrative, and the American Cinema, 1940–1950.* New York: Columbia University Press, 1986.

Rosenbaum, Jonathan, ed. *This Is Orson Welles: Orson Welles and Peter Bogdanovich.* New York: HarperCollins, 1992.

Ross, Murray. *Stars and Strikes: Unionization of Hollywood.* New York: Columbia University Press, 1941.

Sarris, Andrew. *The American Cinema: Directors and Directions, 1929–1968.* New York: Dutton, 1968.

———. *"You Ain't Heard Nothing Yet": The American Talking Film; History and Memory, 1927–1949.* New York: Oxford University Press, 1998.

Schatz, Thomas. *Boom and Bust: American Cinema in the 1940s.* Berkeley: University of California Press, 1997.

———. *The Genius of the System: Hollywood Filmmaking in the Studio Era.* New York: Henry Holt, 1988.

Sikov, Ed. *On Sunset Boulevard: The Life and Times of Billy Wilder.* New York: Hyperion, 1999.

Thomson, David. *Rosebud: The Story of Orson Welles.* New York: Knopf, 1996.

Vaughn, Steven. "Poltical Censorship During the Cold War." In *Movie Censorship and American Culture,* edited by Francis G. Couvares, 129–159. Washington, D.C.: Smithsonian Institute, 1996.

CHAPTER 6:
MOVING TOWARD A NEW HOLLYWOOD (1955–1967)

Doherty, Thomas. *Teenagers and Teenpics: The Juvenilization of American Movies in the 1950s*. Philadelphia: Temple University Press, 2002.

Lev, Peter. *The Fifties: Transforming the Screen, 1950–1959*. New York: Scribner, 2003.

Lewis, Jon. *Hollywood v. Hard Core: How the Struggle over Censorship Saved the Modern Film Industry*. New York: New York University Press, 2000.

———. *The Road to Romance and Ruin: Teen Films and Youth Culture*. New York: Routledge, 1992.

Levy, Shawn. *King of Comedy: The Life and Art of Jerry Lewis*. New York: St. Martin's Press, 1997.

McCann, Graham. *Marilyn Monroe*. New Brunswick, N.J.: Rutgers University Press, 1987.

McGilligan, Patrick. *Alfred Hitchcock: A Life in Darkness and Light*. New York: Regan Books, 2003.

Menand, Louis. "Paris, Texas: How Hollywood Brought the Cinema Back from France." *New Yorker*, February 17 and 24, 2003, 169–177.

Miller, Frank. *Censored Hollywood: Sex, Sin, and Violence On Screen*. Atlanta: Turner, 1994.

Monaco, Paul. *The Sixties, 1960–1969*. Berkeley: University of California Press, 2001.

Pomerance, Murray, ed. *American Cinema of the 1950s: Themes and Variations*. New Brunswick, N.J.: Rutgers University Press, 2005.

———, ed. *Enfant Terrible: Jerry Lewis in American Film*. New York: New York University Press, 2002.

Sterritt, David. *The Films of Alfred Hitchcock*. Cambridge, U.K.: Cambridge University Press, 1993.

Truffaut, François. *Hitchcock*. In collaboration with Helen G. Scott. New York: Simon and Schuster, 1967.

Warshow, Robert. "Movie Chronicle: The Westerner." In *The Immediate Experience: Movies, Comics, Theatre and Other Aspects of Popular Culture*. New York: Atheneum, 1970.

Wright, Will. *Sixguns and Society: A Structural Study of the Western*. Berkeley: University of California Press, 1975.

CHAPTER 7:
A HOLLYWOOD RENAISSANCE (1968–1980)

Bach, Stephen. *Final Cut: Dreams and Disaster in the Making of "Heaven's Gate"*. New York: New American Library, 1987.

Biskind, Peter. *Easy Riders, Raging Bulls: How the Sex-Drugs-and-Rock 'n' Roll Generation Saved Hollywood*. New York: Simon and Schuster, 1999.

Brunette, Peter, ed. *Martin Scorsese: Interviews*. Jackson: University of Mississippi Press, 1999.

Ciment, Michel. *Kubrick*. Translated by Gilbert Adair. New York: Holt, Rinehart and Winston, 1982.

Clover, Carol J. *Men, Women and Chainsaws: Gender in the Modern Horror Film*. Princeton, N.J.: Princeton University Press, 1993.

Cook, David A. "Auteur Cinema and the 'Film Generation' in 1970s Hollywood." In Lewis, *The New American Cinema*, 11–37.

———. *Lost Illusions: American Cinema in the Shadow of Watergate and Vietnam, 1970–1979*. Berkeley: University of California Press, 2000.

Corrigan, Timothy. "Auteurs and the New Hollywood." In Lewis, *The New American Cinema*, 38–63.

———. *A Cinema without Walls: Movies and Culture after Vietnam*. New Brunswick, N.J.: Rutgers University Press, 1991.

Eaton, Michael. *Chinatown*. London: British Film Institute, 1997.

Friedman, Lester. *Bonnie and Clyde*. London: British Film Institute, 2000.

Grant, Barry Keith, ed. *The Dread of Difference: Gender and the Horror Film*. Austin: University of Texas Press, 1996.

Grist, Leighton. *The Films of Martin Scorsese, 1963–1977: Authorship and Context*. New York: St. Martin's Press, 2000.

Jacobs, Diane. *Hollywood Renaissance*. Cranbury, N.J.: Barnes, 1977.

Jancovich, Mark, ed. *Horror: The Film Reader*. London: Routledge, 2001.

Kolker, Robert. *A Cinema of Loneliness: Penn, Stone, Kubrick, Scorsese, Spielberg, Altman*. New York: Oxford University Press, 2000.

Lewis, Jon. *Hollywood v. Hard Core: How the Struggle over Censorship Saved the Modern Film Industry*. New York: New York University Press, 2000.

———. "If History Has Taught Us Anything . . . Francis Coppola, Paramount Studios, and 'The Godfather' Parts I, II, and III." In Browne, Nick, ed. *Francis Ford Coppola's "The Godfather" Trilogy*. Cambridge, U.K.: Cambridge University Press, 2000, 23–56.

———. "Money Matters: Hollywood in the Corporate Era." In Lewis, *The New American Cinema*, 87–124.

———, ed. *The New American Cinema*. Durham, N.C.: Duke University Press, 1998.

———. "Trust and Anti-trust in the New Hollywood." *Michigan Quarterly Review* 35, no. 1 (1997): 85–105.

———. *Whom God Wishes to Destroy . . . : Francis Coppola and the New Hollywood*. Durham, N.C.: Duke University Press, 1995.

McDougal, Dennis. *The Last Mogul: Lew Wasserman, MCA, and the Hidden History of Hollywood*. New York: Crown, 1998.

McGilligan, Patrick. *Robert Altman: Jumping Off the Cliff*. New York: St. Martin's Press, 1989.

Modleski, Tania. *Studies in Entertainment: Critical Approaches to Mass Culture*. Bloomington: University of Indiana Press, 1986.

Morgenstern, Joseph, and Stefan Kanfer, eds. *Film 69/70: An Anthology by the National Society of Film Critics*. New York: Simon and Schuster, 1970.

Neale, Steve, and Murray Smith, eds. *Contemporary Hollywood Cinema*. London: Routledge, 1998.

Nelson, Thomas Allen. *Kubrick: Inside a Film Artist's Maze*. Bloomington: University of Indiana Press, 2000.

Prince, Stephen. *Savage Cinema: Sam Peckinpah and the Rise of Ultraviolent Movies*. Austin: University of Texas Press, 1998.

Pye, Michael, and Linda Myles. *The Movie Brats: How the Film Generation Took Over Hollywood*. New York: Holt, Rinehart and Winston, 1979.

Schatz, Thomas. "The New Hollywood," In *Film Theory Goes to the Movies*, edited by Jim Collins, Hilary Radner, and Ava Preacher Collins, 1–8. New York: Routledge, 1993.

Slocum, J. David. *Violence and American Cinema*. London: Routledge, 2000.

Tasker, Yvonne. *Fifty Contemporary Filmmakers*. London: Routledge, 2002.

Taubin, Amy. *Taxi Driver*. London: British Film Institute, 2000.

Thomson, David. *Overexposures: The Crisis in American Filmmaking*. New York: Morrow, 1981.

Wasko, Janet. *Hollywood in the Information Age: Beyond the Silver Screen*. Austin: University of Texas Press, 1995.

Wood, Robin. *Hollywood from Vietnam to Reagan*. New York: Columbia University Press, 1986.

Wright, Will. *Sixguns and Society: A Structural Study of the Western*. Berkeley: University of California Press, 1975.

Wyatt, Justin. *High Concept: Movies and Marketing in Hollywood*. Austin: University of Texas Press, 1994.

CHAPTER 8:
A NEW NEW HOLLYWOOD (1982–1999)

Balio, Tino. "'A Major Presence in All of the World's Important Markets': The Globalization of Hollywood in the 1990s." In Neale and Smith, *Contemporary Hollywood Cinema*, 58–73.

Bart, Peter. *Fade Out: The Calamitous Final Days at MGM*. New York: Morrow, 1990.

———. *The Gross: The Hits, the Flops—The Summer That Ate Hollywood*. New York: St. Martin's Press, 1999.

Björkman, Stig, in conversation with Woody Allen. *Woody Allen on Woody Allen*. New York: Grove Press, 1993.

Britton, Andrew. "Blissing Out: The Politics of Reaganite Entertainment." *Movie*, nos. 30 and 31 (1986): 1–42.

Bukatman, Scott. *Blade Runner*. London: British Film Institute, 1997.

———. "Zooming Out: The End of Offscreen Space." In Lewis, *The New American Cinema*, 248–274.

Cook, David A. *Lost Illusions: American Cinema in the Shadow of Watergate and Vietnam, 1970–1979*. Berkeley: University of California Press, 2000.

Elsaesser, Thomas. "The Blockbuster: Everything Connects, but Not Everything Goes." In Lewis, *The End of Cinema As We Know It*, 11–22.

Fleming, Charles. *High Concept: Don Simpson and the Hollywood Culture of Indulgence*. New York: Doubleday, 1998.

Gomery, Douglas. "The Hollywood Blockbuster: Industrial Analysis and Practice." In Stringer, *Movie Blockbusters*, 72–83.

———. "Hollywood Corporate Business Practice and Periodizing Contemporary Film History." In Neale and Smith, *Contemporary Hollywood Cinema*, 47–57.

Griffin, Nancy, and Kim Masters. *Hit and Run: How Jon Peters and Peter Guber Took Sony for a Ride in Hollywood*. New York: Simon and Schuster, 1996.

Guerrero, Ed. "A Circus of Dreams and Lies: The Black Film Wave at Middle Age." In Lewis, *The New American Cinema*, 328–352.

———. *Framing Blackness: The African American Image in Film*. Philadelphia: Temple University Press, 1993.

King, Geoff. *Spectacular Narratives: Hollywood in the Age of the Blockbuster*. London: Tauris, 2000.

Kleinhans, Chuck. "Independent Features: Hopes and Dreams." In Lewis, *The New American Cinema*, 307–327.

Kuhn, Annette, ed. *Alien Zone: Cultural Theory and Contemporary Science Fiction Cinema*. New York: Verso, 1990.

Lax, Eric. *Woody Allen: A Biography*. New York: Knopf, 1991.

Levy, Emanuel. *Cinema of Outsiders: The Rise of Independent American Film*. New York: New York University Press, 1999.

Lewis, Jon. "Disney after Disney: Family Business and the Business of Family." In *Disney Discourse: Producing the Magic Kingdom*, edited by Eric Smoodin, 87–105. New York: Routledge, 1994.

———, ed. *The End of Cinema As We Know It: American Film in the Nineties*. New York: New York University Press, 2002.

———. "Following the Money in America's Sunniest Company Town: Some Notes on the Political Economy of the Hollywood Blockbuster." In Stringer, *Movie Blockbusters*, 61–71.

———. "Money Matters: Hollywood in the Corporate Era." In Lewis, *The New American Cinema*, 87–124.

———, ed. *The New American Cinema*. Durham, N.C.: Duke University Press, 1998.

———. "The Perfect Money Machine(s): George Lucas, Steven Spielberg, and Auteurism in the New Hollywood." *Film International* 1 (2003), 12–26.

———. "Trust and Anti-trust in the New Hollywood." *Michigan Quarterly Review* 35, no. 1 (1997): 85–105.

———. *Whom God Wishes to Destroy . . . : Francis Coppola and the New Hollywood*. Durham, N.C.: Duke University Press, 1995.

McClintick, David. *Indecent Exposure: A True Story of Hollywood and Wall Street*. New York: Morrow, 1982.

Miller, Mark Crispin, ed. *Seeing through Movies*. New York: Pantheon, 1990.

Miller, Toby, Nitin Govil, John McMurria, and Richard Maxwell, eds. *Global Hollywood*. London: British Film Institute, 2001.

Neale, Steve, ed. *Genre and Contemporary Hollywood*. London: British Film Institute, 2002.

Neale, Steve, and Murray Smith, eds. *Contemporary Hollywood Cinema*. London: Routledge, 1998.

Pfeil, Fred. "From Pillar to Postmodern: Race, Class, and Gender in the Male Rampage Film." In Lewis, *The New American Cinema*, 146–187.

Pierson, John. *Spike, Mike, Slackers and Dykes: A Guided Tour across a Decade of Independent American Cinema*. New York: Hyperion, 1995.

Polan, Dana. *Pulp Fiction*. London: British Film Institute, 2000.

Prince, Stephen. *A New Pot of Gold: Hollywood under the Electronic Rainbow, 1980–1990*. Berkeley: University of California Press, 2000.

Redding, Judith M., and Victoria K. Brownsworth. *Film Fatales: Independent Women Directors*. Seattle: Seal Press, 1997.

Rhines, Jesse Algeron. *Black Film / White Money*. New Brunswick, N.J.: Rutgers University Press, 1999.

Rosen, David. *Off-Hollywood: The Making and Marketing of Independent Films*. With Peter Hamilton. New York: Grove Press, 1990.

Ryan, Michael, and Douglas Kellner. *Camera Politica: The Politics and Ideology of Contemporary Hollywood Film*. Bloomington: University of Indiana Press, 1990.

Sayles, John. *Thinking in Pictures: The Making of the Movie "Matewan."* Boston: Houghton Mifflin, 1987.

Stringer, Julian, ed. *Movie Blockbusters*. London: Routledge, 2003.

Tasker, Yvonne. *Fifty Contemporary Filmmakers*. London: Routledge, 2002.

Turan, Kenneth. *Sundance to Sarajevo: Film Festivals and the World They Made*. Berkeley: University of California Press, 2002.

Wasko, Janet. *Hollywood in the Information Age: Beyond the Silver Screen*. Austin: University of Texas Press, 1995.

Wyatt, Justin. *High Concept: Movies and Marketing in Hollywood*. Austin: University of Texas Press, 1994.

CHAPTER 9:
THE END OF CINEMA AS WE KNOW IT (1999–2006)

Lewis, Jon. *The End of Cinema as We Know It: American Film in the Nineties*. New York: New York University Press, 2002.

Miller, Toby, Nitin Govil, John McMurria, and Richard Maxwell, eds. *Global Hollywood*. London: British Film Institute, 2001.

Neale, Steve, ed. *Genre and Contemporary Hollywood*. London: British Film Institute, 2002.

Stringer, Julian, ed. *Movie Blockbusters*. London: Routledge, 2003.

Glossary

A

Academy aperture, also called **Academy ratio.** The **frame** size established by the **Academy of Motion Picture Arts and Sciences** in 1932 to standardize sound film and used until 1952. The Academy aperture indicates an **aspect ratio** of 4:3, or 1.33:1. Non-widescreen televisions still use this ratio. See also **widescreen.**

Academy of Motion Picture Arts and Sciences (AMPAS). A professional organization of more than six thousand motion-picture professionals founded to advance the arts and sciences of motion pictures, foster educational activities involving the professional community and the public at large, and most famously, to recognize outstanding achievements with the annual Academy Awards.

accelerated montage. A **sequence** of shots of increasingly shorter length that creates an atmosphere of excitement and tension. See also **shot.**

action editing. Frequent cutting that uses multiple camera positions to create an action **sequence.** See also **cut; editing.**

actioner. An industry term for an action film.

Actors Studio. An acting school founded in 1947 in New York City by Elia Kazan, Cheryl Crawford, and Robert Lewis. The Actors Studio became the most famous, if not the foremost, acting academy for American stage and screen actors. Emphasizing "the Method," Actors Studio teachers Lee and Paula Strasberg famously tutored Marlon Brando and Al Pacino, among many others. See also **Method.**

actualities. From a French word referring to current events; short nonfiction (silent) films made at the end of the nineteenth century in France by two brothers, Auguste and Louis Lumière.

ADR. See **automatic dialogue replacement.**

aerial shot. A **shot** from above, usually from a plane, helicopter, or crane. See also **crane shot.**

A features, also called **A films, A movies, A pictures.** The term used to describe expensive studio features made with top-flight talent (writers, directors, and actors). See also **feature.**

Allied Artists. A subsidiary of Monogram Pictures, a Poverty Row producer and distributor of **B films,** founded in 1946.

alternating focal lengths. Using different lenses in a **sequence** to present a given subject from a variety of points of view. See also **lens; point of view.**

ambient sound. Sound that emanates from the ambience (or background) of the **setting** being filmed and is recorded during **production** or **postproduction.**

America First Committee. An organization formed by isolationists in 1940 to persuade President Franklin Roosevelt to support the 1939 Neutrality Act and keep the United States out of World War II. Its most famous spokesman was the aviator Charles Lindbergh.

American International Pictures (AIP). A production and distribution company, founded in 1956 by James Nicholson and Samuel Z. Arkoff, that specialized in **exploitation films.** Best known among its more than five hundred releases are *I Was a Teenage Werewolf* (Gene Fowler Jr., 1957), *The Trip* (Roger Gorman, 1967), and *Three in the Attic* (Richard Wilson, 1968).

American Mutoscope and Biograph Company, also known as **Biograph.** An early film outfit, founded in 1896, that was the principal rival of the Edison Manufacturing Company in the early years of American cinema.

analog format. One of two ways of storing recorded monaural or stereophonic sound (the other is **digital format**). Analog format involves an analogous (or 1:1) relationship between the sound wave and its stored version; in other words, the recorded sound wave is a copy of the original wave.

anamorphic lens. A **lens** that squeezes a wide image to fit the dimensions of a **35mm** film **frame.** In projection, an anamorphic lens on a projector reverses the process and projects the wide image on the **screen.** See also **widescreen.**

animatics. An animated **storyboard** composed of rough drawings or computer-generated characters that are composited with video recording or live-action scenes to give both actors and digital artists a guide for the positioning of animated characters and other **digital effects** in the final composite.

animation. The techniques that make inanimate objects move on the **screen,** including drawing directly on the film, photographing animation cells individually, and photographing objects one **frame** at a time while adjusting their position in between photographs. See also **stop-motion photography.**

animatronic puppetry. Electronic puppetry—controlled by hand, a remote device, cable, or computer—used in a live-action shoot.

answer print. The first combined print of a film, incorporating picture, sound, and **special effects,** which the **editor** views to determine whether further changes are needed before creating the **final cut.**

antagonist. The major character in a film whose values or behavior is in conflict with that of the **protagonist.**

antimontage. The film theory that holds that the ground zero of cinema is the **shot** and not the **cut** (as purported by the **montage theory**).

antirealism. A **treatment** that goes against the dominant tendencies of **realism.** However, realism and antirealism (like realism and fantasy) are not strictly opposed polarities. See also **expressionism; mise-en-scène.**

aperture. The opening in a camera's **lens** that defines the **exposure** of each **frame** of film. See also **f-stop.**

arc light. The source of high-energy illumination on the movie **set** and in the film projector; also, the principle source of film lighting used during the 1920s and in three-strip **Technicolor.** Arc light is produced by an electric current that arcs across the gap between two pieces of carbon (the direct-current carbon arc) or, more recently, by mercury that arcs between tungsten electrodes sealed in a glass bulb.

Arriflex. A light, portable camera first used in the late 1950s. The Arriflex was essential to the mobile, handheld photography of the **New Wave** and is essential to most contemporary cinematography. The **Mitchell camera,** however, is the film industry's workhorse.

art director. The person responsible for a film's **set** design and graphics.

art houses. Small theaters that sprang up in the major cities of the United States during the 1950s to show "art films" as opposed to "commercial films"—a distinction that can no longer be made so clearly because of the mechanisms of international funding and the studios' acquisition of independent distribution companies.

aspect ratio. The ratio of the width to the height of the cinematic image, or **frame.** Contemporary widescreen ratios vary, but the most common are 1.66:1 in Europe and 1.85:1 in the United States. Anamorphic processes such as **CinemaScope** can range from 2.00:1 to 2.55:1. See also **Academy aperture; anamorphic lens; widescreen.**

associative editing. The cutting together of shots to establish their metaphoric or symbolic—as opposed to their narrative—relationship. The prehistoric bone that becomes a futuristic space station in Stanley Kubrick's *2001: A Space Odyssey* (1968) is a prime example. See also **cut; editing; match cut; shot.**

asynchronous sound, also called **contrapuntal sound.** Sound whose source is not clear from the film image. Contrast with **synchronous sound.**

Audion tube. Lee De Forest's vacuum tube, a device that first permitted the amplification of audio signals.

auteur. A **director** or other creative person with a recognizable and distinctive style who is considered the prime "author" of a film.

auteurism, also called **auteur theory.** A film theory and historical methodology based on the idea that the **director** is the sole "author" of a movie.

automatic dialogue replacement (ADR). Re-recording done electronically. ADR is a faster, less expensive, and more technically sophisticated process than that involved in recording sound live.

B

backlight. Lighting, usually positioned behind and in line with the subject and the camera, used to create highlights on the subject as a means of separating it (or him or her) from the background and increasing the appearance of three-dimensionality.

back lots. Large tracts of open land that were owned by the studios and used to simulate various locations.

backstory. A fictional history of the situation exposed at the start of a main story.

beats. An industry term borrowed from music to refer to moments of significant action in a film.

best boy. The first assistant electrician to the **gaffer** on a movie production **set.** The term is also used to refer to a production's gofer, or errand boy (or girl).

B films, also called **B features, B pictures, B movies.** Films made cheaply and quickly, often reusing **sets** and costumes from more expensive productions. B films were used to fill the bottom half of a double bill when double features were the industry standard. See also **feature.**

biopic. A film biography.

bit player. An actor with a small speaking part in a film.

blacklist. The industry-wide purge of alleged Communist influence between 1947 and 1959. All told, about three hundred writers, directors, producers, and actors were rendered unemployable due to often unfounded accusations regarding their political and/or union affiliations.

Black Maria. The first movie studio: a crude, hot, cramped shack in New Jersey where Thomas Edison and his staff began making movies.

blaxploitation. **Exploitation films,** popular in the early 1970s, featuring African American actors and themes. Important blaxploitation titles include *Shaft* (Gordon Parks, 1971) and *Super Fly* (Gordon Parks Jr., 1972).

blimp. An awkward soundproofing cover for movie cameras that was used in the early years of sound. Most cameras today are constructed with internal soundproofing.

blind bidding. A system no longer in use, in which theater owners were forced by the studios to bid on films without the benefit of exhibitor screenings.

block booking. The practice whereby distributors forced exhibitors to rent its films in large groups, or "blocks," in advance of production, with the blocks tied to several desirable titles. Initiated by Adolph Zukor in 1916, block booking became fundamental to the monopoly structure that was prevalent in the studio era. Block booking was ruled illegal by the U.S. Supreme Court as part of the 1948 *Paramount* decision.

blockbuster. A film that is enormously popular or was so costly to make that it must be enormously successful to make a profit. The first blockbusters were probably Italian spectacles like *Cabiria* (Giovanni Pastrone, 1914), followed by D. W. Griffith's epics *The Birth of a Nation* (1915) and *Intolerance* (1916). During the 1920s, films like *The Thief of Bagdad* (Raoul Walsh, 1924) and *Ben-Hur* (Fred Niblo, 1925) were conceived and marketed as blockbusters, as was David O. Selznick's *Gone with the Wind* (Victor Fleming, 1939) in the 1930s. In the 1950s and 1960s, the epic-scale widescreen blockbuster—for example Cecil B. DeMille's *The Ten Commandments* (1956)—became a veritable genre. More recent examples include *Jaws* (Steven Spielberg, 1975), *Star Wars* (George Lucas, 1977), *Raiders of the Lost Ark* (Spielberg, 1981), *Batman* (Tim Burton, 1989), *Jurassic Park* (Spielberg, 1993), and *Pearl Harbor* (Michael Bay, 2001). See also **film spectacle.**

blocking, also called **theatrical blocking.** The physical and spatial relationships among figures and settings on the stage or in a **frame.**

blue-screen photography. A special-effects process that involves shooting live action, models, or miniatures in front of a bright blue screen, leaving the background of the shot unexposed. The resulting footage can be composited with other elements, such as traveling mattes, in the primary film. Blue-screen photography is now often supplanted by **green-screen photography,** used in **digital effects.**

boom. A mechanical device for holding a microphone in the air, out of range of the camera. A boom can be moved in almost any direction.

broadcast. The transmission of an electromagnetic signal over a widely dispersed area.

C

cable television. The transmission of television signals via wire instead of broadcast radio waves. Although it was originally developed to permit TV transmission to special geographic areas, cable television has become a popular alternative to broadcast television.

Cahiers du cinéma. A Paris-based film journal founded by André Bazin, Jacques Doniol-Valcroze, and Joseph-Marie Lo Duca in 1951 that featured important articles by future directors of the **New Wave.** In the late 1950s, *Cahiers du cinéma* promoted *les politique des auteurs,* the auteur theory, which became enormously popular with filmmakers and film students in the late 1960s and the 1970s in the United States. See also **auteurism.**

cameo. A small but significant role often played by a famous actor.

camera angle. The perspective that the camera takes on the subject being shot. **Low angle, high angle,** and **tilt angle** are the three most common.

camera crew. The technicians on a film **set** concerned either with the camera or with electricity and lighting.

camera obscura. Literally, "dark chamber"; a box (or a room in which the viewer stands), into which light enters through a tiny hole (or a **lens**) on one side and projects an image from the outside onto the opposite side (or wall).

camera operator. The member of the crew who operates the camera.

camera point of view. The moments in a film when the camera takes on the physical vantage point of a character in a **scene.**

Cannes Festival. An international film festival that has been held annually in Cannes, France, since 1939. Cannes is generally held to be the most prestigious film festival in the world.

casting. The process of choosing and hiring actors for a movie.

cel. A transparent sheet of celluloid or similar plastic on which drawings or lettering may be made for use in **animation** or **intertitles.**

celluloid roll film, also called **motion-picture film, film stock, raw film stock.** Long strips of perforated cellulose acetate on which a rapid succession of still photographs can be recorded. One side of the strip is layered with an emulsion consisting of light-sensitive crystals and dyes; the other side is covered with a backing that reduces reflections. Each strip is perforated with **sprockets** that facilitate the movement of the stock through the sprocket wheels of the camera, the processor, and the projector. Manufactured in several standard formats. See also **frame; still.**

CGI. See **digital effects.**

chiaroscuro. The use of deep gradations and subtle variations of light and dark in an image.

cineaste. An artistically committed filmmaker. See also **director.**

CinemaScope. The trade name used by 20th Century-Fox for its anamorphic widescreen process. *CinemaScope* is frequently used today to refer to all anamorphic processes. See also **anamorphic lens.**

cinématographe. A compact, portable hand-cranked machine invented by Auguste and Louis Lumière and first exhibited in Paris in 1895. It was a camera, a processing device, and a projector all in one.

cinematographer, also called **director of photography (DP).** The person responsible for camera technique and the lighting of a movie during filming.

cinematography. Motion-picture photography.

cinema verité. Literally, "cinema truth," as originally used in 1950s France by the filmmaker Jean Rouch; a kind of nonfiction cinema that utilized lightweight camera and sound equipment, small crews, and direct (and often confrontational) interviews. The term now often refers to a visual style characterized by handheld camerawork and live recorded sound.

cinephile. A person who loves cinema.

Cinerama. A **widescreen** process invented by Fred Waller that requires three electronically synchronized cameras. First used in the 1952 film *This Is Cinerama,* Cinerama was abandoned in 1962 in favor of an anamorphic process marketed under the same name.

clapper board, sometimes called **clapboard.** Two short wooden boards that are hinged together, on which essential identifying information—some of which changes with each **take**—is written in chalk. The person handling the device claps the boards together in front of the camera and says the number of the take. The resulting reference marks, on the photographic film and the sound-recording tape, facilitate the rematching of sounds and images during **editing.** The "clap" has been widely replaced by electronic syncing devices.

close-up. In its precise meaning, a **shot** of a human subject's face or other object alone; more generally, any close shot.

color timing. The color balance of an image or **scene** or any process used to color-correct or balance an image or scene so that color continuity is maintained throughout a film.

colorization. Digital technology used, in a process much like **hand-tinting,** to "paint" colors on the **film stock** of movies that were meant to be seen in black-and-white.

compilation film. A feature or short subject composed of stock or found footage from other films.

computer-generated character. A film character that is completely computer generated. Computer-generated characters are often integrated into live-action scenes—such as the withered Gollum of Peter Jackson's *Lord of the Rings* trilogy (2001, 2002, 2004)—and are made to star in **CGI** environments—such as the "synthespians" of Andrew Adamson and Vicky Jenson's *Shrek* (2001) and Hironobu Sakaguchi and Moto Sakakibara's *Final Fantasy: The Spirits Within* (2001).

computer-generated effects. Special effects created by digital technology and transferred to film. See also **in-camera effects; laboratory effects.**

computer graphics. Electronically generated **animation.** Used since the late 1970s to provide credit **sequences** and **special effects** for theatrical films, television commercials, and network logos.

continuity. The final editing structure of a completed film. Also, the arrangement of events by **editing** so that they appear to have occurred continuously when, in fact, they were shot out of sequence.

continuity editing, also called **invisible editing.** The seemingly imperceptible **editing** of shots so that the action of a **sequence** appears to be continuous. Film historians use the term *invisible editing* to describe this aspect of the classical Hollywood style, in which the **directors** endeavored to mask marks of authorial control. Classical Hollywood films seem simply to unfold before the viewers' eyes without any showy film techniques distracting from the seamless flow of the picture. See also **shot.**

crane shot. An **aerial shot** taken from a mobile crane.

creative geography. The notion that a **director** can create through **editing** a semblance of the real space attended in a given film.

credits. The list of the writers, actors, technical personnel, and production staff involved in making a film.

crosscutting, also called **intercutting** or **parallel editing.** The **editing** of shots from two or more **sequences,** actions, or stories to suggest **parallel action** in a single scene, as in D. W. Griffith's *Intolerance* (1916). See also **cutting; shot.**

crossover. An industry term used to describe a film made for a certain (usually small) target audience that has success in (and thus "crosses over" into) another (usually larger) market.

cut. A direct change from one **shot** to another; that is, the precise point at which shot A ends and shot B begins. See also **cutting; shot.**

cutting, also called **splicing.** The joining together of two shots. The **editor** must first cut (or splice) each shot from its respective roll of film before gluing or taping all the shots together. See also **editing; shot.**

D

dailies, also called **rushes.** Usually, synchronized picture-sound work prints of a day's shooting that can be studied by the **director, editor,** and other crew members before the next day's shooting begins.

day for night. The technique used to shoot night scenes during the day. The effect is created by stopping down the **aperture** or using special lens filters. Compare with **night for night.**

deep focus. A technique that exploits **depth of field** to render subjects both near the camera **lens** and far away with equal clarity and permits the composition of the image in depth. Orson Welles's *Citizen Kane* (1941) was one of the earliest films to use deep-focus shots as a basic structural element.

denouement. The resolution, or conclusion, of a narrative.

depth of field. The range of distances from the camera in which an object remains in sharp **focus.**

desaturated. Color-film images that are dull, washed out, and gray.

diegetic sound. Sound that originates from a source within the world created by a film, such as on-screen and offscreen sounds heard by characters. See also **ambient sound; nondiegetic sound.**

digital effects, also called **CGI (computer-generated imagery). Special effects** created by computer imaging, so that the image is generated and/or manipulated by computer software.

digital file. The series of binary numbers converted from the original light signal during digital-image recording and then stored on a disc. A digital file can be used to reconstruct an original image, or it can be manipulated electronically by mathematical formulas to create a new one.

digital format. The term used for a certain way of storing information; with regard to film, digital format refers to the conversion of aural and visual information into binary, numeric form. The result is a final print that is pristine and does not degrade.

Digital input device (DID), also called **dinosaur input device.** A metal puppet armature with electronic sensors at its pivot points that can generate a digital wire-frame model in a computer when put through a series of maneuvers. The DID was developed by Craig Hayes and Phil Tippett to assist stop-motion model animators in creating computer **animation** for Steven Spielberg's *Jurassic Park* (1993). See also **stop-motion photography.**

digital intermediate process. The process by which a film **negative** is converted into digital files in order to undergo digital manipulation (such as **color timing** or the addition of **computer-generated effects**) before being converted back into film.

digital matte painting. The use of computer "paint" software to create photorealistic matte paintings (images that are intended to be integrated with live-action footage) electronically, as opposed to traditional matte paintings, which are made by hand.

digital set. A completely malleable digital environment, or **set,** within which computer animators can control such variables as lighting, camera position and movement, and the movement of objects. See also **animation.**

direct-cinema documentaries. The predominant **documentary** style in the United States since the early 1960s. Direct-cinema documentaries are similar to (or, some argue, the same as) **cinema verité** in that they use light, mobile equipment and stringently avoid narration. Unlike cinema verité, however, most direct-cinema documentaries eschew participation on the part of the filmmaker.

director. The person who generally (a) determines and realizes on the **screen** an artistic vision of a **screenplay;** (b) directs actors' performances; (c) works closely with the **production designer** to create the look of the film, especially by choosing locations; (d) oversees the work of the **cinematographer** and other key production personnel; and (e) in most cases supervises all **postproduction** activity, especially the **editing.** See also **auteur.**

director of photography (DP). See **cinematographer.**

director's cut. The version of a film preferred by its **director.** Usually the director's cut is longer, more graphically sexual, or more violent than the **release print** of the film. Director's cuts are often included in boxed sets of DVDs to encourage consumers to buy or rent the DVD version of a film they already saw in a theater.

dissolve, frequently called **lap dissolve.** A transitional or expressive device that superimposes a **fade-out** over a **fade-in** so that one image seems to overlap another. See also **soft cuts.**

distribution, also called **theatrical distribution.** The distribution of films through normal commercial agencies and theaters.

documentary. A term coined by John Grierson in the 1920s to describe formally structured nonfiction films like those of Robert Flaherty. *Documentary* has come to refer to any film that is not entirely fictional.

Dolby. A system (named for its inventor, Ray Dolby) for audio recording and playback that reduces background noise and improves frequency response.

dolly. A wheeled support for a camera that permits the **cinematographer** to make noiseless moving shots. See also **dolly shot.**

dolly shot, also called **traveling shot.** A **shot** taken by a camera fixed to a **dolly.** See also **tracking shot.**

double exposure. A **special effect** in which one **shot** is superimposed on another. The effect may be expanded to create a **multiple exposure.**

DP. See **cinematographer.**

DTS. The abbreviation for *digital theater systems,* a multichannel, digital surround-sound format used in movie theaters and better home theater systems.

dubbing. The recording and **postsynchronization** of dialogue or **sound effects,** as, for example, in foreign-language films. See also **sound track.**

duration. The time a movie takes to unfold on-screen. For any movie, three kinds of duration can be identified: story duration, plot duration, and **screen** duration. Duration has two related components: **real time** and cinematic time.

E

ECU. See **extreme close-up.**

editing. The process by which an **editor** combines and coordinates individual shots into a cinematic whole. See also **shot.**

editor. The person who supervises the **cutting** of the shots of a film to create its final structure. See also **shot.**

electronic compositing. The manipulation of film images in digital **postproduction** using nonlinear editing systems to retouch shots, composite synthetic images, or integrate separate photographic elements into one.

ellipsis. Generally, an omission of time—the time that separates one **shot** from another—to create a dramatic or comedic impact.

emulsion. A thin, light-sensitive coating of chemicals covering the base of **film stock.**

ensemble acting. An approach to acting that emphasizes the interaction of actors, not individual movie stars. Robert Altman's films, such as *MASH* (1970) and *Nashville* (1975), famously feature ensemble acting.

establishing shot, also called **master shot** or **cover shot.** A **shot,** usually a **long shot,** that orients the audience in a film narrative by providing visual information (such as location) for the **scene** that follows. It is also called a *master shot* or a *cover shot* because the **editor** can repeat it later in the film to remind the audience of the location, thus "covering" the **director** by avoiding the need to reshoot.

experimental films, also called **avant-garde films.** A term implying that such films are in the vanguard, ahead of traditional films. Experimental films usually feature unfamiliar, unorthodox, or obscure subject matter and are ordinarily made by independent (even underground) filmmakers, not studios, often with innovative techniques that call attention to, question, and even challenge conventional filmmaking practices.

exploitation films. A negative term for mostly low-budget films designed to succeed commercially by appealing to the baser instincts of the moviegoing public.

exposure. The amount of light allowed to strike the surface of a film. Film can be underexposed to create dark, murky images or overexposed to create lighter ones. See also **aperture; f-stop.**

expressionism. An artistic (including cinematic) style originating in Germany in the early twentieth century that sought to use images to express an emotional state or subjective responses to objective and social reality. Expressionist films were usually characterized by **antirealism** or an explicitly psychological **mise-en-scène** and hard, **chiaroscuro** lighting.

external sound. A form of **diegetic sound** that comes from a place within the world of the story that viewers and the characters in the **scene** hear but do not see. See also **ambient sound.**

extra. Usually, an actor who appears in a nonspeaking or crowd role and receives no **screen** credit.

extreme close-up, sometimes abbreviated **ECU.** A very close **shot** of a detail, such as a person's eye, a ring on a finger, or a watch face. See also **close-up.**

extreme long shot, sometimes abbreviated **ELS.** A **shot** that places the human figure far away from the camera, thus revealing much of the landscape.

eye-level shot. A **shot** that is made from the observer's eye level and usually implies that the observer's attitude is neutral toward the subject being photographed.

eye-line match, or **eye-line match cut.** A type of **match cut** that joins **shot** A, a **point-of-view** shot of a person looking offscreen in one direction, and shot B, which shows the person or object at which the person in shot A is looking.

F

fade-in. A transitional device in which a **shot** made on black-and-white film fades in from a black field (or, on color film, from a color field). See also **soft cuts.**

fade-out. A transitional device in which a **shot** made on black-and-white film fades out to a black field (or, on color film, to a color field).

falling action. The events that follow the climax and bring a narrative to its conclusion (the **denouement**).

fast motion. Action filmed more slowly than the standard sound-film speed of 24 **frames per second** so that when the processed film is projected at normal speed, the action appears to be accelerated. Most silent films were shot at nearly 16 frames per second, so they display unintentional fast motion when projected at sound speed, as they frequently are today.

feature. The main film in a program of several films or any film that is more than 4 reels (approximately 45 minutes) long. The standard theatrical feature length is 90 to 120 minutes. Contrast with **short.**

fill light. A secondary light or one that illuminates areas not lit by the **key light.**

film clip. A short section of a movie that is usually shown for the purpose of reviewing or previewing. Film clips are also used to make **compilation films.**

film gauge. The width of **film stock,** measured in millimeters (mm). Standard commercial film is 35mm, although 16mm is also used, especially in lower-budget films made before the advent of digital video; 70mm film produced from 65mm negative stock is often used for epic productions; Super 8mm is basically the province of amateurs; and 8mm is now obsolete. See also **format.**

film noir. Literally, "black film"; a French term for American films that were first made in the 1940s and share certain "dark" characteristics, such as a sordid urban atmosphere, **low-key lighting,** night-for-night shooting, shady characters, and labyrinthine plots dealing with violent crime. See also **key light; night for night.**

filmography. A list of films, their **director,** and their release dates. A filmography is similar to a bibliography.

film spectacle. A term originally used to describe silent-film epics but used more recently to refer to any film that depends on spectacular **special effects.**

film stock. The basic material of film, made of cellulose triacetate and coated with photographic emulsions.

film stock speed, also called **film speed** or **exposure index.** The rate at which film must move through a camera in order to capture an image correctly. Very fast film requires little light to capture and fix the image; very slow film requires a lot of light.

filter. A plate of glass, plastic, or gelatin that alters the quality of light passing through a **lens** and thus the tone or intensity of its illumination.

final cut. A film in its completed form. See also **director's cut; rough cut.**

fine cut. The result of the fine-tuning of a film's **rough cut** (through as many versions as necessary) by the **editor** in consultation with the **director** and the **producer.**

first-person camera, also called **subjective camera.** Camerawork in which the camera adopts the **point of view** of a character in the film.

first run. Before 1980, the **distribution** of a new film to a limited number of showcase theaters. On its second run a film is usually distributed to a large number of theaters in less exclusive locations. After 1980, *first run* referred to the initial release of movies, many of which were released to thousands of theaters nationwide on the same weekend.

fish-eye lens. A radically distorting **wide-angle lens** with an angle of view that approaches 180 degrees.

flashback. A **shot**, a **scene**, or **sequence**—or sometimes a major part of a film—inserted into the narrative present in order to recapitulate the narrative past.

flash-forward. Like a **flashback**, a **shot**, a **scene**, or a **sequence** outside the narrative present, but in this case one that is projected into the narrative future.

flatbed. A pre-digital machine used for **editing,** or a table across which footage on reels is pulled horizontally from left to right.

flat character. A character who is one-dimensional and easily remembered because his or her motivations and actions are predictable.

flat shot. A **shot** executed at a right angle to its subject.

floodlight. A lamp that produces soft (diffuse) light.

focal length. The distance, in millimeters, from the optical center of a **lens** (a point midway between the front and rear elements) to the emulsion surface of the **film stock** when the lens is sharply focused on "infinity"—that is, an extremely distant object. A lens with a short focal length is called a **wide-angle lens**; one with a long focal length is called a **telephoto lens.**

focus. The clarity and sharpness of an image, limited to a certain range of distance from the camera.

focus puller. An assistant **camera operator** responsible for following and maintaining the **focus** during shots. See also **shot.**

Foley sounds. A special category of **sound effects,** invented in the 1930s by Jack Foley, a sound technician at Universal Studios. Technicians known as Foley artists, or footstep artists, work in specially equipped studios, where they use a variety of props and other equipment to simulate the sounds of footsteps, opening doors, jingling car keys, cutlery hitting a plate, people or objects being punched or kicked, and so on.

formalism. An artistic style that focuses on form rather than content. The philosophy of formalism posits that meaning is a function of the formal features of a discourse (usually **editing**).

format, also called **gauge.** The dimensions of a **film stock** and its perforations, as well as the size and shape of the image **frame** seen on-screen. Formats range from Super 8mm through 70mm (and beyond, to include specialized formats such as IMAX), but they are generally limited to three standard gauges: Super 8mm, 16mm, and 35mm. See also **film gauge.**

frame. The smallest compositional unit of film structure; the individual photographic image both in projection and on the filmstrip. *Frame* also designates the boundaries of the image as an anchor for composition.

frames per second (fps). The number of still images that pass through the camera or projector per second. Sound film usually runs at 24 fps, video at 25 fps. See also **still.**

framing. The process by which a **cinematographer** determines what will appear within the borders of the moving image (the **frame**) during a **shot.**

franchise films. Films produced with (a series of) sequels in mind—for example, *Star Wars* (1977, 1980, 1983, 1999, 2002, 2005) and *Batman* (1989, 1992, 1995, 1997, 2005).

freeze frame. A **shot** that replicates a **still.** The effect is achieved by printing a single **frame** many times in succession.

f-stop. The setting on a **lens** that indicates the diameter of the **aperture** (for example, f-1, f-1.4, f-2, f-2.8, f-4, f-5.6, f-8, f-11, f-16, f-22, f-32, f-45, f-64). The size of the aperture determines how much light the lens will transmit to the **emulsion** surface of the film and therefore determines the visual quality of the image imprinted on the **negative.** The larger the f-stop number, the smaller the aperture and the greater the **depth of field.**

full shot, also called **full-figure shot.** A **shot** that includes a human subject's entire body and often a three-fourths view of the **set.**

F/X. See **special effects.**

G

gaffer. The chief electrician on a movie production **set.**

gauge. See **format.**

gel. A sheet of colored material placed in front of the lighting instruments on a movie production **set** to act as a filter, altering the tone, color, or quality of the illumination.

genre. A category used to classify a film in terms of certain general patterns of form and content. Examples include western, the horror film, and the gangster film.

green-screen photography. A special-effects process that involves shooting live action, models, or miniatures in front of a Chroma-key green screen, leaving the background of the shot unexposed. This produces footage that can later be composited with other elements and images.

grip. The person who rigs up equipment on a movie production set, such as lights and props, and makes sure they function properly.

gross. The total amount of money a film makes in ticket and rental receipts before costs are deducted.

H

handheld shot. A **shot** made with a portable, single-operator camera.

hand-tinting. A rudimentary color process used in the silent era to literally stain black-and-white film. A specific section of the positive print of a film—a key scene, for example—is dipped into a transparent aniline dye solution. When projected, the stained image appears to be in color (though the film was shot with black-and-white film stock).

high angle, also called **downward angle.** A high-angle **shot** is made by placing the camera above the action. See also **camera angle.**

high-concept entertainment. An industry term for a film that can be described in twenty-five words or fewer based on "ideas that you can hold in your hand," (according to the high-concept filmmaker Steven Spielberg). These films are developed and produced with an eye toward marketing schemes; they are often pre-sold properties (made from popular novels, comic books, or sequels) and routinely feature popular movie stars. *High concept* is sometimes used by film critics as a perjorative term for films that seem to appeal crassly to the (dumbest) tastes of the broadest popular audience.

high contrast. Having sharply distinguished hues; a term used to describe color **film stock.**

high-key lighting. Lighting that produces an image with very little contrast between darks and lights. Its even, flat illumination expresses virtually no opinions about the subject being photographed. See also **key light.**

Hollywood style. A general and informal descriptive term used for the look of films made during the classical Hollywood or studio era (roughly, 1928–1945). The Hollywood style was characterized by linear, third-person storytelling and a seamless, practical visual style that aimed to make audiences forget they were watching a movie.

holography. A modern photographic technique that uses laser beams to replicate three-dimensionality.

horizontal monopoly. A business enterprise that controls the production of a product from development through **distribution.** Contrast with **vertical monopoly.**

I

IMAX. An immersive, big screen alternative to the multiplex experience first introduced in the early 1970s that became significantly more popular in the late 1990s as studio action features were screened in select IMAX venues. The standard IMAX screen is over 72-feet wide and 52-feet high.

immersive. A term from (computer) gaming culture that refers to works (games, films, amusement-park rides) that immerse the viewer-participant in a fictive world.

improvisation. Acting in which the actors' extemporize—that is, they base their performance (especially the delivery of their lines) only loosely on a written script. Improvisation may take place by design (the director John Cassavetes encouraged actors to improvise, as does Martin Scorsese), or it may be the result of a lucky accident, as when actors forget their written lines or stage directions but nonetheless produce moments interesting enough that the director uses them in the film.

in-camera effects. **Special effects** created in the production camera (the camera used for shooting a film) on the original **negative.** One example is **split screen.** See also **computer-generated effects; laboratory effects.**

inciting moment. The event or situation during the exposition stage of a narrative that sets the rest of the narrative in motion.

intercutting. See **crosscutting.**

interior monologue. One variation on the subjective **point of view** of an individual character that allows the viewer to see a character on-screen and somehow hear (via **voice-over**) that character's thoughts. See also **first-person camera.**

International Film Importers and Distributors of America (IFIDA). The trade organization for companies importing films to the United States.

intertitles, sometimes called **title cards.** Printed titles that appear within the main body of a film to convey dialogue and other narrative information. Intertitles are common in (but not essential to) silent film.

invisible editing. See **continuity editing.**

iris-in, iris-out. Optical wipe effects in which the wipe line is a circle. The terms are named after the *iris diaphragm*, which controls the amount of light passing through a camera lens. The *iris-in* begins with a small circle, which expands to a partial or full image; the *iris-out* is the reverse. See also **wipe.**

iris shot. A **shot** in which a circular device that masks the **lens** contracts to isolate, or expands to reveal, an area of the **frame** for symbolic or narrative visual effect.

J

jump cut. A **cut** that is made in the midst of a continuous **shot** or a mismatched cut between shots (the opposite of the apparent seamlessness of a **match cut**). Jump cuts create discontinuity in cinematic time and space and draw attention to the medium itself, as opposed to its content.

K

key light. The main light on a **set,** normally placed at a 45-degree angle to the camera-subject axis, mixed in a contrast ratio with **fill light,** depending on the desired effect. See also **high-key lighting.**

Kinemacolor. An early two-color film process invented by Charles Urban and C. Albert Smith.

Kinetograph. The first viable motion-picture camera, invented in 1889 by W. K. L. Dickson for the Edison Manufacturing Company.

Kinetoscope. Thomas Edison's peephole viewer, in which short, primitive moving pictures could be seen.

L

laboratory effects. **Special effects** created on a fresh piece of film **stock.** Laboratory effects include a wide range of procedures, such as the **dissolve** and complex multiple-exposure techniques. See also **computer-generated effects; in-camera effects.**

Latham loop. In early projection systems, a set of **sprockets** that looped the **film stock** to keep it from breaking as a result of its own inertia.

lens. The optical device used in cameras and projectors to focus light rays by means of refraction.

letterboxing. The process of blacking out the top and bottom of a television's Academy ratio **frame** to reproduce a **widescreen** image. See also **Academy aperture.**

Licensing Corporation of American (LCA). A subsidiary of Time Warner that enforces the copyrights on the entertainment conglomerates' trademarked characters, including especially the comic-book figures featured in the Time Warner subsidiary DC Comics.

line producer. The person, usually involved from **preproduction** through **postproduction,** who is responsible for the day-to-day management of the production operation.

live sound, also called **wild sound.** An industry term for sound recorded live on the movie production **set.** With so many **postproduction** options for producing good, clean sound, live sound is often replaced in the **final cut.**

location shooting. Any shooting that takes place **on location**—that is, shooting that does not take place in a studio or on a studio's **back lots.**

locked print. The crucial stage in **editing** after which no further changes are made; the **editor** cuts the original **negative** to conform to this print.

long shot. A shot that generally includes the subject's entire figure (head to toe, if a person) and a good deal of background.

long take. A single unbroken **shot,** moving or stationary, that describes a complex action that might otherwise be represented through **montage.**

looping. See **re-recording.**

low angle, also called **upward angle.** A low-angle **shot** is made by placing the camera below the action. See also **camera angle.**

low-key lighting. A term used to denote the position (not the intensity) of lights used to illuminate a film scene. Low-key lights are placed below and in front of the action depicted.

M

magic lantern. A device for projecting images onto a wall or **screen,** consisting of a powerful light source, a transparent slide, and a magnifying lens. First described by Giovanni de Fontana in the fifteenth century, the magic lantern was later integrated into elaborate theatrical shows featuring fantastic images and **special effects.** A *stereopticon* combines two or three magic lanterns to focus several images in one area, allowing for combinations of images or dissolves between them. See also **dissolve.**

magnetic recording. One of two ways of recording and storing sound in **analog format** (the other is **optical recording**) and for years the most popular medium and the one most commonly found in professional production. In magnetic recording, signals are stored on magnetic recording tape of various dimensions and formats (open reels, cassettes, and so on).

marketability. An industry term used to describe a film that can be easily and successfully marketed. *Marketability* is often used as an antonym of **playability.**

master shot. A **shot,** usually a **long shot** or a **full shot,** that establishes the spatial relationships among characters and objects in a dramatic **scene** before being broken into closer, more discrete shots through **editing.**

match cut. A **cut** in which two shots are linked together by visual and/or aural **continuity.** See also **shot.**

medium close-up. A **shot** midway between a **close-up** and a **medium shot**—for example, a human subject from face to chest.

medium long shot, sometimes abbreviated **MLS;** also called **American shot** or *plan américain.* A **shot** of a human subject from the knees up, including most of a person's body.

medium shot (MS). A **shot** of a human subject, usually from the waist up.

Method acting, also called the **Method.** A naturalistic acting style, loosely adapted from the ideas of the Russian director Konstantin Stanislavsky by the American director Elia Kazan and the acting coach Lee Strasberg, that encourages actors to speak, move, and gesture not in a traditional stage manner but in the way they would in their own lives. See also **Stanislavsky system.**

mise-en-scène. Literally, "putting onto the stage"; a term that describes the action, lighting, decor, and other elements within a **shot,** as opposed to the effects created by **cutting.** Purveyors of **realism** generally prefer the process of mise-en-scène to the more manipulative techniques of **montage.**

Mitchell camera. The standard Hollywood studio camera of the 1930s, 1940s, and 1950s, introduced in 1921 to compete with the Bell and Howell 2709, the industry standard from about 1920 until the introduction of sound.

mixing. The work of the general sound editor, who refines, balances, and combines various sound tracks into what is called "the mix." See also **sound track.**

mock documentary, also called **mockumentary.** A film that combines stylistic elements identified with the **documentary** while delivering a fictional or largely fictional (and usually comic) story. Audiences can sometimes be tricked into believing in the film's authenticity, or the effect can be used to heighten the film's verisimilitude. *This Is Spinal Tap* (Rob Reiner, 1984) is an early and especially good example.

model shot. A **shot** that uses miniatures instead of real locations. Model shots are especially useful in disaster and science-fiction films. See also **optical effects.**

modeling. In computer graphics, the process of digitally creating three-dimensional objects, environments, and scenes.

mogul. The head of a Hollywood studio. The term was used more frequently during the classical Hollywood era but is still used today.

montage. From the French verb *monter*, "to assemble or put together"; in Hollywood beginning in the 1930s, a term used to refer to a **sequence** of shots, often with **superimpositions** and **optical effects,** showing a condensed series of events.

montage theory. In the 1920s Russian formalist directors like Sergei Eisenstein and Vladimir Pudovkin argued that meaning in film was constructed entirely by montage (shots cut together to form a scene).

morphing. The digital-effects process whereby one image is gradually transformed into another. See also **special effects.**

motion capture. The process whereby the precise movements of an actor or an object are recorded and converted into digital information that can be used to construct and animate wire-frame skeletons. There are three types of motion-capture systems: magnetic (which track variations in a moving object or a person's magnetic field via transmitters whose signals are used to calculate the position of the person or object in space); optical (which rely on finding markers that are embedded at key points on the object or person with one or more video cameras); and mechanical (which use instruments like potentiometers to measure the relative position of the moving object or person).

Motion Picture Association of America (MPAA). Since the mid-1940s, the name of the film industry's principal trade organization. See also **Motion Picture Producers and Distributors of America.**

Motion Picture Patents Company (MPPC). The film industry's first of many cartels that have rather completely controlled the business of making, distributing, and screening motion pictures. Founded in 1908, the MPPC trust included the Edison Manufacturing Company along with nine of its "competitors": Biograph, Vitagraph, Essanay, Kalem, Selig Polyscope, Lubin, Star Film, Pathé Frères, and Kleine Optical.

Motion Picture Producers and Distributors of America (MPPDA). Predecessor of the **Motion Picture Association of America,** the trade organization formed by the Hollywood studios in 1922 after the notorious star scandals prompted a call for regulation of the film industry. At the outset the MPPDA was headed by Will Hays, a former postmaster general of the United States.

Motion Picture Production Code, also known as the **Hays Code.** A film-industry censorship code written in 1930 by a Jesuit priest (Daniel Lord) and a Catholic pro-censorship journalist (Martin Quigley) at the behest of the **MPPDA** and enforced rigorously after 1934 by the Production Code Administration (headed by Joseph Breen). The Hays Code regulated film content until 1968, when the industry-wide voluntary movie rating system was adopted.

Motion Picture Theater Owners Association (MPTOA). A trade organization for owners of American movie theaters, founded in 1922.

motion toys. Mid-nineteenth century devices that transformed the **magic lantern** (which projects still images) into a pre-cinema projector. Motion toys included the *thaumatrope* (a round card with multiple images held on a string), the *Phenakistoscope* (a platelike slotted disc spun to simulate moving images), the *zoetrope* (a bowllike apparatus with slots for viewers to peer through), and the *praxinoscope* (essentially a zoetrope using mirrors).

Moviola. For years the most familiar and the most popular upright machine for **editing.** A portable device operated by foot pedals, leaving the **editor's** hands free, the Moviola is based on the same technical principle as the movie projector and contains a built-in viewing **screen.**

N

narrative films. Movies whose structure follows a story line of some sort.

National Association of Theatre Owners (NATO). The largest film-exhibition trade organization in the world, representing more than 29,000 movie screens in the United States and additional cinemas in more than forty countries worldwide.

National Board of Censorship. A self-regulatory apparatus of the **Motion Picture Patents Company** that supervised censorship of American films between 1909 and 1921. See also **National Board of Review.**

National Board of Review. The successor of the **National Board of Censorship** as the film industry's principal censorship apparatus from 1921 to 1934.

National Endowment for the Arts (NEA). A federal agency supporting the arts, founded in 1965 as part of President Lyndon Johnson's vaunted Great Society. Many contemporary independent films and **experimental films** have been produced in part with grants supplied by the NEA.

naturalism. A concept in literature and film that assumes that the lives of the characters are biologically, sociologically, or psychologically determined. Erich von Stroheim's *Greed* (1924) is a classic example of naturalism in film. (Frank Norris's 1899 novel *McTeague,* on which the film is based, is a classic of naturalism in fiction.)

negative. A negative photographic image on transparent material that makes possible the reproduction of the positive image.

negative cost. The cost of producing a film, exclusive of advertising, studio overhead, and distribution prints.

negative cut. The penultimate stage of **editing,** in which a specialist **editor,** often called the *negative cutter,* cuts the original **negative** to conform to the **locked print,** resulting in the **final cut.**

negative pickups. An industry term for films that studios purchase ("pick up") after they are produced independently and, often, screened at one of the big film festivals (the Sundance Film Festival, for example).

neo-noir. A term used by film reviewers and film critics to refer to contemporary films that borrow the stylistic or narrative propensities of **film noir.**

neorealism. A post–World War II movement in filmmaking associated primarily with the films of Roberto Rossellini, Luchino Visconti, and Vittorio De Sica in Italy. Neorealism was characterized by leftist political sympathies, **location shooting,** and the use of nonprofessional actors. It profoundly influenced many of the important postwar American directors of **narrative films** and **documentary** films.

newsreel. Filmed news reports shown along with the main **feature** in American theaters in the 1930s, 1940s, and 1950s. Newsreels were eclipsed by television news.

New Wave, or **nouvelle vague.** Often referred to as the French New Wave. A group of French critics for *Cahiers du cinéma* who turned to filmmaking in the late 1950s after the neorealist director Roberto Rossellini advised them to stop writing about films and start making them. Key directors of the New Wave include Jean-Luc Godard, François Truffaut, Louis Malle, Claude Chabrol, Eric Rohmer, Alain Resnais, and Jacques Rivette. Many important American filmmakers in the 1960s and 1970s were profoundly influenced by the New Wave filmmakers.

niche films. Movies made with a specific (and relatively narrow and/or small) audience in mind.

nickelodeons. From *nickel* (the price of admission) plus *odeon* (Greek for "theater"); the first permanent movie theaters, usually housed in converted storefronts.

night for night. The technique used to shoot nighttime scenes at night, used especially to evoke the harsh realism of film styles such as **film noir.** Contrast with **day for night.**

nondiegetic sound. Sound that originates from a source outside a film's world—for example, a musical **score** or a **voice-over.** Contrast with **diegetic sound.**

O

oeuvre. A term used by auteur critics to denote the collected and complete works (films) of a **director.**

offscreen sound. A form of **diegetic sound** or **nondiegetic sound** that derives from a source the viewer does not see. When diegetic, it consists of **sound effects,** music, or vocals that emanate from the world of the story. When nondiegetic, it takes the form of a musical **score** or a **voice-over** by someone who is not a character in the story.

offscreen space. The cinematic space outside the **frame.** Off-screen space is used evocatively in horror films as audiences are led to wonder (and feel anxiety about) what lies outside the arbitrary rectangle of the film **screen.** Contrast with **on-screen space.**

omnidirectional microphones. Sound-recording equipment that responds to sound coming from all directions. Contrast with **unidirectional microphones.**

180-degree system. The method of filming action that ensures **continuity** in the spatial relationships between objects on-screen. The camera must stay on one side of an imaginary 180-degree line, or axis of action, that runs through the center of the **set** or from one side of the **frame** to the other.

on location. In an interior or exterior location away from the studio. See also **location shooting.**

on-screen sound. A form of **diegetic sound** that emanates from a source the viewer sees.

optical effects. **Special effects** that are created with a special camera, an **optical printer, animation, rotoscoping,** or motion-control devices and cannot be displayed in front of a camera. Unlike **digital effects,** optical effects involve some manipulation of the photographic process. They include front projection, the **model shot,** and **rear projection.**

optical printer. A machine that performs many **postproduction** optical tasks, such as producing a **dissolve,** color balancing, and creating some **special effects.**

optical recording. One of two ways of recording and storing sound in **analog format** (the other is **magnetic recording**) and until the 1950s the standard method. In optical recording, sound waves are converted into light, which is recorded photographically on 16mm or **35mm film stock.**

option contract. During the classical Hollywood era, an actor's standard seven-year contract, reviewed every six months. If the actor demonstrated box-office appeal, the studio picked up the option to employ him or her for the next six months; if not, the studio dropped the option and the actor was out of a job.

order. The arrangement of plot events in a logical **sequence** or hierarchy. Across an entire narrative or in a brief section of it, the plot of any film can be arranged by one or more methods, such as chronological order, cause-and-effect order, or logical order.

outtakes. Material that is not used in the final cut but is nonetheless cataloged and saved.

overlapping sound, also called **sound bridge** or **sound transition.** Sound that carries over from one **shot** to the next and is heard before the sound of the second shot begins.

P

pan. From *panorama;* any pivotal movement of the camera around an imaginary vertical axis running through it.

Panavision. The anamorphic process most commonly used today, having replaced **CinemaScope** in the early 1960s. Super Panavision (originally called Panavision 70) uses 70mm **film stock** to produce a 65mm **negative** without squeezing the image. Ultra Panavision produces a 65mm negative anamorphically compressed in filming by an **aspect ratio** of 1.25:1. The process now referred to as Panavision 70 is an optical-printing method that allows a 70mm **release print** to be blown up from a 35mm anamorphic or spherical negative. Panavision is also the trade name of a widely used camera based on the design of the **Mitchell camera.** See also **anamorphic lens; film gauge.**

panchromatic stock. Black-and-white **film stock** that is sensitive to all the colors of the spectrum, from red to blue, but is less capable of achieving great **depth of field** than the orthochromatic stock it replaced in 1927. The introduction of **widescreen** processes in the 1950s greatly enhanced panchromatic depth of field.

parallel action. A narrative strategy that uses **crosscutting** of two or more separate actions to create the illusion that they are occurring simultaneously. See also **accelerated montage.**

parallel editing. See **crosscutting.**

Paramount **decision.** A 1948 United States Supreme Court decision that effectively broke up the studio trusts by forcing divestiture, the sale of the studios' much coveted movie theaters.

persistence of vision. The physiological foundation of the cinema. An image remains on the retina of the eye for a short period of time after it disappears from the actual field of vision; when a successive image replaces it immediately, as on a moving strip of film, the illusion of continuous motion is produced.

pixilation. A technique used in **animation** whereby models are photographed one **frame** at a time. Pixilation can also be applied so that the illusion of continuous motion is disrupted, an effect achieved either by **stop-motion photography** or by cutting particular frames from the **negative.**

playability. An industry term for a film whose quality is such that the film will succeed independent of clever marketing. A film that possesses playability succeeds by filmgoers' word of mouth and critics' buzz. Contrast with **marketability.**

point of view (POV). The position from which a film presents the actions of the story, including not only the relation of the narrator(s) to the story but also the camera's role in seeing and hearing the story.

point-of-view editing. The joining together of a **point-of-view shot** with a **match cut** to show, in the first shot, a character looking and, in the second shot, what he or she is looking at.

point-of-view shot. When the camera seems to share the subjective position of a character in a film, and audiences are led to believe that the camera sees exactly what the character sees.

politique des auteurs. Literally, "authors' policy"; the idea that a single person, most often the **director,** has the sole aesthetic responsibility for a film's form and content. François Truffaut first postulated the idea in his article *"Une certaine tendance du cinéma français,"* which appeared in the January 1954 issue of *Cahiers du cinéma.*

positive. A print, produced from a **negative,** in which the light values of the film correspond to those of the recorded **scene.**

postproduction. The third stage of the production process, consisting of **editing,** sound mixing (of sync dialogue, dubbed sound, **sound effects,** and music), and **special effects.** See also **preproduction; production.**

postsynchronization, also called **dubbing**. The **synchronization** of sound and image after a film has been shot. Postsynchronization was an important step forward in liberating the early sound-film camera from its glass-paneled booth.

Poverty Row. Small-time independent studios like Monogram, Republic, Chesterfield, Tiffany, and Mascot clustered in a small section of Hollywood near the corner of Sunset and Gower (called by those in the business "Gower Gulch") in the early sound era. These B-movie outfits made mostly genre films on the cheap.

preproduction. The initial, planning-and-preparation stage of the production process. Preproduction is followed by **production** and **postproduction.**

principal photography. An industry term used to refer to the period of time during which a film is actively being shot.

process shot. A **shot** filmed live against a background that is front- or rear-projected onto a translucent **screen.**

producer. The person who guides the entire process of making a movie, from its initial planning to its release, and is chiefly responsible for the organizational and financial aspects of the production, from arranging the financing to deciding how the money will be spent.

production. The second stage of the production process: the actual shooting. Production is preceded by **preproduction** and followed by **postproduction.**

production designer. A person who works closely with the **director,** the **art director,** and the **director of photography** in visualizing the movie that will appear on-screen. The production designer is both artist and executive, responsible for the overall design concept—the *look* of the movie—as well as individual **sets,** locations, furnishings, props, and costumes and for supervising the heads of various departments: art, costume design and construction, hairstyling, makeup, wardrobe, and location.

production values. The amount of human, financial, and physical resources devoted to the image, including the style of its lighting. High production values are often associated with slick, expensive films; low production values are associated with **B films** or independent films.

protagonist. The major character in a film who serves as the "hero" or is singled out as the primary figure with whom viewers will identify positively. Contrast with **antagonist.**

R

race films. An industry term for films made by and/or marketed to a particular ethnic group.

rack focus. A technique of **shallow focus** that forcibly directs the vision of the spectator from one subject to another. The **focus** is pulled and changed to shift the focus plane.

ratings. See **voluntary movie rating system.**

raw film stock. See **celluloid roll film.**

reaction shot. A **shot** that cuts away from the central action to show a character's reaction to it.

realism. In cinema, a term often used to describe filmmaking that attempts to be faithful to the nature of the subject and avoids obvious creative manipulation or interpretation. Filmmakers said to have a realist style concern themselves with reproducing a sense of the actual by privileging the **long take, location shooting,** and a naturalistic acting style over more artificial studio effects in an effort to produce the impression of unmediated authenticity.

real time. The time it takes for an event to occur in reality, outside cinematic time. In rare instances, however (Fred Zinnemann's *High Noon*, 1952, for example), real time and cinematic time coincide precisely. See also **duration.**

rear projection. An **optical effect** in which a **scene** is projected onto a translucent **screen** located behind the actors so that they appear to be in a specific location.

reel. The casing and holder for the **film stock**, or tape. The feed reel supplies the film, and the take-up reel rewinds it. A **35mm** reel holds up to 1,000 feet of film or tape. At sound speed (24 **frames per second**), a full 35mm reel runs about 10 minutes; at silent speed (16 frames per second), it runs between 14 and 16 minutes.

reflector board. A piece of lighting equipment, but not a lighting instrument because it does not rely on bulbs to produce illumination. Essentially, it is a double-sided board that pivots in a U-shaped holder. One side is a hard, smooth surface that reflects hard light; the other is a soft, textured surface that provides softer **fill light.**

release print. The final print used for screening and **distribution.**

Rembrandt lighting. A style of lighting taken from portraiture (in both painting and photography) in which the main light is positioned high on the side of the face that is away from the camera. Combined with the three-quarter view of the face, the lighting creates a very flattering effect, slimming the face and highlighting the cheekbones.

re-recording, sometimes called **looping** or **dubbing.** The replacing of dialogue, which can be done manually (with the actors watching the footage, synchronizing their lips with it, and re-reading the lines) or, as is more likely today, by **automatic dialogue replacement.**

resolution. The ability of a camera **lens** to define images in sharp detail.

reverse-angle shot. A **shot** taken at a 180-degree angle to the preceding shot—a practice rarely used. Instead, filmmakers have adopted the **shot–reverse shot.**

rotoscoping. The technique of isolating an object a **frame** at a time by tracing its edges to create a silhouette, which can be replaced by another image during **postproduction.**

rough cut. The first completed version of a film prepared by the **editor.** A rough cut is often longer than the **final cut** or **release print** and may not include all the planned **optical effects** and **sound effects,** and other aspects of **postproduction.**

rule of thirds. A compositional principle that enables filmmakers to maximize the potential of an image, balance its elements, and create the illusion of depth. A grid pattern, when superimposed on the image, divides it horizontally into thirds that represent the foreground, middle ground, and background planes and into thirds vertically that break up those planes further. Generally, objects of interest are placed where the horizontal and vertical lines of the grid intersect.

rushes. See **dailies.**

S

scale. The size and placement of a particular object or part of a **scene** in relation to the rest, with the relationship determined by the type of **shot** to be used and the placement of the camera.

scene. A vague term that describes a unit of narration. In film, a scene may consist of a series of shots or of a single **sequence** shot in one location.

Scope. An abbreviation for **CinemaScope** or any other anamorphic process. See also **anamorphic lens.**

score. The musical **sound track** for a film. The word is also used as a verb.

screen. As a noun, the specially treated surface on which a film is projected; as a verb, the act of projecting or watching a film.

screenplay. The script of a film. A screenplay may be no more than a rough outline that the **director** fills in, or like most Hollywood studio scripts of the 1930s and 1940s, it may be detailed, complete with dialogue, **continuity,** and camera movements.

screen test. A **scene** on camera that actors seeking the opportunity to appear in a given film are asked to perform during the **casting** process. The **producer** and **director** review the performance and decide whether to cast the actor.

screwball comedy. A type of romantic comedy that was popular in the 1930s and is characterized by frantic action and a great deal of verbal wit.

script supervisor. The member of the film crew who is responsible for ensuring **continuity** throughout filming. Although script supervisors once had to maintain detailed logs to accomplish this task, today they generally rely on the **video assist camera.**

second unit. In an elaborate production, a supplementary film crew that shoots routine scenes not shot by the first unit. Background shots and establishing shots, for instance, are usually shot by the second unit.

sequence. A series of edited shots characterized by inherent unity of theme or purpose.

series photography. A series of **still** photographs shot by a battery of cameras and then mounted and framed (as a series of photographs) or placed in a **motion toy** to simulate movement. The most important purveyor of this late-nineteenth-century, pre-cinematic art form was Eadweard Muybridge.

set. The location where a **scene** is shot, often but not exclusively constructed on a **soundstage.**

set pieces. A term used by critics and filmmakers to describe a carefully constructed **scene.**

setting. The time and space in which a story takes place.

setup. One camera position and everything associated with it; the position of the camera, lights, sound equipment, actors, and so on. Whereas the **shot** is the basic building block of the film, the setup is the basic component of the film's **production.** The number of different setups that a film requires can be an important financial factor.

shallow focus. A technique that deliberately uses a shallow **depth of field** in order to direct the viewer's perception along a plane of **focus.**

shooting angle. The level and height of the camera in relation to the subject being photographed.

shooting ratio. The relationship between the amount of footage shot and the amount of footage used in the completed film.

shooting script. A guide and reference point for all members of a **production** unit in which the details of each **shot** are listed, to be followed during filming.

short. A film whose running time is less than 30 minutes. Contrast with **feature.**

shot. A continuously exposed, unedited piece of film of any length: the basic unit of film structure.

shot/reverse shot. One of the most prevalent and most familiar of all **editing** patterns, consisting of **crosscutting** between **shots** of different characters, typically in conversation or confrontation. The angle separating the two perspectives is usually between 120 and 160 degrees. The French call such sequences *champ contra champ,* "(visual) field against field." When used in **continuity editing,** the shots are typically framed over each character's shoulder to preserve screen direction.

showcase theaters. The select urban movie palaces into which studios released their biggest films, especially during the classical Hollywood era. The studios made a lot of money at showcase venues, so the theaters were a key to the studios' (and a given film's) profitability. After this **first run,** studios released their films more widely. Today, the norm is so-called saturation releases, in which a film is released to as many theaters as possible nationwide.

shutter. A device that blocks light from entering the camera at the **aperture** while the film is moving from one **frame** to another.

sight-line cut. An industry term for a **cut** that follows the sight line of a character in a film.

slapstick. A type of comedy that relies on acrobatic gags and exaggerated pantomine rather than verbal humor. Slapstick was the dominant comic form during the silent era.

slate. The board or other device that is used to identify each **scene** during shooting.

slow motion. Photography that decelerates action by photographing it at a faster than normal rate.

social-realist filmmaking. An aesthetic doctrine that originated in the Soviet Union in the late 1920s and insisted that all art be rendered intelligible to the masses. This ideal was adopted by **documentary** and other politically minded filmmakers in the United States.

soft cuts. An industry term for editing techniques that present smooth (as opposed to abrupt) transitions—for example, the **dissolve** and the **fade-in** and **fade-out.**

soft focus. The blurring or softening of a subject's definition by means of lens **filter,** special lenses, or even petroleum jelly smeared directly on a **lens,** producing a dreamy or romantic effect (and often making an actor appear younger).

sound bridge. See **overlapping sound.**

sound crew. The technicians on a film **set** who generate and control the movie's sound physically, manipulating its properties to produce the effects that the **director** desires.

sound design. A term coined by the film **editor** Walter Murch, to describe the combination of the crafts of **editing** and sound **mixing.** Murch coined the term to emphasize the importance of sound.

sound editor. The post-production technician responsible for the final "mix" of the various sound fields: dialogue, music, and sound effects.

sound effects. Sounds that are artificially created for a **sound track** and have a definite function in telling a film's story.

sound track. A separate tape for the sound recorded for a movie. One sound **track** is recorded for vocals, one for **sound effects,** one for music, and so on.

soundstage. A windowless, soundproofed shooting environment that is usually several stories high and can cover an acre or more of floor space.

special effects, sometimes abbreviated **F/X.** A term used to describe a range of synthetic processes used to enhance or manipulate the cinematic image. Special effects include **optical effects;** mechanical or physical effects such as explosions, fires, fog, and flying or falling objects or people; makeup effects such as **animatronic puppetry** and the use of blood bags and prosthetics; and **digital effects.**

splicer. An **editing** device with an edge for cutting film evenly on a **frame** line and a bed on which to align and tape together **cuts** that will be invisible to the audience.

split screen. The **in-camera effect** of dividing the **screen,** either in the camera or during editing, to tell two stories simultaneously. Unlike **crosscutting,** which cuts back and forth for contrast, the split screen can tell multiple stories within the same **frame.**

sprockets. The evenly spaced holes on the edge of a filmstrip that allow it to be moved forward mechanically; also, the wheeled gears that engage these holes in the camera and the projector.

stand-ins. Non-actors who substitute for movie stars during the tedious process of preparing a **setup** or taking light readings. Stand-ins need not look just like the actor for whom they stand in, but they need to be about the same height and weight.

Stanislavsky system.   A system of acting developed by Russian theater director Konstantin Stanislavsky in the late nineteenth century that encourages actors to strive for realism, both social and psychological, and to bring their past experiences and emotions to their roles. It influenced the development of **Method acting** in the United States.

Steadicam.   A camera suspended from an articulated arm that is attached to a vest that is strapped to the **camera operator,** permitting him or her to remain steady during handheld shots. The Steadicam removes jumpiness and is now often used for smooth, fast, and intimate camera movement.

stereophonic sound.   The use of two or more high-fidelity speakers and **sound tracks** to approximate the actual dimensionality of hearing with two ears.

still.   A photograph that re-creates a scene from a film for publicity purposes; also, the enlargement of a single **frame,** made to look like a photograph.

stock footage.   Standard, often used shots (such as World War II combat or crowds on the streets of New York City) taken from an archive and inserted into a feature film.

stop-motion photography.   A technique used for trick photography and **special effects,** reputedly devised by George Méliès, in which one **frame** is exposed at a time so that the subject can be adjusted between frames.

storyboard.   A scene-by-scene (and sometimes shot-by-shot) breakdown that combines sketches or photographs of the way each **shot** is to look with written descriptions of the other elements that are to go with each shot, including dialogue, sound, and music.

story conference.   One of any number of sessions during which a **treatment,** or rough draft of a **screenplay** is discussed, developed, and transformed into a more polished work

studio directors.   The men (and, in rare cases, women) who directed the vast majority of films during the classical Hollywood era, whose job involved executing the studio style (making the movie look the way the studio wanted it to look). That a director might put his or her personal stamp, or signature, on a film (as a so-called **auteur**) was frowned upon. The term is also used pejoratively by film critics and film historians to denote a filmmaker whose primary skill was to make a movie according to a studio's plan.

studio era.   A term used to describe the classical Hollywood era, roughly beginning with the advent of sound (1928) and ending with the end of the Second World War (1945).

stunt persons.   Performers who double for other actors in scenes requiring special skills or involving hazardous acts, such as crashing cars, jumping from high places, and riding (or falling off) a horse.

subjective camera.   See **first-person camera.**

subrun theaters.   Movie theaters that screen films well after the intial release.

subtitle.   A printed title superimposed on the picture, usually at the bottom of the **frame,** used mostly to translate foreign dialogue.

Sundance Film Festival.   The premiere American film festival held annually in Park City, Utah. Founded in 1981 by the actor and director Robert Redford, Sundance began as a venue for smaller, independent films. Sundance now functions more like a film marketplace than an indie-film festival; it is *the place* where deals are made and careers are launched.

superimposition.   An optical effect created as one image is literally placed over another.

surrealism.   A movement in painting, film, and literature, originating in Paris in the 1920s, that aimed to depict the workings of the subconscious by combining incongruous imagery or by presenting a situation in dreamlike, irrational terms. More generally, surrealism may suggest a fantastic style of representation.

swish pan.   A **pan** that moves from one **scene** to another so quickly that the intervening content is blurred.

synchronization, also called **sync.**   The use of mechanical or electronic timing devices to keep sound and image in a precise relationship with each other.

synchronous sound.   Sound whose source is made clear by the image track. Contrast with **asynchronous sound.**

T

take.   Each version of a **shot** in a given **setup.** A director shoots numerous takes, only one of which appears in the final version of the film.

take-up spool.   A device that winds the exposed film inside a movie camera.

Technicolor.   Founded in 1915 in Boston by the engineers Herbert Kalmus, Daniel Comstock, and W. Burton Wescott, Technicolor was involved in the earliest experiments in two- and three-color film processes. Technicolor remains a thriving company—the industry's premiere color lab.

telephoto lens.   A **lens** with a long **focal length** that functions like a telescope to magnify distant objects. Because its angle of view is very narrow, it flattens the depth perspective.

theatrical blocking.   See **blocking.**

theatrical film.   A film made primarily for viewing in a motion-picture theater, as opposed to films made for television or some other specialized delivery system.

35mm.   The standard **film gauge** for cinema stock since the late nineteenth century.

three-point lighting scheme.   Perhaps the best-known lighting convention in feature filmmaking, a system that employs three sources of light—**key light, fill light,** and **backlight**—each aimed from a different direction and a different position in relation to the subject.

tilt angle.   A tilt **shot** that is made with the vertical movement of a camera mounted on the gyroscope head of a stationary tripod. Like the **pan,** it is a simple movement with dynamic possibilities for creating meaning. See also **camera angle.**

time-lapse photography.   A kind of extreme fast-motion shooting that compresses **real time** by photographing a subject at a rate, for example, of one **frame** every 30 seconds. Time-lapse photography is used primarily as a scientific tool to photograph natural phenomena that occur too slowly for normal observation. The opposite type of time-lapse photography would expose film rapidly to capture movement that occurs too quickly to be seen by the naked eye.

Todd-AO. A **widescreen** process very popular in the 1950s and 1960s that used a 65mm **negative** printed on 70mm film in combination with a high-quality six-track **sound track.** The final projected print had a 2.35:1 **aspect ratio.**

track. A single recording channel on a **sound track** that can be mixed with others and modified to create a variety of effects.

tracking shot. A **shot** produced with a camera that moves smoothly alongside, above, beneath, behind, or ahead of the action. A tracking shot is made possible by mounting the camera on a set of tracks, a dolly, a crane, or an aerial device, such as an airplane, helicopter, or balloon.

travel matte. Used in digital editing to match images and text, often in credit sequences.

treatment, also called **synopsis.** An outline of the action that briefly describes the essential ideas and structure of a film.

tungsten incandescent light. The main source of soft or low-intensity, illumination on a movie **set;** also, the principle source of film lighting during the early sound period, owing to its relative silence. Like household lighting, tungsten incandescent light is produced within a bulb when a tungsten filament is made incandescent by electric current. In contemporary incandescent film lighting, ordinary glass bulbs have been replaced by quartz halogen globes.

two-reeler. A film running about 30 minutes, the standard length of silent comedies.

two-shot. A standard Hollywood shot in which two characters appear. Ordinarily, a two-shot is a **medium shot** or a **medium long shot.**

typecasting. The casting of actors based on their looks or "type" rather than their talent or experience.

U

undercrank. To run a camera at a speed of less than 24 **frames per second.** When an undercranked film is projected at normal speed, the subject appears to be in fast motion.

unidirectional microphones. Sound-recording equipment that responds, and has great sensitivity, to sound coming from just one direction. Contrast with **omnidirectional microphones.**

V

VCR. The abbreviation for *videocassette recorder.*

vertical monopoly. A type of trust or cartel that links the providers and buyers in a single industry. The studios were all vertical monopolies in the 1930s. Contrast with **horizontal monopoly.**

video assist camera. A tiny device, mounted in the viewing system of a film camera, that enables a **script supervisor** to view a **scene** on a video monitor and thus compare its details with those of surrounding scenes to ensure visual **continuity** before the film is sent to the laboratory for processing.

videocassette. A sealed two-reel system of videotape generally used for private recording and viewing.

videodisc. A plastic disc on which audiovisual information is encoded by a laser beam for decoding by a corresponding laser beam on the playback unit.

videotape. Magnetic tape used for recording video images and sound.

viewfinder. On a camera, the little window that the **camera operator** looks through when shooting a film or video; the viewfinder's frame indicates the boundaries of the camera's **point of view.**

VistaVision. A nonanamorphic **widescreen** process developed by Paramount to compete with Fox's **CinemaScope** in 1954. It ran **35mm film stock** through the camera horizontally rather than vertically to produce a double-frame image twice as wide as the conventional 35mm **frame.** The **positive** print could be projected horizontally with special equipment to cast a huge image on the **screen,** or it could be reduced anamorphically for standard vertical 35mm projection. Because the process was very expensive, VistaVision has been used since 1961 only for **special effects.** See also **anamorphic lens.**

visual-effects (VFX) supervisor. The person in charge of the technical and creative aspects of special-effects production, including **digital effects, blue-screen photography** and **green-screen photography,** and the use of miniatures.

voice-of-God narration. A term used by film critics and film historians to describe a particular type of **voice-over** narration denoting authority. Voice-of-God narration is often employed in documentaries but is occasionally used in feature films as well.

voice-over. A voice **track** laid over the other tracks in a film's sound mix to comment on or narrate the action on-screen. Voice-over is often used as a cinematic substitute for the first-person narration of literature.

voluntary movie rating system. A rating system developed by Jack Valenti, president of the **Motion Picture Association of America,** and adopted industry-wide in 1968 to replace the archaic and far more restrictive **Motion Picture Production Code.** Movies are rated with an eye toward suitability for certain age groups. The system initially comprised four categories: G (suggested for "General Audiences," M (suggested for "Mature Audiences," parental discretion advised), R ("Restricted"—persons under sixteen not admitted unless accompanied by a parent or adult guardian), and X (persons under sixteen not admitted). The M designation was replaced by PG ("Parental Guidance Suggested: Some Material May Not Be Suitable for Children") and PG-13 ("Parents Strongly Cautioned: Some Material May Be Inappropriate for Children under 13"), and at the other end of the scale, NC-17 ("No One 17 and under Admitted") was added for adult-themed, adult-content films.

VTR. The abbreviation for *videotape recorder,* used to refer to a reel-to-reel or cassette tape.

W

walk-on. A role even smaller than a **cameo,** reserved for a highly recognizable actor or personality.

wide-angle lens. A **lens** whose broad angle increases the illusion of depth but distorts the linear dimensions of the image.

widescreen. Sometimes reserved to describe any flat (nonprocessed) **format** with an **aspect ratio** of 1.66:1 (the European standard) or 1.85:1 (the American standard); also, any format that produces a **screen** image wider than the **Academy aperture** of 1.33:1, whether processed or not. Most widescreen processes are anamorphic, but some, such as **Panavision 70** and **Todd-AO,** employ wide-gauge film, and others, such as **Cinerama,** employ multiple camera processes.

wipe. A transitional device in which shot B wipes across shot A, either vertically or horizontally, to replace it. Although (or because) the device reminds us of early eras in filmmaking, directors continue to use it, especially in video effects.

wire removal. The use of digital painting or compositing techniques to eliminate cables, rigs, or harnesses that were used to execute stunts or **special effects** during **production.**

work print. Any **positive** print (either print or sound or both, but not yet timed or color corrected) intended for use in the initial trial cuttings of the **editing** process.

Z

zoom-in. A **shot** in which the image is magnified only by the movement of the camera's **lens,** without the camera itself moving. This magnification is the essential difference between the zoom-in and the **dolly shot.**

zoom lens. One of the four major types of lenses (the others are the short-focal-length lens, the middle-focal-length lens, and the long-focal-length lens). The zoom lens allows for continuous motion toward and away from the subject being photographed; it has a continuously variable **focal length.**

zoopraxiscope. An early device for exhibiting moving pictures, consisting of a revolving disk with photographs arranged around the center.

Credits

Every effort has been made to reach the rights holders for each image. Please contact W.W. Norton with any updated information.

Front Cover: © United Artists/Courtesy Everett Collection; **Back Cover:** Courtesy Everett Collection; **Title Page:** Chaplin/United Artists/Kobal Collection; **Author Photo:** Courtesy Sam Leinen; **p. vii:** Edison Production/Courtesy Everett Collection; **p. viii:** (top) Courtesy Everett Collection; **p. viii:** (bottom) Courtesy Everett Collection; **p. ix:** (top) Courtesy Everett Collection; **p. ix:** (bottom) Courtesy Everett Collection; **p. x:** (top) Courtesy Everett Collection; **p. x:** (bottom) © United Artists/Courtesy Everett Collection; **p. xi:** (top) © Miramax/Courtesy Everett Collection; **p. xi:** (bottom) © Warner Bros/Courtesy Everett Collection.

CHAPTER 1

p. 2–3: Edison Production/Courtesy Everett Collection; **p. 6:** Hulton-Deutsch Collection/Corbis; **p. 7:** Hulton-Deutsch Collection/Corbis; **p. 8:** Hulton-Deutsch Collection/Corbis; **p. 8–9:** (bottom) Hulton-Deutsch Collection/Corbis; **p. 9:** Corbis; **p. 10:** Jerry Tavin/Courtesy Everett Collection; **p. 11:** *Edison Einetoscopic Record of a Sneeze*, 1894, William K. L. Dickson, Edison Company; **p. 12:** Hulton-Deutsch Collection/Corbis; **p. 13:** *Arrival of a Train at La Ciotat*, 1896, August Lumière & Louis Lumière, Lumière; **p. 14:** Corbis; **p. 15:** Bettmann/Corbis; **p. 17:** Corbis; **p. 18:** (bottom) Photo courtesy of American Mutoscope and Biograph Company; **p. 18:** *McKinley at Home*, Canton, Ohio, 1885, Edison Company; **p. 19:** *Airy Fairy Lillian Tries on Her New Corsets*, 1905, American Mutoscope and Biograph Company; **p. 20:** MPPC/Courtesy of The Bison Archives; **p. 22:** Bettmann/Corbis; **p. 23:** Courtesy Everett Collection; **p. 24:** Courtesy Everett Collection; **p. 25:** *Serpentine Dance*, 1895, William Heise, Edison Manufacturing Company; **p. 26:** Bettmann/Corbis; **p. 28:** *La voyage dans la lune*, 1902, Georges Méliès, Lubin Manufacturing Company; **p. 29:** Jerry Tavin/Courtesy Everett Collection; **p. 30:** *Life of an American Fireman*, 1903, Edwin Porter & George S. Fleming, Edison Manufacturing Company; **p. 31:** *The Great Train Robbery*, 1903, Edwin S. Porter, Edison Manufacturing Company; **p. 32:** *The Girl and Her Trust*, 1912, D. W. Griffith, Biograph Company; **p. 33:** Courtesy Everett Collection; **p. 34:** Courtesy Everett Collection; **p. 35:** Bettmann/Corbis; **p. 36:** Courtesy Everett Collection; **p. 37:** Courtesy Everett Collection; **p. 38:** *Making of an American Citizen*, 1912, Alice Guy, Solax Film Company; **p. 39:** Courtesy of Jon Lewis; **p. 40:** Bettmann/Corbis.

CHAPTER 2

p. 42–43: Courtesy Everett Collection; **p. 45:** (bottom) Courtesy Everett Collection; **p. 45:** (top) Rykoff Collection/Corbis; **p. 46:** Courtesy Everett Collection; **p. 47:** Jerry Tavin/Courtesy Everett Collection; **p. 48:** Courtesy Everett Collection; **p. 49:** Courtesy of Jon Lewis; **p. 50:** Courtesy of Jon Lewis; **p. 52:** Courtesy of Jon Lewis; **p. 53:** Bettmann/Corbis; **p. 54:** Courtesy Everett Collection; **p. 55:** Courtesy Everett Collection; **p. 56:** (top) Courtesy Everett Collection; **p. 56:** (bottom) Courtesy Everett Collection; **p. 57:** Courtesy Everett Collection; **p. 58:** Courtesy Everett Collection; **p. 59:** Courtesy Everett Collection; **p. 60:** Jerry Tavin/Courtesy Everett Collection; **p. 61:** Courtesy of Jon Lewis; **p. 62:** *The Cheat*, 1915, Cecil B. DeMille, Jesse L. Lasky Feature Play Company; **p. 62:** (bottom) Courtesy Everett Collection; **p. 63:** Courtesy Everett Collection; **p. 64:** Jerry Tavin/Courtesy Everett Collection; p. 66: Jerry Tavin/Courtesy Everett Collection; **p. 67:** Courtesy Everett Collection; **p. 68:** © 20th Century Fox Film Corp./Courtesy Everett Collection; **p. 69:** © 20th Century Fox Film Corp./Courtesy Everett Collection; **p. 70:** (top) Courtesy Everett Collection; **p. 70:** (bottom) Jerry Tavin/Courtesy Everett Collection; **p. 71:** Courtesy Everett Collection; **p. 72:** Bettmann/Corbis; **p. 73:** John Springer Collection/Corbis; **p. 74:** Jerry Tavin/Courtesy Everett Collection; **p. 75:** Courtesy Everett Collection; **p. 76:** Courtesy Everett Collection; **p. 78:** (top) *The Gold Rush*, 1925, Charles Chaplin, Charles Chaplin Productions, United Artists; **p. 78:** (bottom) *The Gold Rush*, 1925, Charles Chaplin, Charles Chaplin Productions, United Artists; **p. 79:** Courtesy Everett Collection; **p. 80:** Jerry Tavin/ Courtesy Everett Collection; **p. 81:** Courtesy Everett Collection; **p. 82:** *Sherlock Jr.*, 1924, Buster Keaton, Buster Keaton Productions; **p. 84:** Courtesy of Jon Lewis; **p. 85:** Bettmann/Corbis; **p. 86:** Courtesy of Jon Lewis; **p. 88:** Courtesy Everett Collection.

CHAPTER 3

p. 90–91: Courtesy Everett Collection; **p. 93:** Courtesy of AT&T Archives and History Center; **p. 94:** Jerry Tavin/Courtesy Everett Collection; **p. 95:** Courtesy Everett Collection; **p. 97:** Courtesy Everett Collection; **p. 98:** Courtesy Everett Collection; **p. 100:** Bettmann/Corbis; **p. 101:** Courtesy Everett Collection; **p. 102:** (top) Courtesy Everett Collection; **p. 102:** (bottom) Courtesy Everett Collection; **p. 103:** Courtesy Everett Collection; **p. 105:** Courtesy of Jon Lewis; **p. 106:** Courtesy of Jon Lewis; **p. 109:** Courtesy Everett Collection; **p. 110:** Courtesy Everett Collection; **p. 113:** Courtesy of Jon Lewis;

p. 114: Courtesy Everett Collection; **p. 115:** Courtesy Everett Collection; **p. 116:** Courtesy Everett Collection; **p. 118:** Bettmann/Corbis; **p. 119:** Courtesy of Jon Lewis; **p. 120:** Courtesy Everett Collection; **p. 121:** Courtesy of Jon Lewis; **p. 122:** Courtesy of Jon Lewis; **p. 123:** Courtesy Everett Collection; **p. 124:** Courtesy Everett Collection; **p. 125:** Courtesy Everett Collection; **p. 126:** Courtesy Everett Collection; **p. 127:** Courtesy Everett Collection; **p. 128:** Courtesy Everett Collection; **p. 129:** Courtesy Everett Collection; **p. 130:** Courtesy of Jon Lewis; **p. 132:** Courtesy Everett Collection; **p. 134:** Courtesy Everett Collection; **p. 135:** Jerry Tavin/Courtesy Everett Collection; **p. 136:** Courtesy Everett Collection; **p. 137:** Courtesy of Jon Lewis; **p. 138:** Courtesy of Jon Lewis; **p. 140:** Courtesy of Jon Lewis; **p. 141:** Courtesy Everett Collection; **p. 142:** Courtesy Everett Collection; **p. 144:** © 20th Century Fox Film Corp./Courtesy Everett Collection.

CHAPTER 4

p. 146–47: Courtesy Everett Collection; **p. 149:** © 20th Century Fox Film Corp./Courtesy Everett Collection; **p. 150:** Courtesy Everett Collection; **p. 151:** Courtesy Everett Collection; **p. 152:** Courtesy Everett Collection; **p. 153:** Courtesy of Jon Lewis; **p. 154:** (top) Courtesy Everett Collection; **p. 154:** (bottom) Courtesy Everett Collection; **p. 155:** Courtesy Everett Collection; **p. 156:** Courtesy Everett Collection; **p. 157:** Courtesy Everett Collection; **p. 158:** *Citizen Kane*, 1941, Orson Welles, RKO Radio Pictures, Warner Bros.; **p. 159:** Courtesy Everett Collection; **p. 161:** *Citizen Kane*, 1941, Orson Welles, RKO Radio Pictures, Warner Bros.; **p. 162:** Courtesy Everett Collection; **p. 163:** Jerry Tavin/Courtesy Everett Collection; **p. 165:** Courtesy Everett Collection; **p. 166:** © Walt Disney Co./Courtesy Everett Collection; **p. 167:** (top) Courtesy Everett Collection; **p. 167:** (bottom) Courtesy Everett Collection; **p. 168:** Courtesy Everett Collection; **p. 169:** Courtesy Everett Collection; **p. 170:** *Now, Voyager*, 1942, Irving Rapper, Warner Bros.; **p. 171:** Courtesy of Jon Lewis; **p. 172:** Courtesy Everett Collection; **p. 173:** (top) Courtesy Everett Collection; **p. 173:** (bottom) Courtesy Everett Collection; **p. 174:** Courtesy Everett Collection; **p. 176:** (left) Courtesy Everett Collection; **p. 176:** (right) Courtesy Everett Collection; **p. 177:** Courtesy of Jon Lewis; **p. 178:** Courtesy Everett Collection; **p. 179:** Courtesy Everett Collection; **p. 181:** Courtesy Everett Collection; **p. 182:** Courtesy Everett Collection; **p. 184:** Courtesy Everett Collection; **p. 185:** Courtesy Everett Collection; **p. 186:** Courtesy of Jon Lewis; **p. 187:** Courtesy Everett Collection; **p. 188:** Courtesy Everett Collection; **p. 189:** Courtesy Everett Collection; **p. 190:** Courtesy Everett Collection.

CHAPTER 5

p. 192–93: Courtesy Everett Collection; **p. 195:** Bettmann/Corbis; **p. 196:** (left) Bettmann/Corbis; **p. 196:** (right) Hulton-Deutsch Collection/Corbis;

p. 197: Bettmann/Corbis; **p. 198:** Courtesy of Jon Lewis; **p. 199:** Courtesy Everett Collection; **p. 200:** Bettmann/Corbis; **p. 201:** Courtesy Everett Collection; **p. 202:** Courtesy Everett Collection; **p. 204:** Courtesy Everett Collection; **p. 205:** Courtesy Everett Collection; **p. 206:** Courtesy of Jon Lewis; **p. 207:** Courtesy of Jon Lewis; **p. 208:** Courtesy Everett Collection; **p. 209:** Courtesy Everett Collection; **p. 210:** Courtesy Everett Collection; **p. 211:** Courtesy Everett Collection; **p. 212:** Courtesy Everett Collection; **p. 214:** Courtesy Everett Collection; **p. 215:** (top) Courtesy Everett Collection; **p. 215:** (bottom) Courtesy Everett Collection; **p. 216:** Courtesy Everett Collection; **p. 217:** Courtesy Everett Collection; **p. 218:** Courtesy Everett Collection; **p. 219:** Courtesy Everett Collection; **p. 220:** Courtesy Everett Collection; **p. 221:** Courtesy Everett Collection; **p. 222:** Courtesy Everett Collection; **p. 223:** Courtesy of Jon Lewis; **p. 224:** Courtesy Everett Collection; **p. 225:** (top) Courtesy Everett Collection; **p. 225:** (bottom) Courtesy Everett Collection; **p. 226:** © 20th Century Fox Film Corp./Courtesy Everett Collection; **p. 227:** Courtesy Everett Collection; **p. 229:** Courtesy of Jon Lewis; **p. 230:** Bettmann/Corbis.

CHAPTER 6

p. 232–33: Courtesy Everett Collection; **p. 235:** Courtesy of Jon Lewis; **p. 236:** H. Armstrong Roberts/Corbis; **p. 237:** Bettmann/Corbis; **p. 239:** Jerry Tavin/Courtesy Everett Collection; **p. 240:** Courtesy of Jon Lewis; **p. 241:** (top) Courtesy of Jon Lewis; **p. 241:** (bottom) Courtesy of Jon Lewis; **p. 242:** John Springer Collection/Corbis; **p. 243:** Courtesy Everett Collection; **p. 244:** Bettmann/Corbis; **p. 245:** Courtesy of Jon Lewis; **p. 246:** Courtesy of Jon Lewis; **p. 247:** Courtesy Everett Collection; **p. 248:** Bettmann/Corbis; **p. 251:** Courtesy Everett Collection; **p. 252:** Courtesy of Jon Lewis; **p. 254:** Courtesy Everett Collection; **p. 255:** Courtesy Everett Collection; **p. 256:** Courtesy of Jon Lewis; **p. 257:** Courtesy Everett Collection; **p. 258:** Courtesy Everett Collection; **p. 259:** Courtesy of Jon Lewis; **p. 260:** Courtesy Everett Collection; **p. 261:** Courtesy of Jon Lewis; **p. 263:** Courtesy Everett Collection; **p. 264:** Courtesy of Jon Lewis; **p. 265:** Courtesy Everett Collection; **p. 266:** Courtesy Everett Collection; **p. 267:** © 20th Century Fox Film Corp./Courtesy Everett Collection; **p. 268:** Courtesy of Jon Lewis; **p. 269:** Bettmann/Corbis; **p. 270:** Courtesy Everett Collection; **p. 271:** Courtesy of Jon Lewis; **p. 273:** Courtesy Everett Collection; **p. 274:** Courtesy Everett Collection; **p. 277:** Courtesy Everett Collection; **p. 278:** Courtesy Everett Collection.

CHAPTER 7

p. 280–81: © United Artists/Courtesy Everett Collection; **p. 283:** Bettmann/Corbis; **p. 285:** Courtesy Everett Collection; **p. 286:** Courtesy Everett Collection; **p. 287:** (top) Courtesy of Jon Lewis; **p. 287:** (bottom) Courtesy of Jon Lewis; **p. 288:** Bettmann/Corbis; **p. 289:** Courtesy Everett Collection; **p. 290:** Courtesy Everett Collection;

p. 291: Courtesy Everett Collection; **p. 292:** Bettmann/Corbis; **p. 293:** Courtesy Everett Collection; **p. 294:** Courtesy of Jon Lewis; **p. 296:** Courtesy Everett Collection; **p. 297:** Courtesy Everett Collection; **p. 299:** *The Godfather*, 1972, Francis Ford Coppola, Paramount Pictures; **p. 300:** Courtesy Everett Collection; **p. 301:** Courtesy of Jon Lewis; **p. 302:** Courtesy Everett Collection; **p. 303:** (top) Courtesy Everett Collection; **p. 303:** (bottom) Courtesy of Jon Lewis; **p. 304:** © United Artists/Courtesy Everett Collection; **p. 306:** Courtesy Everett Collection; **p. 307:** Courtesy Everett Collection; **p. 309:** Courtesy of Jon Lewis; **p. 310:** Courtesy Everett Collection; **p. 311:** Courtesy of Jon Lewis; **p. 312:** Courtesy Everett Collection; **p. 313:** Courtesy Everett Collection; **p. 315:** Courtesy of Jon Lewis; **p. 316:** Courtesy of Jon Lewis; **p. 317:** Courtesy Everett Collection; **p. 318:** © Paramount/Courtesy Everett Collection; **p. 320:** Courtesy of Jon Lewis; **p. 321:** Courtesy Everett Collection; **p. 323:** Courtesy of Jon Lewis; **p. 324:** © United Artists/Courtesy Everett Collection; **p. 325:** Courtesy Everett Collection; **p. 326:** Courtesy of Jon Lewis; **p. 328:** Courtesy Everett Collection; **p. 329:** Courtesy Everett Collection; **p. 330:** Courtesy of Jon Lewis; **p. 332:** Courtesy Everett Collection; **p. 333:** Courtesy of Jon Lewis; **p. 334:** Courtesy of Jon Lewis; **p. 335:** (top) Courtesy Everett Collection; **p. 335:** (bottom) Courtesy of Jon Lewis; **p. 336:** Courtesy of Jon Lewis; **p. 339:** Courtesy of Jon Lewis; **p. 340:** Courtesy of Jon Lewis; **p. 341:** Courtesy of Jon Lewis; **p. 343:** Courtesy of Jon Lewis; **p. 344:** Courtesy Everett Collection; **p. 345:** Courtesy Everett Collection; **p. 346:** Courtesy Everett Collection; **p. 347:** Courtesy of Jon Lewis; **p. 348:** Courtesy Everett Collection.

CHAPTER 8

p. 350–51: © Miramax/Courtesy Everett Collection; **p. 353:** Reuters/Corbis; **p. 355:** Hulton-Deutsch Collection/Corbis; **p. 356:** Courtesy of Jon Lewis; **p. 357:** Najlah Feanny/Corbis SABA; **p. 358:** Courtesy Everett Collection; **p. 360:** Courtesy of Jon Lewis; **p. 361:** © Warner Brothers/Courtesy Everett Collection; **p. 362:** (top) Courtesy of Jon Lewis; **p. 362:** (bottom) Courtesy of Jon Lewis; **p. 364:** Courtesy of Jon Lewis; **p. 365:** © Warner Bros./Courtesy Everett Collection; **p. 366:** Courtesy Everett Collection; **p. 367:** Courtesy Everett Collection; **p. 368:** © 20th Century Fox Film Corp/Courtesy Everett Collection; **p. 369:** © Warner Bros./Courtesy Everett Collection; **p. 370:** (top) Courtesy of Jon Lewis; **p. 370:** (bottom) Courtesy of Jon Lewis; **p. 371:** © 20th Century Fox Film Corp/Courtesy Everett Collection;

p. 372: Photo by Ilpo Musto/Rex USA; **p. 373:** © Andora Pictures International/Courtesy Everett Collection; **p. 375:** Courtesy of Jon Lewis; **p. 376:** © DreamWorks/Courtesy Everett Collection; **p. 377:** Courtesy of Jon Lewis; **p. 378:** © Universal Pictures/Courtesy Everett Collection; **p. 379:** © Warner Bros/Courtesy Everett Collection; **p. 380:** Island Pictures/Courtesy Everett Collection; **p. 381:** © Universal Pictures/Courtesy Everett Collection; **p. 382:** Courtesy of Jon Lewis; **p. 383:** (top) © Paramount Pictures/Courtesy Everett Collection; **p. 383:** (bottom) De Laurentis Group/Courtesy Everett Collection; **p. 384:** © Paramount Pictures/Courtesy Everett Collection; **p. 385:** Courtesy Everett Collection; **p. 386:** © Miramax/Courtesy Everett Collection; **p. 387:** © Miramax/Courtesy Everett Collection; **p. 388:** © 20th Century Fox Film Corp/Courtesy Everett Collection; **p. 389:** Island Pictures/Courtesy Everett Collection; **p. 390:** Courtesy of Jon Lewis; **p. 391:** © Gramercy Pictures/Courtesy Everett Collection; **p. 392:** © Gramercy Pictures/Courtesy Everett Collection; **p. 393:** Courtesy of Jon Lewis; **p. 394:** Miramax/ Courtesy Everett Collection; **p. 395:** (top) Courtesy of Jon Lewis; **p. 395:** (bottom) Courtesy of Jon Lewis; **p. 396:** Courtesy of Jon Lewis; **p. 397:** Courtesy of Jon Lewis; **p. 398:** Courtesy Everett Collection.

CHAPTER 9

p. 400–01: © Warner Bros/Courtesy Everett Collection; **p. 403:** Reuters/Corbis; **p. 404:** (top) James Knowler/Reuters/Corbis; **p. 404:** (bottom) Frank Trapper/Corbis; **p. 406:** *Die Another Day*, 2002, Lee Tamahori, MGM, United Artists, Danjaq, Eon Productions; **p. 407:** © Buena Vista Pictures/Courtesy Everett Collection; **p. 409:** Lieutenant Amy Render/Corbis; **p. 410:** Richard Cummins/Corbis; **p. 411:** Courtesy of Jon Lewis; **p. 412:** © Warner Bros/Courtesy Everett Collection; **p. 413:** © Warner Bros/Courtesy Everett Collection; **p. 414:** © 20th Century Fox Film Corp/Courtesy Everett Collection; **p. 415:** © Universal Pictures/Courtesy Everett Collection; **p. 416:** (top) Reuters/Corbis; **p. 416:** (bottom) Courtesy of Jon Lewis; **p. 417:** Courtesy of Jon Lewis; **p. 418:** © Universal Pictures/Courtesy Everett Collection; **p. 419:** (top) © Focus Features/Courtesy Everett Collection; **p. 419:** (bottom) Nick Cornish/Rex Features/Courtesy Everett Collection; **p. 420:** Natacha Connan/People Avenue/Corbis; **p. 421:** © Focus Features/Courtesy Everett Collection; **p. 422:** © Paramount Classics/Courtesy Everett Collection; **p. 423:** Courtesy of Jon Lewis; **p. 424:** © Lions Gate/Courtesy Everett Collection.

Index